THE
LAWYERS

MARTIN MAYER

THE

LAWYERS

HARPER & ROW, PUBLISHERS

New York, Evanston, and London

Grateful acknowledgment is made for permission to reprint excerpts from the following:

"Prison Folklore" by Bruce Jackson. Published in the *Journal of American Folklore*. Reprinted by permission.
The Changing Practice of the Law by Harrison Tweed. Reprinted by permission of The Association of the Bar of the City of New York.
Law and Computers in the Mid-Sixties by the ALI-ABA Joint Committee on Continuing Legal Education, © 1966 by the American Law Institute. Reprinted by permission.
The Lawyers Know Too Much. From *Smoke and Steel* by Carl Sandburg, copyright, 1920, by Harcourt, Brace & World, Inc.; renewed, 1948, by Carl Sandburg. Reprinted by permission of the publishers.
Adams-Jefferson Letters. Thomas Jefferson and Abigail and John Adams. Edited by L. J. Cappon. © 1959 by University of North Carolina Press. Published for the Institute of Early American History and Culture at Williamsburg, Virginia.
The Supreme Court in United States History by Charles Warren. © 1922, 1926, by Little, Brown and Company. Reprinted by permission of Little, Brown and Company.
Listen to Leaders in Law edited by Albert Love and James Saxon Childers. © 1963 by Tupper and Love, Inc. Reprinted by permission of Holt, Rinehart and Winston, Inc.

K-R

For HENRY MAYER and
RUBY P. MAYER of the New York Bar

CONTENTS

"WHEN I THINK THEN OF THE LAW,
I SEE A PRINCESS MIGHTIER THAN
SHE WHO ONCE WROUGHT AT BA-
YEUX, ETERNALLY WEAVING INTO
HER WEB DIM FIGURES OF THE EVER-
LENGTHENING PAST—FIGURES TOO
DIM TO BE NOTICED BY THE IDLE,
TOO SYMBOLIC TO BE INTERPRETED
EXCEPT BY HER PUPILS, BUT TO THE
DISCERNING EYE DISCLOSING EVERY
PAINFUL STEP AND EVERY WORLD-
SHAKING CONTEST BY WHICH MAN-
KIND HAS WORKED AND FOUGHT ITS
WAY FROM SAVAGE ISOLATION TO
ORGANIC SOCIAL LIFE."

—HOLMES

(in steel letters on marble at Boalt Hall, Law School of the University of California, Berkeley)

"The most interesting case I had when I was County Attorney? Well, I had a case of sodomy with a goat. Very interesting—very unusual. You see, there are so few *goats* these days in Appanoose County. . . ."

—Midwest lawyer

"Law . . . begins when someone takes to doing something someone else does not like."

—Karl Llewellyn

PREFACE

"Truth emerges more readily from error than from confusion."
—FRANCIS BACON

1

Shortly after the publication of *The Schools* in 1961, I ran into a cousin who was assistant professing education at New York University. He said nice things about the new book—people you meet on the street will say nice things about your new book even if they aren't cousins, and even if they haven't read it—and asked what came next.

I said, "Lawyers."

He made a moue. "That," he said, "is the big leagues."

And so it is. No other enterprise I have attempted to investigate has yielded so often the pleasant sensation of contact with a first-rate mind working on a first-rate problem. During the course of more than five years on this job, I have come to feel that one can on occasion thoroughly understand how a lawyer thinks about a given situation and still believe there are more productive ways to think about it—indeed, that there are areas of human experience where lawyerlike habits of mind positively inhibit understanding of what is actually happening. But I have not forgotten that this is the big leagues.

2

Quite apart from the variety and complexity of the subject, law and lawyers present a unique obstacle to the reporter. Normally, in hunting the Snark, the reporter is the Bellman, and the people

he interviews will crew for him; they may have reason to regard
his book as really a Boojum, they may not like each other much,
but they are willing to take on faith the notion of a joint venture.
Looking for law and lawyers, the reporter feels himself rather the
Butcher of the crew, who has admitted to specializing in Beavers.
Thereafter, you will recall,

> Whenever the Butcher was by
>   The Beaver kept looking the opposite way
> And appeared unaccountably shy.

In the summer of 1965, on the occasion of the elevation of Abe
Fortas to the Supreme Court, the *New York Times Magazine* asked
me to write an article on the Washington law firm formerly called
Arnold, Fortas & Porter. A letter was sent to Thurman Arnold,
formerly a judge on the federal Court of Appeals and senior partner
of this firm; and the following reply was received:

Of course, I would be glad to let you see my house. It has historical
significance, being the headquarters of Lafayette on his triumphal tour in
1824. I am sorry that I cannot be of any greater assistance to you in writing your article than that. The Bar is quite sensitive about practicing
lawyers cooperating in articles about themselves. . . . I would anticipate
criticism if any member of our organization cooperated with you in giving
you information with respect to the operation of the firm.

I hope you understand the situation and do not consider that I am
being ungracious about it.

Sincerely,
THURMAN ARNOLD

As Judge Arnold has kindly given consent for the publication of
this letter, it would be ungentlemanly to stress (though it is not
quite possible to avoid) the fact that he had recently published a
personal memoir which included a chapter entitled "Arnold, Fortas
& Porter." He could reasonably reply that he retained full control
over what went into that chapter, while he would be at the mercy
of the outsider if he cooperated in an article or a book. And the
grounds on which his letter rests are as solid as can be.

Canon 27 of the Canons of Professional Ethics adopted by the
American Bar Association states that

It is unprofessional to solicit professional employment by circulars, advertisements, through touters or by personal communications or interviews not warranted by personal relations. Indirect advertisements for professional employment such as furnishing or inspiring newspaper comments, or procuring his photograph to be published in connection with causes in which the lawyer has been or is engaged or concerning the manner of their conduct, the magnitude of the interest involved, the importance of the lawyer's position, and all other like self-laudation, offend the traditions and lower the tone of our profession and are reprehensible.

Canon 27 has produced about as much trouble as all the other forty-six put together. It has been amended six times since its adoption in 1908, though the second sentence in the quotation, which is the key matter, has remained roughly the same throughout. Among the Canon's official interpretations is one "on all fours," as lawyers say, with the problem presented to Judge Arnold:

"A law firm may not acquiesce in the publication by a magazine of a laudatory history of the firm, or allow itself to be listed as counsel for a community chest."

On this basis, a firm of young lawyers who cooperated with a naïvely admiring picture story in *Life* were severely censured by the Appellate Division in New York in 1963. Obviously, punishments are not meted out with a precisely even hand—a Louis Nizer, a Melvin Belli, a Jake Ehrlich are permitted to pass unrebuked after publishing self-laudation of a kind that might be regarded as ludicrous in an opera singer. But the rules are there. Because laymen are hopelessly incapable of judging the quality of professional services, and because competitive advertising can tear the fabric of a professional community, the rules can even be justified, up to a point. It must be said, though, that by denying the society important information about what lawyers do and how they do it, professional secrecy has both protected the bar from criticism of the kind that improves performance and stimulated criticism of the kind that shakes confidence. For this reporter, the Canon has been, inelegantly, a pain in the neck.

No worse than that: in one way or another, I was in fact able to interview nearly all those I asked to see. Many prominent lawyers felt what Louis D. Brandeis once called "The Duty of Publicity" as strongly as they felt Canon 27. Some understood that in books as in courtrooms anonymous testimony should not be permitted, and raised no objection to being quoted. Others (perhaps because of government training) were quite unconscious of the irresponsibility inherent in a situation where one talks for quotation but not for attribution. Still others started an interview on a normal basis, but would end it with an offhand remark to the effect that of course everything had been off-the-record.

Such situations raise ethical problems for reporters. Where an interview was granted on a "background" basis, of course, quotations have not been attributed unless specific consent to do so was obtained on completion of the manuscript. Where the request of anonymity was made early in an interview, it has been granted as though it were a condition of the interview. Where it seemed to me, however, that a man was making a request at the end of an interview from mere abundant caution, because he thought he had said something that might damage him, I have used my own judgment. In those situations where a request was made only at the end of the interview and a senior partner in the same firm had made no objection to the use of his name (so the firm name, which is the valid Canon 27 objection, would appear anyway), I have felt free to ignore what was not a contract but merely a self-serving declaration—subject, of course, to Canon 1 of my business, which is that a reporter does not use the courtesy of an interview to punish the man who granted it.

3

Technicalities:
The word "lawyer" has been preferred to "attorney" throughout, partly for the same reason that the word "reporter" was preferred to "journalist" in the preceding paragraphs, partly because the Yellow Pages list lawyers under "Lawyers" and what's good enough for the telephone company is good enough for me.

The term "judge" is used consistently for judges of trial courts and intermediate appellate courts, and the term "Justice" is used consistently for judges of state supreme courts and the U.S. Supreme Court. This usage contradicts correct form in New York State, but consistency seems to me a more important value. Indeed, I was tempted to use "judge" for all judges, following the precedent of Charles Warren's classic study *The Supreme Court in United States History*, but newspaper pressure is too great for that.

A single convenient term for a kind of court—juvenile, family, probate, criminal, civil, supreme, small claims—has been applied throughout, except where the reference is to a specific incident, when the local term ("Recorder's in Detroit, "Surrogate's" in New York, etc.) seems required to avoid local confusion. Similarly, "state" has been used throughout, though some states are "commonwealths." Where membership in the bar association is compulsory, the words "state bar" have been used; where it is voluntary, the words "bar association."

Bibliographical notes are in the rear. As the notes deal exclusively with the provenance of the quotations and statistics, the pages of the book have not been pimpled with superscript numbers, and the citations are identified in the notes by the key phrase. Virtually all quotes appearing without citation are from interviews or personal correspondence.

4

I am deeply grateful to the many lawyers whose names appear in the succeeding pages, and almost as grateful to many others whose names do not appear. I owe special thanks to several men who introduced me to lawyers in their areas, and helped me organize my time: to Felix Stumpf of the California Continuing Education of the Bar project; the late Professor Harold W. Solomon of the University of Southern California; Professor Morris Janowitz of the Sociology Department of the University of Chicago; Victor Collette of the New Hampshire Council on World Affairs; James Milani of Centerville, Iowa; Rufus Poole of Albuquerque, New Mexico; Richard A. Green of the ABA Project on Minimum Standards for the Administration of Criminal Justice; Norris Darrell, Leo Gottlieb, Paul DeWitt, Sidney Faber, Stuart Speiser and

Monroe Singer of New York. I hope they are not unhappy about the results.

I am grateful, too, but for much more than merely his help with this book, to John Cancian of Boston, a partner in the firm of Bingham, Dana & Gould, a dear friend for twenty-three years, a man of vast charm and life-enhancing gusto, who had beaten off polio and all resentment of the need to walk on crutches, who loved the battles of the trial court and was achieving full maturity as a counselor when he was killed in an automobile accident on January 20, 1967. None will forget who ever enjoyed the pleasure of his company.

I should like to pay separate tribute to several men whose writings served as a continuing and invaluable guide after my interviews with them were over: to Chief Justice Roger J. Traynor of the California supreme court; Judge Henry J. Friendly of the federal Court of Appeals for the Second Circuit; Judge Giles Rich of the Court of Customs and Patent Appeals; Commissioner Lee Loevinger of the Federal Communications Commission; Dean Francis A. Allen of the University of Michigan Law School; Professor Henry M. Hart, Jr. of Harvard; Professor Herbert Wechsler of Columbia; Professor Harry Kalven, Jr. of Chicago; and Professor Alexander Bickel of Yale. The number of those who gave me unusually cogent and valuable interviews is too large to permit a listing of names; but surely they know who they are, and I thank them. I am deeply grateful to the Association of the Bar of the City of New York for five years' use of its fine library.

The following have been kind enough to read some or all of this book for me in manuscript: Edward Q. Carr, Vern Countryman, Sidney Faber, Alfred W. Gans, Leo Gottlieb, Richard A. Green, Marc Gross, Geoffrey Hazard, Jr., Robert Hodes, Delmar Karlen, Lee Loevinger, David Riesman, Stuart Speiser, Felix Stumpf, Herbert Sturz and my father. Their generosity with their time and comments has saved me much embarrassment; and what embarrassment remains, of course, is my fault entirely—as are all the opinions.

Parts of Chapters 1 and 2 have appeared in *Esquire* Magazine; part of Chapter 3 in *Harper's Magazine*; parts of Chapters 5 and 6 in *The Saturday Evening Post*; part of Chapter 7 in *Redbook*;

part of Chapter 10 in *TV Guide*. Paragraphs from an earlier article for *The Saturday Evening Post* have been incorporated in several chapters. I am grateful to Harold Hayes, Jack Fischer, Otto Friedrich, Bud Hart and Roger Youman for their help and hospitalities—and to their magazines, of course, for releasing the material.

I am grateful again to Marguerite Munson of Harper & Row for her patience and charity and astonishing editorial skill; and always to my wife, for putting up with it, for the clarity of her intelligence, and for taking the time from her own work to fight about her husband's. My boys are now old enough that I can be grateful to them, too, for the good cheer with which they accepted all the dislocations created by Daddy's Book.

For those who know my parents, the reasons for the dedication will be immediately obvious; for those who do not, no explanation could be adequate.

MARTIN MAYER

PART I

IN GENERAL

CHAPTER 1

A NUMBER OF LAWYERS:
THE PROFESSION FROM
A DISTANCE

"True, we build no bridges. We raise no towers. We construct no engines. We paint no pictures—unless as amateurs for our own principal amusement. There is little of all that we do which the eye of man can see. But we smooth out difficulties; we relieve stress; we correct mistakes; we take up other men's burdens and by our efforts we make possible the peaceful life of men in a peaceful state."
—JOHN W. DAVIS

"All the attorneys I have ever seen have the same manner: hard, cold, incredulous, distrustful, sarcastic, sneering. They are said to be conversant with the worst part of human nature, and with the most discreditable transactions. They have so many falsehoods told them, that they place confidence in no one."
—LORD MELBOURNE

"I have a high opinion of lawyers. With all their faults, they stack up well against those in every other occupation or profession. They are better to work with or play with or fight with or drink with, than most other varieties of mankind."
—HARRISON TWEED

"But the lawyer is always in a hurry; there is the water of the clepsydra driving him on. . . . He is a servant, and is continually disputing about a fellow-servant before his master, who is seated, and has the cause in his hands; the trial is never about some indifferent matter, but always concerns himself; and often the race is for his life. The consequence has been, that he has become keen and shrewd; he has learned how to flatter his master in word and indulge him in deed; but his soul is small and unrighteous . . . from the first he has practiced deception and retaliation, and has become stunted and warped. And so he has passed out of youth into manhood, having no soundness in him; and is now, as he thinks, a master in wisdom. Such is the lawyer, Theodorus. . . ."

—PLATO

"I would rather have clients, than be somebody's lawyer."
—LOUIS D. BRANDEIS

1

A lawyer is a man carrying a briefcase, and in the briefcase there may even be a brief. There will certainly be legal-size paper, 8½ x 13, flimsy typed stuff stapled together through a blue backing, printed forms, lined yellow scratch pads, the top sheets already annotated with scrawled information, guidelines for the meeting to come, summaries of questions to ask, notes on facts or law already acquired somewhere.

The lawyer is not going about his own affairs: he is on a mission for someone else. Of all mankind, he is the most removed from what Kingman Brewster, Jr., president of Yale (and a former law professor), has called "that happiest figure in the law, a servant on a frolic of his own." Ontologically, the lawyer without clients does not exist. The lawyer is an "attorney"—that is, someone other people have "turned to" in the corruption of the law-French that came to English-speaking countries with the Normans. (In France the word is *"avocat,"* the "advocate," someone who speaks for someone else; the Anglo-American term, like the Anglo-American practice, is broader.) If no one turns to the lawyer, he finds another way to make a living; he ceases both in theory and in fact to be a lawyer—but not in form, because admission to the practice of law is good for life unless specifically revoked. (In some states a lawyer must pay annual dues to the state bar.) The monumental annual Martindale-Hubbell *Law Directory* defines a lawyer simply as a "person who has been admitted to practice in one of the states or the District of Columbia." A few years ago, in one of their periodic looks around, the editors discovered they were including a few people they hadn't really thought of as lawyers, like Branch Rickey and Lanny Ross.

Admission to practice is, simply, the privilege of participating in an almost exclusive right to manipulate one of the three coordinate branches of government. (The right is *almost* exclusive because anyone can go to court by himself—*in proprio persona,* or "pro se," as the lingo has it. He just doesn't have much chance of winning, because he doesn't know what the court is looking for.) The privilege is granted in each state for that state only, by the courts themselves, in recent years on a highly routinized basis, following certification by "bar examiners" whom the judges (at least formally) appoint. There is no other way in—for a while legislatures used to admit people to practice by passing private laws for their benefit, but the courts in most states have ruled that such laws are void— and there isn't anything much the legislatures can do about it unless they abolish the bar examination altogether.

From the fertile soil of this privilege to enforce the law on a client's behalf springs the entire lush garden of the lawyer's work. Wherever there is a human activity that may produce disputes that a court is empowered to settle—between heirs about a will, landlord and tenant, driver and pedestrian, husband and wife, buyer and seller, the state and its citizens—only a lawyer can give people that confidence in the security of their positions that most of them need if they are to function effectively in a time of stress.

Because the world is a chancy place (and nobody knows it better than the lawyer, who sees lots of his clients lose), there are limits to the security the lawyer can offer: "Why are you lawyers always so *equivocal?*" a lady impatiently asked a New Hampshire practitioner, and turned away in disgust when he replied, cheerfully, "Oh,

I don't know about that." Any good advice must often be negative: "About half the practice of a decent lawyer," Elihu Root once said, "consists in telling would-be clients that they are damned fools and should stop." Ideally, as Justice Felix Frankfurter once put it, echoing Justice Louis D. Brandeis, "A lawyer is a counselor, an adviser. He isn't just a hired man to do the bidding of his clients, but he must exert the independence of his mind and understanding upon the conduct of his client's business."

Most clients, of course, do not want such services at all. Their attitude is that which God proposed as proper in the relationship between Moses and Aaron: "And he shall be thy spokesman unto the people: and he shall be, even he shall be to thee instead of a mouth, and thou shalt be to him instead of God." There is something they wish to do—or something they are afraid will happen to them—and they want the lawyer to take care of it. They expect him to be on their side; and they are forever asking him to do things he can't (maybe won't) do: Eugene Rostow, formerly dean of the Yale Law School, says that lawyers like to work in Washington (which has about five times as many lawyers per capita as any other city in the country) not for love of practice before federal agencies but "because they don't have to see their clients." Even in cases where nothing is involved but a business contract, the client's emotional demands may be heavy. Where someone has suffered a personal injury in an accident, a high order of sympathy must be displayed; and in domestic relations the demands may be even heavier. As a divorce specialist said to the sociologist Hubert J. O'Gorman, "The woman in many cases hasn't anyone else to talk to. The husband may have been the only man in her life, even though he was no good. You are her defender. She is grateful, lonely, and, if you are lucky, she's ugly."

Because of his sympathy for his client (naturally felt, because he is so much closer to his client's side of the story, or forced, because his client is the one who pays his bills), the lawyer is rarely conscious of the face he turns to the outside world. For in fact he is not merely helping his client; he is harming his client's adversary. "The bringing in of a lawyer," says Geoffrey Hazard, Jr., the young executive director of the American Bar Foundation, "is like bringing up the tanks—it's a violent threat." To the opponent, the lawyer is simply a symbol of the fact that someone "called the law on me"—a law which compels, which does not from the loser's point of view provide a just result, from which there is no escape. (Sometimes, amusingly, unsophisticated lawyers see this aspect of their role only too clearly: Justice Michael Musmanno of Pennsylvania has written of his distaste for "breaking bread" with the lawyer on the other side, who is "deliberately seeking to injure my client.") At the very least, the man who gets himself a lawyer forces his opponent to get a lawyer of his own, an expense that may be far out of proportion to the stakes in the dispute. And "he that goes to law," as Burton wrote in *Anatomy of Melancholy,* "has a wolf by the ears."

The lawyers, it is held, know too much; they can twist the system to get things done that ought not to be done. The Philadelphia lawyer and Senator George Wharton Pepper wrote of John C. Johnson, perhaps his most eminent colleague, that he took "an impish delight in successfully making the worse appear the better reason." (This is the same Johnson who turned down an appointment to the U.S. Supreme Court with the words, "I would rather talk to the damned fools than listen to them.") More's Utopia had no lawyers. George Washington in his will provided that any dispute over its contents was to be resolved by a panel of three arbitrators, who would not hear lawyers. Rhode Island, while a colony, tried the experiment of prohibiting lawyers from membership in the legislature. The constitution of the Illinois Grange in 1872 provided that anyone could be a member except actors, gamblers and lawyers. A nineteenth-century dictionary explained that a "lake-lawyer" fish got its name from its "ferocious look and voracious habits." Carl Sandburg put the Western attitude most savagely:

> . . . When the lawyers are through
> What is there left, Bob?
> Can a mouse nibble at it
> And find enough to fasten a tooth in?
>
> Why is there always a secret singing
> When a lawyer cashes in?

Why does a hearse horse snicker
Hauling a lawyer away?

> The work of a bricklayer goes to the blue.
> The knack of a mason outlasts a moon.
> The hands of a plasterer hold a room together,
> The land of a farmer wishes him back again.
> > Singers of songs and dreamers of plays
> > Build a house no wind blows over.
> The lawyers—tell me why a hearse horse snickers
> > hauling a lawyer's bones.

And the attitude persists. "I always used to stay at the same place," says Arthur Godfrey on a radio show, talking about himself and a hotel in Miami Beach. "Used to own a piece of it."

"Not any more?" says his interlocutor.

"You know how it is—eventually the lawyer gets everything. So now the lawyer owns the hotel."

These views are not necessarily the product of ignorance. Public opinion polls invariably show that people who have had occasion to be represented by a lawyer think less well of the profession than people who have never hired legal services. Of those laymen interviewed in a Missouri bar study who said their opinions rested on their experiences in court, less than one-third had emerged with a favorable attitude. A survey by Columbia's Bureau of Applied Social Research, sponsored by the Association of the Bar of the City of New York, showed that people who had once gone to a lawyer for help with a personal-injury claim were more likely to try to handle the claim themselves if they ever got into another accident—and the higher the income and education bracket, the more likely they were to avoid a lawyer the second time. For a while in 1966, the best-selling nonfiction book was a faintly preposterous collection of forms, by no means equally usable in all states, compiled by a mutual-fund salesman named Norman F. Dacey and entitled *How to Avoid Probate*. Especially in the light of Jessica Mitford's far superior style and sense of fun, the fact that this essentially technical tome has outsold *The American Way of Death* argues strongly that middle-class people who have lived through a death in their family feel even more suspicious of lawyers than they do of undertakers.

Much of the unpopularity of the lawyer simply reflects his proprietorship of a mystery—all professions, as Bernard Shaw once put it, are conspiracies against the layman, and are perceived as such. "Does your heart warm to the surgeon," Karl Llewellyn once asked Columbia Law School students, "as he draws on his rubber gloves and asks you whom to notify?" Much of what remains is resentment of the constraints of law, because law makes people do things they don't want to do and keeps them from doing as they please—and any direct involvement with the legal process, from a traffic ticket to an antitrust suit, will devour time for which the layman is not paid and the lawyer is. The client's disaster is often the lawyer's bonanza: the best years for lawyers as a class, relating their income to incomes in general, were 1930 and 1931 (then the lawyers too began to suffer, perhaps more grievously than anyone else, from the Depression). "Blessed," says the old legal adage, "are the troublemakers." Anything that involves appearance in court, even by a winner, will be more or less traumatic: "[A]s a litigant," Judge Learned Hand once said, "I should dread a lawsuit beyond almost anything else short of sickness and death."

Suspicion and dread are, of course, only one corner of the story. The respondents in the Missouri survey who had a low opinion of lawyers in general mostly thought their own lawyer was capable and honest; the middle-class New Yorkers who tried to handle their own accident claims dealt cheerfully enough with other lawyers in their business life. If lawyers seems to make trouble, they also ease it; disturbed people in this society are probably more likely to go to a lawyer for advice than to a clergyman or a psychiatrist, though this preference is dying—older people are much more likely to feel it than younger people. As the new law offices in the poverty program are discovering, the average American brings with him on his first trip to a lawyer's office a fearfully flattering notion of what a lawyer can do for him.

Another tradition is operative, too. "In America," Tocqueville wrote in the 1830s, at the height of the Jacksonian effort to disseise the legal profession, "there are no nobles or literary men, and the people are apt to mistrust the wealthy; lawyers consequently form the highest political class and the most cultivated portion of society.

... If I were asked where I place the American aristocracy, I should reply without hesitation that it is not among the rich, who are united by no common tie, but that it occupies the judicial bench and the bar." Having devised the trust, the institution by which property is held and managed by one person entirely for the benefit of another, lawyers are the nation's trustees, carriers of the burden of good faith that makes a human society something more than a monkey house; and violations of such "fiduciary" obligations are among the rarest crimes.

Lawyers are community leaders throughout the land: they serve on (often chair) the boards of trustees of our educational institutions, museums, orchestras, hospitals; they donate their services to charities, to civil liberties causes, to the defense of poor people charged with crime (even where courts have budgets to pay lawyers assigned to such work, the payments typically cover 10 percent or less of what this kind of case costs a successful corporate lawyer). Most remarkable, perhaps, is the service to the law itself—the unpaid work as an arbitrator, the teaching of practical courses for young lawyers, the articles for law reviews, the endless committee meetings at the bar associations. "I estimate," George Wharton Pepper wrote in 1944, "that through the years about half of the whole amount of my activity has been gratuitous nonlegal service to the Church, to the University, to the Profession, to the Community, and to individuals; and that of the other half, which represents my legal work, about a quarter has been done without charge."

Not all this activity is entirely disinterested. In the words of *A Lawyer's Practice Manual* (a book enthusiastically endorsed on publication by the then president of the American Bar Association), "The corporation president with whom you work on the orphan's milk fund drive may soon need a lawyer. If you impressed him favorably and gained his liking in your work together on the charity drive, he may decide you are just the man to handle the important transaction his corporation is going to undertake." Still, even lawyers who when young look for charitable labors only to help them build a practice usually get bit by the bug of social utility (or just prominence), and give much more than they receive.

Lawyers are the great public servants of America: as Dean Erwin

Griswold of Harvard has put it, they "carry a large part of the load of self-government in the United States." The late Robert P. Patterson liked to say that when he went to Washington to work in the War Department, shortly before the Second World War, "the entire membership on the secretary level was made up of lawyers."

"If you take someone into international work from the American civil service," says Francis Wolf, general counsel for the International Labor Organization in Geneva, "seventy percent of the time you get a lawyer; from the English civil service, seventy percent of the time it's someone from history or literature or classics." The French financier and international organizer Jean Monnet once noted, according to Dean Acheson, that American corporate lawyers "seemed peculiarly able to understand at once the uniqueness of unprecedented situations and immediately to set about devising new and practical ways of dealing with them."

John J. McCloy, who was U.S. High Commissioner in Germany as well as chairman of the Chase-Manhattan Bank and a partner in the Wall Street firm of Milbank, Tweed, has listed the lawyer's advantages in the "extracurricular" world:

> He has learned to gauge human emotions and to make due allowance for them, for in his practice he has seen them flare and subside; his training has taught him the practical necessity at least of assessing the other side's point of view if not of conceding its merit; it has similarly given him the ability to judge what are the important and what the less significant facts of a situation. I think that practice in explaining matters clearly and concisely and in drafting documents which are to be read and understood by others, sometimes others at a far removed point of time as in the case of a will or deed, also has important use in these situations. . . .
>
> The lawyer who has faced the give and take of the courtroom, who has debated before the appellate court with lawyers of equal skill and resourcefulness, or who has run the gamut of conferences with counsel for opposing sides has usually a rich background with which to face [the negative comments] of public life.

Also, McCloy noted, somewhat grimly, "Those in government and business who are responsible for final decision come to place heavy reliance upon one who has trained himself and accustomed himself, and, I may add, his wife, to the habit of irregular hours."

Twenty-three of the thirty-six Presidents have been lawyers, and half of the governors elected since the Civil War; and lawyers account consistently for about 60 percent of the U.S. Senators and Representatives. Again, the question is more complicated than apologists for the profession sometimes say. The American tradition permitted men in public office to continue in the practice of law (Lincoln maintained his law partnership while he was President). As is often demonstrated when a lawyer-politician dies and his estate is admitted to probate, public service does not inevitably involve a financial sacrifice for a lawyer. Prosecuting attorneys in all but four states are permitted to retain private practice. In 1958 a county attorney in New Mexico (unsuccessfully) sued his county to compel it to pay him fees for legal advice on a bond issue, on the grounds that such advice was part of his private practice. "Around here," says a lawyer in rural Iowa, "the county attorney gets most of the divorce business."

When the renewal of the charter of the Second Bank of the United States was pending before Congress, Senator Daniel Webster wrote his client Nicholas Biddle, president of the Bank (for which Webster had tried and won forty-one cases before the Supreme Court), "I believe my retainer has not been renewed or *refreshed* as usual. If it be wished that my relation to the Bank should be continued, it may be well to send me the usual retainer." There probably would not be anything as raw as this in the correspondence of today's Senators and Representatives, but the spirit of Daniel Webster is by no means dead. Most lawyers do take a financial licking, however, when appointed to office in the executive branch, because here Congress requires that all private connections be severed, to avoid any possible "conflict of interest."

In the words of Elihu Root, who was in and out of public office at considerable cost to himself throughout a long life, law is a "public profession." Institutionally, there are the hundred New York law firms each of which volunteered a man when the Supreme Court ruled that every convict was entitled to one appeal as a matter of right, and the dozens which responded to a plea from President Kennedy to send men south so the civil rights demonstrators would not lack counsel. Privately, there are the individuals who went on their own from Wall Street and LaSalle Street, taking a summer month in the unbearable heat of Mississippi because they knew that just the presence of a lawyer, even if he couldn't practice in the state courts, would give the yahoos pause.

The leaders of the bar, which does not necessarily mean the presidents of the bar associations, have mostly been men of quite extraordinary probity and dedication. If one must note William Nelson Cromwell of Wall Street requesting close to a million dollars from the company that built the Panama Canal for his services in persuading Theodore Roosevelt to back the company-sponsored independence movement in Panama, one must also observe Henry L. Stimson of Wall Street as Secretary of State refusing to look at the information gathered from breaking the Japanese code, on the grounds that "gentlemen do not read each other's mail"; and Charles Evans Hughes of Wall Street suing on behalf of the five Socialists denied their seats in the New York State Assembly; and John W. Davis braving the American Legion to demand citizenship for an immigrant lady who said she would not bear arms in defense of the United States; and Stephen Strong Gregory of LaSalle Street demanding habeas corpus to prevent the execution of the poor lunatic who had murdered Chicago Mayor Carter Harrison in the aftermath of the Haymarket Riots; and Joseph Welch of Federal Street putting his head in the mouth of Joe McCarthy, not only donating his time but paying his own expenses between Boston and Washington to restore decency to American government.

Even Carl Sandburg, feeling all the savagery of his poem, made an exception for Abraham Lincoln.

2

Give or take some tens of thousands of men now doing other things or more or less retired, there are 300,000 lawyers in the United States—one for every 250 of the labor force. No other nation has anything like so many lawyers, either in absolute numbers or in proportion to population. "Our society, now more than ever," Felix Frankfurter wrote shortly before his retirement from the Supreme Court, "is a legal state in the sense that almost everything that takes place will sooner or later raise legal questions." Great

Britain, whence so much of our law and so many of our legal attitudes derive, has one-quarter our population and only one-tenth as many lawyers.

About three-quarters of the active lawyers are "in practice"—the place where they work has their name on the front door, they represent clients, and presumably they live on their fees. The presumption, however, is often false. "In the real small towns," says Perkins Bass of Peterborough, New Hampshire, a sophisticate, once a Congressman, Republican National Committeeman and candidate for the Senate, "the lawyers are also insurance men, real-estate men. It all works together—he does the real-estate deal, searches the title, and his agency writes the insurance."

The late Charles Belous of New York once estimated that "at least 75% of the attorneys who have made substantial monies during their practice have done so strictly outside of their law work. Either they dabbled in real estate, stocks, some business venture of an impecunious client who subsequently made good, or in a defunct corporation subsequently reorganized and revived by some client's business genius." Norman Bingham, one of the founders of the large Boston firm of Bingham, Dana & Gould, liked to tell of an incident in his early practice when a friend in Detroit sent him a collection job, and when he collected told him that the client was poor—would you like to take some of his stock, or he can afford $50. Bingham took the $50, and the client's name, of course, was Henry Ford. Many lawyers have similar stories, but they don't always tell about the times they took the stock.

The other quarter of the active lawyers are employed, two-fifths of them by private interests (in positions ranging from president of the company to claims investigator), three-fifths by the government (as judges or prosecutors or legislators or at agencies, in states and cities, boards of education or water supply and so forth). The fastest-growing category of lawyer is the "corporate house counsel," whose work is often indistinguishable from that of the lawyer in an office, except that his only client is his employer. Indeed, his internal office communications are privileged: the normally confidential relationship of lawyer and client will be protected by the courts even within the walls of the company. A federal court, refusing to give the government access to an employed lawyer's memoranda, noted that the only "apparent factual differences between these house counsel and outside counsel are that the former are paid annual salaries, occupy offices in the corporation's buildings, and are employees rather than independent contractors. . . . The distinction is chiefly that the house counsel gives advice to one regular client, the outside counsel to several regular clients." This is probably a little strong, though some house counsel enjoy a very variegated practice—especially in those companies (like Prudential Insurance, with 150 men in its Law Department and a law library of more than 40,000 volumes) where management encourages its lawyers to keep a small private practice on the side to handle the personal problems of employees. Job and income security in these positions is virtually total, which may mean, as a report by two law school professors recently suggested, that "the minimum tolerable level of performance is rather low—one house counsel said that in order to be fired in his department, a lawyer would have to be caught raping his secretary."

The practice of law in the United States is sliced geographically fine. Admission to the bar is good only in one state; people who wish to move must make new arrangements, and sometimes it isn't easy (the requirements are particularly brutal in Florida). To appear for your client in the courts of another state, you must normally retain a local man to be "attorney of record," to whom you are officially a mere associate. Even if you are admitted in both states, you may be excluded: Kansas, barring from its courts a lawyer who was also admitted in Missouri and maintained offices in both states, has ruled that nobody who practices in any other state can also practice in Kansas. The basic subdivision is the county, with its county courthouse in its county seat. The geographical divisions help protect the local lawyers, who can often, however, take good care of themselves. "In a little state like this," says a New Hampshire lawyer, "if you show up with New York counsel, well, my God . . ." In Pennsylvania, until 1965, lawyers had to be admitted separately to practice in each county; in Indiana, still, the state legislature through budgetary control forces lawsuits outside of Indianapolis and into the counties.

Law looks like a highly urban profession—and, of course, even a small county seat is a population center for its area. But the law is by no means an exclusively big-city profession; nearly one-half the nation's practitioners have their offices in cities and towns with under 200,000 population, while fewer than 40 percent work in cities with a population of 500,000 or more. These proportions have remained stable for at least a dozen years. Many a town that has severe problems finding itself a dentist will have two or three lawyers in residence.

Law is not a young man's profession: there are more lawyers over seventy than there are lawyers under thirty, and the median age is about forty-seven. Lawyers are eligible for the "Junior Bar Conference" of the American Bar Association up to the age of thirty-six.

About one lawyer in forty is female; less than one in a hundred is Negro. More than a fifth are Jewish; in New York City more than three-fifths are Jewish.

Internal Revenue Service data from 1963 (the most recent year available at this writing) show 132,891 solo lawyers and 21,418 law firms filing tax reports. Ten of the firms had gross incomes of more than $5 million; 164 grossed between $1 million and $5 million; and 1,985 between $200,000 and $1 million. Four solo practitioners grossed more than $1 million, 43,078 grossed less than $5,000. Almost 12,000 soloists and 1,500 partnerships lost money. Of those with net profits, almost exactly two-thirds showed expenses which were less than half their income, and one-third expenses which were more than half their income.

The median income of the individual lawyer in 1966 was probably about $13,000, which is generally regarded as unsatisfactory—and all such figures, of course, conceal wide disparities within the profession. Vast ranges of income have always characterized the law: in the 1850s, when most lawyers made less than $1,000 a year, William Evarts in New York and Judah Benjamin in New Orleans earned $50,000 a year—as lawyers. (Evarts' income became part of the inheritance of his grandson, Harrison Tweed, a national figure at the bar, perhaps the best-loved lawyer in the generation which started practice in the 1910s.)

Offices vary accordingly, from the magnificence of professionally decorated tower suites in the newest skyscrapers to second-floor rooms above the drugstore that once were and may be again home to a small pool parlor. Particularly in new suburbs and near the criminal courts, lawyers who seek a transient trade use store-front offices, the plate-glass windows revealing a receptionist and an impressive if obviously unused array of old lawbooks. In San Francisco, in an old converted beer hall, the window yields a view of Melvin Belli himself, busy at his desk. A few large firms (the most striking is Washington's Arnold & Porter) have purchased and converted to elegant offices former private mansions not far from the business district.

Lawyers who are in practice by themselves average only about half as much income as lawyers who are part of a partnership. (Both Jews and Catholics, incidentally, are more likely to be "solo practitioners"; and Negroes are rarely anything else.) Though there is a point of diminishing returns, because of the difficulty of controlling costs in very large law offices (an Indiana study in 1963 showed that the optimum firm—the one with the lowest ratio of overhead to fees—was four lawyers), up to twenty-five lawyers or so it is almost universally true that the larger the firm, the higher the income of its partners. In his large-scale survey of the New York bar, Jerome Carlin (a politically minded sociologist who was trained as a lawyer) found that 70 percent of the partners in firms with fifteen lawyers or more earned at least $35,000 a year, while only 11 percent of the solo practitioners hit that figure. Since World War II there has been an accelerating trend toward partnership rather than solo practice, and at some point before 1970 the balance will tip for the first time in the nation's history in favor of the partner and the employed "associate" in his firm.

Law partnerships were a creation of the American nineteenth century (in Britain's bifurcated legal profession, barristers are not permitted to have permanent associations of this sort, though solicitors are). At first they were two-man operations, yielding the convenience of an "office lawyer" (the British solicitor) and a "court lawyer" (the barrister), but with the growth of industry, and particularly with the bankruptcy of the streetcar companies at the turn of the century, clients' problems grew too complicated for any individual to handle. By the mid-1960s there were fifty or so law firms

with more than fifty lawyers, about half of them in New York. Up
to the 1950s the ratio in such firms was normally one partner to
three or four "associates," usually young lawyers, though senior
associates are by no means unknown. With the competition for legal
talent that has characterized the 1960s, the ratio has been changing
to meet the demand of law school seniors for something better than
the one-in-ten chance for a partnership that used to characterize
these offices. Many large firms are now nearing (a few have passed)
the point where there are as many partners as associates—though it
should be kept in mind that the word "partner," like the words
"vice president" in an advertising agency, may cover a fairly junior
and essentially salaried person who has a title rather than a real
share of the proceeds.

The institution of the law partnership is among the most
attractive aspects of the profession. Lawyers who will prepare
sixty-page contracts for their clients (because they know that businessmen can't be trusted) will organize their own office on a scrib-
bled piece of notepaper that may not even be signed by anybody
(because they know they can trust their partners). Daniel J. Cantor,
a management consultant specializing in the problems of law firms,
says that 55 percent of the nation's law partnerships have no written
agreement whatever. Law firms do break up, sometimes because two
clients come into conflict with each other and neither of the partners
who have primary responsibilities for these clients is willing to give
up his friend, more often because there are disagreements about the
proper division of the firm's income. (The dispute is usually between
the man who brings in the business and the man who does the
work.) But many law partnerships endure for the professional lifetimes of their members, who come to know each other in breadth
and depth, through one of the most intimate relationships known
to a commercial society. "I can't talk to my friends in other firms
about how they handle some of these questions," says a young
partner saddled for a term with management responsibilities in a
Boston firm; "it would be like asking them how their wife was in
bed."

"It's a real brotherhood," the Bostonian Reginald Heber Smith
said shortly before his death in 1966. He was the theoretician of the

profession and doyen of its missions to the lay public; he first came to prominence half a century ago as the author of a book on *Justice and the Poor*, and he always and hugely enjoyed the practice of law. "A man loses a father or a sister or a child, he's back in the office the next day, because he knows he'll get sympathy. Your liability is unlimited: any one of my partners [in Hale & Dorr, Boston's second or third largest firm] could bankrupt me today. And I've never lost a moment's sleep about it."

Oddly, the question of whether lawyers in a community practice as soloists or as partners is a matter of historical accident. The states where lawyers are most likely to be partners are Alabama, Idaho, Iowa, Louisiana, Nebraska, New Hampshire, North Carolina, Washington and Wyoming. The states where lawyers are most likely to be operating alone are Alaska, Arkansas, California, Hawaii, Kentucky, Maine, Maryland, Massachusetts, Michigan, New Jersey, New York, Oklahoma, Rhode Island, Texas and Vermont.

3

Department of Commerce figures indicate that more than $4 billion were spent in 1966 for legal services. It is almost unbelievable, but true, that nobody has any very precise notion of what is done for the money. A relatively few large offices, using computer systems, know where their fees come from and where their money goes, but many law firms—even law firms with a dozen partners—are run like a momma-poppa store. Even so simple a question as which lines are profitable is often beyond the resources of the accounting system. A Maryland "Economic Survey" concluded that most of the lawyers interviewed "were not even able to make an educated guess with respect to the number of hours they worked."

Since the early 1950s a few state bar associations have tried to do simple statistical compilations of the profession's activities, and their appropriations for this purpose have been enough to support the small management consulting firm of Daniel J. Cantor, who also edits a quarterly magazine on *Law Office Economics and Management*. A reasonable guess at the sources of lawyers' income would be that roughly two-fifths come from commercial operations (from vetting mortgages for banks and collecting debts to making mergers and fighting antitrust suits), and three-fifths from private parties (mostly claims for personal injuries, personal real-estate transactions, divorce suits and the creation and management of wills and estates).

Legal services are sold on three different bases—by the hour, by the job or as a proportion of the amount of money involved in the matter. Many large law firms bill by the hour, with a time charge which is some multiple of the actual cost to the firm. Associates cost the client three times their hourly salary (calculated at 1,500 hours a year); partners about 1.5 times their anticipated hourly income (calculated at 1,000 hours a year). The result of the arithmetic is a "profit hourly cost rate." A senior partner in one the largest of the Wall Street firms recently told a seminar that "A number of the firms have nicknamed the profit hourly cost rate 'progress,' and in those firms 'progress' is their most important product."

Billing by the hour requires record-keeping of the highest quality; a managing partner in a Wall Street firm with about fifty lawyers says his office must sort and bill 100,000 items a year. Hours may appear in quarters or as six-minute bits, because one-tenth is an easy fraction to work with, and for each of these six-minute periods each lawyer (and in firms which bill clients for stenographic services each secretary) is supposed to keep an accurate diary of telephone calls, letters dictated, cases looked up in the library, as well as meetings, court appearances, etc. In the big firms the charge for the time of a young associate runs about $30 an hour; for a young partner, about $50; for an older partner, what the traffic will bear—which can be quite spectacular for defeated presidential candidates, former Attorneys General or other cabinet officers, ex-Senators and the like.

Clients are not normally informed of the breakdown by lawyer in their bills; rates are averaged out and even a detailed bill will show, say, $15,247.70 for 412.1 hours of lawyers' time at $37 an hour. Partners of large law firms hope to get 1,500 to 1,600 billable hours from associates, 1,000-1,300 from partners, every year. Given 10 holidays, a 48-week year and a 35-hour week, 1,600 would mean a bill for every working minute, which cannot be achieved; so associates in firms which intend this target seriously are worked on a 50-

hour week. Getting partners to keep really detailed time records is by no means easy. "We talk about it frequently at the firm lunch," one partner told his seminar audience, "and find that by criticizing the younger men whose diaries are not in on time, we generally get through to the senior partners."

As a practical matter, most lawyers who work alone or in two-man partnerships cannot count on more than 1,200 billable hours a year. Recommending minimum fee schedules to their members, most state bar associations set $20 as a rock-bottom figure per hour, and some have gone to $25. Many lawyers representing little people, however, can't get that much and won't try. "Take an ordinary farmer," says Robert Valentine of Centerville, Iowa; "five dollars an hour sounds like a lot to him." Lawyers dealing with private problems, moreover, must take a lot of time finding out from prospective clients whether in fact they have any services to offer. It's hard to bill much for these first preliminary visits; and if the upshot is that the lawyer *can't* help, it's hard to bill (or collect) anything at all. Most lawyers can expect that about 5 percent of their bills won't be paid. They can sue for their fees and sometimes do—but, of course, it's terrible publicity.

Small businessmen and plain people usually prefer to deal with a lawyer on the basis of a flat fee for a specified job. The criminal defendant, the home buyer, the man drawing up his will, the couple adopting a child, the inventor seeking a patent, the storekeeper incorporating—all know in advance how much their lawyer is going to cost them for this specific job (the criminal defendant will have to pay in advance, too). Surprisingly often, lawyers will set a flat fee on such potentially time-consuming business as handling a matter—a contested application, say, for a broadcasting license—before a federal regulatory agency; but the thought here is that the price can be renegotiated if the job turns sticky.

For such work, too, the state bar associations have been adopting minimum fee schedules—$150 to $250 for uncontested divorces or adoptions, $15 to $75 for drawing up a lease on residential property, $25 to $50 for drawing up a simple will, $200 to $300 for incorporating the grocer (or disincorporating him, or superintending his bankruptcy). These schedules are practical matters in many law offices;

they are widely (and probably correctly) regarded as the best way to avoid arguments with clients, particularly before the client is securely in hand (and hard experience has convinced the profession that fees should be established in advance). "If packaging is important for commodities," *A Lawyer's Practice Manual* suggests, "it certainly should be for the fee schedule. A fee schedule should be in an attractive folder, preferably evidencing a degree of dignity and substance. A black leather cover with gold lettering, or even a dignified, all-black cover, is more desirable than a plain, though neat, paper cover. The appearance of the schedule will add to its prestige and importance or detract from it in the eyes of the client. . . ." Another authority advises the practical lawyer to study Internal Revenue Service rulings about tax deductions for legal fees, "not only because he should know the law, but also because his chances of collecting the fee are greatly enhanced if the client is advised of this Government subsidy."

The aim of the fee schedule is to prevent that "shopping around" among lawyers which many regard as the reason why the legal profession has failed to keep pace with the doctors in income growth over the last generation. The schedules are probably not enforceable, though the question may come up some day in the twenty-six or twenty-seven states which have an "integrated bar," an association to which every lawyer in the state must belong, by law. Setting its schedule in 1961, the state bar of New Mexico commented: "[I]f the lawyer sets a fee below the minimums here adopted, he is acting either with reckless disregard of the costs of operating a respectable law office or he will have a strong determination to cut corners, thus endangering the rights of his client and bringing further economic chaos to the profession as a whole." An ABA pamphlet has said that "the lawyer member who consistently undercuts the schedule" may be engaged in "solicitation of employment on a basis not ethical under Canon 12." In Wisconsin the state supreme court has taken judicial notice of the minimum fee schedule, but no one has ever been punished for its violation.

In one way or another, despite schedules of hourly charges and minimum fees, the lawyer's income from any matter tends to be a function of the amount of money involved. Such proportionate shares are often set by statute. Seeing an estate through a probate court, for example, normally calls for

> 7% of the first $1,000
> 5% on the next $4,000
> 4% on the next $10,000
> 3% on the next $60,000
> 2½% on balance over $75,000.

This is primarily an accounting job, involving accurate listing and appraisal of the assets in the estate, and the fee of $2,470 on an estate of $75,000 is a profitable piece of legal business. Where the estate runs to $1 million, the fee on such a schedule (normally enacted as a maximum, but serving also as a minimum) will be almost $26,000, often with not much work to do for it. From the point of view of the beneficiaries, this initial lawyer's fee may be only the beginning, because the estate will also have fees for other administrators and for special guardians appointed by the court to take care of the interests of minors, and perhaps for others (including, sometimes, a lawyer who brought suit to break the will, for his services in clearing up confusion). Thus the willingness of lawyers to write wills for very low fees (and to prepare people's tax returns for virtually nothing) in expectation that they will work on the probate of the estate. Thus, too, the popularity of Dacey's *How to Avoid Probate* (which, in fairness, mostly echoes with new and nasty overtones criticism of the current probate system published by the ABA itself).

Fees will also be set as a percentage of value in real-estate work—where, for example, in upstate New York, a lawyer will receive one percent of the mortgage for his labors in searching the title to the property. In divorces judges usually award lawyers a percentage of a settlement—probably ten weeks' alimony; both the wife's and the husband's lawyer will receive the same percentage, and the husband pays for both. (This is not always understood: in a circuit court in Detroit, a judge sits in front of a curved marble wall on which is inscribed, "THE BUSINESS OF THE JUDICIAL PROCESS IS TO ENFORCE OUR AMERICAN SENSE OF FAIR PLAY," and explains to a young Negro that he must indeed pay $150 to his ex-wife's lawyer: "It may not be fair, but that's our law.")

In collection cases lawyers generally receive a proportion of the recoveries (the Commercial Law League of America recommends 18 percent on the first $500, 15 percent on the next $500 and 10 percent on everything over $1,000). In condemnation proceedings, where a government is trying to take over somebody's land for a highway or a school or some other public purpose, the lawyer's fee can be as high as 50 percent of the difference between the original offer made by the government and the final award by the court. In tax cases the lawyer's fee is often a proportion of what the taxpayer saves.

Several of these examples present cases where the fee is not only proportional to the client's gain from the action but also contingent on his winning. Nothing about the practice of law in America is more surprising to lawyers elsewhere than the general approval of the "contingent fee," which in effect makes the lawyer a party to his client's action. This sort of fee comes up most often, of course, in connection with claims against somebody with insurance who has been negligent (in the glorious language of the law, a "tortfeasor") and has thereby "caused" an accident which produced personal injuries. Such fees range from 20 percent (the statutory maximum in claims against the federal government) up to 50 percent (after deduction of the lawyer's expenses). General opinion in the profession outside New York City seeems to be that fees in these matters should run one-quarter for a case settled before trial, one-third for a case that goes to trial, and two-fifths for a case taken on appeal. In New York, prior to the late 1950s, 50 percent was normal. The Appellate Division in the First Department (Manhattan and the Bronx) then established rules of court limiting the lawyers to a sliding scale which could go as high as 50 percent only in the smallest cases. Harry Gair, a peppery, aggressive, leather-skinned little man who has become one of the city's most successful negligence lawyers despite the fact that he never went to law school, claimed the Appellate Division had no authority to make such rules and took the question to the Court of Appeals, the state's highest court, which ruled against him.

There will be occasion later (see Chapter 7) to consider the morality, the utility and the future of the contingent fee; for now it is enough to observe that most legal fees are to some extent contingent. Even where time records are religiously kept, the partner responsible for handling the client simply will not permit his firm to charge a fee that yields the firm a profit when the result of the matter was a loss to the client. A lawyer at the PLI seminar referred to this problem as "the busted issue point. No one expects to bill at a normal margin when the merger falls through."

Income from the practice of law is always somewhat uncertain, even in the absence of contingent fees, because so much of the work is on a one-shot basis, with new clients every month. "The lawyer," says Felix Stumpf, Administrator of the Continuing Education of the Bar program in California, "is a little like a building contractor. He doesn't have an annual wage, so he charges too much for the jobs he gets, and takes too many jobs because he's afraid to turn things down." A New Hampshire lawyer, his chair surrounded by the debris of current cases, says, "You want the reservoir, and at the same time you want to convince the client you're working for him. So you're always putting out fires, which isn't good. One case may be worth ten thousand dollars, another one hundred and fifty—but if you're conscientious they both demand the same amount of work."

The incomes of even large law firms fluctuate considerably from year to year, but large firms tend to have continuing clients who can predict fairly well the volume of legal service they will require. Where these predictions can be made (or where a company wants to make sure it will have instant access to competent and informed outside legal advice), clients customarily pay their lawyers an annual "retainer," which will come into the office whether there is relatively little or (within limits) relatively much work to be done that year. Despite the security of the retainer, not every lawyer is entirely happy about the notion that he is committed in advance to defend whatever a client does, or about the dependence that can be the obverse of security. (The lawyer who might be willing to give up the client if it were only his own income at stake may also worry about what would be fair to his partners.) "Out here," says Judge Gibson C. Holliday of Des Moines, thinking back on his thirty-odd years of practice, "lawyers are very careful not to be married to a few particular clients. My firm used to turn down retainers for that reason."

A final source of income for individual lawyers, though obviously not for the profession as a whole, is the payment from one lawyer to another, for services rendered. All British barristers live on such payments: they have no relationship, financial or otherwise, with the people whose cases they argue in court; they look for their business and for their fees to the solicitors, who handle all dealings with clients. A few American trial lawyers, functioning essentially as barristers, will work on a similar basis, though they usually handle much more of the preparation of the cases themselves. (Defense counsel for insurance companies and assistant district attorneys prosecuting criminal cases will often work from a brief given them by, respectively, the claims department and the police.) The significant payments, however, go the other way: they are "forwarding fees," which a lawyer who does bill the client directly will pay to the lawyer who first sent the business his way. (Lawyers are absolutely forbidden to split fees with nonlawyers, though this cat has been known to be skinned.) The phenomenon is especially common in personal-injury lawsuits, where a garden-variety lawyer who finds himself with a potentially big case, because the victim is family or friends, will turn over all responsibility to a specialist who becomes the attorney of record entitled to the lawyer's share of the recovery. Normally, one-third of that lawyer's share will be funneled back to the lawyer who first found the client; and there are disturbing numbers of lawyers in most cities for whom this windfall referral fee, essentially an unearned increment, annually makes the difference between prosperity and despair.

CHAPTER 2

A NUMBER OF LAWYERS:

SKILLS AND FUNCTIONS

"You have everything that goes into life: they get married, get divorced, they have children, they buy property, they sign contracts. The law is the only profession I know of which is from before the cradle to after the grave. That's why it's such a satisfying way to spend a life."

> —MARTIN GANG of the California
> Bar, discussing a Hollywood
> practice

"Early in my career in government, I had the personal experience of seeing the distinguishing marks of a good lawyer manifest themselves graphically. I had worked hard on a problem, one I felt was important. I had worked out the law, but I was assailed by doubts of many kinds, and I had only a few minutes to explain all this to my boss as we walked down the corridor to a group meeting, outlining all that I could of the problem after my days of research and reflection. Troubled by my own doubts and misgivings, it seemed certain to me that my boss, after such a meager briefing, would not be able to handle the meeting. But it did not turn out that way at all, because this lawyer knew his trade. . . .

"He did not need to know the law until I told it to him, because a lawyer's judgment told him where he wanted to come out and a lawyer's skill told him how to get there. Judgment told him when to talk and when to keep quiet, what to emphasize and what to

[27]

de-emphasize, when to agree on a small point to win a big one, when to press and when to withdraw, which technicalities were important and which ones were not. By a lawyer's skills, he worked out the result and persuaded others to accept it."

—JOHN K. CARLOCK, Assistant
Secretary of the Treasury

"[O]ne can scarcely imagine a speaker at a meeting of a county medical society discussing the possible elimination of some disease by public health measures, and then qualifying his observations by the statement that many practitioners make a living out of treating the disease in question; and that unless the physicians are vigilant to prevent the adoption of such measures, this source of business will be taken from them. Yet speakers at bar association meetings are frequently heard to make similar observations about the effect of proposed reforms."

—PROFESSOR ARTHUR E. SUTHERLAND, JR.
of the Harvard Law School

1

Lawyers who have read this far may have found the preceding chapter distasteful, and perhaps shocking. The practice of law, they have been told since their first days in law school, is not a business but a profession; the lawyer's satisfactions come not from his income but from the services he renders. Yet by any objective criterion it is also true, as California's Felix Stumpf puts it, that "a lawyer's fee is the price of a commodity just as much as the numbers stamped on a can of beans are the price of a commodity." Somewhat more gently, Harrison Tweed once took occasion to remind the Association of the Bar of the City of New York that "the law is a profession, but its clients are also customers." Not the least handicap confronting anyone who seeks to get a grip on what lawyers do in this society is the failure of the profession to consider (as distinct from defend) its own economic foundation. "[L]awyers," as Tweed said, "should pay some attention to themselves and their brethren. As a generality they have failed to do so and with unfortunate consequences."

If discussion of the income sources fails to reveal what lawyers do to earn their fees, it is largely because lay ignorance and professional dignity have combined to make these two elements almost independent of each other. Easy jobs command high fees ("It's amazing," says a spokesman for a liability insurance group, "how much money a lawyer will think he's entitled to, just for writing a letter"), and hard jobs are done for relatively little money (by labor lawyers, for example, who will sit endless nights in negotiations and write incredibly detailed contracts as part of the service due under a modest monthly retainer). But it is also true that many (maybe most) lawyers would rather do the hard but interesting job for little than shovel in the fees by processing long chains of automobile accidents at intersections.

Lawyers' activities break down most conveniently into four categories: fighting, negotiating, securing and counseling. Not infrequently, all four skills are involved in a single job for a client; but few men are equally accomplished at all of them.

The fighter par excellence, of course, is the trial lawyer. "If you are not a fighter by disposition," the St. Louis lawyer Lon Hocker once told an American Bar Association meeting on trial tactics, "you should hire a fighter to try your cases." This is the lawyer of popular image: the man in court, questioning witnesses, objecting to another lawyer's questions, appealing to juries. And the courtroom is still the fundament of legal work. Once legal action has begun, only a court can end it: all the guilty pleas, negotiated settlements in personal injury cases, divorce arrangements, wills, agreements to drop the suit—all must be registered by a court, if only to make sure that the matter is really closed and cannot be started up again. The negotiated settlements are not simply agreements between the parties; they rest on what courts have been deciding in similar cases. Moreover, as New York's Morris Ernst says, "The guy who's never tried a case is a lousy negotiator." But the time is long past when nearly every lawyer considered himself a trial lawyer; litigation is now a specialty, and in the lives of most lawyers an actual trial (as distinguished from an appearance in court to confirm something already done elsewhere) is rare enough to be an event. Even the men who work frequently in court are not really trial lawyers in the older sense—barristers prepared to argue a case in any area of the law. They are specialists in one area, which happens to take them to court.

"A cause célèbre today," Judge Aron Steuer of the New York Appellate Division wrote at the close of his biography of his father Max Steuer, perhaps the greatest of all New York trial lawyers in the first forty years of this century,

is most likely to be a revolting crime of violence or a contest of ideologies either presenting no field for trial ability or one that the former generation would have scorned with every evidence of distaste. A trial man today must be a specialist in either accident cases, taxes, patents or some similar field. This specialization produces experts but not the trial lawyer who formerly dominated the courts. One of the factors that has tended to bring this about is that bane of so many institutions: rising costs. Only the very rich and those who have nothing to lose can afford to litigate. So that when the dramatic case does occasionally appear, it is no longer the arena where the titans do battle. There are no Titans; there is no place where exercise can develop them.

Though a Louis Nizer or a Melvin Belli can make his name almost a household word by writing a book about himself, no one would seriously disagree with Judge Steuer about the decline of the trial bar. And everyone recognizes, too, the crucial importance of rising costs in diminishing the number of trials. "Particularly those disputes between neighbors," says a Midwest lawyer cheerfully, "which turn so nasty. They share a common driveway; one of them builds a curb down the middle. The other one says the curb's on his side; he comes to your office, he's going to take the s.o.b. to court. You tell him it will cost him a thousand dollars for three days in court, and then he wants to compromise it."

But there are other causes, too. Certain fertile sources of lawsuits have been eliminated or restricted by legislation. The breach-of-promise-of-marriage case, which kept the gutter press interesting through the first twenty years of the century, has been eliminated by law. Labor injunctions, always hard fought, are gone. Accidents to workers on the job are now on the docket of a commission rather than a court. The growing file of data available on private persons has discouraged the dubious claimant under a will. The professionalization of the police and the prosecutor's offices has given the accused criminal far less reason to take his chances with a jury (particularly in commercial frauds: "Before Dewey became DA," says the New York criminal lawyer Harris Steinberg, talking about thirty years ago, "the New York District Attorney's office had no accountants on its staff—it was full of Tammany hacks. Now you have a staff of ten CPAs—and you can't live in this world and do business without leaving a trail of paper"). The routine contract case, the buyer trying to get out because prices have dropped since he made his deal, has disappeared into the less costly and less public chambers of the arbitrator. Moreover, the growth of the expert bar means that a general trial lawyer may come to court at a disadvantage against the specialist, whose twenty years of work (in, say, a manufacturer's liability for his product) will give him resources of argument the general man cannot match from a month's preparation.

Another factor may also be operating. Fifty years ago a young man made his mark in the law, and assured his future, by his performance in a courtroom. Other lawyers noticed him; and so did the general public. The obvious reward was high office (William Howard Taft, Calvin Coolidge, Thomas E. Dewey and Earl Warren, not to mention Pericles, made their first reputations as public prosecutors); but equally important was the attention of possible clients and of the leaders of the bar. Thinking back to the early days of his own career in the 1920s, Paul Carrington of Dallas has written that "corporate executives choose lawyers to serve corporate enterprises . . . for the same reason that I was chosen for my first corporate employments, because I had impressed someone favorably in connection with the trial of lawsuits." Today an academic ladder has replaced the courtroom. Everyone goes to law school, and by far the most efficient way to make a start toward the top of the profession (nearly the only way, these days) is to go to a good law school, become an editor of the school's law review, and win a reputation for brilliance while a student. The trial has lost its appeal for the best of the younger men, because it has lost its function in the formation of their careers.

The life of the trial lawyer is immensely demanding, both physically and psychologically. It also requires a more systematic office than many trial lawyers have; in January, 1966, Continental Casualty revealed that 46 percent of the legal malpractice insurance claims pending in that one company involved lawyers' failures to remember when a court had told them to get something done. "Have you," Francis L. Wellman of New York demanded in 1910 of a hypothetical young lawyer, "the physical requirements of the advocate? Have you the healthy frame capable of enduring the long-continued exertion of mind and body, the confinement of study, the excitement of public speaking, the long day of labor, the work by night, the excited, broken sleep that follows a prolonged trial in a stifling court room? It is almost impossible to exaggerate the physical strain of court work." Joseph Millimet of Manchester, New Hampshire, in charge of litigation for one of the largest firms in a small state, says, "I run a mile every morning; if I don't I can't try cases. You find a trial lawyer, unless he's a big bruiser (and many of them are), he has very good personal habits—doesn't drink much, doesn't smoke."

Nervous energy is drained by the repeated need to make decisions on the spot, some of them drastically affecting the client's future. "It's not like a movie," says New York's Raphael Koenig. "You can't make it over." Trial work presents in the most nerve-racking form what Millimet calls "the problem of any intellectual activity—when you have to say, 'My God, I'm all by myself—have to settle this one all by myself. My father's dead, my senior partner doesn't know anything about it.'" And Millimet's work is entirely in civil trials ("There isn't anything in New Hampshire worth stealing"), where his client at worst will lose money. For the criminal lawyer who takes his work personally, the strain is that of the surgeon; and just as the surgeon knows he will live whatever happens on the table, the lawyer knows he will go home; both, for self-protection, need a hard shell. A wrong question at the wrong time can make a case hopeless. Edward Bennett Williams tells a prize story of this sort, about the defense lawyer who has established from a witness that he did not in fact see the defendant bite off the victim's ear, and then asks how the witness can have the effrontery to testify against his client. "Because," the witness says, "I saw him spit it out." According to Wellman, an English barrister who had asked a wrong question of this kind, because the client's solicitor had insisted it be asked, turned to the solicitor after the answer and said, "emphasizing every word, 'Go home, cut your throat; and when you meet your client in hell, beg his pardon.' " In the American pattern, this release is denied the trial lawyer; he has no one to blame but himself.

"I would come home and talk about a case," says San Francisco's Irving Reichert, now retired to the relative calm of educational work. "I'd dream about it at night. The case would be over and done, won or lost, I'd dream about it until the next one came. When I was on trial, I'd eat breakfast and then throw it up before I left the house. I'd work all night, bring home the record, all weekend. Finally my doctor said to me, 'Look, what are you proving?' "

In a complicated case just the information retrieval is a monstrous job. Every good trial lawyer becomes, for the period of the trial, one of the world's experts in any technical subject that is crucial to the issue. And then he has to arrange his information with great clarity, because the jurors (or the judge) to whom he is speaking must be made to follow him. "I have an associate who's very capable," says New York's Milton Pollack, one of the few British-style barristers in American courtrooms (that is, all his clients come to him from other lawyers). "Basically, he's a librarian; he keeps everything in order. But I just can't play the other fellow's notes; you can't get the conductor of the orchestra to rely on the first fiddler; he's got to know that score and know it perfectly. I take everything apart and put it back together for myself." And when this trial is over, there's another, presenting (for someone like Pollack, if not for the criminal lawyer or the personal-injury lawyer) an entirely different set of issues and pattern of facts. "I have a bathtub memory," Pollack says. "I can fill it up, and then when it's over I pull the plug and all this stuff drains right out. In a matter of days. It isn't until years later that I can remember any of the details of a case I've tried."

The New York firm of Milbank, Tweed has listed the subject matters of its antitrust cases: aluminum (which took twenty-four years to dispose of), "sardines, masonite, wood alcohol, abrasives, car wheels, cement, batteries, pharmaceuticals, electric tools, dairy products, hoisting machinery, precipitators, cameras, chickens, fire alarm devices, books, dry cargo vessels, typewriters, charcoal and watches." Such cases turn essentially on questions of fact, not law; and a fairly small litigation department handled all of them.

Finally, an actor's temperament is necessary, and a gift for self-deception. The trial lawyer *must* bring himself to believe in the justice of his client's cause. "A practicing lawyer," as Boston's Charles P. Curtis put it, "will soon detect in himself a perfectly astonishing amount of sincerity. By the time he has even sketched out his brief, however skeptically he started, he finds himself believing more and more in what it says, until later, when he starts arguing the case before the court, his belief is total; and he is quite sincere about it. You cannot very well keep your tongue in your cheek while you are talking." Judge Steuer recently recalled an episode from a case where he had assisted his father, and had suggested that his father fiercely cross-examine a witness whose testimony had been highly damaging and seemed to have holes. Max Steuer said, "No—then it will come out that the reason he's bitter is that they didn't cut him in on the swag." Fearing his interlocutor would take this story wrong, Judge Steuer added, "That doesn't mean my father was capable of objective judgment of his clients—once he took a case, he was committed. But tactics might be another story."

Judge Harold L. Medina of the federal Court of Appeals ("Me-*deena*," he likes to say, "rhymes with hy*ena*") remembers from his own trial days another example of Steuer's tactics: "He had a way of kind of whispering, and I noticed he was always on my left side, I couldn't hear him. I got ahold of a doctor to test my hearing; he told me, 'You've got a ten percent deficiency in the left ear.' Steuer *sensed* it."

Because trial lawyers identify closely with their clients, they enjoy their practice only when they win, and nobody wins all the time. Recalling his own days as Steuer's assistant, a now prominent New York lawyer said recently that "There's grown to be a legend that none of Steuer's clients was convicted. That's nonsense, and no honor to Max. A good half of them were convicted—but nearly all of them were guilty. . . ."

Much of the time, there is considerable question about how much difference it makes whether the trial lawyer is first-rate or routine.

The British bar seems fairly well agreed "that of every hundred cases, ninety win themselves, three are won by advocacy, and seven are lost by advocacy." The recent study of *The American Jury,* by Harry Kalven, Jr. and Hans Zeisel of the University of Chicago Law School, comes to the conclusion that in criminal cases a superior defense counsel will cause a jury to acquit when a judge would convict in almost exactly one percent of all cases where such disagreements occur. In the personal-injury field, however, where the trial talent has now concentrated, it seems likely that the size of the award by a jury is influenced by a lawyer's ability to build sympathy for his wounded friend. A lawyer is not invariably a help, however. "Any man who comes into court with a lawyer on a pure nonsupport case is a fool," says Mortimer Getzels of the Legal Aid office in Harlem. "The judge just says, 'If you can afford a lawyer, you can afford support.'"

Trials and trial work are least common in the East and Middle West, becoming more frequent as the traveler passes South and West. Where the "litigation department" of a large New York firm will employ a tenth to a quarter of its lawyers, the litigators make up a third or more of the large Los Angeles firms. "People in the West," says a Los Angeles lawyer, "like issues decided with precision and decision." For criminal trials, there are statistics: the range is from 144 for every 100,000 of the population in Georgia to 3 for every 100,000 of the population in Connecticut and Minnesota. For civil trials, there is as yet no evidence other than the opinions of mobile lawyers. One such, in Albuquerque, says happily that New Mexico is the national capital of court work: "These are the most litigious people in the world." Robert Emmet Clark, then acting dean of the University of New Mexico Law School, did not like the comment. "There are two parts to this story. First there are the natives, up in the hills, where not too much is happening. A trial is a drama and a ritual and a ceremony for them. A day in court is a one-act play. And they've had to deal for a long time with slick gringos who've taken their land and some other things. Then, in Albuquerque, this is a boom town. These people who have made this beautiful place look like Kansas City—sure, they're litigious. They're all con men. . . ."

2

Trials are simply ways to get something settled; they have neither virtue nor evil in themselves. If the trial mechanism becomes too cumbrous or too expensive, the legal system finds something else —in the United States of the 1960s, the negotiated settlement. Because the courts retain ultimate jurisdiction, and no settlement is meaningful unless it can survive a challenge in a court, lawyers retain a quasi monopoly of settlement work, even in a negotiating society.

There are a few lawyers and judges who look back wistfully to the good old days, to the drama of the trial and the clear-cut decisions at its conclusion. Most do not think of the matter one way or the other, because lawyers take the practice of law as they find it. To students of the law, however, the change is almost entirely positive. Nearly forty years ago, Karl Llewellyn looked forward to negotiated settlements in his parting speech to seniors at the Columbia Law School: "[T]here is nothing sacred, there is nothing immanent, there is not even great utility, in this whole-hog-or-none approach which is so typical of law. . . . There is some trend, then, toward a more intelligent adjustment, toward the discovery of the more *workable* result."

A Yale Law School study published in 1933 saw the process already well advanced in New Haven: 83 percent of all contract disputes and 84 percent of all accidents filed with the court never came to trial. Relative certainty of the result at trial contributed to the drive for settling: 82 percent of all contract cases and 75 percent of all automobile cases tried were won by the plaintiff. (Probably because an even smaller proportion of cases is tried, plaintiffs do not do so well at trial today.) James Willard Hurst suggested "that judges had their widest influence on the disposition of people's disputes by exerting background pressure for the parties to settle cases by negotiation."

Today the lawyer representing one party in a dispute is primarily a negotiator. The criminal case will end, four-fifths of the time, in a guilty plea bargained out with the DA against a reduced sentence or reduced charge or both. Even the big antitrust case is most likely to be settled by a plea of *nolo contendere* in exchange for a fine or a cease-and-desist order (and the locking up of the government's evidence, so private litigants cannot use it for triple-damage suits). About four out of five claims for personal injuries will be dropped or settled even before a suit is filed with a court; of the fifth that survive, only about one-quarter will come to trial, and of that quarter, only one-half (about 2.5 percent of all the personal-injury claims) will be tried through to a decision by judge or jury. (These proportions vary erratically around the country, and are greatly influenced by local custom even within a state; in Los Angeles, according to the fairly limited data available to the Columbia Project for Effective Justice, more than half the suits filed result in trials; while in San Francisco only a fifth of the suits produced a trial.)

"The adjustment of differences," says New Hampshire's Joseph Millimet, "is the lawyer's job; and that kind of law is administered in lawyers' offices, not in courts. In most of the work I do, there isn't any law, there's no place I can go to find the law; it's all in my head." Lincoln agreed. "As a peace-maker," he wrote, "the lawyer has a superior opportunity of being a good man."

Courts increasingly see their central role as the promotion of settlements. Pretrial hearings at which the lawyers must agree on the issues dividing their clients, "discovery" procedures which permit each party to learn the opponent's case before trial, the appointment of "referees" in bankruptcy and estate proceedings, the reliance on arbitrators (who have to keep peace in an industry) for contract disputes—all these devices are primarily ways to promote settlements outside the courtroom.

Even lawyers and judges who believe profoundly in the importance of negotiated settlements are not always happy with the use of the courts in achieving them. "You find a judge who hates to make a decision, and if he has to he gets very cross indeed," says Robert P. Bass, who left the excitement of the CIA for the suavity of academic international economics, and then returned home to be a state-capital lawyer in Concord, New Hampshire. "He'll force a settlement." Other lawyers have deeper suspicions.

"The judges around here," says one in the rural West, "are not qualified in evidentiary rules, so they cajole to get a settlement." A judge as distinguished as New York's Bernard Botein has warned about "changing the courthouse from a dignified forum for the deliberate resolution of legal disputes to a market place for bargaining of cases."

On the other side, California's Chief Justice Roger J. Traynor particularly admires a judge in Long Beach who "is a genius at settling cases. On one occasion he called Lloyd's of London to get them to raise their offer. Part of his technique is that he promises the lawyers that under no circumstances will he try their case, so they don't have to worry about what they tell him." And New York's Harry Gair, speaking of trial judges rather than appellate judges like Judge Botein, comments, "The judge who says, 'A court is not a marketplace; we try it and justice is done'—he has a complex, Freud should look at him."

Tax lawyers talking things over at the Internal Revenue Service, patent lawyers swapping licenses with one eye on the Antitrust Division and the other on the fantastic expense of patent litigation, bankruptcy lawyers making arrangements with the creditors to keep the business going and get it out of court, corporate lawyers setting up mergers—for them the knowledge of law and the normal adversary skills of the lawyer are merely background to the job at hand. Probably the most extensive use of the lawyer as negotiator, however, is in divorce practice. For divorces in America, except in New York State (and soon in New York, too, once the judges get used to the divorce statute of 1966), are in fact though not in law granted by the consent of the parties. Even in New York Hubert J. O'Gorman found that the more matrimonial work a lawyer did, the more likely he was to say that "It isn't really law."

Reno and Las Vegas are famous for their factory processing of divorces (in clerks' rooms rather than in open court, with little JP marriage chapels interspersed among the bail bondsmen's offices on the streets near the courthouse); but their fame derives more from the easy residence requirements which allow out-of-state customers to win a quick divorce and remarriage than for anything special about their procedure. The normal process elsewhere is described in an article about the situation in Utah prior to that state's Marriage Counseling Act (and after the Act's failure):

An attorney would file the necessary pleadings specifying mental cruelty as the ground for divorce and would get a waiver of service signed by the defendant. The plaintiff would then be taken to the courtroom of the district judge who happened to hear divorce matters. After waiting her turn in the courtroom while other divorces were being granted, the plaintiff would be examined as a witness by her attorney, and the judge would interpose a few questions. There would be no other witnesses, nor would anyone appear to represent the interests of the State or of the children. The hearing would last not more than ten minutes. A divorce decree would issue immediately, including custody and property awards.

"Uncontested" divorces are granted everywhere on the basis of whatever story may be fashionable at the moment. "Ninety-nine out of a hundred divorces in Massachusetts," says Boston's Harold Katz, "are 'cruel and abusive treatment.' The wife perjures herself: 'He slapped me; I ran to the neighbor.' The neighbor perjures herself: 'Yes, she came over; she had a mark on her face.' There are other grounds for divorce in this state, but lawyers would have to open a book to discover them."

"Contested" divorces, on the other hand, are hard to get everywhere, even in Nevada, unless one party can prove severe misbehavior by the other (and purity in himself or herself: if both of them can be shown to stink, the court in its wisdom will insist that they remain married). "If you have to go to court in a contested situation," says a New England lawyer, "you want to know about the judge's private life." These cases are most likely to involve adultery, which is grounds for divorce in all states, and in Canada.

In Victoria, British Columbia, for example, a small, rather ineffective-looking truck driver is trying to get a divorce from his pretty, blonde, rather blowzy wife; and he wants custody of the children. She has been haunting beer halls at night, and he has had her followed. On the stand is an inoffensive young bachelor she picked up at one of the beer halls ("I never had any idea she was married"), and as the story proceeds, the young man chivalrously trying to protect the girl, it develops that they rode around in his car awhile and then parked a block or two from her home. They were intertwined on the front seat when the detectives and the husband opened the door and dragged the girl away.

"You've heard the evidence, haven't you, as to your fly being open?"

"Yes."

"What do you say?"

"If this had been so, I had forgotten about it."

"Now or then?

"What do you mean?"

"Did you forget about it now or then?"

"What?"

"Now, did you or did you not open your fly when you were with Mrs. D———?"

A clerk enters the courtroom from a back door, bows formally to the wigged judge, who is busily taking notes, and proceeds snickering to a clerk's table.

"All right. You were sitting there in the car with Mrs. D———, when the door opened and three men dragged her out. What did you do?"

"I drove off."

"Was that a gentlemanly thing to do?"

"Well, she seemed to know them. . . ."

This sort of thing feeds the newspapers well, and it is indeed entertaining to people who have a taste for cruelty, or for those who do not see and cannot imagine Mrs. D——— and her weeping father sitting on the front bench. But think of the lawyer who has to put a witness through such paces! Negotiation is better.

Most divorces start off contested, and in many the parties are only too eager to destroy each other. As a Los Angeles lawyer specializing in celebrities puts it, "The husband wants to demolish the wife, and the wife wants to castrate the husband." Then, says Robert Valentine of Centerville, Iowa, "you explain to the client that he or she won't get the divorce unless they agree on property settlement, custody of the children and so forth. If they want the divorce bad enough, they'll try pretty hard." The fights are most often over money, occasionally over the children; they are negotiated and settled by the lawyers, dragging their principals behind them. "You always," says a New York theatrical lawyer, "get to be friends with the lawyer on the other side in a divorce case: you've got the same problems."

For some lawyers, divorces are the simplest way to make money that the working day can offer. "It's easy," says a Los Angeles lawyer who supplements a more interesting practice with such work, "and you get paid outrageously well. There are two categories: one, Mickey Mouse; some lawyers handle on a volume basis, have a couple of hundred cases pending all the time, and take fifty to a hundred dollars on the front end; two, the good case, always defined by property, no problem to give some to Mums and grab off five hundred dollars on the way by."

For other lawyers, including some who specialize in this area, divorces are all agonizing. "If you approach this thing as something more than a piece of business," says Chicago's Benjamin Davis, earnest, distinguished and bald, with forty-odd years of experience in matrimonial affairs, "these are people in trouble, and every one of these things is at least to some extent tragic. A lawyer has a duty to satisfy himself that what is done is correct; we're professional people, not just mechanics. Some of my time in *every* case goes into conciliation. I think the Catholic Church does a magnificent job; when Catholics come in here, I always want to make sure they've gone through the Chancery Office procedure. Many times they don't come back here, which so far as we're concerned is just as well. I think it would help if the young lawyers were psychoanalyzed, the way analysts are psychoanalyzed."

Negotiations in a divorce practice, like those in labor relations, are greatly helped by the feeling of the parties that they *must* come to an agreement; as Ambassador Arthur J. Goldberg likes to say, comparing his work at the United Nations with the work he used to do for Philip Murray at the Steel Workers and at CIO, "There everybody was operating in the same frame of reference: labor movements want *more* but not different. That's not true in the international community."

The personal characteristics that push a man toward law and the traditions of the profession both work against the talent for negotiation. The investment banker, the labor leader, the industrial psychologist, the sales manager, the dean of the faculty, are all more likely than the lawyer to be well equipped for negotiations. Because the talent is so scarce, and so important to business enterprise, the lawyer-negotiators as a group are probably the most highly paid people in the law. By and large, incidentally, they miss litigation ("I'm sure I'd be a better lawyer if I were in court more often"); and being mostly very intelligent men who enjoyed law school and did well at it, they sometimes wish their work had a little more law in it.

3

The most legal of the lawyer's skills is his provision of security for his clients, through the documents he drafts. As the small-claims courts demonstrate, the representation of litigants is not essential to the maintenance of a legal system, and the work of negotiating and counseling came to lawyers for reasons of convenience and efficiency rather than for any virtue residing exclusively in the profession. The one necessary societal function of the lawyer —the reason why it is necessary to license lawyers and to demand that all entrants to the profession pass a bar examination—is that the lawyer writes enforceable contracts. Communal life in a modern society rests upon pieces of paper that tell people their rights, privileges, powers and immunities, duties, liabilities and disabilities. When challenged, these pieces of paper—wills, trust agreements, mortgages, deeds, certificates of incorporation, leases, agreements to purchase or to sell, warrants and so forth—must stand up. The lawyer assures that they will.

Indeed, this "surety" function soon becomes too important to be left to the accidents of lawyers' training and judges' views. The only way to be really certain that a document will stand up is to make it identical with other documents that have stood up. For the more common legal arrangements, there are printed forms, supplied by private publishers or officially. In addition to its volumes of legal encyclopedias and practice tips, the American Jurisprudence series ("AmJur") provides book after book of forms, for the lawyer to use as a "model" in virtually the entire range of possible client problems. Because judges are subject to reversal on appeal, many of them at the end of a case will simply read most of their charge from the safe "Pattern Jury Instructions" locally in use. Except on the highest levels, it's a rare lawyer's office that doesn't have somewhere within easy reaching distance some published book of forms. (On the highest level the office has its *own* book of forms.) Clients do not see such things, of course; the lawyer's secretary types a fresh original for each customer.

Even the trial lawyer makes contact with this side of the law; court actions must be started in a formally correct manner. Young lawyers are therefore advised to go talk to the clerks at the court and get a copy of a similar complaint filed recently. Milton Pollack remembers a case in federal court, tried before Judge Simon Rifkind shortly before Rifkind resigned from the bench en route to becoming senior partner in what may be New York's most politically influential law firm. "One of the lawyers objected," Pollack says, "that the complaint was frivolous, because it had been copied word for word from a complaint in another matter filed with the court a couple of months before. Rifkind said from the bench, 'Was it a good complaint that he copied?' And when the lawyer admitted it was, Rifkind said, 'You wouldn't want him to copy a bad complaint, would you?' "

Even in matters of the greatest sophistication, lawyers will copy document forms if they can. One Wall Street lawyer recently had occasion to claim credit for designing the first "trust indenture" to sell Japanese securities in the United States, back in the 1920s.

"I was a young associate at the time and I put in a lot of time working on the problem," he said. "I went to Japan. I didn't find anything anywhere I could use. Finally my draft cleared through the senior partners and the bankers, and the indenture was printed and sent out, and I went back to my desk and found that I had left out the date at which the bonds were to be redeemed. I went to my partner and put it on his desk, and he was disgusted, but he relieved my worries by pointing out that the date was, after all, up in the heading, so we were safe. Anyway, the issue was successful and during the next few years a number of other underwriters brought out Japanese mortgage bonds. And the reason I'm pretty sure we were first is that every one of those indentures left out the date for the redemption of the bonds."

The two areas where formal certainty is most demanded by the courts themselves are wills and titles to land, and in both the requirement is clearly reasonable. The right to pass on one's property as one wishes (particularly real property, land) is one of the most extraordinary examples of personal liberty gained by our European ancestors. Prior to the collapse of feudalism, it was understood that whatever a man owned when he died was to be divided according to the custom of the country; whatever privileges his ownership might give him while he was alive, it was unthinkable that he should be permitted after death to disturb the normal organization of society. Modern rules for the division of property owned by someone who has died "intestate" still reflect the organizing principles of a culture; and the legislatures and courts, in permitting control to be continued from the grave through the execution of a document, have hedged the privilege carefully.

This issue apart (and it will seem to most lawyers a more unreal issue than it is), there is the difficulty that a will is the intention of a man who can no longer be consulted as to what he meant; its formal structure *must* be such that the authorities will feel no confusion when they look at the document. Wills that a man has written in his own hand are often as valid as the lawyer's carefully drawn instrument, with its two or three witnesses (depending on the state), its quaint language about "devising" and such. All the rules can be made to bend, because human beings operate them; one of the most heavily publicized wills ever admitted to probate in the United States was accepted (quietly, in chambers) with all sorts of penciled and unwitnessed alterations, because the surrogate who saw it had known the old codger and knew it was all right. But the hand-drawn will is subject to effective challenge, and the lawyer's will, correctly prepared, probably is not.

Where real estate is involved, the law is supremely conscious of a fact nearly every modern American forgets: that whatever else may change in a society, the land endures. Searching about for the sources of the gargantuan development of law in Britain and the United States, as distinguished from continental Europe, a Wall Street lawyer with a speculative turn of mind recently attributed it to the uncertainty about land titles which derived in the one case from the Norman Conquest, in the other from the existence of a continent occupied first by lesser breeds without the law and then by a succession of pioneers and sharp operators. Particularly in the Great Plains, people used land for decades without worrying much about who owned it; and the county offices that registered deeds after the government introduced private property to the West were often inefficient, subject to fire, flood and forgetfulness, corrupt or just inconvenient. "In the early days," says Charles L. Johnston of Centerville, Iowa, "a man would own a little prairie land—and he'd go somewhere and buy five acres of timber for his wood. A man with eighty acres might cut it up into twenty two-and-a-half- and five-acre tracts, but he'd never get a surveyor." A mobile society invented and forgot all sorts of ingenious encumbrances, easements and disabilities which can be revived at any time.

Someone who wants to buy a piece of land needs better protection than a few family letters in the seller's cupboard, and a bank putting out mortgage money will demand proof that the land against which the money is advanced is in fact pledged for the loan. Through much of the nineteenth century the economic foundation of the American bar was primarily in the giving of assurances about "title" to real property. In some states the bar developed a special legal action—the "quiet title" suit—by which courts would give a declaratory judgment that somebody owned a piece of land. ("John Doe" and "Richard Roe" are names deriving from the elaborate fictions British lawyers invented to secure the same result.) But basically the work was digging out the records and getting the county clerk to certify them. "I remember when I was a high school boy working in my father's office in Minnesota," says San Francisco's Burnham Enerson, recently head of the state bar in California. "He was always examining abstracts, sending out letters of opinion at five dollars each: you have a good title, or you don't." The problem was by no means restricted to the countryside. In New York, for a generation, the rigidities of the so-called "Torrens title" directed the development of the city to blocks where all the titles had been more flexibly registered. And even now, in some states, the examination of title abstracts and the preparation of opinions on titles may be a source of support for the younger or less talented members of the bar.

"Probate" and real-estate practice are highly technical, highly repetitive and often highly profitable. ("I have a beef against my profession," says Edward Harris of Rochester, New York, where lawyers certify all titles. "The fee for a title search is one percent of the mortgage. You get a downtown office building that changes hands every few years, and each time you're paid one percent of the new mortgage for a little job you've already done. I think it's unconscionable, and I've said so at the bar association, but they tell me to keep my mouth shut.") The two kinds of practice are alike, also, in their susceptibility to competition from organizations outside the bar. The trust department of a bank (which, of course, employs lawyers) may know a good deal more about estate planning than most lawyers know. And what the purchaser or the bank really wants of a title is less a document certifying its validity than a guarantee that if something does turn out to be wrong any financial loss will be covered. Where state law permits, this guarantee is given by a title insurance company (which also has salaried lawyers). With the broker handling negotiations and the title insurance company guaranteeing the title, the lawyer can be frozen almost entirely out of real estate, as has happened in California, where matters that would elsewhere go through a practitioner's office are sent for decision to "the Supreme Court of Montgomery Street" in San Francisco and "the Supreme Court of Spring Street" in Los Angeles, headquarters for the state's title insurance companies. Lawyers may still get some income out of these situations, through what are in effect agent's commissions paid by the title insurers. These payments are officially unethical but commonplace. In *Lawyers and Their Work*, Quintin Johnstone of Yale and Dan Hopson, Jr. of Kansas report, "In the nineteen forties, one of the big New York title insurers discontinued paying commissions to lawyers, but business fell off so badly that the company had to resume commission payments."

Other areas where lawyers exercise their "surety" function are less routine than probate and title. While forms will take care of most of the difficulties in the usual commercial contract (procedures are being still further routinized in all states with the adoption of the Uniform Commercial Code), and some of the documents required by law for a sale of stocks and bonds are sufficiently repetitive to earn the name "boilerplate" given to them at the large law offices, clients with special problems are likely to need significantly special contracts. Big law firms will throw teams of lawyers into the preparation of these contracts and "registration statements," which may run hundreds of pages and are designed to cover every contingency. "[A]n essential of the good lawyer," Harrison Tweed once said, "is that he visualizes all the possibilities and particularly those that might make trouble." The purpose of these intensely legal documents is to take the matter out of the realm of possible legal dispute. "You'll get a contract drawn up by a trial lawyer," says a senior partner in corporate work at a Wall Street firm, "and you'll look at the proof and say to him, 'What about *that*?' And he'll say, 'Don't worry about *that*—any court will hold . . .' and then you have to say to him, 'That's no good; the whole purpose of this thing is to make sure we stay out of court.' "

Lawyers elsewhere look with some amusement and distaste on these obese documents that come out of the big offices in New York and Chicago; everyone is a little pleased when such a contract turns out not to protect the big firm's client after all (and this happens). "I feel like a barefoot boy when I go down to Manhattan," says Erwin Ellman of Detroit. "They show me a partnership agreement, a two-man corporation, clause after clause, in enormous detail." Then Ellman gives the explanation: "In a town like Manhattan you've never dealt with the lawyer on the other side; you may never see him again, you have to be very watchful. Here, even in a city as big as Detroit, the odds are that you'll know the other lawyers, so we have fairly important deals where the documents are three or four or five pages long." Speaking of the relatively casual attitude toward "surety" practice in New Hampshire, a judge said recently, "There are only about six or seven bastards in the whole state, and we all know who they are."

Ultimately, the security a lawyer offers his clients in the business context is less the technical verbiage of the documents and the access to the courts than the stability of the profession. Geoffrey C. Hazard, Jr. of the American Bar Foundation says that "What a lawyer is saying to another lawyer is, 'I can vouch for my client and his behavior.' Every business needs a foreign secretary." In many ways, the practice of law is built, as Karl Llewellyn once wrote, on the premise "of a town of twenty-five thousand (or, much more dubiously, fifty thousand)—a town with a single high school, where reputation speaks itself from mouth to mouth, even on the other side of the railroad track; and reputation not only of the oldster, but of the youngster. The youngster is watched when he hangs out his shingle; watched if he be a home-town boy, watched doubly if he be not." Where such conditions are not met, the legalisms and standardizations once required only for wills and titles spread to cover every part of the legal system which deals with sums of money large enough to tempt people to write their own Canons of Ethics. Insurance, interestingly, has escaped; the words "You're covered" on the long-distance telephone are better than a hundred notarized papers, for here the courts have demanded *"ultissima fides"*—the highest good faith.

Many lawyers, particularly if their work deals mostly with "human" problems like marriages, regard contract-making as stolid and uninteresting stuff, leaving little opportunity for imagination or invention. In fact, such corporate practice draws the best minds in the profession not only because of the money involved but also because of the challenge, which is nothing more nor less than making new law. Justice Benjamin Cardozo, with that mastery of courtly prose style that was his alone in the American twentieth century, described the situation from the vantage point of the bench:

[I]n the literature of the law there has been a tendency to underestimate the importance of the role that is played by the office adviser, not merely in keeping his client out of jail or in avoiding civil liability, but even in shaping and directing the institutions of the law itself. He is much more than a traffic officer, warning of obstructions and keeping travellers to the travelled path. He is a creative agent just as truly as the advocate or the judge. In our complex economic life, new problems call from day to day for new methods and devices. The lawyer in his office formulates a trust receipt, or stock certificates with novel incidents, or bonds, municipal or corporate, with privileges or safeguards till then unknown to the business world. At times legislation is necessary to make the innovation lawful. More often, the new device establishes itself in practice, is taken up by business men generally as one of the accepted moulds of conduct. When that happens, the function of the court becomes in a sense supervisory and secondary. The innovation must still be tested for possible infringe.

ment of the behests of public policy and justice. Even so, except in rare cases—in cases where the infringement is serious and manifest—the form that has thus worked itself into the methods of business life will be accepted almost automatically as postulates of the legal order. The courts do no more than set the *imprimatur* of regularity upon methods that have had an origin in the creative activity of an adviser, working independently of courts in the quiet of an office.

If Cardozo seems old-fashioned, consider David Riesman, a reformed law professor, who asked mildly a few years ago "why Holmes and Brandeis have been inflated to mythical proportions and have captured the imagination of the young law student, who is unlikely even to know the names of the brilliantly daring and inventive corporate and governmental lawyers who helped build our modern industrial society and its governmental stimuli and curbs."

Here the work of the legal draftsman, making contracts which will be "private law" for the parties, blends with the work of the legislative draftsman who writes the public laws of the state or nation. The techniques involved are very different: the contract, between a limited number of parties in a limited field of action, should be so detailed that it covers all imaginable contingencies; and the law, which will be applied to more people and situations than the legislators can possibly know about, should state public policy so clearly and simply that a lawyer will be able to predict without difficulty where his client would stand if confronted with legal challenge. But the reason to get the thing well written is the same for both: because, in the words of Indiana University's Reed Dickerson, "people can't afford—society can't afford—litigation." The well-drawn contract keeps the client out of court; the well-drawn law makes relatively clear what the judges will have to do in specific cases, diminishing the temptation to take the question to court.

A disciple of Llewellyn's, Dickerson worked sixteen years in Washington, nine of them as head of a team of fifty-odd lawyers who redrafted the entire General Military Law for the Department of Defense, and saw the product through its adoption by Congress as Titles 10 and 32 of the U.S. Code. A large, earnest man, he conceals a sharp wit and wide curiosity under a Rotarian manner. "I am not interested in research or creativity or history or philosophy," he says. "I am a bug on right answers to real problems."

Dickerson and his legion of followers (he is the author of standard books on both legal and legislative drafting) feel little respect for the antique verbiage of the law. (The lawyer and novelist Arthur Train once suggested that the prolixity of older legal documents could be traced to the fact that the "scriveners" who set them out were paid so much per word.) The philosophical position is that the English language is not necessarily ambiguous or vague (words which have different meanings, as Dickerson likes to point out; and generality, which is desirable in a law, is something else again). "The courts' and litigants' normal preoccupation with sick or uncertain language," Dickerson has written, "might lead to the belief that all language is as inherently weak and inadequate as the particular fragments of statutory language that are scrutinized in legal opinions. . . . The professional legislative draftsman knows better." Some flavor of what he is talking about can be gathered from Department of Defense Instruction 5550.7, on language to be used in amending Titles 10 and 32:

> If you want to authorize the Secretary to issue regulations, say "Under such regulations as the Secretary may prescribe." If you want to require him to issue regulations, say "Under regulations to be prescribed by the Secretary." Do not say "rules and regulations". . . .
> Don't say "retirement pay"; say "retired pay". . . .
> Don't say "which" (to begin a restrictive clause); say "that". . . .

James B. Minor, who went from Dickerson's team at Defense to the Federal Aviation Agency and reduced the bulk of its regulations by four-fifths, says, "They used to rely heavily around here on interpretations. I've seen interpretations which said, 'Though we said black, we mean white.' This is not our policy today—now we try to clarify in the regulations. We avoid legalese, avoid the passive voice, use the present tense."

Intellectually, the draftsman's skills are the highest in the practice of law. Judges at bottom need merely reach decisions, and, as the new breed of computer programmers for law have discovered with some horror, the judges are not held to very high standards of explaining how they got there; negotiators and advocates need understand only as much of a situation as will gain a victory for their clients; counselors can be bags of wind because it is only rarely that anyone can successfully pin a bad mistake on a lawyer's advice. But the documents survive, and to draw them up well requires an extraordinary understanding of everything they are supposed to accomplish. In the federal legislative process professional drafters do the work; in the states, except for a handful that have established strong drafting offices as part of the legislative branch, the most important work is farmed out to members of the bar. Probably the greatest compliment a lawyer can receive from his profession (a compliment never publicized) is an assignment to draft a major law.

"One of the most difficult parts of this job," says Edward Craft, chief of the Legislative Counsel's Office of the House of Representatives, "is to find out what it is the member really wants to do." Craft's office, founded almost by accident in the Revenue Act of 1919, offers to Congressmen the services of a dozen or so extraordinarily intelligent young lawyers who will badger them until they get clear in their own minds why they are introducing this legislation, and then will get the thing in shape. Unfortunately, committees of the House and of the whole, Senate discussions and conferences can amend any bill out of all recognition, and while Craft and his crew try to attend the conferences they never control any part of what is done. "It's a lawyer-client relationship," Craft says, "except that all our clients are good clients." In the end, ambiguity may be restored to the Act simply because, as Craft puts it, "there are times when you can achieve agreement on specific language but not on purpose."

At that, it's better than working for a state legislature, where some State Senator may come around to insist, jovially, that you help him draft his bill to require that marriage licenses be renewed every year, like dog licenses or car licenses, or the marriage shall be void.

Keeping the mass of state statutes in order, where any order is kept, is mostly the work of private publishing companies; keeping the mass of rules from regulatory agencies in shape will be done by the agencies themselves or not at all. (The Federal Trade Commission has not the vaguest notion of what it has done with the remarkably ill-drawn Robinson-Patman Act, which deals with relations between manufacturers and sellers, and neither, therefore, does anybody else, including the Supreme Court.) For the body of permanent federal legislation, however, there is a Law Revision Counsel attached to the House Judiciary Committee, which publishes every six years a new version of the U.S. Code. Sixteen of the fifty titles in the Code have been enacted by the Congress as law, superseding the individual acts that made them up; for the others, statement in the Code will serve as "prima facie evidence of the law" when introduced in court, but nobody is bound by the document.

The man in charge of this labor is Charles J. Zinn, who first came to Washington in 1939 to work for the original Committee on the Revision of the Laws. "It was a temporary assignment," Zinn says, running a hand through long gray hair. "I commuted from New York for twenty years before I decided it might be permanent." When Zinn came, there was one volume for the entire Code, plus one volume of supplement; now there are shelves full of books. Sometimes the job of fitting in the new laws is easy—"Especially," Zinn says, "when the drafters make reference to my Code." Sometimes finding the right place is quite difficult, and when the difficulties become extreme, the law is simply slotted into the omnibus supplement to the miscellaneous Title 50. The law may be a seamless web, but the U.S. Code emphatically is not.

To say that the profession as a whole is not enchanted with the work of the Law Revision Counsel would be to understate the attitude. Still, the job is a difficult one ("[E]ven the best draftsman," writes Judge Henry J. Friendly, an amiably sarcastic redhead whose sharpness of mind has terrified the profession since he was Justice Brandeis' law clerk a generation ago, "is likely to have experienced the occasional shock of finding that what he wrote was not at all what he meant"); the staff is small; and the influence of Emanuel Celler, chairman of the House Judiciary Committee, has guaranteed that no appointments will ever be made on a nonpolitical basis. There is also, incidentally, some power residing here. "Every once in a while we change something," Zinn says cheerfully, "to make it conform to a Supreme Court decision." What is meant by that particular vague phrase is decided by Zinn himself.

4

The fourth of the lawyer's skills—counseling—is the one most likely to match most lawyers' image of themselves. In writing the will, the lawyer does not think of the guarantees built into the formal verbiage, but of the differing needs of the son who is launched as a successful surgeon and the daughter who married a handsome fellow who incorrectly considers himself a gifted speculator in the market. Working for a client injured in an automobile accident, the lawyer not only negotiates with the insurance company but advises the client about which offers to accept and which to reject. Lawyers who specialize in divorces, criminal defendants and corporations spend much more time talking with their clients than do other lawyers. In Jerome Carlin's study of the New York Bar, four-fifths of the senior partners in the larger law offices ranked "conferring with clients" as their first activity. "A counselor-at-law," says one of these, "has his clients conditioned to paying his fees the way the Chinese paid their doctors—as long as they stayed well." If the counseling involves tax questions, a tax specialist says, the fees are better, "because you know how much they have."

Much of this advice-giving fits into the category the salesmen have taught us to call "human relations." The Missouri Bar study found that half of the state's satisfied clients "mentioned the word 'friendly' in telling why they were pleased with the way their attorneys treated them; on the other hand, more than half of the dissatisfied clients mentioned that their attorneys had been 'condescending' or 'bored and indifferent.' "

The value of the right personality has never been denied, and nobody has ever said that a business-getting personality demonstrates ability as a lawyer. "I know good lawyers who have no clients," says Harvard's Erwin Griswold, "and lots of bum lawyers who have plenty." But the negative aspects tend to be overstressed. The lawyer who can work up a fair degree of sympathy with his client is better equipped to understand the client's problem and to help him with it. Norris Darrell, president of the American Law Institute and a senior partner in Sullivan & Cromwell, the archetype of Wall Street law firms (it was John Foster Dulles' firm), whose specialty was taxes and who can scarcely be accused of covering up lawyerly deficiencies with charm, likes to say that "The human interest is what makes this business fun. What real lawyer is happy if all he's doing is the cold, dry stuff?" (The attitude is not universal: Justice Abe Fortas, before he ascended the bench, successfully argued before the Supreme Court the *Gideon* case, which established an American criminal defendant's inviolable right to a lawyer; and through the long period of its preparation and the exhilaration of the victory he never met or wished to meet Clarence Earl Gideon.)

In a country practice the ability to look helpful and to get on with people is primary. "If you don't have a good business head and you don't understand people you won't do well in New Hampshire," says Perkins Bass, who keeps on the wall of his small-town office the commission of appointment as U.S. Attorney given to his grandfather by Abraham Lincoln. "And I don't care," he adds, "if you were editor of the *Harvard Law Review*."

While Reginald Heber Smith was in the hospital, a physical therapist mentioned to him that she had a tax problem. "You go up to my office," said Smith, "and see Mr. Powell." The physical therapist said, "I'd be afraid." Smith said, "No, you won't be. You'll see fresh flowers on the receptionist's desk, and Mr. Powell will be right out to make you welcome." The flowers on the receptionist's desk are also a part of the practice of law; and not an ignoble part, either.

Much of a lawyer's most significant counseling falls under the heading Professor Louis M. Brown of the University of Southern California Law School has labeled "Preventive Law." The client who is already in trouble is likely to need (and to want) specific service more than advice. But where there are permanent and continuing relationships, the lawyer can keep his client's business practices and wills and tax liabilities in the area of minimum trouble simply by regular consultation. G. E. Hale of Chicago has given a routine example from the area of antitrust law:

Guiding a trade association is a large responsibility. . . . All publications should be submitted to counsel for approval prior to dissemination. It is easy for a busy trade association executive to write bulletins which suggest the existence of illegal activities. Not long ago one such executive sent an appeal to his membership for prompt payment of annual dues. In doing so, he described the heavy load carried by the executive staff, particularly in "doing the dirty work behind the scenes." By "dirty work" the executive no doubt meant the drudgery of normal association activity, but his language could be read in a less friendly light.

Brown has urged on the lawyers and their clients a regularly spaced "legal audit," based on accounting practice. The bar associations, more status-conscious, advise a "legal checkup," like a medical checkup. How much of this consultation there is, nobody really knows; the big law firms, with partners serving on the boards of directors of big corporations, undoubtedly do a great deal of it, and the rest of the profession does relatively little. Studies in Connecticut and Ohio in the 1930s indicated that people handled their legal problems without legal advice about 80 percent of the time. The Missouri Bar study of the 1960s showed only 25 percent of home buyers employing lawyers—and only 36 percent of those who had been involved in an automobile accident with personal injuries or damages of more than $100. In 1963 the School of Business at the University of Washington did an elaborate study of the use of lawyers by small businesses in that state, and came up with results which are, to lawyers, even more discouraging. Of the 676 businesses that answered, only 72 had lawyers on retainer, and only 109 said that they consulted lawyers "periodically whether or not you have problems." About a quarter said they got their information about new government regulations from a lawyer (68.8 percent mentioned an accountant), and only 15 percent of those who used printed legal forms went to a lawyer for them (24.9 percent simply bought forms at a store). The median annual gross sales of the businesses replying ran about $180,000; the median expenditure for legal services was about $275.

The lawyer's qualifications to give advice vary, obviously, according to the nature of the problem, the ability of the lawyer and the sophistication of the client. "Trial lawyers aren't good at this sort of thing," says a Washington lawyer who has held some of the highest government offices despite a trial background. "If you try cases, you're used to having your mind made up for you." If the question is one of a lawsuit or taxes or the impact of a new zoning law, the lawyer is uniquely prepared to help; if it is one of a divorce or a will or a merger, his knowledge of the relevant law together with his observations of similar patterns over the years make him an obvious choice—though here the psychiatrist, the trust officer at the bank and the management consultant may know a thing or two that the lawyer doesn't know. On more general questions of family relationships, business decisions and public policy, the lawyer may be no better than anybody else—a phenomenon he may or may not understand.

For counseling, while it brings out the most attractive aspects of the profession, can also reveal an almost boundless arrogance. *A Lawyer's Practice Manual,* for example, points out that many clients expect advice on financial matters, and tips off the lawyer that "The New York Stock Exchange and various member firms issue many informative, easy-to-read booklets on the subject." On a much more sophisticated level, a partner in the largest Los Angeles law firm insists that "Most of the company presidents I know are guys who look to me for leadership in intellectual matters. You know—'I don't know what to do until you tell me what I think.'" To the faculty of the Yale Law School and others, the lawyer appears not as the proprietor of technical skill and a professional mystery, who thereby gains what may be useful experience for his clients, but as "the last generalist," the one person in the situation who can pull together all the disparate elements and make the policy decisions.

This control posture is assumed and accepted where the lawyer's significant business clients are celebrities—movie stars, pitchers, golf pros, astronauts, novelists. It is far less real, probably, with professional managers who run corporations. Earl Kintner, formerly head of the Federal Trade Commission and now in practice in Washington, says that "I don't try to tell my clients what to do and what not to do; I tell them how they can do what they want to do. There's always a legal way to achieve any legitimate purpose." New York's James B. Donovan, who first came to public attention when he represented the Russian spy Rudolph Abel and later dominated the headlines when he negotiated the release of the Cuban prisoners left over from the Bay of Pigs, has actually made his living as a lawyer for insurance groups, specializing in policy questions. "In my experience," Donovan says, "as general counsel to two federal agencies and many major corporations, every time I have seen the ultimate decision pass into the hands of the lawyers it has been the indication not of an aggressive lawyer but of a weak executive."

The most usual situation is the one a senior partner at Washington's Covington & Burling remembers from his firm's association with Du Pont: "We'd go down to the board meetings and we'd tell them what we thought. Was it a good idea for Du Pont to bring out *all* the new artificial fibers? No, it would be a damned bad idea. Sometimes they'd listen."

Meanwhile, there are lots of meetings. Lawyers are good at meetings.

5

Of these four central skills, beginning lawyers may have a chance to practice two: drafting (under tight supervision as an employee of a big law firm or a public office) and advocacy (as an employee of a public prosecutor's or defender's office, or as someone hanging around a courtroom to whom a judge can assign the case of an indigent defendant). Few clients will be willing to permit someone with neither business nor law experience to handle negotiations for them, and fewer still will be willing to pay for counseling from such a source. In New Jersey, where the title of "counselor-at-law" is officially available, only lawyers with at least three years' experience can claim it.

During 1965 and 1966 the deans of the ten law schools in New York State sweated over accusations by Chief Justice Charles Desmond that they were not adequately preparing their graduates to practice law. None of them had as many as 10 per cent of a graduating class hanging up a shingle immediately upon passage of the bar exam (NYU had fewer than one percent), but this answer to Justice Desmond's worry could also be interpreted as simply another piece of evidence to legitimize the worry. Nationally, of lawyers twenty-eight and under reported on in *The 1964 Statistical*

Lawyer Report of the American Bar Foundation, about half were employed at least part time by government or business and almost a third were working as associates in a law firm. Only one-sixth were exclusively engaged in private practice either as individuals or in partnership. By contrast, about 60 percent of the lawyers in their forties were exclusively engaged in private practice.

Recently, the large firms and expanding corporate law departments have created a seller's market for the graduate of the twenty or so most highly rated law schools; for the others, life can be hard. Young lawyers are always astonished at how hard it is to get started in the law. To do the thing right requires considerable money. The lawyer who types his own letters is likely to earn a secretary's salary; the lawyer who relies entirely on the library of the bar association or the county courthouse is not available in his office if somebody does show up; the lawyer whose office looks like a shipping clerk's will have no place to interview clients. Even if there are clients whose fees will pay basic living expenses, running capital is required: many fees are contingent, and at best will not be paid for some time after the work is done; there are disbursements for stenotypists, for travel, for copying, for court fees, for telephone calls that will not be collected immediately even from clients whose fees are guaranteed. The Missouri bar study estimated that at any given time the average lawyer in that state was carrying disbursements for his clients amounting to 30 percent of his annual income. Access to at least $10,000 is usually necessary for a young lawyer to set up on his own, quite apart from the fact that a man with a wife and child needs a steady income. Yet the new law school graduate is eager to practice law. Jack Artigues, the young associate editor of the American Law Institute's Continuing Legal Education Project, went from Northwestern to an insurance company to a legal publishing house and then to ALI; he says that "the people I know who went into publishing or insurance companies or government all did so because they needed the money." The head of a loose-leaf service came to publishing after seventeen years in practice as a minor partner in a small firm. "When the boss in the firm sent his little boy to law school—a boy I had seen grow up—I saw the handwriting on the wall."

The most fruitful source of clients for the beginning lawyer is the established lawyer who has taken on more than he can handle, or finds himself with a case too dubious or too unremunerative to justify his time. Coming from the Midwestern state university law schools, the young lawyer will scan the Martindale-Hubbell *Directory* to see which towns seem undersupplied with legal talent, and will go off in that direction. If he guesses wrong, a lawbook salesman, who travels the territory and learns who needs what, can often set him right. In the big cities newcomers will seek introductions through family or friends, participate in the work of the local bar association, seek out charitable and educational activities known to command the interest of busy lawyers.

Where the bar is overcrowded—New York, Boston, Miami, Denver, San Francisco, Atlanta, Cleveland—this tactic is likely to work only fairly well. In places where there are nowhere near enough lawyers—most of them in Texas and California—a newcomer can count on enough work to show whether he's any good or not. Los Angeles used to be the prime example. "We came down from Anaconda, Washington," says Robert H. Newell, speaking of himself and his Stanford Law School classmate and partner, Theodore Chester, "because it seemed Southern California was the land of milk and honey. We'd never been here. And by God it turns out this *is* the land of milk and honey. Our clients came from other lawyers, originally maybe because it was an unpleasant type of case or a tough one—the first couple of years my work was divided between drunk drivers and admiralty, real screwy. [Newell and Chester also taught part time during those first years, at Loyola Law School.] Now the big firms send us good cases that aren't in their line, or that they don't have the manpower to handle. We do public utility work and rape cases. And a college classmate of ours who owns a transportation system has been patient enough to teach us admiralty lore and law."

In *Lawyers on Their Own,* Jerome Carlin reported that the normal way into the profession for the individual practitioners of Chicago was a period as a kind of runner and clerk for a lawyer who had an extra room, and who would pay his new associate with free rent and a few dollars a week. Some crumbs might fall from this table, or from contacts made while going about another man's business. The sort of thing that came along would be

collection matters, evictions, rent cases, "dead" judgments, along with some personal injury, criminal and divorce cases. . . . The most distinguishing feature of such cases is their petty character—the small amount of money involved, the tenuousness of the claim (or its nonexistence)—and the inordinate amount of time required to make any headway at all. In short, such practice constitutes the dirty work, the "crap," the "junk" that no one else will handle, but which the younger lawyer will often have to take if he wants any business at all.

A somewhat different perspective comes from a small-city lawyer: "You get low-level clients. Low-level clients are a hell of a lot better than no clients."

Next to referrals from other lawyers, the most important source of business for the beginner is the political connection, which can be made easily: every clubhouse needs workers. Any degree of prominence in a political club (whether the party is currently In or Out) will guarantee a few pieces of business at the disposal of the courts themselves, or some matters brought to the attention of the precinct leader or county chairman. In the county seats the new arrival makes himself known by running for county attorney, not because he believes he can win, but because it gives him an opportunity to present his business card to every voter, without being accused of soliciting business in violation of Canon 27 of the Canons of Ethics. Any county attorney, moreover, has made himself a number of enemies, and some business will come to his opponent to spite him. The practice of running for county attorney is so common in the rural West that any new lawyer who does not do so may be suspect in the eyes of his colleagues—what other, sinister way does he have to find clients?

The most useful friends to have are real-estate brokers, doctors (and hospital attendants), undertakers, policemen and employees of finance companies; all are significant sources of referrals for a young lawyer. And, of course, as a practice builds, the satisfied client becomes an unpaid business-getter for any lawyer.

In recent years, increasingly, young lawyers come to independent practice through real employment (rather than "space-for-service" in an older lawyer's office), minor public office, or even through jobs with banks or insurance companies or real-estate firms. They make their contacts with clients through the job; when the time comes for them to start out on their own, or in a small partnership of younger men, they have a foundation on which to build. Particularly if their jobs were in the Patent Office or the Internal Revenue Service, the local prosecutor's aerie, an insurance company's claims bureau or some specialized agency of the city or state government, they will be able to offer expertise and useful experience from the day they "hang up a shingle." This path, rather than the one Carlin described, is becoming the norm; and the spread of law offices associated with the poverty program will accelerate the trend, because these offices will have to rely mostly on beginners, who will thereby get a chance to impress the not-impoverished on the other side of the cases, the local political leaders and the mother hens of the organized bar who will incubate these offices very carefully.

In the end, most lawyers who make a decent living build a practice on representing some organization, not necessarily a business corporation. Surveys of the economic status of the bar often come up with the labor lawyer as the best paid, not because unions are lavish with their fees, but because a workingman who has an accident is more likely to know about the lawyer who represents his local than about any other lawyer. In small and even medium-sized cities, the most successful lawyer is likely to be one who represents a bank—"not," says one of them, "because you make any money on a bank, because you don't; but you meet a lot of potential clients." Trade associations will generate for their counsel a lot of business from the members (in flat violation, incidentally, of Canon 35, but nobody cares). Even the Marching and Chowder Society can be useful.

It must be said that all this works a good deal more smoothly in small cities and towns than it does in the metropolis. Justice Robert H. Jackson once wrote in praise of the "county-seat lawyer" that he "understands the structure of society and how its groups interlock and interact, because he lives in a community so small that he can keep it all in view. Lawyers in large cities do not know their cities: they know their circles, and urban circles are apt to be made up of those with a kindred outlook on life; but the circle of the man from the small city or town is the whole community and embraces persons of every outlook." The other side of this picture is that the whole community knows the lawyer, his strengths and weaknesses, and the chance that maybe he can be helpful with some problem. The farmer has a good notion of what you have to pay (not that he won't shop around a little); and even reasonably selfish lawyers will be willing to handle matters for deserving clients who can't pay much (or even at all), because the bread is reasonably likely to return on the waters. There is no great need for specialization because most cases are reasonably simple—and even if they are in fact complicated, nobody who knows that they are complicated is ever likely to hear about what the lawyer did with them.

And the county-seat lawyer, as city slickers often learn to their discomfiture, can be a first-class practitioner. "In the years I was out in central Illinois," says Nathan Pond of the Martindale-Hubbell *Directory*, "I was very impressed—it might have been my imagination—by what I considered the persistence of the Lincoln tradition. They *loved* to practice law; and there were a whale of a lot of good lawyers. I remember Herb Livingston of Bloomington, representing the old Atlas Rail Road. An oil truck ran into a locomotive at a crossing, the truck sued, Livingston counterclaimed, and the railroad won an award from the truck. A group of Texas lawyers wrote him to find out exactly *how* he had done that."

In big cities a lawyer has little chance to build a public reputation; his work, like so much else, is essentially anonymous. And lawyers are not allowed to advertise or to solicit legal business, although, as everyone knows, fairly broad allowances are made within the Canon. (The California Supreme Court once found nothing wrong with a lawyer's going up to a hospital with photostats of checks received by his previous clients, to convince a lady to hire him to handle her negligence case: "We fail to see how such conduct constituted solicitation contrary to the rules of professional conduct. It was merely a showing by petitioner of what the possibilities of recovery were in personal injury cases in order that the prospective client would have a clear understanding of the matter.") The matter was most intelligently put in Boswell's *Life of Johnson*:

BOSWELL: "You would not solicit employment, Sir, if you were a lawyer."
JOHNSON: "No, Sir, but not because I should think it wrong, but because I should disdain it."
This was a good distinction, which will be felt by men of just pride. He proceeded: "However, I would not have a lawyer to be wanting to himself in using fair means. I would have him inject a little hint now and then, to prevent his being overlooked."

None of this, obviously, justifies ambulance chasing (see Chapter 7) or "strike suits"—actions against corporate directors on the part of stockholders with no real reason to complain, malpractice claims against doctors jealous of their reputations, artificial libel suits, attacks on a will on behalf of a lady with a story to tell—in the hope of blackjacking vulnerable people into parting with some money that can be split between the client and the lawyer. This happens, and the lawyers who do it get away with it, because a shadow of a claim for justice can usually be conjured up to support the lawsuit, but it doesn't happen often, because few lawyers are sufficiently self-contemptuous (and few of those are brave enough or clever enough) to look to make a living in that manner.

More pervasive are the problems which arise because a city offers to its residents an infinite range of possible troubles, and little information about how to handle them. Even county-seat lawyers are specialized to some degree, but in county seats people know who knows most about the workings of the milk-marketing service or the liability insurance company. In the cities a lawyer is a lawyer —an attitude insisted upon by the bar associations, which run "lawyer-referral" services for people who know enough to call them, and insist that lawyers who have put their names on this list must be summoned in rotation, whether the case is the sort of thing they have worked on in the past or not. (The reason for the insistence, apart from philosophy, is the fear of many lawyers that otherwise the occasional lucrative personal-injury matter will go to a member of the in-group—which it may, anyway.) There is no publicity value for the big-city lawyer, as there is for his county-seat brother, in handling matters for poor people at much less than a reasonable fee.

While there are more city lawyers than people think who will look across the desk with a first thought of what a lawyer can do to help, most city lawyers are (and economically have to be) interested first in the fees they can earn.

People don't know who can help them in a situation where a lawyer *can* help; lawyers are forever trying their luck in areas of work which they know very imperfectly, if at all, where they either manage their client's business badly or run up his costs by making him pay for their education. (This problem may exist in large metropolitan law firms, too: Johnstone and Hopson write that Wall Street's "feeling of across the board superiority or super-competence . . . may be a myth, and moreover may be causing a reduction in quality and an increase in the cost of much legal service.") And, says the standard treatise on legal ethics, ominously, "There has never apparently been any extensive attempt to remove lawyers from active practice merely because they are or have been obviously incompetent or careless in performing their professional duties."

Predictably, the public turns to people other than lawyers to do what has traditionally been regarded as legal work, and people other than lawyers gleefully accept their new responsibilities— indeed, advertise for them. And the bar is upset. Unfortunately, the lawyers' primary (though not exclusive) reaction to the situation has been to guard the monopoly rather than to improve the service. Throughout the country there are literally scores of bar Committees on the Unauthorized Practice of Law, organized to hale into court (where the victims' fate will be determined by judges who are also lawyers) accountants, banks, real-estate brokers, insurance companies, mutual-fund-selling organizations which are found giving what can be called legal advice. In Arizona, after a state supreme court decision in 1961, it was necessary to pass a constitutional amendment to restore to the public the right to buy real estate without paying a lawyer; the amendment carried by a 4-1 vote.

"Actually," a chairman of the American Bar Association Unauthorized Practice Committee once wrote, "unauthorized practice of law is a swindle upon the public. Whenever it takes place, some person receives either incompetent or unqualified advice, or advice which cannot be honestly disinterested." Thus the citizen should not go for tax advice to an accountant who worked seven years with the Internal Revenue Service; instead, he must go for his own protection to some newly licensed lawyer who never did take the tax course offered at his law school, but needs the business. "There is at least a suggestion in defendant's brief," wrote Chief Justice Taft for a unanimous Ohio Supreme Court in 1965, enjoining a bank from unauthorized practice,

> that defendant is more qualified than the general lawyer to provide the legal advice necessary to reach sound conclusions with respect to estate planning and that there is therefore a public interest in making such legal advice from defendant available to prospective customers. There is nothing to prevent such a customer from getting any benefit he would have gotten from such advice if defendant is enjoined from giving it to prospective customers. The lawyer of a prospective customer will undoubtedly welcome the helpfulness of defendant. . . .

Anything can be dispensed with, except the lawyer's fee.

Not all this agitation is nonsense. A great deal of the legal advice given by nonlawyers is incompetent and reflects the interests of the giver. The real-estate broker wants to make a sale, and may supply a "standard form contract" and a mortgage that work against the interests of the purchaser—and "Representing a home buyer at a closing," as a New Hampshire lawyer puts it, "costs only about twenty-five or thirty dollars on a purchase of, say, thirteen thousand; and can save a lot of trouble later on." The small loan company wants to make sure the bankrupt is still stuck with his payments. Mr. Dacey wants to sell mutual funds, and the insurance broker wants to sell insurance. Even the bank and the accountant may be looking forward to fees for fiduciary work—though it is hard to see how in that case their interest is different from the lawyer's.

Over the long run, in any event, the public will not stand for paying two fees for a single piece of work: one to the lawyer for his license and the other to the specialist for doing the job. "[S]ome of these encroachments on the practitioner's ancient fields," Karl Llewellyn wrote a generation ago, "are like the encroachments of the white man on the Indian: neither right nor law, neither tradition nor stubborn fighting by the gathered tribe, will over long hold up the dispossession."

The more unsavory aspects of the trade-union approach to a profession are hangovers from the 1930s, when lawyers literally starved. "There are more than five hundred attorneys hereabouts," Jacob L. Bernstein wrote of a city of 100,000 in New Jersey in 1936.

. . . They steal in silently, unannounced, like gypsies; every day or so there is a new sign swinging in the breeze. Yet only a dozen local lawyers make money. . . . Lawyers scurry about like newsboys in an effort to drum up business. . . . I and most of my lawyer friends would quickly abandon our practices for a salaried job, if we had the chance. . . . Many barely earn their keep; they walk around with nickels in their pockets. Most of them are receiving assistance from parents, in-laws or wives. . . . Recently a prominent young attorney in my town quit the profession to become a shoe salesman. Others have gone into insurance, bookselling, and storekeeping One is now the happy proprietor of a fruit and vegetable stand.

And there is evidence that the depression hung on somewhat longer in the law than it did elsewhere. Of 2,325 law graduates of June, 1948, surveyed at the end of that year, 30 percent (including a fifth of those who had stood in the top third of their class) were still without full-time legal work, and 9 percent were still looking for some sort of job.

In 1937 the American Bar Association turned to formal "treaties" with competitors, in which the two groups would agree to respect each other's turf. The first such was signed with the collection agencies; there followed insurance adjusters in 1939, banks and publishers of legal materials in 1941, real-estate brokers in 1943, life insurance underwriters in 1948 and accountants (somewhat abortively) in 1951. Many state associations have comparable agreements, plus additional treaties with automobile clubs and teachers' associations about what these organizations can do in legal areas for individual members. These treaties have relaxed some of the pressure: asked in 1963 why lawyers don't make enough money, only 6 percent of Indiana lawyers mentioned "fees charged by non-attorneys" (38 percent mentioned "fees charged by other attorneys"). But the bar has done relatively little to meet competition from lay sources by improving the organization or the quality of service offered by lawyers. The only serious efforts have been made in the title insurance area, where, led by Florida, the state bar associations have set up their own "Lawyers' Title Guaranty" companies.

The way out has been pointed by the Supreme Court in its decision in the *Brotherhood of Railway Trainmen* case in 1964. The Brotherhood had been trying for years to establish a system whereby lawyers known to be competent (and to be friends of the union) would handle the negligence cases of injured railwaymen and their widows. (The stimulus originally was the fact that railroad men, equally scared of the company and the lawyers, were not taking advantage of legislation passed by Congress as early as 1906 to help them sue their employers.) At one point, the scheme had included a kickback arrangement to the union, and the Supreme Court of Illinois had destroyed it on that basis. Even with the kickback feature removed, the Supreme Court of Virginia ruled that the union was stirring up litigation and engaging in the unauthorized practice of law. The U.S. Supreme Court by a 6-2 vote, in an odd decision stressing the union's First Amendment rights of free speech in recommending lawyers, held that Virginia could not forbid BRT's sort of "group legal service." Forty-four state bar associations, four municipal bar associations and the ABA filed a brief requesting a rehearing, which the Court denied.

Meanwhile, the state bar of California had a distinguished committee investigating this question of the extent to which organizations did (and should) help their members get legal services. Previous decisions of the California Supreme Court had declared that lawyers engaged in such programs were subject to discipline. In a subsequent ruling, however, the Court said that a defendant in such an action was entitled to examine all the records of the state bar in considering whether to prosecute similar cases, to assure that he was being treated like everybody else—and the bar was unwilling to allow such records to be opened. General expectation in California was that the new committee (headed by a former president of the bar, who had never shown any enthusiasm for group services) would, like its predecessors, call for more stringent enforcement of the rules against unauthorized practice and solicitation. In the fall of 1964, however, the committee submitted a report urging that group legal services be legitimized and promoted by the bar itself, under appropriate supervision. Though the state bar later refused to approve the report, BRT will keep anyone from interfering with plans to carry out its recommendations, in California or elsewhere.

What the California committee recommended was that all sorts of organizations—labor unions, trade associations, professional societies, property owners' leagues, tenant groups, automobile clubs, consumer cooperatives—should be encouraged to make group arrangements with lawyers whose services would then become available on a known basis to all members of the organization, at least for help with matters related to the purposes of the organization. The committee cited a comment from a California Consumers Cooperatives Association: "These people do not want cut rates. They want to pay the going rate, but they want an assurance of qualified service at predictable cost. They are not interested in the Bar Association's reference service, because it meets neither requirement."

In part of its report, the committee even looked forward to the day when organizations could offer legal insurance as they now offer medical insurance: membership would guarantee that in a certain range of possible legal troubles the lawyers' bills and court costs would be paid by the group. The committee also noted that specialization by lawyers in separate fields of law "appears inextricably intertwined with group legal services, both as a cause and as an effect."

To some extent, this bold and much disliked report ("Many of my friends, Chairman Burnham Enerson told an ABA meeting, "who know me as a rather conservative person, have asked me how I could be associated with any recommendation for such an unorthodox proposal") merely reflected what is already happening in the marketplace for legal services. "I believe," Enerson continued, "that group legal services are now a fact of life . . . the legal profession is losing touch with reality when it concludes that it can avoid any entanglement with this trend toward group activity." In California itself, labor lawyers who are in theory forbidden to have any special relationship with the accident claims of the union members keep their records of such claims on IBM cards that yield daily print-out of the stage of the case. And specialization—reliance upon expertise in a single field of law for at least half one's income

—undoubtedly characterizes the practice of many lawyers in any metropolitan area. An Illinois survey in 1959 showed that more than half the lawyers in Chicago between the ages of thirty-five and sixty-five regarded themselves as specialists.

But the bar is not wholly foolish or reactionary in its reluctance to plunge the profession into what could be a bag of snakes. Specialization, for example, has come to the legal specialists by experience rather than by training: except in a very few metropolitan centers (maybe only in New York, where the NYU Law School takes the matter very seriously) there are no facilities for training specialists; and even the NYU Law School won't do it with law students who are not yet lawyers. "It's a rare case where a man chooses his specialty for himself," said Dean Miguel de Capriles. "His clients force him into it." Stanley Fleischmann of Los Angeles, who has taken half a dozen obscenity cases to the Supreme Court, says, "My entry into the field was pure accident. My cousin had a friend who was having trouble with the Post Office Department. I didn't have much business, he didn't have much money—it was a natural."

Nobody has come up with any very good way to certify that lawyers are, indeed, competent specialists. Leaving to students the decision as to desirable specialties will produce waves of fads. (A Wall Street hiring partner began asking law school seniors in 1966 what field of law they hoped to specialize in, and three-quarters of them said, "International law." Finally he found the answer. "We don't do much of that on Wall Street," he said; "our specialty is mostly civil rights.") Though nobody talks about it much, many lawyers also realize that recognized specialization will reduce some of today's full-fledged lawyers to the status of, say, dental technicians. Particularly because lawyers' incomes have been rising recently more rapidly than the national average, the bar does not believe that there is anything seriously wrong about current procedures for the provision of legal services to the public at large; as organized, it can see nothing but radicalism, change and decay in the pressures toward group practice and specialization. But nothing the bar can do will make these pressures go away.

"Working with the lawyers on the Group Legal Services project," says Murray L. Schwartz of the UCLA Law School, "was a very exciting experience. These men really gave of themselves for eighteen months. We'd talk; they'd say, 'It's the end of the solo practitioner.' And I'd say, 'What's so terrible about that?' After the third time—they were very intelligent men—they began thinking about the problem."

CHAPTER 3

THE LAW SCHOOLS: WHERE THE LAWYERS COME FROM

"No man can be a compleat Lawyer by universality of knowledge without experience in particular Cases, nor by bare experience without universality of knowledge; he must be both speculative and active, for the science of laws, I assure you, must joyn hands with experience."

—LORD COKE

"It is an odd commentary that law education in this country started in the law office and then in large measure forgot it."
—LOUIS M. BROWN, University of Southern California

"Law is what the law professors do."
—THOMAS M. FRANCK, Oxford University

"On one occasion a student made a curiously inept response to a question from Professor Warren. 'The Bull' roared at him, 'You will never make a lawyer. You might just as well pack up your books now and leave the school.' The student rose, gathered his notebooks, and started to leave, pausing only to say in full voice, 'I accept your suggestion, Sir, but I do not propose to leave without giving myself the pleasure of telling you to go plumb straight to

hell.' 'Sit down, Sir, sit down,' said The Bull. 'Your response makes it clear that my judgment was too hasty.' "

    —JOSEPH N. WELCH, in a memorial tribute
    to Professor Edward Henry Warren

1

"That's right—in this case the court held that the rule of *Hadley* versus *Baxendale,* undoubtedly the most famous case on damages we have in the common law—the court held that the rule of *Hadley* versus *Baxendale applies.* Now, can you state in your own words the rule in *Hadley* versus *Baxendale?*"

The questioner is Professor Walter Henry Edward Jaeger, and the gentleman being questioned, a hefty young man with a blond crew cut, is one of about a hundred first-year students gathered together in one of the worn, wood-floor, wood-table, portrait-littered "halls" (classroom is clearly the wrong word) at the antique red-brick law school of Georgetown University on the edge of downtown Washington. (The rule, roughly, is that damages for breach of contract will be assessed only to make up the victim's actual losses on the ruptured deal, not to yield him the profits he expected to make had the contract been honored.) The course is Contracts, and this is its last meeting of the year. Professor Jaeger, a rather small, muscular man with a classic profile and long iron-gray hair, works from a platform raised several feet above the class, running almost the length of the huge room. He wanders up and down on it. He has a rather odd, high-pitched, faintly whining classroom voice—necessary to carry to all the corners of a room which is an acoustical monstrosity. A significant scholar in the law, charged with maintaining the currency of the standard treatise in his field, *Williston on Contracts,* Jaeger is also something more: a first-rate actor and storyteller, and a teacher.

The method, of course, is Socratic: with very few exceptions, American law schools build their first-year programs on a methodology which requires all students to come to all classes prepared to discuss and analyze a group of actual appellate court decisions in real cases, assigned for this day. He must think fast enough on his feet to know which cases he can then cite in answer to a professor's wholly unexpected question—for example, about a situation where "A is juggling dynamite in Harvard Square and. . . ." This cannot be faked; if the case has not been read carefully, annotated, related to other cases and firmly placed in the mind somewhere convenient to the mouth, the student had better avoid the dialogue. His teachers during his first months will see to it that he shuts up unless he has something to talk about; the motto, now out of fashion but not entirely out of practice, was "Humiliate the student—it's good for his mind." Called upon by a professor reading from a seating chart or simply running his eye around the room, the student who is not ready says so, as Jaeger's next candidate does: "I'm not prepared."

A note is made in a notebook at the desk on the platform, and a comment is added to the case, to break the embarrassment, before the next student is called. "This," says Professor Jaeger, "is one of the first cases where we encounter sound in the motion pictures; up to then it was very quiet. . . ."

The next student is ready to talk, but his language is unsteady. Glancing at the notes he has made in the casebook, he runs down a few salient pieces of information about the case, and then shifts gears: "Your client collects if—"

"*Collects!*" says Professor Jaeger, and looks horrified to the ceiling. (An experienced lawyer says "recovers," for "collects" is a separate legal action.) "Collects!" This is, after all, his last class of the year, too. "Collects! Shades of dear old Professor Kegman, who *hangs*—" he points a finger at the floor, indicating the room where the portrait is—"who *hangs* below! He would flunk a man who used the word 'collect.' Of course, we are much more lenient now, and I merely deduct thirty points.

"Collects! Now, there *is* an occasion when that word is proper. As a practical lawyer—and since you use the word 'collect,' I can see you are a practical lawyer—you may sometimes wish to *collect* a fee in advance from a client. What that means is that the practical lawyer does not really want this client: he is a fly-by-night client. The fly-by-night *client* is thereby properly relegated to the graduate of the fly-by-night *law school*. They need the practice. We need the money. . . .

"Continue. . . ."

2

In 1961 the National Opinion Research Center in Chicago collected completed questionnaires from a sample of about 34,000 male college seniors, and followed up a year later to see what they were doing. About 1,200 of those who had said they were going to law school actually went, and most of them reported back from 124 different law schools. Of that quarter of the group who were attending the eight law schools NORC had rated the best, 97 percent said they thought the "caliber of classroom teaching" was "excellent" or "good." Of those at the sixteen schools NORC had slotted in "Stratum II," 92 percent praised the teaching; and even those in the hundred "Stratum III" law schools gave a 75 percent vote of confidence. The author of the report wrote that "It comes as a distinct surprise to this former graduate student of sociology to discover that entering law students overwhelmingly endorse the caliber of classroom teaching to which they are exposed. Perhaps there are differences between graduate and professional training that impose different perspectives on this and other aspects of higher education." Apparently it did not occur to a former graduate student of sociology to go look at some of this teaching himself. If he had done so, he would have discovered that his respondents were not making subjective ratings; they were reporting the truth. Law school teaching is on the average (especially in the first year) more intense and more intelligent teaching than is offered in any other variety of academic institution in the United States.

The recent tendency of the universities to pull together like a frightened spider has brought to the law schools for the first time some of the evils of "publish or perish"; and Dean Erwin Griswold of Harvard has been complaining in his annual reports for the last dozen years about the lack of money to finance research by his faculty. The rise of the administrator has led California's Frank C. Newman to denounce "the squandering of scholars' skills on deans' work, clerks' work and hack work." Consulting jobs have begun to drain the energies of some of the staff—"especially the tax man," says Dean Edward L. Barrett, Jr., of the new California law school at Davis; "he's always under pressure unless he beats them off with clubs." A lawyer who has practiced in both New York and Boston reports a difference between the two: "In New York the Columbia professors come down to Wall Street; in Boston we go out to Cambridge." But by and large it is still true that law school professors have a first commitment to teaching. Insiders boasted proudly of the Harvard Law School as revitalized by Dean Christopher Columbus Langdell in the 1870s that "It turned out not books, but men."

Fresh from his last year at college, with its seminar work and its research papers, its cock-o'-the-walk freedom, the law student comes to twelve or fourteen hours a week of required classes, nearly all of them in large rooms like theaters, each row of desks a step higher than the one before. Each class meeting is organized around an assigned section in a thick textbook that presents mostly the decisions of appellate court judges, who state the facts of the case before them, summarize the arguments that have (and sometimes that haven't) been made by the lawyers who represented the parties, and at some point in the opinion announce a result in the case with the reasoning that lies behind it. Each case must be read several times, to make sure nothing of significance is missed (or, perhaps worse, added); and it is often wise, or even required, to look up in the library some of the other cases cited by the judges in their opinions or by the casebook author in his comments.

Various schools have different work rituals—bound notebook or loose-leaf, little pages of tissue paper with glue along one edge to allow abstracts of cases to be pasted in the lecture notebook, underlining in the casebook with blue, red, green or black ink, or lining through with an almost transparent yellow crayon. The object is to make sure that you have picked out from some four or ten thousand words of judicial comment just those statements of fact and phrasings of opinion that tell you which subsequent cases will be seen to "stand on all fours" with this one and will produce the same result, which rule of law will (or may not) be applied to slightly different sets of facts.

Any educational institution can supply an infinitely long list of its functions and purposes. Like Oxbridge in Britain, the best law schools select future leaders, who emerge marked men. David Riesman writes: "A young student who does 'well' at law school in terms of its unidimensional grading system (barring an aggressively unfortunate personality) is ticketed for life as a first-class passenger on the talent escalator."

Most law professors would agree that the primary target is to make the student "think like a lawyer." Almost nobody comes to law school with such habits of mind—the fact that the man was hit by a truck rather than by a horse cart and suffered a fractured skull rather than a twisted finger seems important to almost every tyro, though it's all the same to the law (and thus to the lawyer who is thinking about the law rather than about his fee). Lawyers at work, as clients discover, do not think the way other people think, and it was usually a law school that made them different from other people.

At bottom, a lawyer thinks in terms of controversies and their resolution. "Actual disputes," Karl Llewellyn said in the lectures he began to give in 1929 to entering law students at Columbia,

call for somebody to do something about them. First, so that there may be peace, for the disputants; for other persons whose ears and toes disputants are disturbing. And secondly, so that the dispute may really be put at rest, which means, so that a solution may be achieved which, at least in the main, is bearable to the parties and not disgusting to the lookers-on. This doing something about disputes, this doing of it reasonably, is the business of law.

But under an adversary system of law the lawyer is not supposed to see the resolution of these disputes as a question of what might be best for the society as a whole. He is an advocate; his function is to see the possible resolution of a controversy in terms of his client's best interests (though he is not obliged to accept his client's view of what these best interests may be). Nobody knows, anyway, what might be best for society; such knowledge can come, if at all, only a fortiori, after the dispute has played itself out, rather than a priori, as part of the terms of reference. The lawyer's approach to a problem, therefore, is *argumentative*. Soia Mentschikoff, Llewellyn's widow and herself a professor at the University of Chicago Law School, gives lectures today to the wives of first-year law students: "I tell them, 'Your husbands are going to change: their personalities are going to change in law school. They'll get more aggressive, more hostile, more precise, more impatient.'" (For a student who started out with this "potential character" David Riesman observes, "his very neuroses become salable in the highest degree and often indeed valuable.")

A lawyer's thinking must be clearly delimited by the standards of relevancy of the legal system and the profession rather than those of some other section of the community. "Does *mens rea* [evil intention] imply cognition?" a student asked Professor Jerome Hall in his freshman course in criminal law at Indiana University; and Hall, an old-timer, shook his head. "I don't know what you mean. What you're asking is a general question, not a legal question. The legal question is: What is the liability?" But this was a first-year student, and in relating words like "malice," "motivation" and "provocation," he was unable to resist the intrusion of psychology. Hall interrupted him: "Just a minute—you're giving us the whole business again. What's the relevancy of this?" The boy, flustered, said, "Well, I suppose it isn't *really* relevant." "Then leave it out," said Hall, and the class laughed.

To think productively, the lawyer needs a highly developed sense of procedure, of the ways the system can be used to resolve the dispute in his client's favor—indeed, this is the heart of his work. A hundred-odd years ago no claim could be put forward in the law unless it fit properly into one of the "forms of action"; and as recently as 1959, in Maine, lawyers were still suing "in assumpsit" or "in case" or whatever the appropriate phrase might be, on peril of being thrown out of court for a wrong choice of procedure. It is easy enough to have fun with these artificial categories, but they related directly to the remedies available from the law and the competence of the courts to give them, and such matters will always be crucial in any legal system. "The forms of action we have buried," as Maitland put it, "but they still rule us from their graves."

Finally, the lawyer reasons by analogy. No client's situation is exactly the same as that of someone whose case has already been decided; the lawyer's job is to find out how the facts presented to him are like (or can be made to seem like) the facts in some decided case that "made law." The client doesn't come into your office wearing a sign reading, 'I am *McPherson* v. *Buick*,' " says Alfred W. Gans, formerly editor of *American Law Reports*. (The case he mentions is the one in which Justice Cardozo allowed a customer to sue the manufacturer rather than the dealer for injuries in an accident caused by a defective car. What he means is not that you need this case to handle your client's automobile accident, but that you need it if a chair he has just bought collapses under him, causing him to slip a disc: can you successfully draw an analogy?) "You have to dig that out. And if you don't learn that in law school, you never learn it."

Even in this day of domination by the legislatures and their statutes, the law often grows by a court's extension to new situations of key phrases from past opinions. To see how the language of past opinions or of statutes can be stretched—or how the facts of the situation can be cut to fit within a phrase—is part of a lawyer's most fundamental skills, whether he is giving advice or pressing a claim through the courts.

Inherent in much of this training is the notion, very difficult for students to grasp, that "law" can usually be found on both sides of a dispute—that when one comes down to actual cases (especially the cases in the law school casebook) there is no "black letter" law, no statement of a rule as opposed to its discussion, which will certainly govern. The law schools, by and large, do not win this one; but, then, understanding that there is good law on both sides of a dispute is thinking like a law professor or a judge rather than thinking like a lawyer.

3

There is something quite odd about the notion that a university is a good place to teach young people how to think like lawyers. In Britain, whence most American legal traditions derive, law was not taught at all in universities until the second half of the eighteenth century, when "William Blackstone, then a disappointed barrister, began to give lectures on English law at Oxford." Even today, though law is a respectable undergraduate study at the British universities, nothing nearly so elaborate as the American law school has been developed, and the aspiring Englishman proceeds through some variety of apprenticeship training under a barrister or a solicitor. Up to the turn of the century most lawyers in the United States followed a similar route to the bar. Most apprentices paid for the privilege, augmenting the income of the lawyer in whose office they "clerked" (which meant that the lawyers most interested in teaching the young were normally those least successful in the profession itself). In addition to the cash payment, and sometimes in lieu of it, the candidate would make himself useful, most often by copying in longhand. When the typewriter and the female secretary came along, the economic function of the apprentice vanished; and, presently, so did the apprentice.

Independent law schools had existed in late medieval and Renaissance England, when the Inns of Court were something more than the uncomfortable offices-cum-restaurants which they later became. "Lawyers of that age," Maitland wrote, ". . . went through an elaborate scholastic course which if not severe was at least prolonged—ten or twelve years of 'readings,' 'mootings,' and 'boltings' [a "moot" was a case proposed by a junior to be debated by everyone; a "bolt" was a case proposed by a senior, for debate by the students on the wrong—the "outer"—side of the bar], of hearing and giving lectures, and the path of scholastic success was the path to profit and to place." It was the decadence of the Inns of Court (and the disappearance of the comparable institutions which had trained men to appear before courts other than King's Bench) which opened the way for Blackstone; and it was with Blackstone in mind that Thomas Jefferson, while Governor of the Commonwealth of Virginia during the Revolutionary War, arranged the appointment of a professor of "Law and Police" at the College of William and Mary.

There was an important independent law school at Litchfield, Connecticut, as early as 1784, and in half a century it produced among its thousand graduates 101 Congressmen, 28 Senators and 14 Governors. Harvard's first part-time law professor was appointed in 1815, and two years later the university incorporated an alleged "law school." But anyone at all with $100 and a place to stay in

Cambridge could declare himself a student at the Harvard Law School and depart eighteen months later proclaiming himself a lawyer.

Modern American legal education dates only to 1870, when Charles W. Eliot, the new president of Harvard, hired the New York lawyer Christopher Columbus Langdell to be first a professor of law and then (a new title) dean of the Law School in Cambridge. Up to then law school everywhere had been an alternative rather than a successor to college, and the program had been mostly scattered lectures by practicing lawyers and judges on the invented disputes of a mythical Flavius and Titus over the ownership of a mythical Blackacre. Langdell hired full-time professors, began to demand undergraduate preparation, and set up a compulsory program (Crime, Property, Contract, Torts, Civil Procedure), the first year of which is still pretty much the standard fare everywhere.

During his first year on the job, Langdell invented and largely perfected the case method of teaching, replacing the old abstractions and rules of law with the analysis of how judges had decided specific disputes that had come before them. "He told me," Eliot later said, "that law was a science: I was quite prepared to believe it. He told me that the way to study a science was to go to the original sources. I knew that it was true, for I had been brought up in the science of chemistry myself." In 1871 Langdell published the first "casebook," containing a collection of decisions on Contract. The printed material, where possible, contained the arguments of the lawyers as well as the decisions of the judges, but Langdell offered almost no commentary—the job of the student was to write his own commentary.

Judge Jerome Frank, the most unhistorical of legal observers (psychology and sociology were the thing for Frank), attacked the long-dead Langdell in 1947 with the comment that "American legal education went badly wrong some seventy years ago when it was seduced by a brilliant neurotic." What drew Frank's wrath particularly was Langdell's statement that "the library is to us what the laboratory is to the chemist or the physicist." Langdell's analogy to science was obviously more fashionable than valid even at the time—Justice Holmes observed calmly during Langdell's tenure that what he was really talking about was a kind of theology rather than the messy reality of law. But the library was indeed the key, because the essence of law is the idea that people shall know what they cannot do unpunished, and such knowledge demands a minimum degree of consistency with the past, which in turn is securely knowable only through written records.

Contrary to the thrust of Frank's attack, Langdell's purpose had been to make legal education more realistic and less abstract, by using the facts of cases and what judges had done with them rather than the treatises and generalizations of book writers. Louis D. Brandeis in 1876 wrote his brother-in-law enthusiastically that "The points thus incidentally learned are impressed upon the mind as they never would be by mere reading or lectures . . . for they occur as an integral part of the drama of life." Frank was shrewder in his criticism (though still unhistorical) when he commented elsewhere that the "facts" as presented in the casebooks through the opinions of appellate court judges are not a mirror of reality but "a censored exposition, written by a judge, of what induced him to arrive at a decision which he had already reached." But it was precisely this prior purification of the "facts" by a judge that eventually made the case method such a brilliant pedagogical tool.

What today's much publicized educational reformers are trying to do under the labels "discovery" and "structure" is simply an application of Langdell's case method to the elementary and secondary schools. What Langdell saw, as the math and science reformers in the schools have seen, is that the materials to be studied must themselves control the student's frame of reference. By presenting several cases with substantially different facts, all resolved by the judges on the basis of a similar *ratio decidendi* (reason for the decision), Langdell could force the aspiring lawyer to see what was and what was not legally relevant. There is also a more profound "case method," of which the late Ralph Baker of Harvard was the recognized grand master. It involves the study of a single large case in great detail and depth, as the men who tried the case had to study it—a procedure which expands as well as refines the idea of relevance.

"DON'T miss taking down the questions your professor poses,

even at the expense of not hearing the answer," says the *Handbook for Entering Students* at the Harvard Law School. "The questions are the things he has given thought to, the answers are often off-the-cuff and tentative." Many law professors never (or hardly ever) provide answers, except in the form of acceptance—for the time being—of what a student has proposed, and even here there is often a question: "What about Moore's clause, men?" Julius Getman calls to an Indiana class that wants him to be satisfied, "Are we ready to put this in boilerplate?"

When some sort of general statement seems unavoidable, the law professor will make it ambiguous, unsuitable for regurgitation on an examination. Chicago's Harry Kalven, Jr., for example, put a class of about a hundred through its paces on that most distasteful facet of Anglo-American law, the fact that nobody is legally obliged to throw a life preserver to a drowning man, or keep a baby from falling into a well, and can become liable for what happens only if he does try to help. "What about the man who sees the baby crawling toward the well, puts down his paper, calls out, 'Wait, baby,' takes seven steps—then decides, the hell with it, and goes back to his chair?" After the students had responded to the series of such questions, something was necessary to wrap this one up and go to "the second cluster of no-duty rules." Kalven, a juggler on a platform, wrapped it up: "If you want the big architectonic rule about affirmative actions in our society, the answer is—you buy it." And, ignoring the glazed eyes of the class, he proceeded to the next set of cases.

Harvard's Warren Seavey once remarked, "I think teaching law is rather like herding sheep. You run around behind the students and bark at their heels, and head off the ones that start for the hilltops, and after a while, if you create enough commotion, they move down the valley and arrive at a destination, without ever knowing how they got there." At worst, the method requires the student to do his own work. At best, when a professor has a gift for posing hypothetical questions, invented cases to supplement the real ones, the method can be fantastically stimulating, pointing out to a student that the rule as he has stated it would produce an impossibly unjust result under other circumstances, forcing attention to subtleties that did not occur to the court that heard the case—if, indeed, they have ever before occurred to anybody.

A great deal of this is just logic-chopping—like a class overheard at New Mexico's fledgling law school, where a professor was insisting that students take seriously the question of whether two robbers could be convicted of murder if the man they had beaten unconscious and hurled down a cliff was in fact alive and viable at the end of the experience, and subsequently died from exposure after crawling about in the desert. But sometimes "a hypothetical" can raise innnumerable questions for students to worry over, like the one cited by California's William L. Prosser in his tribute to Seavey:

"I once heard him, during a visiting hour at Stanford, baffle a class for an entire hour with this problem: You are driving a car down a hill when you discover that your brakes have failed. On your left there is a precipice of a thousand feet; on your right there is an oil tank truck parked at the curb; across the road in front there is a procession of old ladies wheeling baby carriages; in the back of your car is your paralyzed sister. What do you do to avoid legal liability?

"The case is not, I think, likely to arise," Prosser adds; "I do not know the answer, nor, I suspect, did Seavey." And even if Seavey had known, of course, he would not have told. In their pedagogical writing, and sometimes even in their casual conversation, law professors have a special style built around the phrase, "If . . . then *quaere* . . ." It is a very exciting experience for students who have spent sixteen years in classrooms where they knew that if they sat back long enough the teacher would tell them what they should know. For some, the experience is also seriously destructive.

One striking advantage of the case method, noted by educational administrators, is its adaptability to large classes; indeed, there is an argument to be made for the proposition that the impersonality of the large class is helpful to the student called upon to perform under attack for the first time in his life. "I prefer a hundred," says Myres McDougal of Yale. "I will work for a hundred and put on a good show; I'll go to sleep with ten or twelve. After you've taught a subject to a class of a hundred for two or three years, you can anticipate the questions and their timing. When I started, I was told, 'Pick four or five points and keep coming back to them; find the bright students and play them like a piano.' It works."

Thus, while colleges usually need one professor for every ten or twelve students, and some graduate schools must lay on staff even more thickly, the Harvard Law School runs with one professor to every thirty to thirty-five students. And the professors, in American education's most remarkable revelation of commitment and energy, read all their students' papers and exams, unaided. Historically, the large class (coupled with the opportunity to use the practicing lawyer as a part-time teacher on a part-time salary) made law schools not merely self-supporting but profitable. Individual promoters, YMCAs, Catholic colleges that wanted the status of university—all launched law schools once Langdell's model had proved out. By 1910 there were 124 law schools, all using casebooks as their fundamental tool.

The intellectual reputation of Langdell's venture was such that F. W. Maitland, delivering the Rede Lecture at Cambridge University in 1901, could urge a revival of the educational function of the Inns of Court with the phrase, "the glory of Bourges, the glory of Bologna, the glory of Harvard may yet be theirs."

The significance of Harvard has persisted: a quarter of all the nation's law professors are Harvard alumni—and so are 6 percent of the nation's law school graduates. Though Harvard is a middling-sized university, its law school with sixteen hundred students is the nation's largest (Texas is second), and its influence far transcends its size. "We have to do something about the Harvard syndrome," says a Chicagoan, "you know, the attitude that there are just two very good law schools, Harvard and this one."

4

Yet the case method was never universally accepted. To secure its adoption at Columbia in 1890, President Seth Low had to fire half the faculty. Even today, despite Dean Griswold's insistence that the battle "is long since passed[;] the case method has won on all points," many people are troubled by its side effects, and even by its triumphant end product.

"If you have something to say," says Yale's Alexander Bickel, a brightly casual professor who also teaches law to the readers of *The New Republic*, "the Socratic method is time-wasting beyond belief."

Case study is limiting. "Intensive, sustained analysis in group discussion *must* presuppose a narrow, a very narrow, common subject matter," Karl Llewellyn said in his lectures to second-year Columbia students. "Case teaching is graduate teaching in its training in analysis. It calls for ripe powers, it calls for a ripe attention span, it calls for ripe depth of thought. But it is grade school teaching in its method of assigning stuff. . . . Thus the very precondition of case discussion lames initiative."

Columbia's Herbert Wechsler, a rather owlish, witty man with shoulders thrust forward, who is also executive director of the American Law Institute, says that "criminal law through cases is an invitation to close distinctions that don't mean anything and merely point out the incompetence of the law. My interest with law students is the precondition of competence, a cultivated sense of the subject, of the fundamental and abiding problems that inhere in condemnation and punishment. Aristotle had more to say about that than the Chief Justice of this, that or the other court."

To the extent that the law is known, handed down by judges long dead, the cases available only in archaic and uninformative reports, case study is a hard and rather foolish way to get at the rules. "The settled areas of law are not litigated," as David Riesman wrote while he was still a law professor at the University of Buffalo, "and the study of cases teaches the content of the law only as a by-product of teaching how to learn the law as needs arise in practice." Moreover, the emphasis on cases teaches a contempt for statutes, though the legislature can change the rules in every court. "The average lawyer today doesn't start with cases," says Frank C. Newman, who tried four years as dean at the University of California in Berkeley, didn't like it and went back to being a professor. "He starts with statutes, and looks it up there. So we have a new first-year course to start them with real law instead of yakking about cases. If you wait until spring semester, you can never persuade them again that the appellate courts don't determine every-thing."

The quality of the information the student takes from a year of case work is often bad. UCLA's Murray Schwartz reports a moment of terror at the front of a criminal law class when he realized that after half a year's work on this subject his students did not know that 80 percent of all accused persons plead guilty. Similarly, Sanford Kadish at the University of California in Berkeley was distressed to find that second-year students offered fellowships for a summer's work at a district attorney's office were most reluctant to accept—they all wanted to work for the Public Defender, and they had not acquired the very basic knowledge that the chance of really helping any number of accused people is infinitely greater in the prosecutor's office than it can ever be on the defense side.

And some just don't like the case method as a classroom technique. "The law teachers I had," David Riesman said recently, "were ham actors, with a few exceptions. Law school was unbelievably boring, endless cases—this bombastic give-and-take of law-school teaching, which I didn't like then and don't like now: 'Riesman, get up and state such and such a case.' "

Most of those who denounce the pedagogy of the law schools, however, have a more profound and stranger reason for their dis-taste: though their work is to train young men (and occasional women) to think like lawyers, they don't like the way lawyers think. The late Thomas Reed Powell of Harvard once put the matter philosophically: "If you think that you can think about a thing inextricably attached to something else without thinking of the thing which it is attached to, then you have a legal mind."

Usually, distrust of the case method is openly political. "I watched my classmates go in with liberal and generous views," says William Robert Bishin of the University of Southern California Law School, speaking of his very recent student days at Harvard (a West Coast colleague, not unfriendly, calls Bishin "the tallest three-year-old law professor in California"). "And I watched them come out with the attitudes of the corporate lawyer. Here at USC we're concerned about attitudes toward legal education; we feel a lawyer is a public servant."

The objection has its roots in Justice Holmes, who dedicated the Boston University Law School in 1897, in part with the words, "I cannot but believe that if the training of lawyers led them habitually to consider more definitely and explicitly the social advantage on which the rule they lay down must be justified, they sometimes would hesitate where now they are confident, and see that really they were taking sides upon debatable and often burning questions." In Langdell's day the university law school avoided some of this narrowness through its incorporation into the main stream of the larger institution. Henry Stimson remembered that in his time at Harvard "George Palmer, William James, and Josiah Royce . . . were available [to a student] whether he was an undergraduate or in a professional school." The decision to make the law schools exclusively professional institutions blocked the normal flow of ideas and information from nonlegal sources.

Meanwhile, of course, the "public profession" of the law became much more public. Today, more than forty thousand lawyers, 15 percent of the national total, are in government service of one kind or another. For them, and for an unknown percentage of the private practitioners whose time is devoted entirely to counseling people and corporations and labor unions on what they should and shouldn't do, the traditional lawyer's sense of relevancy and irrelevancy can be disabling. The case method presents law as an independent process, which can be intellectually mastered and to a degree manipulated; what these government lawyers and legislators and judges and even business advisers need, it can be argued, is the sense of law as *policy*.

The view of law as an independent process is identified with Harvard; the view of law as an expression of policy is identified with Yale, and to a lesser extent with Chicago—and in both places, probably, it reflects the almost forgotten influence of Robert Hutchins, who was dean of the law school at one and president of the other. These slogans of identification, however, should not be taken too seriously. "The policy orientation of legal studies which we've been talking about here for so long has become highly platitudinous," says Louis Pollak, Yale's new and vigorous young dean, out of place in the dean's big, mock-Tudor office. "The question is, can we put any content in it?"

On the other side, Harvard's David Cavers can say, rather blandly, that "Since American judges, in writing opinions, tend to discuss the political, economic and social policies that bear upon their decisions, students who have made these opinions a principal basis of their work for three years naturally tend to think of the significance of particular legal rules and decisions in terms of policies." The Harvard Law School has sloughed off to separate Graduate Schools of Public Administration, Business and Public Health some of the issues that occupy the third-year men at Yale; but certainly anyone who has passed through the fire of Henry Hart's second-year course in Legal Process, which has become for most Harvard students the centerpiece of their program (and which alumni have carted to at least a dozen other law schools, complete with fifteen hundred pages of mimeographed reading material), can have no doubts that specific policy considerations underlie both the rules and the procedures of law.

Shortly before he left his professorship at Chicago to become dean at Michigan, Francis Allen said, "If you were blindfolded and set down in any of ten or twelve law schools, in a classroom, could you tell where you were? No, you couldn't. We and Yale recruit students who come with the notion that they aren't going to law school at all but to some institute for the practical application of the social sciences. They are dismayed—some of them go across the street [from the jewel-faceted, glass-sheathed Law School which is one of Eero Saarinen's most spectacular accomplishments to the Rockefeller Gothic of Chicago's social science division directly across the Midway]. What we say does attract a thoughtful kind of student— gives a broader range of interest in the classroom. But I'm talking in millimeters, not in feet or yards."

What the argument comes down to in practice is that the orientation shifts at most law schools, some time during the second year, from cases to "problems," as reflected both in legislation and in court decisions. At Yale and Chicago there are a handful of non-lawyers on the faculty, who bring nonlegal perspectives of social control and government intervention; while Harvard, staffed entirely by lawyers, remains supremely conscious that, as Henry Hart puts it, "You are dealing with a legal system that is basically individualistic; rights are for people who assert them, and your means of enforcing them is in the courts."

All larger law schools offer the same subjects in the later years: equity, wills, trusts, labor law, jurisprudence, securities regulation, taxation, bankruptcy, land law, family law, agency, aspects of constitutional law, and the intellectual fashions, currently "conflict of laws" and international law. ("The Uniform Commercial Code put the bills-and-notes teachers out of business," says a Wall Street lawyer cynically, "so they all became experts in international law.") The course in antitrust law may bring in someone from the economics department or the business school; for "law and psychiatry," which can be found at about a third of the schools, some time with the nonlegal perspective is considered desirable. New courses in "poverty law," called into being by the Office of Economic Opportunity, may introduce sociologists. Classes tend to be smaller when the goal is the study of what Yale once rather grandiosely called "policy science"; the reading list is larger and looser—and so, alas, is the class discussion, because questions of what ought to be are not amenable to the tough-minded analysis that can be brought to bear on questions of what is.

The names most intimately associated with the policy approach are those of the psychoanalytically oriented political scientist Harold Lasswell and the Yale law professor Myres McDougal, Mississippian, college classmate and friend of Senator James Eastland and American Bar Association ex-president John Satterfield (who led the Southern lawyers in their fight against the Supreme Court's desegregation decisions). McDougal was the one who got the Rhodes scholarship; and he obviously acquired a different perspective. Still active despite badly deteriorated eyesight, immensely useful in the effort to turn Mississippi into the modern world (he set up the 1965-66 program by which Yale and Harvard professors took two-week tours of duty teaching at the University of Mississippi Law School), hugely respected among his colleagues (in 1966 he was president of the Association of American Law Schools), McDougal in recent years has grown rather bitter about the failure of his own school to adopt the tactics he and Lasswell outlined, as follows, in a famous law review article in 1943:

> If legal education in the contemporary world is adequately to serve the needs of a free and productive commonwealth, it must be conscious, efficient and systematic *training for policy-making*. . . . Policy is defined as the making of important decisions which affect the distribution of values. . . . The supreme value of democracy is the dignity and worth of the individual; hence a democratic society is a commonwealth of mutual deference. . . . Implementation of values requires . . . scientific-thinking . . . to enable us to mould the future. . . . The great contribution of modern specialists on the human sciences is less in the realm of general theory than in the perfecting of method by which ancient speculation can be confirmed, modified or rejected. . . . Throughout the length and breadth of modern society decisions are modified on the basis of what is revealed by means of intensive or extensive observations of human life.

Four years later McDougal announced that the time had come: his speech was called "The Law School of the Future: From Legal Realism to Policy Science in the World Community." The law schools, he said, had been living with a

confusion inherited from a time when people had no realistic understanding of psychology and personality, of how the human mind works . . . from a time when people had a minimal insight into group behavior, social processes, and community institutions, and into the methods by which the conditions and trends, relevant to prediction and control, could be studied . . . when the full role of the lawyer in the community—his impact on policy-advising and policy-making and, hence, on the extent to which a community can achieve its values—was not clearly apparent.

It goes without saying that this is a time which has gone forever. . . . We have a psychology which is daily working new miracles in the understanding of the mind, in disclosing the secrets of personality formation, and in delineating the variables that affect behavior. We know today how to classify values into blue-prints for action. . . . We have today a social science that can achieve enough precision in the study of the environment variables that affect human behavior to found wise policy judgments without requiring impossible and interminable investigations.

But the time McDougal had said was gone forever has come again; and we clearly have none of the assets he ascribed to the world of 1947. It is in a sense cruel to quote such stuff today, because McDougal has retreated some distance—as president of AALS, he was struggling to establish a research foundation, "because you can't teach unless you have something to teach, and we know almost nothing about the relationship between legal process and social process." But the position persists though its foundations have collapsed, and McDougal says rather resentfully that at Yale "there has been if anything retrogression since Lasswell and I wrote twenty-five years ago." Lasswell himself, forward-looking in the manner of the 1930s, still considers "policy science" the wave of the future. Most of those who once agreed feel they have learned better, not only in terms of the basic argument, but also in terms of the values represented by more traditional law school training.

Criticizing the case method twenty-five years ago, David Riesman wrote that

> Discussion is . . . ended at a question-begging phrase about 'competing social policies' at the very point where it should properly begin. . . . Those higher domains where the important truths are examined and revealed are outside the province of a mere legal technician. Thus law, which is the keystone of the arch of public policy, is robbed of vitality and significance . . . the consequence of pedagogic failure which for three years drowns imagination in technique.

Today Riesman says, "Students come to me all the time because they know I left. 'Is there anything wrong?' I say, 'No—there are many mansions.' I can't predict how my students will do. If they do well, they get what I have called the impenetrable self-confidence of the lawyer; they change. But I must say for the law school that those it does not alienate it does not crush, while the students come out of our graduate schools not knowing their own names."

The aborted revolution left its mark: today's casebooks contain more history, more analysis of the social context of the case, more comment by legal scholars on the greater issues raised by the decision. But the only place that seems to retain the first fine careless rapture of the McDougal-Lasswell approach is the University of Southern California, where a bright collection of very young law professors is engaged in remaking legal education because that is the way to remake the world.

As USC the course in Property begins with the sit-ins at the Southern lunch counters, and the course in Crime with the Appalachin case, the meeting of Mafia executives raided by the police. Christopher Stone, a blond young man with a shining smile and a comradely classroom manner with students many of whom are no older than he is, says the course in Contract will be superseded by a "course on Industry and Government. Instead of the contracts, the old cases, no feeling of a problem, I want to take the problem of the distribution of resources. The government's role in shaping transportation, the broad outlines of what the policy ought to be— and then the various devices."

Harold W. Solomon, a lean and earnest New Yorker who died in early 1967 while still in his forties, was the recognized pater- familias of these Young Turks. He liked to talk about lawyers as fitting into three general categories—physicists, engineers and plumbers. USC was to train the physicists, who would, for ex- ample, "see the crime problem as a problem of groups, racial groups, disadvantaged groups," rather than as, classically, a problem in the control of individual behavior. Stone's question in the Constitutional Law class (a freshman requirement at USC) is not "On what authority and by what reasoning do the courts ban wiretap evidence?" but rather "Mr. Collier, do you think the courts ought to allow wiretap evidence?"

"The legal physicists," says William Bishin, "the sort of lawyers I'm talking about, will get the very hardest problems." Pervasive in the conversation of the USC professors (there are about fifteen of them, for about six hundred students) is the concept of the lawyer as the last generalist in a fragmented society, the one figure who can pull together all the expertise and tie up a program. The attitude deliberately ignores the warning recently given by Dean Pollak of Yale, against "the folly of building a law school on some sort of principle of omnicompetence." If a law faculty is not omnicom- petent, after all, who is?

5

Most students, even at Harvard and Yale, are not that over- whelmingly interested in the subtleties of analysis opened up by the case method or the grand sweep of dictum made possible by policy studies. They are at law school because they want to become lawyers, and they see clearly (more clearly than some of their professors) how tenuously much of this work is related to the actual practice of law.

"The profession is committed," say Dean Pollak, "every lawyer you know is deep down committed, to the notion that one handles all these things by intuition. You don't have to go and find out much law." A 1947 sample survey of Harvard Law School alumni asked respondents to rank in order of importance six lawyerly skills: "negotiation, draftsmanship, advocacy, legal planning, 'knowing the law' in a practical sense (the ability to predict how cases will be decided), and ability to secure an understanding of facts and motives." The numerical rankings were then averaged for each skill, and five of them were pretty well bunched; the solitary leader, by a big margin, was the ability to deal with facts and motives. "There are very very few questions of law," says the head of a legal publishing operation, "and if and when they arise they are handled by a very very few members of the bar. Ninety-nine of one hundred things a lawyer handles are fact situations." Students sense this hierarchy without knowing it. They ache for guidance in practical matters, in getting the most for a possible client and out of a possible client; they don't care if they miss some fine points. As one complained bitterly to Indiana's Julius Getman, "You're teaching me to argue with Cardozo, and I'm going to go up before judges who never even *heard* of Cardozo."

Law schools have been a significant growth industry in American education of the 1960s. The 43,000 students of 1960-61 have become almost 70,000 students in 1966-67. This expansion does not reflect population pressure: the postwar baby boom first hits the law schools in 1968. In part, it is the result of the nation's prosperity; in larger part, probably, it traces to the increasing insistence on a law degree for anyone who wishes to practice law. As late as 1951, only thirteen states required such a diploma; by 1963, the number had grown to thirty-seven. By the mid-1970s there may be two hundred law schools, about two-thirds of them affiliated in some degree with a university. By the end of 1968, quite apart from the quasi-proprietary schools that rise and fall in states where the law is indulgent about these matters (most noticeably California, where the largest law school, Los Angeles' Southwest, is not nationally accredited), there will be at least six important, well-financed new state university law schools, in Arizona, California, Florida, Massachusetts, New York and Texas.

The National Opinion Research Center study of college students' plans and performances indicates that the vast majority of college seniors who definitely wish to go to law school can get in somewhere—90 percent of those who said they were sure they wanted to go and 64 percent of those who were "tentatively going" in the spring of 1961 were in fact at law school in the fall of 1961. But the better law schools (defined from a candidate's point of view as those which have produced the most successful lawyers either nationally or in his location) have been under admissions pressure almost continuously since the veterans began returning from World War II.

Like the colleges under similar pressure, they turned to the Educational Testing Service of Princeton, New Jersey, proprietors of the College Boards, to make them a "Law Schools Aptitude Test," a highly verbal, machine-scored, multiple-choice test which is taken by about three-quarters of all college seniors who wish to go to law school. The admissions committees are moderately sophisticated about the use of this instrument. If the applicant has done well at a first-class college—if, say, he stands in the top 10 percent of the graduating class at Amherst—then nobody will pay too much attention to his Law School Aptitude Test scores. If he comes, say, from the University of Chattanooga, he'd better show up well on the test. Yale has a simple formula: there is one list of colleges from which grade-point averages are weighted twice as heavily as test score, and another list in which they are weighted half as heavily. Oddly some law firms will request LSAT scores as part of job applications three years later.

About one-fifth of entering law students were economics or business majors; a fifth were political science or government majors; a fifth were in history or one of the other social sciences; a tenth were in English or a foreign language; a tenth in science or engineering; and a final fifth in one of the God-knows-what subjects in which the liberal arts colleges have specialized. The value of a science-engineering background is widely debated. Dean Edward L. Barrett of the new Law School of the University of California at Davis says that "some of them can't handle ambiguity; and if they've got to have two plus two equals four, then they'll be lost in law school." On the other hand, A. Kenneth Pye, while he was associate dean at Georgetown (where a quarter of the evening school students are engineers, mostly from the Patent Office), said that "while their work has been nonverbal, they've been developing logical procedures rather than memory, unlike so many of the history students. Moreover, they're *never* unprepared."

What the law schools want students to have done in college can be briefly described as "everything." The Chicago suggestions are: "some study of history and of the social sciences, while not neglecting literature, philosophy or other human fields . . . competence in mathematics or the physical sciences [and] a mastery of some foreign language. . . . Perhaps of greatest importance is that the student should have acquired habits of precision, fluency and economy in speaking and writing." Every law school stresses the ability to write, and complains that it is not forthcoming.

"I don't think the law occupies the same position now that it did in the 1930s," says Eugene Rostow, Pollak's predecessor as dean at the Yale Law School. "Nobody went to architecture school then, there was no pull from physics." But Rostow also says that "the level of discourse is very high—higher now than it used to be." Thirty years ago Edward "Bull" Warren of Harvard used to end his welcoming speech to freshmen by telling each of them to look very carefully at the man on his right and then at the man on his left— "because one of the three of you will not be here next year." Now the better law schools graduate at least 90 percent of their entrants, and the 130-odd accredited law schools as a group graduate about 60 percent. The truth probably is that the top hasn't improved (it never does), but the bottom has been eliminated.

Asked about "occupational values," according to the NORC study, the prospective law student is

- 21% more likely than other college seniors to say he wants to make a lot of money,

- 14% more likely to say he wants to work with people rather than with things,
- 13% more likely to wish a chance to exercise leadership,
- 12% more likely to look forward to a job without much supervision,
- 10% more likely to want to help others or be useful,
- 18% *less* likely to want moderate but steady progress rather than a chance for big success or failure,
- and 9% less likely to wish opportunities for originality.

Psychologically, says Myres McDougal, "most people who gravitate toward law have character formation toward power—but this draws the idealist, the reformer and the rebel, too." A student explains that "the practice of law is the application of *my* anxiety neurosis to *your* problem" (a psychoanalyst says this is wrong—it's the student's compulsions that are at work). Though even the top law schools can show at least a few students who may run deep but don't run fast, the operative word for the average student is "sharp." Still, attitudes have been improving. "Ten years ago," says Harvard's Louis Loss, "they were all talking about what they were going to be doing when they were fifty or sixty—it was disgusting. Now they go teach law in Africa."

Law students tend to live together and eat together: like medical students, they form a separate caste at a university. They work hard. "The library closes at eleven," says Harvard's Griswold, "but a number of people have keys." Law schools try to fill extracurricular time with law-related activities, from moot court clubs to legal aid societies, and professors stress the importance of talking over the day's work with fellow students. ("A lone wolf in law school," Karl Llewellyn told his Columbia students, "is either a genius or an idiot.") Through living with each other, and through daily immersion in the same baths, they become increasingly like each other as the years proceed.

Unfortunately, they started rather like each other, too. As Louis Toepfer wrote while he was admissions director at Harvard, "The law seems to do its fishing in restricted waters stocked largely with the product of professional families, private schools, and the upper social strata." About two-thirds of all college graduate law students are from families where the father is a professional, a proprietor or a manager, as against 44 percent of college seniors so situated and 15 percent of the nation; two-fifths are from families where the annual income is over $15,000, as against one-fifth of college seniors, and one-twentieth of the nation.

Jews are enormously overrepresented in the group (20 percent of law school entrants, as against 8 percent of college seniors and 3 percent of the population)—and, contrary to widespread belief, Jews are *more* likely to be in the eight top schools the NORC study slotted as "Stratum I," where they account for almost a third of the entering class. Lance Liebman, president of the *Harvard Law Review* in 1966-67, said rather defensively to a visitor that if he read the list of editors carefully, he'd see that not all the names were Jewish; and one of the other editors said, "Yeah—some guys changed their names." At Harvard, where through the 1920s Felix Frankfurter was the solitary Jewish professor, nearly half the faculty is now Jewish; and the last three deans of the Yale Law School have been Jews.

Of Negroes, however, there is scarcely a trace—anywhere. In a speech to the Association of American Law Schools a few years ago, Walter Gellhorn of Columbia said that in the preceding year the seven law schools associated with Southern Negro colleges had produced among them a total of seventeen graduates; and two professors at one of these institutions estimated (probably incorrectly but within the ball park) that these seventeen were one-half the total output of Negro lawyers in the United States in that year.

Various reasons, none wholly convincing, can be given for the failure of Negro college graduates to try the law schools. A professor at Chicago suggests that law is a predominantly paternal affair, in conflict with the matriarchal Negro community. The two Texas Southern professors who made the estimate of thirty-four graduates across the country say that the community perceives a "general ineffectiveness of the Negro lawyer to handle 'the white man's law.' " In the past, Negro lawyers have not done well financially, with a few exceptions, and have found few chances to build or participate in the partnerships which are the source of substantial incomes in the law: of the graduates of the Howard University Law School who are in private practice, five-sixths are solo practitioners.

In recent years, the "Stratum I" law schools have been beating the bushes for colored students, offering entrance for substantially less performance on the LSAT than they would demand of whites, and scholarships sufficient to pay all expenses—which are otherwise very rare at law schools. There are few takers. Undoubtedly, the recruiting efforts of the law schools are overwhelmed by the management-training opportunities (at good starting salaries) which big business under the Kennedy and Johnson prodding has been waving before the most promising Negro college graduates. Still, it is disturbing to note that the number of Negro law students has fallen absolutely over the last twenty years, particularly at the night schools, which have historically eased the way into the profession for "disadvantaged" groups. Noble W. Lee of Chicago's John Marshall Law School, a last-chance place where the average entrant is thirty-one and many do not have a college diploma, reports that right after the war his student body was almost half Negro—while today he has only a handful.

Lord knows the jobs are waiting. Thurgood Marshall while Solicitor General recently told a friend of a Justice Department meeting called to prepare a report to President Johnson (all government departments must now deliver such reports periodically) on how many Negroes had been hired and promoted in the last months. Somebody observed idly that there wasn't a single Negro in the Solicitor General's office; to which Marshall replied, "I thought there was *one*—but I guess he passed."

6

The decline of the night law school—and not just for Negroes—is among the most important and saddest social developments in the United States since World War II. More than half of today's practitioners were products of such schools; today they have less than a quarter of the law school students, less than a seventh of the graduates (because their dropout rates are high), and less than an eighth of the entrants to the profession (because the graduates of night law schools tend to do less well on bar exams). A number of law schools which have historically offered both day and evening programs are dropping the night division (among them NYU, Boston University and Southern California), and those which maintain both find their night enrollment declining while their day enrollment (and its quality) improves.

The angriest and probably the most effective spokesman for the night law school as it has always been is Noble Lee of Chicago's John Marshall, successor to his father, who was dean of the school from 1909 to 1943. Large, aging, shabby, impatient, with a politician's shaking jowls (he has served as a Republican state legislator), Dean Lee was himself the product of a John Marshall education— but only after graduation from Harvard College and a term of years as a bond salesman ("A lot of little country banks owe their solvency in the depression to my services—I was what is now called an investment counselor"). His school, which has its own buildings in the southern part of the Loop (Olde Englishe decor, complete to Perpendicular Gothic bosses in the ceilings of some of the classrooms), has been approved by the American Bar Association but not by the Association of American Law Schools, mostly because he has refused to meet the AALS standards on minimum salary ("If I can get a qualified man, retired general counsel of a corporation, to come teach for nothing, why shouldn't I?"), maximum hours ("I want a man to teach eight hours a week") and faculty autonomy ("I want a team; last year there were fourteen deanships vacant with no takers, because of the autonomy of the faculty—the dean becomes the butt of faculty feuds").

Lee's case for his sort of law school and against Harvard's rests on three arguments:

1. "I'm simply against closing the door to the guy who wants to work." When John Marshall was founded, the requirement for entrance to law school in Illinois was three years of *high school,* and John Marshall developed a "prelegal" program to take care of that. Later, as ABA requirements lengthened out to two years of college, the school stretched its prelegal course to offer a "college equivalency"—but presently equivalencies were ruled unacceptable by ABA (and State of Illinois) committees. This is a *fait ac-*

compli, but Lee does not accept it gracefully: "It's not healthy in my opinion for the lawyers to be wholly recruited from academicians—high school, college, law school, nothing else. We need men who have something more than just the intellectual equipment."

Until the fall of 1965, when the AALS opened the back door a crack, it had been an unwritten rule of American law schools that anyone who flunked out of one would not be accepted at another—but John Marshal took them. (This worked only fairly well: when nobody could criticize the school for accepting veterans, Lee took two hundred such rejects, and found that "one-third dropped out within eighteen months, one-third we flunked, and a great many of the remainder were second- or third-timers on the bar exam; and since then we've screened them.") Students are permitted to continue trying, on probation, for three terms, to show if they can possibly make it—"but then they leave with goodwill toward the law, unlike those dropped by the flossy schools, all of whom hate the law." Meanwhile, of course, as Lee's antagonists say, they have paid their fees.

2. Law teachers should be experienced lawyers. "We are going through the West catalogue of law teachers; I bet we'll find they don't average two years' experience." At John Marshall nobody is appointed to the faculty—part time or full time—without at least five years' practice as a lawyer. "I'm bitter that the legal profession—the rock of the Republic—can be turned over to people who've never even handled a five-hundred-dollar property transaction."

3. The essence of a law school is to prepare people to practice law where they live—and the courses at the "national" law schools, with their discussions of the "majority rule" (the opinion in most states) and the "minority rule," their old cases from the common law, their policy questions and so forth, will not assist the local garden-variety practitioner dealing with the local garden-variety client in a matter that may come before the local garden-variety judge. "We used to publish a *John Marshall Law Quarterly,* all articles on Illinois practice. [The *Law Quarterly* was closed down by the paper shortage in World War II, and has never been revived.] The *Columbia Law Review* had a fine series on the Soviet Constitution—that's spendid, but what good does it do for the

lawyer in Galesburg, Illinois? Even unindexed, I had to have five hundred reprints made of one of our articles, entitled 'Garnishment of the Contents of a Safe-Deposit Box.' "

In the halls at the night law schools, the students do not talk law, except perhaps bar exam; they talk children, housing, job, food. Nearly all of them are employed full time, and must be. "Those who finish the night program," says Dean John A. Gorfinkel of San Francisco's Golden Gate School of Law, "have all the guts in the world." To deliver the same number of classroom hours as the three-year full-time law school, the night school must run four years, and usually ten months rather than eight. By rule of thumb, half the students will drop out during the first year, and half the remainder before completion—though very selective night law schools like NYU, Georgetown and Philadelphia's Temple, where the entering LSAT scores are far above the national average, will graduate three-quarters of those they accept. And the problem is not entirely restricted to night schools: at the University of New Mexico, a few years ago, normal expectation was that an entering class of fifty would produce ten graduates. "You have to err on the side of magnanimity," said Acting Dean Robert Emmet Clark, explaining the admission standards. "Anyway, most of them fail because they don't care."

At Golden Gate, which began to become selective only in 1955 ("We had thirty applicants; I threw out the worst five"), Gorfinkel says that the reasons for attrition "are only partly academic. The student commutes. He fights with his wife because they never get to the movies. I patch up marriages here. Wives come in and say, 'Is he doing it to get rid of me?' I say, 'Look—do you want to be married to a file clerk, or do you want to be married to a lawyer?' "

Like John Marshall, Golden Gate has its own building, a converted loft on the wrong side of Market Street, achieved only in 1965. ("We did most of the fund-raising at the Bank of America.") Before then, the school had been housed at the Golden Gate branch of the YMCA ("The architect put the classrooms on the fourth floor and the gymnasium on the fifth"). Gorfinkel, who had been teaching part time since 1934, was the first full-time professor, hired as such in 1952. Now there are six (and will presently be seven), and they take care of all the first-year and most of the second-year work, leaving to the active practitioners, the part-time teachers, only the relatively specialized courses of the third year. In 1966 Golden Gate launched its first full-time three-year day program, and within two months of the announcement received two hundred applications, forcing the addition of new sections. By 1970 the full-time program will unquestionably be substantially larger than the night school, which has about 250 students.

Tempers are shorter in the evening, and the classroom atmosphere is a little more tense. For various reasons, teachers at night law schools may lecture a little more and run through the case questions a little less. Fatigue is palpable at the end of any class. But there can also be a greater feeling of comradeship between the law professor (who is not at the top of his profession) and the older students (who are struggling to improve themselves). On the evening of May 2, Golden Gate's Michael Golden, half a dozen years out of Stanford Law School and committed to teaching, greets some sixty students of Property with the question, "You all know what was yesterday?" Socialism is unfashionable in a night law school, so one student timidly ventures, "Law Day?"

"No, no," says Golden, "for this class—for Real Property." After a moment's silence, he supplies an answer: "It's the anniversary of the passage of the Statute of Uses." The class cheers and whistles, and Golden adds, "Our family really lives it up on that day"— and then everybody gets down to work.

Golden's class, except that the answers were less quick and less fluent, was not vastly different from a lot of classes at "Stratum I" law schools; fundamentally, indeed, the similarities between the night law schools and the "flossy" law schools seem greater than the differences. "This course is optional for the law school but required for the bar exam," said a student at the ambitious limestone full-time Indiana University Law School in Bloomington, slipping into Professor Ralph E. Fuchs' class on Domestic Relations; and his peers at the university's night branch in a rotted section of downtown Indianapolis would say precisely the same. For all the talk about local law, the economics of educational institutions forces poorer schools (which include all the night schools) to rely on text-books—and the textbooks, for commercial reasons, are all national in orientation. Because the law is so much bigger than any one lawyer's experience of it, most of what even a veteran teaches he knows only from books. At many night schools, indeed, it is a source of pride that the work is as "national" as that in more famous establishments. "We have a man who studied at Yale," Gorfinkel says; "I told him to teach the course as though he were teaching at Yale. We talk about California law to the same extent we would if we were in Washington."

"One of the things that annoys us most," said Georgetown's Kenneth Pye, defending his school's decision (after prolonged debate) *not* to abandon the evening program, "is this assumption that day students are full-time. The question is the required courses between twelve and four. If all courses are nine-to-twelve, people are working in the afternoon." Of the 667 college graduate law students who filled out all the blanks in the NORC study, 148 held jobs that paid them $400 a month or more; and very few of them, apparently (this information was not specifically requested by the questionnaire), were attending night law schools.

There would seem to be real advantages for the prospective lawyer in getting some apprenticeship while he studies—in work for the trust department of a bank, or the city's welfare department or the Patent Office, or (ideally) as a junior assistant of some sort, even office boy, in a law firm. Still, the deans of the full-time law schools are almost universally opposed to evening programs, and almost every year there have been efforts of varying degrees of seriousness to destroy the night law school. The first of them came in 1921, shortly after the death of a Chief Justice of the United States who was the product of a night law school (Edward Douglass White, a graduate of Georgetown), when the ABA had on the table a resolution which would have forbidden law classes after four in the afternoon. A determined effort was made at the AALS meeting in 1965 to deny accreditation to all evening divisions, and only the forceful intervention of Southern California (which is now no longer interested) prevented a vote on the resolution.

"Good evening law schools can perform a real service to many people," says Harvard's Dean Griswold. "But there aren't many good evening law schools. And four years of evening law school can't be as good as three years full time: the real benefit comes from spending full time at it." Still, Dean Lee is not wholly unreasonable when he inquires what this real benefit is; and Harold Solomon of Southern California was not unrealistic in his division of the community of lawyers into physicists, engineers and plumbers. The man who is going to advise a corporation on a decision to locate a factory in a Common Market country, or help the Solicitor General decide which cases should be appealed by the government to the Supreme Court, doubtless can use the sophistication that comes from the study of law as a liberal art. But the full treatment cannot really be necessary to the man who is going to write little wills and secure collusive divorces, set up two-employee corporations, represent the home buyer at a closing, and perhaps haggle with an insurance company over the cash value of a fractured femur. "The evil," as Alfred Z. Reed wrote in 1921, "lies in the perpetuation of a theory of a unitary bar." Legal education, like so much else in the profession, loses touch with reality whenever it pretends to believe the antique notion that a lawyer is a lawyer is a lawyer.

7

"Every person of good moral character," said the Constitution of the State of Indiana from 1851 to 1932, "being a voter, shall be entitled to admission to practice law in all courts of justice." There were bar exams in colonial Virginia, and between 1776 and 1829 seventeen states established some restrictions on entrance to the profession, but all were swept away by the Jacksonian democracy of the 1830s and 1840s. The first modern bar exam was given by the Supreme Court of New Hampshire in 1880. It is probably significant that New Hampshire did not then (and does not now) have a law school within its borders.

Except in a few states, graduation from law school does not entitle anyone to practice law—that is, to collect fees for giving legal advice and to appear in court for clients. Candidates for the profession must leap another hurdle: the state bar exam, which

may run to as many as three days of writing answers to as many
as two hundred questions about substantive law. Bar exams grew up
mostly as a way to validate apprenticeship (nobody expected that
law school graduates would have much trouble with them), and in
some states candidates could simply come to the examining room
with a fee, as shepherds can come down from the hills in France to
try for a baccalaureate, without presenting any diplomas. Today,
by law in thirty-seven states and custom in others, law school
graduation is required for admission to the exam—but the independent growth of the two institutions still means that they don't
match very well.

In law school, by and large, there are no right answers to a
problem—usually, either side of the hypothetical case presented in
the exam at the end of the course can be defended, with reference
to appropriate authorities. In the bar exam, there is none of this
intellectualizing: the purpose is to assure that someone who pays
money for a lawyer's services will in fact receive advice as to the current condition of the law in this state, and the questions are framed
accordingly. Before tackling such an examination, most law school
graduates will take a "cram course" offered by a local lawyer or
judge or professor (or a syndicate of all three), which outlines topic
by topic the sort of question that will be on the exam, and the sort
of answer (with appropriate references to state statutes and cases)
that the examiners will like.

Though in many states the law school deans have now got the
exam-writers pretty safely in the bag (which was from the beginning
the unstated major purpose of the AALS), there remains a symbiotic relationship between the lawyers and judges who mark the
papers and the lawyers and judges who give the courses. Usually
the appointments to mark papers come from a court, but in thirteen
states they derive from the bar association itself. In New York State almost two thousand people a year take the cram course offered in
five cities by the nonprofit Practising Law Institute; in California
there are fifteen hundred students a year in the "Wicks Course,"
started by USC Professor G. Richard Wicks, and definitely for profit;
the name will probably stay, though Professor Wicks died in late
1966. These are lecture courses supplemented by study outlines to

be memorized, with very little of the question-and-answer routine
of the law school (outside New York City, the PLI course is presented mostly on tape); and they are barbaric.

Fear of the bar exam, which can turn three years' work to ashes,
is the skeleton in the closet of almost every law student. ("They
ought to abolish those night law schools and unaccredited law
schools," said a California student angrily. "Then there wouldn't be
any need for a bar exam.") And in fact the exam does keep out of
the profession a small fraction of law school graduates. When
Harper's Magazine announced a forthcoming article on law schools,
a number of letters came in from failed law students who wanted
to wise up the author on corruption in the bar exam: "The bar
exam is a hoax. It is a device to keep out as many as they can. No
papers are ever marked in some states. . . ." Even the law school
professors are sometimes suspicious. "Bar examinations," Johnstone
and Hopson write, "are a haphazard test of ill-defined knowledge
and skills administered by well-meaning amateurs with fuzzy and
inconsistent notions of what they are trying to accomplish . . . [I]n
some instances, the grading of out-of-staters' bar examination papers
is . . . suspect. But," the professors conclude, "despite all their weaknesses, bar examinations are a necessity, for the law schools cannot
be trusted to do equitably and honestly the full job of professional
selection."

The statistics across the country are that 40 percent of all candidates fail every year, but the statistics are misleading, because
people come back and take the exam again. In the fall of 1953, to
use the most spectacular example, there were about nine thousand
third-year law students in the law schools; in the summer of 1954
twenty thousand candidates took bar exams. In the average year
the number of graduates from law school and the number passing
the bar exam are roughly the same: anyone from a plausible law
school who fails the first time is more than likely to succeed on a subsequent attempt. People who are employed on the basis of their law
school diploma, researching cases at offices, investigating for DAs
and Public Defenders, settling claims for insurance companies, can
usually keep their jobs while they try the bar again.

Having succeeded, and having demonstrated that his past record

is free from publicly known moral turpitude, the student becomes
a lawyer: he is now officially qualified.

But qualified for what? "A law school graduate who passes his
bar examinations," Sidney Post Simpson wrote in 1946,

is not a lawyer. . . . The primary difference between a law school graduate
and a lawyer is that the latter knows how to do the practical things that
lawyers have to do. . . . He has some idea of what to do when his best
client's wife's brother lands in jail for reckless driving, and when he is
asked to draw a simple will or to work out a property settlement incident
to a divorce. He knows where to find the courthouse and how to subpoena
a witness. . . .

This practical knowledge is best imparted by an older lawyer. . . . It is
largely a process of passing on to the neophyte "what every lawyer knows,"
which is also what every law school graduate does not know.

As a law professor puts it, more harshly, "We would never dream
for one moment of putting any of *our* personal affairs in the hands
of the new lawyers we graduate and license every year." A New
England group queried on these matters delivered an "almost uniformly unflattering criticism of law school training . . . directed,
in the first place, at the scope and quality of technical training."
(In passing, one may note that Lincoln thought these practical
questions relatively unimportant. The New York lawyer C. Frank
Reavis keeps on the wall of his office in the Chase-Manhattan building a framed letter to his grandfather from Lincoln: "If you can
read the books and reason and understand them, you don't have to
read *with* a lawyer.")

The problem is known in the business as "bridging the gap." In
five states—Delaware, New Jersey, Pennsylvania, Rhode Island and
Vermont—an apprenticeship of six to nine months in somebody's
office is required before admission to the bar; but Dean Griswold is
undoubtedly justified in his complaint that such rules work more
often to give lawyers a source of sweated labor than to train the
competence of the juniors. The actual work of building these bridges
is done by judges' clerks, who give the bewildered beginner a step-
by-step program of how to involve the law in a client's situation.
"The day I went to work," Alfred Gans recalls, "I knew the Rule in
Shelley's Case. They threw a bundle of papers at me: 'Here. A client

wants to buy this piece of property. Go down and check the title.'
Fortunately, the clerk was a friend of my father's."

The costs of such on-the-job training are often paid, willy-nilly,
by clients. But there are some formal efforts, too.

New York's Practising Law Institute was founded in 1933 by
Harold Seligson, himself then a fairly recent graduate of Columbia,
in hopes of systematizing the advice new lawyers were forever seeking from him. Its first national work was done in the late 1930s,
when the American Bar Association contracted with PLI for a series
of courses and pamphlets on the income tax (then a very new field
for lawyers). After the war PLI expanded both its publishing and its
course work to care for the lawyers newly returned from service,
and ran correspondence courses for lawyers in smaller cities who
couldn't get to the lectures associated with the paperbacks. (The
correspondence courses were dropped at the end of the first GI Bill,
which had paid for them.) "We never issued certificates," Seligson
says, "because lawyers don't want to take examinations and I don't
want to issue certificates without examinations."

About 25,000 lawyers attend PLI lecture courses in hotel ball-
rooms every year, and Seligson stands ready to meet special needs.
(A few years ago PLI offered a course for DAs, police departments
and civil rights lawyers on the legal aspects of demonstrations.)
But most of Seligson's work today is through publishing, and his
books (written mostly by leading authorities as a public service, for
an honorarium of $200 a book) tend to be relatively general dis-
cussions of a lawyer's problems in the area, comments and reminders
rather than instructions. Seligson wants PLI texts to emphasize
"what experienced people think about the field, not what the lawyer
already learned in law school and needed to pass the bar exam. We
go on the assumption that the lawyer knows something."

Felix Stumpf, Administrator of California's "Continuing Educa-
tion of the Bar," the largest state program of this sort, feels that
Seligson is sometimes unrealistically optimistic about his clientele.
Stumpf stresses "office-made law," which is what a lawyer really does
for a living and is often quite different from "judge-made law."
Housed halfway between the handsome university campus and
Berkeley's remarkable Beatnik Row, CEB is self-supporting (PLI
relies to an extent on foundation grants), and grosses about a mil-

lion dollars a year from its lecture programs and the sale of its thick, colorfully bound "Practice Books," which are useful only in California.

Stumpf, an earnest Harvard Law School product in spectacles, says, "We call them lawyers' cookbooks—gourmet cookbooks. We try to organize a book in the form of the chronological development of a transaction. You can tell where a California lawyer is in a matter by the page to which his book is open. Our books aren't in the California lawyer's library—they're on his desk." Every book contains legal forms for most legal purposes: "In a commercial-lease transaction," Stumpf says, "traditionally now, the landlord's lawyer offers our landlord's form, the tenant's lawyer counters with our tenant's form, and then one calls the other and says, 'Let's take CEB's compromise form.' " Most of the books are written by practitioners, then edited by CEB's staff, which in early 1967 included twenty-four lawyers.

One wing of the California Bar regards Stumpf's books as undignified for a learned profession; but nearly half of the bar owns at least one of them (at $35-$50 a book), and most approve of the idea. CEB's 1966 program on the state's new code of evidence drew an enrollment of 9,285 lawyers. The lawyer has to live with his mistakes (though not to the same degree that the client has to live with them), and Stumpf's staff-written cookbooks enable lawyers to work in areas where they have no particular expertise without blowing the client's lifeline. There can be, incidentally, a degree of pressure associated with the selling of such publications: "How much is an injury really worth?" asks the flier for volume 5, *Damages,* in the Michigan CLE's Personal Injury Library. "In this volume the nation's most famed lawyers and legal authorities, by means of trial demonstrations and lectures, show you. . . ."

Nationally, a joint committee of the American Law Institute and the ABA publishes *The Practical Lawyer,* a monthly magazine that can be stuffed in a pocket, plus occasional books that reflect someone's low opinion of the treatises already on the market; the authors are unpaid. Most of the time of the Committee's staff of half a dozen lawyers goes into helping state bar associations plan their own programs. ALI, formed originally in the 1920s to produce "restatements" of common law which would clear up the confusion of judges, is the intellectual epicenter of the profession ("The only adjective the newspapers ever use about us is 'prestigious,'" says Paul Wolkin, director of the education division); here the approach tends to be on a somewhat higher level.

"There's an idea around," Wolkin says, "that the way you get to be a good lawyer is by learning the pat procedures and devices and short cuts of other lawyers. And the first man who thought up using a blackboard in a negligence trial undoubtedly had a very successful technique. But you can give a lot of lawyers all the blackboards in the world, and it doesn't do any good—what you have to do is think through your own case."

Wolkin says that "the law schools are going to have to get into this CLE work," and adds that since Myres McDougal took over the presidency of AALS they have become less hostile to the proposition. In fact, of course, eminent voices have been raised over the years in support of what Judge Jerome Frank called a "lawyer school" rather than a "law school." The current term of fashion at the law schools, copied from the medical schools, is "clinical studies."

8

For one group of their students—the very top—most law schools have for many years offered highly practical experience in the form of editing the school's law review. These student-run publications are the scholarly literature of the law, and they are uniquely American. "There is not so far as I know in the world," Karl Llewellyn once wrote, "an academic faculty which pins its reputation before the public upon the work of undergraduate students—there is none, that is, except in the American law reviews. Such an institution it is a privilege to serve."

At the eighty-odd law schools that publish law reviews, the top 5 to 10 percent of a class are selected at the end of their first year for this privilege. The selection at most schools is strictly by academic ranking, by the grades received in the first-year courses. It is, as Justice Felix Frankfurter put it in his reminiscences,

an automatic affair. All this big talk about "leadership" and character, and all the other things that are non-ascertainable, but usually are highfalutin' expressions for personal likes and dislikes, or class, or color, or religious partialities or antipathies—they were all out. . . . And so I say, as I've said often in talking to the young, the Harvard Law Review in particular and the Harvard Law School in general are to me the most complete practices in democracy that I have ever known anything about.

Depending on whether the law review comes out two, four or eight times a year, the elect will devote from twenty to forty hours a week, and full time for a month or so before the school year begins, to their little magazine. In the process they will acquire a training in legal research and legal writing far beyond anything that can be offered to them in courses. They will also gain access to the best jobs: the big law firms, with their starting salaries of $9,200 and up, recruit almost exclusively from the law reviews, and the most exciting job a young man can hold—a year as clerk to a Justice of the U.S. Supreme Court—is reserved to law review products. (David Riesman, who clerked for Justice Brandeis, doubts the utility of this custom: "It seems to me that this is one more year of law-review-style legal research, in most instances quite arguably under much less severe editorial auspices.")

Law reviews break into two sections: the articles, which are written by lawyers, professors and judges; and the "notes," which are the anonymous product of the student staff. But the students are responsible for everything. "It's an interesting situation," says Lance Liebman, president of the *Harvard Law Review* for 1966-67. "We get a lot of letters asking, 'Would you like to see my article?' And we ask to see *everything*—the burden is on us to read the stuff. And here we are, second-year law students, turning down all this great stuff by big people. We get calls from the faculty—a friend of theirs wants to know why we've held his article three weeks. When the article is by our own faculty, we're judging the work of our teachers."

Actually, the editors do not normally make their decisions completely unaided: most manuscripts will be circulated around the little knot of professors, usually young professors, with whom the law review editors feel most comfortable. But the final responsibility rests with the staff, which will go over each article with incredible thoroughness, and edit with a firm pencil. ("We have to sense how much we can get away with.") Then the manuscripts are returned to the professors, "edited and with pages of queries—our man says the case doesn't mean this—and they're in for a lot of work."

The *Harvard Law Review,* working out of an ancient wood-frame house a few steps from granite Langdell, the massive headquarters of the law school, has a paid circulation of about eleven thousand and an almost invisible free list; alone among the law reviews, it breaks even or makes a little money. As the largest single customer of the company that prints for the Harvard University Press, it gets service; the students boast that every issue comes out on time, which is probably true only of this law review. The normal complement is fifty-eight editors, twenty-five from the second-year class and thirty-three from the third-year class (there are eight supplementary elections at the end of the second year). The president is elected by the staff on nomination by the outgoing class; he appoints his own lieutenants. This election is a peculiarly solemn affair, prefaced by a dinner at Locke-Ober's, Boston's best restaurant, and requiring an entire day's earnest discussion surrounded by Rothko murals in the great hall atop Holyoke Center, the right ventricle of the university.

Most of the work done by the student editors is in the preparation of "Notes" on recent cases or on live issues before the courts. A topic or a piece of a topic, suggested by a professor or an editor, will be assigned to someone for a preliminary rundown and report, which means reading *all* the case literature and significant treatise literature on this matter. Most proposed notes are killed by these preliminary studies, but others are worked up, by individuals or teams, and then sent out to selected faculty members for first readings. "You get all sorts of reactions," says an editor, "everything from 'This is preposterous' to 'Mr. Justice Harlan prefers "that" to "which." ' " Meanwhile, every current reported decision from every jurisdiction in the United States, Britain and the Commonwealth is read by some editor, and commented on in some manner, to swell the files available for the notes. This works out to almost six hundred decisions per year per editor.

The question of who reads these notes is an interesting one. Dean Harno of Illinois wrote flatly that "they are read principally by law teachers," which is probably true. But when the *Harvard Law Review* published an unconscionably long and thorough study of the confession problem in the spring of 1965, its editors received a wire from the California Supreme Court, ordering seven copies. Fifteen somewhat arbitrarily chosen law reviews are included in the "citing material" in *Shepard's Citations,* which means that anyone looking up the career of a court decision will find all references to its use in the notes of these law reviews together with the references to its mentions in subsequent cases. "More than one law review writer," says Chief Justice Roger Traynor of the California Supreme Court, "has been surprised to recognize pieces of his work paraphrased or even lifted in a judicial opinion." But judges set in their ways, Traynor adds, may be unhappy with quotations admittedly from the work of "a boy whose brain has not yet been washed in practice."

None of the law reviews takes any apparent interest in its readership: there are no correspondence columns, or opportunities to correct errors for readers other than the professors who can write replying articles. But the law reviews are not written for readers. "The *Review* is run for the benefit of its members," says one of the Harvard case editors. "We do much more work than we would do if our only purpose were to put out a magazine."

Law review work is exact training for writing the kinds of memoranda these students will be asked to write when they move on, as most of them will, to the giant law firms or the law departments of the big corporations or government agencies. For the very small number of students who will have something to do with arguing appellate cases, there is also some practical training in the traditional "moot courts," at which teams of two to four first- and second-year men argue and present briefs they have written in support of one side or the other on a mythical appeal from a mythical lower-court decision. The moot courts are competitive, with progressive elimination of teams leading to a champion of the school and further regional and national contests between teams from different schools. For the national contest, and for the finals at the most prestigious Eastern law schools, it is traditional that a Justice of the U.S. Supreme Court sits on the mythical bench to hear the argument.

Recently, to get closer to what new graduates may actually be called on to do, some law schools have supplemented their moot courts with mock trials, at which students (or even professors) serve as coached witnesses to be examined by student lawyers seeking to win a mythical case on some accident or broken contract. At the Kansas City branch of the University of Missouri, real cases from the small-claims court are brought into this process. Today, moreover, as was not true forty years ago, students are encouraged to go visit courtrooms and report back on what they have seen. At Michigan a closed-circuit television system permits students to observe trials from a distance; and the lawyers involved then come to the school to discuss the case.

Since the 1930s the law school courses in "legal writing," started as a way to teach research skills and to free professors from the agonies of reading typical collegiate prose compositions, have expanded to include the drafting of contracts which will lock up a given set of facts—and even the drafting of legislation. At Indiana, Reed Dickerson gives his third-year class the job of drawing up a real statute that will become law when they are finished: a zoning law, a law of private swimming pools, a law controlling the operation of an airport, or the development of lake-front property to be created by a dam. Students, he finds, are not much concerned about the significance of the issue. "They say, 'Will our work show up in the final product?'" Such work need not be done on a course basis: Harvard, since 1952, has maintained a Student Legislative Research Bureau composed of those who almost but not quite "made" the *Law Review.* The Bureau holds itself open to requests from governments and charitable organizations for proposed drafts of new laws to meet detailed situations. More than a hundred such requests have been honored.

Some law schools will help students find summer jobs in law offices between terms. But if student lawyers, like student doctors, are to receive any substantial amount of genuine "clinical" experience, they must work, like student doctors, on the problems of the poor.

Most law schools have always had legal-aid adjuncts, staffed by volunteers supervised more or less directly (depending on the condition of the state law governing "unauthorized practice") by a practicing attorney. In October, 1959, the Ford Foundation granted $900,000 to the National Legal Aid and Defender Association to expand student legal aid work. NLADA set up a National Council on Legal Clinics to spend the money, and the Council, with its sponsor's consent, broadened the terms of reference to the entire area of "professional responsibility," the question of the obligations of anyone who has been entrusted by the society with the special privileges of the licensed lawyer. Twenty law schools developed experimental programs under the grant. Wisconsin, for example, assigns students to work on the noncriminal legal problems of imprisoned convicts who will presently be released; Kansas sends them off on tours of duty as clerks to understaffed trial courts. Other law schools have merely added some text material on "responsibility" to the usual courses (this is known somewhat smugly as "the pervasive approach").

One of the most deeply admired of these programs is at Tennessee, where the legal clinic program has been a well-established teaching device since 1947. Here students spend parts of three quarters organized into "law firms" that work on real cases coming to the school's legal aid service, discussing their cases both in the classroom and in "firm meetings."

With the rising concern about poverty, and the rather wide-screen projections of the value of legal services in alleviating it, nearly every law school has substantially expanded its existing legal aid clinics, and a score or so have worked them into optional courses. In thirteen states, mostly under statutes that have oddly hung on from the days of Jacksonian democracy, students can advise legal aid clients and even, under certain circumstances, appear in court for them.

At Boston University thirty student "voluntary defenders" who receive credit for the "course" represent about 350 indigents a year in a district court in the city's Negro slum.

At Yale, in connection with New Haven's highly developed Neighborhood Legal Services program, law students sit in with the lawyers (most of whom were Yale law students themselves a year or two ago), helping out with the interviews as well as with the research. Miguel de Capriles of NYU (which has been battling New York's Legal Aid Society to get for its students assignments other than landlord-and-tenant cases) feels that even greater responsibility could be given to the third-year men: "If I were an accused, I'd rather have a senior for whom I'm his whole life than somebody appointed by a court who's going to get fifty bucks for it."

All these programs seem to be emotionally satisfying to most of the participants, but most law professors feel that their value in other directions has been limited. Ohio State abandoned its required service in a legal aid clinic because the faculty felt that real live people were being injured by the negligence of students whose minds were on other things; as Kenneth Pye of Georgetown told a conference that showed signs of going Gung-ho, "We do not help the poor by providing them with highly motivated young men who do not know what they are doing." Educationally, moreover, the training must be extremely narrow to provide instant competence. Most lawyers who passed through legal aid clinics while students seem to feel that the experience was really important in one direction: it taught them something they had never previously known about the complexity of the task of drawing information from interviews.

"Outside the physical sciences," as NYU's de Capriles says, "you can't control the laboratory." At most law schools there is too stark a contrast between the brilliantly developed and controlled pedagogy of the law classroom and the well-intentioned but embryonic progressivism of law field work.

9

Quite apart from the questionable utility of "practical" experience, however, there is room for doubt that the professors really like it. As critics of society and the existing law, they approve of working for the poor, but not many of them admire the students who hope to pick up purely vocational skills by working in the clinics.

They are an odd group, the two thousand or so law professors. Because the law schools are mostly small, they know each other.

Themselves the most successful students in what a psychiatrist who teaches at a law school has called "an acculturating event that trains people to be more comfortable with conflict situations," they get on well with each other; and they tend not to know people on the other faculties of the university. They are mostly terrifyingly bright, and they appreciate it. "It's as good an approximation as I know," says Harvard's young Paul Bator, "to a field where merit really counts. We live pretty well, get paid pretty well, think of ourselves as a big deal. We get to consult with the government, go to conferences in Japan and West Africa. And you can get to be an unquestioned authority—a Pooh-Bah—at the age of thirty-five."

David Riesman still "despises the childishness of the law schools— the joking about Yale and Harvard—the self-preening complacency of the law-school professors. But there's a nice thing about law schools: I was a full professor of law at the age of twenty-seven. It's the opposite extreme from the British and German system of a chair, or from the way things work at the faculties of arts and sciences. There's no envy of the young, no novelists *manqué,* no *Schadenfreude.* I used to play squash and tennis with my professors at law school. They're sportsmen. They dance. They're charming. They're not competing with their students. And they're not intellectuals."

Among the attitudes they share is one less interesting to describe but more significant in the formation of the law school. "With a few exceptions," says UCLA's Murray Schwartz, "people are law professors because they tried practice and didn't like it. You can't expect them to orient their teaching toward the practice of law." Yale's Alexander Bickel says, not analyzing it, "We very consciously *don't* fit somebody to hang out a shingle and try a case."

Nearly all law professors hate what Arizona's Robert Emmet Clark once called "the show-'em-the-way-to-the-courthouse" school of law teaching, and they suspect its intrusion in any reform proposal. The Ford grant for legal aid clinics was transmuted to academic concern about "professional responsibility." The staff of California's CEB program is part of the University of California but not part of the law school faculty. When a prominent patent lawyer (now a judge) wanted to give a course in his very practical field at Columbia a few years back, he was shunted off to that university's School of General Studies, and law students received no credit for his course.

At bottom, the problem of the law school is that startlingly little is known systematically about the real world of the lawyer, and even less is known about the purposes the society wishes the lawyer to serve in the latter years of the twentieth century. "I'm always wary about sending students out just to get exposure," says Howard Sacks of Northwestern, director of the Ford-sponsored "professional responsibility" project. "They get upset, confused, disillusioned." But there may be something to be said for giving students a chance to become upset, confused and disillusioned before rather than after they leave law school. What the law professors offer in their courses is the best quality of education in America—but in a professional school educational excellence may not be enough.

CHAPTER 4

JURISPRUDENCE:

WHERE THE LAWS

COME FROM

"The prophecies of what the courts will do in fact, and nothing more pretentious, are what I mean by the law."
—OLIVER WENDELL HOLMES, JR.

"Now there are only two subjects of thought—the only two perhaps with the exception of physical science—which are able to give employment to all the powers and capacities which the mind possesses. One of them is Metaphysical Inquiry, which knows no limits so long as the mind is satisfied to work on itself; the other is Law, which is as extensive as the concerns of mankind."
—SIR HENRY MAINE

"He who tries to fix and determine everything by law will inflame rather than correct the vices of the world."
—SPINOZA

1

"No vast literature," the British legal philosopher H. L. A. Hart wrote recently, "is dedicated to answering the questions, 'What is chemistry?' or 'What is medicine?' as it is to the question, 'What is law?' " The subject is singularly elusive, and this chapter does not pretend (God forbid) to get a really firm grip on it. But some first principles will be useful later on.

Law, obviously, is a means of social control: an official assertion of the society's interest in the behavior of its members. It tells people what they must not do and what they must do, secures private arrangements and distributes the benefits of community. It is overwhelmingly and necessarily negative, because its most affirmative purposes can be achieved only by enjoining interference with them. But law clearly does not "prohibit" anything—words can no more prevent a possible human action than King Canute could stop the tides. Nor does law in fact seek to prevent actions in themselves—there is nothing you may not safely do, without risk of interference from law, if you are alone in the middle of the desert. What law says is that if you act in specified ways, in a range of circumstances, you may be liable upon completion of specified legal procedures to suffer specified unpleasant consequences.

The words "may be," "unpleasant consequences" and "legal procedures" are all crucial.

Law is a system of predictions, and predictions (as David Hume pointed out two hundred years ago) must be statistical. Nobody expects that any law will work all the time. The law against murder is quite real even though murder persists, a number of murderers are never caught and some of those who are caught are never convicted. At the other end of the statistical scale, a law prohibiting the washing of store windows during the first three months of the year (New York has such a law) will normally be unknown to either storekeeper or policeman, and thus, presumably, not a law at all. But if some literal-minded young cop finds it in the book, he may hale into court some poor grocer who has taken advantage of a balmy day to get the soot off the glass. (This once happened, before Judge Jonah J. Goldstein; he looked at the policeman astonished after reading the statute which the policeman had handed up to him, and the policeman said shyly, "I'm studying to be sergeant.") In 1944 a lady fortuneteller was convicted in England for violation of the Witchcraft Act of 1735.

Law requires punishment—increased likelihood of unpleasant

consequences for its violations. These consequences need not be officially imposed. "Archaic procedure," Sir Frederick Pollock wrote, "shows us a period in which a suitor may obtain judgment, but must execute the judgment for himself." (This approach can still be found in what it is no longer fashionable to call primitive societies: "When an Akamba court has decided as to the rights of a complaint," the anthropologist Paul Bohannan writes of an African tribe, "the judgment takes the form of a declaration that *A* has been wronged by *B* and *B* should atone or should receive a retaliative sanction at the hands of *A*'s kinsmen. The court leaves the enforcement of the judgment to the kinship groups.") Even today the significant sanction of a divorce action may be the lady's legal right to change the lock on the apartment for which her ex-husband pays the rent. But somewhere there must be punishment. "If you want to know the law and nothing else," Holmes told a group of Boston University students at the turn of the century, "you must look at it as a bad man, who cares only for the material consequences which such knowledge enables him to predict."

Most lawyers, including law professors, would rather restrict the notion of punishment to the criminal law, and stress in other branches of their subject the "remedy" the law offers to someone who without law would be a loser. But one man's rights are no more and no less than other men's duties to him. The meaning of a legal right is that anyone who violates such duties—who alienates the affections of the legally contracted wife or fails to pay his legal debts or runs down the pedestrian legally present in the crosswalk—risks unpleasant consequences by process of law. Whenever these consequences can be insured against, so that the element of punishment is withdrawn, law becomes an impenetrable mess (as we shall see in Chapter 7). Where there are no unpleasant consequences to be feared, there is in effect no law: even Pollock conceded, rather reluctantly, that "to conceive of any part of human conduct as subject to law is to conceive that the actor's freedom has bounds which he oversteps at his peril." Nor is this attitude ethnocentric to the jurisprude: the anthropologist E. Adamson Hoebel will accept a "social norm" as "legal" only "if its neglect or infraction is regularly met, in threat or in fact, by the application of physical force." One of the great difficulties in fitting human or even constitutional rights into a legal order is that they often do not come equipped with "remedies." If the police department does not choose to punish the policeman who breaks down your door, there is nothing law can do to deter him from similar such acts in the future. The remedy then lies in political, not legal, action.

Law requires an established procedure for its enforcement—a body, usually called a court, authorized to assess and supply remedies. As Henry M. Hart, Jr. and Albert M. Sacks of Harvard have put it, "The central idea of law [is] . . . *the principle of institutional settlement.*" The existence of presumably neutral forums to determine whether or not a law has been violated makes it possible for us to differentiate by definition between law and arbitrary state action. In Pollock's pregnant phrase, "Law is enforced by the State because it is law; it is not law merely because the State enforces it." At bottom, what Pollock means is purely procedural: a rule enforced through a court or similar agency will qualify as law, while a rule enforced without recourse to such a forum will not. On the other side of the same coin, if you can get into position to see both sides at once, lies Holmes' famous aphorism quoted at the head of the chapter—that law is merely the prophecy of what the courts will do (or, more exactly, in Pound's formulation, the set of bases for such prophecies).

2

Caveat lector: In passing from a theoretical definition of law as a means of social control to a working definition of law as a prophecy of what courts will do, something of great importance is lost. Law performs its most significant social function as a set of guidelines for good men, not as a set of warnings for bad men. The finest statement of this significance comes from Benjamin Cardozo:

Life may be lived, conduct may be ordered, it *is* lived and ordered, for unnumbered human beings without bringing them within the field where the law can be misread, unless indeed the misreading be accompanied by conscious abuse of power. Their conduct never touches the borderline, the penumbra, where controversy begins. They go from birth to death, their action restrained at every turn by the power of the state, and not once do they appeal to judges to mark the boundaries between right and wrong. I am unable to withhold the name of law from rules which exercise this compulsion over the fortunes of mankind.

The influence of law on the law-abiding is a great unexplored subject. It is not relevant here, because those whose conduct never touches the penumbra of law have no need for lawyers.

3

We find it deceptively easy today to answer the question of where the rules come from: laws, obviously, are made by authorities who have been empowered to make laws. Sovereignty over territory normally carries the power to make law: Gaullist France enforces a large body of statutes legislated in the days of Pétain. We are concerned about the institutional arrangements through which law-making authorities are chosen, and about the procedures they follow, but a very high degree of arbitrary action will be required before we deny that the rules these authorities lay down and enforce through their courts are law. And it is disgracefully clear that in making law these authorities are not necessarily bound by considerations of morality and justice.

Our ancestors found the same question much more difficult, because they saw the world as an ordered whole rather than as a series of transient atomic arrangements. There was, then, a law of nature which should govern human affairs; and the authority of merely human law had to be derived somehow from its consonance with the law of nature. Even Blackstone, who was a practical lawyer, saw the law of nature as "binding all over the globe, in all countries, and at all times; no human laws are of any validity, if contrary to this; and such of them as are valid derive all their force, and all their authority, mediately or immediately, from this original."

In a society ruled by an anointed king or by a class of priests, the law of nature was passed on through those whom God had ordained for this purpose. Acceptance of this absolutism disappeared long before anyone thought of questioning the validity of the law of nature, and a new transmission belt was required. In England, ingeniously, the royal judges argued that through much study and contemplation (of the kind the judges did) what Blackstone called "municipal law" could be correctly deduced from natural law by what Coke called "right reason." This is, roughly, where Blackstone came out. Law to him was, in Holmes' scornful phrase, "a brooding omnipresence in the sky." Law, in Blackstone's theory, was declared by the judges through their decisions in the cases they heard. But they did not *make* law—how could they? They simply, through their trained reason, *found* law which had always been there to be found.

Consistency is the first demand that trained right reason will make on natural law. "It will not do," as Cardozo wrote, "to decide the same question one way between one set of litigants and the opposite way between another." Maitland pointed out that the judges themselves were originally less than enthusiastic about the doctrine of "precedent," which limited their powers. Precedent was forced upon them by the growing professional caste of lawyers, the "sergeants," who kept up with the rulings so they could make the judges apply on behalf of their clients the same rules that had been found in similar cases.

By the same argument, identical questions must be decided identically in different parts of a kingdom (nothing can be done, of course, about the dirty habits of foreigners). Judges in Cornwall and judges in Northumbria may not be permitted to find different law just because they are at different ends of England. Once the royal authority enters, there must be a "common law" which applies everywhere the royal writ runs, supplanting whatever local law may have been created by local authorities.

Finally, if law is to be stable, it must be either memorized in the same form by everybody (ancestral recollections of this need account for much of the insistence on verbal forms that continues to the present day) or it must be written down. Laws that are promulgated by a king or a priesthood or a legislative assembly will be written— most of the oldest writing we know is law: somebody may even find some day the tablets Moses brought down from Sinai. The decisions of the judges can become "common law" only if they are reported case by case. Hence the eight hundred years of English Law Reports, the longest continuous chain of historical information man has ever put together.

By contrast with the convincing paraphernalia of legislative investigation and debate and voting, judicial decision looks like a painful and risky way to make law—but it is by no means foolish or archaic. Chief Justice Harlan Fiske Stone wrote approvingly only thirty years ago of the common-law "method of marking out, as cases arise, step by step, the line between the permitted and the forbidden, by the process of appraisal and comparison of the experiences of the past and of the present." As John Chipman Gray wrote,

> The knowledge that a decision will have direct consequences, often of the serious character, to actual human beings, is a tremendous sanction for rendering right judgment. . . . The temptation of professional men, judges and jurists alike, is to subordinate the welfare of persons subject to a system of law to the logical coherency of the system itself, and there is more danger of yielding to this temptation when the question is whether an imaginary Numerius Negidius shall be condemned in a sum of imaginary sesterces, than when it is whether a real John Jones shall be mulcted so many real dollars.

(It should be kept in mind, incidentally, that this process draws its virtue from the reality of the disputes; thus courts mostly will not hear hypothetical cases or give advisory opinions, and will insist that a plaintiff have "standing to sue," something to gain or lose by the decision of the court.)

Of the essence of natural law is the idea that God would want justice done in the individual case; the ingenuity of the common-law judge must be employed to find law which supports the just result. But sometimes the only law he can find among the precedents leaves evil triumphant, and then he is in trouble. Every once in a while, of necessity, a judge in a common-law tradition must take his courage in his hands and declare that the precedents are wrong: his predecessors found the wrong law.

Any change in judge-made law raises important practical problems. If judges merely find law, then judicial decisions are retroactive—i.e., the law is held to have been always as now stated, even though previous judges had stated a contrary law. Anybody who relied on the previous rulings is now out of luck. In 1928 the Supreme Court found unconstitutional a Massachusetts statute taxing royalties from copyright. Four years later, the Court overruled itself and upheld a similar statute from another state. The playwright Elmer Rice had earned considerable royalties in the interim, and the State of New York now came around to collect back taxes from him. The New York courts not only held him liable for the taxes, but assessed him interest for late payment.

In the 1960s the Supreme Court has had to face squarely this question of whether its decisions change the law or merely declare what the Constitution always said, really. In two cases that were legally but not practically very similar, the Court went in opposite directions. Where it had declared that convictions could not stand if a defendant had not enjoyed the right of counsel at his trial, the Court held that its decision merely expressed the Fourteenth Amendment as it had always been—thereby relieving the taxpayers of the State of Florida of the expense of maintaining many prisoners in the penitentiaries. Where, however, it had declared that convictions could not stand if they were based on confessions which the police had gained from suspects who had not enjoyed the right of counsel in the station house, the Court held that its decision made new law, and that convictions entered before the date of the decision were still valid. The reason was that the impact of retroactivity would be very different in the two situations: all but a handful of states had managed to pony up some kind of counsel for defendants in serious cases before the Court spoke, but no state had extended the full protection the Court now demanded in confession cases. Given a choice between logically unjustifiable conflict in its rulings and practically impossible consequences, the Court calmly chose to avoid the consequences.

In fact, of course, there had always been something faintly lunatic about the notion that judges merely found law that had always existed. "What," Gray asked irreverently seventy years ago, "was the Law in the time of Richard Coeur de Lion on the liability of a telegraph company to the persons to whom a message was sent?" But something was lost, too, when judge-made law could no longer claim extra authority by descent from God-given natural law.

Lord Radcliffe, generally regarded as the most profound of contemporary British appellate judges, sees plainly that "the history of judge-made law is largely the history of the judges themselves." Still, he cannot easily accept what logically follows. "Historically," he writes,

it has been one of the strong bonds of society that the law should be regarded as expressing and being controlled by some higher value than mere command, or custom, or logical reason, or the say-so of the judge; and if the liberal political society has cut itself free from all these old and potent associations by assigning to law a position of irrevocable neutrality, it has thrown a strain upon the social fabric which may, of course, be endurable but of which we should at least take anxious notice.

Lord Radcliffe speaks as an English judge who has seen his job lose much of its historic function with the disappearance of belief in some tie between common law and natural law. Americans will find it easier to sympathize with him if they consider the change that would occur in the situation of a Justice of the Supreme Court if someone took away from him the authority of the Constitution, which is the American substitute for "natural law." But these eggs were always going to be broken. In a developed social system, which demands of the law rapid adjustment to changing statistical norms through the use of democratic processes, the dominance of judge-made law was inevitably doomed by three of the common law's most admirable characteristics: precedent, case-by-case development and aristocratic detachment.

In Cardozo's exact metaphor, "The power of precedent . . . is the power of the beaten track." Given a good enough reason (knowledge that the beaten track is booby-trapped), a good enough man may make his own new track, but the evidence must be overwhelming and the individual powerful. Men have made their plans relying on the stability of law. It is one thing for a duly constituted legislature to insist that these plans must be changed and something else again for a single aristocratic judge, who boasts that he is above the battle, to tell conflicting forces he has changed the rules in the middle of the game. Finally, the very need to decide cases one by one limits the vision of any individual judge. He may not inquire into the influence of his decision in cases not before him: indeed, he may not hear testimony not directly relevant to the dispute in court. Yet the rules he finds to settle this dispute will be applied to others, where the situation of the parties may be vastly different. "Hard cases," says the slogan, "make bad law."

The system of judge-made laws was not without devices to mitigate its rigidity. The royal courts had grown up originally on the theory that the king was the fount of justice. As the common-law rules hardened, supplicants returned to the king to argue that they were not receiving justice at law, and in Tudor England there grew up in the Lord Chancellor's office a separate Court of Chancery empowered to hear matters in which it was claimed that the law courts would not or could not do justice.

Chancery had three great advantages over common-law procedure. "Pleadings," the formal statement of the claim and the defense, could be entered in a much more common-sense manner at Chancery, and there was no need (as there had been at law) to show an existing property interest in the dispute before a judge would hear the case. The chancellor (unlike the common-law judges) could compel the parties to testify, and could therefore inquire much more effectively than ordinary courts into questions of "fraud, mistake and breach of trust." Finally, while the common-law courts could only award damages or possession of land, Chancery could make defendants live up to their part of a bargain, or stop damming the stream on which the plaintiff relied for water, by issuing "orders commanding restoration of the rightful situation." These orders were called "injunctions," and the court which issued them became known as a court of "equity" rather than of law. Separate courts of equity grew up not only in England but in many of the American states (New Jersey still had them until after World War II); and even today, in a "unified court of general jurisdiction," a lawyer will seek for his client "equitable remedies" as distinguished from legal remedies. While there were two sets of judges, relations between the courts were often rather uneasy. But both, of course, were equally the proprietors of judge-made law.

To mitigate the danger that a judge would see a dispute only from a remote and aristocratic point of view, the common-law courts relied on juries. The question of whether a given individual has behaved improperly can be answered fairly only through comparison of his behavior with some standard; and juries were better placed than judges to decide how an ordinary reasonable man would behave in the situation that had given rise to the case. Judge Learned Hand saw this device as pure evasion of the legal issue: "We hide our incapacity to dispose of a future controversy," he wrote, "by deputing it to the putative choice of that factitious ghost, 'the reasonable man.'" But a jury of ordinary people was an invaluable way to protect justice in the case from the possible rigidities of law. Not the least of its advantages was the fact that a jury verdict could not be a precedent in another case.

The doctrine of "the reasonable man" became so deeply embedded in English law that judges without embarrassment extended reasonableness to other animals. Baron Bramwell was confronted with a lawsuit by a man whose property had been damaged by some pigs which had escaped from the defendant's pig pen. Query: how strong a pig pen need a farmer build to be free of liability in such a case? Answer: a pen strong enough to restrain pigs

of average vigour and obstinacy . . . Nor do we lay down that there must be a fence so close and strong that no pig could push through it. . . . One could scarcely tell the limits of such a requirement, for the strength of swine is such that they would break through almost any fence, if there were a sufficient inducement on the other side. But the [owner is] bound to put up such a fence that a pig not under any excessive temptation will not get through it.

One further corrective was built into the system of judge-made law: acknowledgment of the supremacy of the legislature. "What the Parliament doth," Blackstone wrote, "no power on earth can undo. . . . To set the judicial power above the legislature . . . would be subversive of all government." The natural law which sustained the judges was, after all, a moral law, and there were many rules to be made that had no relation to morality. Not even the most insular of English judges could pretend that the Americans had found the wrong *moral* law when they decided to order people to drive on the right rather than on the left. If a warehouse has been destroyed by lightning, the question whether the owner of the stored merchandise or the owner of the warehouse shall bear the loss is not one we can reasonably refer to God for solution. When the law deals with contracts, with questions of "which promises shall be enforced," the best rules are those most convenient to the business community as a whole, whether or not these rules embody the finest feelings of a man of the highest moral sense who is not in business. (Once the rules are laid down and known, of course, their violation *does* raise a moral issue: driving on the wrong side of the road is clearly punishable behavior; and so is failure to live up to a contract on which another man has reasonably based his own plans.)

Admittedly, it was always possible that under a system of precedent the first judge to rule on a question with moral content had got the wrong answer, and that later judges had felt constrained to follow his beaten path. The barons of the Exchequer in Elizabethan England agreed cheerfully to examine legislation with an eye to finding "the mischief and defect for which the common law did not provide" and the "remedy the Parliament hath resolved and appointed to cure the disease." Then "the office of all the Judges is always to make such construction as shall suppress the mischief, and advance the remedy."

Wholehearted judicial acceptance of legislative supremacy rested, however, on the premise that the legislature would not interfere too often. For if a judge really believes that he is in tune with the infinite, and that the rules he lays down in the cases he decides are reflections of a divine natural law or "constitutionality," he cannot also believe in the propriety or morality of promiscuous legislative review. When the Industrial Revolution worked vast changes in the normal relations among people (and between people and property), a judge-made common law based on precedent became more and more unsuitable to more and more of the disputes that created lawsuits. Legislatures moved in on the lawmaking authority, and the lawyers and judges fought back bitterly.

The arguments against legislative "codification" of the common law rested in fact (though not always in words) on surviving belief in natural law. The judges, James C. Carter wrote as part of his temporarily successful fight to kill a proposed New York Code, apply "the national standard of justice, [which is] the product of the combined operation of the thought, the morality, the intellectual and moral culture of the time. Under our present unwritten system of law, it is ascertained and made effective by the judges, who know it and feel it because they are part of the community." Time had undermined the argument, as the weak last sentence reveals. Either the judges could successfully claim the status of priests or the community of which they were a part would refuse them the special authority they claimed.

Still, they fought, through the nineteenth and well into the twentieth centuries. The doctrinal weapon was an assertion that statute laws which changed the common law were to be "construed strictly"—that is, the legislature was to be assumed not to have wished to change the common law unless it said so inescapably. The high point of this judicial sabotage was reached in the United States in 1902, when the Circuit Court of Appeals for the Eighth Circuit ruled against a railway conductor who had lost a hand trying to couple together a locomotive and a railway car which would not couple automatically. Under the common law (as misinterpreted by the House of Lords, which did not control but profoundly influenced American judges), the conductor would have been held to have assumed the risk of losing his hand when he accepted his job. But Congress had passed a statute requiring railroads to equip their cars with automatic couplers, to put an end to just such accidents. The Court admitted the controlling force of the statute, then pointed out that both cars were in fact equipped with automatic couplers (though of different designs which would not lock together automatically), and that one of them was a locomotive rather than a car, and if Congress had wished to include locomotives in the law it could have said locomotives. So the statute didn't apply and the railroad was not liable.

The Supreme Court reversed: by 1902 both British and American judges had once again accepted the theory that in construing and enforcing statutes they should think about what the legislature had wished to accomplish by passing them. A last rebellion in the United States, sustained into the 1930s, took the form of construing statutes so broadly that their results (in certain hypothetical cases) would become unconstitutional, at which point the court would throw out the whole thing. Legislatures thereupon made sections of laws separable to avoid total destruction by judges, Congress chipped away much of the power of federal district judges as individuals to declare either state or national statutes unconstitutional; and eventually, after a last flurry of protest against the New Deal, the judges accepted their fate.

4

Second *caveat:* Jurisprudence comes after the event. The judges acquired the power to make law not because Englishmen by some affirmative gesture accepted the idea that they were especially equipped to find law but because they were royal officials working in a period when the royal authority was slowly but surely stamping out the power of the feudal barons. The courts of equity were created at least in part (the history is disputed) because the common-law judges had grown independent of the king, who by manipulation of Chancery would restore his control over them. Juries were demanded not as correctives to law but because their empaneling had been originally an exclusive royal prerogative: they were built into the system for political reasons. American judges threw out legislation not because they felt constitutional scruples but because they disapproved of the objectives of the legislation.

Institutions acquire their philosophical underpinnings not in the course of their construction but after they are in place and come under attack.

But the historical argument claims too much. Whatever their origins, institutions are maintained later by something more than mere inertia and the difficulty of finding a substitute. The quality of the "jurisprudential" arguments that can be found for the maintenance of a given rule of procedure is highly significant in maintaining this part of the system. Historians perform a great service when they demonstrate that the reasons for starting a social institution have nothing to do with the reasons now given for keeping it: everyone, but especially a judge, tends to confuse antiquity with validity. But the reasons for retaining, say, the "rule against parol evidence" (the refusal to hear testimony as to what somebody who signed a contract now says he thought it meant, when the words of the signed document are clear) are quite independent of the social conditions that created it.

In considering the shift from judge-made law to legislation, it should be kept in mind that American and English commentators have always exaggerated the differences between the two, and pretended that somehow the common law was different *as law* from the "civil codes" descending from the Romans, which dominated the European continent. There was, indeed, a major philosophical difference: because Anglo-American law, unlike the law of the Romans, grew out of decided cases, its emphasis was always on the relations of people rather than on abstract principles for the governance of society. As Roscoe Pound wrote,

> The Romanist speaks of the contract of *societas*. He develops all his doctrines from the will of the parties who engaged in the legal transaction forming the partnership. . . . We speak instead of the partnership relation and of the powers and rights and duties which the law attaches to that relation. Again, the Romanist speaks of a letting and hiring of land and of the consequences which are willed by entering into that contract. We speak of the law of landlord and tenant and of the warranties which it implies. . . . The Romanist speaks of family law. We speak of the law of domestic relations.

But ultimately the continental codes become real law only as they are applied by judges, and the skilled analyst of cases knows the rules that a common-law judge is likely to apply about as well as the Roman lawyer could know the practical force of his codes. "At the present moment," Sir Henry Maine wrote a century ago, before the wave of statutes had engulfed England,

> a rule of English law has first to be disentangled from the recorded facts of adjudged printed precedents, then thrown into a form of words, varying with the taste, precision, and knowledge of the particular judge, and then applied to the circumstances of the case for adjudication. But at no stage of this process has it any characteristic which distinguishes it from written law. It is written case-law, and only different from code-law because it is written in a different way.

The greatest single difference is in the status and functions of the legal profession: the more the law grows out of cases rather than legislation, the more important the lawyers and the judges.

5

But the swing from common law to statute law, well advanced now in both Britain and America, does not destroy the role of the judges, and probably increases their work load. Applying a statute to the facts of a case turns out to be no less challenging than applying a rule of common law. At the most rudimentary level, given the rudimentary standards of drafting much of the nation's annual 25,000 pages of new statutes, there is the difficulty presented by the meaningless law. Each commentator has his favorite example. Arthur Vanderbilt of New Jersey liked one from the original fair-trade act in California: "That the vendee or producer require in delivery to whom he may resell such commodity to agree that he will not, in turn, resell except at the price stipulated by such vendor or by such vendee." As Vanderbilt pointed out, this language "was not only grammatically incorrect but utterly lacking in meaning." The section was copied verbatim in Iowa, Maryland, New Jersey, New York, Oregon and Pennsylvania.

Nor is federal legislation immune. The tax laws are peculiarly impenetrable. We shall have occasion in Chapter 10 to note the confusion caused by the Robinson-Patman Act, in which Congress attempted to regulate relations between manufacturers and sellers in the interests of free competition. "Anyone who has had to deal with the Copyright Act of 1909," Judge Henry J. Friendly wrote, "must stand in awe of the ability of the framers to toss off a sentence that can have any number of meanings."

But even when the meaning is fairly clear, its application to the case at bar usually is not. Holmes' comment that "General propositions do not decide concrete cases" applies quite as much to statutes as to common law rules. For a long time it was considered sound doctrine that a judge should attempt to think himself into the position of the legislators who voted for the bill, and ask himself how they would have applied this statute to the point the lawyers had raised. Gray knocked this argument on the head with the fact that "in most [such cases] it is perfectly evident that the makers of the statutes had no real intention, one way or the other, on the point in question . . . [it] never occurred to [them]." Worse, the legislators may have deliberately ducked the problem because raising it would have imperiled the passage of the bill. Harvard's Lon Fuller has also emphasized "the very real temptations a government may have to make its laws vague."

In Britain the rule has been that only the words of the Act may be considered. No committee reports, or debates on the floor, or comments by sponsors may be brought to the attention of the judges, and they may not remake plainly unreasonable laws even if they have the strongest reason to believe that Parliament never intended the language of the statute to mean what, alas, it does mean. In the United States lawyers found they could sway judges by quoting from the legislative debates, and such quotes became so important in arguments and opinions as to provoke "the quip that only when legislative history is doubtful do you go to the statute."

Justice Robert H. Jackson was disturbed on both logical and practical grounds at the way the Supreme Court stretched statutes hither and yon by reference to the legislative history. "It is the business of Congress," he wrote, "to sum up its own debates in its legislation." Moreover, he added,

Laws are intended for all of our people to live by; and the people go to law offices to learn what their rights under those laws are. Here is a controversy [it was a fair-trade law, permitting manufacturers to fix retail prices] which affects every little merchant in many States. Aside from a few offices in the larger cities, the materials of legislative history are not available to the lawyer who can afford neither the cost of acquisition, the cost of housing, or the cost of repeatedly examining the whole congressional history.

Today Congress attempts to get around the difficulty by appending to each piece of legislation a committee report summarizing the reasons why the committee approved the bill. Presumably, Congressmen who voted for the legislation shared the reasoning of the report; but you never can tell. "The hard truth of the matter," Hart and Sacks write, "is that American courts have no intelligible, generally accepted and consistently applied theory of statutory interpretation."

Capable men argue about the extent to which courts should

consider themselves free to make a statute workable by rewriting it, or by revising their own prior interpretations of its language to bring a better brand of justice to new cases. Hart and Sacks have written scornfully of "the flagellant theory of statutory interpretation . . . that it is a court's duty to discipline the legislature by taking it literally." In the case of a criminal law, of course, the courts can generally rely on the prosecutors not to prosecute acts (noncommercial Mann Act violations, for example) which earlier judges mistakenly included within the prohibitions of the law.

Though precedent cannot govern decisions based on statutes because the document is there to be consulted, judges tend to be nervous about changing their interpretations of a statute. What looks like a dubious former ruling (because it had to be made in an extreme case or before enough cases had come before the courts to show how the rule would work) will often be retained on the grounds that the legislature could have changed the law if it didn't like the interpretation. As it did not do so, it can be assumed to have accepted the court's interpretation as its own. Various commentators have pointed out that this argument (which is used many times a year in bodies as august as the Supreme Court) is simply a classic example of the logical fallacy known as the undistributed middle. Legislatures have other things to do, such as passing budgets and taxes. California's Roger Traynor has described as "a mighty assumption" the idea "that legislative silence means applause. It is much more likely to mean ignorance or indifference. . . . There can be idle silence as well as idle talk."

Still, however tightly they feel bound by statutory control, judges in a changing society continue willy-nilly to play a creative role in lawmaking. If they are no longer the ultimate authority, they are usually the authors of the first experiments. The world throws up cases involving new issues much faster than it can produce new legislation. "Emerging problems of social maladjustment," Hart and Sacks write, "tend always to be submitted first to the courts. . . . Legislatures and administrative agencies tend always to make law by way not of original solutions of social problems but by alteration of the solutions first laid down by the courts."

Today, then, the rules of law come from constant interplay between judges and legislatures. It seems an excellent answer to the old jurisprudential question about the source of the law. Unfortunately, the job of getting the machine to work smoothly has not yet been accomplished: large areas of American law are an incoherent mess. Despite some promising beginnings in New York forty years ago under the proddings of Cardozo, we have been unable to establish a procedure for systematic interaction by courts and legislatures. The legal structure still changes only in response to crisis: lawyers and judges, like laymen, are forever crying that there ought to be a law.

6

Every American is governed by two separate and discrete bodies of law, which are enforced in separate court systems. "State sovereignty" and "states' rights" have become such feeble rallying cries in the last generation—and have been so abused on behalf of discreditable conduct by state governments—that people who are not lawyers tend to forget how much of American law is in fact state-created and state-enforced, beyond any possibility of legal interference by the federal government. There can be no "common law" for the United States as a whole, because there is no common sovereignty over its citizens.

The Constitution left to state law and the state courts the overwhelming majority of the disputes that involve ordinary people—crime, contract, property, personal injury, divorce, wills. The state courts have always been the basic suppliers of legal remedies: among them, they handle literally hundreds of times the volume of business done in the federal courts. They can apply a federal law or the law of other states when they find that a case should be decided on that basis. When a resident of a state is suing another resident of that state, except in one of the relatively few cases that directly involve an area of federal law, he may not sue anywhere except in the courts of that state.

What the Constitution awarded to the national government was only that part of business law which affected "interstate commerce," the laws of ships at sea, national defense and foreign affairs, plus certain restraints on state action. (The Congress was also empowered —very significantly, as it later developed—to increase the scope of national law through legislation to "promote the general welfare.") The federal courts originally established by Congress in 1789 were not in fact authorized to hear cases which arose under national legislation: enforcement of national law was left entirely to the states for the first dozen years of the national existence. Apart from the Supreme Court (which was empowered to hear appeals from state courts where it was claimed that the state decision violated—or denied enforcement to—a national law or treaty or the national Constitution), the new federal courts were to hear only cases involving the law of the sea, cases where the United States was suing somebody (nobody had yet thought of the possibility that anyone might sue the United States), cases where one of the parties was an alien—and cases where the two parties were citizens of different states. This last category, the so-called "diversity jurisdiction," provided the great majority of the cases heard in the federal courts.

How to deal with these cases was a real problem. There was no body of federal law which the federal courts could apply: indeed, Congress did not and does not have the power to legislate in most areas of contract, personal injury and the like, which are the areas of law presented by most "diversity" cases. The laws of the states were often different enough to produce different results, depending on which law the court chose to apply. What should the federal court do?

In 1842 Joseph Story, Justice of the Supreme Court, Harvard professor and bank president, found a startling answer to the question: the federal courts were to find their own law, like British common-law courts, ignoring any decisions by state courts. The case involved a six-month note given by a Maine man named Tyson in payment for some lands sold to him by a pair of New York real-estate sharps named Norton and Keith, who had misrepresented the property in the course of selling it. Tyson told his bank not to honor the note, but meanwhile Norton and Keith had handed it over in payment of a pre-existing debt to a New Yorker named Swift, telling Swift they had received it in payment for some valuable lands in New York. Swift sued Tyson for the money in federal court, because he and Tyson lived in different states. Tyson argued that his note was void from the beginning, because his acceptance had been procured by fraud. Swift argued that he had no way of knowing anything of the sort, and was entitled to collect on what looked to him like a perfectly good note.

This is one of those neutral questions on which the law must lay down a rule of the road: assuming Norton and Keith have absconded, which of their victims should bear the loss? The New York courts had ruled in similar cases that men in Tyson's position owed nothing—in effect, that men in Swift's position had to inquire about notes before taking them as repayment of a debt. English courts, following Lord Mansfield, had ruled in similar cases that men in Tyson's position had to pay up—that the greater interest of society lay in the promotion of trade, and that it was therefore wiser to require the Tysons of this world to reclaim their notes when they found they had been defrauded than to require the Swifts to make investigations.

Story decided that Mansfield and the English were right, and the courts of New York State, if they had ruled to the contrary (which he did not quite admit), were wrong. He then had to face the fact that Section 34 of the Judiciary Act of 1789 had provided that "the laws of the several states . . . shall be regarded as rules of decision, in trials at common law, in the courts of the United States, in cases where they apply." Full of Blackstone and self-importance, Story ruled that the word "laws" did not include judicial decisions, which "are, at most, only evidence of what the laws are." Therefore the federal courts were free to apply what they considered the *true* law in this sort of situation. And "the law repecting negotiable instruments," Story announced, "may be truly declared in the language of Cicero." The doctrine of *Swift* v. *Tyson,* that federal courts could make up their own law in cases involving citizens of different states, expanded to cover all kinds of contracts, personal injury cases—indeed, just about everything except real estate, wills and matrimonial problems. And presently the Supreme Court held that federal judges were not bound by state court interpretations of state statutes any more than by state common law, and Section 34 of the Judiciary Act went into the ash can.

It should be noted that Swift could have got his money *only* through Story's ruling. His transaction had occurred in New York. He could have sued in the state courts of Maine, because that was where Tyson was: the Maine courts had jurisdiction. But from the beginnings of foreign trade, courts had held that the decision in a case should not depend on the accident of where a lawsuit happened to be brought: one party to a deal should not later have the opportunity to choose the law that would be applied to it. If a British merchant made a contract in Venice, and his disappointed Venetian partner later sued him in Britain, the British courts consulted with the Venetian Embassy to discover the Venetian laws, which would govern the case. In 1966 a court in New Jersey sent down to Costa Rica to discover the law that should apply in a case against U.S. Steel for injuries suffered in the collapse of a bridge U.S. Steel had built in Costa Rica. On occasion, courts might even invoke the doctrine of *renvoi,* submitting the question to a court abroad for determination under the law of that court. Similarly, it was understood from the beginning that the courts of the American states would apply recognized international "choice of law" rules to each other's laws and decisions. A Maine court hearing Swift's case, even if Maine law favored Swift's position, would have had to apply the New York law and decide in Tyson's favor.

Story, in short, was wrong in principle, in statutory construction and in history. As Karl Llewellyn put it, his opinion was "horrendous as law, unnecessary to the case, and badly argued." Story, Gray wrote musingly some sixty years later (when the doctrine of *Swift* v. *Tyson* seemed "too firmly settled to be shaken"),

was then by far the oldest judge in commission on the bench; he was a man of great learning, and of reputation for learning greater even than the learning itself; he was occupied at the time in writing a book on bills of exchange, which would, of itself, lead him to dogmatize on the subject; he had had great success in extending the jurisdiction of the Admiralty; he was fond of glittering generalities; and he was possessed by a restless vanity. All these things conspired to produce the result.

And the result, as we shall see in Chapter 9, was extremely important. Once corporations were permitted to sue in the federal courts (as they were two years later), they could take advantage of a more property-minded federal "general common law" whenever customers or victims tried to sue them. Lawyers had to learn two different sets of law, one for state and one for federal courts. A suit brought in the state courthouse would produce one decision, while a suit brought across the street in the federal courthouse would produce a different decision on the same set of facts.

Worse, the federal courts could be used deliberately to duck perfectly reasonable state regulation. Kentucky prohibited railroads from giving taxi companies monopoly franchises at their stations. The owners of a taxi company which had such a contract with the Louisville & Nashville Railroad dissolved their Kentucky corporation and reincorporated (same people, same business) under Tennessee law. They then petitioned in federal court to forbid another Kentucky taxi company from interfering in any way with their contract for monopoly rights at the Louisville & Nashville station. The federal courts upheld the contract and enjoined the Kentucky defendants from actions which were perfectly legal under Kentucky law. Justice Holmes hit the ceiling in dissent, denouncing "an unconstitutional assumption of powers by the courts of the United States which no lapse of time or respectable array of opinion should make us hesitate to correct."

In fact, of course, Story did not intend this development at all: he thought the state courts would be forced to change their rules to follow the Supreme Court. At least one modern historian has argued that this compulsion was the intention of the Judiciary Act, but the argument can be sustained only by ignoring all history other than a few documents. The first Congress almost declined to establish any federal district courts at all, and was ultimately persuaded to do so on the grounds that the Admiralty jurisdiction (the ships-at-sea) would require them. And the same men who wrote the Judiciary Act specifically refused to apply the guarantees of the Bill of Rights to the states—an amendment to do so, the proposed Article 17 of the set of amendments to the Constitution considered by the first Congress, passed the House but was rejected by the Senate. If they were not prepared to insist that the states follow Supreme Court interpretations of the Bill of Rights, they certainly were not prepared to insist that the states follow Supreme Court interpretations of Cicero.

In any event, the states did not follow. They ignored the "general common law" of the federal courts across the street, and developed their own bodies of separate common law and statutory interpretation. The differences among the states are considerable, not only in questions like water rights and mineral rights where geography makes different results practical and necessary, but also in fundamental day-to-day legal rules.

Some states, for example, permit unlimited recovery for the heirs of people who die as the result of somebody's negligence; others have set ceilings on the maximum award for "wrongful death." Some states protect charitable institutions from liability for damages (the hospital can sew the scissors into your gut with impunity), while others treat charitable institutions like anybody else. Some states will not permit guests in automobiles to sue hosts or wives to sue husbands; others will. Some states allow wages to be garnisheed to pay installment debts; others don't. Some states regard married women as fully capable of entering into contracts; others retain at least part of the old common-law protection of the *femme couverte*. Laws about what constitutes a valid contract of sale, a valid will, a valid agency agreement, a cause for divorce, even (still) a negotiable instrument—all these vary from state to state, and did through all the years of the reign of *Swift* v. *Tyson*.

That reign ended, after ninety-six years, in 1938, when the Supreme Court heard an appeal by the Erie Railroad against an award of $30,000 to a man named Tompkins who had been walking along a path on railroad property beside the tracks, uninvited, when a train came along and he was hit by a swinging door on a freight car. Under Pennsylvania law he was a trespasser on railroad property, and could not recover; under federal "general common law," the railroad was liable. Justice Brandeis, in a 6-2 decision, reversed the award. "There is no federal general common law," he wrote. "Congress has no power to declare substantive rules of common law applicable in a state whether they be local in their nature or 'general.'. . . And no clause in the Constitution purports to confer such a power upon the federal courts." When cases arose under state law, the federal courts were to apply the law of the state. Period.

Three years later, to the outrage of the federal judges, the Supreme Court went a step further, requiring the federal courts in "diversity" cases to follow not only the precedents of the supreme court of the state in which they sat, but the line of decisions of lower state courts. Judge Joseph C. Hutcheson, Jr. complained that this doctrine made federal judges subservient to "any jackleg judge" of a state. Judge Henry J. Friendly, more recently, has compared the posture of the modern federal judge in "diversity" cases to that of "the little dog seeking to make out his master's voice."

Erie and its companion doctrines brought out of the woodwork a great deal of formerly academic casuistry on choice-of-law problems, and presently the state supreme courts began to act. California appears to have been the leader. As early as 1953 the California Supreme Court abandoned the hallowed common-law rule that the law governing an action growing out of an accident would be the law of the place where the accident occurred. An injured Californian was permitted to sue the estate of another Californian whose negligence, while he was alive, had caused the accident, even though the accident occurred in Arizona, where the death of the guilty party stops all such lawsuits. In 1957 Minnesota courts held the proprietor of the Hook-em-Cow saloon in Minnesota liable for damages under a Minnesota "dram-shop" law when a driver who had got drunk at his saloon went on to have an accident in Wisconsin, which has no "dram-shop" law. In 1963 the courts of New Hampshire permitted an injured wife to sue her husband for negligence in an automobile accident, even though the accident occurred in Massachusetts, where wives are not allowed to sue husbands.

The fastest motion (forward and backward) has been in New York, where the landmark case is *Kilberg* v. *Northeast Airlines*. Here the estate of a New Yorker who had bought his tickets in New York was allowed to recover whatever a jury would award for wrongful death after an airplane accident in Massachusetts, even though Massachusetts law then limited recoveries in such cases to a maximum of $30,000. Similarly, New York approved an award to a New York resident who had been the guest of a New York driver at the time of an accident which occurred in Ontario, even though Ontario has a "guest statute" prohibiting such recoveries. Then, defining its meanings more clearly, the New York court held that a Colorado guest statute *should* apply, barring a suit by a girl against her boy friend when the two New Yorkers had met while they were both summer students at the University of Colorado and had suffered their accident in that state.

In these choice-of-law cases, judge-made law has been set in motion again, and in many of them the quality of the opinions justifies the old reverence for common-law procedures. Meanwhile, the denial of a "federal general common law" has, in Judge Friendly's words, "opened the way to what, for want of a better term, we may call specialized federal common law." The new study of choice-of-law rules has led to questions about the real interests secured by different laws in different states, and the categories of people whose remedies should thereby be protected. The new study of federal jurisdiction has led to questions about those areas where state law may not be permitted to control simply because the significant interests involved are larger than those of any one state. Justice Brandeis himself, in an opinion delivered the same day as *Erie* v. *Tompkins,* brushed aside state statutes and decisions to apportion the water of an interstate stream according to "federal common law."

7

Erie v. *Tompkins* and its successors demonstrate the remarkable resilience of judge-made law in the United States. The tradition is alive: push it down here, it comes up there. The great reason for its persistence, of course, is the ability of American courts to find law in constitutions, superlegislation which can often be construed in ways indistinguishable from those by which the English judges found their common law. During the years of retreat from *Swift* v. *Tyson* in civil cases, the Supreme Court injected federal supervision into criminal law (nearly all of which is state law), partly by insisting that the Fourteenth Amendment had made certain guarantees in the Bill of Rights applicable to state prosecutions, partly by developing the rather odd idea that if a state violated certain procedural guarantees its courts "lost jurisdiction" over the defendant, who therefore could be set free in federal district court through a writ of habeas corpus (literally, bring the person to this court to determine whether you may hold him). In several of the following chapters we shall find lawyers at work to gain from the courts remedies which, in effect, the judges are adding to the law.

Detailed examination of what the lawyers and judges have done must await those chapters. Here it is enough to observe that though we live in a legislative age, when society will not allow strongly felt desires to be frustrated by lawyers and courts, the courts can still speak up, and their voice will be heard if not heeded. Through judicial review under a constitution the courts are also the proprietors of a necessary garbage can for the disposal of laws that were always undesirable and are no longer felt as necessary (laws, for example, for the control of alleged subversives or the prohibition of information on birth control). Finally, though natural law is dead, a community sense of "natural justice" may give significant political power to a court speaking without legislated authorization.

But it is silly to deny that in many directions the drive of the community has relegated the courts to byroads. The power of any legal system is in the hands of those who have authority to exericse discretion. Inevitably, in any large and intimately interrelated modern society, most of this power will be retained by the legislature and the executive. We cannot today afford what any nineteenth-century lawyer would have considered minimum standards for a "rule of law." The influence of today's lawyers on what happens is increasingly independent of legal weaponry.

Our inherited legal procedures are often ill-suited for the effective control of power in other parts of the governmental system—for preventing the award of excessive discretion while permitting what is necessary and will therefore in fact survive, whether courts like it or not. By abdication or by misemployment of its limited power, the legal system of a modern society can easily become merely an ornamental façade for government essentially without law. We have seen it happen elsewhere.

Judges in the United States retain enough discretion to be significant: it is still important to know what the courts as courts will do in fact. In the nurturing and employment of that discretion—in the development of a new "equity" to meet the needs of a polity very different from that which gave birth to our traditional jurisprudence—today's lawyers and judges can keep prominent the ideal of law as central to the structure of the community. They will need more help than they think from the rest of us.

PART II

PEOPLE

CHAPTER 5

CRIMINAL MATTERS:
THE WAY IT IS NOW

"The horrible thing about all legal officials, even the best, about all judges, magistrates, barristers, detectives, and policemen, is not that they are wicked (some of them are good), not that they are stupid (some of them are quite intelligent), it is simply that they have got used to it."

—G. K. CHESTERTON

"Wherever the visitor looks at the system, he finds great numbers of defendants being processed by harassed and overworked officials. Police have more cases than they can investigate. Prosecutors walk into courtrooms to try simple cases as they take their initial look at the files. Defense lawyers appear having had no more than time for hasty conversations with their clients."

—EDWARD L. BARRETT, JR., Dean,
School of Law, University of
California, Davis

1

Part 1-A is a large, squarish room with a high ceiling, on the second floor of the chaste, Rockefeller Center style criminal courts building in lower Manhattan. 1-A is an "arraignment court"—

that is, a place to which prisoners are brought by the police who have arrested them, so that a judge may inquire into the circumstances of the arrest, learn the charge the state expects to prove, hear a lawyer if there is one and assign one if there isn't, set or deny bail or release with orders to return on a certain day. There are seven such arraignment courts in Manhattan, each specializing in a different kind of violation. The specialty in 1-A is felonies, the serious crimes, and the court runs on a "we-never-close" basis twenty-four hours a day, seven days a week. Suspected felons pass through the court at the rate of one every ten minutes. Most cases are adjourned, so the prosecutors and the defense counsel can bargain out a guilty plea; a few are assigned to trial; a few are disposed of on the spot.

The courtroom has four entrances. At the rear, a pair of heavy doors covered in leather swing soundlessly into the center aisle of a public area which occupies about three-quarters of the room, full of long, dark wood benches. The public end is separated from the business end by a hip-high dark wood barrier. Into the working part of the court open three small doors, one at stage right for the lawyers and court attendants and two at the rear, one leading to the judge's robing room and one to the shallow pens where the men are kept, eight or nine to a cell, awaiting their moment in court. Lawyers interview their new clients through the bars. The courtroom walls are wood-paneled to a height of about seven feet; dark brass fixtures hang down from the geometrically ornamented ceiling and give an even, just-bright-enough light, not influenced by what comes through the dirty north windows which look at another wing of the building. During the day both parts of the courtroom are a mess of humanity. In the public area sit several hundred people—those of the accused felons who are out on bail or "on recognizance," their friends and family, complaining witnesses, some policemen, some lawyers. There is a great deal of motion along the rows of seats and up and down the center and both the side aisles. About half of those on the benches are colored, and some of the rest, no doubt, are white Puerto Rican. A buzz rises from the area, though many, perhaps most, sit dumbly and incuriously and wait. People are not allowed to read in courtrooms, and the proceedings up front are only partly audible—and rarely comprehensible—in the rear.

Judge Simon Silver, looking quite small, as judges always do in black robes, sits on a raised chair behind a very long desk on a platform raised perhaps eighteen inches off the courtroom floor. Behind him are flags and *(pace* the atheist set) a raised gilt motto: "N GOD WE TRUST." (The "I" has fallen off.) Below him at a long table sit assorted clerks and probation officers. Over by the lawyers' door is a small desk and some chairs for the young Legal Aid lawyers, three or four of them, who will represent about three-fifths of the defendants. Backed against the wooden barrier is a sometimes empty, sometimes crowded row of wooden armchairs, for paid lawyers. People are forever walking back and forth. On the wall at stage left, where the jury box would be, there are more chairs for policemen, chatting, lounging, waiting to lead their catch to the bar. Beside the clerk's table stands a small raised platform with a small table and wooden armchair, for witnesses. The Assistant District Attorney, a very young lawyer with protruding eyes and a glum expression, stands at a lectern before this platform, slightly stage left. In dead center, facing into the public area, a uniformed policeman, known in the lingo of the court as "the bridgeman," pulls folders from the clerk's table and calls out in a stentorian voice:

"Docket Numbers Twelve Hundred Fifty and Fifty-One, Defendants Michael and Mary . . ."

A young couple come out from the public area to the railing before the bridgeman. They are accompanied by a policeman, who talks to the DA.

"Do you waive the reading of the charge?"

There is confusion at the center: their lawyer isn't present. At the lawyers' row one rather shabbily dressed older man says to a younger colleague, "If you're not here, you get murdered. If you are here, you get murdered."

The younger lawyer replies, "I asked for a reduction; he said I could have it if I plead now; not if I wait till later. I told him we'd go later."

Michael and Mary have returned to their seats, to await their lawyer. A burly white man is at the railing, waiting while his lawyer and the policeman talk with the DA. The DA says, "Your Honor, there's a motion to reduce this charge to assault in the third degree. I have no objection." The case is set for trial. The judge says to the accused, "Would you rather have a three-judge court or a one-judge court?"

A statutory rape case: a small, thin, Puerto Rican boy, a pregnant girl who looks about thirteen, and her mother. "I want him to get his own lawyer," says the judge.

The DA says, ignoring this comment, "We agreed to a rather long adjournment to give the parties an opportunity to get married. I request a *final* adjournment."

They leave. A white man in a ragged tweed jacket, the stuffing coming out the bottom, is standing in the well of the court. He stole $64 worth of jewelry from Macy's; the charge is reduced to petit larceny, and he pleads guilty. The atmosphere changes a little. The judge browses through some papers, the man's "pedigree sheets," a confidential report, and says, "Four months."

"Your Honor, I have a wife and four children—nobody else takes care of them."

"You should have thought of that before." The judge looks down at the flimsy carbons. "You had a year suspended a few months ago. By rights, I should give you that. Instead, I gave you four months—I think I was pretty generous."

Time presses: a very pale, flabby, middle-aged man in a suit and a white shirt and a tie comes up with a policeman holding his elbow. He has laid his hands on a child on the Staten Island Ferry. The District Attorney asks $10,000 bail. "He's on parole from a life sentence for rape in Maryland."

His lawyer objects: "It's academic, anyway—but—he turned himself in."

The DA says again, "He's on a life sentence."

The judge shakes his head. *"He came in."*

"Yes, Your Honor," says the DA.

The judge sets $500 bail, and the man goes off to await trial (or return to Maryland) in the jail: an out-of-towner, he is a bad risk for the bail bondsman. Offhand, to the DA, the judge says, "I'd have let him go."

A tall, broad-shouldered young man comes up with a girl: charge of felonious assault. He and the girl talk with the DA.

The judge interrupts, "Where's your lawyer?"

The man shakes his head.

"Do you want to go back to jail?"

"No."

"Then get a lawyer—you're on bail, you can afford a lawyer."

But the girl with him is the girl he beat up. The DA says, "The People will consent to a reduction to third-degree assault."

The girl speaks to him even more earnestly, and he shrugs his shoulders. The complaint is dismissed, and the boy and the girl go off arm in arm.

Next is another statutory rape: a fat mother, a young man holding his hat in his hands, a hugely pregnant very young girl. Again the judge is annoyed by the absence of counsel. "You're on bail, you're not a charity case, you're not entitled to a free lawyer."

But these statutory rape cases are not meant to be prosecuted— they are the state, as a substitute father, pulling the shotgun out from behind the door. Judge Silver, impatiently, notes: "November 5, parole continued, defendant to retain counsel." He rises a little and leans over the desk to address the family group. "Well, *get married*. Come in here and show us that you're married." As an afterthought, as they turn around to leave, he adds, "Bring the baby."

A rather trim young couple have been shoplifting as a tandem. A low bail is continued—"But," the judge says to their lawyer, "tell 'em to keep out of the stores between now and Christmas, or I'll raise it to five thousand dollars."

A young Negro comes up grinning, the arresting officer with him, and the DA puts the arresting officer in the witness chair. An oath is administered, and then the question is asked: "Officer, did you arrest this defendant in possession of what you believed to be stolen property?" He did; the man could give no convincing explanation of why he was walking down the street at night carrying a television set and four suits of clothes; but nobody had reported a burglary, and the Legal Aid lawyers were raising hell about holding a man against whom no complainant had appeared. In Britain the circumstances and the man's inability to explain them would have constituted a crime; not in America. The purpose of the detective's testimony is to release the man while making a record to prevent any possible suit for false arrest.

Two young men come up, and the judge says with great distaste, "They're lovers, aren't they?" They are followed at the bar by two men, a girl and a policeman carrying a can of film: they want a preliminary hearing and are sent off, the girl miserable despite (or because of) some jollying by the policeman, to an adjoining courtroom where a judge will explore the legality of their arrest.

A colored boy wearing a sweater full of holes comes up to ask an adjournment on a burglary. Legal Aid represents him. Judge Silver continues his bail irritably. "Come back December 4 with your own lawyer—you're not a charity case." The Legal Aid lawyer wants to say something, but the judge won't hear it: "I'm not going to let you state a case. He's on parole. Why should he have a free lawyer?"

A middle-class, decently dressed Puerto Rican stands at the railing sweating, while the DA, a pair of trimly dressed policewomen beside him, describes an indecent exposure charge. Another adjournment.

Next, a conference forms around the DA's lectern, three men and a woman, and the DA, after a few minutes' chatter, looks up to the judge. "Your Honor, there's an application here to withdraw the charge. They were drinking. The defendant with the long record is the complainant's brother-in-law, and this is a family affair. As regards the other defendant, there is no record. I consent to the withdrawal."

A ratty little colored man comes in from the pens, and a detective in plain clothes is put on the stand. The case is felonious assault, a knifing, and the victim is in critical condition in the hospital. The DA, leafing through a folder—for he never heard of the case until thirty seconds before—requests that the man be held without bail. "I should like to point out to Your Honor that there is a fifty-fifty chance the complainant witness will not survive."

At the lawyers' row is an overdressed, overpowdered lady of fifty or so, in a bulging red blouse and a wide-brimmed hat. She mutters, "Now, that's an adverse comment. He could say, 'There's a fifty-fifty chance the complainant witness *will* survive.' He has a negative attitude."

One of the men says, "You got troubles—there are two defendants and a policeman I can't find."

The overdressed lady lawyer says, "I can't stand that DA; he sounds like a grocery clerk."

This is not a pleasant place to work. "You'll notice that a criminal lawyer never wears a hat," one of them says. "You know why? It's because if you put a hat down anywhere in a criminal courts building, somebody steals it."

2

"The problem with being a defense lawyer is that it's like giving your life to the Boston Red Sox," says James Vorenberg, director of the National Crime Commission, who before he went down to Washington was a Harvard professor with children who rooted for the home team. "You always lose."

"Not too many survive in criminal business," says George F. Callaghan, a lean Irishman of dramatic bent who wears the scales of justice as a tie pin and has survived very well on the criminal side of the federal courts in Chicago. "It's a catch-as-catch-can business. Your source is satisfied clients—and satisfied clients are damned rare in the criminal field."

The best of horror stories is that of the innocent man convicted of a crime, and among the most popular of entertainments is the murder which the police have the deuce of a time solving. Both situations are real, too: they happen. But their incidence is statistically invisible in each year's 300,000-plus serious criminal cases where an adult is arraigned before a judge. Substantially more than 95 percent of these defendants have unquestionably done *something* for which they could properly be punished by law; and about 80 percent will in fact be convicted. New quick arraignment requirements will change the percentages, because the police will have to bring before a judge more of the people who used to be released in the station house without insertion into the formal process—but only some numbers will change.

Discussions of criminal procedure in America normally start with a sonorous statement to the effect that all men are presumed innocent until proven guilty. Unfortunately, once this premise is accepted it is almost impossible to say anything either intelligent or relevant about the problem. As the late Charles P. Curtis once wrote, "No one who has been indicted and formally charged with a crime is really presumed innocent by anyone but his friends or well-wishers, or somebody who happens to know that the government was wrong."

An abstract "presumption of innocence" cannot long survive the experience of the courts—except in the form the proposition takes in Britain (and in Curtis' own ideological defense of it), where the phrase means merely that the prosecution carries the entire burden of proof. A federal district judge once observed to Harvard professor Henry M. Hart, "The truth of the matter is that I never see a defendant in a criminal case without assuming he's guilty."

In the great majority of cases, the presumption of innocence is not put to the test in court. Of those arrested on a serious criminal charge, more people are cleared and released by the police themselves than by the entire legal process of arraignment, preliminary hearing, indictment by grand jury (where this custom exists) and trial. A defendant's next best chance is to persuade the DA not to prosecute: six or seven times as many people are released between arraignment and trial as are acquitted after a trial. A good proportion of these will be defendants (like our young man whose girl decided she wanted him even though he had beaten her to a pulp) who have never troubled to deny the charges against them, but for one reason or another it seemed impolitic for the prosecutor to proceed. Of the cases where the prosecutor does decide to press felony charges, something over 95 percent (in Manhattan the figure runs about 99 percent) result in conviction by guilty plea or verdict. "Our system of criminal courts," Dean Barrett has written, "is organized to deal with a situation in which police and prosecutor screen out all but the most clearly guilty."

"The sad fact is that the cops don't go around arresting people indiscriminately," says the New York defense attorney Harris Steinberg, a sober, deeply thoughtful lawyer (and not quite so sober though perhaps equally thoughtful cartoonist) who came into the criminal field largely because there were no other jobs in the late thirties for young Jewish graduates of the Harvard Law School. "And the district attorneys don't go around indicting people indiscriminately."

Nobody is trained at a law school—or prepared by the culture—to operate as a defense lawyer in such a system. It is a true paradox (though probably an inevitable one) that a period when the Supreme Court is insisting on ever-widening representation by lawyers in the criminal process should also be a period when the traditional and popular function of the lawyer in the criminal courts has almost disappeared.

Almost—but not quite. "I have sympathy for these people; they're my clients," says Harris Steinberg. "And there's a great deal the lawyer can do. A man may have had a stroke or a heart attack—he doesn't think it has anything to do with his stealing the money, but I may know the DA has a policy of not indicting someone it may kill. A man may not know that the person who will testify against him is an accomplice whose testimony has to be corroborated, which it isn't. He may not know the statute of limitations has run."

After a brawl in a bar the police will bring in and book the man who's still standing up—and he may regard himself as guilty, because he knifed somebody. But he may have a valid claim of self-defense. A boy who was part of a criminal group but didn't directly do anything may not have committed any crime, even though he identifies with others who are guilty, and the police have brought him in. He needs a lawyer to tell him he is clear.

Moreover, many thousands of people are arrested every year for offenses which are punished severely but which not everyone would consider "crimes." Boston's Harold Katz, whose round face and intellectual manner conceal an adventurous temperament (he settled down to practicing law in Boston only after commanding a ship for Israel during the time when refugees had to be smuggled into British-controlled Palestine), has represented a number of people accused simply of possessing obscene materials. William Devine, a spare old-time New Englander, has represented University of New Hampshire professors hauled in on similar charges; and his firm represented the pacifist Willard Uphaus, jailed for refusal to tell a state investigating committee about his associates. "It's harder here," Devine observes mildly, "because we have a newspaper that identifies the lawyer with his client. The [Manchester] *Union-Leader* still calls my partner Joe Millimet an 'Uphaus lawyer.' "

And the defense lawyer plays an absolutely essential role in keeping the system honest—if they think he's going to have a lawyer, both police and prosecutor are more likely to require verification early in the game to support their inner conviction that this particular s. o. b. is guilty.

Basically, however, the criminal defense lawyer, like lawyers in wildly different areas of the profession, works as a negotiator for his client. The aim of the negotiations is to trade the DA a plea of guilty for a reduction in the seriousness of the charge and/or the promise of a light sentence. "Plea bargaining," as this process is called, is the central phenomenon of the American system of criminal justice. Oddly enough, it has no legal standing.

"Maybe the most common crime in America," says a New York lawyer who takes occasional court-assigned criminal cases, "is the perjury of the defendant who swears before the judge that he hasn't been promised anything in return for his plea of guilty." It is not that the judges do not know what has been going on—normally, they do, and may even have been consulted—but that without such a statement in open court a convict may later take the option of appealing for a new trial on the grounds that his guilty plea was induced. Early in 1967 the American Bar Association Project on Minimum Standards for the Administration of Criminal Justice published a report from a committee headed by Justice Walter Schaefer of the Illinois Supreme Court, calling on the courts to recognize plea bargaining as wholly legitimate, and to find ways by which judges can promote and control negotiated justice.

Trials are a time-consuming and expensive business. "The basic idea of our system," Supreme Court Justice Abe Fortas said shortly before he went on the bench, "is that the citizen has the right to say, 'Thou sayest.' It's a marvelous, thrilling concept." But little or no purpose is served, for the accused individual or for the society that has to supply the courts and jurors, when people who are clearly guilty insist on that right. "The fact is," Judge Henry T. Lummus of Massachusetts once wrote, "that a criminal court can operate only by inducing the great mass of actually guilty defendants to plead guilty, paying in leniency the price for the pleas." More than six hundred people are arraigned every day in one of the seven significant "parts" of the Manhattan criminal courts; and there are fewer than a hundred lawyers in the District Attorney's office. If even one percent of these arraignments were actually to proceed to a full-fledged trial, the system would break down instantly. Similar figures, on a smaller scale, can be found everywhere. A Midwestern prosecuting attorney told an investigator from the American Bar Foundation that "All *any* lawyer has to do to get a reduced charge is to request a jury trial."

Sometimes the prosecutor is not, in fact, paying much for the plea. In a rape case, for example, conviction might be hard to get because of the girl's intense reluctance to testify: reduction to an assault charge in return for a guilty plea may be the state's best result. The stiff mandatory sentences for burglary, which frighten defendants, make convictions much harder to obtain, because juries don't like to slap people in jail for ten years just because they broke into a house; reduction of the charge to breaking and entering at a year or two makes the prosecutor's life easier. Some of the state's evidence may have been illegally seized by the police, and would not be admissible in court; or the state's witnesses may have a criminal record themselves, which gives a jury pause. Often a prosecutor will have brought the maximum possible charge that could be sustained on the evidence, with an eye to negotiating it down at a later period in the process. And always, of course, the defendant is threatened by the prosecution (and the situation) with the maximum sentence in the law—which he would be unlikely to receive even after a jury verdict—and the "bargain" merely assures him what he probably would have got anyway.

For the man who committed the crime and believes he will be convicted (and a guilty man must be highly experienced and sophisticated to give himself much chance of acquittal), even fairly small favors may seem desirable: there is a big difference between eighteen months and three years in jail. The offer that is particularly attractive involves reducing the charge to a misdemeanor rather than a felony, because felony convictions may involve the loss of citizenship rights down to and including the right to hold a driver's license—and because some "recidivist" statutes demand life imprisonment after a fourth felony conviction. The importance of this factor was demonstrated in a recent study of city criminal courts, in which 50+ to 90+ percent of all cases were disposed of by guilty pleas—except in Las Vegas, where the District Attorney did not have the right to reduce charges to misdemeanors, and only 20 percent of accused felons "copped out." Recently, the Las Vegas courts informed the Institute of Judicial Administration that they couldn't supply any estimate of the delay in their court in processing personal-injury cases—they'd just declared a six-month moratorium on *all* civil cases to catch up with the criminal business.

Once the plea is negotiated, everybody tends to lose interest in the proceedings. In Michigan, before 1964, for example, the penalty for breaking and entering in darkness was three times as heavy as that for breaking and entering in daylight; and defendants who had been caught in the act in the middle of the night routinely pleaded guilty to charges of the daytime offense. A report from California tells of a man who heard his name called, came to the bar and pleaded guilty of statutory rape, though the charge against him was grand theft. Asked why, he said, "Well, I thought maybe my attorney had made a deal for me." In Wisconsin the newspapers had some fun with a man who pleaded guilty to driving the wrong way on a one-way street in a town that had no one-way streets; he had agreed to that plea to avoid conviction on a speeding charge that would have cost him his license under the state's point system.

What the lawyer normally seeks for his client in a criminal situation, then, is not the vindication and acquittal of song and story, but a conviction followed by a suspended sentence or immediate parole. "Most clients," says a quiet, very matter-of-fact young man named Roger Koontz, a year out of Yale Law School and handling cases at one of New Haven's poverty-program neighborhood law offices, "feel you've been successful in a criminal matter if they stay out of jail." At the Los Angeles Public Defender's office (in its own way a civilized place, where people take a number and sit on upholstered theater seats rather than wood benches while waiting for a lawyer, and the management supplies newspapers and magazines), a young assistant comes bursting into an interview to tell his boss, gleefully, "You know what Rosy did to my man? Reduced it to simple assault, and let him off with time served."

The negotiation of these pleas is in the vast majority of cases the real contribution the criminal lawyer makes to his client. Some judges will not accept naïve guilty pleas to charges like armed robbery and nighttime breaking and entering, which are *always* reduced on negotiation (the reduction from armed to unarmed robbery is known colloquially as "swallowing the gun"). But there is no question that a lawyer can make a better deal than a defendant can. Moreover, fortunately, this sort of practice takes relatively little talent.

How much money these lawyers make for hanging around the courts is a matter of some dispute. Sometimes, no doubt, they have to split the fees they receive with the bailiff or the bail bondsman (many bail bondsmen offer a package deal, including lawyer); and because their clients are poor people with poor relatives, lawyers can rarely hope for more than $250 for a case that goes to trial, and must often make do with $50. Some lawyers who have occasional, more remunerative practice in the criminal courts feel, however, that sympathy for the regulars is misplaced. The National Crime Commission reported that its investigators, looking into the bull pen, saw "defense attorneys demanding from a potential client the loose change in his pocket or the watch on his wrist as a condition of representation." Boston's Monroe Inker says that "there was a man died here the other day who'd practiced forty years in a district court, and he left an estate of four hundred thousand dollars —all of it from those twenty- and fifty-dollar fees." And, of course, because these payments are cash and unprovable, the Internal Revenue Service need not know about all of them.

In any event, criminal practice is the one branch of the law where lawyers collect their fees in advance. Not long ago, an older New York lawyer with little experience in the criminal courts had a client who had been picked up in another county for drunk driving, and for whom a conviction at precisely this moment would be extremely inconvenient. He wanted a postponement, but knew of no excuse a judge would have to accept, so he consulted with the young assistant district attorney who would be on duty that day. The DA heard the reason for the postponement, which was a good one, and said, "That's all right. You just tell the judge you haven't been able to get hold of your witness, Mr. Green."

"But I don't have any witness, Mr. Green."

The DA looked incredulously at the older lawyer's white hairs and said, "Don't you *know?* It means you haven't been paid. Any judge will give you an adjournment on that."

In Washington, D.C., these matters are handled with greater apparent formality: a lawyer still waiting for his fee comes into court and demands an adjournment "pursuant to Rule I of this Court."

Private lawyers are to some extent paid to be sympathetic. Part of this sympathy comes out in a protective coloration of self-proclaimed corruption, because a criminal likes to hear his lawyer say he has the DA or the judge in his pocket (sometimes it is even true); part of it is simply a more human relationship with criminal clients than most Public Defenders or legal-aid lawyers can maintain. A good symbol of the difference is the office furniture: the visitor to the offices of a Public Defender sits on a rather uncomfortable wooden chair on a level with the lawyer's swivel chair; the visitor to the offices of a private criminal lawyer usually sits on a very comfortable armchair, which leaves him, however, perceptibly lower than the lawyer across the desk. Most people—and especially criminals, whose insights into the human situation tend to be weaker than the normal—prefer the private comfort to the public dignity.

Partly because the public and agency lawyers maintain an essentially correct rather than cordial manner, the legend grows that they don't really *defend,* which is nonsense. Indeed, the private lawyer who lives on small fees from poor people is more likely to sell his client the need for a guilty plea, partly because he considers (usually correctly) that it is in his client's best interests, and partly because he doesn't have the resources to try cases.

Legal aid and defender offices exist in varying strengths (up to 170 lawyers in Los Angeles), supported from tax revenues in many states (and here the salary scale will be that of the DA's office, ranging up to almost $21,000 a year in California), by charity or federal grant in other states (at substantially lower salaries). These offices, despite rumors to the contrary, all maintain a policy of never urging a man to plead guilty unless he admits his guilt. Anthony ("Chick") Marra, head of the New York Legal Aid office in the criminal courts, who has been defending indigents since he left Fordham Law School in 1938, remembers a case where a defendant insisted on standing trial despite an overwhelming case against him. When it was over, and the man had been convicted on a maximum charge, Marra asked him what on earth he'd expected.

"He said," Marra recalls, " 'I was wearing a lucky tie.'

"I said, 'What do you mean, a lucky tie?'

" 'The last three guys who wore this tie were acquitted—so I thought I'd take a chance.'

"I said, 'You know what you can do with that tie? Go around the bars and hang yourself.' "

In *Gideon* v. *Wainwright,* in 1963 (a case superbly detailed by Anthony Lewis in his book *Gideon's Trumpet*), the Supreme Court announced that criminal convictions in felony and serious misdemeanor cases could not be sustained unless the defendant had a lawyer, or had deliberately and consciously waived his right to a lawyer. The decision made new law in fact in only thirteen states, and changed custom in only five, but the publicity attendant on it was carefully noted in the criminal community and made monumental nuisance in the legal-aid offices of the larger cities, who had been representing everybody for years. "As soon as their case was called for trial, they fired their lawyer," Marra recalls gloomily. "They thought if they didn't have a lawyer, they couldn't be convicted. One fellow said to me, 'I have nothing against you, but I have to fire you so I can protect the record for appeal.' " The courts put a stop to this nonsense after a year or so, but while it flourished it reinforced the defendant group's prejudices against a "charity lawyer."

On the ground floor in the New York criminal courts building, Legal Aid runs seminars a dozen times a year for new recruits and for volunteer lawyers, young men who have been given leave for the purpose from a large firm, or who want to make a contribution to justice or the poor, or who simply seek a little trial practice. These meetings are held in the shabby little windowless library of the Legal Aid office, and they are a quick course in the tricks of criminal procedure, given by an experienced Legal Aid staff member to four or five newcomers at a time:

"Your defendant can be held after a hearing or waived to the grand jury after 1-A. In this county you never get a hearing on a homicide; you do in Kings County [Brooklyn]. The hearing tells you some of the DA's case, but you may not want it. *Always* make a note of the address of the complaining witness. If it's out of town, don't be too eager to have a hearing. When you have a hearing, you perpetuate testimony. You have a right to ask the DA whether the purpose of the hearing is the perpetuation of testimony. If the purpose *is* perpetuation, you are entitled to two days' notice. The purpose of the notice is to give you time to prepare for a cross-examination. If you don't get the two days, stand mute. The statement, 'I have no questions,' means you're participating. You must say, 'The defendant stands mute.'

"Remember, your defendant has the right to testify to the grand jury [where defense lawyers are not admitted]. And the grand jury has the power to vote No Bill even though there has been a violation of the law. You use a negative test. Can he help himself is not good—the question is, can he hurt himself? Never have a defendant testify in a crime of violence—grand juries are loath to throw out a crime of violence, even if you have a self-defense.

"The typical case where you say he can't hurt himself is where you have a guilty client. You get the picture—a slob but a harmless slob. Or a statutory rape, if you have a clean defendant: he doesn't have to be Jack Armstrong, he can be José Ramirez. Our legislature has seen fit to set the statutory age at eighteen. Sometimes we get a sixteen-year-old defendant with a seventeen-year-old girl. We get eight out of ten statutory rapes dismissed by the grand jury, with no objection from the DA.

"Don't think a reduction is the best you can get in a case. Sometimes the DA will wish to reduce a statutory rape (which requires corroboration) to an assault-third, where all you need is that the witness be believed. If your defendant isn't an absolute slob, you don't want it.

"We don't owe any more obligation to the court than a private retained counsel. Don't go for this bit that Legal Aid is an arm of the court. Your drug-addict defendant who's up for breaking into a car. He says, 'I didn't take it out of the car, I bought it from a guy.' It's the usual story, but you have to believe it just as much as if you were getting a $10,000 fee. You may very well have an innocent defendant—there aren't many around, but you may have one. Even if it's one in one hundred, the only way you can protect the one who deserves it is by extending the same protection to everybody."

The few large and respectably financed defender offices have teams of investigators who can check out the client's story. Most of the investigators are retired detectives, who can get some help from their old buddies, know how to locate witnesses by nicknames, etc. Particularly in California, where defenders and assistant DAs are assigned to the same courtroom for a year at a time and see each other every day, the "charity lawyer" often has good working relations with the prosecutor. "He knows you're not in it for money," one defender says, "and you're not going to suborn perjury. He'll give us his case, where the private attorney will have to make a motion for a bill of particulars, and even then won't get as much." If the Public Defender comes, troubled, to the prosecutor to say he's pretty sure his client is innocent, he will be taken seriously.

Since a Supreme Court decision in 1963, all convicted criminals have had a right to counsel for one appeal; and this, too, is handled by the legal-aid and defender offices, though not with equal enthusiasm in every case. Before this decision, when the office could pick and choose, New York's Legal Aid had a 55 percent batting average in obtaining reversals. "You can't keep the judges straight unless you appeal," Marra says.

Most defender offices, of course, are nowhere near so well staffed as those in the big cities. And in the majority of courts in smaller cities, lawyers will simply be appointed (sometimes without any fee whatever) to meet the constitutional requirements of counsel. (Federal courts could not offer fees to appointed counsel until the

Criminal Justice Act of 1964.) Their total preparation for the defense may be a ten-minute talk with their unwanted client, after which they take a further ten minutes of negotiation with the DA, and the client is advised to plead guilty. Still (though not for the reasons set forth in the Supreme Court's magniloquent opinions), the defendant is probably a lot better off than if he'd never had a lawyer at all: he's not at the mercy of the court; he's got a deal. Most important of all, perhaps, his lawyer will know (as he will not) which judge he should plead before, to secure the minimum sentence, and will know how to manipulate the situation so he comes before that judge.

3

The first and logically the only cause of crime is the criminal law: no conduct is "criminal" unless authority makes it so. And the criminal law, of course, does not "prohibit" anything: the law can do no more than announce what punishment society will visit upon people who are caught performing certain acts under certain circumstances. "The words of the law," as Llewellyn once put it, "are not: 'Keep hands off the goods of others,' but 'Any person duly convicted of larceny shall be sentenced' to so many years in prison."

Announcing that certain conduct shall be criminal is one of the most solemn rituals of any society. "It is on the perfection of the criminal laws," Montesquieu wrote, "that the liberty of the individual depends." For the citizen to be safe, the criminal laws must be generally known, tightly defined (the courts say "strictly construed," meaning that authority must say very precisely which conduct under which circumstances will be punished), and enforced only upon a high order of proof of guilt. Even so, the society normally feels queasy about depriving its members of life, liberty or even property, and legal theory demands that before a man's actions are called criminal the state must prove *mens rea*—literally, "evil mind," usually translated as "guilty intent," once translated puckishly by Justice Holmes as "actual wickedness." But the theory does not state the fact: as Holmes pointed out, "Acts are rendered criminal because they are done under circumstances in which they will probably cause some harm which the law seeks to prevent." Jerome Hall of Indiana University explains rather lamely that "inasmuch as normal persons share common attitudes regarding the elementary interests protected by the criminal law, it is a fair inference that the doer of a proscribed harm knows that his conduct is immoral." What *mens rea* means in practice is that the jury does not empathize.

In Britain the source of authority for the criminal law was the judges: crimes, like rules for the proper sale and purchase of land, were part of the common law. Indeed, despite the general maxim that people cannot be punished for violating laws that have not been announced and defined, the British courts do in fact retain some marginal power to create new crimes. In 1927 a London magistrate was confronted with a man who had jumped off Westminster Bridge on a bet, whose defense was that there was no law against it. The magistrate convicted and fined him anyway, and the conviction was upheld on appeal.

"It is a principle of English law," said the Court of Criminal Appeal,

that a person who appears in a police court has done something undesirable, and citizens who take it upon themselves to do unusual actions which attract the attention of the police should be careful to bring these actions into one of the recognized categories of crimes and offenses, for it is intolerable that the police should be put to the pains of inventing reasons for finding them undesirable. . . . It is not for me to say what offense the appellant has committed, but I am satisfied that he has committed some offense, for which he has been most properly punished.

No such opinion could be written by an American court (though similar or worse results could be achieved through manipulation of vagrancy, disorderly conduct or breach-of-the-peace statutes). It has been thoroughly understood in the United States since 1812 that only the legislature can create crimes—and even in 1812 Justice Johnson wrote that "although this question is brought up now for the first time to be decided by this Court, we consider it as having been long since settled in public opinion." In both Britain and the United States trial by jury guarantees against the enforcement of criminal laws actually repugnant to the community, because there is no way to prevent a jury from declaring a defendant not guilty, and juries will do so when they don't like the law. (This protection has been watered down in many states and in England by denying defendants the right to trial by jury for lesser crimes.) Circuit Judge Simon E. Sobeloff, while Solicitor General of the United States, once told an American Bar Association meeting of a case where a federal judge had successfully persuaded a jury to return a verdict of not guilty in a case where the defendant was clearly guilty. The defendant was a pharmacist, never in trouble before, who had been brought to trial under the Anti-Narcotics Law for having sold a narcotic preparation to an apparently reputable customer who had assured him, falsely, that a prescription would be forthcoming. Under the law, the judge would have been forced to sentence the pharmacist to two years in prison, and he explained the unfairness of the law to the jury to make sure of an acquittal.

Originally, according to the historians, the purpose of criminal law was to substitute organized state action for the disruptive private punishments that would otherwise be sought. The thief caught in the act in Rome was subject to a penalty twice that given to a thief who was captured later, because "the injured proprietor, if left to himself, would inflict a very different punishment when his blood was hot from that which he would be satisfied with when the thief was detected after a considerable interval." When the state forced the criminal to make a "composition"—to pay money— to his victim, "the Salic Law gave double composition to the Frank, accustomed to right his own wrongs, as compared with the Roman, trained for generations to adjust his controversies in court."

As late as Bentham, students of the subject were arguing that the thirst for retribution was and should be the basis of criminal punishment. Holmes pointed out, however, that "this passion is not one which we encourage, either as private individuals or as lawmakers." The purpose of the criminal law is not to get even with selected individuals, but to discourage certain kinds of behavior.

Calling the behavior a "crime" is not the only way to discourage it—many "wrongs" are left to be remedied by civil lawsuits (see Chapter 7), because the harm done is of a kind that can be reasonably recompensed, because the threat that the malefactor will do it again to other victims seems slight, or because the people most likely to misbehave are people who can pay damages. Most fraud, most trespass, most libel, most carelessness with weapons (including automobiles), most breaches of contract are discouraged by the provision of official channels for private action. When potential miscreants appear unable to pay for the damage they do, however, criminal law will be written. In Macaulay's nineteenth-century Indian Penal Code, for example, it was a crime for a palanquin bearer to abandon his passengers: the bearers "were too poor to pay damages, and yet had to be trusted to carry unprotected women and children through wild and desolate tracts, where their desertion would have placed those under their charge in great danger."

Used imaginatively, the criminal law is one of the great playing fields for social invention. Around the turn of the century, a common swindle was the employment of the new immigrant, fresh off the boat, for an unskilled job. After he had worked at it a week or two, his boss would fire him without paying his wages. The costs of bringing suit, even if the immigrant knew enough to do so, were greater than the wages to be recovered; the east coast Legal Aid societies, which were formed in large part to deal with this monstrous fraud, considered themselves lucky if they recovered for their clients one-quarter as much as it cost the societies to handle the cases. The problem disappeared when nonpayment of wages was made a crime, and collection was enforced in the criminal rather than the civil courts, by agents of the state.

In the 1920s, according to Karl Llewellyn,

The books of the New York Public Library persisted in disappearing. This was a field peculiarly of juvenile delinquency; the opportunity was open to all, but the rewards of theft so petty as to make juveniles the likely prospects. A statute was passed making exhibition for sale of a book bearing a library stamp an offense. The library officials saw to it that every second-hand book dealer in the city received notice of this statute. Promptly the thefts decreased almost into nothingness. The market had become unprofitable. There has never been a prosecution under the law. There is no need.

Conduct that would not normally be criminal can be made so for reasons of state policy. A generation ago, for example, price-fixing was not only tolerated in the United States, it was virtually mandated under Franklin Roosevelt's NRA; but in the 1960s senior executives of major electrical equipment companies, who had started their business careers in the NRA days, went to jail for price-fixing (and deserved it, of course, having shown much *mens rea* in their work). As recently as the latter 1940s, American courts were enforcing "racial covenants," by which the owner of a house had agreed not to sell his property to a Negro. By 1966 the Congress was considering legislation which would make it criminal for anyone to refuse to sell his property because the prospective purchaser was a Negro: it had become obvious that discrimination in the sale of houses could not be stopped without the imposition of criminal penalties.

Unfortunately, the criminal law is also attractive to the legislature as a means of enforcing private morality, business ethics and minor public policy. "Living under free institutions," Ernst Freund remarked, "we submit to public regulation and control in ways that appear inconceivable to the spirit of oriental despotism." Francis Allen gives some illustrations. "The killing of domesticated pigeons, the fencing of saltpeter caves against wandering cattle, the regulation of automobile traffic, the issue of daylight saving versus standard time, to give only a few examples, have all, at one place or another, been made problems of the criminal law."

A more significant and disturbing string of offenses has been categorized and analyzed by Edwin Schur under the general heading *Crimes Without Victims.* Large percentages of every city police force, and days of courtroom time, must be devoted to enforcing these laws against gambling, prostitution (or "lascivious carriage," as New England knows it), drunkenness, abortion, addiction, homosexuality, attempted suicide. "Arresting people for gambling," said Jonah J. Goldstein, a very small, wiry, energetic old man who was a judge of New York's criminal courts for twenty-five years, "is like dusting pictures. You come home, there's a terrible smell in the house. The maid is dusting pictures. You ask her what happened; she says the sewer backed up. And she's dusting pictures."

These crimes without victims (particularly gambling and homosexuality, which opens great vistas to the blackmailer) are the major source of corruption in police departments; they are also the greatest source of injustice to the poor. Herbert Sturz of the Vera Institute has ridden the paddy wagons on the Bowery as the cops picked up drunks, and estimates that half of those arrested (and subsequently lined up in a criminal court) were merely beaten and weary old men, who might have planned to get drunk if they could cadge the price of it but were sober as a judge at the moment of arrest. It is a matter of record that such a police sweep once picked up the father of an Assistant Attorney General of the State of New York, simply walking down the street and minding his own business.

Alcoholism is so obviously a disease that many lawyers have long been troubled about calling drunkenness a crime. In several states and in a few federal jurisdictions, appellate courts have recently ruled that the Constitution prohibits criminal conviction for drunkenness—though of course there is no constitutional bar to compulsory treatment for drunks. Congratulating itself on its fairness and its grasp of modern psychiatric evidence, the legal system within a few years will probably be sending drunks not to jails called jails, where they would be held, cursed occasionally, fed and released, but to jails called hospitals where they will be held, cursed occasionally, fed and released—after they have been forcibly subjected to whatever fads for the treatment of alcoholics are currently bemusing the medical profession.

Maybe something better can be devised. The Vera Institute has a project in the works which would involve voluntary treatment at existing hospitals, with a corps of reformed alcoholics to prowl the street and invite cooperation. There is a value in getting these things out of the courts—and not much worth preserving in a legal system which, for example, compels the judge assigned to this duty in Los Angeles to process sixty thousand drunk cases a year, all by himself.

4

The Hall of Records, Detroit's criminal court, is a grimy building in a grimy section of downtown, a nasty contrast to the air-conditioned river-view modernity of the civil courts building a few blocks away. Recorders' Court is the home of the most organized plea bargaining anyone has yet turned up—a hallway office where a "bargaining prosecutor," permanently assigned to this duty, holds his own kind of court for defense lawyers who line up to discuss their problems with him. Near him in the hall is the pen for those awaiting arraignment or trial; the defense lawyers go back and forth from the prosecutor to the bars of the pen, discussing offers and counteroffers with the state and its putative enemy.

The arraignment system here is unique in the nation's big cities in that one judge will look at everything from vagrancy to homicide: the court is both a city court and a state court, depending on the nature of the offense being considered. The pens in which prisoners wait for the opening of court—big ones, lined with benches —contain every kind of violator. The police simply line them up, and the line snakes into the well of the court, those who are waiting on it forming an interested audience as those at the front talk with the judge. Unlike New York's 1-A, this courtroom has a light attendance in the public area: this court is reserved for the newly arrested; those whose cases are processed here and adjourned will move to docket in a trial court.

The judge on this day was a man now dead, W. McKay Skillman, who had been serving on the Detroit criminal courts for thirty-seven years, and was in point of service the senior criminal courts judge in the United States. In the early 1930s he was chairman of the American Bar Association Criminal Code Committee ("On my staff was a young lawyer named Tom Dewey"). He was not stuck with this line-up all year round: the ten judges of the Recorders' Court rotated the assignment, a month at a time. (It was unpopular duty, because the arraignment court, unlike the others, works Saturdays too.) But after thirty-seven years Skillman was at home with the process.

New York's 1-A is a prosecutor's court: the focus is on the assistant DA at his lectern. Skillman's court was a judge's court. The prosecutor, dressed in a cheerful sports shirt, was present in the well of the court, but the judge himself read from the documents relating to the case, which his clerks handed to him as the defendant's name was called:

"Charged with being drunk. Were you drunk?"

"I'd been drinking."

"What happened? Sidewalk come up and hit you?"

The prosecutor said, "He's been on a drunk for about a month." Skillman browsed several sheets of previous record and shook his head. "I'll give you thirty days."

On either side of the judge was a representative of a charitable organization—Christian Enterprise and the Salvation Army—who had already gone through the pens to see which of today's prisoners seemed a reasonable candidate for salvation rather than incarceration. A note to that effect came to the judge with the man's record.

"Want to go to Christian Enterprise?"

"Yes, sir."

To one of the neat young men: "You want to take him?"

"Yes, sir, he's a good cook."

Several of the drunks asked to be put away for a while: the weather was still cold, and they had no place to go. Some wanted to get out instantly, like a grizzled fat man. "He was staggering down the street, Your Honor," said the arresting policeman. (Detroit knows two categories of drunkenness—"Staggering Drunk" and "Down & Out.")

Skillman said, "You work for Ford's?"

"Twenty years."

"I'll suspend sentence."

The cop said, "You get back to Ford's; they're looking for you," and the man left.

Still others were remanded back to jail overnight, to receive a suspended sentence the next day. "We have a semisobering-up process here," a clerk explained. "If you send this man out, he'll go get three, four drinks and fall on his face again. There's no place to send him, so we keep him a day." One battered old colored man badly wanted out.

"I had an asthma attack."

"What about six days ago? Were you here six days ago?"

"Yes, sir. I was drunk."

"January 27?"

"I was drunk that time."

"But this time it was asthma?"

"Yes, sir. Sometimes it comes over me, I get sick."

"In other words, you don't want to go to jail right now?"

"Yes, sir."

"All right: you're not guilty. But don't let me see you here to-morrow."

A bum had been taken off a bench in a Greyhound terminal.

"No money, no job, no home," said the DA, discouraged.

"Member of the Wayne County Road Commission," said Judge Skillman, and then to the man, "What do you want us to do for you?"

"Lemme out of town," the bum said thickly.

"All right. You get out of town. By tonight."

A thirty-year-old colored woman with four children had had her husband picked up on nonsupport charges. Skillman listened, asked the man if he had a job, found he did, said, "Do you want ninety days in the workhouse or do you want an assignment of wages?"

"I'll take a wage assignment."

"I think you made a wise choice."

There were upwards of a dozen accosting-and-soliciting cases confronting the judge, with vice squad officers in plain clothes and ladies of assorted ages. Here the four or five lawyers who were at the courthouse looking for business had an opportunity to be help-ful: the girls mostly had a little money. Not every case was simple. There was a domestic servant, fat and middle-aged, who said the (colored) policeman had tried to shake her down. Skillman listened to her story and said, saving the policeman (against whom, after all, there was also no evidence), "Not guilty—this time."

A handsome, well-dressed, tall colored girl had been picked up by a detective who registered at a hotel and asked the bellboy some standard questions. "He said," the policeman reported in a flat voice, " 'If you want a French don't spend more than twenty-five dollars.' "

The lawyer, a natty little man in a polka-dot bow tie, intervened: "I'm going to ask a dismiss on the grounds that the officer initiated the act."

Skillman waved an impatient hand and asked the name of the hotel, which was a fairly good one. He made a face. "What was she doing there?"

The lawyer said, "She's hustling on call—that's not like hustling on the street."

Skillman said, "You're getting technical, I'm getting practical." He asked about the girl and received the information: four children, husband behind in payments. She had a previous record. He shook his head. "All right," he said, "I'll give you thirty days' suspended sentence, and put on probation for a year. You get out of that district, they're trying to keep it clean." In an aside to the clerk, he commented, "I don't see how they expect to get convention business for that new hall of theirs if they insist on chasing the girls."

After the parade of prostitutes, a hulk of a white man in a lumberjacket. The DA read the charge: "He stole from the Great Atlantic & Pacific Tea Company."

"What did you steal?" Skillman asked with some interest. "Tuna fish?" This was the week two ladies in suburban Detroit had died of food poisoning after a tuna-fish salad, and the line laughed.

The man from the A & P said, "No—cookies. A box of Kirkman's Butter-Flavored Cookies."

The accused had pleaded guilty. "Why'd you steal them?" Skillman asked.

"I was hungry."

Skillman said, "Yes. Thirty days." There was no wife, no family, no address: in thirty days the weather would be warmer.

A colored boy "stole gas out of Mr. Goldberg's car." He was a high school senior. "Your family on welfare?" Skillman asked.

"No."

"ADC?"

"No."

"What does your father do?"

"He works at Ford's."

"He works at Ford's and you go around stealing gas. What's your juvenile record?"

The boy said, "B and E," meaning breaking and entering.

"Well, I'll put you on probation for a year, and charge you twenty-five dollars court costs."

Next a man caught with policy slips. The lawyer said, "Not guilty. They're his wife's."

The policeman said, "He has two jobs—works in a laundry and at a car wash."

Skillman said, "With policy running, that makes three jobs."

The policeman: "Counting moonshine, four."

"He had moonshine?"

"Quart."

"Fifty dollars!" Except for a really dangerous offense, no employed man ever got a jail sentence in Skillman's court.

Assault and battery: husband, wife and policeman. "He bites me," the wife said.

Skillman said, "Why does he bite you?"

"He must be hungry."

Skillman said, "Interesting. Most men use clubs or fists."

"No," said the wife wearily, "he bites. And he growls like a dog when he does it."

His lawyer identified the defendant as a shop steward in an auto factory. The man had paid $706 in eleven weeks toward the support of his family. "He bit her to keep her from strangling him."

There is obviously more here than meets the eye. Skillman suggests that they all go out and have lunch together and see if they can't settle this by themselves, without the intervention of criminal process. . . .

5

Judge Skillman's court represented a style of criminal justice that is on its way out in the United States; New York's Part 1-A is criminal justice en route to the future. Detroit's Recorders' Court is not to be regarded as archaic: it maintains the largest corps of probation officers in the country. But the virtue of what Skillman was doing rested fundamentally on the human qualities of the judge. ("You've got to be a pretty sympathetic human being to hold down a magistrate's job for any length of time," says Orison

Marden, president of the American Bar Association in 1966 and president of the National Legal Aid and Defender Association before that; and a partner in the Wall Street firm of White & Case before either.) The virtues of 1-A and its ilk will depend on the capacity of the judicial system to assure fairness in a presumed contest between the state and the accused.

And the long-standing "adversary system" of criminal justice is in deep trouble in the United States. The central assumption of the system is, as Lord Eldon once put it in the eighteenth century, that "truth is best discovered by powerful statements on both sides of the question." Because of the inherent disadvantages of the accused, the adversary system in criminal procedures relieves him of the need to state a side; he need merely cast doubt on the prosecution's case. By contrast, the "inquisitorial system" of the European continent placed the state itself in the role of truth-seeker, with an inquiring *juge d'instruction* to gather all the evidence on both sides and determine whether public prosecution should follow. The requirement of public trial at the end was mostly a form of publicity for the administrative procedure, to assure against arbitrary actions of a kind that the state would be unwilling to publicize or actions based on policies that the community was unwilling to support.

An inquisitorial system assumes an efficient and fair administrative procedure in criminal justice, and a defendant whose only real reliance against unfair prosecution is the truth-seeking solicitude of the state. An adversary system assumes that the state may have other goals in view—Chief Justice Warren in 1966 based his insistence that anyone arrested must be warned of his right to remain silent partly on the grounds that "this warning may serve to make the individual more acutely aware that he is faced with a phase of the adversary system—that he is not in the presence of persons acting solely in his interest."

To protect the accused from malicious prosecution, British and American courts and legislatures developed strict rules of procedure. Accused persons could be brought to trial only after "indictment" by a "grand jury," which would establish that there was a case against them and state very precisely the nature of the complaint. Prosecutors were not permitted to amend indictments after they had been filed. In the eighteenth and nineteenth centuries judges in England and the United States demanded such precision in these documents that an indictment for stealing sheep, for example, would be thrown out, and the defendant released, if the proof involved the theft of lambs.

Rules of evidence were created to keep out of the courtroom plausible reports of what someone had reason to believe; only what the witness saw or heard himself could be admitted. (Even then, of course, the system was confronted with the fallibility of human perception. There is a German case on record where somebody identified an assailant who had hit him in a pitch-black room—he had seen the man, he testified, by the light of the sparks he saw when he was hit.) Indeed, all the rules of evidence reflected what Sir Frederick Pollock once called "our ancestors' deep distrust of human testimony and entire disbelief in the power of human judgment to discover the truth, perhaps also in the existence of any impartial will to discover it." Judges severely restricted the use of circumstantial evidence, which creates reasoned suspicion rather than objective proof of a defendant's guilt—though reasoned suspicion may be legitimate, too: "circumstantial evidence" that the murdered man was having an affair with the defendant's wife is simply unavoidable, even if it cannot be conclusive.

At a trial, the defendant had a right to confront and examine his accusers, to produce witnesses in his defense (and later to subpoena them, to secure a court order requiring their presence "under pain" of some judicial punishment), and to challenge the evidence against him. These rights were hard won, mostly in the seventeenth century, and were never really secure until the nineteenth century (Blackstone was still fighting for them). A defendant could not be compelled to give evidence against himself (another seventeenth-century victory), and he had a right to have someone speak for him. He usually could not give testimony in his own defense, however, until well into the nineteenth century, because it was felt he had too strong a motivation not to tell the truth, and lying under oath would be bad for his immortal soul.

These principles of Anglo-American criminal justice were laid down when criminal charges were most frequently brought by individuals who bore the responsibility of gathering the evidence themselves—though they might, particularly if they were servants of the king, gain the authority of a search warrant from a court, and the assistance of the king's friends and flunkies.

The first police force was not started until 1829, when Sir Robert Peel (hence "bobbies") hired one to control the London mob. From the beginning, however, the police department showed alarming signs of independence and self-stimulated growth. By the mid-1830s the London force had spawned an investigatory division, and had assumed the task not only of preventing crime but of "solving" specific crimes—or, in the lingo of all American police, "apprehending the perpetrator." Imperceptibly, during half a century of urbanization, the amateur citizenry abandoned its historic role in law enforcement and acquired what Karl Llewellyn called "that attitude of an age of specialization: let the cop do the dirty work; what else are we paying him for?" As an unexpected and unwelcome by-product of this specialization, the public lost much of its previous interest in the fairness of the administration of criminal justice. Criticism of the police, even when justified, became a radical and somewhat disreputable activity. "We have surrendered," says the defense attorney Harris Steinberg, "to our guilt about these cops who are protecting us from people we don't have the guts or strength to handle ourselves."

Meanwhile, inevitably, the quality of evidence improved. Fingerprints and photography arrived in the nineteenth century; the twentieth century brought the matching of bullets to guns, blood chemistry, spectography, X-ray diffraction, various forms of microanalysis—and, most important, the ubiquitous plain-clothes man, wiretapping, the half-conscious, half-automatic surveillance that oversees the apparent anonymity of the modern city and produces information whenever the administrative net is hauled in.

To complement the police force there arose in the United States the office of the public prosecutor, the district or county attorney, who is in theory charged with protecting the innocent as well as with convicting the guilty. In most places he has unlimited discretion not to prosecute, and will sometimes extend this discretion to his juniors. "I never took the word of the police," says San Francisco's Irving F. Reichert, Jr., a lean, intense former assistant DA now retired to the peaceable surroundings of the California Continuing Legal Education program, because the tension of trial work wrecked his digestion. "I always did my own investigating. There was one inspector whose cases I wouldn't prosecute, because I was sure he trapped people." The most recent full report from the DA's office in New York announces that "the office is ever mindful of its dual obligation and its quasi-judicial function."

Dedication of this sort turns the DA into a French *juge d'instruction*, running an inquisitorial system of criminal justice and merely presenting cases for the ultimate verification, the seal of approval, of a jury. And everyone does, in fact, want the DA's office to operate as a kind of ministry of justice; the harm done to someone who is prosecuted for crime in open court is never healed by an acquittal.

Most close students of the criminal justice system feel that its greatest single need is for a full-time, career service in the DA's office—and that its worst horror is the collection of harried, young, part-time prosecutors, their minds on their fee-producing labors in their own offices, who make the decision to charge a man as a criminal without reading more than the first page of a police report, assuming there is more than one page in the police report. Only in Manhattan (where Thomas E. Dewey established the rules in the 1930s and his successor Frank Hogan has maintained them) and in some major California cities (where the municipal charter includes such a provision) does a local public pay for the services of a prosecuting agency staffed entirely by lawyers who are not permitted to supplement their salaries in private practice. In early 1967 both the National Crime Commission and the ABA Project on Minimum Standards in Criminal Justice strongly recommended heavy infusions of money into the DA's offices, to staff them properly —indeed, the Crime Commission, in what was probably its most idealistic proposal, suggested that where the load in a county is too small to justify a full-time prosecutor, the county should make arrangements to borrow occasionally from elsewhere rather than hire a local man part time.

In the American system of criminal justice, the District Attorney has a fearfully important job. "You walk down Center Street with the commission in your hands from the people of the County of New York," Judge William McAdoo, formerly a Police Commissioner, said at an inquiry in 1913; "they have confided in you by a popular vote that greatest power that any man has in this community. You personify the majesty and power of the State of New York in your office. You have a secret body behind you there with a locked door [the grand jury]; you can go in and tell them anything you want." An extraordinary display of these powers was given in early 1967 by Jim Garrison of New Orleans, who made himself a world figure by using his authority to arrest some people he wanted to accuse of conspiring to kill John F. Kennedy. This, incidentally, is the same Garrison whose defense of a libel action a few years ago made civil liberties history: while pushing for a bigger budget as DA, he said that all the city judges of New Orleans were in league with the town's vice lords or at least subject to their influence. The judges sued and won. In *Garrison* v. *Louisiana* the U.S. Supreme Court threw out the verdict against Garrison, with an opinion which said, in effect, that in discussions of public policy the Constitution protects anything a crusader says about an office-holder unless his victims can *prove* (which is impossible) that he knew for a fact it was false. Clearly, we need more responsible people than we have in some DA's jobs.

But the more convincing the public prosecutor, the less the significance of an adversary system. Even a relatively unprofessional prosecutor, who really represents only the police (because he had neither the authority nor the time to investigate for himself), will make a strong impression on many jurors. He, like them, represents the public. Carl Newton, now a distinguished Wall Street lawyer, remembers his first trial, in 1925, as the newcomer, fresh from a Rhodes Scholarship at Oxford, in the United States Attorney's office in Manhattan.

"You always broke in the young DA on a narcotics case," Newton recalls, "because you weren't going to win it. To get a conviction, you had to have a buy. To get a buy in those days, you had to have a federal narcotics agent with a record of dope. Otherwise, the pushers wouldn't sell. The agent testified he bought this packet, and the chemist says it's dope. Then on cross-examination it would be brought out that the witness had a criminal record. . . .

"I explained this to the jury, and we got a conviction, the first of the day. I talked to the foreman afterward, and I asked him why. He said, 'We thought you were an honest guy, you wouldn't be prosecuting him if you didn't think he was guilty.' Then the foreman got a little concerned. He said, 'You *do* think he was guilty, don't you?'

"I said, 'I don't know.' "

Impressed with the improvement in police techniques and perhaps overimpressed with the DA's offices, the courts in the last generation relaxed many of the rules which had governed criminal cases in the nineteenth century. As the little courts confined their investigations to the question of why the cop believed he had caught a misdemeanant, the larger courts in effect began to question only why the prosecutor thought his man had done it. Indictments were opened for amendment and rules of evidence were liberalized. (In many Western states grand juries had disappeared long before, to be replaced by mere "informations" filed by the DA.) Judges who had long exercised their power to throw a case out of court if they felt a reasonable doubt themselves began leaving everything, or nearly everything, to juries. Privileges against self-incrimination were held not to apply to fingerprints, blood, urine and handwriting specimens, or appearances in police line-ups. It became settled doctrine not only that a man could be interrogated by the police but that his *silence* in an interrogation could be used as evidence against him, on the grounds that an innocent man will cry out when accused!

As early as 1921 Roscoe Pound, dean of the law school first at Nebraska and then at Harvard, who had never been one to "coddle criminals," caught the direction of the wind and did not like it. "The function of securing social interests through punitive justice," he wrote, "seems to be insensibly slipping away from the courts and hence from law and in substance, if not in form, to be coming more and more into the hands of administrative agencies."

By the middle 1950s, then, the criminal process operated roughly as follows: the police would be notified of a crime, would investigate on the scene and gather information from witnesses and possible witnesses and from informers. Having found what Justice Holmes once called "the magnetic point" around which their evidence seemed to cluster, they would arrest a suspect. They could then interrogate at length, and use whatever statements they got from the suspect, provided they kept their hands off him and let him eat and sleep regularly. In several Midwestern jurisdictions a study found that the police generally regarded *three days* as a reasonable time for processing a suspected felon in the station house before producing him in a courtroom for arraignment. In connection with the arrest, the police would search the suspect, and whatever places associated with him they regarded as reasonable sources of evidence. In most states, indeed, they could (and did) search anywhere at all, provided they could find a shadow of an excuse.

The district attorney's office might or might not have been kept informed of these developments; in the most serious cases, they usually were. "Since we're lawyers," said Alexander Herman while chief assistant in charge of homicide prosecutions in New York, "we know what a legal case is; so we direct the arrest." At the arraignment before the judge, the DA would recommend a bail figure— a bond surety someone would have to post as a pledge that a defendant, if released, would appear for trial. The DA's recommendations were almost invariably accepted. In considerably more than half the serious charges—and not much less than a quarter of the minor charges—bail was set at a figure beyond the ability of the defendant, his friends and his family, to meet a bondsman's fee; and he was kept in jail awaiting trial. One study has estimated that 56 percent of all those arraigned for crime stayed in detention awaiting trial.

In the typical felony case of the 1950s, a prosecutor armed with bundles of evidence gathered by the police (including a confession) would make contact with a defendant in court for an appearance between sojourns in a foul local jail, and would negotiate a plea of guilty. Where the prosecutor was prepared to offer a suspended sentence—freedom now—the bargain was absolutely irresistible. (A court official in Cheyenne, Wyoming, reported to a study group, "I think many indigent prisoners plead guilty merely to avoid sitting in the county jail.") But even when a guilty plea would involve a prison sentence, the prosecutor was well placed to bargain, because for most crimes the maximum sentences laid down by American state legislatures run four to ten times as high as the maximum sentences in any other nation in the civilized world. In one recent year, all the courts in England imposed only 588 sentences with a maximum term of more than five years—while 18,000 such sentences were uttered in the United States.

A number of law school professors and appellate court judges (especially Chief Justice Earl Warren, who had been an outstanding district attorney at the beginning of his political career in California, and Justice Felix Frankfurter, who had given ten years of his life to the fight for Sacco and Vanzetti) looked at this system of criminal justice, and decided they did not like it at all. Statistically, what they saw was something like this:

Of every 100 persons picked up by the police on serious criminal charges:

- about 50 were convicted of something (not necessarily the original charge) on a plea of guilty;
- about 5 were convicted after trial;
- about 30 were released without charges being brought;
- about 13 were released by administrative process after arraignment but before trial;
- about 2 were acquitted after trial.

There was no good reason to believe that innocent people were being convicted in perceptible numbers, that the 80-odd percent of persons held for trial who had confessed had not in fact committed the crime with which they were charged (or something very much like it). But the adversary system of Anglo-American tradition was being employed in only about 7 percent of the cases; in the rest, the operation of the police-prosecutor combination had substituted something much closer to an inquisitorial system. And the American people had never formally expressed any desire for this basic change in the most fundamental institution of government.

Something else was involved, too. "There is no value in the limitation of police power merely for the sake of limitation," Judge Irving R. Kaufman wrote in 1960. "The true and ultimate end is to protect innocent persons from false charges." On sober consideration, many appellate judges decided that Kaufman was wrong: that there were independent values in the limitation of police power. Someone had to face the problem of the 30 percent of those arrested, and perhaps a higher percentage of those searched, who are never formally charged at all, and never see a judge. What was happening to them? "The innocent suffer with the guilty," wrote the California Supreme Court, "and we cannot close our eyes to the effect the rule we adopt will have on the rights of those not before the court."

CHAPTER 6

CRIMINAL MATTERS:
THE SEARCH FOR
SOMETHING BETTER

"In England a man is presoomed to be innicent till he's proved guilty an' then they take it f'r granted he's guilty. In this counthry a man is presoomed to be guilty ontil he's proved guilty an' afther that he's presoomed to be innicent."

—MR. DOOLEY

"Excessive securing of the technical rights of accused persons in the nineteenth century produced the third degree just as the excessive zeal of prosecutors, browbeating of witnesses and unreasonable searches of the seventeenth and eighteenth centuries produced the criminal procedure of the nineteenth century. No one who has reflected on the history of the criminal law can doubt that these things in their turn will be followed by some such reaction as that which superseded the executive justice of the Star Chamber by the system of excessive limitations upon prosecutions which became classical in our polity."

—ROSCOE POUND

1

The first line of attack in the Supreme Court's struggle to reassert judicial control over the criminal process was an effort to restrict the policeman's right of arrest without prior judicial approval. The case involved an illegal still in New Jersey. Government authorities, tipped off by the farmer who had leased the land to the moonshiners, slipped an agent into the operation from the beginning: he helped build the distillery and worked at it (turning over his salary to the Treasury Department, of course). When all the sugar and alcohol and bottles and other appurtenances were in place and the line was rolling, the government raided—without a warrant. The Supreme Court upheld the arrest of one man, on the grounds that he had actually been observed in the act of committing the felony, but (with four Justices angrily dissenting) refused to allow the government to use the evidence gathered at the still because no judge had issued them a warrant to seize it. The clear implication was that if the agents hadn't actually seen the man in the act of committing a crime, the arrest itself would have been illegal.

Two years later, in the case of a crooked rare-stamp dealer caught with a drawer full of overprinted stamps he had forged, the previous minority became a majority, admitted all the evidence and told the G-men and T-men that in cases like these they didn't need warrants.

The second line of attack was an effort to give the defense access to the prosecution's files. The case in which the doctrine was most seriously laid down, however, involved national security; and the Congress the next year changed the Federal Rules of Criminal Procedure to make sure the Supreme Court would never try *that* again. There remains, however, a rule requiring the prosecution to make available to the defense any evidence *favorable* to the defendant— "Very hard to enforce," says Richard Green of the ABA Minimum Standards Project, "because the defense has no way of knowing about favorable evidence in the prosecution's files."

At least one committee appointed to revise the Federal Rules has toyed with the notion of giving the defense substantial rights to "discover" the prosecution's case; both California and Minnesota have taken steps in this direction. In New Jersey, where the state supreme court makes the rules for the trial courts, Chief Justice Joseph Weintraub has suggested that some way be found to open cases all the way before they reach trial. The "pretrial conferences" which these new rules would require, however, are hard to fit into an adversary system: like similar conferences in civil cases, they would almost certainly turn into private bargaining sessions. Some discovery of the defense case must be given to balance the situation (new Federal Rules allow limited access to prosecution data only by defendants who will in turn disclose their own "physical evidence and scientific reports"), but such procedures are itchy under the Fifth Amendment. There is also more than a little danger in giving either side in a criminal case uninvited access to all the witnesses expected to testify for the other side.

The Court's third assault came in *Gideon* v. *Wainwright*, the 1963 decision noted in the last chapter, which announced that convictions for crimes of any seriousness could not be sustained unless the defendant was represented by counsel or had deliberately and knowledgeably waived the services of a lawyer. The real significance of the decision was not its explicit guarantee of representation at trial but its implied guarantee of representation in the crucial period between arraignment and trial. "The time a defendant needs counsel most," a federal judge in Utah wrote in what turned out to be a prophetic opinion in 1952, "is immediately after his arrest and until trial." The involvement of lawyers in the administrative process of plea bargaining does not, however, change the essential nature of the process. As the overwhelming majority of defendants at this stage are guilty—and as the defense lawyer has at present no way of discovering whether in fact the prosecution has sufficient admissible evidence to convict them—this formal protection seems more likely to produce a reduction in the average sentence (which is, of course, important) than to reverse the course of history.

Finally, most publicly and most importantly, the Supreme Court and some of the state appellate courts have vastly widened their exclusionary rules, to keep out of trials evidence against defendants that would have been admissible prior to 1960. The reasoning offered to support these decisions rests, perhaps unsteadily (a dissent to one of them said it was "supported by no higher authority than its own rhetoric"), on the Bill of Rights of the Constitution.

Several of the most striking cases in the development of English civil liberties had been decided shortly before the American Revolution—most notably, the John Wilkes affair, in which agents of the King, armed with a "general warrant," had searched Wilkes' home and his printer's shop, arrested Wilkes and some printers and seized everything that might be evidence of their connection with the allegedly libelous publication of Number 45 of *The North Briton*. The victims, later released, sued for damages for wrongful arrest and wrongful seizure of papers, and among them collected from the King's agents no less than £4,300, the equivalent of perhaps $80,000 today. Indiscriminate search and seizure had been among the most resented features of British colonial rule, but nobody had successfully prosecuted the colonial agents on those grounds. The Fourth Amendment, safeguarding the privacy of persons and homes, was designed to assure forever the citizen's right of action against abuse by government agents.

In 1914 the Supreme Court gave the Amendment a new and different interpretation, proclaiming that it formed part of the rules of evidence in the federal courts. If the government was prohibited from making such seizures, then it had to be prohibited from introducing the "fruits" of the seizures in evidence against the victim. The ruling applied only to actions by agents of the federal government, as it had not yet occurred to anyone that the Fourteenth Amendment obliged the states to follow federal constitutional guarantees in their own criminal prosecutions. (Indeed, some very substantial constitutional guarantees, like indictment by grand jury and trial by jury, are not binding in state prosecutions.)

The rule against federal use of illegally seized evidence had a pretty discouraging history. Because the states mostly refused to make a similar interpretation of the similar provision in their own constitutions (Justice Benjamin Cardozo, then of the New York Court of Appeals, thought it bad law that "the criminal is to go free because the constable has blundered."), federal officers could either turn over their evidence to the states for use in state prosecutions or, where state law was not involved, could arrange for the local police to seize and then give the evidence to the federal authorities. This was known as the "silver platter" doctrine. In 1949, largely to eliminate the silver platter, the Supreme Court went a step further, and held in *Wolf* v. *Colorado* that it could if it wished apply its interpretation of the Fourth Amendment to the states— but it didn't wish. Most states said they didn't wish, either; and there the law stood when the police of Cleveland, Ohio, went after Miss Dollree Mapp.

Miss Mapp ran a boardinghouse, and the police believed she had a gambler with a gambling den among her boarders. They knocked on the door; Miss Mapp called her lawyer, who told her not to let them in unless they had a search warrant; she told them to go away; they did. Three hours later they returned, seven of them, and broke down the door. She demanded their search warrant, and one of the officers gave her a piece of paper which was not, in fact, a search warrant; she stuffed the piece of paper in her bosom; and the officer reached into her bosom and took back his piece of paper. The police found no gambler and no gambling equipment, but they did find a trunk full of pornography, which Miss Mapp claimed was the property of a previous boarder. She was convicted anyway, for possession of obscene materials, and appealed, claiming violation of her constitutional rights. The Supreme Court of Ohio found no serious fault with the Cleveland police.

Miss Mapp's lawyers failed to suggest to the U.S. Supreme Court that it might be wise to overrule *Wolf* v. *Colorado*. But this notion did occur to the Court. In *Mapp* v. *Ohio*, in 1961, the state police, too, were informed that they could use the physical evidence they had seized only if their search for it had been justified by a warrant which specified this piece of evidence, if the person whose premises were searched had consented, or if the search was incidental to a valid arrest. The rule was strict: the police could not use their discovery of the evidence as justification for the arrest; if they didn't *know* the man was carrying policy slips or a concealed weapon or an envelope of heroin before they searched him, the fact that their guess was right could not be used to make the arrest valid or the search legitimate. How far the rule carried was demonstrated two years after *Mapp*, when the Supreme Court overturned the conviction of a man arrested after the police broke down the door to his hotel room because they had smelled in the hall the opium he was smoking.

Another kind of evidence commonly used in criminal trials had been bothering the Supreme Court even more than the products of illegal searches: the confession resulting from police interrogation of a suspect. It is a problem that displays all too clearly the damage done to the adversary system by the improved efficiency of the police and the prosecutor. "Sometimes a client comes in to me after he's made bail," says the Chicagoan George Callaghan, "and he tells me he was arrested and told the whole story. I tell him, 'What you need now is not a lawyer but a minister, rabbi or priest.' "

Here, of course, there is a long tradition of excluding the evidence, refusing to allow a confession to be used by the prosecution, because the document for one reason or another looks untrustworthy. Staundford's *Pleas of the Crown*, in 1607, explained that "If one is indicted or appealed of felony, and in his arraignment he confesses it, this is the best and surest answer that can be made in our law for quieting the conscience of the judge and for making it a good and firm condemnation; provided, however, that the said confession did not proceed from fear, menace, or duress." And in the nineteenth century the slightest hint of pressure on the accused was enough to eliminate the confession—for examples: "I dare say you had a hand in it; you may as well tell me all about it"; or "You had better tell all about it; it will save you trouble"; or "You had better tell the truth." Toward the end of the century, a six-man majority of the Supreme Court ruled, once, that confessions could never be admissible in federal trials. This opinion was treated almost immediately thereafter as though it had never been written. Dean John H. Wigmore of the Northwestern University Law School, author of the standard treatise on *Evidence,* asked sternly a generation later, "How much longer will that misguided and unrepudiated opinion continue to cloud the reputation of the Federal Supreme Court?" Then in the 1960s the Court resuscitated the opinion as authority for new rulings on interrogation.

From 1900 to the early 1930s the reports of the Supreme Court are almost barren of confession cases. Federal crimes, except for prohibition offenses, were few and fundamentally uninteresting, the Court refused to hear appeals from state criminal decisions, and nobody then even imagined what is now standard operating procedure: the petition for habeas corpus brought in a federal district court on the grounds that the state courts had behaved so badly in admitting testimony that they had forfeited their jurisdiction over the prisoner. The turning point came with the publication in 1931 of the Wickersham Commission *Report on Lawlessness in Law Enforcement,* which found widespread "use of physical brutality, or other forms of cruelty, to obtain involuntary confessions or admissions."

In 1936, for the first time, the Supreme Court overturned a state conviction because of a coerced confession. It was a Mississippi case, and the admitted facts were that a bunch of white men had beaten the Negro suspects with a steel-studded belt until they confessed. The Supreme Court of Mississippi refused to throw out the confessions because the lawyer for the defendants had failed to move formally for their exclusion. In a Texas case the state conceded that its Rangers had taken a Negro prisoner from jail and out to the deserted countryside at night, to ask him questions; and the Supreme Court of Texas found no intimidation. A rape-murder in Indiana in 1947 was followed by five nights of questioning the suspect until three in the morning, two days of solitary confinement in a cell called "the hole," little sleep, not enough to eat, and no chance to speak with anyone except the six to eight police officers who badgered the suspect in relays until he confessed. Justice Frankfurter wrote, throwing out the confession and the conviction in this case, "There comes a point where this Court should not be ignorant as judges of what we know as men."

After 1949, either because the police had mended their manners or because the state appellate courts were no longer passing such horror stories up the chain of command, the Supreme Court heard no cases where confession was associated with physically brutal treatment. Still, the confession cases came, and they were raw enough: California police announced in the hearing of a suspect that since he wasn't talking they'd just have to arrest his sick wife; New York police sent an old buddy of a prisoner, now a cop, to say that he'd be fired if his pal didn't confess; Illinois police told a lady that if she didn't confess to possession of marijuana the court would take her children away from her. She did confess, with the idea that the police had promised her a light punishment; and a court gave her a minimum of ten or maximum of eleven years in the penitentiary.

By 1957 the Court had tightened up on interrogation in federal proceedings. Relying on the Federal Rules of Criminal Procedure rather than on any constitutional guarantee, the Court in a bootlegging case and then in a rape case ruled that no confession could be admitted if it was the product of questioning that occurred during a period of "unnecessary delay" between arrest and arraignment before a magistrate. In the second of these cases, the "unnecessary delay" had been only two hours; and because the crime was a rape in a dark cellar prosecution was impossible without the confession. (Normally in the United States these "reversals" of conviction do not mean the defendant goes free: the state can try again, omitting the evidence that tainted the first trial, and in the majority of cases a new conviction is obtained. In Britain, by contrast, reversal (except in certain cases, by recent statute) means charges must be dropped; to British lawyers, a second trial would mean double jeopardy. The British appellate courts are therefore much more cautious—some would say responsible—in reversing convictions. The rapist released by the Supreme Court did go free, presently assaulted more girls and wound up in a state prison.)

But there was no Federal Rule 5 (a) which the Supreme Court could apply against state convictions. Year after year, the Court denied the vast majority of petitions for review, and set aside convictions in most of the cases it actually heard, one by one, on narrowly specific grounds—because the defendant was a juvenile, or illiterate, or had been denied the right to let his wife know he'd been picked up, etc. And then, in 1964, there arrived on the docket the case of *Escobedo* v. *Illinois*.

Danny Escobedo was a Mexican-American who was serving a twenty-year sentence as an accomplice in the murder of his brother-in-law. Escobedo, with his sister and two friends, had been picked up, questioned and released. He consulted a lawyer and was advised not to say anything at all to the police. When he was picked up again, his lawyer came to the police station and asked to see him, and the police refused. Presently, Escobedo was confronted with one of the friends, who had confessed to being an accomplice but claimed that Escobedo had actually fired the shot. The trap closed: Escobedo denounced his friend as the actual murderer, thereby dooming himself as an accomplice. Justice Arthur J. Goldberg, who wrote the opinion of the Court's 5-4 majority, made much of the fact that Escobedo, not advised by a lawyer, did not know that under Illinois law the man who pulled the trigger and his partner were equally guilty of murder.

All that Justice Goldberg actually said as a matter of law was that a conviction could not stand if the evidence presented to the jury included a confession given by a defendant who had been questioned without a warning of his rights to remain silent and who had been denied his request for the help of his lawyer. The *Escobedo* argument, moreover, rested entirely on the Sixth Amendment right to counsel rather than on the Fifth Amendment privilege against self-incrimination or the Fourteenth Amendment guarantee of "due process." But while the Court had always before included in its reversals of such convictions some recognition of the legitimacy of the confession if freely given (interrogation, Justice William Brennan, who concurred in *Escobedo,* had written only a year before, "is undoubtedly an essential tool in effective law enforcement"), Justice Goldberg's opinion argued that "A system of criminal law enforcement which comes to depend on the 'confession' will in the long run be less reliable and more subject to abuses than a system which depends on extrinsic evidence independently secured by skillful investigation."

Escobedo raised hopes at the American Civil Liberties Union, and fears in police departments and prosecutor's offices, that the Supreme Court was about to forbid the use of confessions entirely. Because the opinion was so strong and the statement of law so weak, nobody had the faintest notion what *Escobedo* meant. A controversy over what it did mean and should mean divided the bar and produced a spate of private correspondence written for publication, most of it centering on a "Model Pre-Arraignment Code" which the American Law Institute had begun to develop a year before *Escobedo* was decided. This project involved the services of four "Reporters," all law school professors, three from Harvard and one from California (James Vorenberg continued as an ALI Reporter after taking leave from Harvard to become head of the National Crime Commission); plus an immensely distinguished "Advisory

Committee" of forty, including thirteen judges and former judges, among them the three most widely admired state supreme court justices in America—Fuld of New York, Schaefer of Illinois and Traynor of California.

The resulting draft code, published eighteen months after *Escobedo,* took a relatively narrow view of the Goldberg opinion. It forbade interrogation when a suspect had been arrested under a warrant, on the grounds that once the cops got a warrant they were dealing with an accused person rather than a mere suspect; and it followed the letter of Goldberg's opinion in requiring that anyone who had a lawyer was entitled to the lawyer's presence while being questioned. But it did not insist that the police supply suspects with lawyers, and it provided for four hours of tape-recorded and preferably photographed questioning at the station house (more under certain narrowly specified conditions) without representation (unless demanded by the suspect) and without arraignment before a magistrate.

All four Reporters regarded themselves as liberals; and in fact their Code was much stricter than actual practice in any state. But a number of libertarians, led by Circuit Judge David L. Bazelon of the District of Columbia, thought and said the Reporters were scoundrels for their reliance on the letter rather than the spirit of *Escobedo.* Bazelon was particularly upset at the failure to require the police to supply counsel to those who did not come so equipped. "We have to make up our minds," he said, shaking his fine gray head sadly, "whether or not in this society we want to trade on ignorance." Of those arrested for felonies, the overwhelming majority are poor and unintelligent; they don't have their own lawyers on tap. Judge Bazelon once said to Nicholas deB. Katzenbach, waving to a set of Supreme Court Reports on a high shelf, "Up there we have these rights. Some people are tall enough to reach there themselves. Don't we have an obligation to give the others a ladder so they can reach, too?"

The obvious answer was that the rules are laid down to protect the innocent, not to provide the guilty with a better chance of escaping: the fact that Jimmy Hoffa has lawyers who can keep him out of jail for some years after his conviction on criminal charges does not require the state to provide every criminal with a lawyer who can keep him out of jail. As the ALI Reporters wrote, "Criminal justice is not a sport or a game, and notions of fairness derived from the moral structure of games, premised on legitimation of self-interests to the fullest extent consistent with the game, are by no means persuasive. The pursuit of truth is an important function."

Attorney General Katzenbach weighed into the argument with a letter to Judge Bazelon (excerpted on the front page of the *New York Times*), in which he accurately but somewhat nastily pointed out that "In your own court of appeals, the result [of a criminal appeal] is too often determined by the particular panel which hears a case. Thus the consistency, the efficiency and consequently the fairness of justice have suffered." It was one of Judge Bazelon's colleagues on this bench who reacted to a discussion of the rights of suspects with the comment, "Nice people have some rights, too."

In conversation, Katzenbach said, "Let's talk about questioning, not about lawyers. There's only one bit of advice a lawyer who doesn't know his client can possibly give in the station house: keep quiet. There's no need to set up some fancy system of lawyers to give everybody advice—just prohibit questioning." A lawyer must assume as his working hypothesis that his client is guilty—one of the first things any criminal lawyer learns is that his clients will try to maintain the most implausible claims of innocence when talking with him, in hopes of getting him to work harder. An Illinois judge observed sardonically after *Escobedo* that any convict whose lawyer had told him to talk to the police could probably get his conviction reversed on the grounds that he'd had incompetent counsel.

The discussion grew nasty: those who feared the extension of *Escobedo*, wrote Pennsylvania professor Anthony G. Amsterdam, were "the comfortable middle and upper classes . . . who imagine themselves always as potential victims of crime, never as potential victims of a police investigation."

One of the ALI Reporters, Paul Bator, a slim, young Harvard professor with an old-fashioned rhetorical manner, dismissed the opponents of the ALI Code with the comment, "Most of these people don't believe the enforcement of the criminal law serves a social value."

And both, of course, were right.

In June, 1966, in *Miranda* v. *Arizona,* Chief Justice Warren, writing again for a five-judge majority, specifically affirmed *Escobedo* but renounced its reasoning. He informed police departments that, at least for the time being, if they wished to use confessions (or information gathered from interrogation, "the fruit of the poisonous tree") they would have to tell their prisoners that they had a right to have a lawyer with them during interrogation, and that a lawyer would be supplied for that purpose if they wished. Much of the opinion was given over to the Chief Justice's own sketch for a code of prearraignment procedure, but he specifically invited the Congress and the state legislatures to make their own codes. "Our decision," he wrote, "in no way creates a constitutional straitjacket." In *Miranda* Justice Goldberg's Sixth Amendment right to counsel disappeared, and the Chief Justice announced a willingness to approve any procedures "at least as effective" as his sketched code in safeguarding a defendant's Fifth Amendment privilege against self-incrimination. The criticisms of confessions per se also disappeared. "Confessions," the Chief Justice wrote, "remain a proper element in law enforcement."

What the *Miranda* decision means will be worked out over the years, in legislatures and in the Supreme Court. Its future is unpredictable not only because of its inherent ambiguities but also because the four-man minority (which included the two youngest justices) indicated an intention to overturn the opinion if anyone of its persuasion should be appointed to replace one of the five-man majority (which included the two oldest justices). Even as an immediate matter, the impact of *Miranda* is uncertain. Anyone, of course, can waive his right to a lawyer during interrogation. *Miranda,* James Vorenberg commented the day after the opinion came down, "just moves the battleground from the voluntariness of the confession back to the voluntariness of the waiver." Such battles are fought out, of course, in local trial courts, not in the Supreme Court. "The police," Vorenberg said, "have done pretty well with these swearing contests over the years." In the spring of 1967 the New York police (with the cooperation of the Vera Institute and a Ford Foundation grant) began experimenting with tape-recorded interrogations along the lines recommended by the ALI Reporters, with the addition of a taped acknowledgment by the prisoner that he knew of his right to counsel and had waived it.

To date, the experience in states that had established a *Miranda*-like rule before *Miranda* argues that no great changes will occur. The Detroit police report that the percentage of confessions by those arrested fell from sixty to fifty-eight, which is not statistically significant, in the first year after the accused were informed that they could have a lawyer at interrogations if they wanted one. Wilbur F. Littlefield of the Los Angeles Public Defender's office says, "So far as I can see, *Dorado* [the California version of *Miranda*] has made no difference at all—they still cop out all the time. It happens infrequently that people ask to see an attorney. We wish it would happen more often. Last Friday at a quarter to five, we did have a call from the forgery division—they had an arrestee who wanted an attorney. We sent a man over, who told him about the only thing a lawyer can, which was not to tell anybody anything."

Samuel Dash, formerly District Attorney in Philadelphia and now director of an institute on criminal justice at Georgetown Law School, has set in motion a study of the practical effects of *Miranda* across the country. His first returns showed "substantial numbers" not asking for lawyers. "Many people," he explains, "even law violators, when they meet a symbol of authority have a tendency to want to explain themselves, to adjust to the guy in uniform. Most people want to belong, they want society to love them. Even sophisticated businessmen. When I was a defense attorney, they'd call me and tell me Internal Revenue agents wanted to ask them questions. I'd advise them to say nothing, and they'd be troubled: 'But how will I look? I'll look guilty.' "

Ultimately, the question is the effectiveness of an exclusionary rule in changing administrative behavior. The history of police activities after *Mapp* v. *Ohio* argues that the society is highly resilient, but selectively so, in refusing to change its behavior on orders from appellate courts. *Mapp* appeared to threaten police procedure in three types of crimes: gambling, carrying concealed weapons and narcotics. In all three, conclusive evidence can usually be got only by seizing people for searching purposes or by breaking down doors to catch people before they can dispose of the incriminating material. Immediately after *Mapp*, a local judge commented, "The Supreme Court has legalized narcotics traffic in New York."

On gambling, the society was prepared to go along with the Court; nobody was really that interested in convicting gamblers. On concealed weapons, the relevance of criminal prosecution had always been a little dubious: the important thing, after all, is to get rid of the guns. Either through new legislation (in New York) or through administrative decision (in Chicago), the police were empowered to stop anybody anywhere and frisk him—and when they found a weapon they simply took it away. In 1965 Chicago "burned" more than six thousand hand guns, most of them seized in just this manner. This is illegal behavior by the police—indeed, Chicago politely keeps the guns available for a month, in case the people from whom they were seized would like to go to court to replevin their weaponry—but even the predominantly Negro community that is subjected to the indignity of the stop-and-frisk has not protested.

The block against narcotics evidence presented more difficult problems. At the beginning, the police simply won swearing contests. Prior to *Mapp*, narcotics users and pushers were almost universally convinced that if they weren't caught with the stuff on them they couldn't be convicted; when they spotted a plain-clothes man approaching, they would throw the envelopes on the ground. Later, though, in court, the policeman would simply testify that he had seen this defendant throw this envelope on the pavement; and the judge would convict. News of *Mapp* spread through this group with astonishing speed, and the police found for the first time that they had to search—quite illegally—to get the evidence. Fortunately, the judges had been hearing for years about envelopes thrown on the pavement (and were not very sympathetic with the *Mapp* doctrine, anyway); so the police continued to tell the same old story, and the prosecutors continued to win the same old convictions.

This subterfuge was unsatisfactory over the longer pull, and did not cover the cases where the police wanted to get inside apartments and homes. Few judges were willing to accept a policeman's statement that the defendant had let him in voluntarily, really, but "these places are built so rickety the door just came loose in my hand."

Therefore, in California and New York, the two states worst hit by narcotics addicts and the crimes they cause (60 percent of all New York Legal Aid criminal cases involve addicts), the legislature made addiction a kind of insanity, which required compulsory "hospitalization" for periods of up to three years. In civil proceedings of this sort, which are supposed to be for the addict's or the lunatic's own good, evidentiary rules like those of *Mapp* do not necessarily apply—and the police can proceed, usually, in whatever manner seems most suitable to them.

Mapp made a major change in the way lawyers handle criminal defenses. "When we tried our first criminal cases, eight or nine years ago," says Boston's Monroe Inker, "and we made motions for a bill of particulars, motions to exclude evidence, we were regarded as very intellectual. Now everybody does it." Even defendants sense the change. "One of the first things a client will say to you these days," says Chick Marra of the New York Legal Aid Society, "is, 'Make a motion for me.' You ask him what kind of motion he wants made, he says, 'I don't know that—you're my lawyer.'" Two Midwestern law school professors have found nothing admirable about the usual hearing on a motion to suppress evidence:

Defense counsel often present the motion to suppress orally and without articulating any specific ground upon which it should be granted. The police officer is immediately sworn and cross-examined by defense counsel, who, even without preparation, is in many cases able to cast doubt upon the propriety of police conduct. . . . The prosecutor is likely to be frantically examining the officer's written report of the case for the purpose of getting clear in his own mind the circumstances leading up to the arrest and search.

The trial judge never gets it clear in his mind. Most often, if he believes the defendant is clearly guilty, he admits the evidence—and the appellate courts do not have the manpower or, in most cases, the inclination to control the rulings of large numbers of trial judges.

The exclusionary rule, in short, is neither a very intelligent nor a very effective means to control the police. As Thurman Arnold wrote a generation ago, "A moment's reflection would indicate that the temper of the police commissioner is of much more significance on governmental interference with rights of respectable citizens than appellate-court utterances." Five years after *Mapp* "barred" illegal searches and seizures, a federal circuit court found it necessary to issue an injunction against the Baltimore police, in the wake of the illegal search of some three hundred Negro homes by officers looking for the murderers of a policeman. Nearly thirty years after *Nardone* v. *U.S.* forbade wiretapping, various agencies of the federal government were bitterly disputing which should pay the costs of transcribing the endless miles of tape they had recorded with their various bugs, and the district attorney of Las Vegas was threatening to arrest an FBI agent for violating the Nevada antiwiretapping laws. Columbia's Walter Gellhorn has written that the confession decisions, "plainly enough," were "educational effort masquerading as a rule of law."

At best, moreover, exclusionary rules protect only those who are to be accused in court: the police are under no obligation to provide lawyers for people they do not intend to charge. A chunk of the *Miranda* opinion was given over to a memorandum from the Solicitor General, detailing the arrest procedures of the FBI, to demonstrate that interrogation without counsel is not necessary. But in fact the FBI often questions people without lawyers, because the aim of the questioning is to get information about those higher up, and any lawyer the prospective witness might bring would be, in fact, in the pay of those higher up.

To everybody but Americans, the use of exclusionary rules as a way to control the police seems "very odd," as the Australian criminologist Norval Morris puts it. In Australia, as in England, "the evidence is accepted and the policeman is punished. The whole meaning of the exclusionary rule is that Americans have not developed decent police administrative procedures."

Francis Allen, who served as chairman of the Advisory Committee that reported to the Attorney General on the inadequacy of legal services for poor people in the federal courts, comments that "elsewhere in the world there is a major political figure—a Home Secretary who can be held responsible for the effectiveness and the decency of the system. Here we have this extraordinary fragmentation. The Court felt itself forced to engage in supervision of the kind that political scientists feel is most dubious. This day-to-day regulation is the kind of thing the courts do least effectively." In Chicago investigators found that there was a police department employee whose job was to receive appellate court opinions sent over from the prosecutor's office, acknowledge them and file them—unread. If one aspect of the system is completely visible and comprehensible to the ordinary policeman, it is that trial court rulings on exclusion of evidence depend on the nature of the case and the personality of the judge, not on any rule of law.

Certainly, the courts will never be able to prohibit questioning by the police. Interrogation, says Chicago Police Commissioner Orlando W. Wilson, who was an academic criminologist before he streamlined, motorized and computerized the Chicago force, "is the device mankind has used since it learned to talk, the device the courts use, and in many cases the only device there is." A certain irreducible idiocy underlies the argument of some civil libertarians that a cop who finds a man driving a stolen car does not have the right to ask the man how he came by the car.

"Kidnaping," Circuit Judge Henry J. Friendly of New York said in a speech in California in 1965, "raises the issue . . . poignantly. If such a tragedy were to strike at the family of a writer who is enthused about extending the assistance of counsel clause to the station house, would he really believe the fundamental liberties of the suspect demand the summoning of a lawyer, or at least a clear warning as to the right immediately to consult one, before the police began questioning in an effort to retrieve his child?" Whatever the courts may say, Judge Friendly added at the ALI meeting that discussed the proposed model code, "society will not long endure" any system that forbids such questioning.

Nor does a requirement of *public* questioning by a magistrate— rather than station-house questioning by the police—guarantee a higher grade of justice to all. A man who has been accused of molesting a child, for example—by the child herself or, perhaps, by a disappointed ex-girl friend—is better off if the police can clear him quietly than he would be if the law demanded his immediate appearance in open court. But any questions the police might ask such a suspect in private would carry the risk of eliciting admissions from the guilty as well as believable denials from the innocent.

The confession plays a more subtle role in criminal justice than the long pre-*Miranda* debate revealed. As Staundford wrote in 1607, it "quiets the conscience" of those involved in the process. In the absence of a confession, as the hoo-hah over Lee Harvey Oswald brilliantly demonstrates, a shadow of doubt always hangs over the matter—for the police and the prosecutors, as well as for the public. "A good maxim for police and prosecutors," Judge Nathan Sobel of Brooklyn has written, "is, 'Leave well enough alone!' Instead they operate, because they are so zealous of success, on the opposite theory, 'Leave no stone unturned!' " But surely we can all sleep better at night (especially the judges who must sentence convicts) if we are confident that those who investigate crime have left no stone unturned.

There are two dangers in dispensing with confessions. One, detailed by the ALI Reporters, is "pressure to deal with the situation by enormously widening and intensifying general surveillance, with all the hidden costs to the quality of life that may be entailed." Another would be a lowering of the standard of proof that prosecutors require before taking a case to trial—and of the standard required by a jury for conviction.

"From an academic point of view," says Chief Justice Roger J. Traynor of California, "I think there's some question about exclusionary rules—keeping the truth from the trier of facts. Why should a court depart from the standards of evidence, if it's *good* evidence? That was the position I took in *People* v. *Gonzales*. But other cases came. It became clear there was no alternative to the exclusionary rule, because we were being made a party to this dirty business."

But what if the result of repeated and widespread exclusion was to be not merely the inability to prosecute some murderers and rapists but also an increase in the conviction of the innocent? At least one convicted defendant has already appealed to a federal circuit court to order the introduction of the prosecution's wiretap evidence, never offered (of course) at trial, on the grounds that it would show him innocent. Defenders of exclusion can (and, oddly, do) demonstrate that it hasn't made much difference in the results —that the conviction rate of those arrested before the California court adopted a *Mapp*-type rule in 1955 was about 86 percent, and remained at that figure while the number of defendants more than doubled in the next six years. The Chief Justice argues the absence of any need for confessions in a footnote to *Miranda,* pointing out that three of the five defendants whose cases were considered in the opinion "were identified by eyewitnesses." But elsewhere in the same opinion he cites Borchard's *Convicting the Innocent* and Frank and Frank's *Not Guilty* as sources for concern that the criminal process is sending innocent people to prison—and nearly every case in both books was due to faulty identification. Judge Sobel, having proclaimed confessions unnecessary in the third chapter of his PLI manual, goes on in the fifth chapter to say that "coerced confessions have never constituted the major problem in the administration of criminal justice. The major problem, where actual guilt or innocence is involved, has been and is now the problem posed by evidence of eye-witness identification."

In effect, what the Supreme Court has done is to attempt to move the essence of the adversary system back into earlier, administrative stages of the criminal process. The gains from success in this venture would be visible, but there might be losses, too. Restrictions on the evidence available against the guilty make the guilty and the innocent look more alike, and ask both prosecutors and jurors to make finer distinctions. It is at least arguable that the ratio of convictions to arrests is a fact determined by many variables, of which the rules of evidence are not necessarily the most important. Judges can scarcely consider these questions, because they are confronted with a case from the past rather than with hypotheses about what their decisions may mean in the future. Where the legislature will not act, the courts must. But "it's like Alice in Wonderland," says Herbert Sturz of the Vera Institute, "to make changes like these without information."

It is also worth remembering, perhaps, that the adversary system of justice is something less than the noblest creation of man's intelligence. Fifty years ago, Roscoe Pound wrote of

our American exaggeration of the common law contentious procedure. The sporting theory of justice . . . is so rooted in the profession in America that most of us take it for a fundamental legal tenet. But it is probably only a survival of the days when a lawsuit was a fight between two clans in which change of venue had been taken to the forum. . . . The idea that procedure must of necessity be wholly contentious disfigures our judicial administration at every point. . . . The inquiry is not, What do substantive law and justice require? Instead, the inquiry is, Have the rules of the game been carried out strictly? If any material infraction is discovered, just as the football rules put back the offending team five or ten or fifteen yards, as the case may be, our sporting theory of justice awards new trials, or reverses judgments.

Ultimately, what may take care of both the search-and-seizure and coercive interrogation problems is the provision of an Ombudsman —a public official charged with investigating administrative actions that oppress the citizenry, on the Swedish model—or an extension of the function of the DA's office to include a measure of control over the police force. "The logic of events," Yale's Abraham Goldstein writes rather sadly, "has left us no alternative but to pursue the professional model." In the spring of 1967, the Supreme Court took a long step back from *Mapp*, ruling in *McCray* v. *Illinois* that police could use evidence they had seized in the course of an arrest without a warrant, on their own statement that the arrest was made following a tip from some qualified but unidentified informant. Justice Douglas objected for the minority that the new decision left constitutional rights "to the tender mercies of the police." But there is no avoiding it: in the great bulk of cases there is no judicial substitute for the tender mercies of the police. Solutions must be found in administrative procedure, not in rules of evidence.

In the meantime, one may doubt that even the most drastic exclusionary rules would make much difference in the fundamental process of American criminal justice. A guilty man, uncertain of how much evidence the state has or can find against him but knowing the evidence may exist, will still find it hard to resist (whether or not he has confessed) when the prosecution offers a reduction in charge or the recommendation of a light sentence in return for a plea. His resistance will be particularly weak, of course, if he is already in jail. Far more important than *Mapp* or *Escobedo* or *Miranda,* over the long run, will be the bail project Herbert Sturz and Vera launched in 1961. The really significant motion toward decency in criminal procedure comes from reform of the bail system.

2

Louis Schweitzer may be the outstanding modern example of how much a private individual can do—and how much fun he can have —in a fundamentally uncontrolled society, provided he has money, intelligence, imagination, energy and a high order of efficiency. Born into a paper-manufacturing family (Peter Schweitzer & Sons), Schweitzer acquired training as a chemical engineer and then picked up expertise as a manager to the point where Kimberley-Clark bought out his company mostly to secure his services as executive vice-president. Among his accomplishments as operating head of Schweitzer was a contract with the French government during the days when the franc was a soft currency, permitting his company to take out the profits of its French operation in dollars through a separate contract to supply the American cigarettes the state-owned French tobacco industry needed to meet the demands of the tourist trade.

Much of Schweitzer's fun has turned out to be profitable, too. When a one-star restaurant near his Brittany paper factory was about to close, he bought it and reorganized it, to make sure he would have a good place to eat on his visits; and it has turned a profit ever since. Because his wife liked opening nights at the theater, he bought her one of the oldest off-Broadway houses—which opened under the new management with *Threepenny Opera,* giving no further opening nights but rental income for five years. Annoyed by his inability to get cabs after the theater, he bought a medallion and the first Mercedes-Benz taxicab to ride the streets of New York, and turned it over on a successful partnership basis to a cabbie with the interesting name of Louis Schweitzer. The same impatience with lack of service persuaded him once to buy a gondola in Venice (over the objections of his lawyers, who could just see what an Italian court would award to the victim of an accident caused by a gondola owned by an American millionaire). He named the gondola "Lucille," after his wife.

A radio ham who communicates with friends and employees overseas from short-wave transmitters at home and in his car,

Schweitzer grew interested in the problems of providing intellectually respectable broadcast service, bought New York's WBAI, and
presently (because, to his disgust, it had begun to make money) gave
it to the Pacifica Foundation for an experiment in listener-supported
radio. Then, one summer's day, Schweitzer ran into some cases of
poor men arrested on criminal charges and unable to pay a bondsman's fee, who had sat in jail for some months simply because they
were poor.

The situation Schweitzer had stumbled on was (and is) the truly
outrageous aspect of the American system of criminal justice. Anyone accused of (and guilty of) a crime will wish himself elsewhere
than in court on the day his case is called. As the law developed in
England, then, justices of the peace remanded accused people to
jail to make sure they would show up for trial, unless someone was
prepared to stand "surety" in their place—to risk his liberty as a
pledge of their appearance. Later, a pledge of money—a bond that
would be forfeited on nonappearance—became an acceptable
guarantee. In the United States, when there was a frontier just over
every hill, bonds were set high; and there grew up the "profession"
of the bail bondsman, who would pledge the necessary money, charge
the accused a premium on the bond (local custom varies between
5 and 10 percent of the total) and guarantee to the court that the
defendant would be present when wanted.

The immediate result is that people who can afford bondsmen's
premiums can spend the time before trial (and on appeal) in freedom; people who can't afford the premiums must remain in jail.
Once bail rises above $1,000, requiring at most courts a $100 premium, most defendants are locked up. "It's catastrophic," Abe Fortas
said shortly before his elevation to the Supreme Court. "These guys
really aren't *there*—they don't exist." Their time does not exist,
either—if they are convicted, a judge in most states need not consider
in sentencing them the "dead time" they have already spent behind
bars. Meanwhile, they have been separated from family and friends;
if they had a job, they've lost it; and every aspect of the treatment
they receive argues that they are already convicted criminals, like the
others kept in the same cells. The situation can be even worse in
small towns than it is in big cities. "The grand jury in Hillsboro

County meets in September, January and April," said Theodore Wadleigh, a large young man who handled legal aid problems in Manchester, New Hampshire, while breaking into his father's law practice in the early 1960s. "If you're arrested for a crime in April, you can be bound over till September, which may be a longer sentence than you'd get if convicted."

Meanwhile, the bail bondsman becomes a fertile source of corruption in the criminal courts. His best customers, of course, will be professional gangsters—and his best source of the information he needs to track down anyone who doesn't show up for trial (thereby endangering the bond) will be the mob. Because the accused need him, they are only too willing in many cases to take the lawyer he recommends, which produces unwholesome alliances and unethical fee-splitting. His presence at the courts, plus the substantial sums of money that flow through his hands, make him the natural man to ask when anyone wants to fiddle with the system.

Schweitzer discovered all of this quickly, and was outraged. He inquired after the possibility of setting up a foundation that would provide bail without fee. Several law-school professors and judges explained to him the legal and political difficulties that would attend the conversion of a foundation into the kind of insurance company empowered to write bail bonds, and pointed out that nothing of the sort was either necessary or really very interesting. Judges had always had the power to release accused persons "on their own recognizance," without bail. They didn't use this power, partly because they had neither time nor resources to investigate the situation of the man arraigned before them (and the DA, recommending how much bail should be required, had no stake in seeing the man free before trial), partly because they were scared of possible political repercussions if someone they released committed another crime while out "r.o.r." ("released on recognizance").

To investigate what would happen if judges really used this authority, Schweitzer in 1961 established the Vera Foundation (named after his mother; now called the Vera Institute of Justice), and in perhaps the most imaginative gesture he ever made hired a nonlawyer to run it—Herbert Sturz, a young, gangling, quick writer and editor, former graduate student of philosophy, who works with his feet on his desk. Even in 1967, with its missions much expanded, Vera had only a dozen employees, five of them lawyers, and was housed on two floors of the converted private house in Manhattan's East 30s that also holds the offices of WBAI.

Vera's first project was bail in 1-A, and the work was done with the help of the New York University Law School and with additional money from the Ford Foundation. After some early floundering with procedures, a simple mechanism was developed: law students working part time went into the pens behind 1-A and interviewed those awaiting arraignment to find out their previous criminal record, whether or not they were living with their family, whether they had a job or some other source of support, and how long they had been at their present address. These answers were then checked by a few telephone calls, and the students assigned the accused a rating, based on a maximum of three points for each major positive factor. Five points out of a possible maximum of thirteen were enough for a recommendation of "release on recognizance." Completing the questionnaire form, including telephoning, rarely took more than an hour for any prisoner.

"The bail bondsmen had some small political power," Sturz says today, "and if they had taken us on in our infancy they could have knocked us off. But they had seen various academic studies come and go since the twelfth century. They were sure we would be gone soon. And the first weeks of course, in 1961, we had only five a week in one court—that wasn't serious."

By the time the bail bondsmen had collected themselves, the Manhattan Bail Project was arranging the release of scores of accused felons every week, several dozen similar projects had been started across the country, and the Chief Justice was addressing a 1964 National Conference on Bail and Criminal Justice. Presently the administration of the Manhattan program was taken over by the New York City Probation Office, on public funds. At this point the bail bondsmen began to mutter darkly about Communism.

The results of the Manhattan Bail Project were dazzling. Of the 3,505 released on their own recognizance while Vera was running the project, more than 98 percent showed up for trial—as against 97 percent of those who got out by making bail. Even more important, nearly half of those so released were not convicted, as against less than a quarter in a control group; and only 53 of the first 1,214 whose cases were disposed of wound up with a jail sentence. Meanwhile, a parallel study of accused felons who did not have access to the Vera procedures showed that 47 percent of those who made bail and got out were not convicted and only 17 percent went to prison— while only 27 percent of those who stayed in jail after arraignment were not convicted, and 64 percent went to prison. Obviously, the question of whether or not a man was free before trial was closely correlated with the question of his freedom later; and Vera, after extensive study, decided that the answer to the one did in fact cause the answer to the other.

In the spring of 1965 Judge Bernard Botein, presiding judge of the Appellate Division supervising trial courts in Manhattan and the Bronx, an avuncular figure who had made himself Vera's guiding uncle, reported that plans similar to those of the Manhattan Bail Project were in the works or in operation in at least a few juris- dictions in four-fifths of the states; in the spring of 1966 President Johnson signed into law a bill encouraging the federal courts to run such projects on their own, "to weigh the individual rather than his money in the scales of justice." Judge Botein wrote, "In sheer volume, probably never before in our legal history has so substantial a movement for reform in the law taken place in so short a time." Earlier, in 1964, Vera had taken yet another step forward, setting up with the Manhattan police a "summons project," in which people arrested for misdemeanors were re- leased on recognizance at the police station, with a date to show up in court. Of the first few hundred trusted in this manner (shop- lifters, drunk drivers, disorderly persons, etc.), *every one* kept the appointment with the judicial process; over the full two and a half years of the Vera study, before the police themselves took over the idea as standard operating procedure in the summer of 1966, 98 percent came to court unassisted. Though no follow-up in- formation has been compiled, logic argues strongly that this gesture of trust by the society is a useful step in the "rehabilitation" of those summonsed rather than arraigned.

Quite apart from all other considerations, the bail and summons projects represent a substantial saving of public money (the $10 a day and up for housing, feeding and guarding people in detention) and time (the need for the policeman to accompany his captive to arraignment). One would expect rapid and radical amendment of existing procedures along the lines proposed by Vera. But though Vera hears of new projects every week (as of mid-1967 there were 150 r.o.r. programs in various counties), some observers feel the process of change has slowed since Judge Botein wrote in 1965. One reason is the timidity of elected judges, who fear that voters will hold against them any crimes committed by people released on recognizance. In San Francisco the project was briefly in danger of collapse after a Mexican dishwasher o.r.-ed on a drunk driving charge killed his common-law wife and two others, and the newspaper ran a banner headline: " 'SAFE RISK' KILLS THREE." Fortunately, that same day a policeman in jail in Oakland awaiting trial on charges of accepting bribes managed to raise $12,000 bail, went out, and killed the two witnesses against him—thus demonstrating that there is no safety in bail numbers, either. A more serious threat to the expansion of the Vera projects, however, is the fact that the constitutional lawyers have got into the act, and their antics could produce results that the society is not prepared to tolerate.

In theory, bail exists simply as a guarantee that accused people will turn up for trial; and the Eighth Amendment to the Constitution specifies that "Excessive bail shall not be required." (It must be remembered, however, that bail was never allowed in "capital cases," those for which a convicted felon could be executed, and that *all* felonies were theoretically punishable by death when the Constitution was written.) In fact, the bail system has come with the years to serve other purposes not easily transferred to other procedures. The most trivial example is the tendency in many jurisdictions to save the time and trouble of trials and convictions by providing for a forfeiture of bail instead of a fine. Hailed before a justice of the peace or a magistrate on misdemeanor charges, the offender posts a small cash bail as surety of his return for trial, on the general understanding that he will not be seen again. Most traffic offenses are handled this way in many rural areas and small towns; and it was through a record of this posting and forfeiture of bail that the newspapers during the 1964 elections picked up the story that a presidential assistant had been arrested on homosexuality charges at a YMCA. The system is convenient, and words on paper will not easily change it.

Bail is also used—and here the illegality is unquestionable—for punitive purposes. "We don't have a lot of juvenile offenders," Judge Roy Harper of the federal court in St. Louis told the National Conference, "but I will tell you frankly that I put every one of them right over in city jail, where they are kept for twenty-four to forty-eight hours. . . . When they go over there and come back, they tell me they don't want to go back." If this "taste of jail" is the end of the process—if the charges against the youngsters are then dismissed—the procedure makes much more sense than the full panoply of trial, conviction and sentence, or even the less formal "finding" of a juvenile court; it is simply an exercise of judicial discretion comparable to the police discretion represented by the decision not to arrest but to give the kid a cuff on the ear or a trip home to Papa and the suggestion of a spanking. (In cases of conflict between the two, for practical and probably also for theoretical reasons, the rule of *de minimis* takes precedence over the rule of due process.) Nor is it foolish to say, as Judge Ruppert Crittenden of Berkeley, California, said at the same conference, that bail gives some "control of the local bum, the local hoodlum. This man comes in and if he is released by me immediately upon coming into court, he laughs all the way out of the courtroom, because this is a joke. Part of setting bail, even a low bail and one that he can get out on, is to impress the accused and the community with the seriousness of the offense." Such procedures are obviously subject to abuse, and they are not easy to control—but even if illegal they are not necessarily wrong.

Finally, bail is used for purposes of preventive detention, an aspect of law enforcement which is universally permitted elsewhere —even in countries like Sweden, which regards the bail system as horrifyingly undemocratic, but holds in detention five thousand of the fourteen thousand arrested annually. Detention has had to be smuggled into American jurisprudence through the bail bond. It is not uncommon to hear a judge set bail of, say, $25,000, and then mutter to his clerk that if by any chance the man finds that big a bond he should be called back to court so his bail can be raised. Take the case of a man with a record of armed robbery, who holds up a bank, shoots and wounds a cashier, then trips while backing out and hits his head on a marble table, so that he can be safely arrested (because he is unconscious) with the gun still smoking in his hand. That this man is "presumed innocent" and therefore should be released on bail, to go out and rob more banks, is a notion unworthy of an intelligent legal system, whatever anybody says the Constitution says. On this issue the lawyer participants in the National Conference on Bail and Criminal Justice began to sound like medieval scholastics discussing the substance of the angels. At a time when the vast majority of persons accused of serious crimes were being held in jail awaiting trial—because Vera-type projects still affect only a tiny fraction of those arraigned—the law professors and judges solemnly debated whether a judge could *ever* be justified in setting an impossibly high bail on a man who, for example, had just brutally beaten up his ex-wife before their children and announced that next time he was going to kill her. If the Constitution forbids such common-sense behavior by a judge (and even so level-headed a commentator as Francis Allen has said that it does), then there should be no great difficulty amending the Constitution.

The remedy proposed by some of the professors (and by the defense attorney Edward Bennett Williams) was civil commitment to a mental hospital for people whose antisocial behavior, as reflected in a series of crimes, makes it dangerous to leave them running around loose. But surely the presumption of sanity is at least as fundamental a right as the presumption of innocence. There is every reason to set up some sort of administrative review within the court structure to assure that a judge is not abusing his power to set bail. But the word games lawyers can play with the Constitution are surely not a good enough reason to abandon what could be made a fair and reasonable system of preventive detention.

Legalisms and wishful thinking have distorted the significance of the Vera statistics, particularly the statistics showing that 48 percent of those released on recognizance were not convicted. The accurate statement is from Sturz himself: "I'm not naïve enough to believe that that percentage hadn't done anything at all. But some of them weren't guilty—not of anything criminal, anyway." Comments seeking to illustrate the advantages the free man enjoys when he comes to trial miss the point completely. There is no good evidence that among that small proportion of accused who come to trial the defendant at liberty does better than the defendant in detention. But in the prior administrative process the man who is out on bail or on recognizance is far less likely to plead guilty unless he is guaranteed a suspended sentence or immediate parole—otherwise his plea represents a clear sacrifice of liberty for incarceration.

The defendant who is free awaiting trial, then, will seek and, if his crime was not too grave, probably gain postponement after postponement. The months pass, and if the man is functioning in society —ideally, holding a job; at least, living with his family and committing no further crimes—even the most bloodthirsty prosecutor may come to feel that no public purpose is to be served by wrenching him from a more or less productive situation and locking him in prison. Charges are then quietly dropped, not because anyone believes or even presumes the man is innocent but because the society has nothing to gain by insisting on his guilt. Similarly, the Roxbury Project of the Boston University Law School arranges supervision by social agencies for those accused of misdemeanors, the judge continues the case for six months, then if all goes well "wipes it off. That way," says Assistant Dean Robert Spangenberg, "you don't add a record to all his other employment problems."

Though ostensibly directed only at pretrial release, what a Vera-style report really says to a judge is that there is no point in incarcerating this particular person—*either before or after trial*. At the beginning, Vera made it easier for such reports to be written by excluding from its coverage the sex offender, the killer, the narcotics addict. Recently, and somewhat tentatively (based on experience with a similar program in Washington, D.C.), the restrictions have been reduced. "The main thing we've done," Sturz says, "is to introduce the system to a job of fact-finding. With facts, we can open up options." The most important of these options is the possibility that all concerned—the defendant, the society and the courts—will be better served by keeping large numbers of offenders out of what criminologists call the "penocorrectional system." Judge Botein, whose original interests were in the fate of the first offender, probably knew from the beginning that the Vera project would produce such results.

3

Part of the definition of a crime is the punishment prescribed for it. While prosecutions were entirely in the hands of private persons, the punishment was usually a fine to be paid to the victim or his family. In the laws of Henry I of England, the murderer of a villein, who is a free man, must pay the family two hundred Saxon shillings and the feudal lord thirty shillings for the loss of service; the murderer of a serf pays the family forty pence and the lord twenty shillings. ("If a man slays his own serf," Maitland quotes, "his is the sin and his is the loss.") When the state intervenes in this process, everybody else loses: the criminal is executed (the death penalty still applied to all felonies in the eighteenth century), his property is forfeited to the king, and the victim receives nothing but a feeling of gratification, maybe.

Prison as punishment—except for debtors and people in political trouble—was unknown until the end of the eighteenth century; as late as 1771 a French criminologist wrote that imprisonment was permissible only in the case of people awaiting trial. Norval Morris, professor of law and criminology at the University of Chicago, awards pride of place as the first modern prison to Philadelphia's post-Revolution Walnut Street Gaol. Today prison is all there is: the death penalty is out of fashion (only one man was executed for crime in the United States after legal process in 1966, although, as Harold Solomon of the University of Southern California liked to point out, four hundred were executed by the police before legal processes began); mutilation survives only in Saudi Arabia, where thieves still lose a hand (the Chief Justice of Pakistan in 1964 said he thought that was a good idea that ought to be instituted in his country, too); transportation is almost impossible because the whole world is politically organized and no nation—not even Italy, which used to be nice about the matter in the case of its emigrants—is prepared to take another nation's criminals. Fines are still assessed against those who can pay them, and every once in a while some ingenious judge finds a uniquely suitable penalty, like the federal judge in California who sentenced a doctor guilty of income tax fraud to a year of working nine to five in a public clinic without salary. But otherwise a modern society's means of punishment is a term in prison, and the legislation that establishes the crime sets up maximum (and sometimes minimum) terms which an offender must serve.

Certain categories of persons have always been declared exempt from punishment (and thus from conviction for crime). The secular courts could not punish the servants of the church; thus, "benefit of clergy," which in late medieval England extended to nearly everyone who could read and write. An idiot or a madman could not be convicted, because he was incapable of understanding the law he broke; in effect, the criminal courts declared that they lacked jurisdiction over such people. Starting in the late nineteenth century, a third category was added: the juvenile offender, whose youth was assumed to keep him from a full understanding of his actions, and whose future had to be considered in a way that the older criminal's future did not. Again, the criminal courts were deprived of jurisdiction, and separate juvenile courts were established. Meanwhile, benefit of clergy as a principle disappeared, though there remains a great gulf between the disposition of educated, middle-income persons and illiterate poor persons convicted of the same crime.

What lawyers call "the insanity defense" is a question which "has attracted more attention and stimulated more controversy than any other question in the substantive criminal law." The chance to plead a defendant "not guilty by reason of insanity" was a matter of great importance at a time when most of the serious crimes were punishable by death, which is even more frightening to most people than years in an insane asylum. It is still important in the United States because so many prison sentences run so long, and the controversy will probably continue for a long time, though at least one crystal ball (property of the psychiatrist Thomas Szasz) shows a major change in the terms of reference. Not everyone will care to risk a possibly unlimited commitment to a mental institution to escape a fairly short jail sentence (indigent defendants have already appealed angrily, and fruitlessly, against their court-appointed lawyer's "victory" in getting them "acquitted" by reason of insanity without their consent). There is something inherently ridiculous about the lawyers and judges who have defended the more "liberal" rules of the Court of Appeals for the District of Columbia with the argument that the average defendant acquitted by reason of insanity in that district spends more time at St. Elizabeth's than he would have spent in jail if he had been convicted.

Essentially, the legal position is that an insane person is not "criminally responsible," and that the law may not convict someone who is not responsible for his actions. The rule for drawing the line between the responsible and the irresponsible is usually that laid down by the judges of England in an advisory opinion to the House of Lords in 1843, after a poor madman named Daniel M'Naghten had tried to assassinate Sir Robert Peel and had actually killed his confidential secretary. (M'Naghten "got off"—that is, he died a madman after twenty years in an asylum rather than on the gallows shortly after his crime.) The M'Naghten rules hold that nobody may be convicted of a crime unless he knew what he was doing and knew that it was wrong. In 1954, in the case of a housebreaker and check-passer named Monty Durham, who had been in and out of institutions (both jails and mental hospitals) for seven of his twenty-four years, Judge David T. Bazelon of the Court of Appeals for the District of Columbia laid down another rule: that nobody could be held "criminally responsible if his unlawful act was the product of mental disease or mental defect."

Both M'Naghten and Durham rest on the notion that the criminal law, expressing the moral sense of the society, has a primarily punitive purpose, and that therefore a *mens rea* (Holmes' "actual wickedness") is required. Reporting a Model Penal Code to the American Law Institute, Herbert Wechsler moved on the problem from another angle, arguing that the purpose of the criminal law is deterrence and there is no point trying to deter anyone if "as a result of mental disease or defect he lacks substantial capacity either to appreciate the criminality of his conduct or to conform his conduct to the requirements of law."

Under any of these definitions a lawyer enters for his client both a plea of not guilty and a plea of not guilty by reason of insanity. One or more psychiatrists are put on the stand to expound the theories which led the defense to call on them, one or more prosecution psychiatrists make rebuttal, and the jury retires to decide whether this particular poor devil should go to the jug or the loony bin.

Professor Monrad Paulsen of Columbia states the assumption simply: "We address ourselves to a system in which some wrongdoers will be punished and some will not because of mental disease or defect." But this is not our system at all. Except in the "irresistible impulse" cases (where the double-murderer who found his wife in bed with her boy friend is acquitted as temporarily insane and triumphantly released) the "acquittal" does not mean that the defendant will not be punished. Whether lawyers wish to admit it or not (and many don't: Geoffrey Hazard writes that "an infant knows the difference between blame and dismay"), involuntary commitment to a mental hospital is a punitive act. The most cursory look at our institutions reveals that some prisons, in Wisconsin, in California and in the federal system, are in fact much *less* punitive than the ordinary state mental hospital. And a man is not likely to be much better off in the job market later if his record shows a civil commitment to an institution for the criminally insane rather than a conviction for a crime.

The fundamental question, as Chief Justice Weintraub of the New Jersey Supreme Court has pointed out, is "the postconviction disposition of the offender." Professor Wechsler cannot argue with any great logic both that "the law must recognize that when there is no black and white it must content itself with different shades of gray" and that the end result must be the sharp black-versus-white decision of conviction or acquittal. The new British formulation of the "insanity defense" calls for the more meaningful plea of guilty but insane. A jury is a fact-finding beast, and here, beyond the question of whether he Did It, there are no "facts" to find. Anyway, as Garofalo wrote a hundred years ago, "When we undertake to ascertain whether a man is really responsible for what he does, we always end by discovering that he is not." Surely a judge, with whatever expert assistance he can empanel and subject to appellate review, is better equipped to deal with the shades of gray than a jury held to a black-or-white answer. In fact, judges probably do handle these questions more often than juries, because the decision that a defendant is too far gone to stand trial at all is made by a judge.

If it is desired to keep the jury determination in the situation, the British Medical Association shortly after the war offered a plausible way to do so. In a statement to a Royal Commission, the BMA proposed that "When a jury find that an accused person, at the time of committing the act, was labouring, as a result of disease of the mind, under a defect of reason or a disorder of emotion to such an extent as not to be fully accountable for his actions, they shall return a verdict of 'guilty with diminished responsibility.' " This suggestion was rejected by British lawyers, except as a way for a jury to get a murder charge reduced to manslaughter, and it has not even entered into the debate in America. But it must make more sense to proceed along these lines than to indulge endlessly in the Talmudic exegesis involved in reconciling the psychiatrists (whose fundamental doctrine holds that "all acts—healthy, sick, or not-sure-which —share one property: *they are predetermined*") with the lawyers (whose entire intellectual structure is based on the notion that behavior is *willed.*) The desire of the legal system not to "blame" people who "couldn't help themselves" stands in the way of progress along what will be at best a long road to rationality in dealing with the nonvicious criminal.

Societally, in any event, "the choice," as Professor Wolfgang Friedmann of Columbia puts it, "is between overcrowding of two sets of institutions, both of them inadequate, qualitatively and quantitatively." Pointing out that there is no purpose to be served in overcrowding the mental hospitals simply to ease the jam in the prisons, Morton Birnbaum, who is both a doctor and a lawyer, has advocated judicial adoption of the medical maxim *"Primum Non Nocere"*—"First, do no harm."

Far more significant than the insanity defense is the exemption given to juveniles. According to the FBI Uniform Crime Reports, 48 percent of all arrests for serious offenses in 1964 were arrests of children under the age of eighteen, and 43.3 percent of all those formally charged with serious crime by the police were referred to the juvenile court for disposition. The peak comes at age fifteen. (Generally speaking, incidentally, the larger the city, the smaller the proportion of those under eighteen in the total number of arrests.) It has been estimated that one-ninth of the nation's children—one-sixth of the boys—make some contact with a juvenile court (usually for a quite minor offense) between the ages of ten and seventeen.

What is meant by the juvenile court will vary greatly from place to place: a study by the Institute of Judicial Administration in the mid-fifties found twenty-one states where the juvenile branch was an administratively separate court with special personnel set aside for family and child problems; in some of the other states it may be just the same JP or magistrate or judge wearing a different hat. But the rules are fairly uniform: the public is barred from the room, neither names nor results are made public, the judge makes all decisions himself, the rules of evidence are loose, the child may be called on to testify, and the proceeding is declared to be "civil" rather than "criminal," resulting in a "finding" based on the preponderance of the evidence rather than a "conviction" based on proof beyond reasonable doubt. The trial is conducted (in a famous formulation that goes back to 1906) to do something *for* the child rather than something *to* him. But the end result may be commitment to an institution that bears some other name but is in reality a prison—sometimes for a term longer than an adult offender would have to serve on the same charge.

Children may also be committed somewhere because they are victims, neglected or mistreated to such a degree that the court feels they must be taken from their parents. Here the process is barely judicial at all—the judge easily accepts a report by a probation officer or other investigator, including a great deal of material that could never be admitted in evidence at any kind of trial. Roscoe Pound, who had been among the leaders of the juvenile court movement in the century's second decade, commented in its sixth decade that "The powers of the Star Chamber were a trifle in comparison with those of our juvenile courts and courts of domestic relations. . . . Even with the most superior personnel, these tribunals call for legal checks." As long ago as the 1930s, a California judge called the

juvenile courts "fascist," which is exactly right—the essence of both
the juvenile court and fascist politics being the notion of the state
as the father.

In recent years, especially in the larger cities, juvenile court procedure has been moving slowly toward that of the criminal courts
in general: accused children are represented by lawyers, judges are
denied access to the probation reports until they have made their
findings of fact, etc. In the metropolitan courts standards of evidence
seem to be rising a little—and will rise further, because the Supreme Court in June, 1967, ruled that juveniles threatened with
imprisonment must have counsel and privilege against self-incrimination. Acquittals here as in the Vera cases, however, are
more likely to be an exercise of discretion than a judicial conclusion.

In fact, whatever the finding, commitment is relatively rare: juveniles account for half the cases sent to court but only a seventh
of the incarcerated population. It is as unwise to concentrate
attention on the cases where criminal sanctions are imposed without
the safeguards of criminal procedures as to concentrate attention
in the adult courts on the infrequent rape and murder cases:
neither makes up any ponderable proportion of the business. Cases
that appear on the juvenile court docket have usually been through
a double screening—by the cop on the beat, who ordinarily has no
love for arresting kids, and by an informal "intake" process manned
by caseworkers who try to conclude the matter by social work rather
than legal action. Sol Rubin, counsel for the National Council on
Crime and Delinquency, whose sympathies clearly lie with defendants ("Almost all of us are criminals"), and who is deeply
concerned about the violation of decent legal procedures in juvenile
courts, writes that "in the great majority of juvenile court proceedings the facts are not disputed and the 'remedy,' which we prefer
to call the mode of treatment, lies in the discretion of the judge."
And this discretion is normally exercised by some sort of probation,
the child returning to his home environment (which was his problem to begin with), but under orders to attend school regularly,
stay off a certain block, report at intervals to a probation officer,
stop smoking marijuana, etc.

Next to the terminal ward of a charity hospital, a juvenile court is the most depressing place in the country. Some of the cases are trivial in fact if not in law, but many involve kids who are already in deep trouble that is sure to get deeper, and nobody, from the parent(s) to the judge, really has much notion of what can be done for them. Thus, for example, in Brooklyn, an undersized twelve-year-old boy tells the judge that he was in the halls of his elementary school, ducking assembly, when he saw some older boys playing truant from the junior high come in with one of the big boys from his own school; and he joined them in breaking down the door to the classroom and stealing $57 from a teacher's purse; he got $2 of it. He is as flat and truthful a witness as anyone could ask; and he is telling his story, obviously, because his mother told him he had to do it. The judge compliments the boy and asks the mother what she thinks ought to be done, and she is in despair: "I can't do nothing with him; he beats up my little ones, I'm afraid he's gonna kill them; maybe *you* could get his father to take him." And the judge says to her, lying like a trooper, "After our investigation we'll know exactly what you should do."

Obviously, a judge in these situations must have a good grasp on what is actually happening. He must know the difference between a car theft for the purpose of joy-riding a girl on a Saturday night and a car theft that really is a car theft (the break usually made is on the question of whether or not the boy changed the license plates). He must be able to distinguish between the girl who stole cosmetics at the five-and-ten and the girl who has been taking her classmates' lunch money. He must know the difference between sassing the police in a threatening way and throwing rocks at them, even if the police don't. He must be able to relate the probation officer's report on the family to the relationship of mother (occasionally father) and child that he sees before him in the courtroom. Obviously, he must be better than the juvenile court judges described by the Crime Commission: "Half had no college degree, a fifth had received no college education at all, a fifth were not members of the bar."

There is also something else. Charles Shinitzky, a somber, quiet lawyer who runs the Legal Aid office at the children's side of the Brooklyn Family Court—the first to offer legal aid to all accused juveniles—suggests a prescription for the ideal juvenile court judge:

"The one outstanding quality is that he be a gentleman. Here you're dealing with people of limited intelligence, different mores, different cultural groups. From being a gentleman there flows a kind of courtesy and patience and understanding, the tone of the courtroom—you can see it when you see the same attendant working for different judges.

"It's the easiest thing in the world to become frustrated. Many of the problems that come here seem so easy to resolve. To *us*, but not to *them*.

"The second qualification is—well, this is a court of law. While there is a social aspect to it, when it comes to the disposition of cases there is a framework in the statute.

"A man who has been in practice has entrenched in him this discipline: he deals in pertinent facts. Someone who is not imbued with this discipline takes a purely social approach—he wants to help the child. Then everything becomes wholly subjective. And when you have thirty-three different judges, you have thirty-three different ways to help the child. And once the diagnosis has been made, you don't know that you're right."

Here the juvenile court becomes like any adult criminal court, because sentencing is an area where no judge can ever know he was right. Deciding on a sentence for *this* criminal who has committed *this* crime is the heaviest responsibility a judge bears. He is doubt-less bound by a range of possibilities laid down by the legislature in defining the crime, but, as Judge Simon E. Soboloff said, "the range between a suspended sentence and 300 years . . . permits considerable leeway for difference of opinion."

In about three-quarters of the misdemeanor cases, the judge before sentencing simply looks at the convict's "pedigree sheet" of past troubles with the law and makes an offhand guess of what's reasonable. In the other quarter of misdemeanors, and in nearly all felonies, he receives from the court's probation officers, a "pre-sentence report," including interviews with family and friends, anything any psychiatrist may have had to say, a personal history of some detail and, in the case of recidivists, what the previous prisons have said. This piece of paper—loaded with hearsay—is for the majority of defendants the really key piece of evidence in their case. In wild contrast to almost everything else in the trial process, it is in most states a confidential document which the defendant may not see, to which public access is not permitted. On the basis of his reading of this report and of how the defendant looked to him during the trial—and of how shocked he is personally by the kind of crime the defendant committed—the judge determines how much time the defendant must or may serve, depending on his luck with the parole board.

Perhaps the most upsetting single piece of information about sentencing procedure—and the clearest rebuttal of any notion that a presumption of innocence exists in American courts—is the recent discovery that judges in sentencing treat those with a record of prior arrest (but not conviction) exactly as they treat those who have a real "criminal record." Statistically, the category "first offender," which entitles almost anyone to considerable leniency, seems to be reserved for those who have never had contact with the police before. At present, arrests which do not lead to conviction are expunged from an individual's record only in Massachusetts (which is why the Roxbury Project can be so cheerful about the administrative decision in the district court to continue a case for six months and then "wipe it off"). In California a notation after an arrest that did not produce conviction will read, "Deemed not arrested"—but the judge may not pay attention to such clerical matters. In most states the arrest record—in the same type face and the same format—appears interleaved with convictions on the pedigree sheet, as though there were no difference.

Simple disparity of sentences is a cause of aggravated misery in the prisons: there is no way to reconcile or "rehabilitate" a man with a ten-year sentence who learns that others similarly situated have three-year sentences for the same crime. And the disparity, even from judge to judge within the same jurisdiction, can be extreme. "A study made fifty years ago of the records of the then forty-one criminal magistrates of the City of New York," Columbia professor Harry W. Jones writes, "revealed that the percentage of cases in which the accused person was discharged without any penalty at all ranged from 74 percent for the most permissive of the magistrates to less than 7 percent for the most punitive and austere of the forty-one."

Matters have scarcely improved since. Harvard's Sheldon Glueck reports a study from New Jersey, analyzing the imprisonment vs. probation or suspension decisions made by six judges in seven thousand cases over a nine-year period. The proportions sentenced to prison terms ranged from 58 percent by the harshest judge to 34 percent by the most lenient. In the federal system, in a single year, the district court in Arizona placed only 5.5 percent of those convicted on probation, while in adjacent Utah the proportion was 67.9 percent. Where prison terms were imposed, within a single federal circuit along the Atlantic, Delaware averaged 13.7 months, while central Pennsylvania averaged 53 months. "The factors which determine this difference in the sentencing tendencies," the New Jersey study concluded, "are to be found outside the circumstances of the crime and those of the prisoner and hence probably in the judge, since he is the other factor which is always present."

With all the concern about the abuse of administrative discretion by the police and the prosecutor, judicial discretion in sentencing goes almost completely uncontrolled. A convicted defendant can appeal and win a reversal on the grounds that a judge erred in admitting information about a telephone conversation only remotely related to his crime, but there are only twelve states where by statute he can routinely appeal his sentence. While appellate courts will labor to keep all in one line the rulings of the trial courts below them in the tiniest commercial matters or the most piddling details of procedure, they will not (in thirty-one states and the federal system, by law, they cannot) attempt even a rough leveling down of the sentences different judges award to similar prisoners for similar crimes. Yet this is the pay-off point, the purpose of the plea bargaining, the real reason for having a lawyer. The National Crime Commission has recommended appellate review of sentences on defendant's motion, giving the appellate court the power to increase as well as reduce the term.

In this area, too, unremarked, is the place of greatest disparity between the rich and the poor—and the most serious locus of corruption and favoritism. It is common knowledge in many cities that one of the ways to get a break in sentencing is to hire so-and-so to be your lawyer before such and such a judge. Many lawyers make a living out of just this reputation. There is always a reason for leniency, and even the thoroughly honest and scrupulous judge is more likely to listen to it when he hears it from a friend. In every other country in the world, some higher court or administrative body casts a second look at sentences, but in thirty-odd American states the trial judge, who is barely permitted to say "Boo" during the trial, for fear he might influence a juror, becomes at the moment of conviction a god in whose majesty all punishment resides. It is, perhaps, one of the penalties paid for the adversary system: he had his chance and he lost; now, to hell with him.

When debates on this subject do occur, they are depressing. Some courts hold seminars on sentencing, which serve mostly to reveal the incompetence of psychiatry. The eager hopes of the nineteenth century, that someone would find the Mikado's magic ways really to make the punishment fit the crime, have left no residue of accomplishment; and time has contradicted Lombroso's optimistic prediction that the society would find the right occupations for people who would otherwise show criminal tendencies ("war or surgery for homicides, the police or journalism for swindlers, etc."). The social sciences have failed. "It is foolish to talk glibly of treating the criminal according to his individual nature," Morris Raphael Cohen wrote, "when in fact we have no means of adequately knowing it."

What *should* be done with the convict is incredibly difficult, perhaps impossible, to discover. "It's a problem," says Francis Allen, "that induces people to go through all sorts of falderal to avoid thinking about it. One develops a whole line of chatter about rehabilitation. It's a repression of reality—when you begin talking about rehabilitation when you don't know how to rehabilitate, you can defend anything you want to do."

But the system certainly need not be quite so brainless as it now is. "If you commit a really heinous crime," says Herbert Sturz, disapprovingly, "society will be careful to try to rehabilitate you, give you some money when you leave. If you're unlucky enough to commit only a minor crime, you get thrown into a sump hole, and you're given nothing except maybe a quarter when you leave. If you're put in in the summer, and you leave in the winter, you don't have clothes." Vera has begun a study of sentencing and of the effects of incarceration, to see if better information can be got to replace the criminologists' big generalization that about 70 percent of all those put in jail avoid future trouble with the criminal law, while 30 percent return to the prisons over and over, certainly till after the age of thirty, and often for their entire lives.

"Prison," Norval Morris has written, "is expulsion from the group; it is banishment to a worse country than exists outside prison. And it is a strange and inefficient banishment because there is normally a return. A new and meaningful life is not possible in the country to which the criminal is banished. Life there tends to sever his cultural roots and to cripple him socially and sometimes psychologically for his return."

To this environment, without thinking much about it, we banish about 100,000 people every year—20,000 of them for sentences of five years and longer, unless a parole board intervenes. What the society wants is an institution that will be punishing to the convicts while they are there, yet will prepare them to return and sin no more on their release. It can't be done—but nobody cares much, because the society is prepared in these matters to accept defeat. There is another choice, which has been taken: to sweep under the rug (the same rug), for as long as possible, the vicious, the stupid, the unlucky and the warped, so that they will not bother others. Meanwhile, the long sentences give the prosecutor leverage in bargaining for a guilty plea to a lesser offense.

Disturbed by the increase in crime, the legislatures regularly increase the jail terms and provide irreducible minimums; disturbed by the administration of the system, the appellate courts seek to restrict the evidence that can be entered against the defendant. We are in a fair way of making the worst of both worlds. Among the few criminological observations nobody has ever contradicted is that of the Marchese de Baccaria, two hundred years ago:

Crimes are more effectually prevented by the *certainty* than by the *severity* of punishment. . . . The certainty of a small punishment will make a stronger impression than the fear of one more severe, if attended with the hopes of escaping; for it is the nature of mankind to be terrified at the approach of the smallest inevitable evil, whilst hope, the best gift of Heaven, hath the power of dispelling the apprehension of a greater, especially if supported by examples of impunity, which weakness or avarice too frequently afford.

By advertising to criminals their sporting chance of escape in an adversary trial, letting the more prominent remain at liberty after conviction while their lawyer hunts in the record for "error" (any error) in the judge's conduct of the trial, and then slugging them as hard as the system can if they fail to escape, the law becomes at the same time inefficient and unjust. Meanwhile, the prosecutor's office, the courts, the jails and the asylums are all starved for funds, and the system must make do with inferior personnel in inadequate facilities.

We now know a little about how the system looks from the bottom. Here, for example—and for contrast against the usual discussions of "rights," "remedies" and "judicial review"—is a "Toast," a Negro narrative poem, collected in the Missouri Penitentiary by the young Harvard ethnologist Bruce Jackson:

Now, that judge looked at me like I was a roach on the floor, and said he
   was gettin' tired a me dartin' in and out a' his goddamned door.
He said, "Johnson, I'm gettin' tired a you fellas runnin' around here doin
   these nickel-assed crimes
   jumpin' up here before me and ain't got a cocksuckin' dime."
I said, "But your honor, I can truthfully say, when the crime was com-
   mitted I was miles away."
Say, "My people bought a home out in California, you know, that's where
   I always be when I ain't got no dough."
'Bout this time the prosecutor walked in and my heart felt like a thou-
   sand dirty motherfuckin' pins.
He says, "Your honor, that's old stick-high jivin' Johnson playin' the part
   of a simp,"
Say, "If you let him out on the corner this evenin', he'll be screamin'
   he's a motherfuckin' pimp."
Say, "If you let him out a' here talkin' that bunk," say, "before sundown
   he'll have his arm full a that no-good junk."
Judge say, "Yeah, I heard about you." Said, "You been playin' these high-
   class broads, these broads a' the upper class."

Say, "I'm gonna see if you can't shake this quarter [25-year-sentence] off
your goddam ass."
I say, "But your honor, how 'bout my children, my sickly wife?"
He says, "Contempt of court. Clerk, change that shit to life."
Now they had me up, they had my ass and they had my feet off the floor,
they was draggin' me out the courtroom door.
Judge say, "You know what, Willie, it's a damned shame, but by this
time tomorrow, I won't know your cocksuckin' name."

CHAPTER 7

P. I. AND OTHER WRONGS

"[W]e have a judge in Boston named Donahue, who is indeed brilliant, but a character. . . . [A] jury case was being tried before him, a personal injury case, and the jury sent a note in to him with a question asking if, even though there was not any liability, they could still give the plaintiff some money. The judge sent for the jury. He said to them, 'I have your written question, and I assume from the question that you have found there is no liability.' The foreman said, 'That is so, Your Honor.' He said, 'All right, sign this slip then.'

"After they had signed the slip, which directed a verdict for the defendant, he said, 'I will now answer your question. You may retire to the jury room and pass the hat.'"

—SAMUEL P. SEARS of the Boston Bar

"If in the whole department of unintentional wrongs the courts arrived at no further utterances than the question of negligence, and left every case, without rudder or compass, to the jury, they would simply confess their inability to state a very large part of the law."

—OLIVER WENDELL HOLMES, JR.

"There's no reason why a lawyer or a banker should not recognize the knavery that is part of his vocation. An honest man is not responsible for the vices or the stupidity of his calling, and need not refuse to practise them. They are customs of his country, and there is profit in them."

—MONTAIGNE, translated by C. P. Curtis

"The basic bread-and-butter of almost all individual lawyers to-day is the occasional negligence case."

—ALFRED W. GANS of the New York and
Ohio bars, formerly editor, *American
Law Reports*

1

Bodily assault is one of the most common crimes, and by no means all the people who commit it are poor. Barroom brawls occur in country clubs as well as in slum saloons. Not infrequently the loser in such a brawl will complain to the police, and a state's attorney will start a prosecution in motion. At the same time, however, the wounded victim will probably tell his own lawyer to begin a suit, seeking damages from the assailant, alleging doctor bills, loss of time at work, pain and suffering, and a broken nose leading to cosmetic disfiguration. And if the civil claim of "personal injury" is settled, if the attacker buys off the loser, the criminal charge will usually be dropped for lack of a complaining witness. Among the privileges of wealth is a defendant's chance to convert criminal actions into civil actions for "wrongs"—or "torts," as the English lawyers came to call them, retaining the law-French that arrived with the Norman conquerors.

Many crimes—the list includes embezzlement, forgery, rape, auto theft—can be bought off in this manner, and often are. And should be, too. The welfare of society is better served by "making whole" the victim of an offense than by punishing the offender, and the civil suit accomplishes both. The man whose car has been stolen may or may not wish to see the thief in jail (it's a question of personality), but he certainly wants his car back.

Crimes in general are merely one, relatively small category in the larger class of wrongs. In Biblical times the division between the two was by the nature of the damage done: "He that smiteth a man, so that he die, shall be surely put to death. . . . [But] if he rise again, and walk abroad upon his staff, then shall he that smote him be quit: only he shall pay for the loss of his time, and shall cause him to be thoroughly healed." Other early societies, including both Rome and the Germanic tribes, restricted the category of crime to offenses against the state itself or against the religion: everything else was a tort. "[N]ot theft only," Sir Henry Maine wrote of the *Commentaries* of Gaius,

but assault and violent robbery, are associated by the jurisconsult with trespass, libel and slander. All alike gave rise to an Obligation . . . and were all requited by a payment of money. This peculiarity, however, is most strongly brought out in the consolidated laws of the Germanic tribes. Without an exception they describe an immense system of money compensations for homicide, and with few exceptions, as large a scheme of compensation for minor injuries.

Restitution, "compounding" for wrongs, did not, however, satisfy that felt need for vengeance which Holmes insisted was the foundation of all legal procedure, and in nearly all societies for which we have records an effort was made to substitute a nonhuman object as a target for hatred. In Exodus the ox that gored a man was to be killed and its flesh not eaten, "but the owner of the ox shall be quit." Plato's Athenian laid down that "if any lifeless thing deprive a man of life . . . the nearest of kin shall appoint the nearest neighbor to be a judge . . . and he shall cast forth the guilty thing beyond the border." In the law of England, an object "responsible" for a death was a *deodand*, something to be given to God through the agency of the Crown, and as late as 1842 a locomotive was forfeited to Queen Victoria because it had killed someone.

Lightning, flood, fire, landslide were Acts of God: for almost anything else, someone or something was at "fault." The head of the household was responsible for whatever was done by his family, his servants or his slaves. When necessary, the law would hunt for someone to blame. "Guesswork perhaps would have taught us," Maitland and Pollock wrote,

that barbarians will not trace the chain of causation beyond its nearest link. . . . All the evidence, however, points the other way:—I have slain a man if but for some act of mine he might perhaps be yet alive. . . . At your request I accompany you when you are about your own affairs; my enemies fall upon and kill me; you must pay for my death. You take me to see a wild-beast show or that interesting spectacle, a madman; beast or madman kills me; you must pay. You hang up your sword; some one else knocks it down so that it cuts me; you must pay. In none of these cases can you honestly swear that you did nothing that helped to bring about death or wound.

As late as 1466 the rule of law was that "if a man is damaged he ought to be recompensed." As late as 1616 English courts laid upon the defendant the requirement to prove that an accident was *not* his fault. But such rules can be enforced only in communities where people know each other rather well, at a time when the actual payments for death or injury are small, more in the nature of a token to buy off vengeance than a true reparation. They become an infernal nuisance if any number of people start moving around, or if judges and juries begin measuring the real damages rather than merely following a conventional schedule—and they interfere with business. Slowly but decisively, the English judges changed the law, and by 1881 Oliver Wendell Holmes, Jr. could write, "The general principle of our law is that loss from accident must lie where it falls, and this principle is not affected by the fact that a human being is the agency of misfortune."

The fundamental change was the redefinition of "fault." By Holmes' time the burden was on the plaintiff to prove the defendant's causal relationship to the accident. "Negligence"—doing something that a reasonable man could see would make trouble, like galloping a horse down a crooked street or failing to repair a broken step on a stairway used by the public—was still a source of fault, but it had to be the immediate cause of the injury, and there were lots of ways in which even negligence could be excused.

One of them was by agreement. When the railroads were new, British courts ruled that nobody had to ride on them, and that the owners had the right to insist that passengers waive any actions for injuries when they bought their tickets (and passengers would be assumed to know they had agreed to such a waiver if it was contained somewhere in the book of tariff regulations on the counter beside the ticket seller).

Another was the "assumption of risk"—everyone knew that coal mining was a dangerous occupation, and if a coal miner was killed or injured in the pit, his family should not be surprised or aggrieved or entitled to damages.

Yet another was "privity"—only a direct relationship with the man who had caused the injury could give an injured person the right to sue. If the head came off the hammer and hit the hammerer in the eye, he could not sue the manufacturer, because his only relationship was with the storekeeper who sold him the hammer. And the storekeeper had no obligation to test the hammer before selling it, so there was nobody to sue.

Injured on the job by a loom started too soon by one of the other workmen, a man had no cause of action against his boss: the injury had been caused by a "fellow servant," and the owner was in no way liable. In 1893, the heyday of the "fellow servant" rule, the Interstate Commerce Commission estimated that a railroad switchman had an average life expectancy of seven years. The railroads didn't care; they could find lots of switchmen where that one came from.

Moreover, a victim could recover only if his own actions had in no way contributed to the accident. In 1809 Lord Ellenborough heard the case of a man who had been driving along a road and had run into a barrier that wasn't supposed to be there. Maybe he could have stopped if he'd been driving slowly or had seen it in time. Although the man who had left his pile of wood on the road should not have done so, Lord Ellenborough proclaimed, "A party is not to cast himself upon an obstruction which has been made by the fault of another, and avail himself of it." This rule that "contributory negligence" forbade all recovery has been denounced by the leading American authority on torts with the words, "Nobody has ever succeeded in justifying that as a policy, and no one ever will." But it spread instantly to the United States, where lawyers and judges were more likely to have access to the English reports than to domestic decisions; and it is still the law in all but a handful of the states.

If a victim actually died as the result of an accident, through much of the nineteenth century, even the most blameworthy and directly responsible "tortfeasor" could not be held for damages, because "personal actions die with the person." The heirs, not having been actual participants in the event, had no standing to sue. What the rule meant, Sir Frederick Pollock wrote in 1912, was that "A man wounds or disables another at his peril, but may kill him outright with impunity"; it was, Pollock added, "one of the most foolish rules that have ever been adopted by the courts of a civilized country."

This cruelty, like contributory negligence, was a late development in the common law, and was also the work of Lord Ellenborough. The new rule fitted so well with the temper of an emergent capitalism that it was almost instantly adopted by major courts all over the English-speaking world. (Alfred Gans, former editor of *American Law Reports*, has dug up the odd fact that the courts of Hawaii alone rejected it.) Among the consequences of the bar against death actions, Professor William Prosser of California has suggested, not wholly deadpan, was the provision of fire axes in railway carriages, "to enable the conductor to deal efficiently with those who were merely injured."

By 1846 the English had had enough of this rule, and Parliament in Lord Campbell's Act created an action for wrongful death. The New York State legislature followed a year later, and all the other American states straggled after, some at a considerable distance. (In 1867 the Supreme Court of Michigan denied possible recovery for death in an accident on the reasoning that "to the cultivated and enlightened mind, looking at human life in the light of the Christian religion as sacred, the idea of compensating its loss in money is revolting.") But the American legislatures, influenced by the railroads in one way or another, limited in their new laws the amount of the recovery the estate could secure. Today, twelve states (Colorado, Illinois, Kansas, Maine, Massachusetts, Minnesota, Missouri, New Hampshire, Oregon, South Dakota, Virginia and Wisconsin) retain such limitations on damages, some as low as $20,000, and Pollock's comment is still appropriate. "When I was a claims agent in Chicago," says a lawyer now working in Philadelphia, "we used to tell the taxi companies and the truckers, sort of half seriously, that if their drivers hit somebody the best thing to do was to back up and hit him again."

Harshness was not quite uniform. People on ships were protected as people on railways were not because the law of admiralty was ancient and unchanging. Here "strict liability" continued: if a seaman stupidly chose one rotted rope from a tangle of fifty good ropes, and was injured as a result, the ship had to pay, because the owner was under obligation to make the ship absolutely seaworthy. Contributory negligence did not bar recovery in the admiralty courts, though they might take it into account in determining whether damages suffered should be paid for in full or only in part (the rule was called "comparative negligence").

Warehousemen and other such "bailees" were not permitted to contract out from under their liability for negligence in handling other people's property: the legend on the parking ticket—that the garage will not be responsible—is legal nonsense.

Under certain exotic circumstances, "privity" was not required: because it is one of the few certainties about law that what can happen will happen, a court one day found itself confronted with the case of a man who had thrown a lit firecracker into a crowd, where others had thrown it away from themselves until finally it went off and put out someone's eye. Even though the man who had first tossed it was far removed from the final injury, he had to be held liable. Again, a court ruled that a drug supplier who had put belladonna in a bottle labeled extract of dandelion was liable to the lady poisoned by it, even though she had purchased it at a retail shop and had no direct relationship with the supplier: people who dealt in poisons should be held to high standards of care.

Finally, in a decision by the House of Lords that caused great agitation in the United States, a man who dammed a pond on his property was held responsible for damages done on another man's property by water that escaped for reasons he could not have known (there was a long abandoned and forgotten mine under the land).

But such cases were freaks. In general, at the turn of the century, an activist society committed to progress was concerned about protecting the creators rather than the victims of a new era.

Into this unhappy situation came populist outrage and liability insurance, closely followed by the automobile. Arizona on admission to the Union placed in its constitution (not just in its laws) a prohibition of the "fellow servant" rule. Justice Benjamin Cardozo in New York destroyed "privity" as a defense in negligence cases by equating a car manufacturer's action in putting a defective wheel on an automobile with a drug supplier's mistake in putting belladonna in the extract of dandelion bottle. By hook or crook, judges were deprived of most of their power to throw plaintiffs out of court by ruling that as a matter of law their behavior had constituted "contributory negligence"; such questions now must normally be left to the jury. (The current Illinois Pattern Jury Instructions, which judges read aloud at the end of a case, say, "The law does not say how a reasonably careful person would act under the circum- stances. That is for you to decide.") The state legislatures passed workmen's compensation laws, by which employers in effect traded their good chance of winning a lawsuit for a schedule of statutory maximum damages they could be forced to pay, whether or not the accident was in any way their fault. By and large, however, the American legal system could not absorb this change, and the award- ing of workmen's compensation damages was entrusted in most states to an administrative commission rather than to the courts.

Movements from "fault liability" toward "strict liability" were usually promoted by an argument somewhat cynically labeled "the deepest pocket." Instead of leaving losses where they fell, the law should see to it that they were borne by those who could most easily carry them. The ancient theory of "vicarious liability"—*respondeat superior,* the master answers for the acts of his servant—was dredged up by a succession of commentators to give legal authority to what would otherwise seem mere social justice. In fact, of course, these developments had been made possible by the spread of liability in- surance, which meant that the effects of "strict liability" could be spread over the entire world of risk-takers rather than imposed on unlucky individual tortfeasors.

Unfortunately, because the law of torts is so closely related to the law of crimes (and because public policy forbids anyone to insure against the consequences of his own crime), the legal system could not really accept the existence of insurance. The guilty driver in an automobile accident case often stands to lose nothing by a judg- ment against him, and he isn't even paying the lawyer; but only in Wisconsin and Louisiana may a plaintiff mention in court the fact that the real defendant is his insurance company. (Something can be done about this elsewhere in the proceedings, in the *voir dire,* the lawyers' selection of jurors, when the plaintiff's lawyer is permitted to ask pointedly whether any of the jurors "works for an *insurance company*.") Decisions in Texas and Tennessee have held that if a juror speaks of insurance in the jury room the award may be voided. In legal theory, the only significance of the insurance company is its guarantee that the "defendant" will be able to pay whatever judgment may be gained against him. Procedurally, however, the insurance company is the beneficiary of an act of grace: although a lay intermediary between the defendant and the lawsuit, it is excused from the charge of unauthorized practice of law. And the plaintiff's lawyers are, of course, interested in the question of how much insurance the defendant carried. When there are two possible defendants, the one with the high insurance is obviously the target of opportunity.

Judges have shown a really astonishing ability to ignore the fact of insurance. Historically, for example, the courts distinguished between different kinds of hospitals. If a nurse in a private hospital gave a patient the wrong medicine, the patient could sue for injuries suffered. If the same incident occurred in a charitable hospital or in a tax-supported hospital, however, the patient had no access to the courts. Public policy denied any right of recovery against a charitable institution, because the community feared that a vital facility might disappear in bankruptcy in the aftermath of a lost lawsuit. And a public hospital was the beneficiary of "sovereign immunity," the right of the state to decline to be sued.

In most states, legislatures or courts have lifted the immunities of both charitable and public hospitals, and the victim of mishandling at a hospital (or his heirs) can now sue for damages regardless of who owns the establishment. And legislators, not being bound by judicial terminology, have freely discussed in their debates the fact that all hospitals can now buy liability insurance. But in the few states where the courts themselves have changed the law, the question of insurance has usually been ducked. The decision that withdrew the immunity of charitable hospitals in California did make passing reference to insurance, but only as an argument that had been raised by losing counsel in a previous case: that "as the hospital carried insurance indemnifying it against such liability, the reason for [immunity] failed. In answer to this contention, the court pointed out that charitable organizations had been relieved from liability upon the principle that a trustee may not deplete the trust fund set aside for charity by using it to pay damages . . . and that the protection afforded by this rule could not be infringed upon by the acts of a trustee in procuring insurance." A later court found that this argument would not wash—that hospitals had always been held liable for automobile accidents involving their ambulances or other cars, and could just as easily be held liable for negligence within the building. But the word "insurance" was not mentioned again.

In 1961 Chief Justice Roger J. Traynor of the California Supreme Court withdrew by judicial decision the previous immunity of that state's public hospitals. The opinion rested on the simple proposition that "Public convenience does not outweigh individual compensation." But if there had been no malpractice insurance available to hospitals, this decision would never have been rendered. What Traynor was saying, really, was, "County hospitals like proprietary and charity hospitals can buy insurance, and should do so"—but even so pioneering a judge as Traynor could not be that direct. Indeed, he could not even mention the fact, rather significant to laymen, that the defendant public hospital in this case *had* bought insurance, and the real defendant was an insurance company claiming sovereign immunity. The judges' insistence that they must ignore insurance companies is especially odd when one considers that in many areas of liability it is not the law but the insurance company—with its experience ratings and preferential premiums—which really enforces safety standards.

Insurance has been equally ignored on the plaintiff's side. The fact that the victim of the airplane crash had just purchased $100,000 of insurance at the airport may not be mentioned in court; neither may the fact that Blue Cross and Blue Shield in fact picked up all the hospital bills for which the victim of an automobile accident is suing. Recovery "from collateral sources" is no concern of the law. A plaintiff's lawyer explains rather smoothly that "the law doesn't wish to penalize the man who had the foresight to buy insurance." In fact, obviously, there is no question here of losses and penalties: the issue is now one of windfall gains and rewards.

This refusal to consider how much actual financial damage a victim has sustained turns medical and life insurance into a counter on a roulette table, which can produce winnings after an accident for which somebody else is found liable. Of course, the plaintiffs' lawyers do not share in the proceeds of life and medical policies— only in whatever can be recovered through law.

All these confusions persist because the law itself is confused; as the historian and law professor Max Radin once put it, "The common law never formulated a general definition of tort." Up to the very end of the nineteenth century, the subject was always approached in English-speaking countries as a disconnected collection of "denominate torts," specific categories of wrongful acts which the plaintiff would have to "plead" before a court would listen to him at all. The question of what purpose the law served could not even be raised, because different pieces of it served different purposes; and they still do.

An obvious purpose is deterrence. People are deterred from negligence because they have to pay for the results. Yale's Guido Calabresi says flatly, as though it were beyond the possibility of argument, that "One of the functions of accident law is to reduce the cost of accidents, by reducing those activities that are accident prone. Activities are made more expensive, and thereby less attractive, to the extent of the accidents they cause." Harvard's David F. Cavers assumes continuing close relationship between criminal law and tort law: "[F]inancial protection . . . is in part a sanction for wrongfully causing harm. As a consequence its purposes include elements of deterrence and retribution even though it may be couched in essentially compensatory terms."

In the tort field generally, these statements are fairly obviously true. Plagiarism, libel, conspiracy in restraint of trade, misrepresentation of securities issues—all are torts, and are opened by the law for private damage suits as the most effective means of stopping such conduct. "Gross" or "willful" negligence opens a door in most states to "punitive" damages, over and above actual harm suffered by the victim. Even in the personal-injury field the purpose of making builders who blast foundations absolutely liable for the side effects of their blasting must be to give them a heavy stake in safe operations. The tort field is also wonderfully fertile in hypothetical problems (one that came up not long ago at an annual meeting of the American Law Institute was damages for an indecent proposal made to a girl sunbathing on a roof by the pilot of a hovering helicopter). On examination, nearly all these hypotheticals turn out to be kinds of conduct the society should try to discourage, raising a question of whether or not the law of torts can be adapted to serve the purpose of discouraging them.

Moreover, tort law *has* worked for this purpose: the railroads began installing safety devices as soon as they were made liable for accidents to the railroad men. The plaintiff's bar is self-interested but not necessarily wrong when it promotes the slogan "Sue for Safety." Lee Kreindler, who represents the families of the victims of plane crashes, told a Philadelphia group recently that "There's a lot to be said for making people careful—for making it expensive for people to be negligent."

This argument has been used with great effect in the quest for punitive damages against the Richardson-Merrell Company for aggressively marketing an anticholesterol drug called MER/29 after research tests on animals had indicated great danger of damage (including cataracts) to those who might take it. William F. X. Geoghan told a jury in White Plains, New York, "You are not the conscience of Westchester County in this case, you are the conscience of the whole country. . . . I say that your award, if it is less than one million dollars, you will not—you will not be telling this crowd who are still there that it should not have happened." As hundreds of people were harmed by the drug, and each is suing separately for punitive damages, the ultimate "fine" assessed by jurors (over and above their evaluation of the actual losses suffered by the plaintiffs) may run into tens of millions of dollars—as against the $80,000 fine imposed upon Richardson-Merrell after a plea of no defense in an action taken by the government on criminal charges.

Not everyone agrees. Richardson-Merrell tells its stockholders that insurance will cover a high fraction of the juries' awards, while the company could not insure itself against a criminal fine. Chicago's Walter J. Blum and Harry Kalven, Jr. write that "Generally speaking, the law has not taken very seriously the possibility of deterring with tort sanctions." Automobile accidents, especially, do not directly cost the careless driver anything if he's bought enough insurance. Writing about contributory negligence, Prosser has pointed out the silliness of "the assumption that the speeding motorist is, or should be, meditating on the possible failure of a lawsuit for his possible injuries"; and he is also not meditating on the possibility of his liability for injuries to others. Moreover, a law that seeks to deter must rely to a degree on *moral* disapproval, which is not common in automobile accident cases: as a committee of the California State Bar recently observed, "Liability is routinely imposed for conduct that the punctilio of the strictest moral sense could not call immoral. The 'negligent' driver of an automobile is not held responsible because he is a bad man."

Here, plainly, the purpose has shifted: tort law now seeks, in this formulation, to compensate, "to secure a man indemnity against certain forms of harm," as Holmes put it, ". . . not because they are wrong, but because they are harms." But *who* is to indemnify him? Any passing stranger? If fault is to be rejected as the governing principle of liability, some wholly new *system* must be created. The invention of such systems—"compensation plans"—has been for a generation one of the most popular parlor games at the law schools. But to all the various plans to compensate for accident losses through some form of social insurance, the working lawyers raise at least one of three objections: costs, the absence of deterrence and morality.

One of the few reforms of the present system that has actually gone into effect anywhere is compulsory insurance: in Massachusetts, New York and North Carolina cars will not now be licensed unless they carry minimum liability insurance. In Massachusetts, which has had such a law longest, personal injury claims in 1966 ran heavier than one for every twelve automobiles on the road, more than three times the rate for the nation as a whole. Nobody knows or can sensibly guess how many claims would be entered and paid under a national compensation plan which provided not only compulsory insurance but also automatic recovery. Injuries from automobile accidents have passed four million a year, and total damages to persons and property are estimated by the American

Insurance Institute at about $11 billion annually. Total automobile insurance premiums paid run just under $8 billion a year—but, as we shall see, something less than half this amount returns to the public in net recoveries. Administrative process in the form of workmen's compensation seems to take care of about 2.1 million job-related injuries through insurance premiums of about $2 billion a year—not lavishly, but without the omissions of the legal system. Still, there is a possibility that an auto compensation plan would substantially increase the costs to be borne by drivers or manufacturers or both.

Workmen's compensation plans promoted industrial safety because employers had previously been almost immune from suit, and because different premium rates could be charged according to the experience of the business: people who run dangerous enterprises are "at fault." Auto compensation plans, however, unless state regulatory authorities allow punitive premium rates, would remove the negligent driver from contact with the consequences of his carelessness, and would lose whatever deterrent effect a fault liability system has. Several promoters of plans have pointed out that tort liability is by no means the only possible way to make people feel concerned about the accidents they may cause. Yale's Guido Calabresi and California's Albert Ehrenzweig have proposed a series of noninsurable "tort fines," a purely criminal sanction, to penalize gross negligence; Michigan's Alfred Conard has sought the same result through dramatic increases in license fees for drivers repeatedly involved in accidents. But it seems doubtful that juries would be willing to vote what would be in effect criminal convictions for merely negligent driving of a kind not penalized by the criminal law itself—and surely the temper of the times is not such that a legislature would establish fee penalties (or insurance premium penalties) which permit driving by the negligent rich but not by the negligent poor.

The deterrence element in existing law is not *necessarily* negligible, whatever the appearances to the contrary. A New York aviation specialist points out that European airlines (which are subject to practically absolute but limited liability for what happens to their passengers) have an accident rate four times that of American airlines (which operate mostly under unlimited liability but only for fault), though both use the same aircraft and equipment manuals. Natural human fright at entanglement with the law may be helping to assure whatever care is now found on our highways.

The morality argument is the hardest for nonlawyers to fathom, or to sympathize with once it is grasped, because its roots lie deep in the relationship between torts and crimes. In its purest form, the argument assumes two individuals; one has been injured; and now society comes to the other, who was innocently involved in the accident, and makes him bear the cost. In the absence of fault, Holmes wrote, "[I]t is no more justifiable to make me indemnify my neighbor against the consequences [of an accident], than . . . to compel me to insure him against lightning." In 1911 the New York Court of Appeals voided that state's first workmen's compensation law on the grounds that compelling an employer to contribute to an insurance fund that would pay out for accidents which were not his fault deprived him of property without due process of law. Dissenting in 1919 from a Supreme Court decision which upheld the right of Arizona to enforce a similar workmen's compensation law, Justice McKenna wrote, "It seems to me to be of the very foundation of right—of the essence of liberty as it is of morals—to be free from liability if one is free from fault."

This argument is obviously strongest when the problem is one of allocating the costs between two innocent individuals; one would expect it to lose some of its force when an insured group rather than a single person becomes liable for the consequences of the collision. Yet Harvard's Robert Keeton, himself the author of a compensation plan, worries about insurance on the grounds that "[E]qual payments per capita would be regarded as grossly unfair to careful persons who cause relatively few of the losses and risks." And Chicago's Blum and Kalven say that "It is almost a sleight-of-hand to reject the fault principle in seeking to broaden the base for recoveries and at the same time to use the fault principle in compelling motorists to carry insurance. Once the law is liberated from fault, motorists can appropriately ask why they should pay anything." Indeed, once fault is taken out of the system, Blum and Kalven see no reason why victims of accidents should be compensated in any way: they "find unpersuasive the argument that the auto accident is to be preferred to cancer as an object for state welfare intervention simply because, due to the development of the common law liability system, the state is already intervening in the one case and not the other."

With this argument, the balloon of sophistry disappears not only from the ken of ordinary mortals, but from the sight of many lawyers. Back on earth, Americans are maiming each other with automobiles at a rate of more than ten thousand a day. Whatever the law may say, there is no real difference in the situations of a victim who can and a victim who can't prove that the other driver was specifically at fault. A rather conservative committee of California lawyers put a pin in the balloon with an italicized observation that "[*T*]*he question for decision today is not whether fault should continue to be the basis of liability, but whether we should continue to recognize a privilege to inflict harm so long as the driver of an automobile acted with reasonable care.*"

In reality, the point is even stronger, because there are many situations where care itself is irrelevant, where a kind of insanity defense protects the guilty driver's insurance company. "Many states," writes Yale's Fleming James, Jr.,

do not exclude persons suffering from heart conditions, diabetes, or epilepsy, where those diseases are under reasonable control. . . . But even when these conditions are controlled they will occasionally produce blackouts or other lapses and, consequently, accidents. Should the victims of these accidents be denied recovery because the driver was not at fault? Should they pay with their injuries for society's choices to let these people drive?

And the question is not, after all, whether individual drivers should pay—it is whether drivers as a whole are entitled to lower insurance premiums simply because some of the accidents that do harm cannot be precisely pinned on an individual's fault.

Behind all these disputes lies the worry of the lawyers that this huge area of their business will be taken away from the law. Compensation plans are, of course, established by law, and lawyers find ways to work in a compensation framework, too. But the essence of compensation is the reduction of conflict, reduction of concern about behavior, reduction of the need to fit individual cases into legal categories.

Whatever the reasons—history, morality, lawyers' self-interest—Americans live with a system of fault liability, and liability is the organizing principle of the negligence lawyers' world: without it there is not merely chaos, there is nothing.

Let us see how the system works.

2

Romantically, we start with death; specifically, with death in an airplane accident. This is a "clean" case: no one can doubt the reality of the injury suffered, or argue that the plaintiff or his heirs caused it themselves. Nevertheless, the question remains so complicated that nearly half of all the aviation negligence work in the country is done by one of two specialist firms in New York: Speiser, Shumate, Geoghan & Krause; or Kreindler & Kreindler. Most of the work is in New York, which is convenient to the insurance companies and the airlines. In these cases there are usually no witnesses to worry about. Both Speiser and Kreindler, however, also do a fair amount of work out of state (and even out of the country), called in by the local lawyers as "associate counsel."

In Speiser's office there are nine lawyers who were pilots or aviation engineers (another of the lawyers is a doctor). A tall man with an easy smile and a casual manner that almost conceals the tension below, Stuart Speiser is the son of a negligence lawyer, but he started out as a pilot. "I'd had a year of law school before the war. Then I was a B-24 pilot, a test pilot, a radar-flight instructor. For a year I dusted crops, then I went back to law school. A year of dusting crops will send you back to anything." His office holds the record for a wrongful death payment against an airline: a verdict of $985,000 (with interest, $1,172,000), ultimately settled by the insurance company for $975,000. The verdict was a triumph of doctrine, because if there was one woman in America who didn't need a million dollars, it was Speiser's client. Her late husband, Arnold Kirkeby, had been a hotel and real-estate speculator, and had left her and his only daughter (age twenty) both a fortune and a house in Beverly Hills known to millions because it was used by CBS as the background shot in Beverly Hillbillies. Nevertheless, the law on wrongful death sets up "pecuniary loss" as the measure of damages; and the very fact that Kirkeby was making so much money gave Speiser's trial partner, William F. X. Geoghan, a magnificent string of figures with which to stupefy the jury. But it is not only the rich who win: the four children of a young middle-income couple ($15,000 a year) who died in the same accident were awarded $755,000 plus interest by another jury.

Though one wouldn't necessarily think so, the great problem with the airplane accident case is the proof of liability: under a fault system, it must be shown that employees of the airline (or of the control tower or the maker of the plane) failed to do something that should have been done and that would have prevented the accident. The plaintiffs can in theory rely on the doctrine of *"Res ipsa loquitur"* ("The thing speaks for itself"—airplanes shouldn't fall down unless somebody did something wrong); but the success of two specialist firms in the field demonstrates that this sort of simple-minded argument, which the most incompetent legal general practitioner could easily make, has been inadequate over the years. Nor can the nonspecialist count on a free ride: the fact that a jury has decided in one case that the airline is liable does not mean that other juries hearing actions by the heirs of someone else killed in the same crash must give the same verdict. Juries are not bound by precedent.

Speiser says that up to the 1950s "the majority of the cases tried were won by the airlines. Most people in this country don't fly, have never flown and have no intention of flying. They regard flying as inherently unsafe, and they don't assume negligence in a crash: they think it's a natural thing for planes to fall down. There's a kind of philosophy of assumption of risk—people who fly get killed. And if you go to a jury on *res ipsa,* and the airline gives you a couple of weeks of testimony from bronzed pilots, the millions of dollars spent training pilots and maintaining planes, the government manuals they follow to the letter—it isn't easy." If the pilot had a heart attack or got shot by his girl friend's ex-boy friend while at the controls, or the volcano blew up while the plane was passing over it, the airline is indeed not liable; and in the absence of any evidence on the other side, an insurance company lawyer can easily create the impression that the whole thing was just freak bad luck (which may be true, too). The plaintiff can sometimes, however, count on the aid of the judge: in one recent aviation case, where the defense was based on a dead bird found in the runway, which might have hit the windshield of the plane at a crucial moment of its descent, the judge called the defense counsel to the bench and told them, "You're not going to give me *birds*—these are *death* cases."

So the work of the aviation specialist begins with the hearings of the Civil Aeronautics Board to determine the cause of the accident. The pilot-lawyers will sit in the audience section of the hearing room, making notes. One of the oddities of the law that set up the CAB is its insistence that the agency's decision as to fault may not be used in evidence in a private lawsuit, and that CAB investigators may not be asked for their opinions by private counsel. While the publicity given a CAB decision undoubtedly helps some cases, the lawyers must build again, from the ground up. "I've won plenty of cases," says Lee Kreindler, "on theories the CAB rejected."

Indeed, Kreindler beat the CAB at its own game in the first case he ever handled. Though the son of a negligence lawyer, he had come out of the Harvard Law School lusting for politics, specifically for the Congressional seat later occupied by John Lindsay. Then a lady who had been injured in a crash outside Newark Airport came in to see his father, and he got interested in her problem. Though there had been some testimony at a CAB hearing that something might have been wrong with the plane's propeller system, official investigators had dismissed this possibility—instead, they had closed Newark Airport as inherently dangerous. "I went to work in a propeller shop in Mineola," Kreindler recalls, "paid the man to let me fool around, and I found out why the plane had crashed. I amended our client's complaint to *punitive* damages for *gross* negligence, because the maintenance logs showed that the propeller system was defective. Lawyers saw the amendment, and we got eleven more cases from that crash; and I've been at it ever since."

Before the CAB has issued its report, lawyers for the victims and their estates have filed suit against the airline. (Shortly after the war, airlines escaped in some cases because the fine print in the ticket had said that suits had to be brought within thirty days of the crash, and while the courts will no longer countenance such procedural unfairness, lawyers are still in the habit of filing early, just in case.) In the aftermath of the CAB hearings, the manufacturer of the plane and perhaps some of its components, or the Federal Aviation Agency (which runs the air traffic control centers in the airports) may be joined as defendants. There then begins a lengthy round of taking depositions, examining potential witnesses before trial (usually with lawyers for both sides present), "discovery" of documents at all the companies and agencies involved. On one recent case, a particularly difficult one because the manufacturer of the plane had to be found liable for reasons we shall examine presently, Kreindler's office invested "four or five years of man-hours" building the argument. Trial in these situations is an anticlimax, and indeed Kreindler's case (the Belgian plane that went down in Brussels, killing the American ice-skating team) resulted in a settlement of $2 million from Boeing and Sabena to the heirs of the victims.

Where the FAA may be liable for nonfeasance in the control tower, settlement is hard. Any settlement the FAA makes must come out of the agency's own already established budget, while a court action is brought against the government rather than against its agency (*respondeat superior* again), and any award is charged against the government's general fund rather than against the agency. (One of the seats of resistance to the ambitions of Robert F. Kennedy is in the FAA, because Kennedy agreed while Attorney General to a settlement of the cases arising out of a collision over Staten Island, which could be blamed in part on the traffic controllers.) Otherwise, the great majority of airline wrongful death cases, like the great majority of all personal injury matters, are disposed of by negotiation.

Damages in these cases tend to be easier to determine than they are in mere injury actions. All sorts of things are compensable in injury actions (including "loss of consortium," a fancy word for sexual intercourse: courts have even worried deeply about how much a wife is entitled to if her husband's accident deprived him of one testicle). But death in most jurisdictions is measured only by loss of income—how much would he have made over a statistically predictable working lifetime. Where the victim was young, the plaintiff tries to prove that he was just at the start of a big career, while the defense tries gently to show that, though a lovely fellow, he really wasn't much of a businessman. Compensation for the death of a child is impossible to calculate rationally, if only because the plaintiffs are the parents, and the cash value of a child's future support of his parents is highly variable in this society.

Damages are assessed as of the moment of injury; if the lady has remarried, that fact is, except in Wisconsin, none of the jury's business—the judge will call the defense lawyer into chambers before the trial begins and tell him in no uncertain terms that if the lady is addressed under her new name he will declare a mistrial. He sometimes does this reluctantly: "Take a case," a judge said recently, "of a woman married to a man earning ten thousand dollars a year. They have a miserable life—they hate each other. A month after he dies, disobeying her attorneys, she marries a millionaire—and now she wants a jury to make her even richer." Remarried widows, however, almost always want to settle—a defense lawyer says that when a plaintiff's lawyer calls him to propose a meeting to discuss settlement, his first question always is, "What's up—does she want to get married?"

In theory, the jury is supposed to keep in mind the fact that its award is tax-exempt and that money given now will earn interest over the years for which it is given—that $300,000 over twenty years, for example, requires a lump sum of something less than $200,000 now. Judges often do not instruct the jury in either of these matters, doubtless because the jury is *not* supposed to consider the fact that lawyers will get a chunk of the award, and failure to reduce to "present value" or calculate the tax exemption will leave margin for the lawyer's fee. The victim's life insurance, of course, may never be mentioned.

Other ways that the lawyer's fee can be got out of the package without diminishing the arithmetical award have been accepted by some courts. Where minor children are involved, they may be compensated for "loss of parental care and guidance." And in some jurisdictions the heirs are entitled to recover for the pain and suffering of any deceased who may have lingered for a while after the accident. "I had a case once," says the New York admiralty lawyer John Martin, who handles both plaintiffs and defendants, "for people who died after fifty hours in the water, people getting chopped up by sharks all around them. The court allowed $30 an hour; then the appeals court reduced it to $15 an hour. I could never figure out how they hit on either figure."

Recoveries can also, as noted above, be limited by statute to a certain maximum figure; and the aviation injury lawyers, who are the most subject to such conflict-of-law problems, are the ones who have taken the lead in changing the law. It was Kreindler who argued *Kilberg* v. *Northeast Airlines,* which led the way toward an abandonment of the rule that courts must apply the law of the place where the accident occurred. In cases involving the Warsaw Convention, an international treaty which limits the amount a passenger can cover on an international flight (up to 1966 the limit was $8,300; now it is $75,000; incidentally, it applies on domestic flights connecting with an international flight if both are on the same ticket), the lawyers were challenged to find ways to blame the manufacturers, who are not protected by the treaty. Hence, Kreindler's man-hour-years on the Brussels accident. Boeing could be made to pay in ways that Sabena couldn't.

Aviation specialists get their clients almost entirely through other lawyers. People who fly are normally well enough off to have wills, and lawyers ready and waiting to administer the estates; from their point of view, the wrongful death action is one of the assets of the estate. They take the matter to Speiser or Kreindler or someone else, reserving for themselves one-third or so of the contingent fee, which is itself usually a third of the award. By getting together a number of plaintiffs to split the costs of doing exhaustive research, the aviation specialist can handle P.I. matters, in Stuart Speiser's words, "like an antitrust case." The technique can be applied to "product-liability" cases, too, as Speiser has shown in the MER/29 drug litigation.

The lawyer who brings the case to the aviation specialist earns his share of the fee by "conditioning" the widow and the family for the settlement, leaving the expert free to work in his area of expertise. "Really," Speiser says, "the relationship is that of barrister and solicitor—though I don't like that word solicitor, it cuts a little near the bone."

3

For each of the roughly 110,000 people killed by accidents in the United States each year, there are a hundred who are merely injured. And whatever complications there may be in wrongful death actions, the legal consequences of airplane crashes are lucidity itself beside the confusion in the much greater area of personal-injury law.

Everybody who has ever served on a jury has a good story from this branch of the law. Mine is a suit brought by a Turkish rug dealer, who had stumbled getting out of one of those old-fashioned freight elevators which close by means of doors that come up from the floor and down from the ceiling. He broke his right thumb, and perhaps suffered back injuries. It was admitted that the door had begun to close when he started out. The Puerto Rican elevator man said he had called out that he was departing. The rug dealer said he hadn't. The rug dealer's Armenian assistant (no longer in his employ) was called by the plaintiff, but testified that maybe the elevator man had said something. (An effort to have him read his previous statement misfired when it developed he couldn't read.) All three men, of course, were testifying in what was to them a foreign language.

The jury was confronted first with the question of liability— under the New York contributory negligence rule, if the elevator man had announced departure, and the rug dealer had simply been careless, recovery could not be allowed. No juror felt any strong reason to believe any of the witnesses. A little old seamstress disposed of contributory negligence with the comment that "He didn't look where he was going—it could happen to anybody—give him his money." Others were unquestionably influenced by their feeling that this sort of elevator was intrinsically dangerous, and its use ought to be discouraged.

On the question of the extent of the damages, plaintiff's lawyer had been quite convincing about the importance of the right thumb to a rug dealer, who must always be pulling out rugs to show to customers, less convincing about the back injury. (Sophisticates on the jury pointed out that the action had been brought in municipal court, where the maximum recovery allowed at that time was $3,000; and a real back injury would have been worth much more than that.) Three of the jurors were disposed to find for the defendant, and it was necessary to reduce the award below $1,500 (half of the amount asked) to bring one of them around and produce the ten votes necessary for a verdict on a New York civil case. But the drama was not yet over, because when the jury was polled a little seamstress voted against the verdict on the grounds that it wasn't enough money—and only a last-instant shift by a tough Irishman who had been the most vigorous on the defendant's side saved our jury from the ultimate embarrassment.

Though the matter was capably tried before a distinguished judge, there wasn't much law to it. There rarely is in personal-injury cases. "This stuff," says negligence specialist Emile Zola Berman, "doesn't come out of books." The point of the trial is to uncover if possible what actually happened at the moment of the accident; nobody has any significant rights to preserve; and judges are disposed to stretch the rules of evidence.

The work of a lawyer with a P.I. case, then, is in gathering evidence to persuade a jury. In some states lawyers will almost immediately start suit, filing their pleadings (copied from a book of forms: the AmJur series of forms offers "1,135 automobile pleading and practice forms") on the understanding that everything may be amended later on; in others negotiations are begun with the insurance company before suit is officially started, and the courts may or may not be called in at a later point. The overwhelming majority of all claims—well over 90 percent in every jurisdiction—are either dropped or settled without trial; but in order to bargain effectively for a settlement the lawyer must be prepared to go to trial. About 45 percent of the cases that go through to a jury verdict (many are settled during the trial, even when the jury is out) are lost by the defendants, often because their lawyers, confident of a settlement up to the last moment, come to court fundamentally unprepared. Specialists win a much higher fraction. "I try about ten cases a year," says New York's Harry Gair. "But I've sworn in a jury in twenty, and I've been prepared to the eyeballs in many more."

Preparation consists in taking depositions from all available witnesses to the accident (on both sides of the case), working out the story that demonstrates your client could not reasonably be held in any way responsible for what happened, collating the data on the economic loss, and going over the medical situation in massive detail to substantiate claims for continuing impairment, pain, headaches, psychological hardship, etc. Everything, from accusations of recklessness to proof of disability, goes to "money up the award"— the jury can give as much as it likes, up to the amount claimed in the complaint, which is commonly much more than plaintiff's lawyer has actually asked for in the courtroom, and often ten times the final settlement price. In states where the business is divided between courts according to the amount at stake, claims are highly inflated to get the plaintiff into the higher-ranking court, if only because the threat that a trivial claim will be treated seriously makes the insurance company more willing to settle. Every personal-injury lawyer has shelves of medical books convenient to hand, and closets full of "medical atlas" material—anatomical drawings and charts that can be displayed to a jury. A few larger firms include a partner who was a doctor before he became a lawyer; and everyone has stringers in the medical profession, available for consultation on forensic medicine and perhaps for testimony at the trial.

Meanwhile, the insurance company is busy, too, with its own investigators exploring the events that led to the accident, its own doctors examining the victim, its own committee analyzing the case and deciding how much the company should have to pay. "The deposition is very important," says a New Hampshire defendants' lawyer, "gives you a chance to see a person: Is he really hurt? What kind of case is it?" The decision on whether to offer anything at all is a very complicated one, involving calculation of the odds on a successful defense and the costs of making it, the nature of the injuries, the reputation of the lawyer on the other side. The size of the offer is mostly a question of climate: "I just settled a case for $23,000," the San Francisco specialist Ernest Leff said recently. "I had estimated it as worth $15,000—but the attorney on the other side had just dropped $225,000 on a case where his client had refused a $50,000 settlement." Much of the work of defending may be done by company investigators; the defense lawyer receives a fairly complete scenario in which to insert his dialogue.

Plaintiffs' lawyers invariably work on a contingent fee, which means that they get a share of the proceeds if their client collects and nothing if he doesn't. By contract, the fee is assessed on the total award, with all court costs, witness fees, payments to stenographers and such coming out of the client's share, but usually such expenses are deducted before the split is made. Defendants' lawyers, by contrast, work on an hourly basis, plus special fees for days in court.

Nobody has really good figures on lawyers' total income from negligence practice, but some calculations are possible. About $5.5 billion of automobile liability premiums was written in 1966, and about 60 percent of that sum, or $3.3 billion, was paid out to claimants on injuries and property damage. Perhaps one-fifth went to people without lawyers. Of the remaining $2.6 billion, about a quarter went in fees to plaintiffs' lawyers—or $650 million. Non-automotive accidents and workmen's compensation cases must have pushed lawyers' income to $850 million—and the fees to defendants' lawyers (who are not called in on every case, but do handle all the larger cases) cannot have been much short of $200 million. The gross income of lawyers in private practice was slightly more than $4 billion. Negligence work would appear to account for at least a quarter of it.

And these cases are, in the splendid understatement of Chicago's Harold A. Smith, "a chief source of merited uncomplimentary remarks about the profession as a whole."

4

From any angle of approach, the realities of the legal consequences of accidents are an unconscionable mess.

To begin with, large numbers of people injured in accidents get nothing at all. A Connecticut study in the early 1930s showed 38.9 percent with nothing, and 71 percent with less than their out-of-pocket medical expenses. In Pennsylvania in 1959, 46.8 percent received nothing, and another 5.4 percent less than half the "tangible loss." Among those seriously injured, whose out-of-pocket loss was more than $3,000, 66.9 percent received nothing or less than half their costs—and these receipts, incidentally, were calculated *before* the subtraction of lawyers' fees. In Michigan in 1960, 51 percent of all victims made no recovery. Even in New York, where the lawyers swarm most ardently around accidents, 16 percent of those injured in 1957-58 got nothing, and the median recovery for those who did collect on a claim was under $300, leaving less than $200 after payment of lawyers' fees—a figure which is supposed to include the costs of repairs to the car.

The costs of running the system are appalling. In Michigan, "the operating costs of the damage system are about 120 percent of the net benefits that go to the injury victims themselves." In Illinois lawyers' fees resulting from accidents total more money than doctors' fees. By contrast, the costs of running Blue Cross and Blue Shield are only about 8 percent of the benefits.

Meanwhile, a number of people are being enriched. The Pennsylvania study showed 18 percent of all victims (one-third of all who recovered anything) receiving more than five times their tangible losses—though it should be kept in mind that these cases were clustered heavily in the lower brackets. Though high awards can be won anywhere (a quick browse through a recent issue of the *Bulletin of the Iowa Academy of Trial Lawyers* shows $81,432 for a herniated disc, $9,187 for a claim of headaches and double vision not supported by medical testimony, $17,500 for "whiplash"), only in New York do insurance companies have to worry about "compensating psychic injury . . . laymen being much oversold on the liability of the ordinary man to traumatic psychosis." But the size of the settlement or award does not measure the extent of the enrichment—because as the law now stands the victim can collect for expenses which have in fact been paid by his own medical or accidental-injury insurance. And the way of the world is that most of the winners in the claims contests are people who *have* received

insurance payments, which the law ignores, while many of the losers
are made destitute.

To achieve these results requires 85 percent of the time of the
civil courts of the United States. In a recent year in California
3,346 out of 4,074 civil juries sworn were impaneled for personal
injury actions. Though less than 5 percent of the actions brought
ever reach the trial state, what does come into court is more than
enough to clog the system. Two and a half years is the normal
wait in most cities from the day a suit is brought to the day a trial
begins; and many calendars are so far behind (Chicago's, for example) that the *average* delay is five years. There is nothing new
about the law's delay—Hamlet listed it as among the reasons for
suicide, and Goethe abandoned the law because he found a backlog
of twenty thousand cases pending in a court which disposed of only
sixty a year. As we shall see in Chapter 13, heroic measures can
bring calendars up to date even in the most congested court, provided judges are willing to use their office to bludgeon settlements
rather than to try cases. In many jurisdictions, however, delay (itself an injustice) breeds ever more delay, corruption of those in
the court who control the calendar, incredible inefficiency and
universal disrespect for the judicial process, a process we need every
once in a while for more serious matters. "I tell you," says an office
boy, returning from a Brooklyn courthouse to the New York offices
of Berman & Frost (very plain waiting room: negligence lawyers
do not waste money), "that place is a *mess*. I'm telling you, they
lost three orders—either that or there's dirty work, somebody's
sitting on 'em."

Among the worst aspects of the court delay is the last-minute waiting around which seems to be its inevitable concomitant. Because the
courts are behind, it is unthinkable that there should be vacant
time in the courtroom, so the calendar is set to make sure another
case is ready to come in the minute the one being heard is finished.
But the next case in line, though it may be more or less ready for
trial, may not be ready at that moment—a lawyer or a witness may
have another engagement—so the court keeps several waiting, just
in case. The friction is vastly increased by the concentration of
many negligence cases in the hands of a few law firms. Much litiga-

tion is against the city or a municipal agency, with a limited staff of "corporation counsel"; nearly all the rest is against insurance companies, each of which typically operates through one or two law firms. A study in Philadelphia indicated that eleven firms handled 40 percent of the entire trial list for the defense.

Plaintiff's cases are less bunched, and a New York study indicated that fifteen thousand lawyers in that city handle negligence matters every year—but three hundred of these lawyers appear to handle no fewer than two thousand such cases. In Pennsylvania the longest wait during the many processes between accident and judgment came between the day the case was put on the calendar for trial and the trial itself—the median was five months for a "normal" case, three years and eleven months for the hundred most delayed. "A lot of delay," says New York's Harry Gair mildly, "is because lawyers are lax." David Peck, now a partner in the Wall Street firm of Sullivan & Cromwell, put the matter rather more bitterly while he was presiding judge of the Appellate Department that serves Manhattan: "Delays do not bother lawyers. A busy lawyer with a lot of cases does not care whether the case he is trying is yesterday's case or yesteryear's case."

Delay in the Courts cites a comment by a Chicago judge that it is "not uncommon for judges to call forty or fifty cases in an unsuccessful effort to find one ready for trial"—and the opposing comment by a Cleveland lawyer that trial work requires

adeptness at crystal gazing and legal legerdemain to guess when the case is likely to be called. . . . At the appointed time, although your case is "next to go," you discover . . . that all of the rooms are engaged with the previous day's cases, or you learn that opposing counsel is engaged in another trial or court. And so, you try to entertain the assembled group by treating them to the conditioning process of watching other trials, and by other means at hand to assuage their unhappiness at being called away from their employment and business and being required just to sit around and wait. The net result is that when the case is finally sent into a room for trial, the litigant has all but given up, and the witnesses have "gone home."

The world's record is apparently held by the federal court in Boston, which kept three lawyers and witnesses waiting two weeks for a chance to impanel a jury—while twenty-seven other cases in which these (and fifty other) lawyers were involved had to be postponed in the state courts. This appalling inefficiency, in addition to all its other evils, multiplies the costs of processing compensation for accidents: lawyers who are subjected to this waste of the time that is all they have to sell must charge fees that would otherwise seem larcenous. In New York the plan to compensate victims of uninsured motorists (up to a $10,000 ceiling) calls for arbitration rather than trial, and lawyers were at first very nervous about it but the plan has now won their ardent loyalty, simply because the arbitrators have been able to provide a "date certain" for every case.

Personal-injury actions are notoriously a source of both intellectual and literal corruption, because there is often nothing to them but money. Especially in the smaller cases, when lawyer and client are strangers to each other, nobody on either side is concerned about what the victim of the accident may need: the entire process, negotiation and trial, focuses on what he can get. Insurance companies promote adjusters who can reach victims (or even victims' widows) before a lawyer gets there, and buy a waiver at a minimum price ("You'll have a hard time with us: we're a lousy insurance company"). In larger actions, insurance companies can "discover you to death," demanding time from counsel and witnesses for examinations before trial, the production of dubiously relevant documents and the like. (In "product liability" cases, where someone is suing for damages suffered through the use of a defective car or dangerous food or dishonestly advertised drug, the defendants can seek to sabotage plaintiffs' "discovery" by supplying too much—in the MER/29 case, the anticholesterol drug which caused cataracts, plaintiffs' motion for discovery produced a trunk packed with microfilms of 120,000 documents.) Because they normally have many cases pending in a court (one insurance company defends a quarter of all the personal injury actions in Brooklyn), insurers "control the calendar," and can manipulate dates to their opponents' disadvantage. In many counties they can in effect threaten a delay of four or five years, and while this threat is somewhat less effective on the victims than is generally believed (most people with substantial claims are getting something from other kinds of insurance in the interim), it can be devastating to the lower class of plaintiffs' lawyers. ("I get calls from the lawyers who refer cases to me," says a specialist;

"they want to discount their share in advance, or push a quick settlement." On the other hand, Robert Gilmore of the American Insurance Association suggests that the companies, because of inflation of awards, dislike delay as much as the plaintiffs: "What's worth a thousand dollars today will be worth fifteen hundred in a few years.") But the poorer the victim, the longer he is likely to wait.

After a case has been tried and a jury has established an award, insurance companies can often force a settlement at a lower price by threatening to appeal, which would probably involve a further delay of anywhere from six months to two years, and would cost the plaintiff's lawyer time and money. Moreover, the victorious plaintiff risks not only a reversal of the verdict, but also in some states a "remittitur," a reduction of the award by the appellate court even though the court affirms the verdict. Though the jurors think they have really finished a case when they deliver their verdict, in fact the verdict can become just another (though a very important) counter in the continuing game of negotiation.

Further problems may be created by the fact that adjusters and defense lawyers sometimes have their own interests to advance. At least two large insurance companies employ adjusters who seek bribes before raising initial offers. "I remember," says a partner in a rather elegant midtown New York office, "we had a client injured leaving this building, and I put it in the hands of one of New York's leading, theoretically most reputable firms in this field. When they sent me the accounting, I was informed I was terribly naïve to question a $2,000 disbursement, because everybody knows you never settle with this company until you *schmeer* the adjuster." This is one of the reasons lawyers are called in only at the end by some insurance companies. But the lawyers themselves are not always without stain. A Pennsylvania survey found that the way defense lawyers are paid significantly delays recoveries: "There is evidence that a significantly large number of cases in Allegheny County are settled only after a jury is sworn in order to allow the attorney to collect his fee for a 'day' in court."

The insurance companies' attack on the plaintiffs' bar begins with questions about the contingent fee. Boston's Reginald Heber Smith wrote fifty years ago that

The contingent fee . . . attracted undesirable persons to become members of the profession. Because the stakes were high and the players essentially gamblers it induced the unholy triumvirate of lawyer-runner-doctor conspiring together to win fraudulent cases. It has degraded expert testimony and served as a cloak for robbery through extortionate fees. Unquestionably, it has done more than anything else to bring the bar into deserved disrepute.

Courts enforce contracts for these fees—often, indeed, the money is paid to the lawyer, who passes on the victim's share. In several states the statute law specifies that lawyers must be paid before liens of doctors and hospitals are satisfied. It is by no means easy for a client to get rid of a lawyer with whom he has signed a contract of this sort; though normally a discharged attorney can collect only for the value of the work he can prove he did (his legal action is called *quantum meruit,* or "How much does he deserve?"). California courts have held that a man who switches lawyers in midstream without the consent of his first lawyer may be liable for the *full* fee to both. The problems are many, and they are bad problems.

Within the bar, the main worry (at least the proclaimed worry) seems always to have been "solicitation"—the tendency of lawyers who work on contingent fees to seek out people who might have cases in which the lawyer could, in effect, buy a share. "Ambulance chasing," so called, seems to have started in New York around 1907, when law offices hired newspaper reporters and their friends to get lists of accidents from the police and to follow up the names with visits to the hospitals. Presently this process was short-circuited through direct contacts with ambulance drivers, hospital attendants and doctors. It was a risky business, because the solicitation payroll had to be met and until liability insurance became general there was always a danger that even a good case would yield no pay-out.

Today solicitation is much safer and much better organized. Labor unions and even social clubs are a major source of negligence business—as indeed they should be, despite the Canon of Ethics to the contrary, because at the least they can assure the plaintiff that his lawyer's interests in the matter extend beyond his isolated action. More dubious is the mechanized ambulance chasing of law firms which keep a radio car on the road, manned by a photographer who tunes in on the police and follows along to any major accident.

Word is then passed to the victim or the victim's family that such and such a law firm has pictures of the accident, names and addresses of the witnesses, and is all ready to start on the case.

In slum communities there are recognized brokers for law firms, usually tied in with other rackets. Irving Reichert of San Francisco remembers that when he left the district attorney's office and set up in practice for himself he had a visit from a hood whose admiration he had won while prosecuting him; and the hood said he controlled all the undertakers in town and could deliver a lot of business, and with Reichert's reputation and skill and his contacts they could both make a fortune. He was hurt and quite puzzled when Reichert turned him down. Probably the most frequent runner today, however, is the neighborhood lawyer. "In some cities," MacKinnon wrote in his American Bar Foundation study of contingent fees, "a few attorneys have 'specialized' in locating clients and referring them to others for a share in the fee. These men are not practicing law, and conditions which create such a group introduce a commercial attitude which is detrimental to the bar as a whole." That's a nice way to put it.

To the extent that the people who sign the retainers do have legitimate claims, however, no harm is done to the society by a mechanism which leads the victims of accidents to recover for their injuries. The old horror of "stirring up litigation" ought not to be felt when the litigant is an injured man with a valid claim. Where the difficulty arises is with the fraudulent claim. Such swindles are stimulated by the availability of money from insurance companies more than by the existence of contingent fees for lawyers (they are also common in Britain, where contingent fee arrangements are criminal); but lawyers are more likely to be involved in such jiggery-pokery when they can share the proceeds.

Somewhere between the fraudulent claim and the legitimate lawsuit is the case which is improved by perjury. Anyone who has served on a jury has observed that the witnesses as well as the lawyers are partisans for their side (made even more partisan by counsel's warning about the lawyer on the other side and the way he will cross-examine). The lawyer's job is to pull out of the witness the best story he can pull, and if the resulting testimony stretches the truth pretty far, the lawyer can console himself with the thought that he is, after all, engaged in an adversary proceeding. The theory is that cross-examination will expose lying and lead jurors on the path of truth, so restraints are automatic. It is a good theory, and common-law countries have built much of their court system on it, but it is by no means a demonstrated truth. Judge Joseph C. Hutcheson, Jr. once wrote that "at the end of eleven years upon the Bench, I am more convinced than ever that the shrewdest, smartest liars make the best witnesses."

The perjury problem seems to trace back to Adam and Eve and the snake, and courts have worried about it since there first were courts. Henry Charles Lea has written that wager of battle became popular in medieval Europe "as the most practical remedy for the crime of false swearing which was everywhere prevalent." To the extent that perjury in a negligence case deals with liability questions, it is largely excused—one could say it is dictated—by the stupidity of the contributory negligence rule, which forces people whose claims are valid by all standards other than those of Lord Ellenborough to improve on an already convincing story. Unfortunately, the practice extends to testimony about damages suffered: the money in personal-injury lawsuits has corrupted two professions.

"A sample study of cases in the Supreme Court of New York," David Peck wrote while he was presiding judge of the Appellate Department,

revealed that in a quarter of the cases there were gross errors in the reading of X-rays and that in over a quarter of the cases essential tests to warrant a diagnosis were not made. We may accept with a certain equanimity the controversies presented as to the facts of how an accident happened and who was to blame. . . . It is disturbing, however, indeed disgusting, to find such variations as frequently exist on the professional plane of medical testimony.

Allegedly to speed up trials, but actually to police the ethics of another profession, the New York and later the Los Angeles courts instituted the practice of testimony by an impartial doctor appointed from a rotating panel and paid by the county. This procedure has been opposed, the California Judicial Council reported, on the alleged ground that there is uncertainty and disagreement within the medical profession which causes each doctor to favor a particular school of thought. Thus it is claimed that under the rotating panel a case may be won or lost depending on the view of the doctor next in line. It is also contended that because the jury tends to regard the impartial expert as an arm of the court, effective cross examination is prevented.

Doubts have been expressed that the average level of competence of doctors is good enough for the law to rest so much weight on any one piece of medical testimony: "The members of the Vienna Bar," Chicago's Hans Zeisel once commented, "still remember the case in which the chief anatomy expert of the criminal court, Professor Haberda—this was at the time when Vienna's medical schools led the world—declared with assurance that some dismembered limbs came from the body of a young girl, when they later were quite definitely proved to have belonged to an old man." Advocates of any change in legal procedure are always required to measure the likely results of their reform against a standard of perfection. By comparison with the scandal that results in the absence of impartial medical testimony, however, the reform seems admirable.

Even where perjury is unnecessary, among lawyers who are prosperous enough to accept only good cases, the contingent-fee arrangement places the lawyer under uncomfortable stress. Among the hypothetical situations presented to lawyers in New York by Jerome Carlin in his study of ethics was one where an adjuster tells a lawyer whose clients have a number of claims against his company that there is a low ("almost fair") ceiling on this one but he can make it up on the others. The responses to this item were overwhelmingly negative—few lawyers were willing to say they would ever make such a deal—and of the thirteen hypothetical situations in Carlin's questionnaire this "package deal" was the third most likely to call forth what Carlin considered an "ethical" action: refusal to go along. In practice, if not in talking to sociologists, lawyers do it all the time. The standard phrase is "I gave in a hundred dollars on Roe, you come up a hundred dollars on Doe."

Moreover, if he can trust the claims agent, the lawyer *should* go along, because any gains to his client from taking the case through the entire process to improve an "almost fair" offer are more than counterbalanced by the higher costs, the 45 percent risk of losing on trial and the additional years of delay. Anyway, there is no law (and not even a very enforceable Canon of Ethics) which says a lawyer in this situation cannot make it up to his client by cutting his fee—and this happens all the time, too. (Indeed, the New York negligence bar defended itself against Judge Wasservogel's discovery that three-fifths of all contingent-fee contracts called for a 50-50 split by arguing that in the actual settlements the fees were not collected on that basis.) Still, the situation is awkward, because giving in on one case and getting back on others may yield the lawyer a higher total fee, and he doesn't like the thought that in any of his cases he has a possible conflict of interest with his client.

For the successful negligence practitioner, the conflict is often much more subtle than that. His credibility as a bargainer rests on his ability to try and win cases; once a case is prepared and he has confidence in it, he is tempted to turn down an offer very near what he expects to get from the trial, simply to improve his bargaining power. "The case we tried and won last week," says an Iowa specialist, "will determine the kind of settlements we make over the next three months. Any one client might be better off with a quicker and lower settlement, but all our clients benefit by our reputation for preparation and trial." A deeper and more disturbing conflict is in the lawyer's desire to see the client come into a courtroom in the worst imaginable shape, though this command appearance may be four or five years after the accident. "[T]he law as it now stands," a California Bar committee wrote in 1965, "may positively discourage the rehabilitation of victims of automobile accidents, retarding the time when they can return to useful activity . . . it is more remunerative, as the law is made to appear to laymen, *not* to be rehabilitated." And it is lawyers, of course, who make the law so appear to laymen—they will get a third or more of whatever extra money may be earned by a victim's continued sufferings, and they don't suffer.

For most plaintiffs' lawyers, there is something intolerably unfair about even the hint that their interests might at any time be different from their clients'. They identify with their clients. They live surrounded by the human wreckage which is an ignored but inevitable part of the American Way of Life, and with cynical but accurate knowledge that in most cases nothing of substance will be done for these victims unless their lawyers fight. "Secretly," says an observer from the law schools, "these men are suing society."

"You have to live your case," says Jacob Fuchsberg, a muscular, balding New Yorker with a square jaw, who works in shirt sleeves, his skis leaning against the bookshelves, in the twentieth floor offices of Fuchsberg & Fuchsberg, a negligence firm of twenty lawyers. Fuchsberg was president of the National Association of Claimants' Counsel when that organization changed its name to the more prestigious (and probably more accurate) American Trial Lawyers Association. "When you say a man is objective, you're not describing a good lawyer. When a case is about to come to trial, I'm hard to settle with, because I've come to know the *people*, not just the file. There may have been an estimate of what the case was worth— which I concurred in superficially—but now I know the *people*." A California negligence specialist, who has himself overcome a severe physical handicap, says, "I have this client whose leg was amputated. I get terribly upset when he drinks; he's hurting *my* case."

At the top of the personal-injury bar one does not find the atmosphere of fraud and incompetence so common in the foothills. It is the lawyer who handles occasional accident cases, who regards them as windfall gains which are his right as the proprietor of a license, who is most likely to come to court with a case thrown together from unexplored self-serving testimony by dubious witnesses and doctors; and it is his lack of preparation and bumbling in the courtroom that gives defendants a record of winning 45 percent of jury verdicts. ("People come in," Fuchsberg says, "and tell me a case has turned unfavorable because the witness was a dope or was surprised by the other counsel; ninety-nine times out of a hundred it's the lawyer's fault.") The specialist must have a reasonably good moral reputation, if only because many of his clients will be referred to him by other lawyers, who want their referral fees badly enough, but certainly don't wish to risk being involved in trouble. All good negligence lawyers are dramatists and actors ("It's like putting on a biographical play," Fuchsberg says), but they are also something more.

"One thing a lot of these fellows have in common," says the executive director of an insurance group, invariably on the other side, "is that if they weren't doing this they could be great salesmen. They have a lot of savoir-faire, they're great fun to be with. They all work like hell, and they're very able. You know, many of them would be the leaders of the bar in this country—the presidents of the bar associations, the senior partners of the big firms—except that they didn't go to the fancy law schools, they're Jews, the jobs weren't open to them when they started. I admire them."

In the end, the defense of the contingent fee is that it has secured for myriads of poor, friendless and damaged people a quality of representation no other device can approach. A few years ago the sociologist Jack Ladinsky, in an acticle that has been much copied, stated that

Partly because legal talent from quality law schools has flowed heavily into the large firms for many years, there has been extensive elaboration of legal procedures to handle the problems of corporate enterprises as opposed to those to care for the problems of private citizens. The result has been a high development of corporate protection, often at the expense of individual citizens. In addition, areas of law unrelated to the operation of corporate enterprises have not had the same level of creativity devoted to them. Developments in public and private welfare, personal injury, divorce, home finance, etc. have been less dramatic than developments in corporate taxation, mergers, stocks and bonds, etc.

The fascinating thing about this observation is its almost universal acceptance by lawyers, sociologists, politicians and journalists —even though it is cockeyed. The development of law for fifty years in the United States has been overwhelmingly in the direction of restricting corporations and safeguarding individuals. Particularly in the area of recovery for personal injury, for all the gaps in the coverage, ordinary people in the United States are infinitely better off than they have ever been before, and their protection has increased at an accelerating rate since the war.

Looking back from midstream on a career replete with exciting discoveries of loose screws that proved liability for airplane crashes, Lee Kreindler spoke with particular pleasure of the *Kilberg* case, where New York refused to apply the Massachusetts limitation on wrongful death recoveries in a Massachusetts accident involving a

New Yorker. "All these things," he said, "are distasteful—they're personally and professionally troubling. But I've made a real contribution to a fundamental revolution in choice of law. It's very nice to know I've *done* something."

When Kreindler argued *Kilberg,* his chances of winning it were minuscule. Every major negligence lawyer has cases in his files which he is nearly certain to lose, and which he will fight because a victory would open up large new areas of liability. All over the country, lawyers are probing the law for ways to hold cigarette companies liable in lung cancer. Fuchsberg remembers a case where four ladies were injured in a taxicab which hit a pillar of an elevated transit line. "The driver had only ten thousand dollars' insurance," Fuchsberg says. "The other lawyers *gave* me the case, they thought it was so hopeless. I developed a theory that the pillar was obscured, and the city was liable. We won it, and the Appellate Division reversed; we won it again, and the Appellate Division reversed again. Then I settled it with the city, got a hundred thousand dollars, and the case of Fuchsberg versus the Appellate Division was closed."

The plaintiffs' lawyers have earned their fees. Every study shows that representation by a lawyer improves both the chances and the size of a claimant's recovery. The Pennsylvania survey showed 111 of 117 victims with lawyers recovering *something,* but only 65 of 194 who were unrepresented. In a New York sample of cases which yielded less than $1,000, and were thus least likely to command a high order of legal talent, claimants without counsel averaged only $158, while claimants with counsel averaged $233 after the deduction of the lawyer's fee. These studies are not fully convincing, because their results can be as well explained by lawyers' sagacity in choosing clients as by the value of the lawyers' services. Better, if less conclusive, evidence comes from Boston, where after a few years of experience with a workmen's compensation law which encouraged claimants to appear without lawyers by allowing only impossibly low fees to be paid out of the award, the local Legal Aid Society opened a workmen's compensation division to make sure its clients received reasonable settlements.

Both in terms of making the law more just (or charitable), and in terms of improving the recoveries of individual victims, the negligence bar has performed well. It is shocking to lawyers, but fairly obvious to nonlawyers, that one of the secrets of the success is the willingness of men to fight especially hard when they are fighting for themselves. Two-thirds of the benefits, however, go to people most of whom could not possibly afford to hire legal talent of the quality now available to them. Whatever system replaces the current procedures, the people organizing it should be careful to insure that the new ways do not punish the impoverished victims of a mechanical society.

5

That there will be changes, and major changes, can scarcely be doubted. Even if the P.I. lawyers really are Robin Hood, the fact remains that Merry Men are no longer a satisfactory system for adjusting social inequity. At present, personal-injury law fails to compensate a large fraction of the victims of accidents and unjustly enriches others, clogs the courts so badly that a fundamental institution in the society is degraded, corrupts a good fraction of the bar, the medical profession and the citizenry, and removes a basic question of social welfare and social justice from the realm of public policy to the trivial arena of squabbling among lawyers. The current system is also shockingly expensive to run, quite apart from the lawyers' fees and insurance company profits: Judge Botein estimates that the average accident trial in New York costs $3,000 for the people who work in and around the courts, and that New Yorkers lose half a million days of work a year serving as jurors. A little arithmetic yields for New York alone a cost figure (including lost production) of about $20 million a year, which is not a fortune as governmental budgets go, but does add up to more than $200 for every automobile accident in the city.

"I'm very disturbed about the negligence situation," says Whitney North Seymour, Wall Street lawyer and former president of the American Bar Association. "But whenever I bring it up, they tell me about all the lawyers all over the country who would be forced out of the profession." Reform from inside seems impossible. "[T]o put it bluntly," Justice Walter Schaefer of the Illinois Supreme Court told a meeting of the Chicago Bar, "there are vested interests in the existing pattern, on all sides." But with injuries from automobile accidents running at a rate of more than four million a year, the problem is too large to be dealt with as a question of what might be best for lawyers. "Was it Louis XIV who said, 'After me, the deluge'?" Schaefer inquired sweetly. "Too much of that attitude permeates our bar, and, curiously, the very segment of the bar that has the biggest stake in the current procedures."

Pieces of this chaos are under constant discussion in the law reviews. Projects for reforming the law include compensation plans which would guarantee all victims their actual losses (after medical insurance) up to a maximum of $800 to $10,000 (leaving fault liability for everything thereafter); proposals that the states adopt the most common European principle, that a driver shall be held liable unless demonstrably *not* at fault; even really drastic suggestions that legal arrangements be abandoned entirely and everyone be insured against anything that might happen *to* him. There are at least as many proposals to drain the swamp in the courts by eliminating juries or splitting trials or arbitrating; and we shall look at some of these ideas in Chapter 13.

Changes are most likely to result from developments in the larger world. Improved Medicare and expanded Social Security will lessen (not eliminate) the need for tort compensation; escalating premium rates may make a system of liability without fault look relatively less expensive. Meanwhile the P.I. specialists see two clouds on the horizon. The more remote is the federalization of accident law. In the aviation field some sort of national legislation is clearly needed to assure that victims of a crash receive the same protection regardless of the state they fall into, and that fellow passengers on the same ill-fated plane will not be treated differently according to their state of residence. In the automobile area, the passage of national safety legislation is surely a first step toward a national policy on injuries suffered in accidents—even the existing legislation probably establishes new liabilities to tort action in federal courts by injured people who can trace their injury to the failure of an automobile manufacturer to meet national safety standards. Any large-scale transfer of negligence cases to the federal courts would create an entirely new situation, if only because the political patronage of the courts is much less important to Congressmen than to state legislators.

Nearer to hand is the great expansion of legal aid offices, financed through the Office of Economic Opportunity. Though such offices have never handled "plaintiffs' cases," and are pledged not to begin now, the bar is uneasily conscious of the fact that poor people who see lawyers working for them on other questions will turn to these lawyers (rather than to today's brokers and runners) when somebody gets hurt.

Because of this fear that P.I. business will be lost, objections to the new tax-supported neighborhood law offices have come primarily from the lower levels of the bar. Liberals have been scandalized by the fact that it is the Negro lawyers who have fought the establishment of such offices in Negro slums, to the point of bringing court action in Washington to prevent it. Robert Spangenberg of the Boston University Law School, who has been helping the Office of Economic Opportunity with its problems, says that these worries are wholly artificial: "The man in the automobile accident case finds a lawyer. In Worcester, at a meeting of the bar association, somebody raised the question. I asked the director of legal aid how many automobile cases had come into his office for referral in the last ten years. He said, 'That's easy. Two.'"

Up to now, undoubtedly, the neighborhood law offices have on balance generated business for the negligence bar. "We had a boy come in here," says Gilbert Douglas, a young investigator for a Washington legal aid office; "he'd broken his foot in a parking lot owned by a tire company; and the lawyer for the tire company told him since it happened on private property he couldn't sue! We sent him to a private lawyer." But over the long run parallel legal establishments for poverty cases and poor people's plaintiff's cases cannot survive. Contingent fees may be justified, as Lord Denning once said in a highly critical lecture about the errors of countries not lucky enough to be Britain, when "the arrangements help a poor person to get justice whereas without it he could not afford to take the risk of litigation himself. No such excuse exists in a country which has legal aid."

CHAPTER 8

THE IDEA OF JUSTICE

AND THE POOR

"If we are to keep our democracy, there must be one command-ment: Thou shalt not ration justice."

—LEARNED HAND

"Justice is not free. It's a luxury you have to pay for."

—ROBERT P. BASS, of the
New Hampshire Bar

"Perhaps we shall even find at times that when talking about justice, the quality we have in mind is charity."

—BENJAMIN CARDOZO

"Don't I think a poor man has a chanst in court? Iv coorse he has. He has the same chanst there that he has outside. He has a splendid poor man's chanst."

—MR. DOOLEY

1

Every legal system serves the purposes of its society, though the lawyers within the system may be no more conscious of these purposes than a fish is of water. Even in the most uncomplicated society the purposes are various enough to cause confusion: Deuteronomy was written to meet the needs of a wandering warrior tribe which had difficulty maintaining its separate tribal identity; and the exegesis of the document has absorbed the energies of more than two millennia of highly intelligent men. In modern Europe and the United States, the central purpose has been the promotion of economic production. As Max Weber put it, "[T]he existence of a capitalist enterprise is preconditioned by a specific kind of 'legal order.'"

Historians have never explained satisfactorily how Britain and the United States arrived, half-consciously, at the decision that exclusively private ownership and control of the means of production would yield the greatest output. This conclusion, with its inevitably concomitant downgrading of the state as an institution, formed a political society fundamentally different from that of the European continent, where economic production continued to rest on state monopolies. Reliance on private ownership was carried furthest in the United States: the Fifth Amendment to the Constitution not only protects people against compulsory self-incrimination; it also proclaims that "private property shall [not] be taken for public use, without just compensation." (Every time a highway or a school is built, property owners "take the Fifth.") One need not accept completely the Marxist view of law as merely a "superstructure" expressing the interests of the dominant class to recognize private property as the central institution of the American legal system.

The great rebuke to this institution, from the moment of its triumph in the eighteenth century (when the poet saw "wealth accumulate and men decay"), has been its neglect of the questions most conveniently lumped under the label "social justice." If the most fundamental purpose of the system is the protection of private property, what happens to the propertyless? A key element in the faith of the Founding Fathers was that there would be no such class in the United States: the eastern third of the continent would be large enough to provide property for all. Even before the Civil War, this faith had been proved false.

Roscoe Pound saw the difficulty nearly half a century ago. "American common law assumed that there were no classes and that men normally dealt with one another on equal terms and at arm's length," he wrote. ". . . [O]ur common-law polity presupposes an

American farming community of the first half of the nineteenth century." The essence of this community was not the individuality and independence asserted by Pound (who all his long life distrusted arguments that rested on economics); below these social phenomena lay the fact of virtually universal ownership of property. The debtor so solicitously protected in the West was not propertyless in origin; one did not acquire debts without property in the nineteenth century.

In its bones the system knew what it was doing: it was stimulating production by protecting the producer. Courts refused to hold manufacturers liable for damage done by their products or grant claims against railroads. When the farmers demonstrated that they could increase the yield of the land by fencing it, the cattlemen became outlaws. Producers with employees could not be held accountable for what happened to the labor force on the job. "[T]he basic principle of freedom of contract," Lord Devlin once said grimly, "included freedom to oppress." In the name of an eternal Law, the courts voided the income tax, wage-and-hour legislation, restrictions on child labor, prohibitions on the yellow-dog contract and much, much else. Injustice to the propertyless was considered a low price to pay for unrestricted opportunity to increase production.

Lawyers, of course, did not talk so practically about the matter—particularly in the nineteenth century, which was the heyday of rights and liberties, of logic in the law. It was not until the 1950s that a court explicitly argued (now for the benefit of a new exploiter) that tort risks must be curtailed to serve social policy. The statement was by Justice Stanley Reed, for a Supreme Court divided 4-3 (Justices Douglas and Clark abstaining) in denying the liability of the federal government for the Texas City port disaster in 1947, a disaster that would certainly have been avoided if the fertilizer being shipped out as part of a foreign aid program had been labeled the explosive substance it was. "The decisions held culpable," Justice Reed wrote, "were all responsibly made at a planning rather than an operational level and involved considerations more or less important to the practicability of the Government's fertilizer program. . . . [A]cts of subordinates in carrying out the operations of government in accordance with official direction cannot be actionable." Sovereign immunity having been waived by Congress, the government succeeded to the privileges and immunities of private employers in the nineteenth century, because its purposes were overridingly important.

Not only was the "substantive law" loaded against the property-less man in nineteenth-century Anglo-America; his access to the system in cases where he might have the law on his side was cynically denied by the imposition of high fees before an action could be brought. As late as the 1950s New Haven required a $70 cash bond before a tenant could have a jury trial (or an appeal from a magistrate's ruling) on an eviction notice, and Georgia would not even allow a tenant to file an answer in a rent case without a surety bond double a month's rent. The British phrase was that "the courts are open to all—like the Savoy Hotel."

There was a chance of going to court *in forma pauperis,* an option first opened, quite magnificently, by Henry VII in 1495:

That every poor person or persons which have or hereafter shall have causes of action against any person within this realm shall have by the discretion of the Chancellor of this realm, for the time being, writs or writs original, and subpoenas according to the nature of their causes, therefore nothing paying to your Highness for the seals of the same, nor to any person for the writing of the said writs to be hereafter sued; and that the said Chancellor shall assign clerks to write the same writs ready to be sealed; and also learned counsel and attornies for the same, without any reward taken therefor.

At the turn of the twentieth century, however, such anachronisms had all but vanished from the living law—"if, indeed," Geoffrey Hazard of the American Bar Foundation comments, "they had ever been part of it."

"Denial of justice," the Bostonian Reginald Heber Smith wrote in his landmark book of 1919, *Justice and the Poor,*

. . . actively encourages fraud and dishonesty. Unscrupulous employers, seeing the inability of wage-earners to enforce payments, have deliberately hired men without the slightest intention of paying them. . . . Everywhere [the system] abets the unscrupulous, the crafty, and the vicious in their ceaseless plans for exploiting their less intelligent and less fortunate fellows. The system not only robs the poor of their only protection, but it places in the hands of their oppressors the most powerful and ruthless weapon ever invented.

By the time Smith wrote, it had become clear to most men, though not to the Supreme Court interpreting the Constitution, that an established economy no longer needed such extraordinary protection, and that the rules which had been (subconsciously) promulgated to promote production had begun to serve nonproductive fraud. Elihu Root, conservative corporate lawyer, demanded that the poor receive access to the courts and to justice:

> Our procedure ought to be based on the common intelligence of the farmer, the merchant, and the laborer. And there is no reason why it should not be. I say it not without experience in legal procedure. There is no reason why a plain, honest man should not be permitted to go into court and tell his story and have the judge before whom he comes permitted to do justice in that particular case, unhampered by a great variety of statutory rules. . . . We have got our procedure regulated according to the trained, refined, subtle, ingenious intellect of the best practiced lawyers, and it is all wrong.

Smith and Root were arguing for two separate but related reforms: "legal aid," which would supply lawyers to help the poor man assert his rights, and municipal or small-claims courts, which ordinary people could use without the interposition of lawyers and legal costs. Both were already in existence, though not commonplace; indeed, the small-claims courts were at their apogee, revealing the charm of essentially lawless justice unencumbered by rules of evidence or judicial reticence (Smith was delighted with the judge in Boston who, faced with a dispute between landlady and boarder over the value of a mattress he had ruined smoking in bed, called a local department store to find out how much such a mattress cost); not yet revealing their potential as a cheap and easy way for retail creditors to dun poor debtors. The first Legal Aid Society had been organized as long before as 1876 (as *Der Deutsches Rechtschutz Verein,* obviously for German immigrants)—indeed, by the time Smith wrote there were already fake Legal Aid societies, set up to swindle the poor.

Though some of the Legal Aid societies were established as part of the settlement-house movement, most of them were or-

ganized by the bar association. Among the proudest of the
Canons of Ethics is one that obliges lawyers to accept clients
on the merits of their cases, without regard to whether they can
pay a lawyer's fee. Psychologically, the Legal Aid bureaus relieved
lawyers of their guilt at failing to live up to their code ("The
lawyers willing to represent the poor," Eustace Seligman of Wall
Street's Sullivan & Cromwell said in 1949, "have gradually become
limited to those with a high sense of public duty or those who take
the cases in order to squeeze a few pitiful dollars out of the poor
man and his family"); practically, the bureaus gave lawyers a place
to which they could refer people whom as human beings they could
not simply kick out the door. As recently as 1963, Orison Marden,
who was president of the National Legal Aid and Defender Association before he was president of the American Bar Association,
estimated that about one-third of the annual budget of the nation's
Legal Aid offices (then about $8 million) was being met by con-
tributions from lawyers as individuals or through their bar associations. The lawyers' contributions were a microtithe of about one-
tenth of one percent of the profession's fee income.

The day-to-day function of these Legal Aid offices was to protect
people who were being overreached by landlords, salesmen, employers or just plain crooks. A broader function was to get laws
and court procedures changed, and to make official governmental
bodies undertake the enforcement of legal rights which poor people
could not uniformly assert for themselves. To Smith in 1919, it seemed
that what enabled thieves to take people off the boat and work them
without paying them was the problem of court costs (filing fees
were often greater than the money to be recovered) and court procedure, which required a lawyer. But even the provision of a free
lawyer and free access to the courts proved insufficient, because the
employer could still try his luck. Legal aid, having demonstrated
its own ineffectiveness, could then successfully promote legislation
which made it a crime not to pay wages, and placed the enforcement of the law in the hands of a public officer (usually a labor
commissioner of some sort). It was the experience of the New York
Legal Aid Society with landlord-and-tenant law that led to the
legalization of rent strikes in New York State, and the inability of

Legal Aid to protect people from gouging by retailers and small-loan companies (despite the usury laws) that produced the reform of laws relating to installment buying in New York in 1957-58. The fundamental change is that an installment contract must now precisely describe the goods purchased, giving the buyer an out if they are not what was promised. Meanwhile, of course, individual clients by the thousands were helped in individual ways.

2

At 125th Street and Lenox Avenue, in the heart of Harlem, stands a three-story walk-up office building with wooden stairs and a damp smell. Since 1950 the New York Legal Aid Society has had a branch here, and a large one, about fifteen lawyers in individual cubicles made by wood-and-glass partitions through which one can (but just barely) hear the mutter of voices next door. There is a large reception room with rows of folding chairs, and against one wall a bilingual, English-Spanish receptionist sits at a metal desk. A big air-conditioning duct system hangs incongruously from the pressed-metal ceiling. As people arrive, the receptionist takes some basic data on a card and gives a number and some reading matter: "The attorney will call you *today* any time after registration. You must have patience. Otherwise, if you cannot wait, please come back another day. Thanks."

Most of the people in the folding chairs are glum. A few are reading, a few are whispering to each other; but mostly they just sit, as the poor will in America, not reading, not talking, not sleeping, just sitting. All are poor—Legal Aid societies everywhere restrict their clientele to people whose income is below $60 a week (even as low as $45 a week in some places), plus $10 a week for each dependent. And even within this group, the society will reject people with "plaintiff's cases," damage suits which a private lawyer would be prepared to tackle on a contingent fee.

The cases are in one way all different, because the people are different. Legally, they are highly repetitious. Two-fifths are family problems, even though New York's, like most Legal Aid societies, is immensely reluctant to process divorces.

"He's living with another woman. . . ."

"He down in D.C.; he supposed to send thirty dollars a week for the children, but he don't do it, you know. . . . He say he got no job but there's that retirement fund. . . ."

And on the other side, too:

"She won't let me see the children—it says I'm to see the children, but she won't let me. . . ."

"It's six years I been livin' with somebody else, we never got no divorce, now my older kid's ready for school, I want him legitimate. She don't know I got kids now; she always wanted kids and we never had 'em, and I been scared to tell her. . . ."

Second in importance are landlord-and-tenant complaints, where the persistence of the rent-control laws in New York give Legal Aid a handle that does not exist elsewhere. If the cause of the eviction is nonpayment of rent, payment of the rent plus $4.50 costs for the eviction notice automatically puts a stop to the action. If the landlord argues that the tenant is for some reason undesirable (dirties up the halls, peddles dope, fights with the neighbors, etc.), the case must in theory be proved in court (in fact, because courts can consider only the evidence before them and the tenant doesn't show up, the landlord's uncontested statement is often proof enough). New York has also broken with the old pattern of landlord-and-tenant law by which a landlord's violations of a lease could be effectively protested only by court action—that is, the tenant owed the rent whether or not the place was habitable, and could put pressure on the landlord only by taking him to law. Now a group of tenants can "strike," paying their rent to a court rather than to a landlord, building a fund which the landlord can be forced to spend on repairs. Such "rent strikes," however, turn out to be heartbreakingly difficult to organize and sustain.

In Washington, by contrast, says Julian Dugas, who runs that city's Neighborhood Legal Services Project, "people are tenants by sufferance. Landlord can put a padlock on the door, take over a person's goods, there isn't much she can do about it." Elsewhere, significantly, matters may be better not because the law is better but because its administration is more humane. "In nonpayment of rent," says Theodore Wadleigh, Jr., the one-man volunteer Legal

Aid office of Manchester, New Hampshire, "the landlord has to give notice the length of the renting period, usually a week; then they give a landlord-and-tenant writ, and in another week there's a hearing. But the district court will look for all the technicalities of law, try to throw out the writ. And the sheriff is good about it—as a practical matter, he won't move people out. Or he'll wait till he has two eviction notices, and he'll switch the tenants."

Quite apart from its notorious impersonality, New York has problems in these areas that other places don't have. All evictions begin with the filing of an application in a court (often by the landlord himself, following formulas drawn up by the lawyer for the real-estate owners' association), and the tenant must then be notified to appear and defend himself. The requirement in New York is "nail and mail"—one copy of the notice must be nailed to the door and another mailed to the occupant. The person who nails to the door is a city marshal, a political appointee whose income derives from the fees he is paid for this and similar jobs. As an official, he carries authority when he says he nailed the notice to the door; but much of the time he didn't do it, partly because it is easier to make money when you collect fees for work you haven't done, partly because the nailing of eviction notices to doors in some parts of New York City is dangerous work for which people would be entitled to more money than marshals actually receive. The jargon for what the marshal does is "sewer service"—the notice is thrown down the sewer. By the time the tenant shows up at Legal Aid, a few days later, having received a mysterious notice in the mail, a dispossess order may have been issued. The Legal Aid lawyer can usually get a quick "order to show cause," which gives a day's delay and may reopen the case. But the job is not made any easier by the tendency of the tenants in the slums to fear and secrete official-looking pieces of paper.

"It's remarkable," says Edith Lorraine Miller, wife of the editor of *Christian Herald,* who works in Legal Aid's Harlem office, "how they clutch a piece of paper. You'll say, 'Do you have the dispossess?' And she'll say, *'In casa.'* She has it well hidden."

Next on the case list in New York—and ahead of housing in many cities, where installment buying is less well regulated—is the con-

sumer problem. Here the evils of sewer service are compounded. The
ritual is that a finance company sends an employee or a lawyer (one
lawyer handles a quarter of all this work in Brooklyn) to file in
court a complaint against somebody who hasn't paid. The complaint calls for an answer in court by a certain day, and must be
served by a process server. On that day the complainant or his
lawyer turns up with an affidavit from the process server to say the
document was handed to the defendant. (Sometimes the affidavit is
quite demonstrably false: in a recent case in Manhattan, the process
server swore to a story of ringing the bell, identifying the defendant
and handing him the paper, when the defendant was in fact in
jail.) If the defendant has made no answer to the complaint, judgment for the plaintiff is entered by default.

A study made by the pioneer poverty agency, Mobilization For
Youth, found that only a third of the defendants were ever notified
of the action at all. (Though there is no doubt the practice is
routine, MFY's percentages are suspect, because the investigators
could find only thirty of the three hundred people they chose from
court records as their sample; and a statement by a defendant that
he was never served may not be quite such objective and indubitable
evidence as the Mobilization analysts assume.) Cheating does not
end there. The marshal, upon receipt of a copy of the judgment,
is supposed to go to the debtor's home and seize sufficient assets to
pay the debt; and only on the marshal's affidavit that the home
doesn't have the assets is the creditor allowed to attach, or "garnishee" the debtor's wages. In the MFY sample, twenty-two of the
thirty had wound up in this position, their employers ordered by
a court to deduct debt payments from wages, and seventeen of them
said that this announcement from the boss was the first they
knew there was any legal action against them. (The director of this
study, the sociologist David Caplovitz, has written elsewhere that
"garnishee . . . may well be one word in the language that the poorly
educated are more likely to know than the better educated.") The
final horror of this situation until 1966 was that many employers
(including charitable enterprises like, say, the YMCA) would automatically fire anybody whose wages were garnisheed. Now a state law
prohibits dismissal for a first garnishment of wages.

The institutional structure invites fraud. Sellers under an installment plan do not themselves advance the money to the purchaser. Instead, they sell the contract to a finance company; the goods are now paid for from the merchant's point of view, and he removes himself from the picture if he can. Usually, he can. The finance company now owns a "chattel mortgage" on what the customer bought—plus, in effect, a mortgage on everything else the customer owns, and on his future earnings. If the goods are damaged, or not as promised, the customer may have a legal action against the seller—but he has to keep paying off to the finance company, anyway. And, of course, he can't afford the legal action. While law limits the interest rates that can be charged, nothing limits the price of the merchandise. In slum areas much of the selling is done by door-to-door peddlers almost as poor as their customers, who in effect place yet another layer of legal shielding around the actual supplier of the goods.

Both price and quality problems are common in furniture purchases (the merchandise delivered to the customer is not what she saw in the store), in television sets (reconditioned older receivers are sold as new), in hi-fi equipment, in food freezer plans and, most pathetically, in the sets of encyclopedias, programmed instruction, books of "Negro heritage" and so forth which ignorant poor people buy in hopes that their children will have chances they didn't have. Major appliances and automobiles are standard brands, but prices will be inflated; and here repossession will pay off for the finance company, because the merchandise is resalable, so the victim may be and often is left with no car or washing machine, but with payments still due under the installment contract, to make up the difference between the debt and the resale price.

Incidentally, this situation can be even worse in Britain, where the "hire-purchase" scheme gives the buyer no equity at all in his purchase, except under somewhat spotty statutory coverage. If the buyer falls behind in his payments, the finance company can "snatch back" the property at any time, and the buyer must still pay 50 percent of the price. A British county court judge once said that "hire purchase consists in being persuaded by a man whom you don't know to sign an agreement you don't read to buy furniture you don't want with money you haven't got." In 1938 a British judge ruling against a defendant remarked, "If anyone is so foolish as to enter into an agreement such as this, I do not know that his case can be considered harsh."

Every Legal Aid society has its favorite criminal swindles to report. In Albuquerque, where the Legal Aid office is run by Mrs. Mary Dunlop, who resigned as judge of the small-claims court to take the job ("I don't care if it's impossible; we'll try it anyway"), a traveling salesman went through the Negro community selling "the right to be buried" (*not* burial plots) in a certain cemetery. "The salesman," Mrs. Dunlop recalls, "generously threw in the down payments. Then the contracts were discounted to the First National Bank, and the people got due books from the bank—'Thank you for this business; please make your payments.' We won that one."

"Sometimes," says Mortimer Getzels, director of the Harlem office, "a man may come in and say, 'I never signed it—that signature is a forgery. Albert D. Osborn is our questioned-documents man. He gives us a written opinion, with blown-up photostats. He doesn't charge Legal Aid for his services, unless he has to go to court; if he does, we pay him $25. Usually, we just have to send his report to the opponent."

For the rest, the Legal Aid cases are thoroughly miscellaneous. There is, for example, the aging but immensely vigorous Puerto Rican lady who wants the government to send her the allotment checks from her son which she was entitled to during the Korean War, and never got. The usual game of Twenty Questions reveals that she doesn't know where her son is now ("somewhere in Puerto Rico"), that the Red Cross has already checked the matter out for her and reported that he had ordered his allotment check transferred to a girl who had borne his child ("that whore"), and that it was properly paid to her. There are the people who co-signed notes for "friends," thinking they were merely giving a reference. Particularly in New York, there are immigration cases. There is, of course, a great bulk of criminal work. Every once in a while, someone comes in to ask a Legal Aid office to check up on the lawyer who has been handling his or her negligence action and who has, according to local rumor, settled the case without sending on the money.

"You have to make decisions on the merits of it," Getzels says. "Sometimes we can make a fast judgment, sometimes we have to suspend judgment, sometimes we just muddle around in doubt. Does he have a cause of action? Can you trust him? The sad thing is the person who's so disturbed you can't tell." Then, finally, there are the litigious poor: "It's a kind of mania, the people who want to use the society to persecute other people." There are more of those than most commentators seem to realize.

Lawyers come to Legal Aid offices from all sorts of backgrounds, most often, probably, from a local law school and a first job with a government agency. Some leave private practice because they'd rather do something they believe worth doing (Edward Q. Carr, director of New York's Legal Aid, started with the Wall Street firm of Cravath, Swaine & Moore). Though jobs in Legal Aid offices are supposed to be full-time, many lawyers undoubtedly supplement their salaries in one way or another; salaries are low, rarely more than $10,000. By and large, except for married women and a few unusually dedicated men, it is not a career service, though there is some tendency for veterans to drift back after a few years of private practice. Though much of the work is frustrating and disheartening, there are few jobs that can leave a man at the end of the week with so certain a feeling that his presence on earth has contributed to the lives of others.

Like any law office, the Legal Aid societies must take great quantities of time in "Mickey Mouse," the keeping up with dockets, waiting around courtrooms, writing memos, convincing people there's nothing a lawyer can do for them, processing forms through the offices of the judges' clerks. And, again, like any law office, the Legal Aid societies when they actually can do something work primarily by negotiating for their clients. But, unlike other law offices, they must put an inordinate amount of time into an intake process, simply talking with great numbers of people whom a lawyer can't help. Of the fifty thousand-odd civil cases that the New York Legal Aid Society processed in 1965, nearly three-quarters involved a single visit. Most of the time there is simply nothing to be done— no fraud, no overreaching, just wretched bad judgment by the prospective client. Professor Lawrence Cremin of Teachers College once took a class of future teachers to visit Brooklyn Family Court, to get a little better notion of what the world is really like. The judge told the teachers, "Whatever else you teach them, *please* make sure they learn one thing: if you make the first payment, you've got to make all the other payments."

3

In 1948 a survey by the Iowa Bar Association showed that 76 percent of the population of the state did not know there was such a thing as legal aid. "The fundamental defect in legal aid service today," Raynor Gardiner, then general counsel of the Boston Legal Aid Society, wrote in 1952, "is that, from a national point of view, it hardly exists. It is true that nearly all of the larger cities in this country have legal aid organizations, good, bad and indifferent, but the great majority of our citizens have no access to legal aid and to pretend anything else is just pompous nonsense."

Gardiner was commenting on Emery R. Brownell's report, *Legal Aid in the United States.* Ten years later, Brownell in a *Supplement* announced that expenditures on legal aid had tripled over the decade, and that of 196 metropolitan areas with populations of more than 100,000, only 12 were without Legal Aid offices and only 23 of the others had offices inadequate by the rather minimal standards of the National Legal Aid and Defender Association. In 1965, four years after Brownell's *Supplement,* Mary Tarcher of the New York Legal Aid Society estimated that expenditures had doubled again, and that legal aid commanded the services of a thousand lawyers and spent $10 million a year on their offices. Yet Gardiner's criticism had been at most blunted, not denied. Private facilities for supplying legal aid continued to be inadequate.

The office sponsored by the bar had never been the only device for providing legal service to indigents. For criminal matters public defender offices have been run on tax revenues in California for the better part of this century, and at the time of Brownell's supplement there were four *civil* Legal Aid offices, with paid staffs, on municipal budgets (in Dallas, Kansas City, and Bridgeport and New Haven, Connecticut). In six other cities (Chicago; Erie, Pennsylvania; Jackson, Mississippi; Lansing, Michigan; Richmond, Virginia; and St. Paul, Minnesota) legal services were given, as they had been in the early years of the movement, as part of the work of private social agencies. And in every large city, of course, there are political clubs which offer some minimum (but not necessarily ineffective) legal services on a charitable basis.

The start of a new pattern of "neighborhood law offices," which has now achieved a budget of nearly $40 million a year in the federal antipoverty program, can be traced to the Ford Foundation's imaginative efforts in New Haven in the early 1960s. Among those to whom the foundation and the local sponsors showed the plans for their new Community Progress, Inc. (CPI) was Professor Joseph Goldstein of the Yale Law School. "Joe looked over these descriptions of what a 'community school' and a community action program should be like," says Fred Danforth, now director of the New Haven Legal Assistance Association, "and he wrote the word 'lawyers' in a few places." When CPI was formed in 1962, there were lawyers in the "community schools," ready to help. The CPI legal services program (though a near disaster itself) became a model for similar operations in Boston, Washington and New York's Lower East Side; and plans for law offices were built into the Office of Economic Opportunity's community action proposals almost from the beginning.

Now that money was to be made available by the government, the Legal Aid societies came under attack from both right and left. The right disapproved of the idea of a bureau with employees who would receive the entire appropriation: it wanted "Judicare," under which poor people would pick their own lawyers (as they pick their own doctors under Medicare) and the government would simply pay the lawyers' bills. This procedure would also minimize the profession's losses if legal aid took over the processing of personal-injury cases. Only one such program was set up, in rural Wisconsin (similar procedures are in effect at one of New Haven's neighborhood offices), and the report on its first months indicated that more than four-fifths of the cases paid for by government funds had been divorce actions—a result profoundly disapproved in Washington, because such actions could not "get at the legal causes of poverty."

Criticism from the left was more significant and influential, and though most of the OEO's legal services money eventually went to established Legal Aid societies, a fair fraction was used to fund new, essentially competitive organizations. Some of the criticism was specific, directed at the societies' refusal to handle matters like bankruptcy and divorce ("My secretary," Albuquerque's Mary Dunlop reports, "says that we don't handle divorces unless she's bleeding on the floor"). Most of it, however, was more theoretical, blending with the sociological arguments underlying the policies if not always the practices of OEO.

As stated by Jerome Carlin and Jan Howard of the Center for the Study of Law and Society at the University of California, the serious objections by the left fall into three basic categories:

1. The Legal Aid offices are too closely related to the local Establishment: "[F]inancial dependence on local business interests that may be threatened by effective legal action on behalf of the poor client is a major structural weakness of the Legal Aid system that seriously undermines its capacity to provide adequate legal representation."

2. By concentrating on service to individuals, in their relations with other private parties or businesses, the Legal Aid societies lose their most significant opportunity to serve the poor and change the structure of society—they do not see themselves, for example, as the organizers of rent strikes or the reformers of administrative procedures in the welfare department or the housing authority. In the hands of the Legal Aid societies, as the Mobilization For Youth proposal to the poverty program put it, "poor man's law was peculiarly defensive."

Another aspect of this problem is the usual location of the Legal Aid office somewhere near the courthouse, which saves a lot of time for the lawyer or lawyers but requires poor people (by definition fearful of and hostile to all parts of the city other than their own neighborhood) to travel considerable distances. Nearly all the projects funded to date by OEO have been "neighborhood law offices," and originally most of them were slum store fronts, on the theory that people who saw the door at street level would walk in on impulse. This doesn't happen—more than 90 percent of the cases handled by these offices turn out to be referrals of one sort or an-other—and as the program ages, the offices tend to move to the lower rents upstairs.

3. "One of the principal drawbacks of the Legal Aid system is its welfare orientation. This tends to undermine the very awareness of rights and capacity for asserting rights that is so crucial for over-coming apathy and promoting full participation in the legal order. It also seems to discourage a legal approach to problems. If we are to encourage the dignity and full enfranchisement of the poor, legal services must be provided them as a matter of right."

On a more technical level, critics of no particular political per-suasion were unhappy about the isolated situation of legal aid—its lack of relationship to other social agencies. Charles J. Parker, a matter-of-fact New Haven lawyer who was chairman of the Munici-pal Legal Aid Committee when CPI was first bruited about, and took the lead in setting up its legal component, remembers "a hope that these lawyers would be more than lawyers—that instead of treating superficial legal problems they would be an entree into multiproblem families. Take an individual from a family living more or less together—he has civil and criminal problems. You settle with his creditors for two cents on the dollar, and get him suspended sentences on the criminal charges. Then you, full of satisfaction as a lawyer, go away—and the family comes back next year. What have you done?" Legal aid had to work that way: the law office that was part of a community-action program could be more effective. Parker's approach, of course, intensifies the left-wing objection to legal aid by proposing an even stronger welfare or-ientation for the new offices.

In the central question of philosophy, however, all the opponents and all the supporters of legal aid were as one: they agreed that The Law itself was fundamentally "just"—did not, could not in its majesty, discriminate—against the poor. The problem, apart from legislative errors here and there, was simply that the poor had insufficient access to the lawyers who alone could make the law work on their behalf. As William R. Vance of Yale said in 1926, "What does it profit a poor and ignorant man that he is equal to his strong antagonist before the law if there is no one to inform him what the law is?" Provide what Columbia's Maurice Rosenberg has rather nastily called "cradle-to-grave counsel" and the oppression of the poor would cease.

4

At this writing, only four of the new poverty program legal projects have been around long enough to have a history—Boston, New Haven, New York and Washington. All have discovered that whatever legal aid's weaknesses might be, the neighborhood law offices shared them. The new lawyers could do no more than the old ones to help the poor in most landlord-and-tenant, consumer and criminal cases. Where the fact of representation by itself might persuade a finance company or a shoddy landlord that some fundamentally dishonest matter should be dropped (the Mobilization For Youth offices in New York virtually put an encyclopedia-peddling group out of business by persuading finance companies not to sue on the basis of its contracts, and thus not to discount such paper in the future), the new offices did as well as legal aid; where actual questions of law were involved, the poor were stuck. As a Legal Aid lawyer told the *New York Times*, "We have no law on our side; all we have is *chutzpah*."

(The one exception—perhaps a very significant one—was the success of Washington's Neighborhood Legal Services Project in voiding an installment contract on the grounds that the arrangement was "unconscionable." This decision did not break new ground [a similar argument had been used successfully by a private lawyer in New Hampshire shortly before], but it did lift the one available precedent out of the freak category. In essence, the Washington and New Hampshire courts ruled that finance companies which wanted to collect through legal process would have to investigate the sales that created the pieces of paper they discounted. Such a rule, if it became general, would be one of the most significant pieces of social invention in the last generation; it would in effect compel the financial institutions to police the retailing business, which they would do much more effectively than any Legal Aid society or consumer frauds division in any district attorney's office.)

With success stories hard to come by in the private sector, the poverty program law offices have concentrated their work on the representation of people who are entangled in one way or another with government agencies. "The Board of Education, Housing, Welfare, Social Security, Unemployment Compensation," says Harold J. Rothwax, an aggressive but tough-minded young lawyer who came over from the criminal branch of Legal Aid to run the Mobilization For Youth office, "touch the poor much more closely than the courts do." As resourceful middle-class people know from their enraged frustrations over traffic tickets, no citizen has really satisfying remedies when public officials use discretion against him; and the poor man is that much more defenseless.

Some of the assistance lawyers can give people in these relationships is simply advisory. "People come in who just operate in an area of what I call no-knowledge," says Henry Jones, who runs one of the Washington neighborhood offices, working at a desk under the stairway in a windowless hall that paint alone cannot clean, on the ground floor of a tenement. "They just don't know where to go or what to do. They're people whose jobs have ended, but they haven't applied for unemployment insurance because they lost the Social Security card. They're eligible for veterans' pensions and they don't know it. Much of what we do is legal only in a collateral sense; we're directing people where to go."

More often, the neighborhood offices have put themselves in adversary positions against the public agencies. "We represented this girl who was expelled from school because she was pregnant, three weeks before graduation," says Julian Dugas of the Washington project, "and she was married, too. They took her back." All the neighborhood offices have had substantial success in restoring welfare clients to the rolls after they (and their children) had been removed because an investigator, poking around outside the window with a flashlight at two in the morning, found a man in the house. (The theory is that any man in the house, husband or not, could be contributing to the lady's support, thereby relieving the taxpayers. In Arkansas and Georgia the state authorities have blandly announced a rule of constructive adoption—that any man living with a woman was automatically a "substitute father" for her children, who thereby didn't need public assistance any more.) Other offices have got unemployment insurance restored to clients who had been denied it because former employers said, without evidence, that they had been fired for drunkenness or dishonesty.

Housing situations have been harder. "Every public housing authority has a month-to-month arrangement," says Edward Sparer, an ardent, round young man in horn-rimmed glasses who founded the MFY office and is now director of a Center for Social Welfare Policy and Law in the Columbia School of Social Work. "It can evict on thirty days' notice, without explanation. We claim a public housing tenant has a right to know why he is being evicted, and a right to a hearing. One of the lease provisions requires a tenant who has an illegitimate child to, one, notify the authority; and, two, get out. We claim that violates the equal protection clause."

Where welfare clients are involved, just getting them to accept a lawyer's help can be difficult; they feel that they desperately need the goodwill of the agency. A 1962 report to a state commission investigating public welfare in New York described the process of establishing one's suitability as a recipient of public moneys: "An applicant becomes eligible for assistance when he exhausts his money, gives a lien of his property to the welfare department, turns in the license plates of his car and takes legal action against his legally responsible relatives. When he is stripped of all material resources, when he 'proves' his dependency, then and then only is he eligible." Even then, eligibility is easily lost. Most welfare authorities forbid clients to have a telephone, or a typewriter, or anything that might give evidence that public money is being spent "unwisely." If anyone in the household chances to make some money—if a boy picks up a few dollars delivering groceries—the proceeds are supposed to be reported and deducted from benefits. Investigators have almost unlimited power to enter the home at any time and search for fancy lingerie or liquor. "This process of proving and maintaining eligibility," as the report to the New York commission put it, ". . . tends to produce a self-perpetuating system of dependency and dehumanization."

The intrusion of a lawyer into such a relationship unquestionably makes an enormous difference to the attitudes of both the welfare client and the welfare department. An application for a "fair hearing" on a decision against a client is often enough to get the decision reversed. (Similarly, just the presence of a civil rights lawyer in a Southern town, even if he isn't admitted to practice in the local courts, will improve the behavior of the sheriff's deputies.) What discourages the lawyers is that, while they win the individual cases, they do not normally change the agency's policies or its climate. "[H]earing decisions," Sparer added in a footnote to his optimistic report to a 1964 conference sponsored by the Department of Health, Education, and Welfare, "do not always have the precedent effect they should." Rothwax, two years later, put the matter more strongly: "Test cases don't accomplish a hell of a lot. The administrative agencies will buy us out—give us what we're asking for, moot us out of court. And if we win a policy change, it may not do any good because the rulings are given grudgingly and can always be distinguished."

The hostility of neighborhood legal service offices to the public agencies set up to help the poor often comes as a shock to politicians —and to social workers. And there is indeed more than a little irrationality in the attitude of the Sparers, that the real enemies of the destitute are the public authorities that feed, house, clothe and educate them. But it is also true that this is precisely the context (replying to a correspondent who had urged that the King and the Pope should be presumed to mean well) in which Lord Acton uttered his axiom that power tends to corrupt and absolute power corrupts absolutely. The welfare authorities have far too much unsupervised power over their clients' lives. In theory, at least, a lawyer can give the poor recipient a dollop of countervailing force against the awesome authority of the agency. It is worth noting in passing that the necessity for this sort of service has risen with the decline of the urban political machine; much of what the neighborhood law offices actually do for poor clients in their relations with City Hall is just what the ward heeler used to do for the immigrants. The elimination of corruption from government and the magnification of bureaucratic cruelty are often—perhaps inevitably—two sides of the same coin.

Ultimately, there are limits on what lawyers can accomplish. Administrative agencies are established to exercise discretion, to make rules where the legislatures (and the courts) feel themselves without the requisite experience or expertise. And wherever discretion is permitted, those it is exercised against will be sure the decision is arbitrary (remember the traffic ticket). Some intrusion upon the dignity of the recipients, moreover, is inherent in the very notion of public assistance. Wolfgang Friedmann of Columbia has written, "It is, in many ways, easier for the 'negative' State (which confines itself essentially to the minimum functions of defence, police and the machinery of justice) to be just to the individual— at the expense of active concern for his social and economic welfare. Such active concern means of necessity interference." Friedmann adds, "On balance, such interference is beneficial; otherwise it would not have been adopted by one State after another during the present century."

5

Unfortunately, the advocates of vastly extended legal services for the poor become trapped in a rhetoric of "rights," most of which is inapplicable to the problem. Carlin and Howard, for example, cite as evidence that "lower-income families have little understanding of their legal rights or of how to exercise them" the following passage from Caplovitz:

Many consumers have almost no idea of the complex set of legal conditions embodied in the contracts they sign. The penalties that can be brought to bear on them, such as the loss of possessions already paid for, the payment of interest on money owed, the payment of lawyer and court fees, are matters that some families become rudely aware of only when—for whatever reason—they miss their payments.

But there are no rights for the poor in this passage, just liabilities. Indeed, what Caplovitz's book buttresses is not the argument that the poor are systematically deprived of rights but the "assumption," which Professor (now Judge) Marvin Frankel of New York denounced as the cardinal weakness of the Legal Aid attitude, "that poor people are afflicted with special forms of stupidity or fecklessness to which the affluent are immune." Nobody really argues, of course, that any social class is immune to stupidity. A New Hampshire lawyer likes to tell a story of a middle-class widow lady who put a down payment on a house by mail, closed her deal after a visit during which a truck delivered huge bottles of spring water, and then tried to get her money back because the well was no good; when the lawyer asked her if she hadn't suspected something fishy after the arrival of the spring water, she said, "They told me it made better Kool-Aid." The lawyer comments, "Such people don't need a lawyer; they need a guardian." Statistically, though, the poor *are* more likely to behave stupidly in the marketplace—that's what we mean, ultimately, when we use the word "ignorance." Legal Aid's attitudes, which are not quite so shabby as Judge Frankel implies, derive from experience, an experience soon shared by the lawyers in the neighborhood offices. "Most consumer matters are not fraud," says Washington's Henry Jones glumly. "They're a lack of intelligence, a lack of a sense of proportion in buying." Observing from afar and wanting to help, the professors denounce a deprivation of "rights."

The false emphasis on "rights," which is merely self-confusing in the private sector, becomes a handicap to rational planning when the OEO-sponsored lawyers come to deal with the public agencies. Led by Professor Charles Reich of Yale, they tend to assert that the poor have "rights" in public assistance, and that the goal must be recognition of these rights. "Only by making such benefits into rights," Reich argues, "can the welfare state achieve its goal of providing a secure minimum basis for individual well-being and dignity." Professor Harry W. Jones of Columbia, in an earlier and more carefully reasoned paper, has said that "I see no reason why the word 'rights' with its unique emotive power, should be deemed inappropriate for these new expectations and preempted for use only in connection with such traditional interests as tangible property." But Jones was talking about Social Security and unemployment compensation, where the recipients have made a contribution to a fund which is supported by such contributions rather than by the general revenue. Such a fund, governmental or otherwise, can be compelled by court order to pay out to a claimant. What a court cannot do is compel a legislature to appropriate money. Sometimes the prohibition is specifically stated—Congress has, for example, forbidden judicial review of denials of benefits by the Veterans Administration. But it is always true in general that courts can grant welfare benefits to applicants only within the terms of the law passed by the legislature; it cannot award them any natural-law "rights" the legislature has not seen fit to establish.

Edward Sparer has insisted (successfully, in individual cases) that welfare departments may not violate a person's natural-law "rights" even at the fairly plain behest of the state law under which they operate. The 1961 New York legislature voted to forbid welfare payments to people who had come to the state for the purpose of obtaining such payments, and in the first ten months that the law was in effect some 2,730 persons were denied aid. "I talked with Ed Carr," Sparer says, "and he said, 'Well, that's the law.' Legal Aid had discussed the problem with welfare, and had concluded that the law was being fairly applied. But they were presuming that if you came without a job or visible means of support you automatically had to have come to get welfare."

Sparer and the social workers (including the then Commissioner of Welfare in New York City) were convinced that nobody did in fact come to New York for the *sole* purpose of receiving welfare, and that this was the only proper interpretation of the law. (A lady with four small children and no possible income who came to New York to be near her sister, another lady with four small children who was living on welfare, could be said to have come for family reasons, not to get welfare.) What they were demanding, in effect, was that the welfare department rule administratively that the legislature had deliberately passed a nullity—and that any other ruling would violate applicants' *"right* to entitlement." With the help of a sympathetic commissioner, the argument was won in all the individual cases where lawyers appealed within the department. But the policy, of course, did not—could not—change. Administrative discretion does not extend that far.

What the argument of rights ignores in all contexts is the question of the social policy which presumably the law is to serve; there is not much point in encouraging "the legal approach to problems" if the problems are not legal. In the private area, emphasis on rights has kept the theoreticians of the movement from exploring the economic realities of the present situation and the best directions to follow in seeking a less unfair result. The fundamental question, to which no one knows the answer, is whether today's slumlords, retailers and finance companies, apart from the dramatic but relatively infrequent cases of fraud, are in fact making heavy profits from the higher payments of the poor. The Mobilization For Youth study of judgment debtors may be more significant for its failure to locate 270 of the 300 in the sample than for its revelation that 22 of the 30 actual respondents say they were never served with papers. How many of these 270 missing debtors had, in fact, paid what they owed? To what extent are the high interest rates and prices paid by the poor as a class a reflection of the fact that the risks of making such loans are high? And if the result of randomly tightening the legal procedures in this market were to deprive the poor of the chance to buy television sets and washing machines on the installment plan, would poor people be happier?

Similarly, in housing it is vital to document the costs of providing slum housing before adding to them with legal harassments. (Mobilization For Youth has noted with sardonic pleasure that its neighborhood law office is well regarded by local lawyers, because it has forced landlords to hire lawyers of their own—but if the profits of the enterprise are not high enough to absorb such added costs of legal representation, then the poor will simply have to pay more rent so their landlords can fight back.) To deprive a landlord of the opportunity to evict the really undesirable tenant (the prostitute, the drug-supply house, the gang headquarters) doesn't help the other tenants in the building. Decent housing for the poor requires major government subsidy, but does it really hasten government subsidy to drive out the better landlords (always the people reached first by any campaign) and keep out (because the atmosphere is uncomfortably heavy with conflict) people who might be prepared to invest private money in the slums?

Urging a new program of essentially confiscatory fines as the only way to "enforce" a housing code, Judah Gribetz and Frank P. Grad admitted in the *Columbia Law Review* in 1966 that "one of the results of firm code enforcement . . . is that the cities will become the landlords of a great mass of uneconomical, deteriorated buildings. . . . A government that has dared to speak of the coming of a great society must, indeed, accept these consequences." But surely if slum landlords are to be expropriated, the decision should be made openly; and if the government is to increase greatly its appropriations for housing, the money should be voted in pursuance of public policy, not merely as a grubby consequence of "enforcing" laws which defendants admittedly cannot comply with. Few observers today give housing anything like first priority on the funds available for improving the conditions of the poor; nearly everyone would place higher value on the creation of jobs, education and training for jobs, and improvements in health and diet. Of the three possible results of the proposed "enforcement" program—greatly increased public appropriations for welfare, diversion of money from other purposes to housing, or establishment of municipal government itself as the slumlord with the most violations—the first is by no means the most likely outcome, and neither is the second.

Such questions have not even been asked—let alone answered—by the leaders of the OEO legal services programs. They are lawyers: they want to assert "rights." But rights, like everything else, can be very expensive for poor people. If the lawyers keep the school system from discharging the boy who knifed a classmate (because the law requires the public schools to provide education for all, there is no other facility where the boy can be placed, and the juvenile court has released him on probation), it is the poor children in the slum neighborhood and not the offspring of Mr. Moneybags who suffer the terror of his next attack. To make divorce free and easy does not necessarily contribute to the welfare of the children, and the results of encouraging personal bankruptcy can be seen in those Western states where ridiculous garnishment laws leave the poor no other way out of their problems. (In Oregon, which leads the nation with more than 200 bankruptcies a year for every 100,000 of the population, a creditor could before 1965 attach *all* a debtor's wages, and can now take half; in New York, where only 10 percent can be attached, there are only 31 bankruptcies per 100,000; and in Florida, North Carolina, Pennsylvania and Texas, where wages cannot be garnisheed, the figure is ten or lower.) Lenders cluster around those emerging from bankruptcy court, who have been stripped of their marketable possessions, are eager to replace the lost car and TV set, and have become somewhat safer risks because they cannot escape again through bankruptcy for six years. "The unscrupulous loan company or furniture dealer whose debt supposedly was discharged in bankruptcy," two University of Chicago law students wrote in 1966 in an article entitled "Schlockmeister's Jubilee: Bankruptcy for the Poor," "will approach the bankrupt to urge him to reaffirm his old debts in return for a renewal of credit. . . . In no time the creditor has the bankrupt back in debt with the additional advantage of having a six-year period in which to collect."

The disabilities of the poor are not fundamentally legal disabilities; the law problem is simply one of the bumps in the pie plate: push it down here and it comes up somewhere else. What the poor really require is not greater involvement with that corner of the law that might be construed as "on their side," but less involvement with the law altogether. As former Attorney General Nicholas deB. Katzenbach put it, "For rights to be worth anything, they must be honored—without lawyers." Institutional structures which promote decent behavior by merchants (like a requirement that the finance companies police their loans) or by landlords (a bonus for the provision of decent facilities rather than a penalty for code violations) or administrative agencies (some semi-independent investigatory branch like the Scandinavian Ombudsman, to take care of citizen complaints)—social inventions that provide earned income for people now apparently unemployable—such ventures will offer much more than any number of lawyers to the well-being of the poor. By concentrating on paper rights, as Geoffrey Hazard of the American Bar Foundation has warned, "the neighborhood law offices may be sweeping under the rug the public recognition of real conflicts in social policy."

On the scene, of course, despite their theoreticians, the lawyers in the OEO-sponsored neighborhood offices mostly dispense legal aid, fighting a little more with the public agencies than the old Legal Aid offices did, but basically performing the same functions. Sometimes, as demonstrated by the success of the Washington office in preventing collection by a finance company on a note which grew out of an "unconscionable sale," they may win a victory of significance wider than the individual case. Even the rhetoric of rights can contribute on occasion to the more fundamental improvements lawyers are ill-trained to consider. And like the private Legal Aid societies, the OEO offices may demonstrate to the legislatures the need for new law of the kind that only legislatures can make.

6

By and large, unfortunately, the foundations and OEO have not been content to see the lawyers they pay doing what lawyers can do. Among the first results of their insistence that the neighborhood law offices must be used to change the social system was the refusal of the New York courts to permit the OEO program to operate in that city in 1966. Revised applications have been prepared.

The first proposals for neighborhood law offices were negotiated between the city's lawyers and the new OEO "poverty corporations" over a long, hard year. The lawyers themselves were by no means united; the Wall Street firms were almost unanimously for the program, while the lawyers who actually drew some business from poor people were against it; the Bronx and Brooklyn bar associations were particularly bitter about any extension of free legal services. The city's Negro and Puerto Rican lawyers were also mostly opposed to anything but a "judicare" plan, but their opposition was psychologically difficult for them to maintain, and was eventually compromised through an arrangement where newly formed "Harlem", "Bedford-Stuyvesant" and "Puerto Rican" bar associations would receive a disproportionate voice in the management of the new legal assistance corporation.

What the various bar associations finally agreed on were neighborhood services to be run mostly by the Legal Aid Society, with supplementary services run by the neighborhood poverty corporations. OEO rejected this agreement because it failed to assure "maximum participation of the poor," and substituted a remarkable organizational monster of contracting and subcontracting legal-service corporations, open-ended in that new groups could get grants to start their own services at any time. To function in New York State, however, the corporation required a license from the Appellate Division, and in November, 1966, the First Department unanimously refused to issue any such license. The opinion by Judge Charles Breitel (presently to be elevated to the state's highest court) criticized the OEO proposal from many viewpoints, and was especially severe on its "indiscriminate mingling of social goals and legitimate legal practices."

Considering how busy these judges are, it was an astonishingly well-informed opinion. For among the most serious dangers to the growth and effectiveness of poverty-program law offices will be, bluntly, the contrast between the morality of the politically active and the morality of the rest of the world.

Among the most severe criticisms of the Legal Aid societies by the doctrinaires of the poverty program was that Legal Aid insisted on examining the merits of its clients' cases in situations where a private lawyer might gladly proceed for a rich man who could pay his fee. The new offices would do for the poor whatever a lawyer would do for the rich. As Professor Frankel put it, "If there is any fixed principle of equal justice, it is that 'rights' for the well-to-do must not be alchemized into mere 'privileges' for the poor." But the cost factor which dissuades a man from suing his neighbor over a petty quarrel—and keeps common criminals from exploiting the full resources of evasion available to Jimmy Hoffa after conviction—will not exist in the neighborhood law offices. It is sound public policy to make litigation expensive for the considerable numbers of people who would selfishly assert what lawyers used to call every jot and tittle of their rights. "We lawyers know well," Pollock once wrote, "and may find high authority for it if required, that life would be intolerable if every man insisted on his legal rights to the full."

Because a rich man may be able to find a lawyer who will help him press unfair charges against public servants does not mean everybody must enjoy such luxuries. "Genuine grievances do indeed exist," Columbia's Walter Gellhorn wrote in 1966 about the experience of the European Ombudsmen and official administrative critics, "but they are far outnumbered by complaints by the chronically querulous, the psychopathically hostile, and the simply mistaken. Only when sober sifting has been undertaken can proper attention be paid to the truly aggrieved and, at the same time, proper support be given to those who truly serve." By criticizing Legal Aid's insistence on investigating its cases, and by demanding that the new offices identify with what one of the applications to the New York Appellate Division called "the consumers of injustice," some of the leaders of the OEO legal-services program have equated themselves with the unscrupulous private mouthpieces whose distortions of legal process have been the scandal of the profession.

Unless carefully supervised, some of the lawyers in the OEO offices will use the compulsory processes of law not for their clients but to express their own compulsions, to "punish" a society they regard as corrupt, from which they feel alienated. They are especially subject to the deformation Charles P. Curtis once warned against: "Lawyers' cases are devoted to particular events. When they start thinking that they are dealing only with the properties of these events, they lose touch, they take their eyes off the ball, they start making gestures. They could do no worse."

New Haven's own original legal-assistance project was almost wrecked at its inception by "making gestures"—indeed, it was only by transferring the neighborhood legal services from the umbrella of Community Progress, Inc., to control by a separate board of corporate lawyers that the program was saved at all, and even then the New Haven County Bar Association voted to disapprove the project. Two descriptions of the incident that triggered the crisis make an illuminating contrast:

The first is from the chairman of the legal-assistance program:

"One of the neighborhood lawyers was consulted by a woman whose son was charged with rape of a white nurse. At her request, the lawyer agreed to assist the public defender in the preparation and trial of the case. At the trial, the claim of consent was raised by way of defense based on evidence which was rather unsubstantial. This shocked the court and the community."

The second is by the lady lawyer who ran the defense:

Neighborhood groups reacted with hostility to [my] participation in the defense of a Negro charged with the rape of a white woman. The Negro community was deeply ashamed and mortified by the prosecution, viewing it as a confirmation of the stereotypes which they themselves had internalized. Members of the community were brought, only by degrees, to understand in some measure the meaning of the presumption of innocence and the right of every accused person to a vigorous defense. At last the willingness of a lawyer to champion the cause of the accused acted in some manner to lessen their own sense of shame and guilt and to enable them to understand that only the accused and not the entire Negro community was on trial.

The boy got a maximum sentence: thirty years—that's why a lawyer representing an accused rather than a theory would worry about adding willful insult to criminal injury of the victim in such a case. Many lawyers, moreover, would feel a certain squeamishness relating to the "rights" of the nurse not to have such protected libel thrown at her in a courtroom. Unrestricted advocacy is by no means in the highest tradition of the bar.

Another incident of that sort in New Haven would have killed the neighborhood law offices in infancy; in most communities the program would have been strangled at birth. If the neighborhood law offices are to perform *any* services in the years ahead, they must be protected from that brand of fiery advocacy which is masochistically self-consuming. The temperament and political views of the lawyers most likely to be attracted to these offices will make the policing job difficult and uncomfortable, replete with cries of fink and brutality, but the survival of the program requires that it offer legal assistance, not a collection of newly manufactured and unseaworthy "rights." A century of hard fighting was necessary to free democratic policy-making from the crushing incomprehension of the courts; and the legislatures are not now going to give up their powers because radical like conservative lawyers can employ the artificial logic of natural-law rights to promote judicial supremacy. The battle to improve the condition of the poor as a group (as distinguished from the fate of individual poor people individually oppressed) must be won in the legislature, not in the courts, and it is confusing and cruel to the poor to pretend otherwise.

PART III

BUSINESS

CHAPTER 9

PIECES OF PAPER

"*What wud I be doin' in a smelly coort room talkin' up to a man that was me chief clerk last year?' says he. 'No, sir, th' law is a diff'rent profissyon fr'm what it was whin Dan'l Webster an' Rufus Choate an' thim gas bags used to make a mighty poor livin' be shoutin' at judges that made less. Th' law today is not only a profissyon. It's a business. I made a bigger honoraryum last year consolidatin' th' glue interests that aftherwards wint into th' hands iv a receiver, which is me, thin Dan'l Webster iver thought was in th' goold mines iv th' wurruld. I can't promise to take a case f'r ye an' hoot me reasons f'r thinkin' ye're right into th' ears iv a larned judge. I'm a poor speaker. But if iver ye want to do something that ye think ye oughtn't to do, come around to me an' I'll show ye how to do it,' says he.*"

—MR. DOOLEY

"*[The corporate lawyer] must become familiar with the history and methods of a great manufactory, the sources and costs of its raw material, the markets for its finished product, the elements of its success or failure, the difficulties and hopes and fears and ways of thinking of its managers. Next week he may go through the same process with a railroad company, and the next week with a banker and the next with a merchant, or a ship owner, or a contractor, or a charitable institution, or a church.*"

—ELIHU ROOT

"*The function of those of us who serve industry, trade and finance is not alone to keep them technically within the law, but to do our part toward keeping them functioning smoothly, contributing to our national prosperity and our high standards of living and furnishing the individual opportunity which has meant America."*

—ROBERT T. SWAINE

1

The modern American lawyer in apotheosis is a man in an office with windows down to the floor, high up in the new monolith of the Chase-Manhattan Bank Building, a block from Wall Street in New York. On the walls are pictures of the resident in some form of casual connection with Presidents, cabinet ministers, governors, Senators, perhaps heads of foreign governments, maybe generals. The desk, though probably not neat, is much less cluttered than one would find in the offices of an old-fashioned lawyer, because there is a large staff to file and retrieve the junk. The telephone has four or five buttons on it, and there may be an intercom with twenty switches. Under normal circumstances, this lawyer can be found in his office; clients hate to pull him away if they can avoid it. He spends several hours each day on the telephone, and takes most of the rest of the information he needs from pieces of paper. He is never in a trial court, and if he goes to an administrative agency in Washington, it will almost always be for a conference with the general counsel rather than for a hearing. He rarely gathers information himself; though he browses the advance sheets from the courts and the loose-leaf services, his time is too precious to be wasted by close study of the kind that must be done in a library, and it is of course out of the question that he should ever interrogate anyone below a policy-making level in a client organization. Every once in a while an old client may have a personal problem, which the senior partner will (with great feelings of satisfaction, incidentally) explore personally; otherwise, his information is largely the product of staff work. Perhaps the most important single reason why there is a staff of a hundred lawyers supporting this senior man and his two to six senior colleagues is the need that this information be absolutely first-class.

On this level—say, perhaps $100,000 a year—the lawyer is paid for his judgment. He contributes not only that feeling for relevance which is the essence of his profession, but a sense of priorities, which is the next step up from relevance. He knows the applicable law (and will have an associate check him out on it, anyway), but in addition he knows the problems in public policy which the law raises. And he can make a shrewd judgment of the capacity (i.e., the combination of ability and energy) of his client and of the others in the situation. By and large, he has been a specialist in the law (financing, taxation and antitrust are the only specialties that count), but he no longer has time for that. He receives his enormous fees—and brings into the firm the business that supports the other lawyers—almost entirely because it is believed that his advice is worth buying. This does not mean that the advice will always be accepted (or even that it will always be correct—lawyers tend to know about finance, not about engineering or marketing), but that he will be able to see in many situations implications that have escaped other people.

At first sight—particularly the first sight of a contract emerging from a Wall Street firm, seeking to cover every possible contingency, up to and including nuclear war—it seems that these newly found implications are overwhelmingly negative. Harrison Tweed (formerly a polo player, subsequently a counselor at law and husband of the poetess Michael Straight) paid tribute to James Byrne, his first boss: "No one could possibly have taught me as well as Mr. Byrne did that an essential of the good lawyer is that he visualize all the possibilities and particularly those that might make trouble. He had the imagination of a child alone in the dark and when he had time he could think up the most dreadful of possibilities." But this collecting of horrors is for the juniors; the senior man must know about them, and then forget them.

Arthur A. Ballantine, later to be the brain trust of the Republican right wing through the Roosevelt era, wrote with some annoyance in 1920, addressing himself to the man who sought to get ahead by inventing trouble: "It is a very common thing for attorneys to spend a great deal of time finding out the answers to questions which are not involved." Recently, speaking to lawyers who would wish to protect the computer secrets of a company, New

York's Lawrence Boonin suggested, "The trick is to get high enough up in the organization and say, 'Look, we're giving you our life's blood. We want to retain some rights in this.' That guy who came out of the stock room two weeks ago and is working in purchasing is going to be much more legalistic than the general counsel of the company on a point like that. Climb as far up the ladder as you can." The same advice, with different terms of reference, applies in negotiations with the Wall Street law firms.

Speaking to students at the Harvard Law School in 1920, Paul D. Cravath, perhaps the first major figure in American law who was only an "office lawyer," listed the prerequisites for the work: "good health, ordinary honesty, a sound education and normal intelligence," plus

character, industry, and intellectual thoroughness, qualities that do not go to make for charm but go far to make up that indefinable something we call efficiency. . . . Brilliant intellectual powers are not essential. Too much imagination, too much wit, too great cleverness, too facile fluency, if not leavened by a sound sense of proportion, are quite as likely to impede success as to promote it. The best clients are apt to be afraid of those qualities. They want as their counsel a man who is primarily honest, safe, sound and steady. . . . I would also add . . . the ability to distinguish the essentials from the nonessentials, to concentrate on the things that count and not waste effort and thought on things that are simply interesting.

Since Cravath's time the purely mental demands have increased. He worked in a period when mergers were accomplished mostly by power plays and stock-market raids, when the important negotiations were with investment bankers who would be, on the whole, partners in the final enterprise, when the lawyer's most difficult and longest-range challenge was the management of a bankruptcy and the reorganization of the business. Now the Internal Revenue Code and the Robinson-Patman Act draw the businessman and his lawyer into a trackless quagmire; and the potential adversary to be feared is often the government, for which litigation is costless and painless. The government, as Chesterton wrote in Mohammed's tribute to the Crusader, "is he whose loss is laughter if he counts the wager worth." (Even in the small firms of the small towns, the constant presence of the government has multiplied the demands on the lawyer. "In the old days," says George Milani of Centerville, Iowa, who has been around long enough to have an experienced son in practice with him, "nobody knew if you made a mistake. The tax laws have changed that.") Yet Cravath's program of requirements still holds; the great leaders of the corporate bar are still, in David Riesman's phrase, "highly intelligent but not intellectual."

Some seek money; some, power; some, freedom. The route to all is a reputation not for shrewdness but for wisdom.

2

God can make a tree; only lawyers can make a corporation. For the corporation is a creature of the law, and draws its very being from documents. Where the law constrains the activities of "natural persons," and leaves them free apart from these constraints, it establishes and empowers and continually controls corporations. "In creating a capital structure," Robert Swaine of Cravath, Swaine & Moore once wrote,

counsel make the facts inherent in the structure, but must make them with strict regard to the extrinsic facts and with strict conformity not only to legal precedent but also to legal trends. Whatever may be their personal views . . . of relevant decisions of the courts of last resort . . . counsel in a creative corporate matter are more rigidly controlled by these decisions . . . than is any judge sitting in a court of first instance."

Blackstone knew only one reason for forming a corporation: to maintain an activity beyond the lives of the persons who began it. The activities he had in mind were important: those of the Throne, the Church, the cities, the charitable foundations and the colleges. Society requires that such institutions continue to function regardless of private fates.

From Elizabethan times on, however, less vital enterprises had gained corporate status, and not only for the sake of immortality. As a practical matter, despite the English debtors' prisons, the law had always recognized that nobody could be liable to anyone else beyond his resources—"*Ex nihilo nihil fit,*" the maxim ran, meaning, "You can't get blood from a stone." If the corporation was an independent artificial person in the law, its liabilities were inevitably limited by its assets. A man doing business by himself or in partnership could be bankrupted, his home and his lands and all his other property seized, because he had guessed wrong in the course of his work as a trader or a shipper or a builder. Moreover, every member of a partnership would be fully liable, personally, for all losses. If the business was done in the name of the corporation, however, then the worst that could happen was the loss of the money already invested: the creditors or victims, not the proprietors, would be stuck. The corporation, in Britain, became known specifically as a "limited liability company," and put "Ltd." after its name. On the continent the title was some version of "anonymous society," to give a grimmer warning.

Limitation of the risk also made it possible to gather money from many investors. A man with a colony to promote or an invention to exploit, later a railroad to build or a mine to dig, could acquire fantastic leverage through the right to sell shares to the public. Indeed, quite apart from the scandals—the South Sea Bubbles and Credit Mobiliers—the corporation offered its promoters a quick and guaranteed profit from the mere organization of the business. For a long time—up through the 1920s—it was commonplace for a new corporation to be organized in such a way that its indebtedness equaled its assets, and the sale of ownership shares was commission for the proprietor. When trouble arrived, the stockholders would be squeezed out, the bondholders would become the owners, and the creditors would become the bondholders. Railroad companies and public utilities in particular were likely to go through this process, because they were most like the corporations Blackstone had in mind; their services were too important to be eliminated even if the companies were broke. The structure invited fraud, and fraud which was harder to get at because the instrumentality was independent of its beneficiaries. As Blackstone pointed out, a corporation cannot "be committed to prison; for its existence being ideal, no man can apprehend or arrest it. . . . Neither can a corporation be excommunicated; for it has no soul."

Obviously, only a sovereign power could create bodies with such privileges and immunities; and for centuries in England the right to operate businesses in this manner was a special favor granted by the Crown only to special favorites. In Blackstone's time corporate charters could be secured only by Act of Parliament, and the powers of the body thus created—the kinds of business in which it could engage, the purposes it was to serve—were narrowly established in the Act. This procedure was inherited by the American colonies, and the right to license corporations was among the sovereign powers of the several states. (The federal government, it later developed, did have the right to charter corporations in areas particularly important to its own financing and to interstate commerce: banks and railroads.) These state powers were at first relatively neglected. Before 1800 there were only 213 corporations in the country, and only eight of those had been organized for purposes of manufacturing—the rest were banks, turnpike and canal companies.

Before 1818 the value of a corporate charter was limited by the power of the legislative body which had issued the charter to revoke it or amend it in whatever way a new legislature thought politic. Then, in the *Dartmouth College Case,* the Supreme Court ruled that a corporate charter was a contract between a state and the proprietors of the corporation. By Article I, Section 10 of the Constitution, a state was forbidden to pass any "Law impairing the Obligation of Contracts." Thus a corporate charter, once passed by a state, became to all intents and purposes embedded not merely in law but in the Constitution. (Congress, incidentally, was under no such disability, the prohibition being only on the states.) Partly because an educational institution was the beneficiary of the decision, partly because the New Hampshire legislature had been in fact attempting to destroy the independence of the college, and partly because of the pathos of Daniel Webster's argument ("It is a small college, but there are those of us who love it"), the case has gone into the schoolbooks as one of the great victories of the rule of law in American history. In fact, its effects were pernicious, too, because protection went to corrupt and vicious as well as to virtuous enterprises. Worst of all, because the "purposes" described in the charters were often vague, it could be (and was) argued that a legislature had granted a monopoly to, say, the first railroad company that came along, on the grounds that authorization of a rival railway corporation would diminish the value of the first charter, thereby impairing the contract.

This last interpretation was scotched by the Court in 1837 (Webster losing an argument), and in 1854 Chief Justice Roger Taney gave the full rationale:

[I]t is a matter of public history, which this Court cannot refuse to notice, that almost every bill for the incorporation of banking companies, insurance and trust companies, railroad companies or other corporations, is drawn originally by the parties who are personally interested in obtaining the charter; and they are often passed by the Legislature in the last days of its session, when, from the nature of our political institutions, the business is unavoidably transacted in a hurried manner.

Even if the charters were granted only upon careful and honest consideration, as Senator Benjamin Tappan of Ohio pointed out, legislators were fallible humans:

The chartered powers which they have conferred may prove to be powers of mischief and destruction, instead of being used to promote the public interest and welfare; guided by a private cupidity, they may be used to corrupt the morals of the people and sap the foundations of our government, and yet upon this theory of vested rights, there is no remedy—the enslaved people must submit.

Nevertheless, the rule survived into this century; and exactly what Tappan had predicted came to pass. "Consider," Elihu Root said in 1879, in his early years as a successful corporate lawyer, "the influence of great corporations, how they are represented in Congress and state legislatures; how they control and corrupt legislatures; how they sometimes mold and sometimes defy the law; how they stifle investigation; how they pervert public franchises; how grasping and unjust they are."

In a national economy with a federal legal system, state power to charter corporations made trouble from the very beginning. The corporation was an artificial person: did it have a state citizenship? Marshall, very firmly, said No: "That invisible, intangible, and artificial being, that mere legal entity, a corporation aggregate, is certainly not a citizen." As the corporation itself was not a citizen of any state, it could not take advantage of "diversity jurisdiction" and sue or be sued in a federal court unless *all* its stockholders lived outside the state of the person on the other side of the case. The growth of the railroads, with the violent feeling against them in many farming communities, made this denial of the federal courts a clear hardship, and in 1844 the Supreme Court changed the rules of the game, announcing in the *Letson* case that for jurisdictional purposes a corporation would be treated as a citizen of the state in which it was chartered. The logic of this was later explained as a "legal presumption" that all the members of the corporation were in fact residents of the state which had chartered it. Herbert Wechsler of Columbia has labeled this presumption "the only outright legal fiction that survives in modern jurisprudence."

As a practical matter, Taney's decision in the *Letson* case gave corporations a reason to incorporate themselves *away from* the state in which they did most of their business. "Foreign" status gave them the right to "remove" to the federal courts all suits against them. Federal judges were appointed rather than elected, and much less subject to local passion—not to mention the fact, important to the railroads, that the federal courts were located in the cities rather than in the county seats. For ninety-four years, moreover, the federal courts applied their own "common law," in many ways more favorable to corporations than the laws of the states. The fees for incorporating and for maintaining the charter were a pleasant supplement to tax revenues for smaller states, which were often willing to grant charters with somewhat broader powers and fewer obligations than might be offered and demanded elsewhere. Lawyers in Delaware, particularly, acquired a profitable, labor-free sideline in acting as a letter drop and keeper of the corporate seal for companies which transacted all their real business elsewhere.

In 1868 the Fourteenth Amendment, aimed at ending the realities as well as the forms of slavery in the Southern states, forbade the states to "abridge the privileges and immunities of citizens of the United States" or to "deprive any *person* of life, liberty or property, without due process of law" or to "deny to any *person* within its jurisdiction the equal protection of the laws" (italics added). Now, the corporation was not a citizen for substantive as distinct from procedural purposes—Marshall's rule on that matter was definitively upheld in *Paul* v. *Virginia* in 1869. But the corporation *was* a "person," albeit an artificial person. In the most remarkable piece of sleight-of-hand ever accomplished by lawyers in the United

States, a group of corporate lawyers headed by Senator Roscoe Conk-ling of New York (who argued several of the cases in the Supreme Court himself) sold the Justices on the idea that this Amendment in referring to "persons" was designed also to protect corporations— and in the process, by the way, sold Charles A. Beard and other historians of the period between the world wars the notion that the men who drew up the Fourteenth Amendment had engaged in a great conspiracy to cheat the American workingman.

The fact is that in his appearances before the Court Conkling was lying and knew it. As a member of the Committee of Fifteen which had drawn up the Amendment, he was in an excellent posi-tion to tell the Supreme Court what the committee had meant by the use of the word "person." "Through ingenious implication and by his dramatic use of the *Journal of the Committee of Fifteen* to create deliberately a false impression," as Joseph James recently wrote, Conkling convinced the Court that this question had been studied in the meetings of the committee; and the evidence is now quite clear that it hadn't been. Conkling stressed the journal entries showing that the committee distinguished carefully between "citi-zens" and "persons"; but James points out that the purpose of all these motions and votes had been to make sure that the Amend-ment did not work to penalize the Northern states with their large and growing class of aliens. Nobody had ever so much as mentioned corporations in this connection until Conkling took a fee.

Obviously, any restriction on the potential profitability of an enterprise—by enforcing maximum hours or minimum wages or by prohibiting child labor or by requiring sanitary conditions in fac-tories—could be seen as depriving the business of property. Cor-porate lawyers used the Fourteenth Amendment mercilessly to overthrow on constitutional grounds all attempts by state govern-ments to regulate the conduct of business in the United States. In the process the corporate lawyer acquired a reputation in society which he has not yet been able to shake.

3

"Every big law firm has a cornerstone," says New York's James B. Donovan; "and then there's this mysterious accretion." Most often, the cornerstone is a bank. Every bank, as its advertisements testify, is in the business of lending money; but equally important to its prosperity is the business of getting back the money it has loaned. This second business is greatly facilitated if the loan contract gives the bank a cheap, convenient and quick legal process to compel repayment. Over centuries of trial and error, lawyers have developed standard clauses ("boilerplate") to make sure the courts will respond correctly if they are needed. But special situations of one sort or another are always coming up, and lawyers must examine them, negotiate slightly different arrangements, and locate the right pieces of boilerplate to express them precisely. Every once in a while, the question of plausible legal protection has to be substantially re-thought—in dealing for the first time, for example, with pipeline companies or computer services or public authorities building high-ways to be financed by tolls, or companies that are nothing more nor less than operating subsidiaries of foreign governments (like airlines).

If the loan goes sour, the lawyer will be put to work negotiating with the borrower and its other creditors about its impending bank-ruptcy. A really big bankruptcy, with all its questions about selling off assets or keeping the business in being, enforcing the bankrupt's own claims on others and so forth, can yield a bank's lawyer fees well into the hundreds of thousands of dollars, and support many other lawyers, too. Even the bankruptcy of a crook—like Tony di Angelis, whose vegetable oil swindles wrecked two Wall Street brokerage houses and shook the giant American Express—will give reason for sober satisfaction in the skyscraper offices. Fowler Hamil-ton of the firm of Cleary, Gottlieb, Steen & Hamilton once estimated that the reorganization of Paramount Pictures in the 1930s had required more than a hundred man-years of lawyers' time.

On the paper-and-pencil or adding-machine level this work is just as dull as the word "boilerplate" implies, but the negotiations are often replete with personality. A lawyer who handles such problems for a bank remembers a recent case where the bank was displeased with the financial statement of an electronics company headed by several college professors, and sent him over to break the news that they were out of business. "It was pretty confusing for a while. I kept looking at the conference table and the heavy glass ashtrays and wondering how much we could sell them for, eying the pretty secretaries in their tight skirts and wondering who was looking for a girl in his office; and they kept telling me the bank ought to lend them another two hundred thousand dollars. They'd lost three hundred and fifty thousand on a subcontract; and in their financial statement they'd capitalized the loss as research and development, on the grounds that they'd learned a lot. It wasn't until I told them they could go to jail for this kind of bookkeeping that they began to take me seriously."

Banks are trustees, with fiduciary obligations to those who benefit from the trusts: they need constant legal opinions about how this money can be invested, how the stock can be voted, how the funds can be paid out. Even if they know what to do, they need legal opinions, because the presence of such documents can greatly reduce if not eliminate their liabilities. Banks work all over the world, and must stay on the right side of foreign exchange regulations, treaties on negotiable instruments and the like. Banks are regulated by both the federal government and the states, and sometimes caught in a squeeze among conflicting policies of the Federal Reserve System, the Comptroller of the Currency and the state banking commission. And banks have all the usual worries about corporate organization, taxes, antitrust dangers, labor relations, responsibility for the acts of subordinate officers, etc. The world's largest law firm, New York's Shearman & Sterling, with 180 attorneys, rests securely on the foundation of New York's First National City Bank; and few firms of twenty-five lawyers or more are without a significant banking client. Banks, moreover, are probably the best source of out-of-town business clients; a man from a small city who needs a lawyer in the big city is more likely to get a recommendation from his bank's correspondent bank than from anyone else, including his own local lawyer.

Banks are all over; if money were merely a matter of banking, the big law firms would not have clustered so around Wall Street. But since the late nineteenth century corporations have raised much of their long-term capital by selling securities to the public, and lawyers have been needed to serve the companies and their "underwriters." Before the Great Crash, these services were very largely in negotiating the terms on which the underwriters would handle the paper, and in drawing up the indentures which would iron-clad the bonds offered to a more sophisticated public of banks and insurance companies. There were also dangers that disgruntled purchasers might sue corporate officers or underwriters who profited too spectacularly from securities that later turned out to be worth less than advertised, and lawyers were needed to advise on how the documents should be drawn to avoid such suits.

With the arrival of the securities acts in the early days of the Roosevelt Administration, all the rules changed. Suddenly securities issues could not be sold to the public at all unless a governmental body passed on the comprehensiveness of formal statements offering the stocks or bonds; and any misstatements would later subject both corporation and underwriter to liability in private suits. Because so many corporate lawyers at the time were bitter about the New Deal, it was not understood then by the public and it is not understood now by most lawyers that the real law in this area was made by Wall Street lawyers, both those who had gone to Washington with Roosevelt (himself originally a product of Walter Carter's lawyer nursery at Carter, Ledyard & Milburn) and those who were steering their clients past the new shoals. William Ward Foshay of Sullivan & Cromwell says, "Back in those days every registration statement was a first time. Every question you ran into had never been answered. The amount of midnight oil was monumental, you never got home for dinner. It's too bad for the young lawyer today; registration statements now are just updating."

Registration statements are today the classic "boilerplate" of the large law office. The status of the new issue with relation to existing securities must be detailed precisely, every item of information that might help a customer decide to buy or (especially) not to buy these pieces of paper must be presented clearly, and this information may include references to the sad experience of other companies in the same line of work (thus Cinerama had to point out that no other process of this nature had ever made money). Speed is important, because the underwriter wants to hit the market just so; and the SEC can move forward or backward the date when the registration statement becomes "effective" and the stocks or bonds can be sold. Around the turn of the century, Edward C. Henderson of Cravath & Henderson used to write out the terms of securities offerings himself, in pencil on yellow pads. Now teams of young lawyers put together the document and will often get it set in type before it goes to a senior man as "The Proof." Normally a registration statement goes through eight or ten proofs before everything has been cleared with clients and other law firms; and the Ad Press near Wall Street maintains a snack bar—and for a while ran a bowling alley —for the young lawyers who wait around while the corrections are being made.

Then the document goes down to Washington, where SEC lawyers and other experts sniff at it, weigh it, examine the accounting procedures employed to produce the figures, check through their own enormous files of data that publicly owned companies are required to file with the Commission, and finally send a "deficiency letter" detailing what the staff feels should be added to the statement. These deficiencies must be corrected; the SEC is not to be trifled with. Once again there are proofs, and late nights at the printer, and consultations; and then the final version goes off with a request that the SEC now permit instant sale of the securities. Intent of Congress or no, by the way, there is still some advertising in this business, because the name of a new company can exert a pull on buyers—especially a real scientific name with good onomatopoeia. No example can be given, because a smart young Wall Street lawyer gobbled them all up, creating corporate shells and registering the names, for the purpose of selling them to promoters.

During the period shortly before and shortly after the sale of new securities, lawyers govern absolutely what corporations do and say in public; the slightest hint of actions designed to influence the sale can produce cancellation of the registration statement. Around the year, the lawyers must approve reports to stockholders, proxy forms, financial statements and so forth, all of which require seals of formal acceptability from the SEC. And, of course, the negotiations with (or for) underwriters in setting up the contract which underlies all securities issues can be a matter of months of work for gangs of lawyers.

The area of new securities, incidentally, is one of very few in which a lawyer may be financially responsible for the *quality* of his advice. His approval of an inadequate registration statement makes him liable to the corporation if it is later sued by its stockholders on that basis. Most lawyers who work for large corporations in the financial market carry attorney malpractice insurance, usually to guard against catastrophe (the policy may cover losses up to $10 million, with the first $50,000 or so deductible). The costs of malpractice insurance for law firms doing SEC work have risen dramatically since the Transitron case, where several million dollars were returned to losers because the registration statement failed to discuss the possibility of a patent infringement suit, even though threats of such a suit were lying all over the company's files. Quite apart from cash liability, lawyers' reputations rest on their expertise in preparing financial documents, or "green goods" (as the late Joseph Cotton once called them).

Nearly all significant contracts with suppliers and customers must pass through a lawyer's hands, to make sure the company isn't falling afoul of the antitrust laws or otherwise violating other laws or contracts. Contracts with the government are particularly tricky, because they can be renegotiated—and no corporation can ever afford to forget that lawsuits cost the government nothing. A couple of years ago, when then Supreme Court Justice Arthur J. Goldberg suggested that governments should reimburse the costs of their defense to criminal defendants who had been found not guilty, a Wall Street lawyer rather bitterly asked whether these reimbursements would extend to defendants in antitrust actions.

The biggest contract problems arise in mergers, or diversification by the purchase of other companies—though simply assuring a steady source of supply at a fixed price for, say, a steel mill can produce an immensely tricky legal document. A few years ago, a consortium of steel companies and banks negotiated for the exploitation rights on the enormous Labrador iron deposits. As the date for closing the contract approached, the Grand Ballroom of the Hotel Astor in midtown New York was hired to hold the piled-up printed documents and the dozens of lawyers from different firms who were working to get everything in shape. Coming out of the theater late one night, a partner in one of the firms involved dropped in on the ballroom to see how his associates and their friends were doing, and shook his head at the mass of miserable sweating humanity working past midnight on the damned pieces of paper. "Why don't we," he said cheerfully, "do the deal on a handshake?" But nobody laughed. And eventually the deal fell through.

Tax work involves litigation—and litigation against what an Internal Revenue Service lawyer once called "the largest specialized law firm in the world. . . . We have over 650 working in direct attorney capacities. . . . We handle 28,000 direct tax cases every year." Anyone who draws any number of contracts will find himself in court or before an arbitrator on occasion, seeking to make his clauses stand up. Several large firms handle the defense of personal-injury actions either for insurance companies or for manufacturers large enough to be self-insuring. Part of any corporate practice is the defense of the corporations themselves and/or their directors from suits brought by disappointed stockholders. But to most large law firms, the word "litigation" connotes an antitrust suit, not because the number of such cases is large but because each of them represents so enormous a quantity of work.

Fundamentally, the difficulty is that the government can and will empty the papers from every section of every honeycomb in the corporation, looking for evidence to prove the very vague (but necessarily vague) charge of restraint of trade. So the lawyers, too, must know every piece of paper, and must be prepared to explain anything that looks like a gesture toward eliminating competition. (Morris Ernst says cynically that "the only art of the antitrust lawyer is going through the file and taking out everything harmful without getting caught.") Normally more than one company is involved, but the work cannot be consolidated because the prosecution presents different degrees of peril to the different defendants and each wants a defense based on his particular problem.

Coming to trial in an antitrust suit, a corporation must stand prepared to defend every one of its actions in every one of its markets over a period of years. Preparing such defenses is one of the largest information-retrieval and information-reorganizing jobs in the society, and the work must be assigned in its pieces. Some of the Wall Street firms will assign the same piece to different young associates, to make sure a point gets examined from all angles; and competing memos of law will wind through channels up to the man who is organizing the case for the man who will try it. . . . A large staff is needed simply to supervise the work of what may be a hundred "document analysts" temporarily hired just for this case. There is a problem of what you do with all these people when you don't have a difficult case. "The Wall Street partner in the antitrust field," says Earl Kintner, formerly general counsel and chairman of the Federal Trade Commission, who now works on such cases for corporations, "heads a staff of lawyers who have to be kept busy; they do a lot of leaf-raking."

At best, however, the business is paralyzingly time-consuming. Taking the depositions and reading the documents lead to motions for the exclusion of evidence and dismissal of specific charges, hearings on the motions, appeals after the hearings; and then the trial itself drags on and on and on, and its results are appealed. Timothy Pfeiffer in his history of the Milbank, Tweed firm tells a piece of the story of the great case against Alcoa for monopolizing the aluminum business, which required twenty-six months to try, produced a record of forty thousand printed pages of testimony, and endured through various appeals and reopenings for almost twenty-four years. Three partners in the firm (which represented a subsidiary defendant, not Alcoa itself) were in the courtroom the entire first year; one was there for all twenty-six months.

A big antitrust trial is one of the sights of America, sometimes with literally dozens of defense counsel representing different defendants, sitting at rows of tables in the well of the courtroom. A moment sticks in the memory from the 1964 trial of the kosher meatpackers for price-fixing (they were acquitted; their alleged partners in crime, the makers of frankfurter rolls, had previously pleaded *nolo contendere* and been fined). An aging delicatessen owner was on the stand in one of the dark first-floor courtrooms in New York's skyscraper Federal Court House. An eager young Assistant U.S. Attorney was cross-examining him. Casting a knowing eye at the jury, the young man said, "In October, 1945, did you know a man named J. M. Levine?" At the defense table, fourteen white-haired, highly paid lawyers rose in a wave—not all at once, because they did not all have the same reaction time: "Object on the grounds that there is no evidence such a person exists. . . ." An irritated judge waved them down. And the witness said despairingly, "There are so many Levines. . . ."

Not the least of the oddities in this courtroom was the bleary-eyed jury of fifteen (three alternates because you can't count on people's lasting through months of a trial like this: they sicken, sometimes die). Prohibited by the rules governing juries from making notes on the fantastically elaborate cases for both prosecution and defense (because the juror who has made notes becomes too influential in the jury room, and there is no way to control the accuracy of his notes), they were supposed to keep straight in their heads material which the lawyers could organize only with the help of staffs of trained assistants. At the end, locked into a jury room, they would have to decide on what could scarcely be better than vague feelings whether they wished to impose a *criminal conviction* on these businessmen. The entire situation was a brilliant *reductio ad absurdum* of the jury system or of the imposition of criminal penalties on violations of the antitrust statutes, or of both.

One of the reasons for going after criminal convictions in the antitrust field is that they open the door for private lawsuits, by which the victims of efforts to restrain competition can secure awards triple the damages they suffered. Any evidence laid out in open court is available to private plaintiffs, and a conviction (by judge, jury or guilty plea) becomes evidence of liability for the assessment of damages. To avoid such convictions, and also to avoid the enormous costs of defending the suits, many defendants plead *nolo contendere* (Do With Me What You Will) in these cases, and then bargain out the terms of the penalties to be assessed.

The final court orders will over the years produce continuing business for the lawyers, who must interpret what are often vague prescriptions, and sometimes convince a judge of the correctness of their interpretations. Looking back on the 1930s from the eminence of an ambassadorship to the United Nations, Francis W. Plimpton remembered working on behalf of National Cash Register, "which was under a consent decree from 1917—we had to get permission to go to the bathroom." Where the government feels strongly that really heavy punishment should be meted out, the prosecution will not accept pleas of *nolo contendere* and will insist, as in the electrical-equipment conspiracy cases of the early 1960s, that the defendants plead guilty.

The conviction of General Electric, Westinghouse and others for conspiracy to fix the prices of heavy-duty transformers and switching equipment launched the corporate bar on the greatest beano in the history of American law. Public utilities, government agencies, other manufacturers brought no fewer than 1,880 suits in federal court. Separate trial of the suits would have removed the federal court system as a whole from the consideration of any other matters; separate pretrial examination of the defendants' officers could not possibly have been accomplished in their lifetimes, even if they did nothing else. In 1962 twenty-five federal district judges met in Philadelphia and resolved to coordinate the cases. "It wasn't," says New York's Bethuel Webster, whose firm represented forty-four of the plaintiffs, "an easy thing to do—they had to call in a professional adviser," who was Dean Phil C. Neal of the University of Chicago Law School. Meanwhile, eighty plaintiffs' lawyers met and formed a "plaintiffs' steering committee." The judges issued "National Pretrial Orders," thirty-four of them by March, 1964, and set up a proceeding for "national depositions," by which pretrial testimony could be taken at one time by all the plaintiffs in all the districts. At the first such session, 150 lawyers showed up to question one officer of General Electric.

After the third round of depositions, the testimony ran to 25,000 printed pages. More than a million documents called for by discovery proceedings were stored by the defendants in a warehouse in Chicago; more than 200,000 documents were stored in a plaintiffs' depository in New York. The plaintiffs set up an organization called "LEAD." Webster says, "It stood for Library of Electrical Antitrust Something or Other. We had a paid employee whose job was to collect transcripts, a girl, bright young lawyer. She made weekly, sometimes daily reports, sent them to all the lawyers." Earl Kintner says disapprovingly (not of Webster), "An awful lot of leaf-raking went on. We finally told our client we wouldn't attend all these meetings—it wasn't fair to him to pay for all that time." In May,

1967, Chief Justice Warren announced that to his pleased surprise the mobilization had worked: all the cases were settled. Recoveries probably totaled nearly $100 million; lawyers' fees were probably around $25 million.

No litigation is as dry as such figures might indicate; the proper handling of witnesses is as important in an antitrust case as in any other. An added element of drama is that for most of the defendants and most of the defense witnesses the case is their first entanglement with the law, and they are terrified as they will not be again until their deathbeds. "[I]n an antitrust case," the New York lawyer Phil E. Gilbert recently told a meeting, "I think the witnesses can sometimes become uneasy about losing their jobs."

Big firms generally have far more personal contact with their clients than the outside world realizes. Some of this is in the course of business. Minor matters, Harrison Tweed explains,

are considered and discussed and decided by a junior partner and a subordinate corporate officer. The relationship between them is almost precisely the same as that between the old-fashioned general practitioner and his client-friend of long standing. It is true that the corporate officer is not receiving advice on a personal matter but on a corporate question. But the interest of the corporation in the solution is much more indirect and remote than the interest of the officer. His job depends on his ability to get the right answer.

[T]he relationship becomes as intimate a one and contains as much reliance and confidence as any attorney and client relationship can yield. . . . It generally happens that as the corporate officer goes up in the hierarchy so does the lawyer. Frequently the close business and legal association and the personal intimacy exist for twenty-five years or more. And it remains very intimate and thoroughly typical of the traditional ideal even when it exists between the highest officer of the corporation and the senior partner. . . . [T]he lawyer's satisfaction comes from having dealt successfully with the problem presented and that was the problem of the individual who headed the corporation.

It is by no means unknown for these business relationships to continue in the country club, the cocktail lounge and even more interesting places. Indeed, one of the requisites for the partner who is to handle certain clients is a capacity for a quantity of liquor, and sometimes a strong stomach in other ways, too. But such clients are a fairly small minority. "Some practices," says Norris Darrell of Sullivan & Cromwell, "are supposed to require entertaining, but I've found they come to you because they think you're good. If someone is a social friend, I'll turn his matter over to another partner. People will say things to him they wouldn't say to somebody they're likely to see for dinner."

Personal relationships do, however, lead to personal work—the corporate officer's son has been picked up for drunk driving at college, his daughter has disappeared into the wilds of New York with a football player, he wants a divorce. "Nearly all lawyers," says Elihu Root, Jr., looking back on sixty years of corporate practice, "have from time to time clients who get into matrimonial trouble—but the serious work is done in Reno." Clients' sex life also enters into the wills and estates practice, which is where the real personal business lies. Robert T. Swaine wrote of "liaisons . . . unknown even to the client's intimates until death revealed a contract to provide for the lady during her life, or a bequest for her in a will, or an account held for her benefit with a brokerage firm" —and added in a footnote an example of the way a lawyer's advice can benefit a client even after death: "Often the provision in the will was a bequest to a third party, who was requested, in a letter outside the will, to use the bequest to take care of the decedent's friend."

Until recently, wills and estates practice was a great convenience for a large firm, because it supplied a place where the firm could employ the client's brother, its own senile partners, and the socially prominent but not terribly bright lawyers who might be useful in getting business. Wills are the most ritualized documents in the law, and provided the client can be discouraged from trying anything unusual any lawyer could fill in the blanks clearly enough to produce a piece of paper that would stand up in court. A bad job was unlikely to be uncovered, because nobody could ask the deceased what his intentions had been, and socially established people mostly dislike battles in the probate court. The real work of operating the estate, and much of the work of setting it up, could be done by a bank. Many clients, moreover, like the idea of discussing will problems with a scion of a great family; and because some of these clients definitely did not like the idea of spreading their personal situation before a Jew or an Italian, wills and estates practice provided an excellent excuse for the ethnic discrimination that was commonplace in the big firms until after the Second World War.

Those days, however, are gone. Tax considerations rather than personal preferences now dominate the writing of wills, and clients, though still uncomfortable about discussing the problems of their daughters' husbands with someone they consider a social inferior, are likely to care more for a lawyer's cleverness than for his acceptability. There is still some tendency (especially in Boston) to keep the Jew or the Italian or the Pole in the back room while someone of longer domestic lineage discusses the will in the front room; but recently the boys in the back room have been getting partnerships, too.

4

In a gesture of high generosity, the sociologist Erwin O. Smigel has defined large law firms as institutions "which depend for their success upon the quality of the men they hire rather than on the new clients they enlist." The statement reflects the self-image of the corporate lawyers, and it is certainly true of those firms which already have a lot of stable clients. Few large firms will take a partner from the outside world more than once a decade; virtually all the partners are men who started with this firm fresh out of law school (or following a brief apprenticeship with the government) and worked their way up. But a firm with a hundred lawyers may have no more than half a dozen *real* partners, and taking an aggressive or powerful man from outside into this circle can drastically change the character of the firm: one a decade may be a lot. Three defeated Presidential candidates—Willkie, Dewey and Nixon —subsequently became senior partners and chief business-getters of previously established Wall Street firms. For a firm which has been declining, the quality of a man is often defined by the quality of the clients who come with him.

Law firms decline for various reasons. In this age of corporate mergers, large clients can simply disappear into the maw of someone else's larger client. (And it is worth noting, for those who believe lawyers incapable of disinterested actions, that many firms have successfully negotiated mergers and acquisitions which deprive them of a major source of fee income.) More firms than most lawyers like to admit are built fundamentally around the talents of one or two men—especially litigators, who draw a great volume of antitrust business—and can be severely damaged by the death or retirement of a single partner. By no means all large firms are equally good; several of the largest have a surprisingly slight reputation with out-of-town lawyers who have sent them business and seen it ill-managed. It was a large law firm which (erroneously) advised a joint-stock insurance company that it could legally sell its stock in New York though it was not qualified to write insurance in the state; and an almost equally large firm which recently wrote for a Southern client a mortgage on a New England factory which turned out not to be a mortgage after all. There are erasers on the pencils in the large law firms, too, and quality control problems which grow in severity as the firms get larger.

Nor is the decision about which young lawyers to hire entirely dominated by their apparent abilities. Other things being near equal, the man with a prep school background gets the edge—though purely social considerations have always been much more important outside New York. (John J. McCloy—after a career which included a partnership in two New York firms, the presidency of the World Bank, the chairmanship of the Chase Bank, public service as High Commissioner to Germany—still remembers with some bitterness his return to his native Philadelphia following his graduation from Harvard Law School: "I was born north of Market Street; my mother had to go to work to keep us in school when my father died. I couldn't get the smell of a job. I went in to see George Pepper, who'd met my mother, and he said, 'Oh, Jack, I don't think you should try to practice law here—this is a *family* town.' I went right from his office to the train, and right off the bat that afternoon I had an offer of a job in New York.") But other questions do arise. A partner in one of New York's large firms touched on one of the difficulties in reply to a question at a lawyers' forum: "I would like to see our firm adopt a policy of not taking our own sons. We would do everything possible to open another firm's door to them and would reciprocate. That way every man who comes along will know that if he prospers, he does so on his own merits. There is also the problem of what to do with the sons, nephews or godsons of your clients. I don't have the answer to that one."

By and large, however, the large law firms want the cream of the crop from the best law schools, about five hundred top new men every year, across the country. The fishing is done in a rather restricted pool. Smigel's study shows that 70 percent of all partners in Wall Street firms come from one of three law schools—Harvard, Yale or Columbia. In the Midwest, Michigan and Chicago would show up more heavily in the sample; on the West Coast, California and Stanford; in the South, the University of Virginia. In terms of the law school background, the partnership roster is probably an accurate reflection of the pattern of hiring associates: except for the handful hired annually to do semiclerical repetitive chores, the men who are taken from a less than elite law school must be so good to begin with that their chances of reaching a partnership are if anything a little better than those of the ordinary associate.

Thirty years ago, the law school senior would come to New York or Chicago during the Christmas vacation, armed with a letter of introduction from one or more of his professors, and make the rounds of the offices. Now the large law firms vigorously recruit at eight or ten law schools across the country. As Felix Frankfurter put it shortly before his death, "The New York firms send their drummers up with their sample trunks." Harvard tacks up on the bulletin board every year about three hundred announcements that somebody is coming from such and such a firm (or corporate legal department) and would like to speak with any third-year (sometimes second-year) student who would like to speak with him. Usually the interviewers arrive in pairs—a younger partner and a recently employed associate, if possible both alumni of this law school. If the man's grades are good, he can supply plausible recommendations and he looks respectable, the interviewers will invite him to visit their office and meet some more people. Some firms interview second-year students and invite them to work for the

summer (at $125-$150 a week), with the thought that at the end of
the summer both the student and the firm will know whether they
are interested in a permanent proposition.

Most firms pay expenses for students invited down to meet other
partners. California firms, which are vigorously raiding Eastern law
schools, will set up a weekend's entertainment: "One of our younger
associates," James B. Tucker of Rutan & Tucker in Santa Ana told
a rather incredulous group of New York lawyers,

will meet the man at the plane, bring him to the firm, and escort him
through the two-day period. . . . We try to get the applicant to spend the
night in a young attorney's home. Many of the firms in Los Angeles put
up students at a hotel. We think the students prefer to spend the night
in the home of a young attorney. They may say to themselves, "In a few
years, maybe I can afford this kind of house." Incidentally, we ask the
wives to come with the applicants, and we pay their expenses. Wives
probably influence the applicant's choice as much as anything else. On
Friday, they are taken care of by some of our younger attorneys' wives who
can tell them about housing, schools and other subjects in which they are
interested. On Saturday morning or Saturday afternoon, the students and
their wives take a limousine tour of the area.

This sort of recruiting has been made necessary by the reluctance
of many men at the top of their class to tie their futures to the
chance of a partnership in a big city. "At the thirtieth reunion
of my law school class," D. Nelson Adams of the New York firm
of Davis, Polk said, "five distinguished members of the class were
asked to speak at a symposium. One was a justice of a high state
court; one was a United States Senator from Hawaii; another was
the president of a corporation; the fourth was a banker; and the
last was a successful song writer. None of them became lawyers in
large offices. We must recognize that only a small part of each graduating class are interested in us."

"I tell the young lawyers," said Morris Ernst, " 'Why come to
New York? Go to the Delaware Water Gap. There's a drunken
lawyer just died down there. You can have his library. Your wife
can teach school, and you can go skiing in the winter afternoons."
A young man a year out of Yale Law School and working with a
New Hampshire firm said in 1964, "New York offered me seventy-
two hundred, and here I get six thousand—but it's a lot easier to

get an apartment, life is less complicated and expensive, and people know each other."

There is sympathy where one would least expect it for the young lawyer who does not wish to risk burying himself in a large firm. "When I got out of law school, the one thing I wanted to do was to try cases," says George Leisure of New York's large Donovan, Leisure, Newton & Irvine. "I went with [Charles Evans] Hughes; they promised me trial experience. But when you came right down to it, a partner would say, 'Of course, it's okay if he wins it; but if he loses it, we lose a client'; and I didn't get the experience." Around the Chadbourne, Parke office there is a favorite story about a young man who had been an associate for six to eight months and was encountered in the halls by a kindly partner:

"How do you like it here?"

"Oh, I like it fine."

"How are you getting on?"

"Oh, I think I'm getting on very well."

"How do you think you're doing?"

"I'm going right on up."

The partner nodded, very pleased with the young man's enthusiasm; and the young man added, "I've had nothing to do here since I came but that damned Brooklyn sewer case—I've *got* to go up."

Young men are expected to work hard; and while nobody holds a clock on partners, they have often acquired habits they don't shake. The classic story tells of Hoyt A. Moore of Cravath, Swaine & Moore, to whom someone had suggested that new associates should be hired because the current staff was overworked. "That's silly," Moore replied. "No one is under pressure. There wasn't a light on when I left at two this morning." Harrison Tweed has written about an episode in his apprenticeship with James Byrne, who

demanded to know why [a memorandum] was not ready and I humbly pleaded that I had not had time to finish it. He glared at me and asked, "What time did you go home on Friday night?" I replied, "Three o'clock in the morning." "What time did you go home Saturday night?" I told him that I had quit at two o'clock in the morning. Then came the final "What time did you go home Sunday night?" And I had to confess that I had done so at eleven o'clock; whereupon he pounded the desk and said: "Don't tell me that you didn't have time to finish that memorandum. Tell me the truth—that you wanted to go home early Sunday night."

Such incidents are much more fun in retrospect than they were at the time, and senior partners now go out of their way to assure possible candidates that the horror stories are now history. But the young associate will usually be expected to work an evening or two every week, and more than occasional Saturdays. For a man with a wife and a baby in the suburbs, the schedule is uncomfortable, particularly because a reputation for keeping at it is the one absolute necessity if a man is to be made a partner. One of the respondents in Erwin Smigel's study referred to "a lot of men who lost their partnership on the New Haven Rail Road."

By and large, the new associates do much the sort of work they were doing for their law reviews; instead of writing "notes" on a point of law for the consideration of the other editors, they write memoranda for a partner (or for a senior associate). There is no particular concern about when associates pass the bar exam and become licensed attorneys—nothing the firm will require from them in their first year or two will demand admission to the bar. Most firms make an effort to move an associate around during his first year, to find out how he works in the different branches of what Felix Frankfurter called "department stores" (a much better image than the conventional "law factory"), and to let a number of partners take a look at him. The man who gets stuck on a single job, however—preparing an exhaustive memo of law to defend marketing practices challenged under the Robinson-Patman Act, or going through the question of exactly what must be negotiated with the union if the client wants to close one of his plants —may come more quickly to the attention of a partner who can be useful to him.

What the large firms offer the young men, primarily, is money. A man looking to get his experience in a small firm may "clerk" for $25 or $50 a week—or even, in states like Florida and California, to which tyros flock from all over the country, for nothing, to establish a residence and make a few contacts. The starting salary on Wall Street in 1967 was $9,200 a year, and it was the same in all firms: one of the most blatant price-fixing conspiracies in America is that of a number of the large New York law firms which delegate a partner to go lunch with his brethren each year and set a maximum salary for all new law school graduates. (Los Angeles broke the price line in 1967, offering $10,000 for the guaranteed grade-A merchandise.) This salary is not so lavish on an hourly basis as the casual observer might believe—a beginning teacher in New York, who will on the average work no more than 35 hours a week for 37 weeks a year, makes $6,100, which works out to $4.71 an hour for 1,295 hours; the beginning lawyer on Wall Street will work 50 hours a week 46 weeks a year (assuming that he really takes 10 holidays away from the office), which works out to $3.91 an hour for 2,300 hours. But the normal bonus is a month's salary; and the first raise, of at least $1,000, will come after six months; and very few men five years out of law school are making less than $15,000 a year in the large law firms. Fifteen years after its graduation, the Harvard Law School Class of 1949 published a report on how its members were doing. Twenty-three of the 246 graduates who reported themselves in full-time private practice were partners in firms of fifty or more lawyers. Their average income was $46,000 a year.

But money is by no means the only lure. Large law firms give young men a unique chance to be lawyers as the law schools have brought them up to define the word. The overwhelming emphasis on law school grades in hiring men into these offices is justified by the impedance match between academic work and the first years as an associate. Even in later years the lawyer in a big office is protected from the nuisance of law as a business. Others rent the offices and hire the secretaries (find the girl you like in the pool); others supply unlimited stenographic, copying, library and research services; others send out the bills and keep track of whether they have been paid; others take care of the filing and retrieval. (Maybe; the filing problem sometimes gets out of hand. "About ten years ago," Lawrence B. Morris of White & Case told a meeting, "the head of our filing department was a very elderly lady. Sending a paper to the file room was like burning it —you probably would not see it again. For all practical purposes each lawyer started his own filing system. It has taken us about ten years to root out this practice.") Clients are rarely obtrusive; the young lawyer gets his instructions from older lawyers in the firm rather than from clients, and sends back his advice through the same channels. (Associates may talk to clients, but they are almost never authorized to sign letters of opinion.) Younger men especially can work on nothing but law all day long—and there are innumerable opportunities for arguments back and forth about the law which are what most of the men who do well in law school like best about law school. The purely business requirements are keeping the diary entries accurate so the accountants can make up bills, and sending different communiqués about a matter on different colors of paper, so the file clerks can work fast.

Within two years the new associate begins working steadily with only two or three partners, normally in one specialty of law; within three or four years he moves to the window seat of a two-man office and acquires a degree of supervisory responsibility over the newer man who sits near the door; within five or six years he gets an office of his own and begins traveling around to see clients on their home grounds; and within seven or eight years the senior men begin thinking (as he himself has never stopped thinking) about whether he should be made a partner in the firm. The focus shifts: "In the early years," a partner in a large firm told the PLI Seminar, "we focus on technical things like legal ability, drafting ability, or the way the man thinks things through. When we begin to consider a man for a partnership, however, our focus changes to the man's ability to take on and discharge responsibility. The question is not whether you would like this man to work for you next year, but whether you would be willing to let this man replace you in handling clients."

Some of the men who will reach this stage will have had a couple of years out of the office in the interim. For a man who is going to work primarily on problems relating to Washington agencies, the firm often thinks it is a good idea that he get himself some experience working at the agency. (Not a wholly good idea, however. "People who start with the government," says a young partner, "can get this enormous belief that what the government says is the law, is the law. You have to start teaching him that this ain't necessarily so.")

Most men leave before the time to parcel out partnerships arrives. Some don't like the hours; some decide they want to practice law on a more personal basis; some are tempted away by offers from corporate law departments at much more money or chances to join a new partnership of younger men at much more excitement. By and large, the big law firm takes care of its own, sends them business if they go out into little law firms, helps them get set in the corporate law departments of client corporations. ("If there is an opening in the legal department of a client corporation with which we have friendly relations," one partner says, "we would much rather see it filled by our good loyal alumnus than by a good loyal alumnus of another firm.") Out of every ten associates hired from law school, four or five will drift off in this manner or to government before they are even considered for a partnership.

The other five or six thereupon come into unavoidable and inadmissible competition for what are probably two or three possible partnerships. In part, the decision among them reflects merely what the military calls the accident of assignment—an associate who goes into an area where the firm's practice is expanding stands a much better chance than an associate saddled with work which is becoming progressively less important to the firm's income.

A client's special pleasure with a man's work (which may or may not mean a judgment on its quality *qua* work) can be very helpful when the day comes. Business-getting ability has not been important to the man as an associate (some firms will split the fees with an associate who brings in business, some will not; but men under thirty-five rarely control really significant business). Now a judgment on whether he can pull his weight in the acquisition of clients— either because of his connections or salesmanship or because his quality in his specialty forecasts referral business from other lawyers —will become a matter of considerable importance. A few men stay without partnerships, becoming "permanent associates," an economically secure but psychologically precarious position.

Departure from a large law firm without a partnership is by no means necessarily a kiss of death. A browse through the list of those who left Cravath in that condition reveals the names of William Ivins, for years the incomparable curator of prints at the Metropolitan Museum; Basil O'Connor, president of the National Foundation; former Secretary of Air Thomas Finletter; former Governor John Lodge of Connecticut; Federal Court of Appeals judge and Columbia professor Paul R. Hays; former Dean of the Yale Law School and Under Secretary of State Eugene Rostow; Congressman Jonathan Bingham; and Edward Carr, executive director of the New York Legal Aid Society.

The addition of new partners makes obvious complications in the internal economics of a law firm. Partnership shares are expressed as percentages, and at any given time 100 percent of the profits are being divvied up. Any new man's share must come out of older men's shares, and even if the growth of the firm is such that less is more, some men are both proud and greedy. (A story about Paul D. Cravath, not in Swaine's history of the firm and possibly apocryphal, recalls a day when a restless committee of partners waited on him in hopes of persuading him to reduce his 50 percent share of the net. They began by saying they thought it was time the question of partnership shares should be reopened, and he heartily agreed, and proclaimed his willingness to approve any arrangement they made, provided it was understood that his share remained 50 percent.)

Persuading a man who is eighty and not very active that he should make way for youngsters is a more difficult job than non-lawyers are likely to realize. In recent years some of the large New York firms have faced this dilemma directly, and rather shocked the conservatives of the bar by requiring new partners, in effect, to buy out the older men. The actual procedure is a compulsory deduction from the new man's partnership share to make up a "retirement fund" to which not all the established partners contribute.

What makes any of this possible is the simple arithmetic that calculates one percent of a $3 million partnership net to be $30,000. So even a one percent share, trivial in the management of the firm, represents a decent living for a man still under thirty five. The smaller shares are more like salaries—they are usually guaranteed at a minimum figure, whether or not the firm's profits would justify them—and the new partner's condition is not really much better than that of an employee. (He may be a "nonparticipating partner," which is a contradiction in terms and in status.) His war is not over. Though some of the old firms worked on the principle that all men admitted to the firm at the same time should receive the same percentage, everybody growing at the same rate as the group got older, the business-getters eventually refused to put up with this equality. Over the long run, a man's share of the firm (and his importance in its management, if he cares) will reflect the significance of the clients he controls. Shifts in partnership shares as new business arrives will normally give two-thirds of the added profit to the man who found the business (and who is also, of course, the lawyer actually advising the client), one-third to the man who works on it. In most firms a partner is expected to put all his earned income in the pot, including anything he receives as trustee of an estate or author of a book; one firm in the Southwest is reputed to require its partners to hand over *all* their income, including dividends and interest.

In most offices clients are served by separate "teams" organized around senior partners; some look like a mere aggregate of individual offices, sharing a switchboard, a library and technical services in the form of tax, litigation and estate specialists. Most junior partners and associates will be on more than one team, and the assignment of men can be a source of dispute. Not the least significant technique in running such an office is the art of getting disputes into the open, fast. Most firms have weekly lunches at which any difficulties are raised in a civilized manner, and the teams are kept in touch with each other's work (reports arc always made on new matters coming into the office, to avoid that most fearful revelation, the case where the firm has been engaged by both sides of the dispute).

People's judgments of each other tend to be influenced to a surprising degree by behavior toward the subordinate staff; nothing is so likely to annoy a partner as the discovery that one of his hardest-working associates has been unjustly chewed out by another partner. It is not required that all partners like each other, but a high level of respect is necessary on horizontal and descending lines within the partnership (that is, men need not feel any great admiration for their superiors, because the structure takes care of that relationship, but they must have confidence in their peers and the younger partners). The conversational manner, contrary to the usual image of lawyers, is brisk and candid; there is time in the big firms to be flamboyant, to sing hymns over a drink after hours or tell a scatological story at the annual firm banquet, to back a Broadway play or to own a racehorse—but not to be neurotic.

Everybody tries to hold down a little, if he can, the bill to his own clients. Though time sheets are always necessary for internal accounting, billing practice is by no means cut and dried. "I am horrified to hear from people," Frank Dewey of Western Electric told a meeting of lawyers, "that there is a range of profit and that manufacturing companies are at the top." Legal advice, Dewey said, "is probably the only service we buy without some kind of survey of alternate cost. I don't know how much longer lawyers can operate in this way." (Indeed, the threat may be more serious than that: respectable authority has recently argued that the growth of corporate law departments drastically cuts down the amount of business from big corporations that goes to big law firms, and has claimed that "Outside of New York City, some big private firms are now moving heavily into auto accident cases and some even into marital practice, fields they formerly shunned.")

Large law firms will not haggle about fees; if the client questions the bill, he is usually invited to send whatever he thinks would be fair. Indeed, there is occasional survival of the old tradition of asking the client to send whatever he thinks the service was worth. In the nineteenth century Clarence Seward wrote to a gas company for which he had lobbied in Albany: "Please send me a check for any amount that the company is willing to pay, and I will make out a bill and send a receipt for it. I have been paying gas bills in this city for some thirty-odd years, and I would like to get as much back as possible."

Lawyers are never removed from deadline pressure, but once a man is made a partner in a big firm he regains that control over his time which was taken from him when he was an associate. Personal tastes and professional logic often impel him into public service and charitable enterprise, with increasing prominence as his status with his clients rises. Not many men of the quality of those who achieve a partnership in a large firm are fully satisfied in human terms by the exercise of their intelligence on behalf of a business. The same sense of relevance and clarity of expression that make a man valuable to a client give him a function in politics, or on the board of an educational or cultural or charitable institution. If he is senior enough, he can also offer such institutions free legal services from his firm; and his influence with men who are making wills may be cherished by friends in nonprofit organizations. Clients and prospective clients, meanwhile, like the idea of having their affairs in the hands of a publicly prominent attorney. All occasions conspire to make the partners in the large firm leaders of the society's extracurricular activities.

Milbank, Tweed, Hadley & McCloy recently listed the institutions to which its partners had contributed their services in recent years. Among those where partners had been president or chairman of the board were the Carnegie, Ford and Russell Sage foundations, Vassar, Sarah Lawrence and Teachers colleges, the New York Public Library, the Metropolitan Opera, the Welfare Council, the New York School of Social Work, the State Commission on Reorganization of the Courts, the Institute for Crippled and Disabled, and International House. And there were thirty or so such institutions where partners were merely members of the board. Whatever else it may be, the large law firm is a civic asset.

Some specific tribute should also be paid to the most extraordinary talents, intellectual and human, of the leaders of the corporate bar. Especially in New York, their acquaintance and knowledge often cuts through an astonishing variety of activities, and makes them genuinely wise counselors as well as smart lawyers. Others say that the heads of large firms elsewhere are not quite on the same level. "I had lunch in Chicago with a big firm," Eugene Rostow said while dean of the Yale Law School. "All able. But I suddenly thought there wasn't one man there you'd make Assistant Secretary of State. In a similar group in New York there would be four." This story was presently improved by President Johnson, who made Rostow Under Secretary of State.

5

In June, 1934, Supreme Court Justice Harlan F. Stone, formerly a partner in two large Wall Street firms, delivered a commencement speech at the University of Michigan, and relieved himself of a number of observations about "The Public Influence of the Bar." Possibly because he was daily engaged in watching his former colleagues sabotage the New Deal with nothing to put in its place (and the sabotage was then easily accomplished, because at that time any federal district judge could declare an act of Congress unconstitutional), he did not like what he saw.

"The changed character of the lawyer's work," Stone said,

has made it difficult for him to contemplate his function in its new setting, to see himself and his occupation in proper perspective. No longer does his list of clients represent a cross section of society; no longer do his contacts make him the typical representative and interpreter of his community. The demands of practice are more continuous and exacting. He has less time for reflection upon other than immediate professional undertakings. He is more the man of action, less the philosopher and less the student of history, economics and government.

The rise of big business has produced an inevitable specialization of the Bar. The successful lawyer of our day more often than not is the proprietor or general manager of a new type of factory, whose legal product is increasingly the result of mass production methods. More and more the amount of his income is the measure of professional success. More and more he must look for his rewards to the material satisfactions derived from profits as from a successfully conducted business, rather than to the intangible and indubitably more durable satisfactions which are to be found in a professional service more consciously directed toward the advancement of the public interest. Steadily the best skill and capacity of the profession has been drawn into the exacting and highly specialized service of business and finance. At its best the changed system has brought to the command of the business world loyalty and a superb proficiency and technical skill. At its worst it has made the learned profession of an earlier day the obsequious servant of business, and tainted it with the morals and manners of the market place in its most anti-social manifestations.

Four years later an article by Ferdinand Lundberg in *Harper's Magazine* opened with Veblen's remark that "The lawyer is exclusively occupied with the details of predatory fraud, either in achieving or in checkmating chicanery"; and later charged that "[M]ost of the deeds and misdeeds [of the robber barons] were in actuality the mere projection of lawyers' schemes."

A good deal of this comment was simply naïve. The leaders of the American bar, as working lawyers, had always been closely identified with business interests. Brandeis in a talk at Harvard thirty years earlier had complained that "The leading lawyers of the United States . . . have, to a large extent, allowed themselves to become adjuncts of great corporations." Though Brandeis thought the lawyer had held a higher "position with the people . . . seventy-five or indeed fifty years ago," in fact the period he looked back upon was the time when Jacksonian democracy undertook what Roscoe Pound called the "deprofessionalization of the practice of law," when state constitutions were written to permit any citizen to practice law in any court.

The interest on municipal bonds is still tax-free, to the great benefit of the rich (and, of course, of the municipalities), because Webster persuaded Marshall to utter his catchy dictum that "The power to tax is the power to destroy." (Justice Holmes much later pointed out that the question of whether a tax is confiscatory is relatively easy for a judge to answer, and commented contemptuously that "The power to tax is not the power to destroy while this court sits.") The corporate lawyer Conkling maneuvered corporations under the umbrella of the Fourteenth Amendment by pure dishonesty; the corporate lawyer William D. Guthrie rigged a collusive lawsuit to rid his clients of the tyranny of a 2 percent federal income tax. Corporate lawyers throughout the country when Stone was young had exploited the Supreme Court's strange decision in *Ex parte Young,* which in 1908 empowered any federal judge to enjoin railroad rate regulation by a state. At one point, according to a debate in Congress (which presently removed this authority from the federal judges acting as individuals), there were no fewer than 150 such injunctions by which lawyers had frustrated state taxes or legislation aimed at regulating corporate activities.

Nothing the lawyers were doing in Stone's time was more anti-social than their general pattern of activities on behalf of corporations for a full century before. By the 1930s, at least, the lawyers had grown conscious of their own biases: John Foster Dulles, then a partner in Sullivan & Cromwell, warned his colleagues that

The lawyer dealing with a commission should not carry into his work prejudices and resentments which are perhaps natural but which, in justice to the client, must not be allowed to color the lawyer's judgment and action. He should, for example, be very sure that he does not unwittingly encourage the client to fight a commission because this will afford the lawyer a chance to vent his general feelings against commissions as such.

Indeed, when Stone spoke in 1934 there were more corporate lawyers serving Roosevelt's New Deal than had served the three preceding Republican administrations put together.

And the problem was never that the lawyers were controlling their clients. Indeed, when asked for their own views, they would often respond in a far less conservative manner than anyone expected. Quizzed at a Congressional hearing on railroad securities, Cravath expressed doubts about the wisdom of much of what his clients had done, and replied to an incredulous follow-up question with the words, "In acting as counsel for gentlemen in these transactions, it has been my duty not to give advice about political economy, but as to the law; and when I speak of economic facts here, I do it as a citizen, and not as anybody's counsel. I may hold views totally at variance with those of my clients on such matters."

This said, there remains the sting of Stone's description of the corporate lawyers as "servants"; and the sting has never been drawn.

Elihu Root represented Thomas Fortune Ryan in the appeal against a streetcar franchise law which he had helped Theodore Roosevelt steer through the New York State legislature; and Roosevelt, he recalled, disapproved of his efforts. Root lost in the Supreme Court—"quite properly," he said.

Roosevelt never could see that a lawyer could argue a case under a law which gave his clients rights and not be responsible for the policy of the law. Of course you can't deprive a client of his rights under the law just because you think the law ought to be repealed. When a lawyer is in a case he is looking out for his client's rights, and if they rest on statute he is bound to give him the benefit of them and he isn't thinking of the policy of the statute.

This argument had been observed before, used by criminal lawyers who will squeeze every procedural teat in the hope of keeping out of jail clients whom they know to be gangsters, by negligence lawyers who will dress up the X-rays to money up the award for accident victims, by poverty-program lawyers who will fight to keep a whore in her apartment after she has lured the next-door neighbor's daughter into the business—all for the sake of rights and justice. But the argument doesn't do in other contexts, and it won't do here.

Karl Llewellyn spoke savagely to Columbia Law School students about the uses of the philosophy that every client is entitled to his full measure of rights:

[T]here may be a pleasant paunch upon your client. His wallet may look fat. Suppose now that his case does not at first blush seem appealing. Then what to do? Courage, my friend, there is that admirable ethic of the profession which makes it clear that the lawyer is neither judge nor jury; that the lawyer has neither duty nor right to usurp the constitutional function of the judicial tribunal. . . .

For your totem, for your ideal, you then can take the squid, the cuttlefish. Spine he has not, but O, a beak he has. The spine is absent, but the beak is strong. There are ten counted legs, each leg alive with suckers, all waving through the water after prey. The world, the whole world, offers hope for prey. When pressed some time too hard by enemies, most lawyer-like he hides himself behind a cloud of ink. *Why does a hearse horse snicker?*

All laws are more or less ambiguous in language, even when the intent is clear. Upon the corporate lawyer there rests, unsought but unavoidable, an obligation as great as that to his client, to deal with the intent of the law, to make his client law-abiding to the extent that his advice is followed. Charles Horsky of Washington's Covington & Burling says, "The Government is entitled to the tax lawyer's help in explaining to taxpayers the necessity and reasonableness of many provisions which taxpayers must inevitably dislike."

Mostly, the corporate lawyers do look for ways that their client can function within the purposes of the law, rather than for ways that the law can be circumambulated for the purposes of the client. Older men, though they may be more conservative, are less likely than younger men to cherish the values of cleverness in lining up the client with the law, more likely to take seriously Holmes' comment that "men must turn square corners when they are dealing with the government."

Norris Darrell of Sullivan & Cromwell worries sometimes about the bright young men who have not learned the difference between staying within the law and staying within the intent of the law. "Pure technicians," he comments, "may say something is all right, when viscerally it smells bad." But such considerations do not by any means bother everybody. "Short of advising that something is, for example, subject to a negligence penalty or fuzzy enough to create possible exposure to a civil fraud penalty," Charles W. Davis of the Chicago firm of Hopkins, Sutter, Owen, Mulroy, Wentz & Davis told a meeting, "it is not incumbent upon the outside counsel to impose his own standards of tax morality and compliance on the corporate client." From this attitude, much can flow.

Sometimes it gets worse than that. With a bitterness one can only guess, Robert T. Swaine wrote of his partner Hoyt A. Moore's devotion to the interests of one of his clients, "No lawyer ever unreservedly gave more of himself to a client than Hoyt Moore has given to Bethlehem." It will not be apparent from this sentence, though it could not have been far from Swaine's mind, that along the way to earning the tribute Moore participated in the bribery of a federal judge, who had control, via previous bankruptcy proceedings, of a growing steel fabricating company Bethlehem wanted to buy for cheap. Indicted on the charge, Moore escaped trial through the statute of limitations. He was never censured by the bar association, and Moore remained part of the Cravath firm name. But a House Investigating Commitee found, Joseph Borkin writes, that "Moore kept the record of the distribution of $250,000 'administration expenses' on the back of a manila envelope in his own handwriting. 'For approximately six years Moore kept memoranda concerning these fees in his personal desk apart from the regular office files.' No one in the Cravath firm, not even his secretary, could learn what was going on from the regular files."

At least two of the large New York firms (neither mentioned in this chapter) have reputations among their colleagues as "fixers." It is amazing how rarely the whistle is blown on a crooked judge or a taking tax agent by a member of a large law firm. When Mortimer Caplin became director of the Internal Revenue Service, a number of Wall Street lawyers had him to dinner and told him something about the mare's nest he would find on taking office; but they wouldn't become involved themselves. In California, where a generation of nonpartisan gubernatorial appointment of judges has made the state courts the envy of the nation, lawyers are appalled at how often their brethren from large firms in New York and Chicago, sending on West Coast business, will call them confidentially to ask which judges you can appear before without worrying that your opponent has put the case in the bag. The large firms take the world as they find it; they see their job as turning situations to their clients' advantage, not as policing any part of the society.

These questions of responsibility are magnified when the partner in the firm becomes a significant stockholder or a director of a client company. Many Wall Street firms have rules against owning stock in a client, if only to avoid dissension in the ranks. A partner in a large firm told a meeting, "We disapprove of a partner who has been working on a matter—and it may have been a very small matter when it started—buying a large block of stock while the firm ends up with a small fee." Most firms, too, would greatly prefer not to have their partners on corporate boards. "Our experience," the same partner says,

has been that the corporations are better off if the partner who attends their meetings is not a member of the board. It reduces problems, avoids conflicts of interest, facilitates decision-making, and gives the participating lawyer more independence. . . . [B]ut competition prevents any individual firm from establishing such a policy. The fear of turning around some day and finding a lawyer from a competing firm on the board leads you to keep one of your own partners there.

Every corporation runs into occasional situations where the penalties for breaking a contract or violating a law seem less forbidding than the costs of living with one's obligations. Backing out on a sale because the value of the thing to be sold has increased so greatly since the contract was drawn, infringing the patent of a competitor whose new product is clobbering you in the market, closing down an unprofitable division quickly without consulting the union—

such activities may commend themselves to a corporate board even though legal action may later impose penalties. No lawyer should ever be a party to such conduct; but there is a limit to how often a member of a board can say "No" to decisions that appear on balance to be genuinely in the stockholders' interests.

There can be no serious doubt that the corporate lawyers work overwhelmingly to keep business clients on the straight and narrow in an economy where a businessman's quality is measured by his superiors or stockholders exclusively by the annual increase in his profits. "[P]rivate lawyers," Horsky wrote, "such as the Washington lawyers who specialize in the antitrust field, do more toward enforcing the antitrust laws than ten times as big a government could ever do." But sinners are not usually credited for all the times they did not sin: we do not excuse the cutpurse because on the very day he was caught he passed up so many attractive purses. What is demanded here is antisepsis, not a high average level of cleanliness. And the suspicion persists that in the inviolate files of many corporate lawyers, protected from public examination by the privilege of confidentiality, there are a number of memos that would be embarrassing to the firm if they were ever published. We should know more than we do.

CHAPTER 10

BUSINESS IN WASHINGTON

"If you'll read the Trade Commission Act or the Clayton Act or the Robinson-Patman Act, you'll know that you can't tell what the law is by reading the Act."
     —JAMES McINNES HENDERSON, General Counsel,
             Federal Trade Commission

"In a sense the term 'government regulation' is quite misleading. It suggests an impersonal, mechanical operation which is far from reality. In a realistic sense there is no such thing as regulation by government, there is only regulation by government officials."
     —COMMISSIONER LEE LOEVINGER,
       Federal Communications Commission

"The Securities and Exchange Commission's report on mutual funds has many virtues. But it also suffers from a major defect. . . . [The] inadequacy is the result of the S.E.C.'s orientation, which is legal, not economic. . . . Given its traditional, built-in legal orientation, it is doubtful that the S.E.C. would be more rational in its solutions even if it had more facts."
     —M. J. ROSSANT in the *New York Times*

1

The idea of business—of producing for sale, employing, trading—is virtually impossible without an idea of law to govern the relations of the parties. And business law, like other law, has to be enforced or it will be meaningless—"government regulation" is inherent even in the most Platonic ideal of business. Roman law had proceeded far down the path of contract and public responsibility before the barbarians came; the *Institutes* of Justinian are full of philosophy and sound advice on the subject. In Europe, where developing legal systems looked to the Roman paradigm, there was never any question about the state's power to regulate business, though the ways in which the state intervened were often controversial and questionable enough.

But Anglo-American law derives from a medieval society which saw the Devil himself in many of the questions the Romans considered routine. Even as late as Blackstone, the word "contract" is a rarity in English (and thus in American) law. When it became necessary in the eighteenth and nineteenth centuries to develop a large body of business law and to place government action within it, the British and American legal professions had no anchors to clutch, and drifted way out to sea. It took two generations to drag them back.

In medieval England actions for Debt or Detinue (to get money owed or recover goods not paid for) were proved by "wager of law" —that is, the defendant swore that he owed nothing, and brought his friends with him to swear that his oath was true. "If they safely get through this ceremony, punctually repeating the right formula," Maitland wrote, "there is an end of the case. . . . They have not come there to convince the court, they have not come there to be examined and cross-examined like modern witnesses, they have come there to bring upon themselves the wrath of God if what they say be not true." The action for Covenant, which enforced contracts under seal, could not be brought when the remedy sought was payment of a debt. Wager of law survived in the British courts on actions of Debt and Detinue *until 1833*—indeed, a defendant offered to "wage his law," thereby frustrating the case against him, as late as 1824.

Obviously, the Renaissance businessman could not rely on this kind of law to protect him—but he had no need for "common law"; he needed only a law for his own trade in the places where he followed it. Each market town developed its own unofficial *"pied-*

poudre" courts to handle the day-to-day problems of traders, quite apart from the royal courts. The boroughs used their charters of autonomy to create *statuta,* elaborate and often catastrophic economic regulations which needed no common-law courts for their enforcement. The guilds and later the grand corporations—East India, Hudson's Bay and the like—made their own rules for their own affairs. Because these guilds and corporations were monopolies which owed their position to the Crown, they had to be more or less amenable to the dictates of whatever passed for public policy. "Government regulation" was commonplace in Tudor England, but it was all from the lawyers' point of view informal and nonlegal.

The boroughs ultimately were absorbed by the authority of the Crown and Parliament, the guilds decayed, and the independence of the trading companies became noxious. Through the seventeenth and eighteenth centuries, the "law merchant" developed by these autonomous bodies was gradually absorbed into the common law— most responsibly by Lord Mansfield, who would hear commercial cases with two knowledgeable men from the business as invited guests beside him on the bench, to advise him of the customs of the trade.

Contract cases were brought into the Court of King's Bench through a curious extension of tort law—the man who breached a contract did a wrong by depriving his opposite number of the "consideration" which had persuaded him to sign the contract (hence the surviving forms which begin "for one dollar and other good and valuable consideration . . ."). This wrong could be related by analogy to the wrong of Trespass, which allowed a writ to be issued to the "injured party" so he could sue for damages. Meanwhile, the Court of Exchequer took jurisdiction over actions for debt, through the fiction that the plaintiff owed a debt to the king which he was kept from paying because the defendant hadn't paid *him.* The Exchequer could also roll up all the heavy artillery of the courts of equity—injunctions, commands for specific performance and the like—on behalf of the businessman.

In fact, despite Mansfield, the new legal processes were ill adapted to most commercial purposes; law is too sharp and final for any business relationship that is supposed to survive the lawsuit. The documents Wall Street lawyers draw today are supposed to keep people out of court not only because litigation is expensive but also because its results are likely to be tangential to the real dispute. For private law purposes, less formal means of adjustment were required and were eventually discovered in arbitration, which has ousted the modern American courts from most cases of the sort Mansfield heard. But through the nineteenth century no replacement was available for the public regulation of business that had once been accomplished through the royal monopolies. Practical, technical and legal obstructions prevented the growth of substitutes for such old half-official, half-private institutions as the Staple, the Merchant Adventurers, the Goldsmiths, the Stationers, etc. One such institution survives, incidentally, as a model in praise of the good old days: Lloyd's of London, whose members need no recourse to law courts.

In Britain the courts had limited staying power in their efforts to prevent government interference with "liberty of contract." Parliament was supreme, and could simply overturn judicial decisions. In the United States, however, the judges were given second wind by their exclusive custody of a written Constitution, which forbade state actions that might "impair the obligations of contract" and reserved most areas of government to the states.

The initial log jam broke in 1877, in *Munn* v. *Illinois,* in which the Supreme Court, rather surprisingly, upheld state legislation fixing the rates of railroads and grain storage depots. Then the battleground shifted from the power of the legislature to regulate by law to the power of the legislature to delegate its regulating authority to the executive department or to an administrative agency or commission. Legislatures physically could not handle this volume of rule-making themselves; to deny the right to delegate (as a violation of "due process of law") was in effect to deny the regulatory power.

Refusal to permit the legislature to delegate was logically preposterous; as Professor Louis L. Jaffe points out, "[E]very statute is a delegation of lawmaking power to the agency appointed to enforce it." In real life the criminal laws turn out to be a delegation of power to the district attorney. But in legal philosophy the question was genuinely difficult. So tolerant a judge as Learned Hand wrote unhappily in 1916 of "the movement to intrust broad powers to administrative commissions . . . which establish . . . a customary law through the slow accretion of their own precedents. Such functions should more properly lie with courts." The essence of administrative action is the exercise of discretion; the essence of "the rule of law" is the compulsion to eliminate discretion. Bench and bar were committed to the rule of law, for reasons of faith and morals as well as for reasons of self-interest. Judges could uphold statutes empowering administrative agencies to "make law" only through the exercise of self-restraint. And as with the monks of whom Gibbon wrote, who proved their sanctity by tempting themselves with naked dancing girls, "outraged nature occasionally vindicated herself."

Between 1889 and 1918, the Supreme Court declared unconstitutional no fewer than fifty-six state statutes regulating the rates of public utilities. The high point in judicial prohibition of administrative discretion was reached, however, in a state court, in Arkansas in 1924, when an examination to license plumbers was declared unconstitutional because the legislature had delegated the writing of the exam to an expert body; if the lawmakers wished to license plumbers, they would have to outline the exam themselves.

But there was no avoiding delegation. Elihu Root, speaking as chairman of the New York State Constitutional Convention in 1915, urged the participants "to make it impossible for any legislature ever to abandon the system of regulating public service corporations through a commission or commissions, and to go back to the old method of leaving public service corporations unregulated, except by the passage of laws in the legislature." To regulate business effectively, to overcome what Root called "very great and real evils," a governmental body had to be expert, quick and flexible, none of them an adjective that could honestly be used to describe either legislature or court.

Fortunately, the first of the federal agencies, the Interstate Commerce Commission in 1887, was the result of an unusually specific piece of legislation, which told the new Commission precisely what sort of activity the Congress wished it to stop. Moreover, the actual power to *fix* rates was not given to the Commission until 1906, by which time its strong early leadership had demonstrated great ability at interpreting the law to forbid illegitimate rates (rebates, discrimination against certain shippers, charging the little man more for the short haul than the big man was charged for the long haul, etc.). Eventually, as is always the solution, judges were appointed from backgrounds in administrative regulation. Jaffe tells the story of a case in which a lower federal court had held unconstitutional a law empowering the Secretary of the Interior to set grazing fees on public lands, and to apply criminal penalties for failure to pay the fees. The Supreme Court, then shy one Justice, affirmed the lower court decision by an evenly divided bench. But during the next year there were three new appointments, "among them Van Devanter, fresh as federal attorney and judge from the Wyoming plains. On reargument, a unanimous Court upheld the law! Had the early experience of the new Justice broken the crust of the old dogma?"

By 1927 Felix Frankfurter could write triumphantly (as a professor professing administrative law) that

hardly a measure passes Congress the effective execution of which is not conditioned upon rules and regulations emanating from the enforcing authorities. . . . The control of banking, insurance, public utilities, finance, industry, the professions, health and morals, in sum, the manifold response of government to the forces and needs of modern society, is building up a body of laws not written by legislatures, and of adjudications not made by courts and not subject to their revision.

That same year Chief Justice Taft gave agencies and executive departments their Magna Charta, holding that administrators were constitutionally empowered to set their rates and issue their regulations whenever "Congress shall lay down by legislative act an intelligible principle to which the person or body . . . is directed to conform."

Then the Depression came, and intelligible principle, with much else, went down the drain.

2

Before the New Deal, there had been a small specialist bar in Washington—patent lawyers, practitioners before the General Land Office which was awarding quarter sections to pioneers, specialists in promoting private bills through the Congress. An 1895 notice in a legal directory touted a Washington firm: "Pensions secured for soldiers, sailors, widows, parents and minor children. Write for particulars." Then depression and the New Deal brought to Washington hordes of lawyers, needed to write the new regulations and to do battle on behalf of the regulated. With about three-tenths of one percent of the nation's population, Washington now has about 4.7 percent of the nation's lawyers. Nationally, the chance that an adult white male you meet on the street will turn out to be a lawyer is about one in 150; in Washington, it is about one in ten.

About three-fifths of the Washington lawyers work for the government. Many of them became lawyers here; George Washington University Law School ranks third in the nation (after Harvard and Texas) in number of living alumni, and Georgetown ranks seventh. One of the first things a man notices when he comes to work for the government is that his boss is a lawyer; and one of the next things he notices is that George Washington, Georgetown, Catholic and American universities all have law school programs with hours tailored to the needs of the government employee.

A fair number of the lawyers who work for the government hold jobs that can be and are done as well by nonlawyers. Patent examiners, FBI men, Internal Revenue Service agents, State Department functionaries, Conciliation Service mediators, Defense Department purchasing agents—all these and others may or may not be lawyers. The law degree is a step toward higher grades of government service, and adds another string to the bow in future possibilities for outside employment. Lawyers who come to government service from the outside often fit into jobs that are purely administrative. "An odd thing about the SEC," says General Counsel Philip J. Loomis, "is that it has lots of lawyers, but only a few of them in the General Counsel's office." At the other end of the scale, there are government lawyers engaged in the most purely legal and significant task the profession offers: sorting through the cases the United States or one of its agencies has lost in the courts to determine which should be appealed, to become a possible basis for nationwide judge-made law.

Government lawyers tend to be young. At his best, Felix Frankfurter pointed out, the young lawyer can supply disinterested enthusiasm, freedom from imprisoning dogmatism, capacity for fresh insight, unflagging industry, ardor for difficulties. . . . He is freed from complicated ramifications of private life; he is diverted by a minimum of vanities and jealousies; he is more resilient, more cooperative in taking orders. . . . A first-rate, well-trained, lively mind of twenty-five is better economy for the government than the services of those who, in the language of Civil Service Commissioner Leonard D. White, "have failed to achieve success in the competitive world, and who in middle life seek refuge in the official world."

The young lawyer also, of course, comes cheaper.

What the government can offer the young lawyers is training in a specialty, belief in the usefulness of one's labors and a feeling of power at an early age. "When I came to work at the SEC," says Louis Loss, now author of the standard work on securities regulation and a professor at Harvard, "there was a staff of a hundred lawyers, all under thirty-five. I was counsel to a division when I was twenty-nine." How important this work is will vary from agency to agency. The occupational deformation of people in Washington is the notion that Washington runs the country; the deformation of youth is the notion that the world is waiting eagerly to hear its message. Still, the Congress is mostly dependent on information from the departments and agencies, and the departments and agencies in most of their work can do nothing but approve what the staff says. A Commissioner in one of the major regulatory agencies says rather irritably, "You get a lot of GS-11 and GS-12 lawyers [i.e., middling-rank civil servants] making very important decisions around here."

John J. McCloy worries about the impact of government service on the young lawyer fresh from law school: "He begins to operate on the basis of the power behind him, not on his own power. A fellow sits with a couple of flags behind him. Everybody who comes in is either a penitent or a supplicant. He's always conscious of those flags." Sensitive older men who come to Washington to major posts sometimes resort to extraordinary devices to avoid oppression by their own importance. Nicholas deB. Katzenbach as Attorney General (working in one of those incredibly huge Washington offices two stories high, with a vaulted ceiling decorated by 1930s-style proletarians exercising their huge muscles on the world's work) kept framed on the wall beside his desk a neatly printed letter on stationery which featured clowns and balloons:

DEAR ATTORNEY GENERAL,

I saw my sister writing to you and she said you are a very important man. Who are you and why are you very important?

Your friend,

DIANE

For one lawyer who has worked both sides of the street, "Representing the government is just like representing a private client—except that when the government is your client the client is always right." But for the young lawyer there is another chance, the chance of a freak moment when something you are doing on assignment becomes an important part of the pattern of governing a nation. Just as lawyers for private parties have to keep their best stories secret because the client's business is confidential, lawyers for the government normally must conceal their role in administrative triumphs because the political leadership needs the credit for itself. A generation later, however, some of the freak moments come to light. For example, Rufus Poole, now practicing in Albuquerque, remembers his early days at the Interior Department:

"The first law I worked on was the Taylor Grazing Law. There were eleven public-domain states, in which there was more land on government ownership in public domain than in private ownership. The government land was being overgrazed, causing soil erosion. The Interior Department had had legislation to control grazing pending for twenty-five years.

"I asked the solicitor, 'Why do we need legislation?'

"He said, 'Everything about public domain requires legislation.'

"I became certain in my own mind that we had the power. I drew up a memorandum to prove we could proceed by withdrawing the land and setting it up under grazing control. It would require a Presidential order. The solicitor said, 'Send it to the Attorney General,' who was Homer Cummings. Cummings held it for weeks, then approved it. I prepared an order withdrawing the whole public lands from grazing, sent it to Ickes. First I knew Ickes had passed it on was, I got a call from his secretary—there was an order on her desk, approved by Roosevelt, that had originated in my department. What did I want done with it?

"I took it up to the Hill—I'd never been on Capitol Hill, though I'd been hired to do this work. I opened the *Congressional Directory,* looked under 'Public Lands,' saw the Chairman of the Committee was Key Pitman, who was also President Pro Tem of the Senate. I went to the cloakroom, sent in my card and he came out.

"I told him what I wanted to do and he reached out and put his arm around me. 'You're a young man,' he said. 'I don't want you to get discouraged. This bill will never pass Congress—you go back to the Secretary, tell him to put you on something easier.'

"I said, 'Has it ever occurred to you that the President has the power?'

"He said, 'I couldn't conceive of a President who was such a political idiot as to exercise the power.' Then he looked at the order. You never knew Pitman. He was from Nevada, time in Alaska, belt line of maybe twenty-seven, twenty-eight inches. He turned white. He said, 'Young man, I hope you're not in a hurry.'

"He walked back, adjourned the Senate, asked me to report to all the Senators from the West, meeting in the Post Office Committee room. I had a feeling my career in Washington was at an end.

"I was called into Ickes' office the next morning. He said, 'What in hell were you doing yesterday afternoon?'

"I said, 'Sir, it's the only way we'll get legislation.'

"He yelled at me. 'Do you think the United States Senate is like the Illinois legislature? Do I have to *tell* you to get out?'

"His secretary called through—it was Senator Carey from Wyoming, wanted to see Ickes. Carey walked in and opened by saying, 'I'm here to tell you that I think we can work with you.'

"Ickes, without looking at me, hit the table. 'By God,' he said, 'if you don't, *we'll regulate it!*' "

3

Washington's private lawyers are, by and large, alumni of government service. To work effectively with a government bureau, a lawyer must know precisely which of the many subbureaus is likely to be seized with his problem, and what its powers may be. Because the turnover is fairly fast, there is grumbling every once in a while about lawyers learning a specialized practice at the expense of the government and then quitting to go to work in a private firm before the government has got value for salaries—but in fact, of course, public as well as private interest is served when the lawyers are efficient at managing an agency's procedures. A more serious criticism stresses the danger that the man who knows he is going to want a job working for a part of the industry his agency or department regulates will be overly gentle with prospective future clients. "Still," says a Washington lawyer, "I think most guys know that's a bad idea. If a guy has laid down, businessmen feel, if he's been so weak as an advocate for the public, which pays his salary, how can you hire him as an advocate for you?"

The fact that the lawyers come out of government and continue to work with government creates odd psychological tensions in the Washington Bar. The situation is in truth ambivalent because, as noted in the previous chapter, the government is entitled to the help of private lawyers in keeping their clients within the law, while the clients are entitled to lawyers who do not assume that the government is always right. The compromise comes in the informal nature of most of the practice: in Washington, private lawyers are forever lunching with government lawyers, negotiating rules and orders and interpretations to accomplish the government's significant objectives without making life impossible for the client. Both sides gain important information at informal conferences, and can advise their principals with greater confidence. The necessary atmosphere of trust is greatly aided by the fact that the private lawyer knew the government lawyer when they were both on the same side of the table, or once occupied that same chair himself.

Much of the work the Washington lawyer does for a client is to prepare a flow of private insiders' newsletters, describing the direction and strength of the prevailing winds in the staff of an agency. This symbiotic relationship also means, as James M. Landis pointed out, that for an agency "contacts with the industry are frequent and generally productive of intelligent ideas. Contacts with the public, however, are rare and generally unproductive of anything except complaint."

Washington practice requires intense specialization. "A general practitioner," says Earl Kintner, who was chairman of the Federal Trade Commission and now leads the bar that practices before that

agency, "cannot be aware of all the precedents. He will fail to
recognize the possibilities for settlement, because he hasn't kept up
with the day-to-day work of the agency." Even the most specialized
lawyers, of course, will occasionally do (or at least supervise) other
work, because lawyers don't normally turn down business. Typically,
they wind up liking their own garden best. "I avoid the SEC," says
a communications lawyer. "It's like working as an inspector for the
Department of Agriculture, counting rat droppings in the bushel
of wheat. You shake out the rat droppings and then you go to
market."

What specialization means in the end is that lawyers represent
issues rather than clients. When they enter objections to a proposed
new rule or appear before the Congress or lunch with a staff member, they do so on behalf of some dozens of clients. Often they will
feel more strongly about an issue (network ownership of television
programs, for example) than their clients will (because the clients
are independent stations, and don't much care who owns the programs the networks send). "You have to decide what's good for your
client," one specialist says. "He doesn't know. For the agency, it
makes for a great confusion of inputs, because there are so many
people who speak for no one but themselves."

Specialization also means that the Washington bar is fragmented.
"Washington lawyers," Charles Horsky wrote, "are disposed like the
spokes of a wheel. They practice down the spokes against the hub
which is the common opponent—the government—but seldom do
their activities extend to what is doing on another spoke."

The Washington lawyer's remote relationship with his client implies a further practical burden. Conferences have to be fitted in at
odd hours. "I'm glad I got out," says a Midwesterner newly released
from a Washington practice. "They come in on Friday, and they
expect you to work all night with them over the weekend. To hell
with it."

4

Lawyers' work in smoothing the relations of business and government is by no means confined to Washington. Practice before administrative agencies regulating insurance companies, public utilities

and banks is a feature of state law, and is in no way different from similar practice under federal law (except that the chances to proceed by corrupting government officials are much better). There are more tax and antitrust lawyers in New York than in Washington, the patent bar is scattered where the big corporations have their Research and Development divisions, and men with a chance to try a case before the Supreme Court no longer refer it to a small group of experienced appeals lawyers in Washington. (The dilution of the Supreme Court bar under the impact of air travel and affluence has complicated the work of that Court, which can no longer count on the presentation of issues in a form which helps the Justices decide them.) Many Washington lawyers, meanwhile, are merely dealing with the government as lawyers for suppliers deal with purchasers anywhere, regarding the Defense Department (perhaps inaccurately) as just another, unusually difficult, unusually large customer.

Some Washington lawyers are lobbyists, and many find it hard to resist dropping the names of their old friends the committee chairmen when a client is around to listen, but that doesn't have much to do with law. "I know three or four people from Washington offices for whom that sort of thing is bread and butter," said Charles Horsky while on leave from Covington & Burling to help the Johnson Administration develop a poverty program for the District of Columbia. "But almost all the lawyers I know would be delighted not to have any of it. It's not satisfying. You can try a case, write a brief, get a decision. In Congress you never know if your work made any difference." Still, as Horsky himself pointed out, clients need lawyers to keep an eye on, for example, the introduction of a bill "which on its face means nothing; let us say that it reads like this: 'The fourth proviso of subsection (b) of Section 1 of the Act of March 2, 1937, is amended by deleting the words following the word 'assessment,' and changing the comma which follows said word to a semi-colon.' " A bill like that could mean a whopping increase in an industry's taxes, and the time to find out is before Congress passes it.

There are a few really exotic specialties practiced in Washington —for example, exploring the arcana of military pay regulations, leading to lawsuits at the Court of Claims on behalf of retired officers who want more. When one speaks of Washington lawyers generically, however, the type is the man who practices before one of the eight major independent regulatory agencies—AEC (Atomic Energy Commission), CAB (Civil Aeronautics Board), FCC (Federal Communications Commission), FPC (Federal Power Commission), FTC (Federal Trade Commission), ICC (Interstate Commerce Commission), NLRB (National Labor Relations Board), and SEC (Securities and Exchange Commission). All have more or less different problems and more or less different procedures, but they are brothers under the skin. Commissioner Lee Loevinger of the FCC has listed four functions that the agencies share: "(a) to regulate economic conduct by issuing orders or licenses to individual enterprises; (b) to regulate economic conduct by promulgating rules . . . specifying prohibited and permissible conduct . . . ; (c) to investigate and initiate proceedings rather than merely to respond to the actions of others as the courts do; and (d) to promote and encourage economic and technological progress."

The agency which most directly touches the public is the FCC, which has large and by no means well-defined responsibilities in the area of broadcasting. It was started in 1927 as a Federal Radio Commission, because something of the sort was clearly necessary. Two broadcast signals on the same (or nearly the same) frequency will instantly interfere with each other if they carry into each other's territory. What administration of frequencies there was in the early years of broadcasting drew its authority from the Radio Act of 1912, passed when the great question was how best to keep in contact with ships at sea, and the job was in the hands of the Secretary of Commerce. His power was to assign frequencies for broadcast use, but not to assign them as franchises to broadcasters. Required by law to issue licenses to people who promised to remain on a given frequency, he could not legally refuse licenses to new broadcasters, or control the power the new broadcasters would put on their transmitters. Nothing could result from free competition on these terms but cacophony complicated by static.

The new Commission's first job, then, was to bring some sort of order to the broadcast spectrum. It declared all licenses temporary under the new law, and weeded out about 150 of the 732 stations that were on the air. This, incidentally, was not easy to do, because Congress had written the Court of Appeals for the District of Columbia into the administrative process, authorizing the Court to hear the whole case over again and change the Commission's ruling simply because the Court didn't agree, not because the Commission had violated any procedural or substantive law in reaching its conclusions. When the Radio Commission tried to restrict General Electric's Schenectady station to daytime broadcasting, to leave a clear channel at night for stations elsewhere, the Court of Appeals simply reinstated GE's station to all its rights and privileges; and the Supreme Court held that as the law was written nobody could review that decision. Congress changed the law.

In 1934 a Federal Communications Act extended the jurisdiction of the Commission to all interstate electronic message-carrying, by telephone, telegraph, radio or television. As presently organized, the Commission consists of seven Commissioners appointed by the President with the consent of the Senate. Each Commissioner has both an engineering assistant and a legal assistant to keep him from becoming totally dependent on the agency's staff. A Commissioner's term is seven years, and his salary at this writing is $27,000 a year; the chairman, separately appointed by the President, makes $28,500. No more than four of the Commissioners may belong to the same political party. The total staff of the agency runs to about fifteen hundred people, the majority in Washington, others scattered around the country checking up on whether or not the communicators are living up to the terms of their licenses. Counting the police cars and the hams, the FCC had in 1967 about 1.6 million licensees, who ran 5.7 million transmitters. In the broadcasting field, no license may be given for more than three years; then it comes back to the Commission for renewal.

The FCC has a bewildering variety of responsibilities. It allocates broadcasting frequencies to individual applicants for all except the little toy transceivers; decides how long stations can be on the air, what power they can put on the transmitter and which direction they must aim the antenna; establishes quality standards for the broadcast signal, approves or disapproves technical innovations up to and including color television and communications satellites; supervises the rate structure of long-distance telephone and telegraph services; upholds the American end in international conferences on telecommunications.

The Commission's authority over *what* is broadcast is an interesting question. In general, broadcasting like publishing is protected from government interference by the First Amendment, and Section 326 of the Communications Act specifically forbids the Commission any "power of censorship." But other sections prohibit the broadcasting of obscenity and of lotteries; and in the famous Section 315 the Commission is instructed to command stations which carry a political broadcast free of charge to offer "equal time" to every other candidate running for the same office, no matter how minor his chances or how trivial his party. This section had to be suspended by Congress to permit the Kennedy-Nixon debates in 1960; and the refusal of Congress to suspend it again in 1964 meant that the networks would not have given time for President Johnson to debate Barry Goldwater even if the President had wished to do so (which of course he didn't, which was why Congress refused to suspend the law).

From time to time the Commission issues statements of policy, rules and orders. By far the most significant for the industry was the order requiring NBC to sell off one of its two networks (the orphan became ABC), which the Supreme Court upheld in 1943. Another of continuing importance has been the limit of five VHF stations (and two UHF stations) as the maximum any one company can own. (This limit is now to be reduced to *two* VHF stations, but all the existing owners of more will be "grandfathered in"—a phrase deriving from the post-Reconstruction South, when tough requirements were established for voting privileges for everybody who could not prove that his grandfather had voted.) Yet another was the prohibition of "option time"—the contract provision by which networks obliged their affiliates to carry the network shows during key hours (as many as nine hours a day). In the radio frequencies, the Commission in 1966 required broadcasters who owned both to run different programs on their AM and FM channels at least half the day.

Some of these policy decisions have been quite seriously wrong. Only the Korean War and the resulting freeze on television licenses and construction saved the FCC from saddling the nation with a color system which could not be received in black-and-white on existing sets. (And saved it, too, from some of the errors in its original assignment of frequencies, which ignored clear engineering warnings of tropospheric interference.) By giving all communities both VHF and UHF frequencies the Commission doomed the technically inferior but much more capacious UHF band, greatly restricting the possibilities for competition among television broadcasters and diminishing the industry's incentive to improve UHF transmission and reception. (Eventually, Congress had to compel the set manufacturers to include UHF capacity in all receivers, to bail out the Commission.) The elimination of option time, which came just as Hollywood was releasing huge backlogs of movies for sale to television stations, added to the pressure on the networks to supply the stations only with sure-fire heavy-audience flimflam to get the necessary "clearances" to keep the network alive.

These rules grew out of staff study, good or bad, and staff work is the normal procedure. But the Commission also listens to feedback from the audience. The rule limiting the decibel level of the commercial to that of the program was stimulated by public complaint, and letters from the outside world—from plain people as well as from lawyers—are taken much more seriously than one would expect. "We get letters," says William Ray, director of the Commission's complaint bureau, "simply saying that there's too much crime and violence, or that there shouldn't be wrestling on television. We recommend that they make their views known to the licensee, and we send the station a copy of the letter. Sometimes, when the complaint is specific—on such and such a commercial at such and such an hour the sound was too loud—we get action: the station writes back that it screened the commercial, the sound *was* too loud, and the advertising agency has been notified that this commercial will not be shown again. All complaints go into the folder to be looked at when renewal application comes in."

The Commission's powers to enforce its rules are limited to a slap on the wrist (a fine of up to $10,000) or a death sentence, little in between. The death sentence is deprivation of license; the in-between, a warning rather than a punishment, is a short-term renewal. The Federal Communications Act specifically provides that nobody is to have a "property right" in a license, and all applications must waive any future claims in that direction. The Commission can always revoke (in 1966 there were two revocation proceedings pending, out of seven thousand radio and television station licenses), and it need not renew at the end of the three-year license period. But in fact no court will uphold a refusal to renew unless a station has been doing something wildly different from what other stations have been doing. When the Commission tried to dump an ownership which had been nationally involved in one of the rigged quiz-show programs, on the grounds of payola to disc jockeys in their local operation, the Court of Appeals reversed on the argument that the action was rank discrimination among licensees.

The severity of the punishment the Commission theoretically can impose means that no station owner can risk ignoring it; even if a refusal to renew is ultimately overturned by the courts, the ex-licensee has huge legal bills, loses his credit at the bank and experiences difficulty selling to advertisers. "They're worried about their licenses daily, weekly, monthly," says a Washington lawyer who earns his living basically by feeding information out of the FCC to station owners across the country. "When the inspector walks into their offices, they want to know exactly what he'll be looking for."

This fear makes possible a great deal of program regulation by lifted eyebrow. When Newton Minow became chairman of the Commission in the early days of the Kennedy Administration, he let it be known that he and the President and the President's brothers and sisters were all distressed by what their children watched Saturday mornings and at the cocktail hour on the weekdays, and the networks hustled to supply the Kennedy children and their friends with more intellectual entertainment.

A year before, Chairman John C. Doerfer had carried "informal" regulation to its high-water mark by inviting down to Washington for a private conference the president or chairman of all three networks. Doerfer had no rules to propose; indeed, he had never discussed with his fellow Commissioners what he was about to say. But he was insistent—and he noted that President Eisenhower agreed with him—that each network must present a public affairs program every week in evening time at an hour when no two such programs would conflict. The network officials had known that something of this sort was in the wind (their lawyers had tipped them off; "The FCC is a sieve," one of them says), and they were prepared. The anti-trust laws, they said sympathetically, forbade any such collusion among them; indeed, their lawyers were concerned that they were meeting together to discuss programs at all, even under such distinguished auspices as those of Chairman Doerfer. At this point, Doerfer reached into his desk and pulled out a letter from the Attorney General, an official opinion by the boss of all government prosecutions that collaboration among the networks for this purpose would not violate the antitrust laws. Presently, without any formal action by the Commission, the networks were (briefly) following Doerfer's suggestion.

Program regulation is an issue that splits the Commission and always has. The outstanding regulator is Commissioner Kenneth Cox, who was brought in from a private practice in Seattle to run hearings for the Senate Commerce Committee in 1956 while still in his thirties, and brought back again to the FCC by the Kennedy Administration. ("Ken Cox," says a Washington lawyer admiringly, "lacks one of the fundamental things in our society: he isn't a complete man; he isn't greedy.") Cox, who is still youthful and casual despite the strains of a difficult and frustrating office, says, "I think the Commission was created for the purpose of regulating. Right now, part of that regulating should be to make the networks establish program categories and use them. If we don't have the authority, the courts will tell us; if our policy is wrong, then Congress should change the statute. I don't want any letters from chairmen of committees, I want law. Otherwise administrative agencies are useless."

On the other side of the war, Chairman Rosel Hyde says with some annoyance that "The law forbids *me* from interfering in programming, even if it doesn't forbid some other Commissioners." Commissioner Loevinger, a lean and formidably intellectual Minnesotan, is not particularly fond of either the broadcasters or their programs, but he believes both that he doesn't and that he shouldn't have the power to tell the broadcasters what to broadcast. "What the regulators are saying," Loevinger argues, "is that we don't want to censor, but people have to be responsible for what goes out. Implicitly, they're saying that the FCC must make the judgment of what is responsible. That's just the kind of censorship other governments have over broadcasting—and the Congress, the Court and the people have repeatedly said that they do not want the FCC given that authority." Writing about this question recently, Loevinger added that "popular as well as unpopular entertainment and ideas may need and deserve some protection against official disapproval." One of the Commission's very few efforts to kill a program type involved "Stop the Music" and its ilk, on the grounds that they were lotteries; Chief Justice Warren said they weren't lotteries. Later the networks had occasion to wish the FCC had won.

Whether the FCC has any power over networks is a hard question, and the fact that the Commission has for years been asking Congress to give it authority to license networks makes a *prima facie* case that under the existing law there isn't much the Commission can officially do. But much of the profitability of any network is in its "owned-and-operated" affiliates, and like other stations these can have their licenses taken away simply by refusal to renew when the three-year period is up. The grounds for such discipline theoretically could be the station's failure to live up to the promises its owners made (heavy local coverage, attention to public affairs, service programs, etc.) while arguing for the original license or for a previous renewal. "In my time there," says the Washington lawyer Paul Porter, who served as FCC chairman shortly after the Second World War, "my old friend Cliff Durr was playing left end, and when renewals came up Cliff would make this comparison between promise and performance. If there was a raving disparity, as there often was, Cliff would say we should have a hearing; I would go along. It got so we had half the industry on temporary licenses, we didn't have enough hearing examiners to handle the business. We discovered that of twenty-six clear channel [radio] stations, only one or two had farm directors; we made a lot of jobs for county agents. Then we issued a blue book—*Public Service Responsibilities of*

Broadcasters—and said, 'Go and sin no more.' It had a short-term salutary effect."

But in these areas, as a network official puts it, "the Commission is trying to enforce something it can't even define. You can't make a crime out of a mystery—that's Kafka." At one point, to help lawyers draw up license applications, the Commission listed fourteen program categories that should be covered; the fourteenth and last was "entertainment." The promises are always elegantly satisfactory, because the lawyers know they create no obligation; even the Commission has recognized in an opinion that "we would be deluding ourselves and the public, if we concluded that the program proposals will be produced exactly as represented." In fact, the staff tells the lawyers what they will have to put down on the form to get the license.

About the only requirement that the Commission has taken seriously is one demanding a few hours a week for locally originated live programming other than news. Not everybody is happy with this rule—not even the chairman at this writing, Rosel Hyde, who came to the brand-new Radio Commission as a clerk in 1928, went to law school in Washington, and rose through the staff to a Presidential appointment. "Why should we sit here and tell the folks they have to see what's going on in the county," Hyde says, "when the whole opportunity of broadcasting is the wider experience?" Judge Friendly has commented acidly on this requirement by asking "whether the Commission is really wise enough to determine that live telecasts—of local cooking lessons, for example—so much stressed in the decisions, are always 'better' than a tape of Shakespeare's histories."

The worst of the FCC's anguish is now presumably over, because virtually all the VHF television frequencies have been assigned and additional radio stations can be squeezed into the AM band only by very clever engineers. Until recently, however, the Commission was under the fiercest kind of pressure from competing applicants for the scarce channels, some of which, in the larger cities, were worth literally tens of millions of dollars. The FCC's performance in making these allocations was literally a national scandal, including what Judge Friendly has called "boudoir episodes" (one of the FCC Commissioners died while under indictment for having taken a bribe in connection with applications for a Miami channel). The problem was made worse by the strong local interests in each allocation, which made it almost impossible for Congressmen to keep their hands completely off, and by the very low quality of many of the appointees of the Eisenhower Administration, which regarded the regulatory agencies as an excrescence on the body politic but for that very reason a good place for Sherman Adams to dump people who had a political claim on the Republican Party.

But even under the Roosevelt Administration, in the heyday of idealism about administrative agencies, the FCC had performed poorly in picking winners of broadcasting franchises, just as the CAB has consistently performed poorly in picking winners of air routes. The difficulty is and always has been the absence of secure and publicly known criteria which the agencies will follow in making their decisions. Where there are no generally known criteria, and money is to be made on the results, agency decisions inevitably become subject to illegitimate pressure.

Some lawyers who represented applicants at these hearings, which meant running around to drum up all sorts of support for your boy, found them ultimately hateful. "Once a man who wanted to win a TV license took me out to dinner," says a broadcasting lawyer. "I knew he was going to offer me fifty thousand dollars for what might be a seventy-five-hundred-dollar job, because there were eleven contestants and he didn't figure to be one of the best. I brought a young partner along with orders to turn over the table if the war horse in me rose and I reached to accept his check. You never get paid in these cases for the third of your stomach you sell.

"When I got out of the Harvard Law School," he continued, "the dean, James M. Landis, advised me (as everybody else did) to go to Washington and practice administrative law. 'That's where the excitement is,' he said. 'Don't get bound into conventional practice, dreary courts, precedent-bound judges.' Then a few years later Landis came down himself to be chairman of the CAB, and there was a big blow-up and he resigned.

"We gave him a party before he went back to Cambridge, and I remember him standing there, a martini glass in each hand. I went up to him and asked him whether he'd give me the same advice again, and he said, 'Hell, no. I'd tell you to stay in the courts, where decisions are made by judges with tenure rather than by the guy who came around most recently to the back door of the White House with a big black bag of money."

5

Attacking the regulatory agencies is one of the easiest sports to master, and there are always horror stories available to back up the attack. For the outstanding characteristic of the agencies is the sheer volume of business they do. The FCC processes almost 3,000 applications of one kind or another *every day*, the ICC approves more than 200,000 tariffs and schedules every year, the NLRB disposes of more than 25,000 unfair labor practice charges a year, the FTC receives about 800,000 printed advertisements and commercials every year, and refers more than 40,000 of them to its legal staff for review. The champion is the Veterans Administration: between 1950 and 1961 the VA had an average annual "adjudicated case load" of 2,600,000 applications, which produced about 40,000 appeals to the Board of Veterans Appeals. (This administrative Board, incidentally, is the last stop; Congress has forbidden judicial review of these cases, and the courts have not tried to intervene.)

"While courts handle thousands of cases each year and the Congress produces hundreds of laws each year," Loevinger writes, "the administrative agencies handle literally tens and hundreds of thousands of matters annually. The administrative agencies are engaged in the mass production of law, in contrast to the courts, which are engaged in the handicraft production of law." To speak of making administrative agencies more like courts, at a time when they can't handle their case load with their existing procedures, is to speak nonsense. To be shocked that the agencies handle some of these many matters very badly indeed is to be either naïve or political or both. The problem is that the agencies seem to be at their worst in handling their most important matters.

On his resignation from the Civil Aeronautics Board in 1959, Louis J. Hector sent President Eisenhower a memorandum about what was wrong in his agency, and told the story of the processing of the application for air routes in the upper Middle West, a matter that went under the heading of *Seven States Area Investigation*. To begin with, the problem was handed over to an examiner, who worked two years with the help of one secretary, and was never at any time in the two years in touch with the Board. The examiner heard 194 witnesses who filed a thousand exhibits, and he reported to the Board with a 684-page plan for allocating the routes among the competing airlines. Objectors to the plan filed "an eight-inch pile of briefs and argued orally to the entire five-man Board for four solid days, a total of 21 hours and 35 minutes." Then the five members of the Board retired, each with one personal assistant, and the ten men wrote a new plan. "They did not have time, of course," Hector wrote, "to review five and one-half feet of testimony and exhibits in the case. They worked mainly from briefs and from their memory of the long oral argument." Then, of course, the case went on into the courts.

One of the elements that made this case so hopeless was the great reform in the Administrative Procedures Act of 1946, which established the independence of the hearing examiners for all the agencies. Up to then the American Bar Association had been complaining about the injustice of the typical administrative situation where an agency makes a policy, hauls somebody in for violating it, and then tries him on the basis of its own information—acting, in short, as legislature, prosecutor, judge and jury all at once. The first remedy was to declare the hearing examiner, who in the great majority of cases will make the final determination, a kind of judge, not subject to discipline from the agency. But when the hearing examiner's conclusions are appealed, as they will be in the more serious cases, the very independence of the parties makes for irrationality. The examiner's report is merely "advisory," and the Commission begins all over again, hearing argument and considering new information. The record of the testimony before the examiner need not be the basis for the Commission's decision. In the *Seven States* case, Hector explained to a Congressional committee, the examiner's report *had* to be worthless:

> The Board had in its own thinking come around to the conclusion that any town which had any reasonable chance of producing 5 passengers a day should have a chance to see if it could do so, and if it could then it

should have an airline. The hearing examiner did not know this, because he is independent, and the Board could not talk to him. So he spent 2 years hearing evidence and turning out a 500-page opinion. It came up to the Board, and the Board's first reaction was, "This wasn't what we had in mind at all. We were thinking of a much more extensive route pattern."

Any substantial "judicializing" of procedure inevitably means even more time per case; and as of the date of Dean Landis' report to the newly elected John F. Kennedy, the CAB was thirty-two months behind, the FTC was considering 118 cease-and-desist orders recommended by its staff more than a year before, and the Federal Power Commission had announced that it would need thirteen years to clear up its backlog. For institutions that had originally been promoted as speedy, it was a sorry record; and while both the Kennedy and Johnson Administrations have wrought great improvement at the agencies (largely through a much higher quality of appointment) delay is still common in important cases at all but the SEC and the NLRB. Moreover, the closer the procedure approaches that of a court, the more the agencies become caught in the trap of adversary presentations with all their little time-wasting tricks and automatic negativisms. The work of the ICC has become virtually impossible since the Congress told the agency to set minimum rates for rail, truck and water traffic to make sure that no one form of transportation sought to knock off the others through price competition. One immediate result was that new rates for anything were opposed as a reflex by the other kinds of carrier. A disgusted trucker in Chicago filed a rate for the carriage of yak fat from Omaha to Chicago, and instantly a railroad lawyer filed an objection, making the matter a docket item for the ICC.

Moreover, even when individual cases are up for decision, regulatory agencies are fundamentally fact-finding and legislative bodies rather than courts. While a court exists fundamentally to decide specific disputes, and lays down general principles only incidentally to this activity, an administrative agency is fundamentally (at least in theory) making rules to govern others. For this purpose it must know more than just the bare facts of the current case.

Because the volume is so heavy and the rules must be so different, the courts are in the end no better placed to control the administrative agencies than they are to control the police. In the first two years of the New Deal, the Supreme Court did, indeed, rectify a great deal of administrative misbehavior. The appalling performance of the Court in the first six months of 1936, when a great deal of badly needed and reasonable legislation was declared unconstitutional by a 5-4 vote, in opinions of sweeping generality, has obscured with poetic justice the great services the Court rendered in 1934 and 1935 (mostly by unanimous vote) in striking down Franklin Roosevelt's mistaken notion that what the nation needed was a version of Mussolini's corporate state. The National Recovery Administration, for example, had issued in 18 months some 546 codes and 185 supplemental codes, plus "over 11,000 orders interpreting, granting exemptions from, and establishing classifications under provisions of individual codes." Most of these codes were not published for a year or so after their promulgation, and even then, Professor Jaffe reports, "it was not uncommon for the White House to retain orders which it preferred to keep from public view. And the executive orders embodying the codes (in many instances) were not even at the White House but here and there in the desk drawers of NRA officials."

The case in which most of this came out was an appeal from an injunction to prohibit violations of "fair competition" under the Petroleum Code. When the brief for the government came to be written, Professor Jaffe recalled a dozen years later, "it occurred to the brief writer to examine the originals (which were found after some difficulty). He discovered the sickening fact that by reason of a mistaken use of terms—the Code had been amended out of existence."

What had happened, as Merlo Pusey put it, was that "men had been arrested, indicted, and held in jail for violating a law that did not exist." Justice Brandeis, after listening to this incredible story, asked from the bench, "Well, is there any way by which one can find out what is in these executive orders when they are issued?" And the government counsel admitted, "I think it would be rather difficult." One does not have to be fanatical about the values of the rule of law to be shocked by this sort of governing.

The petroleum case produced an almost immediate reform—the

institution of the *Federal Register,* in which all codes and administrative rulings are published together with acts of Congress and executive orders. Had the Court not chosen in 1936-37 to stand and fight and lose on the fundamental issue of the government's power to govern, some orderly development of other administrative work habits might have been accomplished through case law. Certainly, if the Supreme Court had not started throwing out *everything,* Congress could have been compelled to give the agencies those "intelligible principles" Chief Justice Taft had demanded. Instead, the Court presented the Congress and the public with a choice between all or nothing, and though Roosevelt's court-packing plan was defeated, the Court presently found itself with nothing.

It should be recognized that these questions are very difficult, and that the agencies consciously or unconsciously make them more difficult. Because the courts cannot hear all over again the cases the agency has decided, the most they can require is that agency determinations be based on "substantial evidence" and that a "fair hearing" be given to the losing side of the dispute. There are very few real disagreements where "substantial evidence" cannot be produced on both sides ("Substantial," Justice Traynor once asked, "in relation to what?"), and the agency by asserting that it has considered arguments for the losing side can disarm the courts. The typical device of the anonymous opinion, issued on behalf of the Commission as a whole and written by an opinion-writing division rather than by a Commissioner, condemns the courts to impotence and the Congress to ignorance of how the decision was actually reached. Hector describes the process:

The job of the opinion writers is to draft an appeal-proof document which will support the result already reached by the Commissioners. An important part of this process consists of having an attorney go through every brief and make a list of every point made by every party. Each point of significance is then mentioned in the opinion, often by the formula: "We have considered the contention of ———— to the effect that ————, but we find that this does not alter our conclusion."

Reversals by the courts have been fairly frequent, even in recent years. (Lawyers hunt out a circuit where the Court of Appeals has been unsympathetic to regulatory agencies, and go try their case there. The recent appeal against the FCC's rule on wired CATV—community antenna television service with wires running to homes—was taken to Arkansas, though all the lawyers involved lived in Washington and the D.C. Circuit Court had an equal jurisdiction.) Typically, however, the courts can only remand the matter to the Commission, because the Commission's law, not its findings of fact, is what the court can reverse. Then the Commission simply offers new reasons for the conclusions it reached last time. The station owners whom the FCC evicted for participation in a network quiz-show scandal were compelled to sell their local franchise even though they had won their legal point in the courts. Sometimes the Commissions do not even bother to invent new arguments; they simply ignore the courts. "These guys around here," says a Commissioner, "don't even read Supreme Court opinions." Landis in his report to Kennedy wrote of "the unwillingness of the [Federal Power] Commission to assume its responsibilities under the Natural Gas Act and its attitude, substantially contemptuous, of refusing in substance to obey the mandates of the Supreme Court of the United States and other federal courts."

In 1961, appealing to the Supreme Court against an adverse ruling in the Court of Appeals, the Federal Trade Commission announced that if the Court refused to hear its appeal (thereby leaving the Court of Appeals ruling in effect), the Commission would continue its old interpretation as though no court had ever spoken. A public fuss was kicked up by this announcement—mostly, apparently, on the grounds that the Commission was trying to force the Supreme Court to hear a case, which is Not Done—so the next time the FTC was in a similar situation it announced it would not appeal. The Commission would, however, "continue to adhere to its own interpretation of the Robinson-Patman Act," whether the Court of Appeals liked it or not.

In fairness, both the Supreme Court and Congress have a long history of conspiring against the FTC. The original Section 5 of the Federal Trade Commission Act (which Commissioner Philip Elman, a former Frankfurter clerk and protégé, would like to substitute for the prolixity of Robinson-Patman) said merely "That unfair methods of competition in commerce are hereby declared unlawful." The

Supreme Court, speaking through Justice McReynolds, thereupon announced that "The words 'unfair methods of competition' are not defined in the statute and their exact meaning is in dispute. It is for the courts, not for the commission, ultimately to determine as a matter of law what they include." (Note the sneaky use of the word "ultimately.") The one amendment Congress produced for this section was an addition of the words "and unfair or deceptive practices," to eliminate a decision of the Supreme Court that in the original form the Act authorized the Commission to move only when it could prove a competitor had already been hurt. Congress failed to give the Commission power to issue rules interpreting the section, and up until 1938 provided no way by which the Commission could enforce its findings other than by suing a violator in the Court of Appeals. Even now, an FTC order in this area (dealing with any commodity except cosmetics and drugs) is automatically stayed by a petition for review in the Court of Appeals.

When the Commission announces its intention to adhere to its own interpretation despite the disapproval of the Court, all it is really saying is that it expects to try again. But this is cold comfort for the businessman who must fear the costs of an appeal of an order the courts have already said the Commission shouldn't issue.

By 1940, only four years after the administrative *Götterdämmerung* of 1936, the Supreme Court had backed away from the review problem. The case was one of a Pennsylvania group that had been denied a broadcasting license allegedly because the FCC found that Pennsylvania law ruled them out. They had won an opinion from the Court of Appeals that the FCC was wrong on Pennsylvania law, and were now faced with a return to the Commission to lose again for some other alleged reason. They wanted the courts to order the FCC to give their application priority, and a unanimous court could offer nothing but best wishes: "[C]ourts are not charged with general guardianship against all potential mischief in the complicated tasks of government. The present case makes timely the reminder that 'legislatures are ultimate guardians of the liberties and welfare of the people in quite as great a degree as the courts.' Congress which creates and sustains these agencies must be trusted to correct whatever defects experience may reveal."

And Congress must in fact shoulder most of the blame for the current chaos in government regulation: the laws have failed to provide intelligible principles, permitting quite arbitrary and inconsistent actions by the agencies. "The Investment Company Act," says a lawyer who works before the SEC, "is banana-peel legislation—you're always slipping and falling on your tail. You know what something means only through a memo in a senior staff assistant's desk drawer."

There might have been some sense in telling the ICC to approve rail lines and rates to serve "public convenience or necessity," but nobody could really have expected the FCC to be guided in awarding broadcast franchises to one of several competing parties by an instruction that the award must serve "public convenience, interest or necessity." As Kenneth Culp Davis put it in his standard treatise on administrative law, "Sometimes telling the agency to do what is in the public interest is the practical equivalent of instructing it: 'Here is the problem. Deal with it.'" An agency can hardly be expected to be independent of outside pressures if Congress has failed to supply a firm direction in the name of public policy. Democracy demands, as Justice Frankfurter wrote, that "final determination of large policies must be made by the direct representatives of the public and not by the experts."

The horrible example is the Robinson-Patman Act, under which the Federal Trade Commission with lawyerlike ignorance of the significance of actual marketing practices has been unsystematically stifling what little competition remains in the American economy. In dealing with tires and canned milk, for example, the Commission ruled that manufacturers could not sell the same merchandise at different prices, depending on whether or not they put their brand on it; on another occasion, dealing with gasoline, it ruled that a manufacturer could not lower the price of his branded gas to that of his unbranded gas because that would be unfair competition. Nobody, from the Supreme Court on down, even pretends to understand the law. (Justice Harlan has called it "a singularly opaque and elusive statute.") The FTC, having failed to index or even collate properly its own previous decisions, has only the vaguest notion of how it has ruled on these questions in the past, and seems to start each case fresh. (A Court of Appeals has commented on "the Commission's construing the Act inconsistently from one case to the next, as appears most advantageous to its position in a particular case." In fairness, the comment was made in a case the Commission was later to win on appeal in the Supreme Court.)

Robinson-Patman has been the subject of endless law review articles, court cases, speeches before bar associations, amendments to treatises. Judge Henry Friendly has commented rather bitterly that "The tiniest fraction of the time spent by lawyers, legal writers, administrators and judges in an unsuccessful effort to elucidate the obscurities of this statute would have sufficed to put the house in order once the problems were revealed; but that time has not been spent." At this writing, this appalling piece of legislation has reached its thirtieth birthday, and Congress has never changed a word of it —"because," one lawyer says, "Congress wants vigorous competition, which does not, however, result in driving anyone out of business."

Yet the agencies are to blame, too, for failing to systematize their interpretations or explain their decisions sufficiently to tell Congress what guidance they need. "The legislature," Harvard's Henry M. Hart, Jr. says, "is supposed to be able to depend on the administrative agencies." Instead, the agencies send over to the Hill every year for new legislation on their own terms, and don't get it. Lee Loevinger has shrewdly noted that "Most agencies develop an institutional bias which, on the one hand, favors extending the power and authority of the agency but, on the other hand, favors avoiding political controversy where possible." Any coherent statement of rules and agency policy invites political controversy; arbitrary actions extend real power and authority.

"You know," the chairman of the CAB once told a House Committee, "we keep talking about philosophy. We keep talking about the philosophy of the Board. Well, the philosophy of the Civil Aeronautics Board changes from day to day. It depends who is on the Board as to what the philosophy is. You cannot say that the Board as a whole has a fixed philosophy for any very fixed period of time because [philosophy changes] as the members come and go, and they do come and go pretty fast down there."

In much the same manner, Chairman Paul Rand Dixon of the

FTC—a stout, choleric Tennesseean almost entirely lacking the ability to believe that anyone who disagrees with him may be honest, yet saving his fanaticism with a real sense of humor—told a meeting in 1965:

> [E]ven our adversary or "cease and desist" order proceedings are actually *educational* in character. In fact, you might call them private tutoring. . . . When a processor of, say, grocery products is sued by the Federal Trade Commission . . . we all go back to school. When the course is over—and that usually means when the Supreme Court has denied someone's petition for a rehearing—both the Federal Trade Commission and the party in question have been pretty thoroughly instructed. . . . Now our grocer, wanting no further trouble with the law . . . naturally consults his lawyer, His lawyer, having read all the Commission's recent opinions . . . is of course thoroughly confused.

The statuary outside the FTC building in the federal triangle shows a man wrestling with a horse, and the FTC's public brochure quotes the artist as explaining the "Symbol of the Horses" with the comment, "Man, by his intelligence, controls the horse as he controls trade." It may be significant that the man in the statue has nothing to work with but his bare hands.

Two agencies have managed to escape the administrative malaise: the SEC, where the routine informal procedure really is routine and generally accepted, leaving the Commission time to think about policy; and the NLRB, where the rule-making power has been permitted to atrophy, decisions have been solidly rested on opinions stating interpretations of the law, and when the direction changes the change has been openly admitted. It is probably significant that at both agencies the facts of life in the outside world—the need to get the securities to market and run the exchanges, the pressure to hold the representation elections and bargain out the contracts—have forbidden delay and quickly and cruelly revealed inconsistencies in the application of the law. Technicians also admire the odd organization imposed on the NLRB by Congress shortly after the Second World War, in the separation of the General Counsel's office from the Board itself, to the point where the President separately appoints and the Congress separately confirms the occupant of the office.

Commissioner Loevinger and Judge Friendly agree, in different terms, on the future needs of the agencies. Loevinger phrases it as "an administrative common law . . . in the original, literal sense of a body of legal principles which is common to numerous jurisdictions." Friendly points to the fact that "administrative agencies are creating, or ought to be creating, a body of substantive law, requiring constant critical analysis, almost as important as that produced by the courts." He asks that this new and expanding body of law be taken seriously, first by the commissions themselves in writing their opinions ("What would you think of a court that regularly said, 'We have decided thus and so—our law clerks will find reasons to support this later'?"), then by the law professors and perhaps their colleagues in the social sciences, and finally by Congress, which should force its standing committees to review the whole body of such law "each ten or fifteen years." Loevinger and Friendly feel that the key institution in straightening out the maze will be the recently formed Administrative Conference, which Congress has forced on the agencies as a permanent standing body, and which will generate reforms over a period of time if only through simple self-disgust. Indeed, with a little luck the Conference might turn into a kind of administrative court on the French model, which such a distinguished scholar as Wolfgang Friedmann regards as "providing better protection for the citizen than present-day common law."

But it is hard to see where the reform movement will find its head of steam. Businessmen mostly have learned to live with arbitrary behavior by the regulatory agencies; greed—it is the ultimate resource of capitalism—adapts to any circumstances. Congressmen find their personal positions rather enhanced than otherwise by their opportunities to influence individual decisions in the regulatory agencies; and Congress as a body inevitably finds it easier to turn problems over to agencies than to slog through the competing interests to a legislative command. And for the lawyers, the confusion is a source of considerable income. A fictitious European lawyer is quoted in a recent *Harvard Law Review* article as saying of the Robinson-Patman Act that "In Europe, the business community would not tolerate that kind of work-program for lawyers." The chaos in many of the agencies makes practice before them, in a way, intellectually demanding and satisfying; and the bar is distressed by the rather obvious fact that any significant reform in administrative law will require a substantial reduction in its legal component. The extent to which the lawyers stop chattering about judicial review and turn their attention to the real job will be a good measure of the public responsibility of the corporate bar in the years ahead.

CHAPTER 11

A SMALL BAG OF SPECIALISTS

"He wouldn't know anything about broadcast licenses," said a lawyer who practices mostly before the FCC, speaking of another lawyer who practices mostly before the FCC. "He does common-carrier work"—meaning the law of telephone, telegraph and the like.

Especially in an adversary system, specialization breeds ever more intense specialization. If there is any reason to believe that an opponent may gain an advantage through employing a lawyer who is particularly experienced or knowledgeable, a client will demand for himself a lawyer with similar skills. The four fields of law which the great majority of lawyers practice are real estate, divorce, wills and debt collections. Each of them also has a rather small specialist bar which does this work only, in volume, and will be consulted by other lawyers when large sums or hard problems are in the case. Where work is less routinized, specialists become more plentiful and important—and should, too. "This is a business," says a bankruptcy lawyer. "If you do a lot of it, you ought to be better than people who do only a little."

The classic specialist is the admiralty lawyer, who handles everything that happens to, by, for, with or on a ship. The federal district courts were set up primarily to handle admiralty matters, which seemed clearly beyond the jurisdiction of the individual states: historically, federal courts have always had a "law side" (which includes the equity jurisdiction) and an "admiralty side," which follows considerably different rules of procedure and enforces a substantive law much of which dates back some hundreds of years. Admiralty actions are *"in rem"* rather than *"in personam"*—that is, the case is in form against the ship itself rather than against its owners. The claim is expressed by a "libel" on the ship, and there are various complicated safeguards to make sure that commerce can continue but that the shipowner cannot escape. Recent modifications have made the procedure less exotic, but lawyers who have not practiced on the admiralty side before still find themselves lost. "We have a client," says a corporate lawyer, "a gas station by a river. They had a little rowboat moored there. A Chris-Craft came along and hit it, and they were sued. You know, we couldn't help our client at all—couldn't even figure out what the lawyers on the other side were talking about. We had to get him special counsel, an admiralty firm."

In recent years more and more of the practice of the admiralty firms has been in personal-injury cases under the Jones Act, which Congress passed to give added protection to seamen and longshoremen, and which has become the largest single category of "federal question" lawsuits in the district courts. Many of the cases have involved dividing the liability between the ship and the stevedoring company or the ship repairers, which is terribly complicated both under admiralty law and under the statutes. By extension, some of the admiralty firms have also become counsel for airlines. But most of the business is still what it always was: lost or damaged cargo, failure to load or unload, late delivery, accidents at sea, salvage rights and so forth. The Supreme Court in the early nineteenth century decided that the admiralty jurisdiction also included the inland waterways, and a good fraction of admiralty practice today deals with barges.

Within admiralty is perhaps the tightest specialty in the law: the customs lawyer, who practices before panels of the nine-judge Customs Court in the port cities, to challenge duties applied by customs inspectors. This court always has the largest backlog of cases in the country, hundreds of thousands of "protests," because each shipment is in theory a separate case; but one decision may dispose of ten thousand cases at a time. About a hundred lawyers handle all the customs business in the country, and they do well. The procedure is not, in fact, very complicated (though the law itself is a mess), and a visitor recently said to one of these lawyers, "You must have a lot of young men coming in to compete." The customs lawyer shook his head. "No," he said, "they'd starve. You see, this is all contingency work, and it's five years before you're paid." That's another way to preserve a specialty for those already in it.

In the years just before and just after the Second World War, the specialty of choice for the young men coming out of law school was labor law, which typically comes in two varieties: employers' and unions'. (A handful of men practice on both sides, in different industries, but by and large the choice is one or the other.) Work in the labor field reaches mountainous peaks at contract negotiation time, when the lawyer sits with his clients either at the negotiating table or in a separate hotel room, caucusing, counseling, drafting, arguing, drinking, often all night long—while mediators run back and forth between the parties. Considerable preparation and intellectual agility are necessary to be effective in this kind of negotiation, because there are enormous numbers of possible swaps that can be made—extra sick leave for less increase in the pension, etc. Good labor lawyers also keep in mind that this particular contract is not a solitary venture between the parties, and often the most significant single question in any one negotiation is its impact on subsequent negotiations.

One part of labor practice is administrative agency work before the National Labor Relations Board, which administers a law forbidding "unfair labor practices" and conducts representation elections to determine which union (if any) shall speak for the workers in bargaining with their employer. NLRB decisions as to the size and scope of the "bargaining unit" will often, in effect, determine the winner of the election, and lawyers spend a good deal of time marshaling evidence for the hearing examiner who will make this decision. After the election, a loser may try to upset the result on the grounds that an employer unduly helped the winner, which may involve further hearings and appeals. Unions which are getting nowhere in negotiations may be able to persuade the NLRB to investigate and commence proceedings to order an employer to bargain. Historically, one of the NLRB's most significant powers was its policing of what an employer could and could not do during an organizing drive, and its right to issue cease-and-desist orders, reinstate dismissed employees with back pay (subject to appeal to the courts), and generally put an end to antiunion practices. The South-ern Democratic-Republican coalition of the Truman and Eisen-hower eras made a large dent in these powers, however, and the agency has been of only limited assistance to union organizing drives since the early 1950s. In recent years the agency and the Department of Labor have also been empowered to investigate and restrain cer-tain internal and external misbehavior by unions, particularly with relation to union elections and administration of funds. This power tends to be exercised in a rather gingerly fashion—still, the fact is that more union leaderships have been overturned by vote of the membership during the 1960s than in the entire previous history of the American labor movement.

The generation of corporation labor lawyers who grew up fighting unions is now just about dead. Though lawyers sometimes counsel flight to the unorganized South, and help companies adjust their plans to minimize the legal consequences of a fast exit, most labor lawyers for corporations are engaged in more sophisticated forms of counseling, for example, in advising on the areas the contract should cover. (The general rule is that anything you would give anyway—improvements in rest rooms or safety equipment or scholarships for workers' children—ought to be in the contract, because the long-term goal is to build worker confidence in an "acceptable" union leadership rather than to puff up the boss.) But there are still clients who want to know only what the law allows them to do, and still lawyers who feel no higher duty than the supply of such informa-tion. And on the other end there are lawyers whose main stock in trade is a close knowledge of the personal weaknesses of the union leaders and the ways to reach the members of the bargaining com-mittee; that's labor relations, too.

What the union's lawyer does is a more fascinating question. Arthur J. Goldberg was amused at the people who expressed sur-prise at his efficiency in running the bureaucracy of the Labor De-partment (and then the smaller but still sticky bureaucracy of the UN Mission). "You know," Goldberg said, "Phil Murray used to get sick a lot, and I had a lot to do with running the CIO. I got re-laxed about administration." During the 1930s, when uneducated and inexperienced workers were trying to set up effective labor unions, lawyers were their most continuous contact with knowledgeable advice. Questions of how to handle organizing drives, what to do about jurisdictional disputes, how to manage dissidence within the union, how to keep up the momentum of a strike, what to settle for—all the politics of an organization, as well as its legal problems, came across a lawyer's desk. With the passage of time, the unions have built up nonlegal staffs of professionals in the field of labor relations, and the elected leadership has acquired savvy. The day of the lawyer as the *recognized* spokesman for the union has passed. In many unions, however, it is probably still true to say that no major decision is made without the lawyer's advice on the political as well as the legal consequences. And when the leadership of a union changes, the lawyer is likely to change, too; the relationship between the deposed chief and the lawyer was too intimate to be easily transferred to his conqueror. Almost every labor lawyer handles the personal legal problems of the leaders of the unions he represents (often without fee); many labor law offices wax fat through handling (with fee) the personal-injury suits of the union's members.

Much of the day-to-day work of the labor lawyer is in the interpretation of the contract, to guide his client in processing the grievances that arise in any employment situation, and that lie near the heart of the ordinary collective bargaining agreement. Annually, about twenty thousand grievance proceedings produce a formal arbitration, a trial of an individual case before an agreed-upon neutral party (sometimes flanked by a pair of nonneutrals, one from each side). These are quasi-judicial proceedings, with witnesses, cross-examination, validation of documents, arguments about the meaning of clauses in the contract which is the "law" to be applied to the case. Most of the time, the arbitrator is himself a lawyer. But he is not restrained by rules of evidence—he can even, to the horror of many lawyers, hear testimony that the original negotiators really understood a phrase to mean something other than what Harvard's Archibald Cox once called "the pretty plain meaning of an agreement that purports to speak for itself."

In the absence of fraud, there is virtually no appeal from an arbitrator's ruling; the courts will routinely enforce his "award."

Gerald Aksen of the American Arbitration Association says, "Sometimes they say, relishing it, that's the risk you took when you signed that contract; you made your bed, now lie in it." Surprisingly often, courts will even accept without question an arbitrator's decision as to whether or not a matter is arbitrable under the contract—work loads, for example, or decisions to subcontract part of the work. Basic decisions on wages and hours may also be put out to arbitration, when the parties cannot agree but neither is willing to risk a strike.

Arbitrations are often very ill-mannered, with lawyers yelling at each other and at each other's clients and witnesses. Because the matter has already passed fruitlessly through negotiation or internal conciliation machinery, and because the contract under which the arbitration occurs was often signed by both parties under the misapprehension that it would eliminate this particular problem, the emotional atmosphere can be heavy. Not infrequently the lawyers play up to it. "Spokesmen for both parties," Sylvester Garrett wrote, "put on a seemingly endless display of histrionics, insults and pettifogging. Either because of accidental mutual insight or implied understanding based on long experience, the respective spokesmen mutually contrive to put on a great show for their clients and constituents. . . . Viewing life as it is—rather than as some might like it to be—we cannot assume that such spokesmen do not perform a service for those they represent." (This sort of "litigation by regulated abuse," as the anthropologist Paul Bohannan calls it, is not confined to capitalist industrial relations. Bohannan particularly likes "the juridical drum songs of the Eskimo. . . . Each party has a turn at singing a song, to the accompaniment of drums, in which he heaps abuse and mockery upon his adversary, reciting his version of the dispute, and seeking to bring shame upon the other. The songs are composed in advance, but follow traditional styles . . .")

More serious problems may arise when the arbitration is understood by all as a formal show to validate an agreement already reached. Such a case might involve a popular union member who was the bookmaker for the shop, and management caught him with the goods and fired him. The union has never been happy about the gambling on the floor (which introduces a gangster element that imperils the leadership in more ways than one), but the membership would never stand still for acquiescence in the firing. So the matter goes to arbitration. The interesting question now is whether or not the arbitrator is let in on the deal, and what effect it has on his fees. Though the average is closer to $200, some arbitrators receive as much as $500 a day, not only for their time hearing the dispute but also for the time they say they were thinking about it or writing up their award. Large fees for arbitrating no-contest "disputes" are a true scandal, and there is no doubt that the scandal occurs.

"A number of years ago," writes Judge Paul R. Hays of the Court of Appeals for the Second Circuit,

> when I was comparatively new at arbitration, two lawyers, one representing the employer, the other representing the employees' union, requested that I arbitrate a wage dispute for them. They offered me $5,000, which was in that day an excellent fee. I was pleased and quickly expressed my willingness to accept the arbitration. I was then informed that it would be unnecessary for me to hold any hearings or even to prepare an award. The award, it appeared, had already been prepared, and all I was required to do was to sign my name to it. . . . I declined to sign. I heard afterwards that two or three other arbitrators had declined. Then a fourth arbitrator signed. I have never particularly begrudged him his fee of $5,000, but I have always felt that it was going a bit too far to give him a dinner and a medal for making the most important contribution to arbitration for that year.

These rigged wage arbitrations may mean that the union leaders have been bribed; the rigged discharge arbitrations may mean that union and management are working together to get rid of the leader of a rival faction in the union. But the discharge may, as noted, be legitimate; and the wage agreement may be in fact the most the boss can pay, though the leadership could not sell this proposition to its members. Regardless of the underlying reasons, Judge Hays contends, "the rigged award . . . is a shocking distortion of the administration of justice. It displays the arbitrator as the creature of the parties, a marionette operated by them, a ventriloquist's dummy."

Judge Hays is also upset, as most commentators are, by the extent to which arbitrators may be swayed by their need to generate business for themselves. A man who is "impartial arbitrator" for an

industry, or permanent arbitrator under a contract, is under constant political pressure. His position is secure only until the next
contract, which is rarely more than two or three years away. If he
deeply offends either side, he may find himself without a job; there
have been strikes over a demand to change or retain an impartial
arbitrator whom one side or the other has vowed to eliminate at
the earliest opportunity. And the free-lance arbitrator knows that
every award he makes influences his chances of being chosen for
similar employment in the future; there are published services which
rate his every performance as "pro-labor" or "pro-management."

The remedy for much of this, Hays feels, is to reverse the doctrine
that in the absence of obvious odor a court will enforce an arbitration award. His book is in large part a reaction to Justice William
O. Douglas' eulogy of labor arbitration and "the common law of
the shop" when what is involved, obviously, is the statute law of
the contract. It is also in part, however, a lawyer's professional
disavowal of what is at bottom a nonlegal proceeding. Unfortunately, Judge Hays' alternatives to enforcement of the award are a
set of special labor courts, a vast increase in labor cases before
existing federal courts, or a you-guys-fight-it-out approach. The
existing courts have neither the time nor the competence to hear
these cases from the beginning, and, in any event, it cannot make
arbitrators *more* responsible if they rule on cases with the feeling
that a court will hear the whole thing over again. And the notion
that the parties themselves will be more responsible if they are
deprived of a tribunal is an argument for the abolition of all courts,
not just labor arbitration.

Both these suggestions ignore the political context in which all
legal labor relations decisions must be taken. Just as a legislature
must be allowed to put vague language in a statute (because agreement cannot be got on specifics), negotiators seeking to avoid or
end a strike must be allowed to put vague language in their contracts. This language must then be interpreted in the light of the
history of the situation, and the rules of evidence would exclude
much of this history from a trial in an ordinary court. Seen in this
light, the fact that the arbitrator must find a way to satisfy both
sides or lose his job is by no means a condemnation of the proce-

dure. There is a baby in this bath water. Most Americans who have looked at both do not agree with Judge Hays' preference for the external politics of the European governmental labor court over the internal politics of American labor arbitration. Whatever the infelicities of Justice Douglas' phrasing—and Justice Douglas is, of course, a master of the pop art of making a slogan appear to do duty as a *ratio decidendi*—improvement in the nation's handling of its labor disputes will surely require more rather than less arbitration. Everybody—including all the labor lawyers—would like to see an improvement in its quality.

2

Many lawyers are specialists not in a branch of law but in an industry. A typical example would be a firm that represents the trade association of restaurateurs in a city. This firm will know everything about real-estate leases for restaurant purposes, about government regulation of health and food and liquor, about any applicable sales taxes and the income taxation of people much of whose income may come in tips, about unemployment and compensation insurance in the restaurant trades and liability insurance to protect against people who slip on banana peels or find snails in their ginger beer, about labor relations with unions of waiters and chefs and dishwashers, about the collection of delinquent charge accounts and the proof that individuals were authorized to sign for their companies, about the warranties given by food suppliers, about the bankruptcy and reorganization of restaurants. They may have intimate alliances with insurance companies which specialize in these problems, with brokers who buy and sell restaurants, with banks which like to handle receiverships in the food trades.

From the lawyers' point of view, such firms are not specialists at all—they practice over a very wide range of law. But they *are* specialists, just the same, the proof being that mostly they cannot successfully transfer their knowledge of restaurant law to other industries, even though the legal headings are the same. This sort of specialization is a natural result of the fact that much of any successful lawyer's business (most lawyers estimate about one-third of the year's new business) comes to him by word of mouth.

One of these specializations is so much fun, and involves such intimate relations with the business itself, that the lawyers who concentrate in it are constantly abandoning the practice of law and becoming entrepreneurs and somebody's clients. For want of a better description, this field can be called arts and entertainment, covering literary, theatrical, musical, cinematic, broadcasting and graphic property. What ties them together is the fact that the big money is in movies and television, so that a man who thought he was just representing authors finds himself involved with producers and then, often enough, with actors. The work often turns out to involve everything from scouting jobs and commissions for one's clients, through swatting out divorce settlements, to arguing cases in constitutional law before the Supreme Court. Like Arthur Krim of United Artists or Leonard Goldenson of the American Broadcasting Company, the lawyer who becomes intimately involved with entertainment may wind up running the business himself. Others wind up running the lives of people who are highly talented in one direction but need nursemaids in several others. "The day I stopped arguing," one of these lawyers says, "was the day my client said to me, 'Look, I get paid a hundred thousand dollars a week when I work, because of what I do to people. Do you think I can turn it off when I'm not in front of a camera?' "

The law here starts with copyright, a subject that is historically fascinating and legislatively confused. Initially, copyright was part of the control machinery that protected the government from the printing press; members of the Stationers Company were awarded exclusive rights to print certain works on the understanding that they would print only material previously licensed by the Crown. The Acts had expiration dates, and Members of Parliament disliked the law for various reasons. Some disapproved of the "prior restraint" involved in licensing (following Milton, who wrote *Areopagitica* to condemn this practice, though he had nothing against punishing people who abused their privileges to publish treason, heresy, Popery or obscenity; if books after publication "be found mischievous and libellous," he wrote, "the fire and the executioner will be the timeliest and most effectuall remedy, that mans prevention can use"). Others, with friends who could not join the Stationers Company, disapproved the idea of monopoly in the printing trades. Among them, the opponents of the Printing Acts killed the law in 1694.

The result was chaos and depression in the printing trade, to the point where Parliament in 1709—in what was, if one stops to think about it, a most remarkable abdication of governmental power—granted every printer the right to copyright what he printed, giving him a monopoly on a particular book even though nobody in authority had read and approved it. The term was fourteen years, because it took seven years to train a printing apprentice. In the United States, for this antique reason, the copyright law has always read in multiples of seven. As of this writing (a bill is pending in Congress to grant more liberal protection), American copyrights run twenty-eight years from date of publication, with the right to renew for another twenty-eight years.

Originally, copyright in America was by the states; Noah Webster became an itinerant peddler partly to copyright his speller in every state. Connecticut passed the first copyright law in 1783, including a provision that anyone who felt the price of the copyright material was too high could petition a court to force the publisher to reduce it. The Constitution specifically authorized Congress to pass a copyright law, which it did in 1790; and the purpose now was to protect the author rather than the publisher. Foreign authors and composers were not protected, and complained bitterly; but the failure to grant copyright to works published abroad did at least as much damage to American authors and composers and playwrights, who were forced to peddle their wares in a market depressed by a large supply of foreign literary and musical property which a publisher could have for nothing. Not until 1891 did the United States grant copyright to foreign works (Mark Sullivan credited this Act of Congress for much of the American literary renaissance in the 1890s). Not until 1954 did the United States become one of the signers of a major international copyright convention.

The mere acquisition of a copyright presents no problems. Herman Finkelstein, general counsel of ASCAP, says that "when I first went into the field, I called in my secretary and gave her the forms and said, 'If anybody comes in and wants anything copyrighted, fill these out.'" Provided the material is original with the author, it need not have anything new in it at all. Learned Hand wrote "[I]f by some magic a man who had never known it were to compose anew Keats' Ode on A Grecian Urn, he would be an 'author,' and, if he copyrighted it, others might not copy that poem, though they might of course copy Keats's." Gaining an injunction or damages against somebody who is infringing the copyright may be a little trickier, because the owner must show that the infringer knew of his work, had access to it and copied substantial parts of it. Actual piracy is required. And the law is full of little gimmicks (down to and including a failure to print a "c" in a circle before the owner's name on every copy) by which copyright can be lost.

Copyright is the basis, because copyright is what the author or dramatist or composer has to sell (or lease). The performer's talents, too, acquire value in broadcast or film largely because they become part of a production which is copyright in its entirety. Lawyers are necessary to defend the property. Plagiarism suits are fairly common in the musical and theatrical areas. (Unsuccessful playwrights, the Court of Appeals for the Second Circuit once noted, are "commonly obsessed with the inalterable conviction that no situation, no character, no detail of construction in their own plays can find even a remote analogue except as the result of piracy. 'Trifles light as air are to the jealous confirmation strong as proof of holy writ.' ") Music publishers will often refuse to open the envelopes in which unknown composers send their wares, to make sure that the defense of "no access" remains open to them.

Literary properties are subject to suits for libel, which can occur by accident as well as by design (printing an innocent man's name, for example, where the guilty man's name should have been); Justice Holmes once wrote that publishing is "very like firing a gun into a street." The proportion of libel suits that plaintiffs will (or can) win is quite low; but a lawyer with a client can put a publisher to great expense defending them, which stimulates "strike suits" looking for a few hundred dollars as a bribe to go away.

A literary property or a movie with gamy sections may also require protection against the government; every state, many cities and the federal Post Office Department administer laws against "obscenity." These cases get in the newspapers because they make good reading, and because the appellate courts have such trouble handling them. (The Justices of the Supreme Court since 1954, when they first attempted to lay down a constitutional standard of what would and what would not be protected by the First Amendment, have had to read more filth than has been read by any other comparable group of normal males in America.) Justice Potter Stewart, in a case involving an attempt to suppress the movie *The Lovers,* was driven to a personal statement about hard-core pornography: "I shall not today attempt further to define the kinds of material I understood to be embraced within that short-hand description, and perhaps I could never succeed in intelligibly doing so. But I know it when I see it." This, incidentally, was a 5-4 case; and Stewart's was the swing vote which permitted the film to be shown in Ohio.

These cases have opened up a considerable field for creativity by lawyers. Justice William Brennan had written that he felt no reluctance to see Samuel Roth go to jail because what the villain had published was "utterly without redeeming social importance." Lawyers for defendants in subsequent cases insisted that this phrase now marked the line of demarcation between punishable and protected behavior. New York's Charles Rembar and California's Stanley Fleischmann both claim credit for wrenching the phrase out of its original context and making it a positive argument; it was to Rembar that Justice Brennan once addressed the rather puzzled question as to the origin of the line, only to be informed that he had written it himself.

Courageous clients have been as important as capable lawyers in advancing the freedom to publish what has come to be called "high pornography." Rembar, who represents Grove Press (he was briefly its president), was particularly proud of its owner, Barney Rosset, in the *Lady Chatterley's Lover* case: "Barney didn't want to win it on the grounds that the Post Office had violated the Administrative Procedures Act; he wanted to win it on the ground that the book was a good book." Still, Rembar does not insist that the Justices read all his clients' output to determine whether the book is good or not. Defending *Fanny Hill* on appeal, he proposed that its social importance had been sufficiently demonstrated by the witnesses who had said they liked it at the original trial. Fleischmann, whose clients are harder to defend (he has appealed mostly on behalf of still and moving nudes), feels that all this question of quality is really irrelevent. "For years," he says, "I was practicing on the assumption that there was a line, and the question is, Where do you drawn it? Now I don't think you can draw a line. Take sexual perversions—fellatio is often one of the grounds for divorce. The grounds for divorce are public policy; and the First Amendment certainly prohibits any interference with discussions of public policy."

These arguments are not really helpful to judges who have to decide real cases. There is no pornographic trash so foul that some Ph.D. cannot be found to give expert testimony that he enjoyed it and recommend it as bedtime reading for his twelve-year-old daughter. And the Fleischmann argument that there are no rules (which is roughly the argument of Justices Black and Douglas) is merely a value judgment of the kind which the society has not deputed to the courts. We shall touch on this question again in Chapter 15; for now it is enough to point out that after rulings by the Supreme Courts of the United States and the Commonwealth of Pennsylvania that *Tropic of Cancer* is not (legally) obscene, the book still cannot be bought in a Philadelphia bookstore. To tell people they can't have a law they badly want is often nothing more than an invitation to them to behave lawlessly.

The New York lawyer Leon Friedman, who believes the Supreme Court should find a way to protect "established publishers and sellers of erotic material," has admitted that "almost anything can now be published and the old danger of serious fiction and social commentary being suppressed has all but vanished." The Supreme Court has played a vital (though not an isolated) role in this progress. Under the circumstances, to criticize Justice Brennan for the verbal infelicities of his opinions is more than a little ungenerous—and cruel, as it is obvious that the angels did not bring to Justice Brennan's cradle any particular gift of clear expression.

Perhaps the best statement of the issues involved was by Learned Hand in 1936, in an opinion now forgotten and perhaps therefore worth reprinting:

As so often happens, the problem is to find a passable compromise between opposing interests, whose relative importance, like that of all social or personal values, is incommensurable. We impose such a duty upon a jury, because the standard they fix is likely to be an acceptable mesne, and because in such matters a mesne most nearly satisfies the moral demands of the community. There can never be constitutive principles for such judgments, or indeed more than cautions to avoid the personal aberrations of the jurors. We mentioned some of these in United States v. One Book Entitled Ulysses: the work must be taken as a whole, its merits weighed against its defects; if it is old, its accepted place in the arts must be regarded; if new, the opinions of competent critics in published reviews or the like may be considered; what counts is its effect, not upon any particular class, but upon all those whom it is likely to reach. Thus "obscenity" is a function of many variables, and the verdict of the jury is not the conclusion of a syllogism of which they are to find only the minor premiss, but really a small bit of legislation ad hoc, like the standard of care.

(Incidentally, in this case, where he reversed a conviction, Hand thought the book was pretty hot stuff: he described it as "a work of fiction of considerable merit . . . [which] would arouse libidinous feelings in almost any reader.") These decisions are *always* "jury" decisions: the reason the Supreme Court has looked so bad in the obscenity cases is that in such matters it can never be more than a jury of nine, deciding cases by majority vote and trying to look like an appellate court.

The money for lawyers in the entertainment industry lies not in the libel or obscenity cases, of course, but in the making of contracts to license the use of copyrights or to rent personal services. Lawyers here are in direct competition with agents, and the two get along badly. Most lawyers do not understand literary practice or entertainment well enough to know where positions are traditionally and interestingly flexible; most agents do not know anything about a contract except the sums of money and percentages written in the blanks, and the traditionally negotiable clauses.

In all truth, literary and entertainment contracts are peculiar documents. It has long been understood that equity cannot compel the performance of a personal-service contract. What it can do, however, is forbid the artist who has broken an exclusive-service contract with one entrepreneur to work for anybody else in the same jurisdiction (the leading case involved an opera singer). In the days when all American movies were made in Hollywood by banks, this possibility of a wholly legal blacklist was a gnarled club that a producer could use on a performer, but today its force is much diminished. Anyway, the interests of both parties lie normally in a resolution of the dispute rather than in even the most delicate judicial adjustment of rights and remedies. The contracts signed, therefore, are usually evidence of a rough agreement rather than enforceable documents. The book you are holding in your hand was contracted for delivery in October, 1963, and was finished more than three years late. At no time did its author hear from its publisher about his violation of a contract, though the violation was plain as day.

The vague nature of entertainment and literary contracts is sometimes hidden from the participants (and even from their lawyers) by the sheer length and complexity of the documents, which deal of necessity with speculative future interests. A contract for a television series may run well over a hundred pages, covering everything from responsibility for a short circuit to responsibility for paying the insurance premiums on possible breakage of the gun arm of the actor who plays the hero.

Even so, show business being what it is, the contract always turns out not to have covered all the contingencies. The man who negotiated the contract by which "Superman" was made into movies in the 1930s recently recalled the six months of meetings around a table that were necessary before the papers, including thirty amendments to the original, could be signed. But nobody had thought of the possibility of color movies; and when color came, there was no hint in the document of who should pay for all the new costumes and sets that would be required; and the whole deal had to go back to the drawing board.

"In this field," says Joel Katz, a young lawyer who went off after some years with a talent agency to become a program producer on his own, "you find a lawyer who's technically superb, and you pick up a piece of his work, and it's just drafting; and you say, 'God, he's *terrible*.' But the contract you *like* may be very sloppy. It always surprises me that there's so little litigation, considering the sloppy way things are done. I know shows that have been on the air three years and canceled before the contract was signed. I know one case where a network paid three hundred thousand dollars to cancel a contract nobody had ever signed—the whole deal was in the notes of the people who were at the meeting."

In this shadowy realm of nonenforceable contracts, the services of a lawyer are particularly valuable; without them, a man is likely to sign an *enforceable* contract, and really be in trouble. Lawyers throughout the business world, as noted earlier, serve a "surety" function. Specialists in literary and entertainment law serve that function less by their drafting than by their physical presence. It's a profitable field.

3

Three more: patents, where the specialty is created by the law and its administration; taxes, where the specialty has been hand-crafted by lawyers; and bankruptcy, where it results from a unique combination of law, economics and politics.

Most people think of patent lawyers as the invisible men across the wall from the reception room where an eager nut sits with a bulging box containing some machine that is already wriggling ominously. The image is misleading, because a patent lawyer is even more likely than other lawyers to make his living serving a large company. About half the present patent bar is employed in corporate offices (Eastman Kodak, with an in-house patent firm of eighty, is reputed to have the largest collection) or works for a law firm which is billed as independent and will in fact have a few out-side clients but is fundamentally a dependency of a company like U.S. Rubber or Minnesota Mining. Some executives argue that the real nut in the patent field is not the inventor but the patent attor-ney. "They're mathematical," Sol Linowitz said a little uncomfort-ably while general counsel and chairman of the board of Xerox. "Of the twenty-six we have, perhaps two could have gone into any other kind of practice. They work alone, have nothing to do with the usual amenities. We had one here for years who carried a metal lunch box to work every day."

Patent practitioners number between six and seven thousand, and on an IQ test they would on the average probably outrank the servants of any other major legal specialty. Their average income is probably higher, too. They are also, incidentally, the most loyal adherents of Canon 27, which forbids publicity; until the late 1950s patent lawyers were permitted to advertise, and the field got a bad name for unscrupulous selling, which its leaders are trying hard to live down.

Few patent lawyers ever planned to be patent lawyers; indeed, few of them planned to be lawyers at all. "They thought of themselves as engineers," says the head of one large patent firm, "and then decided there was more future for them in being parasitic than in being creative or inventive." Most of them studied their law at night while working in a corporate research department or for the Patent Office (which at this writing pays $6,400 to start). "The best of them," says one patent lawyer, "are the physicists—they're like internists: they don't know anything but they know everything." It is not uncommon for a patent law firm to ask a client company to release an engineer who has done an unusually good job of writing up an invention, so the patent firm can make him a lawyer.

Except for those who have worked four years for the Patent Office as an examiner, all lawyers who wish to represent clients at the Office must pass an examination certifying their competence in at least one of the "arts" (meaning sciences) and in Patent Office procedures. It is not a law exam. This is the only area of law where lawyers are in direct and admitted competition with nonlawyers for the exact same business, because a man can be a patent *agent*, registered with the Patent Office, without being a patent *attorney*. Advising "the general practitioner" to be sure he refers patent business to attorneys rather than to agents, a Wisconsin lawyer recently gave as the first reason the fact that communications with a patent attorney are "privileged," while communications with a patent agent are subject to subpoena by a court if the patent or the client later gets into trouble. This is known as protecting the public against the unauthorized practice of law.

The Patent Office grants about 45,000 patents a year, and is rapidly sinking in its own paper. "It's not a pioneering agency at all," says a Boston patent lawyer. "It's always trying to spend the least money. Never developed its rule-making powers—every case is a new problem. If the Office had done its work of classifying technical information, it could have saved the nation billions of dollars of duplicated research efforts. But that would cost money, and the fact is that if the Patent Office came to Congress with a request for a hundred million dollars, Congress would abolish the patent system." A case can be made here for the proposition that the Good Old Days were really better—under the Act of 1790, patents were issued by a committee consisting of the Secretary of State, the Secretary of War and the Attorney General; and Thomas Jefferson as Secretary of State examined every application himself.

Most applications require two to three years for processing ("Patent Pending"). No other country in the world requires so elaborate an application: the papers must describe the invention in such detail and include such complete drawings that a skilled reader could make the thing for himself; up to 1870 a working model was submitted, too. Obviously, only what is new in the device can be patented, and the patent attorney (or his Washington correspondent) must make a search to find out what is already in the files. "You get flocks of patents on a product," says a lawyer. "If it is a new battery, you'll get separate patents for the positive electrode, the negative electrode, the electrolyte, the way of sealing the casing. They all may be separately useful." Only the inventor himself may apply, by contrast with European procedure, which permits the company employing him to get the patent directly.

The papers are registered on arrival, and assigned to one of the several thousand slots by which the "arts" are classified; and a patent examiner who lives in that slot receives the material. "His job," says a lawyer, "is to help you get a patent. That's what the Patent Office says, and some examiners believe it. The first thing he does is tell you to narrow the scope of your claim. You file an 'argument,' and go down to talk it over with him. Then you reduce your scope, and you get another letter. The 'argument' will be part of the record if you're sued. The writing of these arguments and of the amendments to the application is the real art of the patent lawyer."

All applications are kept secret until they are granted, when they are announced in an "Official Gazette" and the whole claim is made available to anyone who sends in fifty cents. If an application looks to an examiner like a violation of somebody else's existing patent or prior application, he will notify the other party of his right to file an "interference," at which point the question of who got there first will be litigated within the Patent Office itself. (Sometimes patent lawyers deliberately copy other people's claims, to force an "interference," which is much less costly than an infringement suit later.) A man who is denied a patent for any reason can appeal first to a board within the Office, and then to the Court of Customs and Patent Appeals, newly housed in an elegant red-brick Washington home after some years on an upper floor in an antique office building. In 1965, for the first time, the Supreme Court ruled that the CCPA was indeed a "constitutional court," its judges were "constitutional judges," and its decisions could be appealed all the way up. An alternative route is to sue the Commissioner of Patents in a federal district court to force him to issue your patent. While the CCPA decides cases on the record made before the Patent Office, the district court will try the case *de novo,* permitting the lawyer more leeway, especially if he has errors to correct.

Once a man has a patent, what exactly does he have? In theory he has (though patent lawyers hate the word) a monopoly for seventeen years on the production of anything incorporating this patented feature. Most significant patents are taken by big companies which the Antitrust Division won't permit to seek a monopoly of anything, and the purpose of the patent is purely defensive. "It means you got there first," says a New York patent lawyer, "and nobody can drive you out." Patents also make possible crushing counteroffensives. Nothing electronic can be made without infringing some of the patents held by GE, Westinghouse, RCA and AT & T. Thus anyone who comes up with an electronic improvement will have to make his invention available to these giants, because part of any device he could make himself would be covered by one of their patents. There is also some danger that the expense of patent litigation will enable a giant to strangle a competitor by means of a piece of paper the Patent Office should never have granted. One authority notes that "Invalid patents, in the hands of unscrupulous and powerful men, are worth money." But it is also true that the system does give the inventor (or, much more likely, the inventive little company) a degree of leverage on the giants.

And sometimes the system works just as it is supposed to work, the classic cases in the postwar era being Polaroid and Xerox. Sol Linowitz said that Xerox, which was invented, incidentally, by a patent attorney, "is almost a model case of how the patent system should work. This process had been turned down by all the large companies in the United States. One little company wanted the rights, and it was a resistible idea. But we were hungry, we were willing to gamble, we could put millions of dollars into disappointment after disappointment because we knew we'd have protection, we could build protection for secondary patents when the basic patent ran out.

"The reason we're in such a pleasing position today is the quality of the working relationship between the research people and the patent lawyers. We were careful not to overclaim, not to tie our patents to nonpatentable things, not to extend them too far. It wasn't easy."

Though normal procedure is to search the files and redesign around another man's patent, some companies planning a new product will not trouble to make a patent search—they have too much invested in the effort to pull back because of a possible patent infringement. At worst, they may have something on their own shelves that they can hang on the company which sues them. And they can also simply gamble that they can get away with it, because nothing in the law is so thoroughly unpredictable as the reaction of the courts to a patent infringement suit.

About eight hundred such suits are brought every year, and about 150 of them come to trial in a district court. "The judges are scared stiff of patent cases," says a New York patent lawyer. "In Brooklyn, where they've got eight judges, the one with the least seniority gets the patent cases—they're shoved on him." Suits can be brought in any district where the defendant operates, which gives a man suing a big corporation a virtually free choice. The expense of these trials runs about $10,000 a week, and most of them require a number of weeks. "Patent infringement suits," the head of the ABA Section on Patent, Trademark and Copyright Law told a Senate committee in 1965, "cost at a minimum on the order of $50,000, and they go up from there. They go way up from there." Almost half the decisions are appealed; appeals look cheap in the patent field. Plaintiffs pick a place to sue according to their lawyers' analysis of the views of the circuit judges who will hear the case on appeal. In the period 1953-63, in those Courts of Appeal which heard fifty or more such appeals, the proportion of plaintiffs' victories (patents held valid and infringed) ranged from 43.8 per cent in the Fifth Circuit (South) and 43.6 percent in the Fourth Circuit (Chicago) down to 14.4 percent in the Second Circuit (New York). For the nation as a whole, the Circuit Courts invalidated 57.4 percent of all the patents they examined in the course of an infringement suit, and in another 13.6 percent of the cases ruled that the patent, though valid, had not been infringed by the defendant.

One of the difficulties has been the reluctance of the courts to approve monopolies, even when they are created by a public policy in favor of invention. Another, more serious, has been in the word "invention" itself. This difficulty started in 1850, in the "doorknob case," when the Supreme Court approved a charge to a jury that a patent should not be upheld on something (in this case, the attachment of a clay rather than a metal doorknob to a metal shank) which anyone experienced in the trade could make. The device this patent sought to protect was merely "the work of the skilled mechanic, not that of the inventor." From this opinion derived first a "requirement of invention" and then a "standard of invention"—which, in the words of Judge Giles Rich of the CCPA, "the courts pretended was being raised and lowered like an elevator, as though it were something tangible." In 1941 Justice Douglas raised this standard out of sight by requiring that before a patent could issue "the new device . . . must reveal the flash of creative genius." The proportion of patents upheld on appeal under this requirement dropped to about 15 percent.

For eleven years the patent bar struggled to move the Congress to establish new rules which would not lend themselves to interpretation by slogan. The roadblock was the word "invention," which is defined in the standard textbook of the field as "the result of an inventive act." Finally, in 1952, a new patent act was procured which eliminated the word "invention" from the requirements for patentability, substituting the phrase "non-obvious subject matter." The section concluded with the words, "Patentability shall not be negatived by the manner in which the invention was made"; and the report of the House Committee which brought forth the bill explained the phrase as a desire to permit patents whether the device resulted "from long toil and experimentation or from a flash of genius." The patent bar then learned with a shock something other lawyers could have told them from sad experience: that many judges don't read statutes at all, and that many of those who do read them read with such blinders of language that they are incapable of following the plain letter of the law. Decision after decision continued to talk about a "standard of invention," though the law contained no license for such a phrase. Among the circuit judges, only Learned Hand immediately saw the difference and set to developing case law around the concept of "non-obvious subject matter." The Supreme Court may not have seen it yet: despite Justice Clark's attention to the idea in *Graham* v. *John Deere Co.*, he concluded that "the revision was not intended by Congress to change the general level of patentable invention."

Still, the proportion of patents sustained began to rise, reaching a peak of 45.8 percent in 1961. The subject is one in which Justice Abe Fortas has taken a particular interest. (Shortly before his appointment to the bench Fortas had submitted a batch of petitions for certiorari in patent cases, in which he accused his future colleagues of avoiding their duty in patent matters, which was probably true; Justice Frankfurter had said publicly on a number of occasions that he didn't think the Supreme Court was competent to hear patent appeals.) In 1966, for the first time in twenty-two years, the Supreme Court specifically upheld the validity of a patent.

Ultimately, of course, the future of the patent system will be controlled not by the personalities and opinions of judges but by developments in the economy as a whole. One of the most remarkable facts about the patent lawyers is that almost alone in the legal profession they are conscious of the troubles to come. "The patent system," says a Boston patent lawyer, "is supposed to be an incentive to invent, but now there's all that government R & D money as an incentive. The most significant justification of patents is that they force people to publish inventions to get protection, which makes the information available quickly to other scientists and inventors. But the government makes you publish everything you find with government money—and, anyway, the Patent Office information retrieval system has broken down. There are millions and millions of patents, and nobody knows where they are."

Meanwhile, the great opening up of the international patent field has made life more interesting for large numbers of lawyers. In 1965 even the Soviet Union, where public policy abhors the idea of property rights in socially beneficial ideas, signed the Paris Convention for the Protection of Industrial Property. Russia now files several hundred applications a year with the U.S. Patent Office, and for some time the Soviet Union has been granting patents to Americans who seek them in Russia. A 1965 report from the Department of State notes that "the U. S. Government knows of no instance in recent years of Soviet copying or 'pirating' of an American invention patented in the Soviet Union." Generally, the conventions provide that filing for a patent in any country yields priority in every other country, provided the inventor applies within one year of his original filing at home. It makes for interesting extensions of patent practice in an age of jet travel.

And there is still the fun of the nuts, who are real enough. There was, for example, the day when Wilhelm Reich appeared in the offices of a New York patent lawyer to patent his orgone box, in which sexual energy was concentrated to help cure the ills of man. The patent lawyers looked him up and found out he was a prominent disciple of Freud and a recognized, if controversial, analyst. One of the lesser partners in the firm asked him into the office, and reconstructs the episode as follows:

"Now, what's in the box?"

"Orgone."

"Can you measure it?"

"No."

"Can you see it?"

"No."

"Can you smell it?"

"No."

"Well, let's open it up, let me see exactly what's there."

"Can't do that: the orgone will get out."

"Oh, really?"

Nevertheless, one of the younger men was deputed to go out to Reich's Long Island country home for a weekend and investigate. He held long conversations with his host, and sat for some hours in the large orgone box. Then he delivered a legal opinion: "You'll have to come into our office and make orgone there in some way that we can tag or identify it. Otherwise, forget it." Dr. Reich could only comment on the antiquated notions of science that pervaded the American patent system.

4

Until 1966 tax lawyers, like patent lawyers, had to be specially registered with the administrative authorities in Washington to whom they owed their professional opportunities. At one time, indeed, the Internal Revenue Service imposed formal requirements, which could be met by accountants as well as lawyers. (In Britain tax practice is largely in the hands of accountants.) But tax work became too important. Today the representation of clients beyond the level of first negotiations is pretty much restricted to lawyers, and anybody admitted to the bar in his home state is welcome at IRS. The major work is done, however, by people who know what they are doing; a tax lawyer recently estimated that three-quarters of all the tax cases, not necessarily the most important, are handled by alumni of the Internal Revenue Service itself.

Though Washington, Chicago and Los Angeles have thriving groups of tax lawyers, a high proportion of the specialist tax bar is concentrated in New York, because taxes and the money market are closely related. Other cities are lightly supplied. Detroit, for example, has only thirty-odd "full-time, practicing tax attorneys. We know the number," one of them says, "because we have a luncheon when the tax court judges come here on their little white donkeys from the head of the realm, and we see who's there." The real specialist these days tends to concentrate in only a branch of taxation—estate planning, or charitable foundations, or corporate financing.

What makes tax law so pervasive are the twin facts that income taxation is self-assessed and that the one universal desire of mankind is to feed buckshot to the government's frog. The law necessarily makes a sharp distinction between tax evasion (which is cheating) and tax avoidance (which is merely planning one's activities so as to incur the least tax). An usher who gives his church a check for the cash on the collection plate so the church doesn't worry about keeping all the money in the rectory until Monday and then deducts the total of his checks from his taxable income as a charitable contribution is engaging in tax evasion. (This seems to be a widespread practice, by the way.) On the other hand, a member of a hospital's board of directors who owns a piece of property across the street from the hospital which cost him $50,000 but now has a market value of $150,000 because the hospital has raised money for an expansion program and will need the land, may give his property to the hospital and deduct the full $150,000 without fearing a visit from the fisc. A policeman may deduct the cost of his uniforms, but a musician may not deduct the cost of his tails. These distinctions are very firm, and the absence of ordinary (or economic) logic in many of them means that men need lawyers. "The tax law," one of them says sternly, "is immutable, inflexible and immoral."

Complications arise through administrative interpretation, judicial opinion and Congressional action—taxes are the one area of administrative law that Congress really looks at every year. A law review article was written a dozen years ago about "the casual remark of a Washington lawyer who asked, 'What is the point of litigating a tax case when we can have the statute amended for the same outlay of time and money?" Judge Friendly found occasion to ask in 1965 whether it is

truly civilized to have an income tax statute more than 500 pages long—the length of a good-sized novel—implemented by over 2,000 pages of regulation, in which almost every principle has an exception, every exception has an exception to the exception, and many exceptions to exceptions are also subject to exceptions, so that a judge needs a computer to determine whether he is dealing with an odd or even number of exceptions.

Fewer complications arise through actions by the Congress to give selected taxpayers special favors than through rules laid down in hard cases by the IRS itself or by the courts. The new rules, in the hands of the tax lawyers, turn out to give more breaks to more taxpayers than the Treasury wishes to benefit. "The Service sees," says a New York tax lawyer, "that Mary has a pimple on her nose. The first solution is, kill Mary. Then the parents come in and say, 'Don't kill Mary.' So you start narrowing it down. You get this terrible statute, which doesn't really take care of Mary's pimple but adds that much more verbiage to the Code, and then you start writing regulations."

Much of the law is in Revenue Rulings, which the IRS issues either in the course of processing tax returns which contain an unacceptable gimmick or in response to a direct query from a lawyer. The benefit of the ruling is guaranteed, however, only to the man who actually made the request for it; the Service can later change its mind and its ruling, and apply the new rules to everybody else. Tax lawyers therefore can offer even less certainty than other lawyers. "In tax law," one of them says, "it's what happened this morning that counts. So you have to hedge and say, 'If we do this, I think we can get away with it.'" Taxes are one of the few fields in the law where the lawyer's opinion to a client will probably be verified; not the least of the reasons why the tax bar is so intelligent is the constant "reinforcement" of its learning through the rewards-and-punishments system of the Internal Revenue Service.

Counseling is the bread-and-butter of the tax lawyer; the "jelly and tuition," as one of them put it, is the litigated case, often taken on a contingent fee, at negotiated percentages. ("There are some cases," says a tax lawyer, "where if you win the fee is *grotesque*.") Litigation comes only after a long period of informal administrative review, conferences with agents and with senior agents, more conferences at which agents not previously involved in the case will look over documents and even hear testimony to make an independent judgment of whether the Service is being completely fair in the case, and then a "30-Day Letter," telling the taxpaper to pay up within thirty days or file a formal Protest. (Throughout this process the outside world knows little of what has been going on, which presents obvious temptations; but here it will be assumed that everybody is Caesar's wife.) The matter then moves from the District Director's office to the Appellate Division in the office of the Regional Commissioner, where new people look at it. Finally, a Statutory Notice of Deficiency, a "90-Day Letter" is sent, and the taxpaper can either take an appeal to the Tax Court or pay what the Service says he owes and then sue for a refund in an ordinary federal district court or in the Court of Claims. If he does nothing, the Service will enter a lien on his property at the end of the ninety days and seize whatever is required to make up the deficiency.

The Tax Court, with judges who travel around the country, is part of the Treasury Department, and it is not a "constitutional court" from which appeals lie to the Supreme Court. In effect, it determines only government policy for the particular case; the Commissioner of Internal Revenue is not bound by its rulings, and may formally announce a "non-acquiescence," stating an intention to continue applying the rule that was just rejected in the Tax Court. Still, any published decision has some precedent value, because a judge is always reluctant to overrule himself or his colleagues. Nine-tenths of the cases taken to the Tax Court are settled before a judge hears them, if only because IRS does not have the staff necessary to prosecute all of them. These cases, moreover, often turn on idiosyncratic factual questions, such as whether a gift taxed at gift tax rates was really made by a deceased citizen "in contemplation of death," to avoid the higher estate tax rates. At least one promising young tax lawyer recently quit practice and turned to teaching because he had spent two whole months gathering opinions on the significance of the X-rays of the colon of a rich man now gone. "That isn't," he said, "what I went to law school for, and it isn't how I want to spend my life."

The Chief Counsel's office decides which of the pending cases raises a "prime issue," and cases in that category normally cannot be settled; IRS wants them tried. Often the "prime issues" are mat ters which IRS has lost in the past, and wishes to see reversed, which reduces the value of the precedent for the taxpayer. "IRS," says a tax lawyer, "will litigate and lose and lose and lose, and the courts are obviously wrong. One day some judge will say, 'Hey, fellas, these guys have been right all along.' Other judges read it, and soon you have a new body of law."

Claims for a refund in the federal district court are tried like any other suit against the government (the taxpayer can even have a trial by jury, if he wishes), with defense counsel supplied by the U.S. Attorney for the district rather than by the Treasury Department. They can be taken on appeal to the circuit Court of Appeals, and thence, if the Supreme Court agrees to hear the issue, to the top.

Claims for a refund in the Court of Claims are heard initially by a "Commissioner" from that court, who will go to the taxpayer's home town or anywhere else for the purpose, and will remain available for the introduction of new evidence. "Lawyers," says a man at that court, "can think about the case, recoup a mistake, find new witnesses—some of them like that." Then the matter goes to a five-judge panel of the seven-judge Court of Claims, where it will be heard as an appellate case, solely on the record made before the Commissioner with arguments by the lawyers. Though the tax jurisdiction of the Court of Claims has existed for a long time, it is only recently that many lawyers have gone there for adjudication. The basic reason for the new popularity is that the Court of Claims has been fairly consistently kinder to taxpayers than the Tax Court or the district courts and fairly (not invariably) loyal to its own precedents.

All the courts are bound by decisions of the Supreme Court, but the Court of Claims is not in any way bound by decisions of the Tax Court or the circuit Courts of Appeal, just as these courts are not bound by each other or by the Court of Claims. This equality of alternative courts does not ease confusion. Tax cases from the Court of Claims are virtually never reviewed by the Supreme Court, and conflicting results in different circuits may "mature" for years before the Supreme Court agrees to clear the air. Meanwhile, IRS can always try the same arguments again and again.

The tax lawyer counseling his client, then, has the incredible statute, Revenue Rulings, Treasury Regulations and the decisions of three lines of courts to guide him. District and regional and national authorities are forever making decisions, and publishers provide services to keep the lawyer in touch with them; most tax lawyers find that they must do at least eight hours a week of reading current material simply to keep in touch, quite apart from the time spent finding ways to use the material for clients. The odd part of it for an observer is that the whole process seems quite normal to the normal tax lawyer; the only change the lawyer sees on the horizon (and he is probably right) is automation, which will put at his command great quantities of additional and even more confusing information. (The process by which IRS itself is automating its legal business is described in Chapter 12.)

"I went down to a meeting on law and computers in Washington," says a man newly arrived in the law publishing business. "There were 275 tax lawyers there, a whole elite group grown up because taxation has become so complicated. They weren't interested in taxes—they were interested only in procedures. They don't want the tax law to get any simpler; they're starting a new business. After two days I began feeling sorry for the poor taxpayer who doesn't have a computer of his own; they will *force* him to go to a tax lawyer."

5

"I remember when I was a child," says Asa Herzog, a small New Yorker with a gray crew cut and a bristling gray-brown mustache who is chairman of the National Conference of Referees in Bankruptcy, "there was a week when everybody was referring to Sam in a very hushed and solemn way. I asked what was wrong with Sam, had he died, and they told me he'd gone bankrupt. Here he'd supported a family and dozens of creditors for twenty years and now he was almost a criminal because he'd gone broke.

"We know better today. The bankruptcy statute is a rehabilitation statute, not a penal statute. We accept that a man can be honest and still have his troubles, he has a right to a second bite on the apple. What the hell—it's only money."

George W. Treister of Los Angeles, who was a *Yale Law Review* editor and clerk to Justice Hugo Black, wound up in a bankruptcy practice "against the advice of nearly all my friends. But there is no more fascinating field. A little bankrupt comes in here, everybody's after him, he wants to kill himself. There is no greater civil suffering than severe financial troubles. Well, I can get a lot of his bills dismissed, get him started again. There's not much money in it—maybe two hundred dollars—but it's very satisfying."

The modern bankruptcy law is one of the great humane accomplishments of the twentieth century, relieving mankind of what had been since antiquity a great source of involuntary servitude. It is important to keep this accomplishment in mind, even while noting that the little rings of bankruptcy lawyers who cluster around some of the federal courts may be the most rapacious community in the legal profession in America. They are also the most protected: the law under which they operate provides that the first slice of the assets of a bankrupt are to go not to the people to whom he owes wages (though failure to pay wages is in some states a crime), not to the people from whom he has borrowed money or bought supplies without paying, not to the governments to which he owes taxes, but to the administration of his bankruptcy. Lawyers' fees must be paid.

The Constitution authorized Congress to pass national bankruptcy laws, and three efforts were made in that direction (the laws survived from 1800 to 1803, 1841 to 1843 and 1867 to 1878) before the Act of July 1, 1898, found a formula which, with about fifty amendments, has remained viable. The need for federal control was clear from the beginning—American states had almost as much trouble as South American republics in resisting the temptation to write bankruptcy laws that would enable local debtors to escape distant creditors. But some state rules remain, declaring local public policy on what the courts can and cannot take away from a man to satisfy his creditors. In Connecticut, for example, the exemptions are "2 cords of wood, 2 tons of hay, 5 bushels each of potatoes and turnips, 10 bushels each of Indian corn or rye or the meal or flour manufactured therefrom"; in Texas they include 200 rural acres or $5,000 worth of unimproved urban property.

The major distinction is between voluntary and involuntary

bankruptcy. The first is a declaration of insolvency and a cry for help to a court; the second is a motion by a creditor to have the court take over what assets the debtor may have left, alleging an "act of bankruptcy" (most commonly, because this is what scares a creditor, the payment to another creditor of an undue share of what looks like shrinking assets to another creditor). The aim of the voluntary bankruptcy petition is often to get the business or the individual reorganized so it or he can stay alive; the aim of the involuntary bankruptcy is usually to liquidate the business and distribute the proceeds equitably among the losers. In either case, the heart of the proceeding is the appointment of a trustee or receiver to sell off what remains or to reorganize the business: the bankrupt totally loses control over his own affairs.

But the loss is temporary, for at the end of the process he will be "discharged," he will leave the court either without debts or (in the case of a reorganization or a "Chapter 13" personal bankruptcy) with debts reduced in amount or extended in time to the point where the court feels he can carry them in reasonable comfort. In the wage-earner bankruptcies, which are court-ordered stretch-out plans and which are all that is available in large chunks of the South (where bench and bar morally disapprove of anybody really getting out from under, epecially if he is Negro), a court's opinion of how much of his salary a man can sacrifice to pay old creditors is likely to run as high as $20 or $25 out of $80 a week.

At the height of the Depression, bankruptcies in the United States ran at a rate of about 70,000 a year. By 1946 the rate was down to 11,000. Now every year sets a new record: in fiscal 1966 there were 192,000 of them, more than nine-tenths of them voluntary personal bankruptcies, and about nine-tenths of those the bankruptcies of people classified as "employees." The total of creditors' (possibly inflated) claims runs near $2 billion a year, of which close to $1.9 billion must be written off.

The lawyer comes into the bankruptcy case in one of three ways: by making the petition for the bankrupt (here, as in criminal cases, the lawyer tries to get his fee in advance), by representing a committee of creditors, which he usually puts together himself after an approach from one of them, or by appointment, from the referee

in bankruptcy to whom the matter is referred by the district court
once the creditors have demonstrated that the fellow really is
bankrupt. Until 1946 referees were paid by a fee for each case;
now they are salaried, but their courts are supported by filing fees
and shares of the recoveries. "Unlike any other part of our federal
judicial system," Harvard's Vern Countryman writes, "the bankruptcy system is still required to be self-supporting."

The economics of the situation are hard to get straight, because
almost every bankruptcy lawyer gets saddled every year with a
number of "no-asset" cases, at least some of which provide no fee
at all. On the other hand, every once in a while it proves possible
to collect a number of outstanding debts to an apparently closed-out
bankrupt company, and the lawyer's share of that collection may
run as high as a third. Meanwhile, there are receiverships for businesses which are to be kept going, where the receiver supervises the
day-to-day operation of the business and may be awarded as much
as 2.5 percent of the cash flow as his fee ("Quite a patronage plum,"
says one bankruptcy lawyer mildly, "when it's a supermarket").
There are the creditors' claims to be proved, and an inquiry into
when the lucky creditors with *secured* claims received their security.
When the business is in receivership, the law allows it to continue
borrowing money as needed, with the new loans forming a prior
claim on the assets. The basic job of the referee is to compromise
the matter—to get the creditors to agree on how much there is to
be recovered, and how they should divide it up among themselves.
His ultimate power is to force a minor fraction of creditors who
don't agree with the settlement to accept the result that has been
approved by the rest.

Some cases come into bankruptcy court fully formed—a lawyer
has organized a committee of almost all the creditors, they have
decided who shall be the trustee or receiver, and the referee merely
puts their plans into action. (Sometimes—it is professionally and
in terms of social utility the triumph of the bankruptcy lawyer—
the whole deal can be made privately, the willing creditors buying
out a few recalcitrants, and bankruptcy can be avoided altogether.)
In others, the referee must make decisions between competing groups
of creditors, each represented by its own counsel. The receivers

and the lawyers who are to collect their fees from the "estate" submit their bills to him, and he must approve them, subject to appeal to the district judge and then possibly the circuit Court of Appeals.

Recently some of the Courts of Appeals have been insisting that the only valid way to calculate the lawyers' and receivers' fees is by the hours they have devoted to the matter, which Referee Herzog considers preposterous: "Is an attorney to be penalized because his mental agility enables him to accomplish the same results in half the time?"

The reason the Courts of Appeal are looking to the time clock is that they want some control, and they don't have it. Invitations to fraud litter the situation in terms of favors to creditors (in evaluating their claims) and to the bankrupt (in determining which assets are in the picture) and to the lawyers and receivers (in fees charged) and to the agreed-upon purchasers of the assets. "You know there's something you want to buy at a bankruptcy sale," says a lawyer who has looked in on these questions occasionally, "and when you get there you can never find it." Reorganizations are an open invitation to leaf-raking at large firms. Every temptation is made stronger by the fact that everybody in the case knows everybody else and can do favors now to get favors later. Counsel for committees appoint banks who appoint lawyers who suggest receivers who need outside counsel, and so forth.

About one bankrupt in eight has assets to reorganize or distribute; and the average recovery in distribution cases is about eight cents on the dollar. In addition to those eight cents, the bankrupt's dollar will provide about two (in the official figures) or almost two and a half cents (in Vern Countryman's figures) for the administration. It looks a high proportion to most observers, including Chief Justice Earl Warren, who makes a special, worried report every year on the costs of bankruptcy administration. And, of course, the percentages are not uniform. In the big chain-store and consumer-credit and manufacturer's case, distributions in the millions may be made to creditors, and the fees in the hundreds of thousands (which are reserved for politically prominent law firms) will represent a small proportion of the recoveries. Meanwhile, Countryman reports, "what few assets there are in most personal bankruptcy cases wind up entirely in administration costs—the creditors frequently don't even bother to show up."

In 1965 the Ford Foundation gave the Brookings Institution a grant of $314,000 to study the bankruptcy courts. It is a rather eerie experience to wander around a field of law that is about to be hit by a tidal wave which is already visible on the horizon, and to observe how resolutely people can ignore their own impending disaster. Mind you, they do have some worries. One referee, from Detroit, wrote an article in 1966 on "The Image of the Bankruptcy Court." He was pleased that the referees had recently been authorized to wear black robes: it "has contributed materially to the dignity of the court, and to improving the attitude of litigants and lawyers toward the court." But he was still concerned about one aspect of the proceedings: "Somehow or other it seems undignified for the Referee to act as a crier in opening his own court each day."

PART IV

INFRASTRUCTURE

CHAPTER 12

WHO HAS SEEN THE LAW?

BOOKS, BINDERS AND BITS

Now entertain conjecture of a time, and see a young man in Louisville, four years out of law school, hep to the rules of civil procedure, a friend of a judge's clerk—at this moment newly returned from lunch after a satisfying morning spent helping a local haberdasher collect from a customer for a suit with two pairs of pants. The young lawyer is picking his teeth and contemplating a newspaper when into his office walks his sister's husband's niece, looking like hell with a bandaged jaw and a black eye and two fingers in a cast. It seems that five nights before, her young man, who travels, was in town with the company car (which is registered in Ohio), and the two of them went across the river to Indiana for a party. Around midnight, on their way back, their car collided with an Indiana jalopy that three boys had "borrowed" from a "friend." The young man was unharmed, and the boys were only shaken up, but the young lady was thrown from the car when the door on her side sprung open. She has just got out of the hospital; she may lose her job as a ticket-seller for a movie house; and plastic surgery may be required before other young men take her to parties in Indiana. The lawyer, as her uncle's wife's brother and a licensed attorney, signs her up, gives her assurances he does not entirely feel, and wishes her Godspeed. What does he do next?

It was remarked earlier that there isn't much law to personal-injury actions, but there may be law to this one. The factual part of the case will be difficult, because the young lady will have to sue her young man's employer—there isn't much hope of getting money out of three adolescents in a swiped car—and it will be necessary to prove that the gentleman caller was at least partially responsible for the accident. But even after the factual hurdle is surmounted, no insurance company is ever going to settle unless the lawyer can prove that under applicable state law the corporate owner of the car is responsible for its employee's negligence even when he's off on a frolic of his own, and that the court where she will bring her action will let the young woman recover for her injuries even though she was a guest in the vehicle. In Indiana and Ohio, by statute, a non-paying guest may not sue a host for injuries unless he has been guilty of "gross" negligence; but in Kentucky she can. The reason she can in Kentucky is that the state's highest court ruled its "guest statute" unconstitutional, and that happened only recently. There are lawyers in Louisville who have been busy with other things, and might assume from the start that the case was hopeless because a statute barred recovery.

More often than anyone likes to admit, a lawyer will deal with legal problems of this complexity by a telephone call to another lawyer, who knows something about this area of the law and who owes him a favor. *Arguendo* in this case, however, the young lawyer wants to do the job himself. He goes looking for law.

The legal realists of the 1920s and 1930s insisted that most cases turned on questions of fact, that judges can always find rules to apply to whatever conclusions they reach on the facts, that the only intelligent attitude for the practicing attorney is one of "rule skepticism." What they were saying at bottom is that there is no such thing as law; and an argument can be made for this position if one is talking about what happens in courts. Being judges and law professors with little experience in practice, the "realists" were oriented toward courtrooms and public records. But the law lives not in courts but in law offices; and in law offices the law comes out of books. Arthur Vanderbilt, while Chief Justice of New Jersey, made a little list for students at the Michigan Law School: "the judicial decisions, constitutions and statutes, administrative rules and rulings, and the mass of secondary authorities such as digests, encyclopedias, annotated cases, volumes of citations, treatises, restatements, and law reviews. . . . The first thing about our legal system that strikes a European or Latin-American lawyer is its sheer bulk."

Most times, the lawyer looking for law will first dip into this bulk through the "annotated statutes" of his state. This set of books will vary by state from half a dozen to a hundred volumes, and at least one is published for every state. The books give not only the text of the statute as passed by the legislature but also the key phrases from opinions in which judges have considered its scope. They are not, however, so helpful as you might think, because legislatures publish their enactments year by year and somebody has to "consolidate" them or at least index them before you can be sure of what you'll find. In most states the consolidation (if any) is out of date, and the indexing is sloppy. This first search, then, is largely for negative information: a statute which a court has held to apply against the argument you would like to make for your client will certainly keep an insurance company from offering a settlement, and will probably signify a lost case (maybe on motion before a judge without even the gambling chance of a trial).

Our hypothetical accident case, moreover, lies in an area of the law where statutes can be understood only by reference to the old judge-made common law which they codify, supplement, modify or replace. Certainly the meaning of the terms used can be followed only by reference to what judges have done in the past. The lawyer doing his own work, then, must turn to sources of information about the details of the law of personal injury in general, and vehicles in particular.

Here he can get a rough view from a distance by reading in one of the sixty- to one-hundred-volume encyclopedias of the law— *American Jurisprudence* (AmJur, for short) or the elegantly named *Corpus Juris Secundum*—or he can study the American Law Institute's *Restatement of Law, Second, TORTS,* a briefer work which has, however, been vetted section by section by some of the nation's leading authorities. A large step up in thoroughness would be an "annotation" in American Law Reports (ALR), three hundred or so fifteen-hundred-page books published serially at the rate of six a year, each containing about fifty to seventy explorations which

take off from a recent decision by an appellate court (and the arguments used before that court by the lawyers in the case) and examine
the law in one of its (usually narrow) branches. The ultimate in
detail would be a "treatise," a geographically and historically exhaustive study of what has been done by courts in this sort of case.
In the matter the Louisville lawyer was trying to handle, the treatise
of choice would probably be Frumer, Benoit and Friedman on
Personal Injury, eight huge volumes divided into "150 titles," each
of them in turn divided into four sections: "(1) Choice of Law and
Remedies (2) Elements of Cause of Action and Necessary Allegations
(3) Damages (4) Defenses." In all these books except the *Restatement,* care has been taken to cite cases from *all* domestic jurisdictions.

Treatises and ALR articles can be cited in briefs, and will go
down well with many judges. (Law school professors say that Am-
Jur and *Corpus Juris* are chancier, like a footnote reference to a
Reader's Digest condensed book in a scholarly article.) But for
safety's sake in negotiation or trial—and for power in appellate
argument, if the case gets that far—a lawyer had better read for
himself the cases on which the reference books say he can rely.
These "reported cases" are almost entirely the decisions of courts
of appeal (trial courts are not required to pay any attention to
each others' rulings, but all are presumably bound by the decisions
of the appellate courts in the jurisdiction). Most state supreme
courts have appointed an "official reporter," who makes up a brief
"syllabus" of the case to print before the opinion, giving a sketch
of the facts and the decision on all challenged points, classifies the
case under legal topics for index purposes, and arranges with a
local printer to make books of collections of the cases. In some
states the judges write their own syllabi; and in Ohio it is the
syllabus rather than the opinion which presents "the law" for that
case. Until the 1940s, the official reporter for the U.S. Supreme Court
also summarized the arguments of the lawyers, to make a frame for
the opinion; now these arguments are printed only in the unofficial
"Lawyers' Edition," published by the same company that puts
out AmJur and ALR.

In most states, the reporting and printing contracts are a pleasant but not major piece of judicial patronage. The syllabus material may be copyrighted; the opinion itself is in the public domain. One of the in-group lawsuits of the early nineteenth century was fought between two reporters for the United States Supreme Court, one of whom was republishing as part of his own series the texts of the opinion handed down during his predecessor's term. The Supreme Court ruled rather reluctantly that his predecessor could not stop him.

Opinions like legislative enactments are simply set down in the order in which they appear. *Kilberg* v. *Northeast Airlines,* for example, is 9 NY2d 34, which means that the report of the case starts on page 34 of the ninth volume of the second series of books of opinions by the New York State Court of Appeals. You have to know where to look; the official index is usually restricted to the book in hand. What the working lawyer needs at most stages of the game, moreover, is not the full opinion but a "headnote" which deals more specifically than a syllabus does with the points of law involved. A good headnote will tell the lawyer quickly what rules the judges relied on to reach their decision. It thus saves the diligent lawyer the considerable labor of reading every word of every opinion that might be relevant (by steering him to those passages which are clearly in point on his case), and it gives the lazy lawyer a ready-made citation. Lawyers who are actually collecting cases, therefore, will tend to use an "unofficial report," a phrase which is misleading, because the texts are exact.

There is only one "national reporter system"—that of the West Publishing Company in St. Paul, Minnesota, which breaks the country into seven regions and publishes a stream of fat books presenting *all* appellate cases in each of the regions, in both state and federal courts, each with headnotes written by West's staff of fifty lawyers, the lot indexed by West "key numbers" into one of 400 topics and 87,000 subtopics. All cases will be cited by their appearance in the West *Reporters* as well as by their local publication: *Kilberg* is 172 NE2d 526 (page 526 of volume 172 in the second series of *Northeast Reporters*) just as much as it is 9 NY2d 34. The existence of the key-number system and the headnotes enables West to publish for many states, without any great additional labor,

a "Digest" of the laws, often running twenty or thirty fat blue volumes, which lists all relevant state appellate-court decisions, in
one-paragraph abstracts, under their appropriate topics. Statutes
being meaningful only as judges construe them in cases, the existence of this Digest would seem to solve all research problems at
a blow, but for various reasons, some of which we shall examine
presently, it doesn't. The uniformity of the topics and key numbers
across the country does, however, help lawyers who must check
both federal and state decisions, or the decisions of several states.
"We publish a book called *Rules of Evidence in Negligence Cases*,"
says Harold P. Seligson of the Practising Law Institute, "and the
case references are all New York; but it's used by lawyers all over
the United States. I once asked a lawyer from another state if we
should annotate this book for decisions in his state. He said that
personally he didn't need annotations. 'I look up the cases cited
from New York, use the Digest system, get the key number, then
look up the cases cited under that key number in my own state
and find out if there's anything that might be objected to here.'
Still," Seligson adds, "I'd like to see that done once in print, so each
lawyer doesn't have to do it for himself."

One further and essential step remains to be taken: it must be
determined that nothing has happened to upset the authority or
change the significance of the case recommended by the reference
book or discovered through the West Digest. For this purpose, the
case must be "Shepardized"—that is, all subsequent reference to
the case in the opinions of judges hearing similar cases must be
checked out in a publication called *Shepard's Citations*, column after
column of numbers and letters. Each reported case that has ever
been cited by another court (or by ALR or by one of the major
law reviews) is listed in boldface type, by volume and page, in the
order in which the decisions came down. Below that boldface reference number will be a string, short or long, of lightface numbers
for subsequent appellate opinions or articles mentioning this case.
So that he who runs may read, *Shepard's* offers a comment on how
the citation was used by a later court: cheerfully, an "a" for "affirmed," an "f" for "followed," a "D" for "appeal dismissed"; or,
worrisome, a "c" for "criticized," a "q" for "questioned," an "m"

for modified, an "h" for "harmonized"; or, fatally, an "L" for "limited," an "S" for "superseded," an "r" for "reversed," an "o" for "overruled." The format permits spectacular economy of space: six to seven hundred citations, reading down eight columns, can be printed on one page, and nearly two million citations a year are added to one or more of the sixty-six *Shepard's* services (fifty states, each West *Reporter* region, Supreme Court, statutes, codes and constitutions).

All this reading may tell the lawyer where he and his client will stand once they get to court, but it does not tell him what to do right now. For that purpose, there are books of "pleading and practice forms," covering what the courts will expect in the line of formalities in every state. A sales brochure from Lawyers Co-operative Publishing ("Lawyers Co-op": AmJur and ALR), ambitiously entitled *The Living Law,* explains that "As a busy lawyer, you can't afford the many hours of research necessary to gather the information to draft your own forms." The forms need merely be copied out of the book, with the blanks filled in and any special instructions followed (the blanks are usually numbered, with footnotes telling the lawyer what goes at each number), and the case is on its way to court. These form books, incidentally, are much better for pleading purposes than for writing contracts, because the publishers usually copy contract forms from old documents which have been through litigation and are thus part of a public record. David Mellinkoff in *The Language of the Law* gives half a dozen examples of contracts with horrendous histories—contracts, for example, which turned out to give *neither* the author nor the theatrical producer the movie rights to a play, or were held "ambiguous" or requiring oral testimony as to the intent of the parties—which are recommended as standard in current books of legal forms.

The lawyer in Louisville had better note at this point that he cannot simply sue the Ohio corporation that owns the car; he has to file additional papers in the office of the Secretary of State, to bring into play the "long-arm statute" by which Kentuckians can apply legal process to out-of-state owners of automobiles. The books will warn him of this requirement and tell him exactly how to go about satisfying it.

An ordinary lawyer in practice for himself will have in his own library some books of forms, a guide to his state's civil practice, the annotated statutes, maybe a Digest, probably a *Shepard's,* and a set of local reports. Depending on how much he has, and how much he bought used, his investment runs between $500 and $2,000. For the rest, he will probably go to a library in the local bar association or the county courthouse. Though Thomas Gosnell, president of Lawyers Co-op, can make a good case for the proposition that his ALR volumes at $15 for fifteen hundred pages are about as good a buy as modern publishing offers, the total cost of a first-rate library is enormous. A complete set of the West *Reporters* runs around $45,000. Twenty years' worth of ALR is $1,800. The Frumer treatise on P.I. lists at $235.50. And the expenses do not end with the single purchase, because these research tools are not usable unless kept up to date. "The whole law publishing field," says Will Garey of McGraw-Hill (which recently got into the field by buying *Shepard's Citations*), "is a razor-blade business." Every year produces about fifty thousand pages of new statute law from Congress and the state legislatures, about thirty thousand reported cases for West.

The usual procedure for keeping the book current is the "pocket part," a new pamphlet every three or six or twelve months, organized according to the page numbers of the book it accompanies and modifying the contents as necessary. Shepard's publishes "Supplements" with a frequency ranging from every six weeks in New York, where both the law business and Shepard's business are brisk, to once a year in Hawaii and Alaska. Most of the publications of Matthew Bender & Company, including the Frumer *Personal Injury* treatise, are bound in loose-leaf form, and any significant changes in what the courts or the legislatures are saying will produce a packet of new pages (including, necessarily, new index pages) for the subscriber to substitute in the binder.

It will be noted that eventually the pocket piece and the supplements grow to the point where convenience dictates new books incorporating this material. "They sell you the pocket parts," says Felix Stumpf, who put California's Continuing Education of the Bar project into publishing because he didn't find the existing books very helpful, "and then they sell you the same stuff again. It's the only business like that I know."

Incidentally, this gargantuan annual output of law in books is uniquely American, and not an inevitable concomitant of the Anglo-American common-law system. "The main body of case law from all the courts in England," writes Delmar Karlen, director of the Institute of Judicial Administration in New York, "grows at only three volumes a year." As against the roughly thirty thousand reported appellate decisions each year in the United States, the English *Law Reports* offer only three hundred. Karlen notes a side effect: despite their rules that they must follow their own prior decisions at all times, the "English judges enjoy a broad discretion in molding the law to fit changing circumstances—broader perhaps than that of judges in the United States, with their power to over-rule earlier decisions. In England, with less voluminous reports, there are fewer precedents to cause trouble or to restrict judicial freedom of action."

2

The entire American system depends upon the West *Reporters;* and West, privately operated and owned and mighty secretive about its revenues and profits, must be one of the dozen largest publishing companies in the United States. "When McGraw-Hill decided to go into the lawbook business," says Fred B. Rothman, formerly librarian of the NYU Law School and now proprietor of the nation's largest used and rare lawbook business, "they went looking to buy West. West laughed and offered to buy McGraw-Hill." Alfred Gans, who spent twenty-eight years with ALR, says that "if you think of Lawyers Co-op as the Ford of lawbook publishing and Matthew Bender as the Chrysler, then West is about half a dozen General Motors."

West's home when visited (rumor speaks of recent renovation) was a joined pair of very large, very decayed walk-up loft buildings beside the Mississippi River in the heart of downtown St. Paul. A false modernistic front had been put on the side of the buildings that faces the town, but it couldn't have deceived a child. Upstairs (on each landing a carefully cleaned sign read: "DO NOT SPIT: SPITTING SPREADS DISEASE"), cast-iron pillars with Y-beams for capitals supported a pressed-metal ceiling ornamented by sprinklers. Wood partitions with windows separated offices that were something less than private rooms. Noise cuts through such partitions like a knife through cream cheese, but there was rarely any noise. Much of the space was devoted (as at all law publishers) to one of the great legal libraries of the world.

Fundamentally, West is a conveyor belt. Decisions get from the courts to West in various ways. Some state supreme courts maintain "public interest lists" of groups to which printed opinions are immediately mailed out. Others make the opinions available at the clerk's office the day they are handed down, and West has stringers at the courthouses who pick them up and mail them to St. Paul. Still others will allow only the attorneys involved to see the actual opinions until the time for rehearing has passed, and in those states West's stringers must keep the calendar and get to the pickup counter on the earliest day. Led by Florida, a small but growing number of states have abandoned the publication of their own opinions and consider the West regional *Reporter* "official." A few others (the first was New Mexico) hire West to print their "official" reports for them in separate volumes, and accept the West headnotes and editorial services as part of their books. Still others, like New Jersey, keep the printing patronage at home but use the West headnotes as their own. For New York, West publishes separate, quicker "unofficial" volumes of the state's appellate opinions (New York *Supplement*) in competition with New York *Reports*. The West volumes also contain opinions from courts of original jurisdiction; the New York Judicial Conference helps West decide which trial-court opinions are worthy of inclusion in New York *Supplement*. Whether or not there is an official relationship, however, says executive vice-president Wayne Davies, "We consider ourselves an agency of the court, and we endeavor to do whatever the courts desire." West also publishes the leading set of New York annotated statutes—*McKinney's,* about a hundred black-bound books with annual "pocket parts" to keep it current; the subscription list is reputed to run fifteen thousand sets of parts a year.

At West, each opinion is read by an editor, who will correct the judge's spelling and occasionally a severe grammatical error, and will see to it that every case he cites actually appears under the name he uses in the place where he says it appears. The editor then writes his headnotes, and gives each note the key number and phrase that will appear in the *Reporter* next to a little drawing of a key and will determine where the case is slotted in the Digest. The opinion (or opinions, if there are concurring or dissenting judges) then goes downstairs to the print shop, where it is set in type. The type will be used first for "advance sheets" which are sent out to subscribers immediately, and then for pamphlet Supplements and yet again for the bound *Reporters*—the outstanding example of what Stumpf calls "selling you the same stuff again."

Law libraries and large firms subscribe to the advance sheets, but the place where they are most eagerly awaited is at *Shepard's Citations*. An off-white *moderne* glass-brick and concrete structure built in Colorado Springs just after World War II, Shepard's sits on a previously residential street atop a bluff that looks out to the magnificence of Pike's Peak. Here, too, the visitor is greeted with a sign: a forceful "NO SMOKING" on the front door. Nowhere in the world has this message been taken more seriously than it is at Shepard's where, according to universal (but perhaps erroneous) belief, the exhaust channel of the air-conditioning system piped into the office of Chairman of the Board W. G. Packard, who would come charging out to investigate if he ever smelled tobacco smoke. The front door at Shepard's opens into a modest reception area with a linoleum floor, the decor featuring a membership plaque in the National Association of Manufacturers and a trophy signifying the championship of the Men's Softball League. Though the building is fairly new, it retains some souvenirs of the company's long residence in Brooklyn—most remarkably, a set of nineteenth-century time clocks, enormous wooden structures of gears and pinions on which *everybody* punches in and out, leaving a permanent record on a huge roll of white paper.

Upstairs, a staff of twenty-five lawyers work in a bull pen, sitting on high stools at reading stands. The day begins at eight; at ten precisely everybody, led by the lawyers, clatters downstairs to the basement cafeteria for coffee; then back to the books in exactly fifteen minutes. A man with another lawbook company, who frequently visited Shepard's, describes the place as "a cross between Dickens and Dachau." McGraw-Hill, the new owners, may change all that, but it's hard to quarrel with success. Like West, Shepard's was privately owned, and released no figures; but the scuttlebutt of the business, much reinforced by the reports of the McGraw-Hill negotiations, says that the company grosses about $3.5 million a year, of which $1 million is profit.

On arrival at Shepard's the West advance sheets are distributed to the clerks of the "extracting department," who prepare a set of green, pink and yellow slips for each case and each statute cited in the opinion. One of these slips immediately goes into the control machinery to make sure that every citation noticed at this step does in fact find its way into the books. The others, different colors for different publications, go upstairs to the lawyers, who read the new opinion and then every one of the older opinions mentioned in the text. Most of the time they simply pass the slips down to the print shop in the basement, where a linotypist will set a new boldface and a new lightface number for the galley proofs being built for the next Supplement (en route to the gigantic file of galley proofs for books, which is the heart of the operation). The fact that a judge cites a case without comment means that he is to some extent relying upon it in the present opinion, and Shepard's can merely list the new case without comment. If the judge in the new case discusses the old case, however, the lawyer may wish to insert on the slug of type one of Shepard's copyrighted one-letter remarks. Some men have authority to make this decision themselves—turnover is low at Shepard's, and the average age of the lawyers a few years ago was fifty-one—but most will check their discovery with a supervisor before noting a comment on the slips.

When the West advance sheets arrive at Lawyers Co-op, a converted old brick factory on the banks of the Genesee in downtown Rochester, New York, they go directly to ALR editor-in-chief William E. Shipley, a lean lawyer with a crew cut, who with one associate reads every reported case and every law review in the United States—"but," he says, "you ought to put 'reads' in quotes. My function is to be a current awareness service for the others. I do it primarily to pick subjects for ALR, but if something seems pertinent to our other publications, the New York and Ohio encyclopedias or AmJur, I'll refer it to them. Your normal pose around here is with your feet on your desk and a Dictaphone in your hand. If a case looks like an ALR annotation, I flag it, dictate a brief note, and letters go out to the judge and the lawyers in the case, asking for their briefs and other material. Judges and lawyers regard it as a feather in their cap to have opinions selected for ALR. We summarize briefs, print the lawyers' names—they like it. Then an editor comes in—'I've finished this job, I need another'—and I give him a file. The editor begins researching, digs up authority from textbooks, encyclopedias, other cases, et cetera. The annotations run from three hundred pages to half a page, and in general an editor will get through fifteen of them in a year.

"ALR is basically a magazine. We publish it on our guess of what the reader interest is, try to balance the fifty annotations in each volume. Each editor signs his article; we don't want this to sound like *Time* Magazine, all written by One Big Lawyer."

After three hundred volumes—twenty thousand annotations— most articles are in large part updating of previous articles, but even so the research burden can be enormous. "It's a tremendous effort," said Robert D. Hursh, a casual young man in a striped shirt who has since moved on from being editor of the company's *New York Jurisprudence* series to running its California subsidiary. "We tell people we have considered every case in the light of every previous case. You have to try to dig up unreported cases. And when you're dealing with a state like New York you have to find the statutes, which is almost impossible because they haven't been published in any rational pattern." Shipley adds, "The statutes are unorganized in most states. The most you can say is that there's a good index, and sometimes there isn't even that. They rush the laws through in the last three days, and nobody knows what their import is."

Lawyers Co-op (the name is a misnomer: the business is privately owned by a few families) employs sixty-five lawyers in San Francisco, many of them working on California cases, for which the firm is official reporter; eighty to ninety in Rochester; and another twenty to twenty-five in New York and its suburb, Mt. Kisco, who put out the tax service of the company's recently purchased subsidiary, Research Institute of America. Like West, it also does a little textbook and treatise-publishing; it puts out "courtroom aids" like big drawings of healthy livers to compare with damaged livers before a jury; it publishes (with West) the largest and most difficult of the digests (*Abbot's New York*) and the most elaborately annotated book of reported decisions, the Lawyers' Edition of the U.S. Supreme Court *Reports*. To a degree, of course, all these things work together. "Any book which is well done," says President Thomas Gosnell (one of very few people at the top of a lawbook enterprise who is not himself a lawyer), "will contribute to any other book."

The West advance sheets are also important for updating treatises at Matthew Bender & Company, in New York, publishers of the Frumer *Personal Injury* books and much, much else, including the twelve volumes of *Collier on Bankruptcy,* now in its fourteenth edition, the nine volumes of *Moore's Federal Practice,* fifteen volumes each for *California Points and Authorities* and *California Forms of Pleading and Practice,* twenty-seven volumes of *Gilbert Bliss Civil Practice of New York.* "We are what's known as a specialty house," says Louis Frumer, a stout, cheerful man with white hair and a high-pitched voice, who is Bender's editor-in-chief as well as one of its authors. "And we are the only company organized by specialty groups—we do not adhere to the theory that a good editor can write on anything."

In addition to an "in-shop editorial staff" of fifty, Bender uses outside authors (among them Arthur Larson, for some years President Eisenhower's favorite exponent of Modern Republicanism, who is the author of Bender's treatise on workmen's compensation). And the purpose is subtly different. Where West will report everything without comment, and ALR will present majority and minority rules (and the rule in Pennsylvania) without expressing any preference, Bender's treatises are at least in part argumentative. "We want our author to cite all the conflicts and then take a stand," says William W. Vanneman, executive vice-president of the company (the president is still a Bender: this was another family operation until the Los Angeles *Times* bought it in 1962). "Otherwise what good is our book to the poor slob without experience who buys it?"

3

Among the differences between a practicing lawyer and an editor at a law publishing house is the fact that the editor invariably reads the actual court opinions that come to him from West, not just the headnotes; and the editor makes his own indices for dealing with the material, ignoring the West key numbers. But many more lawyers read headnotes than read cases; and there are probably more lawyers who use the West Digests than all the other services, treatises and annotations put together. One of the oddities of American law is the considerable influence over the years of this private publishing house in St. Paul. "If they do a headnote wrong," says Robert Hursh of Lawyers Co-op, "it's as though a case has been overruled. Anything they omit is not the law." Oddly, American legal historians have completely ignored the phenomenon.

West began in 1876 with a weekly magazine called *The Syllabi* to print the outlines of opinions of the Minnesota Supreme Court. These outlines, the first issue pointed out, "have heretofore appeared in the daily papers only as it happened to suit the convenience of a reporter, or when a scarcity of news made them useful in filling up space, sometimes being in one paper, and sometimes in another." The new publications would

contain the syllabus (prepared by the Judge, writing the opinion) of each decision of the Supreme Court of Minnesota, as soon after the same is filed as may be practicable, accompanied, when desirable to a proper understanding of the points decided, with an abstract of the case itself, and when the decision is one of general interest and importance, with the full opinion of the Court. . . . We shall endeavor to make the Syllabi indispensable to Minnesota Attorneys, by making it prompt, interesting, full, and at all times *thoroughly reliable.*

Advertising was sold at a price of 75 cents the column inch; and in those easygoing days most of the advertising came from law firms themselves.

The need West met had been created by the long delay, often a matter of years, between the handing down of opinions and their publication in the official state reports; and this problem was shared by lawyers outside Minnesota. As the company moved on to the publication of full opinions and of books, the syllabus system was found to be inadequate, because judges in drawing up syllabi relied so often on the facts of the specific case rather than on the points of law involved. Moreover, there had to be an index. For the convenience of the publisher, if for no other reason, the same index was used as West expanded its operations into other states. In the end, as Robert Hursh puts it, "The West key-number system became the one pervasive entry that we have in this country. The headnoting system is the only way for people to get into cases on a national basis." Even the statutes could be, and were, slotted into West key numbers. "The uniform key-number classification," says West's editor Wayne Davies, "is the contribution we have made to the uniformity of the law."

From the outside the West system looks impressive; even David Riesman, who spent some time on the inside, writes of "the superb index system the legal profession has developed for itself," contrasting it with the sloppiness of sociology. People who research law, for publishers or clients, tend to be less impressed. "If you're doing a products liability book," says Bender's Frumer rather mildly, "you'll find a lot of cases you'd never locate in the West Digest." Jack Artigues, the young lawyer in charge of the American Law Institute's books for continuing legal education, says that "some of the West headnotes read like they were written by first-year law students." Craig Spangenberg of Cleveland told a meeting recently, "I spend a lot of time in upper courts on fine points of law and I tell you most of them are points that we can never find indexed anywhere. The indexer hasn't got this detailed and specific and fine. We read maybe fifty cases hoping to find some paragraph in one opinion where some judge has decided the point, but it isn't in the headnote and it isn't in the index."

California's Felix Stumpf says, "You know the *Palsgraf* case?" (This case, one of Cardozo's most famous opinions, established a limit on how remote from the accident negligent conduct could be and still give a victim a cause of action. A guard helping a man onto a Long Island Rail Road train had dislodged a package the man was carrying, which proved to be firecrackers; the explosion knocked down some scales at the other other end of the platform, harming a lady who was standing there, and who successfully sued the railroad for the alleged negligence of its guard. Cardozo, laying down a rule of "proximate cause," reversed the judgment.) "Well, West didn't put it under 'proximate cause.' The avalanche of head notes under the present classification system makes the digests virtually useless. But West is sitting pretty because its Reporter system amounts to a national monopoly."

How inevitable the West classifications are is a matter of some dispute; Rodney Robertson, a spare Bostonian in half-glasses who heads the lawbook division of Little, Brown, says that "the West Digest is inescapable as much from habit as from necessity." But precedent itself is often little more than habit. Of all the reasons why the *Restatements of Law* of the American Law Institute have failed to move either the courts or the profession, perhaps the strongest is the mismatch between the categories employed by the professors who prepared the *Restatements* and the categories in the West Digests. There is an interesting study to be done on the question of how greatly law reform in the United States is impeded, without any conscious opposition, simply by the work of a small group of unspecialized, ill-paid and overworked editors in St. Paul.

Quality control problems dog all the legal publishers, because so much work must be turned out and it ought to be perfect—really perfect, far beyond what is required of judges. "The work," says Bender's Frumer, "is much more difficult than it may appear; it's hard work and to some extent it's monotonous." Alfred Gans, who left the post of editor-in-chief of ALR to go into private practice again, says that the best of the editors are "like the types in the big firms who are always in the libraries, doing the research for everybody else. They're the types who teach law and run the law libraries, guys who think they're not going to like practice—withdrawn, scholarly, introverted types. It's a personality question; I can show you eight men in this office whom I regard as excellent lawyers, but they'd be climbing up the walls if they had to do what I did with great pleasure for twenty-eight years." All West editors are law school graduates (no publisher admits supplementing the editors with law school students, but everybody says the others do it); not all of them are members of the bar. "They come to us," Davies says, "within a year or two of law school—certainly within five years." Once they come, they stay. Bender says that apart from first-year turnover it hasn't lost a man in five years. "Of course," Frumer says, "anybody you hire, you don't know whether he can or can't do the work you want him to do—maybe he can't write, or can't reason, or has mental problems."

At Bender and at the loose-leaf service publishers like Prentice-Hall and Commerce Clearing House the job of supervising editors' work is eased by the tendency to keep a man in the same branch of law forever. "If a boy sits up here," says the chief of one of the services, "and does nothing but one thing all day, within two years he can hold his own with the biggest expert in the country." The publishers who use a man in all fields must plan tighter supervision —all ALR annotations are done under direction, with outlines and weekly meetings in a supervisor's office. At Shepard's the objectivity of the normal citation is taken as protection: "Shepard's . . . list of cases," says the company's booklet *How to Use Shepard's Citations,* ". . . is not the result of an editor's opinion but is a listing of cases which *physically cite* the particular case or statute."

Especially in recent years, Lawyers Co-op has gone after the law review men at the best schools. "We send our people around to the law schools," Gosnell says. "Of course it serves two purposes. But it's essentially true when we tell them that they will be working at the leading edge of the law." Gosnell will also match, or nearly match, the starting salaries paid by the large law firms, but he can't match the salary progressions. About 40 percent of the ALR staff came directly from law school. Some of the other publishers offer far less money, relying on the terrifying financial insecurity of private practice. "Our editors are recruited by advertising through newspapers in the bigger cities," says Shepard's editor-in-chief Harold L. Wilcox. "You look for a college degree, some experience in practice. We can offer regular hours, eight to five, and the security of a regular salary. We have a man out there with seven children— he's glad to have a regular salary." Most observers believe that only a handful of lawbook editors anywhere make as much as $15,000 a year.

At most of the publishing houses, even those where all the writing is done by employees, the sales staff outnumbers the editors, and the selling effort is pretty violent. "You can sell up to five or six volumes by mail," says Joe Briggs, the young sales manager for Lawyers Co-op. "Above that, no. The man has to be there. We tend to hire people with sales experience, not lawyers. Lawyers love to talk about legal problems; salesmen who are lawyers tend to get into discussions of law, and they don't talk about how the books will save him money."

At best, the lawyer is hard to sell. "You have to reach him at his desk," says Robertson of Little, Brown, which publishes legal treatises (*Wigmore on Evidence, Scott on Trusts,* with pocket parts) as well as law school textbooks and a large line of bookstore books. "If it isn't a book he feels he can buy with firm money and read on firm time, you're going to have a devil of a lot of trouble selling it to him." The argument against buying is usually that the lawyer can use this material as often as he needs it in the bar association library or the county courthouse library. "I sold for a while," says Wilcox, who has been with Shepard's since 1927. "I'd tell 'em that while they were chewing the rag in the courthouse they could have been taking care of three or four clients."

Because legal publishing is a razor-blade business, the established salesmen in an area can count on repeat business for pocket parts and such as the foundation of his commission income. He tends to be stable, and to become an important figure in the legal community of the county seats and smaller cities—he tells people about deaths in another town which have left open a possible practice, he runs a personnel service, he (carefully) retails gossip. Shepard's sales manager Walter Cox, a slight, sober-appearing gentleman with a pencil mustache, says deadpan that his worst problem is "replacing men who've died, gone on to be governor, dean of the law school."

The selling appeal is often naked, vulgar greed. It is unquestionably true that a good office library will make a man a better lawyer, if only by giving him something to browse through on slow days; and it may even be true, as Shepard's salesman William Cunning-

ham says, that "the sales rep gives the lawyer a course in 'legal bib' "
—but that isn't how you sell him books. A large four-color fold-out
brochure for Lawyers Co-op's "Total Client-Service Library" is entitled *Open the Doors to a More Profitable Practice*. Bender promotes *Defense of Drunk Driving Cases* by Richard Erwin with a
statement that the book "makes it possible, easy and wise for the
family lawyer" to handle such problems, and ends with a boldface
paragraph: **"Note: With penalties what they are today, the client
NEEDS a lawyer who knows his ERWIN, and the lawyer who
knows his Erwin deserves a FEE commensurate with the work involved in freeing a client from very serious penalties."** A piece of
Prentice-Hall selling literature, printed to look like a typed legal
document, complete to blue paper folded over and stapled at the
top, offers

immediate fee-boosting help that can turn the tide in thousands of law
offices throughout the nation. . . . Here's just a sample of how your gift
Report can help you dramatically boost the income from your practice—
   1. It tells you 7 simple things you can do that produces [sic] an im-
      mediate flood of top caliber clients. . . .
The information in this Report is vital to the attorney's success. It can
make the difference between a mediocre practice—or a giant thriving
practice. It gives the attorney willing to take the initiative a clear, un-
obstructed path to the top of his profession in terms of wealth, status and
fame.

You couldn't ask for more from a book.

4

West started and thrived because other ways of publicizing legal
actions involved such long delays, and even today its publications
are least entrenched in those states where other ways of getting
complete appellate reports are quicker—especially Ohio, where the
state bar association publishes every week the texts of the state
supreme court's opinions of the week before. For the lawyer engaged
mostly in counseling businessmen about their relations with the
government, even West's minimal delays—measured in weeks for
subscribers to the advance sheets—can be dangerously long. And the
West *Reporters* deal only with court opinions, not with the rulings

of the administrative agencies whose decisions are most of the law for many corporations. (West does report the opinions of the quasi-administrative Tax Court, but the reports are prepared for the exclusive use of the Tax Court itself, and are not for sale.) Lawyers who labor with regulations more than with law find the traditional services incomplete, unsteady and slow.

To serve these lawyers and their clients, upstart periodical publishing houses (the three largest are the Commerce Clearing House of Chicago, Prentice-Hall on the New Jersey side of the Hudson River, and the Bureau of National Affairs in Washington) provide weekly or even daily newsletters, all but one (BNA's *United States Law Week*) devoted exclusively to a single restricted branch of governmental activity. These are big operations, churning out dozens of fifty-page magazines every week. CCH and Prentice-Hall each employs more lawyers than West, Lawyers Co-op and Shepard's put together. Their newsletters and "loose-leaf services" are much more likely than the conventional reports to be read by the senior men in the large law partnerships. "Without the various loose-leaf services that have developed unofficially as the result of private enterprise," Arthur Vanderbilt wrote while Chief Justice of New Jersey, ". . . no lawyer could hope to practice intelligently before the administrative agencies."

The most widely used services are those dealing with taxes and labor relations, though there are also publications for FTC-antitrust, SEC, patents, transportation, copyright, foreign trade and other fields. Some of the services relate directly to what are in effect treatises, the periodic "report bulletins" arriving in a package with sheets to be slotted in binders; one service, Pike and Fischer's *Administrative Law,* is a constantly amended rather general treatise in this category. Others are a more standard kind of Washington newsletter, with a progressive index to make them useful over a longer term. They provide summaries and some full texts of court decisions handed down that week, plus new administrative findings and regulations, discussions of the significance of it all, and opinions ('trends") on where Congress or the state legislatures, or a volatile agency, may move next. Because many of these services are bought by businessmen as well as by lawyers, the bar associations have been nervous about their impact; and somewhere they all carry a legend agreed upon by a joint committee of the publishers and the ABA: "This publication is designed to provide accurate and authoritative information in regard to the subject matter covered. It is sold with the understanding that the publisher is not engaged in rendering legal, accounting or other professional service. If legal advice or other expert assistance is required, the services of a competent professional person should be sought."

In many areas of major concern, the loose-leaf services are the fundamental documents. Generally, they are the only sources of information of any scope and depth about the world of the administrative agencies. Before the Internal Revenue Service developed its computer-based liaison service, men in its regional offices were in the habit of calling CCH to find out what their agency was doing around the country—it was easier than trying to get an information request processed through Washington. The biggest subscriber to most services is the government. "When we point out ways to handle new laws and regulations," says an editor, "the agencies are very interested. Now they know what to do." What reports of labor arbitration results exist come through the services (some are later bound into books). But the services are, and should be, journalistic rather than scholarly. BNA's *Antitrust and Trade Regulation Reports* are to the antitrust bar, as a functional matter, what the wholly nonlegal *Broadcasting* Magazine is to the FCC bar. The fact that practice before the regulatory agencies rests on these necessarily fragmented services, with their stress on practical current procedure rather than on legal continuity, has surely been among the reasons for the American failure to develop what Loevinger calls "an administrative common law."

From the reportorial point of view, probably the most remarkable of the services is *United States Law Week,* which sends out to its 4,500 subscribers (at $120 a year) the full text of all that week's Supreme Court opinions and orders (with a comment on their significance), a summary of proceedings before the Court (including the arguments of counsel and the questions of the Justices in what the editors consider the most important case of the week), and an outline of the issues raised in all new petitions for review by the Court. More remarkably, *Law Week* includes a section of "New

Court Decisions: Significant Opinions Not Yet Generally Reported," taking a look at twenty to thirty new decisions by other courts and administrative agencies all around the country, including on occasion courts of original jurisdiction whose opinions might not otherwise be reported at all, anywhere. "We have more arrangements than you can imagine," says managing editor Mark H. Woolsey. "Clerks, attorneys, newspapermen send the cases; there's an infinite variety."

These opinions, of course, arrive in raw form, without headnotes or syllabus. "I try to pick out cases that mean something. I have to go through every goddamned piece of paper; but I've been doing it since 1945, and after a while you can almost look at the first line and know if there's anything in it. This is a matter of judgment: they pay me for my judgment. The appeal we make is, the ordinary lawyer doesn't have to go through reams of material." Having selected it, Woolsey hands over the case to one of his six associate lawyer-editors, who prepares as brief as possible a digest of it, including significant quotes from the text of the opinion itself, and adds a black-letter one-sentence statement of the decision ("Maintenance and operation of coin-operated milk-vending machines in apartment buildings do not constitute unlawful commercial use in residential zone").

"I get my editors where I find them," Woolsey says. "It's a *rara avis*, the kind of guy I need. If he's got that kind of brains, he can make five times as much. They must be lawyers, and they must be able to write, which is the hardest goddamned thing. We get letters from lawyers when we go off in syntax—there's one in New Orleans who's a dedicated Fowlerite. And they must be able to read a case and decide what's in it. There's a phrase in patent law, 'The claim *reads* on something.' Means that's what the inventor says is his. I use the phrase around here, 'The case *reads* on.' "

The reports of the arguments and questions before the Supreme Court are the only record of this material (which is taped by the Court but not transcribed), and Woolsey gets it because he sends a shorthand reporter over to take notes. This section does not in every line deal with the great issues, the intricacy or the majesty of the law, because Supreme Court Justices have other interests, too. Woolsey's favorite bit of dialogue from a presentation to the Court comes from some years back, one of the earliest cases involving the then newfangled discount stores. Justice Black listened to a denunciation of the trade practices of discounting, asked some questions about how the stores operated, and then said to the government lawyer, "Can you tell me, are there any such places in Washington?"

In the larger cities the law also has its own daily newspaper, reporting what went on in the courts the day before, and maybe (or maybe not) other matters of interest. The largest of them is the twenty-four page New York *Law Journal,* edited until recently by Warren Moscow, formerly (among other assignments) chief of the New York *Times* bureau in Albany, a bulky newspaperman hiding behind a corncob pipe his vast knowledge of who does what to whom in the city's political life. "I can say that most of my friends are judges—I've been a character around this town for a number of years." This is a newspaper with an official franchise, started in 1888 by agreement between the Appellate Division and its owners, whereby the courts would compel everyone who by law had to advertise "designated" items (a foreclosure sale, the hunt for an heir; etc.) to put his ad in the New York *Law Journal*—and in return the publishers would print civil court calendars and rulings in New York, which then meant only Manhattan and the Bronx. In 1937 a separate arrangement was made with the Appellate Department covering Brooklyn, Queens, and the suburban counties, which had given too many hostages to political fortune in local community newspapers to require advertising in the *Law Journal,* but was prepared to pay the costs of setting the type on the decisions of the judges.

To this required body of decisions, orders and calendars, the paper adds two important state or federal appellate opinions on the front page (headnotes by Isidore Blum, retired New York Law School professor), the table of contents of new issues of law reviews so that lawyers working on problems can see what is new in that medium which might be useful, occasional columns of funny stories about the courtroom published under a pseudonym (revealed in early 1967 to have disguised the pen of Judge Aron Steuer), news features (including a superb background story by Moscow himself on the infighting among the bar associations about who should run the poverty program legal services), and important speeches by lawyers and judges, if any. "It's an advantage to me, not being a member of the bar," Moscow said. "It's easy for me to say 'No' to a judge."

5

Among the oldest services publishing to the profession is the "law list" or legal directory, by which lawyers let people (especially other lawyers) know they are in business. Historically, the great use of these lists was by somebody who had a client who wanted to collect from somebody else in another jurisdiction. Fifty-eight select lists for that purpose (and for insurance, probate and banking work) are still published, supported by payments from the listed lawyers, with the approval of the ABA (this is not advertising under Canon 27). But when most lawyers think of lists and directories, they think of the giant four-volume annual published by the Martindale-Hubbell Company. "We undertake," says Vice-President William Hildebrand, Jr., "to list every individual known to be a lawyer—his age, education and address. A great deal flows in, because we've been in business almost a hundred years, and because every lawyer and law student knows about Martindale-Hubbell and that it's desirable to be listed. But we have to dig, too. The admitting authorities send us lists of newly admitted lawyers, with their home addresses. We send a questionnaire, and we must get it back before we will list. There are a few lawyers who have a passion for anonymity."

Martindale-Hubbell was formed in 1930 by a merger between Martindale's *American Law Directory* and the Hubbell *Legal Directory*, the latter a selective list. Martindale had become a little queasy about the implications of a nonselective list, and the new directory presently undertook to "rate" lawyers according to their skill and general reputation. Three skill ratings are given—a, b and c—and only about a third of the profession has qualified for a rating. (Not everyone is eligible: a lawyer must be in practice at least three years before he can be considered for any rating, five years for a "b," ten years for an "a.") A "v," for "very high" general reputation, is also offered, and will be required before any skill rating is given. For lawyers in cities of less than 34,000 population,

Martindale also gives a separate rating of financial reputation, which means how fast he pays his bills. "It's really a carryover of a need that existed forty or fifty years ago," Hildebrand says. "The collection of commercial accounts used to be the main business transferred among lawyers, and you wanted to know if a lawyer would remit promptly what he collected for your client." Martindale's Nathan J. Pond adds, "Lawyers in the Middle West like those ratings—one of them said to me once, 'I like a man who's a good businessman as well as a good lawyer.' That sort of information is a lot easier to get in a small town."

Martindale subscribes to a clipping service that brings all reports of deaths, the formation of new firms, elections to public office and defalcations of lawyers, but its major reliance in information-gathering is on a field staff of thirty, which both sells books (the subscription is $75 a year) and investigates reputations. Many, especially in the big cities, are never investigated at all, and thus never rated. "We would like to have a file on every lawyer," Pond says, "but those who don't come into contact much with other lawyers we don't learn about. Those who do—trial work, negligence and the like— we do learn about." The travelers ask other lawyers and judges about reputations, but no ratings are ever given (or, God save us, lowered) without a written statement in the files from a source of the information. There are acres of strictly confidential files in the company's long, neo-colonial brick headquarters in Summit, New Jersey, and the biggest chore of the 175 to 200 employees is keeping the files current. Martindale, incidentally, is a good place to get a positive view of the profession—many of the "a" ratings, Hildebrand says, "start when a lawyer writes: 'I was just in a case with Mr. So-and-So. I notice he doesn't have a rating (or he doesn't have the highest rating). I formed the highest opinion of him. . . .' "

Lawyers with an "av" or "bv" rating are permitted to buy a "professional card" for their firm, an advertisement in a separate section, in which they may present a *curriculum vitae,* including the clients they represent. They may not list themselves as "specialists" in any area of the law, but the Canon of Ethics does permit them to list "branches of the profession practiced." Oddly enough, this statement can ethically be no more than wishful thinking: there is no requirement, writes the profession's leading authority on professional ethics, "that the lawyer listing it make a specialty of it in his practice."

The fourth volume of Martindale-Hubbell, much used, is a concise digest of the law in each of the states. "A good index," Pond says. "It makes a complete legal service. A client comes into your office, his uncle has died in Nebraska and he thinks he's going to be rich. You look up the lawyers in Nebraska and the law, and you give him some advice, and you get in touch with a lawyer in Nebraska." Hildebrand adds, "It gives you a *writing* knowledge. In some states a trustee is called a 'conservator.' You can correspond intelligently with other lawyers." This digest section is updated annually, without charge, by an outstanding law firm in the state; in New York, to give some notion of the quality sought, the updater is the large Wall Street firm of Simpson, Thacher & Bartlett. "Lawyers don't like to admit they use it for the law of their own state," Pond says. "But they do."

6

A specter is haunting this little world of legal publishing: the specter of computers. At bottom, all the reports, the annotations, the treatises and even the loose-leaf services are information-storage-and-retrieval systems. And if the subscriber to West relies on the headnotes and the digest (which he does), all the systems are devices where, in the words of William Eldridge of the American Bar Foundation, "there are one or more human buffers between the stored information and the man who seeks it." In theory, computer-based legal research could be quicker, more precise, more extensive and cheaper than "hand research." Moreover, to the extent that the law firms' clients have shifted to electronic data processing, like to buy services from up-to-date concerns and share the normal American faith in miracle drugs, lawyers are under a degree of competitive pressure to get with it. There is already a quarterly journal devoted to the subject: *M. U. L. L.*, which stands for "Modern Uses of Logic in Law," and was founded by Layman A. Allen, inventor of the game Wff'n'proof and then a professor at the Yale

Law School (of all unlikely places; he has now gone to Michigan).

Computerized legal research started at the University of Pittsburgh in 1960, when the Health Law Center found that it couldn't function because it couldn't locate the laws relating to health in the Pennsylvania statute books. The solution, devised by director John F. Horty, was to put the entire body of Pennsylvania statute law on a machine. This job is expensive, because no computer can read a book printed, like this one, in "proportional spacing." So every section had to be put on tape or punch cards before it could be stored by the computer. Half a million dollars from the Ford Foundation was necessary to get the project started. Thereafter, however, program design was no problem. Simply by numbering the statutes as documents, sections, sentences and words—in the order in which they were printed in the book—a system could be established whereby the computer would feed out, appropriately tagged, every sentence (or section or document) in which a given word appeared.

The seventy-five volumes of the Pennsylvania statutes reduced to four rolls of tape each 2,400 feet long (you can buy reels that long for a tape recorder). As of 1965, the Pennsylvania statutes contained 6,230,529 words. Of these, 2,815,340 fell into a list of 112 "common" words (articles, conjunctions, prepositions—"a," "and," "with") which the researcher does not need. The other 23,979 uncommon words are potentially valuable sources of law.

For retrieval purposes, Horty designed a "Key Word in Combination" approach. "In a computer search," he wrote, "the entire body of statutes would be scanned. Based on his knowledge and experience the searcher would list in advance the words and phrases which, if found in a section, would cause him to read it more carefully." Horty's example is a search for laws relating to illegitimate children, where the researcher would want all sections in which the words "baby," "child," "foundling," "orphan," "infant," "juvenile," "minor" and the like were associated with words like "father" or "mother" or "parent" or "unwed" or "unmarried" or "natural" or with words like "bastard," "parentage," "putative," "illegitimate," etc., or with phrases in which "wedlock" is associated with "born." Properly informed of what the researcher wants, the computer would feed out the complete body of law, regardless of the day it was passed or the section number it was given, relating to illegitimate children.

Among the uses of this sort of service is a report to legislators considering what to do to amend existing law. (The most obvious and trivial example is a desire to change the name of a bureau: the computer almost instantly locates every sentence where the name appears. Now, consider the grammarian's attitude that every noun is a name. . . .) Senator Earl Brydges of the New York State Senate, confronted with a need to recast the state's totally incomprehensible education statutes, came to Horty with his problem, and New York State commissioned from Pittsburgh a word-index program of its own (this one a little more sophisticated, put together with help from IBM). New Jersey, New York, Massachusetts, Texas and the U.S. Code are already on Pittsburgh's tapes, as is, in a separate project, the enormous bulk of the Comptroller General's decisions relating to purchasing by the Air Force.

Next in line for major use of the computer was the Internal Revenue Service, which not only had to work with an anarchic and internally contradictory code, but had to apply it the same way across a big country in investigating the propriety of literally millions of tax returns. Significantly, in terms of the development and future of the law, the great need here was not to determine the words of the law or the interpretations of the courts, but simply the agency's own position. Work toward computerized stability was speeded by an internal power struggle between the Deputy Commissioner's Office (which had jurisdiction over the government's giant computer center at Martinsville, West Virginia, and thought it would be a good idea to combine legal advice with the growing Automated Data Processing accounting service) and the Chief Counsel's Office, which was afraid of losing its influence within the Service if the Deputy Commissioner became the proprietor of the key legal tool. The Chief Counsel's Office won the race; "The man who was in charge of this job for the Deputy Commissioner," says a close observer of the Service, "is now in *Brazil*."

Again, the first necessity was the development of an index, and this job was done by hand by the lawyers. The result was called a

"Uniform Issue List," which was broken down further into a "Key word in Context" (KWIC) list, and was keyed into the code, the reported cases, *and the lawyers' index words for the cases on which they were currently working.* David T. Link, who was first editor of the List and chief of the Information Retrieval Branch in the Chief Counsel's Office, detailed some of the subsequent problems to a meeting of lawyers:

We now had an inventory of all of our cases and a great deal of information about those cases on a print-out. This computer print-out was about 2000 pages long each month. It stood about six inches thick. We had what the people in the information sciences call a "so-what system." Prior to the installation of this system, all a man knew was that he had a case, he had a problem and he was happy with his problem. Now we had generated a tremendous 2000-page index for him so he could find that ten other people in the country had the same problem. He could find out who these people were and who their taxpayer was, the status of their case, the general position in the case, when they started to work it and how far they had progressed, but beyond that, all he could really say was "so what?" "What do I do about these cases? How do I know that they are inconsistent with me, or, heaven forbid, I inconsistent with them?" So we had to back up this big index with something else.

We began again at the source by asking our attorneys to abstract their cases—simply take a regular eight-by-ten sheet of paper and type something about their case; a little bit more about the issues than they could put down on the indexing form, a little bit more about the facts than they could put on the indexing form and, most important of all, put down on that report, that eight-by-ten sheet of paper, the position of the Commissioner and the position of the taxpayer in the case. It was these latter items that we wanted to coordinate from a pending standpoint; it was these latter items that we eventually wanted to pick up when we were researching.

Now we had a very interesting system indeed. We had a 2000-page computer print-out backed up by thousands and thousands and thousands of sheets of paper. This was becoming an acute problem in itself because it was filling up our office. And the next question obviously was, how do we get this all out of the office, out of the Reports and Information Retrieval Office? . . . The obvious answer was microfilm."

Thanks to the invention of a new automatic microfilm camera and projector, an attorney for the Internal Revenue Service can now in a few minutes at a machine locate and analyze every case like his within the system, to coordinate the government's position on tax issues—and can also generate the complete historical sequence of cases on the point of law. Private tax lawyers, who do not have access to this machinery, are more than a little gloomy about the prospect; and publishers are deeply concerned. To the extent that the indices used by the publishers of tax services do not match the Uniform Issue List, they are likely to become useless. Prentice-Hall (with the help of a computer) has already matched its index against Link's, and found for practical purposes a 90 percent correspondence. Unless the courts forcibly intervene, which they are not likely to do, Link's RIRA system will compel the publishers to achieve 100 percent correspondence and the taxpayers' lawyers to look again at all sorts of problems. Eventually, the publishers of the tax looseleaf services will unquestionably have to offer computer-based research themselves if they are to keep their trade. Publishing in the tax field was never a business for ostriches, however, and it seems likely that the proprietors of the services will be ready to move when they have to move.

The tax situation is unique, because the Internal Revenue Service has the resources and the moxie to force its index system on all the parties, including the outgunned courts. In private litigation— and in litigation with government agencies less luxuriously equipped than Internal Revenue—the prospects for computerized information retrieval are by no means so clear. The Pittsburgh system is much more useful to a state legislator or a scholar than it is to a working lawyer, because only people who know the machinery can coax it to work.

Moreover, Pittsburgh's KWIC system, though a lot of cases have been put into the computer, is designed fundamentally to deal with statutes. "Statutory English is not English," says Stephen Furth of IBM. "It's a standardized language. Judges write literature, they pride themselves on their writing. They will sentence people to death without mentioning the crime." Computerized retrieval of court cases, like human retrieval, can be no better than the index employed, and unless the index for the computer service is better than the West Digest, there isn't really much point in the operation. The cases still have to be read by the lawyers, anyway; the gain in efficiency is slight. Will Garey, explaining why McGraw-Hill bought Shepard's at a time of impending automation, says, "I'm a great believer in computerization and retrieval, but I can't see how you make it much more convenient than Shepard's."

Still, commercially minded people are already trying to sell computerized services to lawyers. Data Retrieval Corporation of America is offering a computerized citator keyed to the Wisconsin Supreme Court Reports and assorted U.S. court reports; more states are being added. In Cleveland the computer has been used for a new kind of service to lawyers—Jury Verdict Research, Inc., which gathers unreported cases from the negligence field and feeds out to subscribers (mostly insurance companies) how the awards are running for various kinds of cases in various jurisdictions. By far the most ambitious effort to date, however, is Law Research Service, Inc., which works out of offices in the decayed grandeur of the Western Union building near the Holland Tunnel in downtown New York, and is "on line" for Western Union's very powerful Univac 491 computer, which means that a subcriber can dial the computer and get case references in answer to his problem in about three minutes.

The service was started by a New York lawyer named Ellias Hoppenfeld in early 1964, and it rests on an index Hoppenfeld calls a "thesaurus." There is a separate thesaurus, a loose-leaf binder with a couple of hundred printed pages, for each of seventeen fields of federal law and eight fields of state law. Each book is supposed to cost $75, but in fact all sales to this writing have been made at the introductory price of $50. The thesaurus is a word list, with a ten-digit number opposite each word. The subscriber finds up to four words that best describe his problem and sends in the four ten-digit numbers on a Western Union Telex (direct from his office if he has such a gadget there). The Univac feeds back to him citations of the ten most recent cases in his jurisdiction involving all four of his key words. If there are more than ten cases on the memory drum, the computer provides yet another ten-digit number (not in the thesaurus), and will respond to that number with another ten references. The charge for each batch of ten cases is $12—$10 for the service, $2 for the Telex. If the lawyer wants the texts of the cases themselves, the computer will print them out at a price of four for $5, and put them in the mail for overnight delivery. Lawyers

who haven't bought a thesaurus can submit a "Special Evaluation
Query" in their own words, and receive ten citations for $20.

Obviously, the quality of the system is a function of the quality of
the thesaurus. Sales manager H. A. Maimon says the thesauri have
been compiled by a staff of fifty experienced, full-time researchers,
and that "the programming for each field costs forty to fifty thousand dollars." Inevitably, the thesauri seem something less than brilliant to the other workers in computerization, and also to some of
the lawyers who have tried the service—though it is possible that
their troubles have derived from their own failure to pick the right
words. Maimon says that the computer itself is now generating the
new thesauri, and that what will appear in subsequent editions will
be computer print-out.

The possibility of generating a really first-rate index through the
computer itself is what intrigues most of the scholars who have
examined the situation, and late in 1966 the American Bar Foundation and IBM wrote a rather sad *finis* to a brilliant five-year study
which had sought unsuccessfully to prove one way or the other the
feasibility of fully computerized law research. The project involved
putting on the computer five thousand cases from West's *Northeast
Reporter*. The first step in the program, designed by Mrs. Sally
Dennis of IBM, was to eliminate all words of no significance, which
were defined as words that appeared much more often than other
words and were randomly distributed across the sample. (If random
distribution had not been a criterion, words like "negligence"
might have been eliminated, too.) Then a table of associations was
developed, through a very tricky program nobody but Mrs. Dennis
can explain, to expand the reference of each word to a cadre of
related words, making sure, for example, that a call for "negligence"
would also produce "negligent," etc.

William Eldridge of ABF then "collected from lawyers and from
appellate briefs filed in the Illinois Supreme Court a list of forty
real-life questions." These questions, as written, without any human
intervention or consultation of a thesaurus, were fed into a computer, which was instructed to analyze the words and phrases of
the question, eliminate the insignificant, associate and expand the
significant, and cite at least twenty-five relevant cases from the five
thousand in its guts. The Bar Foundation then assembled a panel

of lawyers—a senior man with about forty years' experience, a younger man with about twelve years' experience, a law professor and a professional legal researcher. They were given the forty questions and thirty citations for each, without any hint as to which cases had been found by the computer and which by hand research. Each member of the panel was then asked to rate each citation as

- "A," meaning that the case was directly in point and disposed of the issue;
- "B," meaning that the case was relevant but not crucial: the reported decision did not actually turn on the point at issue;
- "C," meaning that the case was related, in the same subject area, but not on the issue;
- "D," meaning that the case was irrelevant, not even in the subject area.

"The panels disagreed among themselves radically," Eldridge reports. "There was more agreement on what was irrelevant, because we had forced the computer to come up with twenty-five cases, which is too many. But there were a number of cases where the four panelists gave all four answers, and a good proportion [apparently between a fifth and a quarter] where they ranged over three of the four answers. There were very few agreements on the top ratings." The only correlations discovered in a year's search of the ratings data were by the experience of the panelist: the older lawyers were more likely to give A's; the younger ones, B's; the professors, C's; and the researchers, D's. In other words, the less likely you were to do research as part of your practical daily labors, the more likely you were to like the computer's cases.

Eldridge was less discouraged than IBM by these findings. "They're scientists," he says. "The scientist attempts to reconcile things, while the lawyer is often attempting to throw a monkey wrench in the works. The scientist who finds four cases agreeing with his point of view and a fifth that doesn't has to do something to eliminate the fifth. For a lawyer, if it's the fifth case that presents his point of view, he may think that's the only relevant case."

IBM's Furth has a simpler explanation: "The lawyers cannot agree on the relevance of the cases because . . . they . . . are . . . *human*."

CHAPTER 13

THE BUSINESS OF
THE COURTS

"A city which has no regular courts of law ceases to be a city."
—PLATO

"Impressed with a conviction that the true administration of justice is the firmest pillar of good government, I have considered the first arrangement of the judicial department as essential to the happiness of our country and the stability of its political system."
—GEORGE WASHINGTON

"[T]ake a short look backward and perceive the effect to date, on both the public and the profession, of the procedural rigmarole and the slow and cumbersome trial process. . . . Until the late 1920s the courts were principally occupied with commercial litigation. Trial lawyers enjoyed a rounded practice with a variety of commercial matters. Today commercial litigation has all but left the courts. . . . [D]isappointed and disgusted, businessmen engaged in self help and created their own tribunals and procedures for handling commercial cases. Now sixty trade associations in this country maintain arbitration tribunals which handle most of the commercial cases, without the benefit of law and largely without the benefit of lawyers. . . .

"[S]uitors seek simplicity and economy of procedure, expertise in

the consideration and expedition in the disposition of cases. . . .
Let us make no mistake about it, the same practices which have
driven commercial litigation from the courts operate adversely on
the litigation which remains and threaten similarly to drive it from
the courts and the profession."

> —DAVID PECK, then presiding judge,
> First Appellate Department,
> New York Supreme Court; now
> of the New York Bar

1

The thing about the courts is that they make decisions.

President Harry S. Truman kept on his desk a sign that read,
"The buck stops here." Still, as his successor demonstrated, the buck
can just lie there after it stops; both the executive and the legislative
branches are fully empowered to be as dilatory as they please in the
face of any problems that arise. Nor is inaction necessarily the
wrong course; in the wise-advice sweepstakes, "This too shall pass"
has always had many intelligent backers. But the option is not available to the judge. In California, by state constitution, a judge may
not draw his salary if he has not yet decided every case that he
heard more than ninety days before. In 1943 an appellate court in
Pennsylvania issued an order to one of its trial judges to clean up
an accumulation of twenty-six cases which had waited from sixteen
weeks to sixteen months for decision, and brushed aside his excuse
of "illness" with the savage comment that the nature of that illness
was "a matter of such general notoriety as to make every reasonably
well-informed person within Westmoreland County and all of the
members of this court well acquainted with it." In France a judge
who unduly delays his decision is held guilty of a crime. Society
places upon the judge one prime responsibility: he must decide.
The only correct temperament is that of Louis D. Brandeis, who
when asked how sure someone has to be before he acts, replied
quickly, "Fifty-one percent."

His power to decide extends only to the cases which are brought
to him; he cannot by his own volition intervene in any dispute.

Alone among the agencies of government, the courts are not self-starting; they are passive agencies until their help is sought by one of the parties to a dispute. And it must be a real dispute, too; nobody can demand judicial decision on a point of law unless he has "standing to sue," which means he has something real to gain by winning. Once the courts are correctly summoned, however, they are the genie from the bottle, and they know no master. They may exert compulsory process to call to their presence anyone whom one of the parties says is necessary to the proceedings; and from their decisions execution issues, backed by the full police power of the state.

We forget how extraordinary these powers are, and how arbitrary. At the beginning, access to the king's courts could be got only through the purchase of a writ from the king, and the writ was addressed not to the defendant in the action but to the sheriff: *"Rex vicecomiti salutem"* ("The king to the sheriff, greetings"). Only those "forms of action" which had been accepted as a reason for a writ would start the judicial machinery in motion. The writ conferred "jurisdiction."

Even so, compulsory process was not really perfected. Different writs allowed different "essoins," excuses for nonappearance at the king's court. Maitland wrote, "The medieval law of essoins is vast in bulk . . . in some forms, the oldest and solemnest, a party may betake himself to bed and remain there for a year and day and meanwhile the action is suspended." When the excuses were used up, however, it was come to court or hide: "The man who did not submit himself to law," Maitland's partner Pollock wrote, "could not claim the benefit of the law; there was no reason why every man's hand should not be against him." We get a word from this principle: the outlaw.

We also get an institution: the summons. Once the defendant could no longer legally delay submission to the jurisdiction, the sheriff was empowered to arrest him: "Someone has said," NYU's Milton D. Green writes, "that in those days if you wished to find out if the court had jurisdiction over the person of the defendant, you looked in the dungeon—if the defendant was there, the court had jurisdiction." But it wasn't really necessary to lock up the defendant in a civil suit; making him accept a piece of paper would do as well. "[T]he physical-power theory [of jurisdiction] was satisfied because the sheriff could have arrested him at the time of the service of the summons."

The notion of jurisdiction is the heart of any court system. If the court has jurisdiction, its order must be obeyed, regardless of whether the order in fact conforms to law. As federal appellate Judge Paul R. Hays puts it, a court "has jurisdiction to be wrong, whatever meaning we may ascribe to the phrase 'to be wrong.' Whether we mean wrong in your opinion or mine or the Supreme Court's or God's, we cannot use the concept of jurisdiction, as it is generally accepted in our system of procedure, in a sense in which it is possible for a court to lack jurisdiction to be wrong."

Power attaches to jurisdiction; and the fact is important. The jurisdiction of local courts in the South empowers them to deal with trespassers and disturbers of the peace; therefore a demonstrator must obey an injunction, whether or not an appellate court can be counted on to dismiss it later. The only remedy is an order from a higher court which in effect enjoins the lower court from exercising its jurisdiction in certain kinds of cases. Similarly, when the Secretary of Agriculture set maximum charges that a stockyard could impose on cattlemen, a company that charged more was subject to the penalties of law even though the Supreme Court later ruled that the Secretary had behaved unreasonably (his office held no hearings on the matter). "But . . . the first administrative order was not a nullity," Justice Stone wrote. "Though voidable, it could not be ignored without incurring the penalties for disobedience inflicted by the applicable provisions of the statute." You ignore at your peril an order however pigheaded or dishonest, from a court or administrative agency of competent jurisdiction.

If the court does not have jurisdiction, however, its action is a nullity, and need not be obeyed. The Permanent Representative of Chile to the United Nations was involved in an automobile accident and was sued for negligence in the normal way in a New York State court; the Appellate Division ruled that there was no reason for him even to answer the complaint: under the Constitution, no state court can have jurisdiction over an accredited diplomat. The difference is between a decision which is wrong and therefore *voidable* and a decision which the court had no power to make in the first place and is therefore *void*.

Ultimately, popular control over the courts is assured by the fact that only a constitution or a statute—a legislative action—can confer jurisdiction on a court. When the federal district courts interfered with state taxation of corporations by declaring the state statutes unconstitutional, Congress took away from the district judges as individuals jurisdiction over questions of the constitutionality of state law; when the same courts made the Wagner Act on labor relations unenforceable by declaring it unconstitutional district by district all over the country, Congress took away from the judges as individuals their former jurisdiction over cases claiming the unconstitutionality of federal statutes. The Norris-LaGuardia Act killed labor injunctions by withdrawing the equity jurisdiction of the federal courts in dealing with labor disputes. The Portal-to-Portal Act of 1947 withdrew the jurisdiction of the federal courts to hear cases (even to continue hearing pending cases) that sought payment for back wages due under the Supreme Court's unexpectedly generous definition of the "work week" as the time a worker spent on company property, including time spent in transit to or from the job.

The first Amendment to the Constitution after the Bill of Rights was passed to deprive the Supreme Court of jurisdiction over cases in which a citizen of one state sued another state. And in one of the most dramatic gestures in American history, Congress by statute, after the case had already been argued, deprived the Supreme Court of jurisdiction over an appeal in a petition for a writ of habeas corpus.

Chief Justice Chase noted that the Constitution gave the Supreme Court "appellate Jurisdiction . . . with such Exceptions, and under such Regulations as the Congress shall make." The case was an ugly one: a newspaper editor in the South being held by the military for the publication of anti-Union articles shortly after the Civil War. "We are not at liberty to inquire into the motives of the legislature," the Chief Justice wrote. "We can only examine into its power under the Constitution; and the power to make exceptions

to the appellate jurisdiction of this court is given by express words.
. . . [T]his court cannot proceed to pronounce judgment in this
case, for it has no longer jurisdiction of the appeal."

The power of the legislature to establish courts and give them
jurisdiction over different kinds of cases has been an invitation to
tinkering. The federal system remains relatively simple. The country
is divided into ninety-two judicial districts (none crossing a state
line), for which Congress has authorized, as of 1967, 337 judges;
and they have jurisdiction over virtually everything that can be
brought into a federal court at all. Appeal can he had from nearly
all the judgments of these courts to one of eleven Circuit Courts of
Appeal in different parts of the country; and further appeal is possible, though unlikely, to the Supreme Court. But even the federal
system has acquired specialized courts (some of them *sharing* jurisdiction with the district courts rather than supplanting them).
There is a Court of Claims, a Customs Court, a Court of Customs
and Patent Appeals, a Tax Court and a Court of Military Appeals;
and during World War II an Emergency Court of Appeals was
established by the Congress with exclusive jurisdiction over all cases
arising under the price-control regulations required by war conditions.

State systems are much more complicated. The foundation is the
"trial court of general jurisdiction," of which there seem to be
about fifteen hundred in the country, served by about three thousand judges (different courtrooms in the same jurisdiction, all
exercising the same powers over the same geographical area, are considered one "court"). Every state has a supreme court of its own
(sometimes called by another name), which is the ultimate source
of interpretation of state constitutions and laws; some matters, raising "a substantial federal question" can be further appealed to the
U.S. Supreme Court. But all states also have trial courts of limited
jurisdiction, ranging from traffic courts and justice of the peace
courts and municipal courts and county courts (where the jurisdiction is limited by the severity of the offense charged or the size of
the monetary judgment sought) to criminal courts, probate courts,
family courts, juvenile courts, courts of claim and the like (where
the jurisdiction is limited by the nature of the issue). "In some

states," the Institute of Judicial Administration reports, "it is not unusual for jurisdiction to be so fragmented amongst the different courts that a litigant may have to go to more than one court to obtain a final decision on all aspects of what he considers a single case." In New York, even under the much-studied simplified organization fought through by constitutional amendment in 1961, there are seventeen different kinds of courts—all but three of them trial courts of more or less specified jurisdiction. A study of the Detroit courts found "one court for the corned beef, one for the cabbage."

If a legislature can control a court's jurisdiction it can also, obviously, write the court's "rules of procedure." The first legislature to proceed systematically along this line was New York's, which adopted David Dudley Field's pioneering code in 1848. As new problems arose, the legislatures tended to add new pieces of procedure (for example, requiring that a stockholder show personal interest of $50,000, or post a bond for the costs of the defense, before bringing a "derivative" action—or strike suit—against the officers of a corporation for abusing their position). In the end, there were books and books of procedural rules that had to be followed before a court could handle precisely the case the lawyer wished to bring. Lawyers don't know all the rules, and neither do judges; if it weren't for the publishers and their books of forms, and the utilitarian clerks in the judges' offices, the entire apparatus would crumble.

Popular influence has intruded itself most strongly, of course, in the selection of judges and in the allocation of so much of the court's decision-making power to the jury. Nowhere else in the world does a court system rely so greatly on juries. Kalven and Zeisel have estimated that the United States "accounts for not less than 80 percent of all criminal jury trials in the world today"; since the virtual abandonment of the civil jury in Great Britain, the United States must account for well over 90 percent of the world's civil jury trials. Article III of the Constitution guarantees trial by jury on all criminal charges, and the words are spoken again in the Sixth Amendment; the Seventh Amendment "preserves" the right to a jury in federal courts "in suits at common law, where the value in controversy shall exceed twenty dollars." None of this applies to the state courts—in New York, for example, defendants charged with "misdemeanors" that may carry penalties as high as a year in jail are offered only a choice between a one-judge court and a three-judge court.

But it is the states themselves that have most greatly exalted the role of the jury and in many places most severely diminished the authority of the judges over actual trials. In two states, Maryland and Indiana, the state constitution provides that the jury in a criminal case is to be the authority on the law as well as on the facts. In twenty states a judge is not permitted even to summarize the evidence for the jury in his own words; and Kalven and Zeisel in their survey found nine other states where the judges in their sample did not summarize, though the rules permitted them to do so. In only eleven states are judges permitted to comment in any way on the weight of the evidence or the credibility of the witnesses. Harry W. Jones of Columbia points out that "the English idiom speaks of a criminal case as tried *by* the judge, while we speak of it as tried *before* the judge."

Indeed, in some states the limitations on the judge's role are even more severe. Though the judge always "charges" the jury on the points of law they are to consider, in some states he is permitted to charge only those points of law submitted to him by the lawyers in the case, and he must use their words. In many jurisdictions he delivers his charge before the lawyers sum up their cases—"though," Arthur Vanderbilt complained, "how the jury could remember the charge after a barrage and counterbarrage of oratory from counsel is difficult to perceive." Often he is expected, if not required, to step down from the bench and stand in the well of the courtroom while delivering the charge, to emphasize that the jury is not to consider his views as any more important than those of the lawyers. The general attitude is perhaps best revealed by a comment from an old-timer in Iowa, who complained bitterly, like a Low Church Episcopalian confronted with a new minister who insists on swinging a censer, that in his state the judges are now beginning to wear robes.

In recent years the trend has been to let the judges make more of the rules for the operation of their own courts. In New York monstrous effort was needed to persuade the legislature to reduce to today's mere six hundred sections the two thousand sections of the pre-1962 Rules of Civil Practice. But now the newly established Judicial Conference may make at least some rules that will go into effect unless the legislature vetoes them. Much of the change was brought about by the triumphant reorganization of federal procedure under the leadership of the Supreme Court after the Congress in 1934, in an extraordinary gesture of respect for Chief Justice Charles Evans Hughes, gave the Supreme Court full authority (subject to Congressional veto never exercised) over the internal workings of the federal courts. The Federal Rules of Civil Procedure, first promulgated in 1938, are a document of pamphlet size. About half the states (not, however, including the most heavily populated and most litigious, where lawyers still have to learn two different sets of court procedures) have copied the Federal Rules, and three dozen states have given the judges an almost free hand in running their own show—complete to budget.

Full authority for the judges is not inevitably a step forward. There are notorious difficulties in the English system of encouraging judges to comment on the evidence: Baron Martin is reputed once to have charged a jury, "The defendant stole the boots. Consider your verdict." Judges, Vanderbilt pointed out, have not historically led "the movement for judicial reform. . . . A weak judge is always afraid of where he personally will end up if changes come; when the reformers speak of scraping off the barnacles on the ship of justice, the weak judge is all too often inclined to think they may be speaking of him. . . . The strong judge . . . often enjoys advantages in the status quo that might be disturbed in any orderly remolding of the judicial system."

As the California Judicial Council admitted in 1961, in part of its biennial request for greater rule-making power, the original practice codes legislated in the nineteenth century "were a great improvement over the common law system," which had made the game of procedure more difficult and time-consuming than the game of substance (viz., Dickens). And to the extent that rules of procedure partake of an administrative quality, the judges are hardly likely to do the job well without help; with a few signal exceptions, they are most inept class of administrators in the country, making the managers of the poverty program look like AT & T.

Speaking to the 1966 meeting of the American Law Institute, Chief Justice Warren remembered that when he assumed office in 1963 he found that all the docket entries on the Supreme Court calendar were still made in longhand, and it took him four years to get the clerk a typewriter. His survey of the federal trial courts uncovered one in "a large metropolitan area" that "was having obvious administrative difficulties." The surveyors noted that one of the deputy clerks made frequent trips out of the room, and that those trips seemed to be in response to a knocking on the wall behind him. Further investigation revealed that the room behind was that of the probation department, and that the knocks were summoning the deputy clerk to the telephone in the probation office. The chief clerk had refused to have a telephone in his offices, as a matter of principle; and knowledgeable lawyers had learned that they could reach the clerk's office by calling the probation office. This was in 1958, a quarter of a century after the federal judges had gained complete control over their own administration, and almost complete control over their budgeting.

In New York in 1953, a state commission observed that "No standard descriptions exist for job titles and there is no general compensation plan" in the courts of that state. Two years later, a committee of the Association of the Bar of the City of New York noted that the costs of operating the New York City courts were greater than those of the entire federal system, and complained that "after much research and investigation it is still impossible to state with any degree of accuracy the size of the clerical and administrative staffs of the New York courts." Among the findings of the committee, published under the title *Bad Housekeeping*, was that court clerks and stenographers in the five counties of the city were paid according to five different salary scales. The Survey of Metropolitan Courts sent out questionnaires about costs of operations, and "A typical answer came from Newark, New Jersey, a state which has achieved maximum court integration and modernization: 'Can't answer; separate payrolls for state, county and municipality.'" Michigan, where the supreme court controls the rules of procedure beyond any power of the legislature to amend, developed one of the nation's messiest court systems.

The management of court systems is an imposingly difficult job, in theory as well as in practice, because everyone wishes to maintain the independence of judges and any judge under tight administrative control is in a position to be punished. Yet something must be done about the inefficiency, if only because it corrupts. In most states the courts are the largest single source of jobs outside the civil service system, and in many states they command great political patronage through their powers of appointment of counsel or executors in cases involving minors, disputed wills, lunatics, bankrupts and the like. Moreover, there is great danger to the rational development of the American political system as a whole in the fact that a visit to so many state courthouses leaves an overwhelming sense of disorder, wasted time and limited talents, especially among the lawyers.

Federal Appeals Judge John J. Parker said in 1941:

If [the lawyer] imagines that the present functioning of the courts is satisfactory to the people, he is simply deluding himself. Workmen's compensation commissions were established very largely because the courts were not handling efficiently the claims arising out of industrial accidents and it was felt that they would not administer the compensation acts as efficiently as administrative bodies. Business corporations are willing, as all of us know, to suffer almost any sort of injustice rather than face the expense, the delay and the uncertainties of litigation. Arbitration agreements are inserted in contracts with ever-increasing frequency; and every such agreement is an implied affirmation of the belief that lay agencies for attaining justice are more efficient than the courts.

Citing this statement in 1955, the Association of the Bar of the City of New York commented, "[T]he situation has grown far worse since then."

The courts are busier than ever, but except perhaps for the Supreme Court, which functions in large part as a third branch of the national legislature, they are visibly moving out of the mainstream of national decision-making. They have declined in part because their extraordinary powers are ill-suited to resolving many of the conflicts in a modern society. In even larger part the harm is self-inflicted, a result of what Vanderbilt once called "the quaint professional notion that the courts exist primarily for the benefit of judges and lawyers and only incidentally for the benefit of the litigants and the state." Even the loyal, ABA-sponsored Survey of Metropolitan Courts found occasion to comment that "the tacit premise that the court system exists for the convenience of the lawyer" is "a luxury we cannot afford." Solicitude for the outside world, when it comes at all, is in the form of worries about the litigants; the idea that some public policy is expressed by the court system, and that some public interest is involved in its behavior, is still regarded by most of bench and bar as an offensive intrusion by a misinformed lay public. Perhaps the strongest assertion of this contempt for what is, after all, an ultimately controlling citizenry comes in the failure of nearly all court systems (California is a brilliant exception) to keep decent records of what they have done.

A professor at the Texas Law School recently wrote, at the conclusion of a research project: "How 'good' is the brand of justice administered by the Texas courts? Do the litigants and the public get a fair deal? . . . Must the answer be that there is no answer— that the system defies analysis? Unfortunately, this may be the necessary reply, unless an even more gloomy one is appropriate." Much the same can be said anywhere in the country.

But meanwhile, let us look about us.

2

Small-claims court in Los Angeles is a large, marbly room with the usual flags and a judge in robes on a high bench. In front of the bench, however, where normally there would be an array of clerks and assistants, there is one of the biggest children's game boards in the United States, with houses and green hills and streets, especially streets, packed with toy cars and trucks and trolleys. Here the participants in small automobile accidents, where nothing was harmed but the vehicles, can *show* the judge what they say happened, saving all concerned from the immensely wasteful process of drawing testimony from inarticulate people. Claims of up to $200 can be tried here. The plantiff simply goes to the courthouse, swears before the clerk to the truth of his statements, and pays one dollar for the affidavit and seventy-five cents for having it sent by registered mail to the defendant. By this document, which the clerk will help the plaintiff prepare, the defendant is ordered to appear at the court on a specified day at a specified hour, roughly two to three weeks from the date the suit is filed. If the defendant doesn't show up, and often he doesn't, judgment enters for the amount claimed.

Attorneys are not permitted. The judge himself conducts the questioning (though either plaintiff or defendant has the right to ask questions, both usually prefer to let the judge take over at an early stage). The most common cases are minor traffic accidents and tradesmen's claims, though a judge in a small-claims court will over the course of a year run into nearly all the aspects of life that cause disputes between neighbors, from the dog in the flower bed to the baseball through the window.

Before the judge are a television repairman and his customer: one has an unpaid bill for $64; the other has a television set which he says still doesn't work. The judge asks questions: "What did he tell you he would do?" "What did you do when you got the set home?" "When it broke down again, did you take it back?" And to the other side: "Did you say it would be good as new?" "How many hours did you work at it?" "Doing what?" "What parts did you use?" The set is nine years old; the repairman did try to sell the customer a replacement. Judgment is entered for $50, after about ten minutes of questioning.

"How many dependents do you have?"

"Wife and two children."

"Does your wife work?"

"Yes."

"What's her net take-home pay?"

"Forty-five."

"What's yours?"

"Sixty-five."

"Let's see—one hundred and ten dollars—what's your rent?"

"Sixty-five."

"Payments on a car?"

"Sixty-five."

"Twenty-five a month is all right. See the clerk and make the arrangements."

Among the powers of a small-claims court is the imposition of payment in installments. Indeed, its function, fundamentally, is to make the sort of arrangements the parties to the dispute ought to have made between themselves. For this purpose, the intermediary does not have to be a judge (in New York the small-claims courts are operated with ordinary lawyers on the bench, donating their services for an evening because they like pretending to be judges); and he need not necessarily be a lawyer (most justices of the peace, who exercise the small-claims jurisdiction in most parts of the English-speaking world, are not lawyers). In Cleveland the small-claims procedure requires a first attempt at conciliation by the court.

Thanks to the simplicity of the situation, the small-claims court reveals aspects of the nature of law normally hidden in clouds of philosophy. To begin with, the court obviously demonstrates the breakdown of normal social intercourse. Law—the coercive power of the state—is summoned here clearly because people do not get along with each other. The power of law is pretty starkly demonstrated, too: simply on a statement by one private person, another is summoned to leave his normal pursuits and appear before a judge, on pain of having the force of the state put automatically behind his opponent's claim; and there is no escape.

Here, more than elsewhere, one can also see some of the less satisfactory aspects of the Rule of Law. Once disposition is controlled by law, compromise and social adjustment become more difficult. Answers based on law are easy to find in the small-claims court, because the litigants have not had the services of lawyers to suggest fraud, duress, ambiguity, technical failure or contravention of public policy as reasons why the obvious law should not be held to apply to this particular contract. But it should be kept in mind that pettifoggery of this kind gets a sympathetic audience from a good judge only when there is something about the case that makes him unwilling to apply obvious law, and he is looking for an excuse; the most important source of "technicalities" in the law is the fear that the easy application of broad rules will produce injustice. The absence of technicalities tends to make the small-claims court more legalistic than other implements of law, and quite possibly more unjust.

"[T]he major number of claims coming before a small claims

court," the Institute of Judicial Administration observes ominously, "have in fact no defense." Not much more than 10 percent of the claims filed are adjudicated in court; most of the time the defendant doesn't show up, and execution of the "default judgment" often winds up by one route or another in the hands of the sheriff. Garnishment of wages probably results more often from small-claims processing than from any other kind of action. Early efforts to keep the small-claims court from being a collection agency have been abandoned in most jurisdictions; this is a "poor man's court," all right, but most of the time the poor man is the defendant. Still, experience in the area of small gambling debts, where legal process is not available for collection, argues that the poor man is probably better off when his creditor has access to law than he would be otherwise.

And, of course, the small-claims procedure in a big city, with real judges inquiring earnestly through the thicket of evidence, is far preferable to the bumbling proceedings of the old-fashioned but still widespread justice of the peace court. These courts are so completely plaintiff's courts that the initials "JP" are translated "Judgment for the Plaintiff." An Iowa lawyer remembers a case where "the JP publicly implored divine guidance in making his decision. Then it was Judgment for the Plaintiff."

JP courts are the foundation of the English legal system. Their occupants, who are only rarely lawyers, are appointed for life by the Crown, serve without pay, and dispose of all but the most important civil litigation and criminal charges. Because the JP system flourishes, England makes do with only 246 paid judges for a nation of fifty million people reared in a common-law tradition that distrusts administrative decision-making. For better or worse, the JP is a squire; but his appointment usually reflects local feeling that he has a well-developed sense of fair play to go with his inevitable conservatism.

America inherited this system of lay judges from its colonial days. According to the Institute of Judicial Administration, forty-seven of the forty-eight states provided for JP courts in their constitutions in 1915, and every state had such courts as late as 1945. But in the United States the JP became a part-time elected official, paid in most states (*not* everywhere) by fees rather than salaries for the work he did. Though some JPs have offices in public buildings, the typical JP holds court wherever he is, most commonly at home but sometimes at work (the back of a drugstore is by no means uncommon, as victims of speed traps the country over can testify). His jurisdiction, in the twenty–odd states where he survives as a significant figure, covers crimes that carry a penalty as great as one year (in Kansas and Kentucky), and civil actions up to $500 (in New York, Pennsylvania and Washington; despite this considerable authority in its JP courts, a recent law review note says that "[N]o one knows how many justices of the peace there are in the State of Washington, much less who they are, where they are located, [and] the extent to which they do or do not function").

As signified in American song and story, JPs marry people. It is by no means unknown for them to divorce people, too, though they have no legal authority to do so, on the sturdy grounds that "If I married 'em, I can divorce 'em." In some circumstances the JP system offers advantages to those who habitually employ lawyers. Appeal from a conviction in a JP court (for drunk drivers, say) requires a new trial in a real court, and DAs often refuse to prosecute JP convictions, claiming that the evidence always has been hopelessly mixed up. Two years after the notice of appeal is filed, in most jurisdictions, the case is dismissed.

The Institute of Judicial Administration in 1965 summarized the weaknesses of the JP system:

"lack of legal training
part-time service
compensation by fee
inadequate supervision
archaic procedures
makeshift facilities"

But this list only hints at the problems. In 1927 it was necessary for the Supreme Court of the United States to inform the State of Ohio that a law that permitted JPs to collect fees only when a criminal defendant was convicted could not meet constitutional standards of due process. Nevertheless, differences in compensation according to the result of the case persisted in Kentucky, North

Carolina, and Michigan for another thirty years and more. The National Crime Commission says they still exist in three unnamed states. And as a practical matter, of course, a JP has immediate access to his piece of whatever he awards a plaintiff. Where the fee system flourishes in traffic courts, it promotes kickback arrangements between the JPs and the police, who usually have a choice of courts into which they can shepherd their offenders.

Though distinguished people serve as JPs in every state, the job is usually a political plum and can go to remarkably unsuitable candidates. In general, both the profession and the public have chosen not to look under this particular rug, but in 1959-60 a committee of the New Mexico State Legislature (headed by then State Senator, now U. S. Senator, Fabian Chavez, Jr.) took sixteen volumes' worth of testimony on the operations of the JP system in that state; and in 1961 published a report that must be the most entertaining public document of the decade. It is devoted mostly to excerpts from the transcripts:

In response to a question as to how the justice of the peace system can be improved, one JP stated, "I know of a lot of justices of the peace that aren't qualified as justices of the peace. They can't even sign their name and can't read or write."

Another JP, the operator of a filling station, maintained that "I can read and the only thing is that I can't explain very well."

In New Mexico, the JPs perform the functions that are customarily performed by coroners in other states. A JP headed an inquest in which a man was shot "three times in the heart and once in the head" and the verdict of "suicide" was rendered. This same JP stated "it worries me such as a man hanging on the tree with his feet flat on the ground. Now according to medical people of which I have asked doctors on my investigation they say a man stretches but sometimes I wonder how far he will stretch." He stated, "I think that 99 per cent of them (the JPs) are not capable of holding an investigation and of medical determination whether a man is dead or not."

A JP, who handles about 1,200 cases a year, stated that "I am not very—possibly not thoroughly—capable of reading the law." He also stated that "I was also very fortunate when I first went in as a JP, of course, my experience in the sheriff's office as an accountant and radio operator helped me a little bit, because I at least knew where the jail was."

A JP, who grossed between $18,000 and $23,000 a year in JP work, believed that a JP should "have at least a high school education."

The New Mexico committee found that most of the state's JPs did not have a high school education. One had held court in a booth in a café, another at a coal mine, another "in an abandoned chicken house." Defendants were rarely found not guilty, and the tendency toward verdicts of guilty was encouraged by the fact that, while guilty defendants had to pay court costs themselves, the bill for innocent defendants had to be sent to the county, which often didn't pay it. Meanwhile, the payment of cash fines gave JPs an interesting opportunity to supplement their fee incomes. "There is no intention here of supplying a manual as to how to embezzle money from the state of New Mexico," the committee report said, explaining why only a few examples of thievery were given. ". . . [T]here are a vast number of other methods, many of extreme ingenuity, used by JPs to take money illegally."

Even the bright side clouded over quickly: "Until recently, few JPs bothered with tampering with receipts. The reason is comparatively simple: many JPs often did not issue receipts at all." Yet another surprising source of income was uncovered in Albuquerque:

A. . . . she peeled the five off . . . and threw it down on the desk and she said, "You're the nicest judge I've ever seen before, and I don't mind telling you I've seen several before."
Q. Got a tip, did you?
A. Yes.

The report concluded, in splendid understatement: "Most JP courts in New Mexico are operated ineptly, incompetently, and inefficiently. On more than a few occasions, they are operated contrary to law." And the desired effect was secured: the 1961 session of the legislature greatly restricted the JPs and established an administrative authority; the 1963 session gave the administrator expanded powers; the 1965 session set in motion a constitutional amendment for the abolition of the JP courts; and in the 1966 election, when reform movements were beaten back at the polls all across the country, the voters of New Mexico abolished the JP courts.

The question of what to do after the abolition of JP courts is easily answered by the experience of the twenty-odd states that have taken this action. "Municipal courts" or "district courts," with salaried judges who must be members of the bar, are given the old JP jurisdiction, and usually considerably more. Delmar Karlen of the Institute of Judicial Administration, who was influential in giving Maine a JP-free court system a few years ago, believes that the JP way of handling local problems is a vanishing phenomenon. This disappearance does not, however, signal the arrival of the millennium. As the Institute points out in its 1965 survey of progress to date, "Many of the minor courts which were created to supplant or supplement the JP courts tended to employ similar low standards of justice."

Where there is not enough business to support a full-time judge, the requirement that the district court judge be a lawyer may be counterproductive. Lawrence G. Brooks, presiding judge of a Massachusetts District Court (a fascinating institution that uses a jury to decide civil matters but not in criminal cases, and produces in misdemeanor cases a "finding" rather than a verdict, with sentence to follow only when the defendant "accepts" the finding), has described some of the problems of the system in his state:

Judges were practising in their own courts, sometimes before their own associates. In one case, a father was Presiding Justice and his son was Special Justice. Judges as lawyers tried cases against insurance companies which were also before them as litigants. One Judge was accused of holding up his decision in a case involving an insurance company with which he was trying to settle one of his own cases. . . . Another serious weakness in the lawyer-judge combination was that the judge's private practice, being more lucrative than his judicial job and more demanding on his time, tended to relegate his judicial duties to second place.

Though Brooks wrote in the past tense, as of mid-1966, a majority of Massachusetts' district judges were still part-time.

Moreover, the extension of more formal procedures down to this level is not necessarily a step forward in the march toward justice. When the JP system came under attack in England in 1888, Maitland protested (unnecessarily, as it turned out) that the JP "is cheap, he is pure, he is capable, but he is doomed; he is to be sacrificed to the spirit of the age." Volume processing is simply inevitable in the lower courts—the JP courts and their replacements, plus the small-claims courts, handle something like 80 percent of all the nation's judicial business even after the exclusion of the traffic offenses (which account all by themselves for 90 percent of the nation's judicial business). The procedural regularity that is the glory of the law cannot be achieved here, and should not be attempted. What went wrong in the JP courts was less the system than the people who manned it. There is more to be gained from a careful choice of individuals for lower-court positions, a training program for lower-court judges, and a close supervision of what goes on in these courts. Common-sense justice ("Cadi justice," as Frankfurter would have it; or, remaining in the East, "the justice of Solomon") does greater service than law on this level (no decision here can be used as a precedent for *anything*); and for this purpose an alert and public-spirited druggist with easy access to legal advice from a centralized clerk's office may be more effective than a third-rate lawyer who couldn't make it in private practice and has been running little errands for a political party.

Even some of the procedural irregularities that so offend the humorless chieftains of the civil liberties movement may do more good than harm. Not long ago, a New Hampshire district judge was talking about his Labor Day weekend, which was somewhat disrupted by a student riot on the beach: "From three-thirty to nine in the morning, with nothing but a cup of coffee, we processed juveniles." Releasing some of the boys in custody of their parents, the irritated judge in clear violation of their civil rights ordered them to return to court for their trials with haircuts, clean shirts and ties. And when they came back, the police couldn't recognize them, so the charges had to be dismissed. . . . *Fiat justitia!*

3

At nine o'clock the lights switch on against the green marble wall at either side of the judge's bench in a second-floor courtroom in the old courthouse of Des Moines, Iowa, and the knot of lawyers at the back of the room quiets down and moves into seats. Judge

Gibson C. Holliday, who practiced law for almost thirty years in this city to amass enough of a private fortune to accept a judgeship (which in Iowa in 1964 paid only $14,000 a year), comes into the court from his chambers; a large, genial man in robes. There are eight judges in the "Ninth Judicial District of Iowa," which means Des Moines; four are assigned to "the law bench," two to "the equity bench," one to domestic affairs and one to criminal matters; to keep from getting bored, they alternate their assignments. This month, Holliday has the additional job of calling the law calendar and assigning cases to the four courts. He calls the cases mostly by the name of the plaintiff's lawyer:

"Mr. Duffield?"

A lawyer rises in the audience.

"Ted, is there any change in *Frank* v. *Jones?*"

"No, it's ready."

"Good. We'll get to that today. . . ."

"Mr. Sloan, hold yourself in readiness because we'll be wanting to clear these cases up. . . ."

"Is Mr. McClintock here?"

"He's out of the city."

"That's right, I saw him yesterday, he told me—he's gone to Burlington. . . .

"*Dalton* v. *Albright*" Judge Holliday points. "George Wright?"

"Ready, Your Honor."

"Attaboy . . ."

Fifteen or so cases are read out; most of them are ready. ("I'm very enthusiastic about our local bar," Judge Holliday says. "They could crucify me. It's only because of their cooperation that we get rid of 132 cases in a six-week term.") Then: "Gentlemen, that concludes the call." The lawyers in the courtroom rise and gather in knots; some light cigarettes (the rule against smoking in courtrooms is for judicial decorum, not for fire prevention). Holliday is leaving the bench when a lawyer comes toward him purposefully.

"What have you got here? What record do you want to make?"

The lawyer says, "Comes now the plaintiff and asks permission of the court to amend the petition as follows. . . ."

This is a court system that works. On the average, cases are tried within eight months of the filing of the first complaint, within four months of the day the lawyers agree they are ready to proceed. Judges are elected on partisan tickets, but they usually start on the bench through interim appointments and thereafter, Holliday says, "The Republicans endorse ours, and we Democrats endorse theirs." The judges eat lunch together daily in full fellowship at a table reserved for them at a nearby hotel restaurant. The lawyers know each other (nearly everyone went to one of two law schools, Iowa U. or Drake). They are by no means unsophisticated—one of them, bearing the fine name Vernon Lawyer, amusing and aggressive like all good negligence lawyers, has pioneered a new technique in P.I. practice, the printing of a slick-paper pamphlet telling the sad story of an accident victim and how the accident wrecked her life, complete with pictures, not so much to prejudice a potential jury as to frighten an insurance company. (Lawyer feels, however, that the old times were better: "When I was a kid in southern Iowa, when the judge came everybody went to the courthouse and decided whom they liked—which lawyers. Now, it's just cases.") It is usually argued that people of Des Moines are less litigious about their accidents and the faulty products they buy—but twenty-two cases a week in Des Moines is the same as 880 a week in New York, and nothing like that number of actual "ready" court cases gets disposed of in a week in New York. And in Des Moines, as everywhere else, personal-injury cases take up three-quarters of the courts' time. It is hard to avoid the feeling that the reason the machine works in Des Moines is that everybody involved wants to make it work, wants to get the business done, believes (more or less) in what he is doing.

The machine itself is the same almost everywhere. An action at law (which means an action for damages or for the possession of land—actions to make people do something or stop doing something or change their legal relationship are actions in equity) begins with the filing of a complaint (a "pleading") which is officially noted at the court and must be "served" on the defendant by the sheriff or a process server, and the defendant then has a certain length of time to answer. The complaint must state a "cause of action"—a pattern of facts which justify recovery under a system of law. The answer may deny the facts, offer other, exonerating facts or deny the applicability of law. The first of these answers may lead to a fairly quick trial, by establishing an issue to be tried. The other two open the door for many motions, which put the plaintiff in the answer business, amending his pleadings or arguing his point of law. If the defendant claims the law gives the plaintiff no cause of action (a "demurrer"), there will be hearings, rulings, sometimes appeals on the rulings.

The horror of the old "forms of action" at common law was that the plaintiff had to get everything just right from the beginning, or he was out of court, regardless of the intrinsic merits of his case. Arguments about the accuracy and formal correctness of the pleadings could go on for years. But the simplified pleadings of today, with their unlimited privilege to amend, turn out not to end the horror stories. David Peck, while on the bench, wrote sourly:

[I]t is a rare case in which the issues get defined in a complaint and answer. The pleadings are apt to be a mere formality, an opening gambit, calculated to say too little or too much, necessitating amplification, clarification or simplification by motions for bills of particulars, motions to make the pleadings more definite and certain, to separately state causes of action, or to strike allegations as irrelevant. . . . The list of motions or cross-motions which are idled through in quite ordinary lawsuits dooms many from the start to delay and expense which impair or destroy the value of the right to prosecute or defend.

The judge barely participates in this shadow boxing; the shadow referee is the clerk of the court, who brings in papers for him to sign, instructing one party or the other to answer what has just been filed. Most of the business pending before the courts is in the hands of the clerks most of the time, and unless a careful eye is kept on the situation the clerks' desks groan at Christmastime with their load of presents from lawyers. "It isn't so much that the clerk can expedite," says California's Felix Stumpf, "it's that he can block you. You're not so much getting a favor as making sure he's in a right mood at all times." If somebody wants a hearing on a motion, he can have one; and all the judges must put some of their time into "motion parts."

It is usually impossible to leave a complicated case in the hands of a judge from the moment it is filed, and have him follow through the entire process; he has other matters to try. In the cities different motions in the same case will come before different judges, none of whom will ultimately try it. The continuity of the case, up to the moment of trial, is in the hands of the clerks; and the judge, who doesn't have time to read all the papers, will often ask a clerk for key information about what goes on here. He gets good information, too; the chief clerk, at least, is often a lawyer and a very capable one; there are cheers from both bench and bar on the infrequent occasions when a clerk is made a judge. A court that has bad luck in its clerks—which can happen, because the appointments are political—will rapidly disintegrate as an effective decision-making tool. With all the attention that gets paid to the selection of judges, it is odd that so little attention is paid to the selection of clerks.

Fifty years ago a case proceeded to trial quickly after the pleadings were squared away. Each side built its own case, and had to guess from the pleadings what witnesses might be called or what documents might be produced to prove parts of a rival's argument. These elements of surprise and trickery, often leading to opposing cases that did not even attempt to meet each other, were widely regarded as a mockery of justice, and over the course of the years the courts developed procedures to compel the opposing sides to define their disagreements and specify their proofs before taking the time of judge and jury.

The two most important of these procedures were "inspections" and "examination before trial"—opportunity for the lawyers to secure well in advance whatever documents they might need that were in the possession of the other side, and to interrogate (under oath) plaintiff, defendant and witnesses. These procedures were also highly productive of motions, because often the court's compulsory process is needed to make someone disgorge documents or produce witnesses. An intrinsic difficulty about this operation is that no judge is present to pass on the admissibility of the evidence that can be drawn from discovery or pretrial examination. In the early years of pretrial procedure, judges were most reluctant to authorize what were universally known as "fishing expeditions"; now the rule in most states is that the lawyers are entitled to uncover information which might not be admissible at the trial, provided they can show that this information leads to other information they might be able to use. Again, disagreement between counsel about the legitimacy of the purpose can lead to requests for rulings from a judge.

At some point in the proceedings, most judges will make an effort to eliminate the case entirely through mediation in a "pretrial conference," an informal gathering in the judge's chambers at which the lawyers are encouraged to put their cases on the table and negotiate a settlement. In the federal system and in many states, these conferences are more or less required; at the least, they give the judge a chance to compel the opponents to pin down the issue between them, to "stipulate" the facts not in dispute and the legitimacy of each other's documents, and to limit the number of expert witnesses either side will call. The agreed-upon "pretrial statement" will then control what can be done at the trial.

Before 1930 most judges would have been amazed to learn that such conferences could be proper or even legal; the thought was that a judge, like a jury, should not know anything but what he hears in open court. Once a defendant has made an offer in a pretrial conference, it is hard for a judge to run a trial which assumes that the defendant may not be liable at all. But Judge Ira W. Jayne of Detroit felt that the gains from getting the case straight far outweighed any possible losses through prejudgment, and he sold his argument first to the courts of Michigan (which made pretrial conferences compulsory in Detroit in 1931, only two years after Jayne began insisting on them in his own court), and then to the Supreme Court, which made pretrial meetings "a fundamental cornerstone of the Federal Rules of Civil Procedure."

In Des Moines court adjourns for a week to put all the cases for the next term through pretrial conferences; in Los Angeles every judge holds a pretrial conference every morning before court opens (and there is also a "special pretrial personal injury settlement calendar" available when both counsel request more detailed mediation). New York has attempted to get cases off the calendar early through pretrial conferences before the lawyers go through the routines of discovery and examination. "[T]his fish-market pretrial," as one judge has called it, has been relatively unsuccessful in itself (though

it may promote subsequent settlement during the long years between filing and trial). A judge wrote to the Survey of Metropolitan
Courts, "After 14 years at the bar and 29 on the bench, I'm giving
my considered judgment. Lawyers will not settle their cases before
the pressure is applied."

At last, an average of almost six years after defendant's answer
was filed in Chicago, more than four years in Philadelphia or
Brooklyn or Westchester, more than three years in Boston, two
and a half years in San Francisco, Phoenix, Detroit, Honolulu,
Cleveland, the personal-injury case that has not been settled comes
to trial. Other varieties of lawsuit often move much faster—often
but not always. The first case cited in *Dispatch and Delay*, a study
of the Pennsylvania courts, was *In the Matter of the Adoption of
Gerald Bair,* where a combination of dilatory tactics and motion-
making had left a baby's fate undecided for four years.

4

"Justice delayed," says a slogan that goes back to antiquity, "is
justice denied." Timing is obviously important if the law seeks to
"make whole" someone who has been mistreated. The importance
of timing is recognized in criminal cases: if a man is languishing in
jail awaiting trial, he has a right to demand a quick prosecution,
usually within thirty days; if he is out on bail, a judge will normally
allow him only so many postponements once the prosecution says
it is ready to proceed. Equity cases—mostly requests for injunctions
—can be heard (and appealed) virtually overnight. In damage
actions, however, if only by mutual courtesy of the lawyers, litigants
have no judicially enforceable right to dispatch. The fact of delay
becomes as important as the facts of the case or the sense of the law
in the negotiation of settlements. And the delay frustrates not only
the quest for "substantial justice," but also the relevance of procedural machinery. If the aim of the process is to uncover the truth
through examination and cross-examination, then the passage of
time, with the inevitable blurring of memories (not to mention the
death or disappearance of witnesses) works against the goal. Meanwhile, everybody develops a bad temper. The authors of *Who Sues*

in New York City? open their book with "A THOUGHT TO START: Enna, Sicily, January 27 (UPI) . . . Giovanni Occhipinti, apparently angered at delays on a civil court case, shot and killed the judge yesterday. . . ."

Judges and lawyers and law professors have been looking hard for more than a decade for procedures that would speed up personal-injury trials within the framework of the existing system. "Viewed as a whole," Columbia's Maurice Rosenberg has written,

the campaign has gone forward with much vigor but no real breakthrough. There has been a definite pattern to the activity. The sponsors of a new device trumpet it as a miracle remedy, manage to get it introduced and almost instantly pronounce it a lavish success. After a time, experience and careful research deflate the premature boasts and then something new is invented. Today it can be fairly said that there is no acceptable evidence that any remedy so far devised has been efficacious to any substantial extent.

The most widely approved device has been the pretrial conference. But when Rosenberg's Columbia Project for Effective Justice investigated the situation in a controlled experiment in New Jersey, the findings were that the settlement rate was no greater with pretrial than without, that trials were no shorter, and that the *elimination* of compulsory pretrial in that state would save "judge time."

In Philadelphia the Municipal Court (with a jurisdiction ranging up to $5,000) instituted compulsory arbitration, in the offices of lawyers appointed by the court (who were paid, but not well, for their time) for all cases under $2,000. The Columbia Project found that by this device between 2,500 and 4,000 trials were spared the Municipal Court, and delay in that court, which had been running 24-30 months, was reduced to 3-5 months. Under the Pennsylvania constitution, which guarantees trial by jury in suits for money damages, this process could not be extended very far, and neither Rosenberg nor Zeisel is happy about its procedural aspects. Zeisel has described arbitration in Pennsylvania as a system "where Ersatz judges work for substandard fees and supply their overhead free of charge." Still, the arbitration procedure does seem to have influenced attitudes in Philadelphia: the 1966 edition of the IJA

Calendar Status Study carries a comment on Philadelphia's 50.8-month delay in its court of unlimited jurisdiction: "Court Administrator advises that the emphasis in this court is on settlement of personal injury cases rather than on trial."

Yet another scheme, in Massachusetts, provided for court-appointed "auditors," who would hear the parties and suggest an award; though this award was not binding on anyone, it could be introduced in evidence at a trial and would obviously exert significant influence on a jury. Both the Columbia Project and a Boston University study come to the conclusion that for the same money Massachusetts could have hired more judges and run more trials, producing about the same reduction of delay.

A new and popular device to speed disposition is the "split trial," where a jury votes on the question of liability before hearing evidence on damages. If the jury finds no liability, then all the time normally devoted to the damage part of the case is saved; moreover, once the jury *has* found liability, settlement can be speeded. This idea was tried out for Zeisel in the federal courts of the Chicago area in 1960-61. The saving in time was 26 percent in the raw data—the average split trial took 3.1 days, while the average regular trial took 4.2 days in these courts through this period—and even after some analysis the saving still appeared to be 21 percent. Only 12 percent of the cases in the separated procedure went to a jury award of damages for the plaintiff (32 percent were settled during trial), as against 42 percent of the cases in the regular procedure (with 24 percent settled). Adding these figures, it will be seen that the jury found defendant liable in only 44 percent of the separated trials, as against 66 percent of the regular trials: the more a jury knows about plaintiff's injuries, the more likely it is to find defendant liable. This change in the results roused Rosenberg's fury: "Definitely not defensible . . . is an accidental or heedless tampering with the adjudicative process in a way likely to distort the outcome in large groups of cases." And, of course, the better the defendant's chances at trial, the more likely he will be to refuse to settle, so the end result of split trials might be more trials, and more delay.

Apart from the provision of new judges ("the conventional

panacea for every judicial emergency," Judge Joseph M. Proskauer once wrote), the most popular approach among judges and law school professors has been the abolition of the jury. Kalven and Zeisel and Buchholz calculated in their study of the New York courts that trials before judges take about 40 percent less time than jury trials. And a number of scholars, annoyed by the fact that the jury's findings never need be explained to anybody, have always been offended by the institution.

"[J]ury trial, at best," Dean Griswold of Harvard has written, "is an apotheosis of the amateur. Why should anyone think that twelve persons brought in from the street, selected in various ways for their lack of general ability, should have any special capacity to decide controversies between persons?" David Peck has described the jury trial as "geared to the assimilation of the unfamiliar by the inexpert." Professor Prosser has even got personal, referring to the "twelve housewives, bakers' helpers and unemployed individuals we get today in the United States."

Juries are chosen in different places by different procedures—from the rolls of voters, from the telephone books, from the lists of houses in census tracts, by selectmen, by county clerks. In New York every literate male may be obliged to serve two weeks every other year, and evasion of jury duty has become a significant talent. (Perhaps the best, if the most expensive, device for evasion is something called the Sheriff's Jury, an elite group appointed to serve in cases where the sanity of a public officer has been challenged. This duty does not take much time—maybe it should take more—and meanwhile those charged with it are excused from service on all other juries. There are three panels, of which the most socially prominent is the Second Panel, which gives an annual banquet at which some judges and the city's leading politicians of all parties are feted and a chunk of the members' $400 dues is refunded to them in the form of an expensive gift.)

In the South the failure of the jury clerks to summon Negroes has resulted in the reversal of criminal convictions; everywhere, judges worry a little about the tendency of the jury lists to be weighted toward the lower middle classes. Jurors are paid between $3 and $12 a day, depending on where they are summoned to serve. Some employers do, and some don't make up the difference between a juror's normal salary and what he is paid by the court. Undoubtedly the fairest means of selection is that now followed, after many reforms, in Detroit, where random number tables are applied to census tracts, the citizens dwelling at those locations are summoned almost beyond the possibility of excuse, service is for a four-week term, and everyone summoned is guaranteed that he will never again be asked to be a juror in Detroit. The most humane is that in New Hampshire, where most excuses are accepted and the average age of the panel runs well over sixty—"We recognize," says a lawyer, "that different people have different uses for their time." Lawyers, doctors, public officials, minors, females, lunatics, convicts and volunteer firemen are excused from jury service almost everywhere.

From this over-all panel, names are picked from a wheel or by some other random means for each trial. The lawyers are then permitted to examine their prospective jurors and find out whether any of them might be prejudiced against a client's case. Each side may reject, usually without limit, "for cause," and may also reject without cause a specified number (normally between two and six) of the prospective jurors. But the courts themselves define acceptable cause, and this definition varies all over. In Iowa the only causes are close friendship with one of the lawyers or the parties to the case, or actual participation in a pending case involving the same issues. The *voir dire,* as it is called, is performed in Iowa before and under the supervision of a judge, lawyers are not permitted to stick notions in the jurymen's heads with hypothetical questions about how they would feel *if,* and at the end each lawyer is permitted three "peremptory challenges" and two "strikes." The whole process is completed in less than an hour. In New York, by contrast, —but nobody can write calmly about the New York system who has ever been compelled to waste literally days of his time while the yahoos of the New York bar (with the consent of the judges, who have ratted out and do not preside over the *voir dire*) run through stereotyped and often illegitimate series of questions, separately for each juror in the box, all for the purpose of frustrating the only excuse there is for a jury trial, that the facts are to be found by an unselected mixed bag of the community. Judge Bernard Botein has written critically of the "prolonged conditioning of jurors under guise of inquiring into their qualifications"; he has never indicated why the New York judges refuse to police it.

Every lawyer who tries cases has rules of thumb about the types he wants and doesn't want on his juries. In some states, where the lists of jurors are published for each term of court, commercial services supply background information on each juror, and a record of how the juries on which he has previously served decided the cases they heard. When damages are substantial, plaintiff's lawyer likes on the jury at least one fairly wealthy person who will not be afraid of big numbers. When liability questions are serious, the range of preference runs from the Jewish mother at one end to the retired New England claims agent on the other. Everybody has learned something through sad experience. "I remember a case I didn't think I'd lose," says an Iowa lawyer, " and after I'd lost it I watched the jury walking out, and I noticed that an old farmer was missing three fingers of his left hand. He looked pleased with himself; he hadn't got any money when the threshing machine got him, and my client hadn't got any money, either. Since then, I always look at their hands." But most lawyers will admit that whatever the statistical probabilities, jurors are fairly unpredictable as individuals, and everybody has his favorite *voir dire* stories. New York's William F. X. Geoghan, Jr. remembers one in an upstate court:

"I believe," said a lawyer, "that you know my learned friend," indicating an opponent.

"Yes, I do."

"Would you say you know him well?"

"Yes, I would."

"Would you say you knew him *very* well?"

"Yes, I would."

"Well, then, you're all right with me!"

Geoghan adds, "I checked up, and that other lawyer *did* have a bad reputation."

Jury trials take longer than trials before a judge alone because the lawyers are forever playing to the jury's emotions and affections, finding petty reasons why a juror should distrust the other man's witness, fighting to get in or keep out evidence that might not be offered before a judge or that nobody would care whether a judge heard or not. It is widely believed by lawyers for both sides that juries are more likely to find for plaintiffs in personal-injury cases, and likely to bring in higher awards than judges would give. The one significant study of this question, by Kalven and Zeisel's Chicago Jury Project, to be published in the latter 1960s (nearly fifteen years after the evidence was gathered: delay in the ivory tower, too), will come up with the conclusion that judges and juries are about equal in their tendency to find the defendant liable (they disagree in a good number of cases, but there are as many where the judge finds liability while the jury doesn't as there are where the jury but not the judge would blame the defendant). But the bar is right in its belief that judges are less generous than juries, by a factor of about 20 percent.

"People who want to keep the jury," says Maurice Rosenberg, a small, brisk, witty law professor in his forties, "make three arguments—political, philosophical and psychological. The political argument is that the jury is democratic, the only place where people assume brief authority. The philosophical argument says that there are many questions which the law raises where there is no really good answer possible—the jury spares the court looking like an ass in attempting to solve these cases, and avoids bad precedents, because jury verdicts aren't precedents. The psychological argument says that often a jury excuses people whom the public would like to see stung, and that lets the judge off the hook."

Lee Kreindler, the aviation specialist, raises a further and perhaps conclusive argument, with implications beyond the courtroom to the settlement process: "Juries fix the community evaluation for a particular wrong in a particular injury. The verdict is a composite of many factors—fault, bias, prejudice, damages—all reduced to a single determination. You get verdict after verdict after verdict, and a standard emerges. Really, what we have is a system of claims evaluations by experts, but the jury statement activates the whole system of claims adjustment." The jury can serve this function in a way that judges cannot, because the jury by definition represents the community. And in the meantime, in individual cases, the juries "legislate interstitially, to fill out the vague general formula" of the law—which also becomes part of the framework for settlements. A New Hampshire lawyer who settles cases for defendants speaks scornfully of insurance adjusters who won't settle "because they had a year of law school and think there really is such a thing as contributory negligence."

But there is no intrinsic reason why the courts cannot eliminate much of the delay and still retain enough jury trials to set the community framework for settlement. California, thanks to "reforms in calendar management," reduced its backlog of cases from 47,616 on January 30, 1963, to 26,884 on June 30, 1965, while *increasing* the number of personal-injury cases tried. In 1962 New York's First Appellate Department achieved full supervisory authority over the trial courts in Manhattan, and Presiding Judge Bernard Botein by 1966 had the personal-injury calendar down from a delay of four years to a delay of eleven months. Botein had been a deeply respected trial judge himself, which probably helped, because his method was simply to keep the pressure unrelentingly on. The key device was the "blockbuster" part, five or six of them in New York and two in the Bronx. To the judge in each such courtroom Botein assigned a block of sixty cases.

"We'll tell them," Botein says, " 'These cases are yours for two months—get rid of as many as you can.' We assign to one part all cases from one insurance carrier, to another part all cases involving the city; then a more responsible claims agent comes in. Instead of taking his regular diet of three cases from the calendar (if one isn't ready, he looks frantically for another), the judge pretrials twenty a day for three days. A lot of them settle, they feel the hot breath of the jury. [Note that under this arrangement the judge *will* try the cases he has heard in pretrial, which gives him great leverage in forcing a settlement.] The rest the judge puts on telephone call—they're to be ready to come in whenever the clerk calls. The result is that the same judge who will normally dispose of nine or ten cases a month will dispose of twenty-seven cases a month in the blockbuster part. They're ashamed to see their part break with a lot of cases still outstanding."

What Botein seems to have demonstrated (though he would not say so himself) is the truth of an observation by a Chief Justice of Pennsylvania: that a lot of delay reflects only "the slothfulness of lawyers and the indolence of judges." Botein himself, however, has recently become greatly disturbed by the impact of his efforts to eliminate delay.

"Like most big-city administrators, I have utilized every device and contrivance I could copy to speed the disposition of cases and have even invented a gimmick or two myself," he told a meeting of the Association of the Bar of the City of New York in 1966,

and now I fear that in doing so we have done the courts a great disservice. . . . Too many judges have been caught up in a consuming campaign against That Old Debbil Calendar. . . . [T]he frenzy with which we try to shorten the long line of cases shuffling toward trial, when it is accomplished by hard-pressed settlements, is highly indecorous and undignified. . . . [I]nstant justice, at the trial or pre-trial stage, can never be a consistent substitute for a true justice, which requires time for brewing, blending and often brooding. In the stark statistics of reducing calendar congestion and delay and keeping most of our calendars current, we have been reasonably successful in the First Department. But how has this been achieved? Regrettably, by converting our courthouses into counting houses.

5

"Among the costs of the obsession with speedier justice," Rosenberg has written, "has been an erosion of the integrity of the judicial process from the viewpoint of the litigants and lawyers, some of whom have the impression that the courts regard their cases as merely counters in a numbers game." Botein is concerned that as part of the pretrials "The judge becomes sucked into the haggling process, blandishing, nudging and I fear at times scolding the lawyers. Hardly a dignified performance." Maxine Boord Virtue, drawing conclusions from her Survey of Metropolitan Courts, worries that "the more sensitive the judiciary grows to the problem of 'delay' viewed as a purely quantitative phenomenon, the more difficult it will be for the judge to discharge his basic function— to see that justice is done in each case." Mrs. Virtue adds later a demand for "cognizance of the litigants' desire to be fully heard and their sense of having had a day in court. Judges and experienced trial counsel will agree, the writer is sure, that this feeling is close to the heartbeat of justice."

These are noble words, but an outsider must wonder whether they mean anything. "Justice," as Rosenberg here defines it, seems to mean either the present pattern of results (thus Zeisel's split trials are unconscionable because the results change) or the present low-pressure procedures. But every empirical investigation (see Chapter 7) demonstrates that the present pattern of results cannot be made to fit into any reasonable definition of "justice"; and the argument that current procedures may not be speeded up without damage to "justice" is available on an abstract level to the opponents of every change—it was used by those in England who sought to perpetuate the system which produced *Jarndyce* v. *Jarndyce*.

Losing litigants after any procedure do not normally feel they have been near the heartbeat of justice; they feel they have been rooked, however elaborate the hearing; if they thought "justice" called for them to lose, they would never have gone to court in the first place. The battle aspects of a trial, moreover, do not really appeal to anybody's sense of justice; too much depends on the skill of the advocates and the luck of the draw. "Every trial lawyer is a ham," says Gerald Aksen, who defended personal-injury cases for some years before he became general counsel of the American Arbitration Association. "He gets such a bang out of winning—particularly the cases he shouldn't win."

What Rosenberg and Botein and Mrs. Virtue are so ardently defending can also be seen as Learned Hand saw it a generation ago:

[N]o rules in the end will help us. We shall succeed in making our results conform with our professions only by a change of heart in ourselves. It is hard to expect lawyers who are half litigants to forego the advantages which come from obscuring the case and supporting contentions which they know to be false. . . . It is important nevertheless that we should realize the price we pay for it, the atmosphere of contention over trifles, the unwillingness to concede what ought to be conceded, and to proceed to the things which matter. Courts have fallen out of repute; many of you avoid them whenever you can, and rightly. About trials hang a suspicion of trickery and a sense of a result depending upon cajolery or worse. I wish I could say that it was all unmerited. After now some dozen years of experience I must say that as a litigant I should dread a lawsuit beyond almost anything else short of sickness and death.

Nobody has seriously suggested that in civil questions, where both sides are usually more or less right, the all-or-nothing, black-or-white determination required by legal proceedings gives a high order of justice.

About the only intelligible definition of justice in personal-injury damage claims is a monetary award that matches the community's sense of a fair allocation of the losses from a specific piece of bad luck. This community sense varies from time to time and from place to place, as any study of jury awards instantly reveals. It is pure word magic to say that under these circumstances justice is more likely to be achieved for a litigant through a trial, which can fall anywhere in the statistical spectrum, than through negotiations by alert and experienced people who know the averages.

The notion that litigants want the present system and would feel aggrieved if they got anything else is fairly conclusively contradicted by the fact that every group of litigants who have had the chance to do so—the businessmen, the labor unions, the theatrical producers and actors, the writers and publishers, etc.—have withdrawn the making of decisions about their contracts from the purview of the courts. An article by a *plaintiff's* lawyer in the *American Bar Association Journal* has proposed removal of medical malpractice suits to arbitration. When the community grows really upset about a problem—the break-up of the family structure, for example —one of the first steps taken is to remove it from the jurisdiction of the traditional courts. Judge Botein has noted "the contagion of indifference, at times approaching disdain, for the forms of judicial trial. How long will the guarantees of the trial process remain vital if other processes, dealing with comparable problems, demonstrate the dispensability of these guarantees?" The answer is, not long— unless the courts bestir themselves to search out what *should* be indispensable and to discard as much as possible of the rest. There will be surprises for everyone once that game is begun.

To say that judges in Botein's blockbuster parts are blackjacking settlements sounds bad, unless one can take a few steps farther back, away from lawyers' concerns, to a vantage point from which one can ask about the function of the civil court system as a whole. *Sub specie aeternitatis,* after all, a judgment in a civil law suit is nothing but a blackjacked settlement, with the state wielding the blackjack. Society supports courts and judges and the accouterments of law so that there will be a place where disputes are settled by an impartial authority who is not influenced by differences in the power and position of the litigants—the ultimate objection, by the way, to arbitration, which normally takes place on the stronger party's home territory according to the rules he was strong enough to dictate into the contract. Neither the society nor the litigants as a class are asking for exact justice (nobody has the faintest notion of what that would be, anyway); everybody except the lawyers and the judges and a neurotic fraction of litigious citizens simply wants to keep life and business going, and sees "the primary purpose of law" as Llewellyn saw it, "to settle disputes which do not otherwise get settled." The lawyers and the judges and the law professors are—or should be—performing a service for society, not engaging in a private search for abstract verities.

CHAPTER 14

THE PERSONALITY OF THE JUDGE

"There is no guarantee of justice except the personality of the judge. . . . [T]he greatest task that can be given a man to discharge, justice, requires a standard of mental and moral greatness far above the common average."

—EUGEN EHRLICH

"Let us face this sad fact: that in many—in far too many—instances, the benches of our courts in the United States are occupied by mediocrities—men of small talent, undistinguished in performance, technically deficient and inept."

—SAMUEL I. ROSENMAN, former judge, adviser to Presidents Roosevelt and Truman, speaking as president of the Association of the Bar of the City of New York, October, 1964

"A judge's life, like any other, has in it much of drudgery, senseless bickering, stupid obstinacies, captious pettifogging, all disguising and obstructing the only sane purpose which can justify the whole endeavor. These take an inordinate part of his time: they harass and befog the bench where like any other workman he must do his work. If that were all, his life would be mere misery, and he a distracted arbiter between irreconcilable extremes. But there is something else that makes it—anyway, to those curious creatures

[488]

*who persist in it—a delectable calling. For when the case is all in,
and the turmoil stops, and after he is left alone, things begin
to take form. From his pen or in his head, slowly or swiftly as his
capacities admit, out of the murk the pattern emerges, his pattern,
the expression of what he has seen and what he has therefore made,
the impress of his self upon the not-self, upon the hitherto formless
material of which he was once but a part and over which he has
now become the master. That is a pleasure which nobody who has
felt it will be likely to underrate."*

—LEARNED HAND

*"If I had me job to pick out," said Mr. Dooley, "I'd be a judge.
I've looked over all th' others an' that's th' on'y wan that suits. I
have th' judicyal timperamint. I hate wurruk."*

—MR. DOOLEY

1

The legislatures keep control over the procedural rules; the
juries deliver general verdicts which express the law (for this case)
as well as the facts; and even when the trial judge sits alone, his
ultimate decision merely ranks as that of a one-man jury. The law
he finds is for this case only—the opinion of a trial judge has little
value as precedent. And in his findings of law he is controlled, as
the jury is not, by legislative statute or appellate court ruling, or
both. "I feel," Kierkegaard wrote in *Either/Or*, "as if I were a piece
in a game of chess, when my opponent says of it: That piece cannot
be moved." One would expect the trial judge to share Kierkegaard's
existential frustration. But he doesn't.

About the trial judge are the trappings of power. He wears a robe.
The state often supplies parking for his car, and a grand license
plate. The court rises when he enters, his entrance impressively
announced. He sits behind an imposing desk on a raised platform,
with flags behind him. He is master of his courtroom far beyond
the imaginings of the most lordly corporate executive cozening his
yes-men. (Judge Botein tells a story about the day he was to deliver
his first charge to a jury, and grew absorbed in some cases he

thought he should read first: "I did not arrive in the robing room until 10:15 A.M. I had adjourned court the preceding afternoon until 10 A.M. 'I'm pretty late,' I said, as I was being helped into my robe. 'I'll apologize to the jurors and counsel for keeping them waiting.' 'Judge,' said the clerk, 'I hope you won't think I'm speaking out of turn. But when you've been here as long as I have you'll know that no matter what time the judge enters the courtroom, it's ten o'clock.' ") In court he is addressed as "Your Honor," and even outside the court some special aura attaches to his presence—and should. He is literally a judge over his people, and the phrase retains its Biblical connotations.

Nor is his power so restricted as a mere reading of the rules might indicate. Where he sits without a jury, of course, he decides the issues; his findings of fact are in most jurisdictions not reviewable by anybody, and to protect them from appellate interference he will come as close as the rules allow to a jury-like "general verdict" intermixing fact and law, to give appellate judges the least possible handle on him. The appellate judges often regard this practice as sheer dereliction of duty, but there is a lot to be said for it: the judge is not making law but deciding a case in which he has heard the evidence. Federal Judge Joseph C. Hutcheson, Jr., in a paper with the title "The Judgment Intuitive: The Function of the Hunch in Judicial Decision," once wrote that a judge "does and should decide difficult and complicated cases only when he has the feeling of the decision. . . . This hunch, sweeping aside hesitancy and doubt, takes the judge vigorously on to his decision; and yet, the cause decided, the way thither, which was for the blinding moment, a blazing trail, becomes wholly lost to view." Judges are entitled to respect from higher courts and from law professors for what Hutcheson calls "opinions lighted and warmed by the feeling which produced them," even if they are not rock solid on the law. On the other side of the same coin, however, negligence lawyer Harry Gair says that "the idiosyncrasies of a judge can create a lot of injustice uncorrectable on appeal."

Even when findings of fact are to be made by a jury, the trial judge by rulings on motions and in pretrial conferences largely determines which of the issues between the parties shall be tried by the jury (and therefore what kind of settlement is likely to be offered or accepted). Once the trial begins, his rulings on the admissibility of evidence determine which facts shall be considered in arriving at a judgment. To the extent that juries are bound by law, he tells the jury what the law is. In criminal cases he may dismiss criminal charges on the motion of defense counsel (though only a jury can convict). In many civil cases he is empowered to dismiss a suit or even in some courts to direct a verdict for plaintiff; and in most jurisdictions he can set aside a jury verdict as contrary to the weight of the evidence. If a jury has brought in what looks to him like an unconscionable award in a damage suit, in many states he can reduce it, offering plaintiff a choice between a new trial or acceptance of the reduced judgment. (In most jurisdictions, however, he cannot increase it—five Justices of the Supreme Court in 1935 ruled that a judge who increased an award deprived a defendant of his right to trial by jury.) All these rulings are subject to review on appeal, and in the new dispensation rapidly increasing numbers of criminal convictions *are* appealed. The clerk of an appellate court reports that recent decisions allowing prisoners nonstop appeals have produced a new kind of prerelease training for ambitious prison inmates. "You get a batch of motions in the same handwriting, from a guy who's amassing a fund for when he gets out by acting as house counsel."

Still, appeals are expensive (in jurisdictions where the entire record of the trial must be printed, usually in at least fifty copies, the printing bill alone can easily run into four figures, and in one recent case in the federal courts the cost of printing the record was $100,000). In most state courts a rather small minority of civil cases, perhaps one in ten, will be appealed. Even then, if the verdict looks about right, the appellate court may overlook "trivial" errors in rulings by the trial judge.

But you can never be sure. Judge Jerome Frank liked to say that the theory of a trial was $R \times F = D$ (Rules times Facts equals Decisions). If a judge gives a jury "the wrong R, then, in theory, the D —their verdict—must logically be wrong. Lawyers thus set traps for trial judges. Decisions, in cases which have taken weeks to try, are reversed on appeal because a phrase, or a sentence, meaningless to the jury, has been included or omitted from the charge." Judge Botein wrote about a group of judges praising a certain lawyer, and the highest praise was: "You can go to sleep when he's questioning a witness. He always protects the record." This lawyer, in other words, would not try so hard to win that he would get in evidence which would later make an appellate court throw out the trial. Even more dangerous to the judge are lawyers who are not really trying to win. The more of a circus a lawyer with a losing case can make of the trial, the better his chances will be that an appellate court will refuse to sustain the verdict. This happens, too—every day.

Though a lawyer must object at the moment of introduction of evidence if he wishes to appeal later on the grounds that it was inadmissible, judges will often supervise these matters even when counsel defaults. ("Does your learned friend know what you're introducing?") Documents must be relevant to a point at issue in the trial and material to some line of argument the lawyer is permitted to pursue, and they cannot be introduced at all unless someone who can be cross-examined certifies their authenticity. Witnesses must not testify as to their opinion (unless they are "expert witnesses"), cannot say what somebody told them ("hearsay"), may be required to respond directly to a lawyer's questions and so on, through the important rigmarole of the rules of evidence familiar, in bastardized form, to anyone who goes to movies or watches television.

Throughout this process, to a greater extent than most people realize, the trial judge is fairly seriously embattled. Decisions on the admissibility of evidence arise constantly, every few minutes, and the problem is often unexpected and intrinsically confusing. Impartiality itself does not help much—quite apart from the fact that, as Lord Hewart observed, "the only impartiality possible to the human mind is that which arises from an understanding of neither side of the case." A judge cannot be prepared for the cases he tries; his matters come up to him in no rational sequence—"like a circus parade," says California's Chief Justice Roger J. Traynor.

In a Detroit courtroom, for example, Judge Charles Farmer was observed wrestling with the evidentiary value of a certificate from Michigan's Secretary of State that he could *not* find a defendant's papers of incorporation in the files. Plaintiff's lawyer objected loudly that while the Secretary of State could by mail testify that a given document was as described, he could not testify without possibility of cross-examination that a document had not been received: "I want to ask him what sort of search was made." There was no precedent; the Secretary of State *always* finds these papers on file. And the situation is ticklish; a wrong ruling here could easily be grounds for reversal.

"Most of the time," federal Judge Charles E. Wyzanski, Jr. has written about the problems of the trial judge, "we do not see the points of difficulty too clearly. With us the pace is quicker, the troublesome issues have not been sorted from those which go by rote, the briefs of counsel have not reached their ultimate perfection." The trial judge asks counsel, "Do you have any law for me on this?" but all he can do is browse the statute or the case proffered to him across the bench; he cannot, like an appellate judge, reserve judgment for long contemplation on the admissibility of evidence from a witness who has other things to do in this world; he has to decide quickly.

And for all the pressure, the repetitive nature of the business may make it hard for a judge to stay alert. "It's so boring," says a law school professor, "to listen to all those personal-injury cases." (There is respectable dissenting opinion here: Judge William Grimes of New Hampshire's Superior Court, now elevated to his state's supreme court, said, "Roughly seventy-five percent of all my time on the bench goes to personal-injury cases. There's an interesting twist to every one.") A Massachusetts lawyer says, "A good judge will really pay attention even though he's bored."

The pay is only fair. Federal district judges receive $30,000 a year, and in New York City the judges in the courts of general jurisdiction make $37,000 a year; but the average across the country is well under $20,000. State judges must often "ride circuit," holding court at different seasons in different county courthouses, which is often uncomfortable (though, one of them says, "The modern motel is a great boon to the circuit judge") and often lonely, because the natural acquaintance of a lawyer is other lawyers, and a judge on circuit usually shuns the local bar until the ceremonial dinner at the end of term. Many judges who thought they were permanent in one location have recently found they are on circuit, too, through the new power of court administrators to order manpower from a court with too little business to a court with too much.

All told, the society asks a good deal of the trial judge—a combination of independence, concentration, patience, decisiveness and efficiency. Where are we to find such people?

2

The Book of Blegywyrd (honest) describes the practice of King Hywel the Good of Wales in the tenth century:

If it is the King's wish to appoint as court judge a person uninitiated in and untrained in law, that person should remain in court with the King, questioning and listening to judges during their visits from the country to the King's court, acquainting himself with the laws and customs and procedures and the King's authorized rulings, and above all the Three Columns of Law, and the value of all domesticated animals, and of the wild beasts with which men are concerned, and listening to plaintiffs and defendants in disputations, and to be in the presence of the judges when they give their verdicts, and to hear their deliberations, and to be attentive when they refer matters to the King because they are in doubt and desire his clarification. Let him spend a whole year in this manner. Then the King's chaplain should take him to the Church, together with the twelve leading officers of the court, to hear Mass, and after the Mass, and an offering having been made to each one present, may the chaplain cause him to swear on the relics, and the altar, and the consecrated elements on the altar, that he will never knowingly give false judgment by yielding to any entreaty or bribe, and neither from the love nor the hatred of any person.

On the European continent a student in law school decides whether he wishes to be an advocate or a judge. If he is to be a judge, he rises through the administrative process rather than through private practice, acquiring at each stage skills and information that will suit him to sit on a bench. In Britain the judges are drawn entirely from the limited ranks of barristers (there are only two thousand of them in all England), and the appointments are made by the Lord Chancellor, who is in a position to know about the candidates. (Sometimes he even knows better. "When Chancellor

Lyndhurst was asked what method he used in making judicial appointments, he replied, 'I look about for a gentleman, and if he knows a little law so much the better.' ") In the United States, as Philadelphia's judge and novelist Curtis Bok once put it, "It has been said that a judge is a member of the Bar who once knew a Governor."

The most likely route to an American judgeship is through a prosecuting attorney's office, and the second most likely is through a state legislature or Congress. Some political activity is almost required; even in the federal system and in states like Massachusetts and Virginia, where appointments to the bench are made by an executive or by a legislature, the choice is normally between people who are known by political leaders to be candidates. (A fine example, of course, was President Johnson's nomination of Francis X. Morrissey, whose only noticeable qualification for the role was his friendship with the Kennedy family.) Only in California, under a succession of remarkably responsible governors from Hiram Johnson to Earl Warren to Pat Brown, has there been a sustained effort to search the bar as a whole, including in the search men who were not looking for the job, before appointing a judge. And in most states, of course, judges are chosen for full terms only at a general election, and must be re-elected at intervals, sometimes (though rarely) intervals as short as two years.

The election requirement is unquestionably a problem. As Justice Lummus of the Massachusetts Supreme Court wrote, "There is no certain harm in turning a politician into a judge. He may be or become a good judge. The curse of the elective system is the converse, that it turns almost every judge into a politician." The words "courthouse gang" refer to the entire system of county political leadership, which has its offices in the courthouse, but judges are normally regarded as part and parcel of what goes on in their courthouses.

The original Canons of Judicial Ethics adopted by the American Bar Association in 1924 called upon judges to "avoid making political speeches, making or soliciting payment of assessments or contributions to party funds, the public endorsement of candidates for political office and participation in party conventions." In 1951, in a rather humiliating retreat, the ABA had to add the sentence, "Where, however, it is necessary for judges to be nominated and elected as candidates of a political party, nothing herein contained shall prevent the judge from attending or speaking at political gatherings, or from making contributions to the campaign funds of the party that has nominated him and seeks his election or reelection." It is generally believed in New York that a contribution of at least $10,000 to a political party is necessary before anyone will be nominated for a judgeship. Across the country, it is quite common for judges not only to be politically active but to run for other office; in 1966, a justice of the Supreme Court of Pennsylvania was a candidate in the Democratic gubernatorial primary, and a justice of the Arkansas Supreme Court ran (as "Judge Jim") for governor.

It is important to pinpoint the real difficulties that come with this political orientation. The worst of them, of course, traces to the fact that the machinery of the political parties is largely controlled by men who are lawyers; and that a judge who is dependent on political favor for the retention of his position (original appointment is far less important) always lies under the suspicion that he can be "reached" by certain of the counsel who practice before him. Less disturbing but nontrivial is the quantity of patronage available to a judge through appointments of special guardians for minors, trustees, receivers and the like; the politically oriented judge (which can easily include judges in the federal system: remember the bankruptcy rings) may become in effect the center of all the political dealing in town. Finally, there is the loss of potential judicial talent because lawyers who might make first-rate judges refuse to serve on courts which operate in an ambiance of political involvement.

Some of the choices made by this process are obviously unsuitable. Every jurisdiction has its favorite stories—the misogynist who won't allow women to wear lipstick in his courtroom, the conservative who rules that wills signed with a ball-point pen are void, the drunk who leans over the bench and hooks a cigar out of the pocket of the lawyer who has come up for a conference (all these are real incidents), the prosecutor in robes. Timothy Pfeiffer of

Milbank, Tweed tells of a difficult moment when his partner, A. Donald MacKinnon, found himself in the strange surroundings of a Brooklyn trial court before Judge Cropsey (after whom a boulevard in Brooklyn was later named). "Plaintiff's counsel began by asking MacKinnon whether he would concede a fact covered by the stipulation. MacKinnon replied that the concession was embraced in the stipulation. Cropsey looked at MacKinnon over his bifocals and said, 'Do you or don't you concede it?' To the reply that it was conceded in the manner stated in the stipulation, Cropsey shouted, 'Sit down. We'll see who's lying here.' "

Timidity can be worse than arrogance. Columbia's Harry W. Jones comments, "The evil that weak judges do, less often from partiality, as commonly supposed, than from simple psychic inability to stand up to abrasive or strong-willed leaders of the bar, is a bitter but largely untold story in the administration of justice." Often the judge has little interest in what the profession is pleased to call the leading edge of the law; Justice Robert H. Jackson liked to tell of the time when, as a young lawyer before an upstate New York judge, he cited in his support a case newly decided by the Supreme Court, and handed up the advance sheets to prove his point. The judge handed them back, glaring, and said, "I don't take no law from no magazines."

"Judge Burnell," a California appellate court wrote in rebuke to a trial judge in its jurisdiction,

apparently delights in exhibitions calculated to deprive the court of the complacency, the disinterestedness, the zeal for truth, the judicial calm and mien indispensable to the avoidance of prejudicial error. The pronouncements of his personal opinions upon counsel and witness impair their efficacy as well as that of the court. Similar behavior by Judge Burnell has been the subject of many reversals during the past 24 years . . . without effecting a reform in his behavior or causing him to conform with orthodox judicial deportment.

In *The American Lawyer*, their 1954 summary of the ABA's "survey of the legal profession," Albert P. Blaustein and Charles O. Porter brought out without comment the fact that only 3 percent of the lawyers trained in law school were judges, while 7.9 percent of the lawyers not trained in law school were judges. Three unsophisticated social psychologists commented that "the bench clearly is not getting the lawyers with the best training."

But here one must call a halt. Judges tend to be older (out of 8,748 listed in *The 1964 Lawyer Statistical Report*, only 828 were under thirty-nine) and more rural (almost 5,000 were in towns of less than 50,000 population), and older and rural lawyers are less likely to have attended law school. Indeed, the end products of the political selection process are not nearly so bad as most legal intellectuals and reformers seem to think. "One of the things that laymen, even lawyers, do not always understand," Felix Frankfurter once said, "is indicated by the question you hear so often: 'Does a man become any different when he puts on a gown?' I say, 'If he is any good, he does.'"

Soia Mentschikoff of the University of Chicago Law School says, "It's true some of the state court judges aren't the brightest people in the world. Why should they be?" Brilliance is an almost impossible burden for a trial judge, who has to sit patiently on his bench while even the best lawyers draw information out of a witness at a pace suited to the slowest wit on the jury (and then sit patiently again while an incompetent hack attorney fails to draw any significant evidence at all out of *his* witness). One of the most deeply admired legal intelligences in the United States sits on a federal trial bench in Boston. Not long ago a Boston lawyer who had to try a case before him headed off gloomily toward the court (upstairs in the old Post Office Building) with the words, "I'd like to open with a statement to the bench: 'Your Honor, I hereby stipulate that you know more law than I do, that you are more conscious of the implications of this action than I am, that you are better acquainted than I am with the customs of my client's industry, and indeed that you understand his cause better than I do. Now will you please permit me to earn my living?' But of course I'll never have the nerve."

An old story tells of the lawyer whose witnesses were constantly being taken out of his hands by an impatient judge, and who grew alarmed at the judge's line of questioning. "Your Honor," he said, "I have no objection to your trying my case for me—but for God's sake don't *lose* it!" In the end, what counts is temperament, a sense of fairness, a willingness to decide—the personality of the judge.

For what trifling value it may have, I must testify that in nearly six years of wandering into courtrooms, and in interviews with some dozens of judges, I have found only one judge drunk in chambers and only one boorish in his courtroom. As a group, they have been courteous, serious, levelheaded, conscious of and proud of the honor their community has given them. As the late Joe Palmer once put it (writing admittedly of the Jockey Club rather than of the bench), you could not catch better men if you set a bear trap in the aisle of a cathedral.

But this is an area, one of very few, where belief and image are more important than reality—and there is no doubt that in several states (especially New York, Illinois and Pennsylvania) the bar is unhappy about its bench. During the late 1950s some clever lawyers in Pittsburgh got into the habit of appointing out-of-state administrators for the estates they represented, so that any substantial actions on behalf of the estate could be taken in federal court on grounds of diversity of citizenship. One out-of-state administrator had been appointed to thirty-three estates in the Pittsburgh area by 1959. Federal courts are not supposed to be involved in estates, and the American Law Institute in its 1963 meeting spent some time devising new rules for "division of jurisdiction" which would put a stop to the practice. At the meeting one lawyer from the area finally blurted, "In the State of Pennsylvania better justice can be obtained from the federal than from the state courts."

"When you have a monolithic machine," says a distinguished New York lawyer who is in daily contact with the courts, "the only way you get to be a judge is by running errands and kissing asses. The guys who've made the campaign contributions, who've helped to elect the judges, later feel they own 'em." Belief that the judges of the separate criminal court in New York are naturally corrupt (perhaps because they are paid $12,000 a year less than the judges of the court of general jurisdiction) has made their lives undignified and uncomfortable. They are shifted virtually without notice from borough to borough, denied a personal secretary, an assigned clerk or permanent chambers, all to isolate them from possible fixers. The cure may be worse than the disease.

Lawyers in other cities are shocked by the attitudes of lawyers from New York and Chicago. "A New York colleague will call to talk over tactics and strategy on something we're to try for him out here," says a partner in a very large Los Angeles firm. "I'll say it doesn't matter much which judge you get. Then they'll call at home —'Well, I understand you don't want to say it at the office.' Sometimes they'll wait until they see me, and they'll say, 'Now, I know, you're worried. Phone taps. But how do you *arrange* things in Los Angeles?' And I'll say, '*You can't arrange things in Los Angeles.*' Often they just don't believe me."

Part of being a trial lawyer anywhere is maneuvering to get on the calendar of the "right" judge; lawyers study judges as children study their teachers. As noted earlier, the patent lawyers carefully pick the circuit in which they will sue for a client who believes his patent has been infringed, and lawyers challenging a federal administrative agency will work their case into whatever circuit seems at the moment least sympathetic to administrative agencies. But the attitude in New York dangerously transcends this normal preference for one courtroom rather than another. Particularly when certain associate counsel are added to the opponent's roster—even in the appellate departments (though not in Botein's)—lawyers become downright frightened about what is going to happen to their client.

Two further observations are necessary: (1) that this fear usually turns out to be quite unwarranted (indeed, it seems to an outsider that the lawyers who worry that their opponent has got to the judge win a remarkably large share of their cases, perhaps because the worry is a function of a touch-all-bases intensive preparation); and (2) that lawyers in private practice never blow the whistle. Quite a number of New York lawyers now say that they knew seven or eight years before DA Thomas E. Dewey forced the issue that Martin T. Manton, presiding judge of the federal Circuit Court of Appeals, was a crook who was selling the judgments of his court to the extent that he could control them. But only one firm—Cravath—seems to have taken any action, and they went only to Judge John C. Knox, who was not empowered to look into the matter. There is much idle chatter about the danger to a lawyer's clients if he turns a judge against him by bringing charges, but there is no reason for the lawyer's identity to be known unless the case is proved: the DA's doors are open for private visits.

Estes Kefauver as chairman of a House Judiciary Subcommittee investigating federal Judge Albert W. Johnson, a notorious bribe-taker, announced that no bar association had been willing to help the committee: "Many times we would meet lawyers who would say, 'We know it is a rotten, crooked setup from beginning to end, but do not quote us, because we have to practice law here.'" Johnson escaped impeachment by resigning and forfeiting his pension rights (he later sued unsuccessfully to get them back); the House Judiciary Committee concluded that "the evidence presented . . . establishes conclusively that Judge Albert W. Johnson is guilty of such high crimes and misdemeanors as in the contemplation of the Constitution ordinarily require the interposition of the constitutional powers of impeachment of this House"; Johnson retreated prudently to a mental institution, then returned to the private practice of law; and presently one of the local bar associations in his State of Pennsylvania elected him its president. Some lawyers get the judges they deserve. Unfortunately, the public gets these judges, too. Law is a public profession, and surely lawyers are under some obligation not to punish the public by protecting the corrupt judge.

For some years it has been an article of faith with the American Bar Association and the American Judicature Society that the remedy for quality problems on the bench is removal of the office from politics, and appointment rather than election of judges. The preferred machinery, first tried out in 1940, is called "the Missouri Plan," and grows out of years of scandal in that state, where the judiciary was completely in the hands of the machine. Two Missouri lawyers have written of that time:

Only twice in the twenty-year period prior to the adoption of the Missouri Plan was a supreme court judge who had served a full term [of four years] reelected for another term. . . . Court dockets were congested, since even the efficient judges had to spend much time with their political affairs and campaigning. Unfortunately, some judges were influenced by political considerations, and many lawyers found it necessary to coemploy attorneys with political influence to offset possible political influence by the opposing party or his attorney. . . . Political reprisals were frequent. . . . At one time the judges in Kansas City refused to pay a 500-dollar assessment levied for campaign purposes. At the next session of the legislature, the judges' salaries were reduced by some 1,500 dollars a year in reprisal.

(This incident, by the way, demonstrates another piece of the wisdom of the Founding Fathers: their constitutional insistence that no federal judge's salary could be reduced during his continuance in office. The prohibition did, however, produce one entertaining abuse of judicial authority. When the Income Tax Amendment was passed and implemented, some federal judges sued to enjoin the government from collecting the tax from them, on the grounds that it would reduce their salary; and the Supreme Court in 1920 upheld them, in a rather embarrassing opinion overruled in 1939. Learned Hand said during the interregnum that this case had given him a working definition of Bolshevism: "A judge of much experience was talking with me one day about it; I was . . . disloyal enough in temper to my class, to say that I thought the tax valid. 'Do you know anything about it?' he asked with some asperity. 'No,' I said, 'not a thing.' 'Have you ever read Taney's letter?' 'No,' I said, for I was innocent of any learning. 'Why, they can't do that,' said he; 'they can't do that, that's Bolshevism.' ")

Missouri's substitute for political control, placed in the state constitution by referendum, provides for a nonpartisan, unpaid panel composed in equal numbers of lawyers appointed by the bar association and laymen appointed by the governor, to recommend candidates for a judicial vacancy. The panel gives the governor three names, and he must choose one of them. At the next general election more than one year from the date of the new appointment, the judge goes before the voters on a ballot which asks simply whether or not he should be retained in office—no opposing candidate is permitted. He then serves to retirement, assuming good behavior. No judge has ever lost such an election.

The plan has been restricted in its home state to judges of the state supreme court and courts of appeals, and the circuit courts for St. Louis and Kansas City. It has been adopted for all significant judicial offices in Alaska, and for some in Iowa, Kansas and Nebraska. In California, Illinois and Michigan sitting judges, whether appointed or elected originally, can be challenged only through a Missouri-style election. In New York City, on his own motion, Mayor Robert Wagner instituted a panel from the bar associations to suggest three names to him for interim appointments within his power, and bound himself to take one of the three—but thereafter the judge is on his own in an election. By and large, in the New England states and Virginia, judges are appointed by the governor or selected by the legislature, and serve for life. All federal judges are appointed by the President and confirmed by the Senate, and serve for life.

Neither the case against the elected judge nor the case for the appointed judge has really been proved. It is simply naïve to pretend that appointments eliminate politics; indeed, Riesman has argued that the federal appointment arrangement "is the source of much dirt in our political system, since many congressmen have partners who itch to be judges." Governors can appoint bad judges, too. (It was in Maine, where judges are appointed and within the memory of living men followed the English fashion of headdress, that a lawyer said after losing a case, "I know how that wig stays on his head: it's nailed on.") Fiorello LaGuardia's famous comment, "When I make a mistake it's a beaut," was delivered in reply to a question about why he had appointed a certain judge. Moreover, if judges are going to be appointed to serve for life, the thing should be done honestly, not through fake elections. Two Utah law professors have written scornfully:

The plebiscite in which the voters are given a choice between a definite proposal ("Should X be retained as a judge?") and an unnamed alternative they cannot control, is the most familiar window-dressing of despotism. "Shall Napoleon be Emperor of the French?" "Shall Louis Napoleon be Emperor of the French?" All such questions cannot but receive huge affirmative votes. . . . Under the Missouri Plan the participation of the voters in the strictest sense is meaningless.

The trial judge's job today is mostly to mediate between the parties in an accident case, grant divorces, assess the correct value of property seized by the state, control the behavior of the police through rulings to exclude evidence in criminal cases and sentence convicted criminals. It is hard to see why removal from concern with public opinion should improve a man's performance in these tasks.

Fairly fundamental to the theory of a democratic society is the notion that public officials are ultimately (though not at every moment) servants rather than masters of the community. Judges live in an atmosphere too insulated from this notion however they are appointed and maintained in office. Some means of challenging a judge on his performance is not necessarily harmful to justice. Some judicial contests, like the Democratic primary in the surrogate's race in New York in 1966, are significant contests of value to the community and to the bench.

The practical needs of the system are not a fancy method of appointing judges from a nondescript bar, but a means of training people who might become candidates for judicial jobs—and of removing those who turn out to be unsuited for the work. The latter problem is hell on wheels, because in most parts of the country the only effective remedy is publicity, forcing resignation, and the bar hates to promote bad publicity about judges. Justice Traynor says, "[A] bad man is as hard to lose, as a good man is hard to find." Philip T. Manly, legislative counsel for New Mexico, said he would strongly object to any effort to introduce the Missouri Plan into his state "because we have enough trouble getting rid of the nogoodnicks now."

Jefferson observed 160-odd years ago that "Experience has already shown that the impeachment the Constitution has provided is not even a scarecrow"—and by that time one of only three federal convictions on impeachment in the nation's history had already been registered. Karlen observes that the impeachment route, indictment by one house of a legislature and trial by the other, "is unsatisfactory for a number of reasons: first, because it tends to be overly political; second, because the procedure is cumbersome, consuming an undue amount of the time of men whose attention and energy should be directed elsewhere; third, because the grounds for impeachment are either excessively narrow, reaching only specified misconduct, or excessively broad and undefined; and finally, because the only sanction is the drastic one of removal."

One of the difficulties has been the failure of the federal system or about half of the state systems to provide compulsory retirement for judges. On the Supreme Court it was necessary for their colleagues to suggest retirement (in interviews of unimaginable delicacy) to both Justice McKenna and Justice Holmes, who had taken to sleeping through the arguments of counsel. The most common device to persuade superannuated judges to leave is a pension on full salary, continuation of free office space in the courthouse, retention of the title of "judge" and liability for continued service as a judge on assignment by the presiding judge of the court. As dockets are always crowded, a judge can then be told of the great favor he does his court by retiring—in effect, he will simply be adding another judge to their hard-pressed bench, because he can continue to serve while someone else is appointed to the chair from which he retires. Then, if you really want to get rid of him, you don't assign him any cases. The opportunities for deviousness in the situation are by no means conducive to calm deliberation in the courthouse.

Only four states—New York, New Jersey, Illinois and California —have any centralized means for disciplining judges, and of the four only California has really designed a procedure to meet the problem. There, constitutional amendment in 1960 set up a Commission on Judicial Qualifications with five judges appointed by the state supreme court, two lawyers appointed by the state bar and two laymen appointed by the governor. The Commission's doors are open at all seasons. In the biennium 1964-65, there were 152 complaints (the Commission has powers of scrutiny over 1,100 judges). Seventy complaints resulted in inquiries, and in forty-seven of them the judges themselves were "contacted," and the upshot was ten resignations or retirements. The other thirty-seven, presumably, involved cases where, as Chief Justice Traynor puts it, "the circumstances do not warrant retirement or removal," and "the Commission communicates with the judge without publicity by way of informal warning." If the judge decides to face the music rather than resign or retire, he is entitled to a hearing before the state supreme court; to date there has been only one such hearing. Something of this sort should surely be part of the administrative machinery of every state, and of the federal court system. Everybody performs better when he feels he is being watched by people he respects.

But removal is only half the scissors, and the less important half.

"Before 1956," Delmar Karlen of the Institute of Judicial Administration writes,

the only training available to American judges was on-the-job training. A man was a lawyer one day and a full-fledged judge the next. Everyone seemed content to operate on the assumption that the donning of judicial robes made a man competent to perform all the duties of office. . . . Today there is almost unanimous agreement that judges need special skills and attitudes that were not necessarily part of their equipment as practicing lawyers, and that they can be helped to acquire these skills and attitudes through schools for judges.

The first two-week seminars at the NYU Law School in 1956 were held for judges serving on appellate courts, which struck Justice Tom C. Clark of the Supreme Court as unresponsive to the problem. Under the sponsorship of a Joint Committee for the Effective Administration of Justice, which Clark helped form, a number of three-day seminars were held from 1961 to 1963, reaching (in the judgment of the sponsors) almost half the trial judges in American courts of general jurisdiction. Starting in 1964, a much more ambitious program, a four-week summer course, has been in operation under the direction of the National College of State Trial Judges, which is a remote wing of the American Bar Association. The course, taught mostly by experienced judges with a leavening of law professors, deals with the management of pretrial conferences, the application of rules of evidence, the use of pattern jury instructions and the sentencing of convicts—but every judge brings his own problems. For the first two years, home base was the University of Colorado; the project is now funded by the Fleischmann Foundation of Nevada, and has moved its headquarters to Reno, which is rather an odd thought. Capacity in 1966 was two hundred judges, one hundred each at Boulder and at Reno, and an East Coast session in 1967 expanded the total enrollment to three hundred. Justice Clark is chairman of the board.

By comparison with the elaborate training and long apprenticeship of European judges, the college looks like too little and too late. Except in New York City, where judges newly elected to the court of general jurisdiction in 1966 were required to attend a two-week institute, the training has always been optional; and many of those judges who need it most will not attend. Perhaps the bar associations and the Supreme Court Justices, who have been so ardent for the Missouri Plan, might achieve more over the long run if they established a continuing academic and apprenticeship program for lawyers who would like to be judges, and restricted nominations for the bench (by a political party or a select committee) to lawyers who had successfully completed such a program. The bar has always accepted the idea that a man who wants to be a judge should work for it; work in a training program would seem to be more suitable than the work of politicking, either in the public arena or in the bar association.

3

Perhaps because the lawyers distrust the trial judges, perhaps because (as the composer Virgil Thomson argues) an "American propensity toward putting off decision has made us a pencil-and-eraser civilization," there has grown up in all but seven states in this country the remarkable doctrine that every losing litigant or convicted defendant is entitled "as of right" to an appeal of the judgment against him. There are probably more appellate judges in the United States than in all the other countries of the world put together. A few statistics: New York State alone (counting the federal Court of Appeals that sits in the city) has more than twice as many appellate judges as England, and Judge Botein's court alone disposes of more appeals than the entire English appellate system.

Whenever the sociologists ask the public to build its little status trees, the appellate court judges are always at the very tiptop. There are about six hundred of them, slightly more than half sitting in "supreme courts," the rest in the intermediate appellate courts which have been forced into existence by the pressure of work in the more litigious states and in the federal system. Generally, appellate judges like trial judges are elected, but the nexus is different, because the public takes the job seriously and a poor candidate for an appellate bench will reflect on political leaders as a poor candidate for a trial bench will not. (Riesman suggests that Tammany "has made a tacit deal with the leaders of the bar to toss them the New York Court of Appeals, where the prestige lies, while holding on to the lower courts, where the money lies.") Very few lawyers would not accept appointment to a federal court of appeals or nomination to the supreme court of their own state, let alone the United States Supreme Court.

Appellate procedure is simple in most jurisdictions. Upon the delivery of the sentence or the award, the losing side files notice of appeal, and moves to suspend the effect of the decision pending the result of the appeal. Within a period of time determined by statute (usually between thirty and ninety days) the "appellant" must file with the appellate court a transcript of the record of the trial, or (recently, in some jurisdictions) of that part of the record on which his appeal rests, plus a "brief" outlining where the trial judge went wrong in his preliminary rulings on the law, his rulings on motions to exclude or admit evidence, his charge to the jury or (where permitted) his failure to set aside the verdict. Sad experience has made most appellate courts restrict briefs on appeal to fewer than fifty pages. The brief must be served on opposing counsel, who will enter an answering brief, and in some courts the appellant then has the right to submit a reply to the answer.

Sometimes the court is asked to rule entirely on the basis of these papers; much more often, the lawyers want a chance to argue their case before the bench. American appellate courts do not allow lawyers to read from their briefs or from the record as part of the argument. In Britain lawyers take days in open court doing nothing else: "[N]o one would ever dream," Lord Jowitt said, "that if they just left it to us to read [the record] we should ever do so."

Arguing an appeal is a special art, because the aim is to get the judges to rule your way on a point of law by stressing all the cases and statutes that support your position; but the argument really must be that the facts in the case favor your client. John W. Davis once wrote about a case where a lawyer, challenging an action of the Interstate Commerce Commission before the Supreme Court, plunged headlong into a discussion of the powers of the commission, and after he had talked for some twenty-five minutes, the Chief Justice leaned over and said in his blandest tone, "Now, Mr. So-and-so, won't you please tell us what this case is about? We could follow you so much better. . . ." The court wants above all things to learn what are the facts which give rise to the call upon its energies; for in many, probably in most, cases when the facts are clear there is no great trouble about the law.

Justice Jackson agreed: "The purpose of a hearing is that the Court may learn what it does not know, and it knows least about the facts. It may sound paradoxical, but most contentions of law are won or lost on the facts. . . . A large part of the time of conference is given over to discussion of facts, to determine under what rule of law they fall." But Jackson added a warning: "Counsel must remember that the function of the Supreme Court is to decide only questions of law. If the appellant, or petitioner, attempts or so puts his facts that he appears to be attempting, to reargue a verdict or findings of fact, he will meet with an embarrassing judicial impatience." The situation obviously offers great opportunities for falling between two stools.

Appellate argument differs from argument at a trial in the conciseness, the scholarship and the level of contention expected from the lawyers. In most courts, oral argument is restricted to about half an hour for each side; there isn't enough time for more if the docket is to be cleared. Though facts are crucial, they can be used only to demonstrate that the case fits into patterns which were decided in a certain way by this court in the past; citations are inescapable. The time goes not to arguing with opposing counsel, but to arguing with the bench, which interrupts to ask questions, sometimes very rough questions. (But, Jackson said, "[T]here should be some comfort derived from any question from the bench. It is clear proof that the inquiring Justice is not asleep.") No successful appellate lawyer simply argues his own case; he must also be a master of the case for the other side, and must take it seriously. "Sometimes, reading the briefs," says California's Chief Justice Traynor, "you get the feeling that the lawyer considers himself in the dentist's chair, trying to get away from the drill. But he must meet the cases on the other side, because the court is going to have to meet them."

Many appellate judges are badly overworked, because the case load is heavy and the job is hard. "In deciding a case," Traynor says, "you simply have to read the reporter's transcript of the trial. You can read the preliminary skirmishing rapidly, but you have to read it to get the feel of the case. The most difficult thing an appellate judge has to do is make up his mind—sometimes you wonder why such miserable human beings are involved in such a beautiful case. The next most difficult is to explain as forthrightly as you can why the fellow who is losing the case has lost it." These are, of course, *collegial* decisions, the view of a majority of three or five or seven or nine judges, who are influenced by each other's arguments in conference and by the internal memoranda of the court as much as by the arguments of the lawyers. The public output of the appellate courts varies enormously from jurisdiction to jurisdiction—in one year not long ago, the range was from 3.57 opinions per judge in Virginia to 78.6 in Kentucky.

In some courts the burden is impossibly heavy. Looking at 1949, when the case load was about 20 percent smaller than it is now, Delmar Karlen calculated that the reading burden on the judges of New York's First Appellate Department was 309,750 pages a year.

Even superior readers, reading for relatively short periods, dealing with merely college level material and satisfied with 80 per cent comprehension, average only 340 words per minute. . . .

If each judge, operating at that fantastic rate of speed, read every record in its entirety as well as every brief in every case in which he participated, it would take him 4,555 hours. That would be more than twelve hours per day for 365 days of the year, including Saturdays, Sundays and holidays. The time so spent would be exclusive of time spent in preparing for and sitting in conference (all day almost every Monday during court terms), listening to arguments (10 afternoons per month on an average), writing opinions (there were 250 written in 1949), deciding motions (there were 1,226 in 1949 [about 1,800 in 1966]), etc.

Karlen's figures deal with the busiest appellate court in the country—and an intermediate court, which need not be quite so concerned that its rulings will make law hard to overturn by normal processes. Still, one of the most important functions of an intermediate court is to get the issues stated clearly for the benefit of the final appellate court. Learned Hand, in his tribute to his colleague Judge Thomas W. Swan, remembered the passage of *Erie* v. *Tompkins* through the Second Circuit:

That involved a tort committed in Pennsylvania, whose common law on the point was different from the great body of decisions elsewhere. At first we were going to follow the Pennsylvania decisions, for we did not know the others, and the briefs—as is so often the case—were inadequate. After much delving, [Swan] found that, if we were to apply the "general law"—as we were then bound to do in a "diversity case"—the Pennsylvania rule did not govern; and so we held and were reversed by the epoch-making volte face of the Supreme Court. Had it not been for his hypertrophied judicial conscience, who shall say that we might not still be worshipping the Golden Calf of Swift v. Tyson.

Hand's speculation was better than he knew, for Chief Justice Hughes' papers were still locked up when he wrote. Later it became known that when the application for certiorari came to the Supreme Court with Swan's opinion, Hughes laid the documents on the conference table with the words, "If we wish to overrule *Swift* v. *Tyson*, here is the opportunity."

Under the subway-rush conditions that prevail in the First Appellate Department's carved and painted, wonderfully ornate courtroom on old Madison Square, even so distinguished a bench as Botein and his colleagues cannot hope to apply this level of scholarship to the matters before them. Indeed, though they write much more than their brothers in the Second Department across the river in Brooklyn, they affirm mostly *per curiam,* by the court, without any opinion at all, and the vast bulk of the opinions are brief memoranda.

In January, 1966, Chief Justice Joseph Weintraub of New Jersey ordered his intermediate appellate courts to stop writing opinions, "in order to cope with the heavy backlog of appeals." Weintraub noted that writing a decision and its reasons "could take a man a week or two. The judge may have to read interminably to determine all the nuances when writing an opinion." But if opinions are not to be published—if the case has no value as a precedent for similar cases in the jurisdiction—what is the function of the appeal? To keep the trial judges honest? There should be cheaper ways than that.

Botein's court, despite general feeling to the contrary, believes its memoranda do have nearly all the values of a more formal opinion. "We give the reasons," Botein says. "Sometimes it seems cryptic—

but it's good enough for Shepard's." The time saved in writing is spent for the benefit of the litigants: this court, with eight judges five of whom will sit on any given case, is a miracle of hard work. "All of us read all the briefs in advance," Botein says. "The bar now knows it. When we come to conference that Monday, we've all worked it."

Even in Botein's court, where decision-making is fully collegial, one judge must be assigned by the court to work out a memorandum statement of the court's reasons for its actions. The important factor is that nobody knows until after the conference who is going to have that responsibility, so everyone must be prepared. When the case goes up from the Appellate Division to the New York Court of Appeals (the state's supreme court), however, it is assigned on the arrival of the papers to one of the justices (simply the next one of the seven in line). That justice prepares a memorandum statement of what the case is about, which is internally circulated on the bench. After the oral argument, says Stanley H. Fuld, the state's new, gentle, scholarly, much-admired Chief Justice (he was nominated by all four parties, including both Liberal and Conservative), "the decision falls to that judge. His is the initial responsibility. He writes a report on the case and circulates it. Not every judge has the full burden in every case."

Procedures similar to this one are the norm in the state supreme courts. There is much to be said for them. They free a judge's time for reading and contemplation and the production of reasoned opinion. It is hard to see how Chief Justice Traynor, for example, could ever read the trial records to get the "feel" of the cases if he had to do so for every case that comes up. Such procedures also enable the members of the court to pick and choose the areas where they will intervene without reducing a supreme court to a group of specialists. After each judge sees a memorandum and a draft opinion, he can decide for himself whether he wishes to look into the matter more deeply rather than go along with his colleague.

In a well-run appellate court it is often true that, as Traynor puts it, the draft opinion "travels a hard road. . . . There are often cumulative intramural memoranda, sharpening the issues, sometimes compelling reassignment if the majority shifts. . . . Such a tempering process is that of a group, not that of a justice alone. One who takes part in it knows the marks of battle in the opinions that bear his name." It is also true, as Fuld points out, that "in eighty to eighty-five percent of the cases there can be only one result." (Cardozo once wrote that "cases where one route and only one is possible . . . make up in bulk what they lack in interest.") But only an optimist can argue as Geoffrey Hazard, Jr. has argued, that these initial memoranda are circulated among the judges merely "to facilitate their reading of the briefs and record and their other preparation for oral argument." The memoranda typically substitute for the reading of the briefs and record.

Arthur Vanderbilt objected violently to this division of responsibility on any appellate bench, calling it "a fraud on the litigant and on the public." Judge Frederick Hamley has protested that "It is contrary to the basic concept of appellate procedure to have the judgment of one trial court judge subject to affirmance or reversal by one appellate court judge." Yet, given the volume of appeals, the choice seems to be between cases which nobody has looked into very thoroughly and cases which rely for decision fundamentally upon the work of the one member of the bench who has studied the matter exhaustively.

Of course, it is possible to take too seriously the lengthy opinions of the state supreme courts. Like other courts, the appellate courts primarily decide cases, and the argumentative stretches in the opinions are *obiter dicta*, incidental words, of no necessary authority. The lawyer who brings a case hoping to establish a point of law (or the organization that submits a brief *amicus curiae*, "friend of the court," for that purpose) will often be disappointed even if he wins. Harrison Tweed tells a story of complaining to Judge Crane of the New York Court of Appeals ("who was rather more practical than intellectual") that a paragraph in an opinion in a case Tweed had won left in a confused state the point his firm had hoped to clear up by taking the appeal. "I learned a lot when I remonstrated with him in chambers. . . . I had the temerity to suggest that the paragraph be dropped out in the final official opinion. Judge Crane told me very good-naturedly: 'The trouble with you lawyers is that you pay too much attention to what we say in our opinions. I had to put that paragraph in to secure a majority in your favor.' I remonstrated no more."

Still, the ultimate fascination of these courts, for laymen and lawyers, is that in their mysterious way they make law. Their rulings as expressed in their opinions are binding on the "inferior" courts within their jurisdiction, and in the case of the supreme courts they have an ultimate power to declare legislation or administrative action unconstitutional by either the state or the federal constitution. Indeed, in their role as lawmakers, they are often excused the responsibility of deciding individual cases; without considering the merits of a case they can reverse a decision and remand for a new trial on the grounds that the judge erred in admitting or excluding evidence or delivered an erroneous charge to the jury.

The origins of this odd doctrine of irresponsibility to the case are little studied, because American lawyers believe it to be a natural phenomenon rather than a local invention. In Britain an appellate court renders a final decision; if it considers the judge's error sufficiently serious, it simply changes the result. Though British high courts can now remand, the notion that a criminal appeal can lead to a new trial still horrifies many. This odd procedure of remanding for a new trial means that cases can bounce back and forth for quite a while between trial court and appellate court; together with the delay in processing appeals (rarely less than nine months in any jurisdiction from the date of filing to the decision), it encourages the use of appeals simply as a stalling tactic; and by excusing judges from any requirement that they deal with the realities of a case it encourages lawyers to make a circus of a trial, to "get error in the record." And, of course, the increased chance of "winning" on appeal creates an ever-growing burden of appeals in an affluent society.

This flood of appeals and of appellate decisions creates problems even on a technical level. Karen writes:

The citation of cases tends to become a habit, almost an obsession, with dozens of cases being cited where one would do, or where the proposition for which they stand is so obvious that no one disputes it. There is also the grave danger that even competent and conscientious judges and lawyers may overlook important cases in the welter of reports. . . . Many of the cases are primarily factual determinations which do not enunciate new principles of law or alter or modify existing principles. Nevertheless, they may be, and frequently are, cited as precedents for future cases. This restricts the freedom of action of judges, for they are called upon to compare minutely the fact patterns in previous cases with the one before them in order to avoid treating one litigant differently from another.

To help with the burden, appellate judges have big chambers with individual libraries, secretarial help (though surprising numbers of them write out their opinions in longhand) and a law clerk, usually a brand-new law school graduate from the top of his class. This institution started with Justice Brandeis on the Supreme Court, who decided he would rather have a young lawyer to assist him in legal matters (as young lawyers had done while he was in private practice) than a secretary to handle his correspondence. His third clerk was Dean Acheson, which continues to be the size of talent which the appellate judges seek. (Federal judges, of course, can fish in a much bigger pond.) Some judges use their clerks merely to filter the citations which look as though they ought to be checked; others demand extensive memoranda of law; others use clerks to do the work the lawyers for the parties should have done but often didn't do (an unlimited right of appeal means that many of the lawyers who come before appellate courts have little experience in this kind of argument and don't raise the significant issues for decision). Some (the clerks' favorite judges) ask their clerks to engage in the kind of dialogue they would have with their brother judges if there were more time for conference and discussion of the cases, bouncing arguments around to see how they sound and what answers to them can be made. It is by no means unknown for clerks to prepare draft opinions, and for these draft opinions to become the decision of the court. Crowded dockets frustrate collegial decision-making.

The problem has been rather starkly outlined with reference to the United States Supreme Court, where every Justice is supposed to inform himself about everything that comes up, and the writing of decisions is not assigned until after the court has read the briefs, heard the arguments, debated the case and voted in conference. (Justice Brandeis once said to Charles Wyzanski, "The reason the public thinks so much of the Justices of the Supreme Court is that they are almost the only people in Washington who do their own work.") Justice Jackson analyzed the time chart of a typical six-hour conference:

360 minutes in which to complete final consideration of forthcoming opinions, the noting of probable jurisdiction of appeals, the disposition of petitions for certiorari, petitions for rehearing and argued cases. The largest conference list during the October 1953 term contained 145 items, the shortest 24, the average 70. A little computation will show that the average list would permit, at the average conference, an average of five minutes of deliberation per item, or about 33 seconds of discussion per item by each of the nine Justices, assuming, of course, that each is an average Justice who does the average amount of talking.

Jackson's figures were a little unfair to his Court, because probably half of the matters on his list were hopeless requests for the Court to hear the case, which would be dismissed with a wave of the hand. But there is further authority for the proposition that the Supreme Court hears too many cases for comfort. Justice Frankfurter in his last years on the Court repeatedly complained that his colleagues' willingness to hear unimportant matters did not leave "ample time and freshness of mind for private study and reflection in preparation for discussion at Conference. Without adequate study there cannot be adequate reflection; without adequate reflection there cannot be adequate discussion; without adequate discussion there cannot be that fruitful interchange of minds which is indispensable to thoughtful, unhurried decision and its formulation in learned and impressive opinions." Professor Henry M. Hart, Jr. commented that "too many of the Court's opinions are about what one would expect could be written in twenty-four hours. . . . Issues are ducked which in good conscience and good lawyership ought not to be ducked. . . . Technical mistakes are made which ought not to be made in decisions of the Supreme Court of the United States. . . . [T]hese failures are threatening to undermine the professional respect of first-rate lawyers for the incumbent Justices of the Court." That was in 1959; later Professor Hart regretted that he had put his displeasure quite so strongly, but he never took it back.

If such strictures can be made by responsible commentators upon the work of the most carefully selected bench in the country, which has been granted full control over its own docket and in fact hears argument in only about 125 cases a year, think what can be said of the work of the other appellate courts! In the end, the doctrine that appeal is a matter of right destroys the status of the trial courts and the quality of work in the appellate courts; and it adds appallingly to the time and money required to manage the work of the legal system. By creating an illusory feeling that injustice below can be remedied above, it relieves the pressure to improve the administration of justice where most of the real decisions are made. Justice Frankfurter once observed that "the right to a judgment from more than one court is a matter of grace and not a necessary ingredient of justice. . . . To be effective, justice must not be leaden-footed." Geoffrey Hazard, Jr. has suggested that appealing should be made perilous—that convicted defendants should risk an increase in sentence, and civil litigants should be made to pay their adversary's costs unless they can show convincing reason for appealing. More feasible, perhaps, would be universal adoption and strengthening of the system now in effect in Virginia and Massachusetts, in the Supreme Court of the United States and in the highest courts of most states where there are intermediate courts of appeal, by which losers can appeal only by permission. A case can certainly be made for appeal as of right when a man's liberty is at stake—though even here once may be enough—but surely the courts should retain an option when nothing has been lost but money.

The shortage of time is made somewhat more severe by the odd American tradition of reverence for dissenting opinions, so that a judge is expected to research and write not only reasoned statements of the law, which can be used by lawyers in other cases and by his successors on the bench, but also personal expressions of dislike for the collective judgment of the court. The tradition grows out of the long period when the appellate courts at all levels were using their powers to declare statutes unconstitutional for the purpose of frustrating popular legislation, and a judge became a hero by standing out against this repression of the political will. Some of its strength, of course, grows from the fact that the dissenting judge can write more personally, more directly and more powerfully than the judge who must state the opinion for the court as a group, and must therefore compromise his language to gain assent to his propositions. But the tradition is odd because, as Justice Jackson wrote,

> Each dissenting opinion is a confession of failure to convince the writer's colleagues, and the true test of a judge is his influence in leading, not in opposing, his court. . . .
> There has been much undiscriminating eulogy of dissenting opinions. It is said they clarify the issues. Often they do the exact opposite. The technique of the dissenter often is to exaggerate the holding of the Court beyond the meaning of the majority and then to blast away at the excess. So the poor lawyer with a similar case does not know whether the majority opinion meant what it seemed to say or what the minority said it meant.

This is not to say that courts should give a false impression of unanimity when the judges are not unanimous. Jackson himself wrote of a need that "the division be forthrightly exposed so that the profession will know on what narrow grounds the case rests and can form some estimate of how changed facts may affect the alignment in a subsequent case." But the sort of dissent once uttered by Jackson himself—"I give up. Now I realize what Mark Twain meant when he said, 'the more you explain it, the more I don't understand it' "—saves a judge's time without implying his agreement. A judge who is really annoyed can choose another form of dissent cited by Chief Justice Fuld: "It is perfectly apparent that the majority here have failed to read either the record on appeal or the reported decisions." Such a comment clears the mind and the spleen, leaving a judge refreshed for more significant labors.

Holmes was in the public mind "The Great Dissenter," but in fact he dissented less often than the average of his brethren. "A dissent in a court of last resort is," Charles Evans Hughes wrote, "an appeal to the brooding spirit of the law, to the intelligence of a future day"; but a decent respect for that future day would argue that wolf ought not to be called too often. Moreover, as Traynor has written, "[T]he well-reasoned dissent, aimed at winning the day in the future, enhances the present certainty of the majority opinion, now imbedded in the concrete of resistance to the published arguments that beat against it." Brandeis not only buried many of his dissents unpublished, but actually cast votes concurring in opinions of which he disapproved, because he could see no point in waging this particular battle.

The problem is not that the dissenting opinion makes the law insecure—the law is always insecure; law is a process, not a thing, and unanimous benches are about as likely to be overruled in the future as one-vote majorities are. Less than 10 percent of Holmes' dissents later became majority doctrine, and most judges fare worse. "Furthermore," as Karl ZoBell noted, "other forums for the advocacy of change in the law are probably more effective, absolutely and relatively. Articles in legal and popular periodicals, pamphlets, and even street-corner speeches have frequently 'become the law.'" But when 90 percent of all opinions in the United States Supreme Court carry a dissent (as against 10 percent in 1930-31), and comparable increases in this speech-making are to be found in the state appellate courts, an observer must wonder whether the appellate judges are not cheating time from their higher responsibility of stating majority opinions clearly and carefully in order to express themselves when in the minority. Voluntary restriction on dissenting opinions would probably increase substantially the work the courts could perform at appropriate standards of craftsmanship.

CHAPTER 15

THE SUPREME COURT:
A CONCLUDING UNSCIENTIFIC
POSTSCRIPT

"Remember what Justice Holmes said about 'Justice.' I don't know what you think about him but on the whole he was to me the master craftsman certainly of our time; and he said, 'I hate justice,' which he didn't quite mean. What he did mean was this. I remember once I was with him; it was a Saturday when the Court was to confer. It was before he had a motorcar; and we jogged along in an old coupé. When we got down to the Capitol, I wanted to provoke a response, so as he walked off I said to him, 'Well, sir, goodbye. Do justice!' He turned quite sharply and he said, 'Come here, come here.' I answered, 'Oh, I know, I know.' He replied, 'That is not my job. My job is to play the game according to the rules.'"

—LEARNED HAND, quoted by
Charles P. Curtis

"There is no use arguing with any man who does not see the drive for justice as a prime good in law."

—KARL LLEWELLYN

"I know of no way we can have equal justice under law except we have some law."

—JUSTICE ROBERT H. JACKSON

[520]

"In addition to the power to hold legislative acts invalid, a written constitution confers another and perhaps as great a power. It is the power to disregard prior cases. . . . A change of mind from time to time is inevitable when there is a written constitution. There can be no authoritative interpretation of the Constitution. The Constitution in its general provisions embodies the conflicting ideals of the community. Who is to say what these ideals mean in any definite way? Certainly not the framers, for they did their work when the words were put down. The words are ambiguous. Nor can it be the Court, for the Court cannot bind itself in this manner; an appeal can always be made back to the Constitution."

—EDWARD H. LEVI

1

By this roundabout route we come to the Spanish Ivory Vein marble palace atop the hill, behind the Capitol in Washington, and to the marvelously ornate, startlingly long carved wooden bench behind which sit, in swivel chairs of their own choice, the nine Justices of the Supreme Court of the United States. This institution is the uniquely American contribution to the theory of government, and there is no shortage of reading matter about it.

The Constitution established the Presidency and the Congress, and instructed the new government to establish a Supreme Court. This was promptly done in the Federal Judiciary Act of 1789, debated more or less concurrently with the Bill of Rights; the Act created a bench of six Justices—a Chief and five Associates. The new Court was by no means strictly a court of appeals, and is not such today. It was to be the trial court in cases involving diplomatic personnel or cases in which a state was a plaintiff or defendant. This jurisdiction, though now restricted by the Eleventh Amendment to suits between sovereigns, is not just a joke; few cases have dragged on so long, or taken so much of the Court's time (even though actual testimony was before an appointed "special master" rather than before the Justices), as the dispute between Arizona and California over water rights in the Colorado basin. But no original jurisdiction beyond these categories *can* be given to the Supreme Court by Act of

Congress—the Supreme Court, for example, cannot issue writs of mandamus or habeas corpus; it can only pass on appeals from the actions of lower courts in issuing (or failing to issue) such writs. Marshall in 1801, in *Marbury* v. *Madison,* declared the Law of the Midnight Judges unconstitutional because Congress had therein presumed to give the Supreme Court an illegitimate power to issue writs of mandamus. Anyway, that's what Marshall said. If the Supreme Court were now to accept a new grant of original jurisdiction not foreshadowed in the Constitution, the whole structure of judicial review would topple.

Mostly, then, the Supreme Court is a court of appeals, in those matters for which Congress gives the Court authority to hear appeals. In 1789 this authority extended to appeals in civil cases heard in the federal courts set up by the same act, provided the amount at issue was more than $2,000, but not under any circumstances to criminal cases. It extended, too—in Section 25, which became the charter of a truly national government on this continent—to appeals from state court decisions that were based on interpretations of the Constitution or federal laws or treaties. (A drafting error left a hole in this jurisdiction, by denying the Supreme Court the right to review a state court decision that a state law was *unconstitutional* under the federal Constitution; this hole was plugged in 1914, after the New York State Court of Appeals ruled the workmen's compensation act federally unconstitutional, and the state found it had no appeal to the Supreme Court.) The Court requires that a litigant have exhausted his possible remedies in lower courts before coming to Washington, but if that exhaustion occurs at a low level, the Court may reach way down to hear the case. A Supreme Court decision in 1912 upheld the circuit court of Hinds County, Mississippi, in awarding $4.76 damages and $25 punitive damages to a company suing a railroad for losing some bottles of vinegar. Another in 1960 reversed the police court of Louisville on a $10 fine for drunkenness.

Up to the 1870s the work of the Supreme Court was largely confined to cases involving disputes between citizens of different states, with occasional arguments about the constitutionality of state or federal statutes. Marshall's great nationalizing contribution was made in the cases involving the "commerce clause"—particularly

Gibbons v. *Ogden* and *McCulloch* v. *Maryland*—which established federal supremacy in regulating business matters that crossed state lines. In 1875, however, Congress vastly extended the jurisdiction of the lower federal courts—which thereupon, as Felix Frankfurter and James M. Landis once wrote, "ceased to be restricted tribunals of fair dealing between citizens of different states and became the primary and powerful reliances for vindicating every right given by the Constitution, the laws and treaties of the United States."

Because the Supreme Court was (and is) primarily a court of appeals from decisions of the lower federal courts, the new rules greatly enlarged its jurisdiction, too. Most of these appeals, unfortunately, were "as of right," and the Court was swamped. Even the creation in 1891 of the Circuit Courts of Appeal, with their own judges, was not enough to save the Supreme Court from delayed dockets and rushed deliberations. In 1925, then, Congress declared the decisions of the Circuit Courts "final" in most cases, with review by the Supreme Court only if the Court issued a "writ of certiorari," a request to the lower court to certify the record of the case and forward it so it could be studied above. In theory, there are still some cases the Supreme Court must hear (especially cases on appeal from state supreme courts), but the only significant modern category where appeal lies "as of right" is the case in which a three-judge district court empaneled for the purpose has passed on the constitutionality of a law or an administrative action.

Cases arrive at the Supreme Court, then, in the form of requests that the Court hear the matter, and nearly 90 percent of these requests are refused. A central doctrine of the Court, of necessity, is that refusal to grant a writ of certiorari or give leave to appeal does not imply in any way approval of the decision or opinion of the lower court (though recently more and more Justices have insisted on giving these denials that significance, by writing their dissents from the refusals—an imposing example of self-defeating judicial egotism). The applications run anywhere from prisoners' scrawls to fifty-page briefs, tens of thousands of pages a year. Primary responsibility for managing this burden lies on the Chief Justice, who is given a third law clerk for the purpose, and in Hughes' time the Chief Justice handled it all himself. Now it is parceled out, though exactly *how* it is parceled out is one of the many well-kept secrets at the Court. Much, perhaps most, of the time at the Justices' Friday conferences (Warren put an end to the Court's traditional six-day week) goes to disposing of these applications, which pour in at a rate of about two thousand a year.

To hear those cases which are accepted, the Court sits Monday through Thursday from 10 A.M. to 2 P.M. for about twenty weeks of the year. Lawyers must be specially admitted to the Supreme Court bar before they can argue a case here, but admission is a formality (and a very pleasant one, because the ceremony is performed in open court by Chief Justice Warren, who is delighted to see the newcomers to the Court and in his warmest manner and brightest smile bids them welcome). Briefs and records have already been submitted and read by the Justices. In most cases, lawyers for each side are allotted one hour of argument (in some, the allotment is only half an hour per side), and by the rules of the Court the argument may not be read from a prepared document.

The lawyer stands at a lectern facing the Court, near the center of the gigantic Egyptian-temple courtroom, speaking into a microphone, and every Justice has his own microphone and can interrupt at any time. The interruptions come out of the hour, and sometimes produce a degree of friction between Justices who are interested in different aspects of the case. Time restrictions are enforced by the Chief Justice, and are virtually absolute: Hughes is supposed to have "called time on a leader of the New York bar in the middle of an 'if.'" The authority that lies behind the question can be pretty terrifying even to the best-prepared lawyer, and he must sometimes swallow comments that are destructive to his case. A favorite story tells of a young lawyer arguing his first case before this bench, who explained his point in response to questions only to be told by a kindly Justice, "But that's not the law." The young lawyer said sadly, "It was, sir, until you spoke. . . ."

On the Friday following the argument, the Court in conference discusses the case (the Chief Justice speaking first, and thence around the table in order of seniority) and votes on a decision (the most recently appointed Justice voting first, and thence around the table the other way). Nobody but the Justices themselves is ever in the conference room (the newest Justice sits nearest the door, so he can open it if someone knocks), and nobody knows what goes on behind the closed doors: there are no leaks from the Supreme Court. If the Chief Justice is with the majority on the vote, he assigns the writing of the opinion to one of his concordant brethren; if he is in the minority, the most senior of the Associate Justices in the majority makes the choice. The minority can decide for itself how the dissent(s) are to be managed. Draft opinions circulate around the bench in proof, and are commented on by both friends and foes (Justice McReynolds used to write in the margin comments like "This statement makes me sick"). Every once in a while, Justices change their mind while writing, or while reading a brother's opinion, and assignments (even decisions) have to be reshuffled. Cases are discussed anew at other Friday conferences. The final opinions are summarized by their authors from the bench in open court, but nothing *said* is authoritative—the only thing that counts is the written document. Until 1965 Monday was always opinion day; now the opinions are announced and released as they are finished, though Monday is still the heaviest day. Opinions are immediately available in print: the Government Printing Office maintains a branch in the basement for the production of "advance sheets."

Most of the business has to do with the interpretation of federal statutes, on which the Court's word is by no means necessarily final; Congress can amend the wounded statute, as it did, for example, when the Court decided that recordings could not be copyrighted because nobody could tell just by looking at them what was on them, or that the FBI had to open its files to fishing expeditions by criminal defendants, or that the Consolidated Edison Company did not have to pay taxes on great gobs of profits that everybody but Con Ed's lawyers had always assumed were taxable. The Court also hears a surprisingly large number of appeals from losers in tort cases brought under federal law and a certain number of criminal appeals which turn on questions of admissibility of evidence and suitability of a judge's charge. In these cases, and in the cases involving government contracts and administrative rulings, it functions very much as the state appellate courts function, except that its power to deny a hearing is greater and is more likely to be exercised. Nor is the Supreme Court's power to interpret the Constitution unique to that body; state supreme courts, too, rule on the fit between state actions and constitutions (including the federal Constitution). What gives the Court its special fascination for the nonlawyer is that on questions relating to the federal Constitution, the fundamental organizing document of our public life, this bench is the ultimate authority. Its decisions, as President Eisenhower liked to say, are "the law of the land."

The men entrusted with this authority are chosen by the President and confirmed by the Senate; and it is only in recent years that Presidential appointments to the job have gone through the Senate more or less as a matter of routine. Marshall became Chief Justice only because the Senate refused to confirm John Rutledge; White became Associate Justice (later Chief Justice) only because Cleveland's bad relations with the Senators from New York blocked his first choices; Owen Roberts was named in 1930 only after the Senate refused John J. Parker. Since the early thirties, however, every Presidential appointment has been approved, and the last battle of real substance was over Hugo Black. Nominations are usually a surprise, because the field in which the President can play is so large. (It is even larger than most people realize or tradition permits: the Justices of the Supreme Court do not have to be lawyers, though all of them have been and will be.) Of the mid-1967 bench, one (Warren) came from a state governorship, two (Marshall and White) from the Attorney General's office, two (Harlan and Stewart) from a Circuit Court of Appeals after distinguished careers as corporate lawyers, one (Black) from the Senate, one (Douglas) from a regulatory agency and a law professorship, one (Brennan) from a state supreme court (New Jersey), and one (Fortas) from private practice, after many years of federal service (in his private office before his appointment he kept an old flag of the Department of the Interior).

They work in oversized offices, too big to be comfortable and too high-ceilinged to be imposing, in a building which (like all courts, but somehow one is surprised) swarms with cops. On the bench, seated before the red velour hangings through which page boys seep with messages, they are individual and uncontrolled, whispering to each other occasionally; they are seated in a pyramid of seniority, the newest appointees at the ends, the most senior beside the Chief Justice at the center, writing (especially Douglas) memoranda which may or may not pertain to the case in hand, swiveling and rocking in their chairs.

Working with a constitution is a hard job—much harder than merely working with law. In Britain the appellate judges could say that their rulings on the law were irreversible in their own courts: Parliament was sovereign; if the judges made a mistake, Parliament could correct it. But in the United States the sovereign was a document, and Marshall had laid down all the intelligible (and conflicting) rules for dealing with it. To begin with, the Constitution is controlling, and where its directions are clear (as Marshall, not very convincingly, said they were in *Marbury* v. *Madison*), then that is an end to the matter. And this is true whether the argument is put piously for the purpose of frustrating legislation by an Owen Roberts ("The judicial branch of the Government has only one duty—to lay the Article of the Constitution which is invoked beside the statute which is challenged and to decide whether the latter squares with the former") or irreverently for the purpose of permitting legislation by a Holmes ("When a state came in here and wanted to build a slaughter house, I looked at the Constitution and if I couldn't find anything in there that said a state couldn't build a slaughter house I said to myself, if they want to build a slaughter house, God-dammit, let them build it"). The second rule Marshall stated as "We must never forget that it is a *constitution* we are expounding," and a constitution is not the same thing as a municipal building code. The Constitution is not often explicit. Where it is not, the Court must consider the fact that all public officials (not just judges) have taken oaths to defend the Constitution, and must assume that a considered public policy is constitutional unless the argument to the contrary is overwhelming.

To manage these conflicts, Frankfurter wrote, "The Court has . . . evolved rules of judicial administration especially designed to postpone constitutional adjudications and therefore constitutional conflicts until they are judicially unavoidable." It will not give advisory opinions, will not hear any case before an otherwise "final" judgment elsewhere, and will not base its decision on the Constitution if any other grounds can be found that will produce the same result. Reflecting on his approach as the Court-appointed lawyer in the case of Clarence Earl Gideon (*Gideon* v. *Wainwright,* which established the proposition under the Sixth Amendment that a state must supply a lawyer for an indigent defendant), Abe Fortas said, "The first question was—could this case be fitted into the established special circumstances rule? If it could be done I would have been obligated to do so, even though it might have meant the Court would never reach the constitutional issue."

But this principle is in tension with another, which is that the Court grants review, as Hughes put it, "in the interest of the law, not in the interest of particular parties." Chief Justice Vinson, fifteen years later, asked the members of the American Bar Association to remember that in cases before the Supreme Court "you are, in a sense, prosecuting or defending class actions; that you represent not only your clients, but tremendously important principles, upon which are based the plans, hopes and aspirations of a great many people throughout the country."

In short, the Court proposes to accept cases only because they involve decisions on the most important points of law, especially constitutional law; and then to avoid deciding them on that basis if any other basis can be found. It is on occasion too much for flesh and blood to bear.

2

There have always been judges who in these situations will see their obligations as lying entirely to the law. "The relation of the United States and the Courts of the United States to the States and the Courts of the States," Holmes once wrote, "is a very delicate matter that has occupied the thoughts of statesmen and judges for a hundred years and can not be disposed of by a summary statement that justice requires me to cut red tape and intervene." The appeal he thereby rejected was for an order delaying the execution of Sacco and Vanzetti.

That was a tougher time, a time when judges were far more

conscious of the truth that "hard cases make bad law" than of its equally valid reciprocal, that "bad law makes hard cases." Today few judges, given the power to do justice in the individual case, will with a good heart apply a law that seems to work injustice in the case. Where possible, because the doctrine of precedent is the anchor of the legal system, justice is done by distinguishing the facts of the current case from those of previous cases. In common-law jurisdictions—and most state supreme courts, despite the largely statutory origin of American state law, retain what is in essence common-law jurisdiction—judges can move the law by opening new categories. "The proper technique," says California's Roger Traynor, "is to open the accordion just a little, and then see what happens." But where a court lacks common-law jurisdiction, it must reinterpret the language of its guiding documents. Then it must follow what Traynor (who, one must hasten to say, is not attacking the Supreme Court) calls "the wrong procedure—to open the accordion all the way and then slowly contract it."

Judges, because they are paid to make decisions, are supposed to be sure. The authority for the Supreme Court's actions rests in the Constitution itself. We have got far beyond the point where anyone speaks of "the plain meaning" of words like "due process" or "equal protection of the laws." When the Court reinterprets the words of the Constitution, it undoubtedly, as Learned Hand complained, assumes "the role of a third legislative chamber. . . . I hope that it may be regarded as permissible for me to say that I have never been able to understand on what basis [this function] does or can rest except as a *coup de main*." The answer to this attack is easy enough: if the Court is to enforce the Constitution, it must interpret the words; and to say that the first Court that gets a crack at the words establishes their meaning *semper ubique et ad omnibus* would be quite serious nonsense. But judges want to feel themselves bound by law; they have taken an oath that they *will* be bound by law. And most of them want the law they lay down to be binding upon their successors.

Justice Hugo L. Black found what looked like a way out of this dilemma. He was interpreting a document which he felt had been wrongly interpreted by his predecessors; but he was a lawyer and he needed law. His authority could not come from precedents; he would find it in the historical context in which the words were originally written. By determining what the words meant at that time, he would be able to overrule subsequent corruptions, and meanwhile fix ruling principles in the galaxy forever. The First Amendment, for example, Black saw in the light of the faith of its original proponents, who "were determined that every American should possess an unrestrained freedom to express his views, however odious they might be to vested interests whose power they might challenge." Its prohibitions against government interference were absolute then, and therefore ought to be absolute today. On this basis, the late Edmond Cahn wrote admiringly, "Justice Hugo L. Black may claim continuity with the original republican tradition. . . . [I]f he should be convicted of deviating from Brandeis, he may still make bold to submit that he is returning to Jefferson."

There are serious problems with this doctrine, one of them being the impracticality of absolute prohibitions. As Learned Hand said of the First Amendment bar against Congressional interference with religion, "We have forbidden polygamy, though it was an honestly entertained article of the Mormon creed. Obviously, we should forbid suttee, hara kiri, or such self-mutilation as in the past was a common practice in the worship of Adonis." And we shall, no doubt, refuse to permit people to circumvent the narcotics laws on a self-serving claim that drug-taking is part of their religion. Another problem lies in Holmes' comment that

when we are dealing with words that are also a constituent act, like the Constitution of the United States, we must realize that they have called into life a being the development of which could not have been foreseen completely by the most gifted of its begetters. It was enough for them to realize or hope that they had created an organism; it has taken a century and has cost their successors much sweat and blood to prove that they created a nation. The case before us must be considered in the light of our whole experience and not merely in that of what was said a hundred years ago.

The worst horrors in the Court's history—Dred Scott, the brief invalidation of paper money, the prohibition of the income tax—were all defended by their perpetrators on the grounds that the

Constitution must always mean what it meant to "the Framers." But the most impenetrable problem about the Black doctrine is that history is always confusing, it yields whatever message those who search it seek to find, and the ease of rigging it promotes intellectual dishonesty.

For example, we have very good evidence about what Jefferson thought of the First Amendment prohibition, at least while he was President. He considered it a jurisdictional limitation on the powers of the federal government, not an absolute protection of the citizen. Writing Abigail Adams about his decision to pardon publishers who had been convicted under the Alien and Sedition Laws for some fairly vicious comments about her husband, he claimed that as President he had an authority coextensive with that of the Supreme Court to declare that law unconstitutional. If the Court alone had that power, he said, the judiciary would be "a despotic branch. Nor," he added,

does the opinion of the unconstitutionality and consequent nullity of that law remove all restraint from the overwhelming torrent of slander which is confounding all vice and virtue, all truth and falsehood in the US. The power to do that is fully possessed by the several state legislatures. It was reserved to them, and was denied to the general government, by the constitution according to our construction of it. While we deny that Congress have a right to control the freedom of the press, we have ever asserted the right of the states, and their exclusive right, to do so.

This letter lay unpublished for a long time, but it was cited from manuscript by Justice Frankfurter at the Marshall bicentenary celebrations in 1954, so it was certainly available to Justice Black at the time of his Swarthmore speech, and to Professor Cahn at the time of his comment.

There is, however, another string to the bow. If one considers Jefferson's letter only from the jurisdictional point of view (which is not easy to do, but you can do it if you try), then his opinion that the First Amendment did not apply to the states could be negated. In his dissent from *Adamson* v. *California*, in 1947, Justice Black noted that he had made a study of the history of the Fourteenth Amendment, which begins with the words "All persons born or naturalized in the United States, and subject to the jurisdiction thereof, are citizens of the United States and of the State wherein they reside. No State shall make or enforce any law which shall abridge the privileges or immunities of citizens of the United States; nor shall any State deprive any person of life, liberty, or property, without due process of law; nor deny to any person within its jurisdiction the equal protection of the laws." These sentences are by no means satisfactory as draftsmanship (the shift from "citizen" to "person" is especially troublesome), and the Supreme Court has had trouble interpreting the Amendment ever since its adoption. "In my judgment," Justice Black wrote, "that history conclusively demonstrates that the language of the first section of the Fourteenth Amendment, taken as a whole, was thought by those responsible for its submission to the people, and by those who opposed its submission, sufficiently explicit to guarantee that thereafter no state could deprive its citizens of the privileges and protections of the Bill of Rights." And he appended a historical analysis based on contemporary reports of the debates in Congress.

Again, there are practical problems with Justice Black's position. As a matter of public policy, application of the *entire* first eight Amendments to the states would cause violent and unnecessary dislocations—the Second Amendment, for example, would destroy all the laws now governing ownership and registration of guns; the Fifth Amendment would throw out the normal criminal process of proceedings on information rather than indictment throughout the Western states; the Sixth Amendment would require trial by jury for all those misdemeanors now handled by judges in the Eastern states; the Seventh Amendment would demand juries in small-claims cases down to $20. . . . And Black's argument certainly is novel. As recently as 1922, Justice Pitney, speaking for a majority which included Holmes and upholding a Missouri law requiring employers to supply reasons why someone had been fired, announced that "the Constitution of the United States imposes upon the states no obligation to confer upon those within their jurisdiction either the right of free speech or the right of silence."

It was not until the *Gitlow* case in 1925 that the Court proclaimed that "For present purposes we may and do assume that freedom of speech and of the press—which are protected by the

First Amendment from abridgment by Congress—are among the fundamental personal rights and 'liberties' protected by the due process clause of the Fourteenth Amendment from impairment by the States." Noting this phrase (which was inserted in an opinion upholding a conviction under the New York Criminal Anarchy Act, in one of those typical throw-away gestures of a judge seeking to show how fair he is), Charles Curtis wrote, "The Court acted as if it were unaware of what it was doing, like a small boy opening a new knife without comment." In recent years the doctrine of "selective incorporation" of the first Amendments into the Fourteenth has made possible decisions like those on evidence in criminal cases. But Justice Black's 1947 dissent, in which he was joined by three others, demanded that the Court apply *all* the amendments to the states.

And once again the historical evidence is bad—much worse in this case than in that of the First Amendment, where Jefferson and Madison can be quoted on both sides. Professor Charles Fairman, then of Stanford and later of Harvard, undertook the weary labor of examining all the contemporary documents. He found that the two speeches on which Justice Black relied had been isolated in the mass of debate, and that their references to the Bill of Rights had not, as Black implied, been widely reported in the press. He found that in none of the debates on ratification in the state legislatures had anyone even raised this question, though many of these states had organized their court systems (in some cases, recently reorganized their court systems) in patterns that did not square with the first eight Amendments. He found that the Confederate States had been readmitted to the Union with constitutions which violated these Amendments. He found that convicted criminals had appealed in the 1870s on the grounds that state courts had not followed all the procedures laid down in the Bill of Rights, and the argument had been brushed aside as nonsense. He found that although Justice John Marshall Harlan (great-uncle of the present Justice of the same name) had raised Black's point in dissent in 1892, it was entirely as an afterthought, for he had dissented on the same logic for years without offering this particular argument.

No doubt the minority in the Slaughterhouse Cases five years after the passage of the Fourteenth Amendment had felt that the majority had savagely constricted its application, but none of them made Justice Black's assertion; and in *Hurtado* v. *California,* sixteen years after the Amendment became part of the Constitution, seven Justices, all of whom had been active as lawyers or judges in 1868 when the debates were proceeding, upheld the right of California to proceed in criminal cases without indictment by grand jury: "Any legal proceeding enforced by public authority, whether sanctioned by age and custom or newly devised in the discretion of the Legislative power, in furtherance of the general public good, which regards and preserves these principles of liberty and justice, must be held to be due process of law."

Professor Fairman wound up shocked by Justice Black's pronouncements. "Sifting evidence," he wrote, "is the everyday business of a Justice. A record of trial is not readily available throughout the country. One counts upon fairness and accuracy in the statement of the case. Here the record lay in a book easily consulted, and one can see for oneself how the evidence was handled." His colleague Stanley Morrison wound up dismayed:

The disturbing thing is not that this piece of judicial research was not more exhaustive, but that such inadequate research should be made the pretext for one of the most far-reaching changes in constitutional interpretation to be seriously proposed in our constitutional history. . . . The real significance of *Adamson* v. *California* was that four of the judges are willing to distort history, as well as the language of the framers, in order to read into the Constitution provisions which they think ought to be there. It is particularly regrettable that the great talents of Mr. Justice Black should be so misdirected.

Morrison was a little unfair to two of Black's fellow dissenters, who announced their agreement only with "much" of his position.

None of this is to say that Justice Black must be wrong in what he wants to do, or that the Supreme Court lacks the authority to make the interpretations of the Constitution which he has persistently demanded (with decreasing support from his brethren) since 1947. The documents argue merely that history, like precedent, must not be used as an escape from the necessity for choice. They also suggest, perhaps, that judges should leave history to historians.

Yale's Alexander Bickel has written brilliantly about this controversy that

> It is not true that the Framers intended the First Amendment to guarantee all speech against all possible infringement by government regulation; but they did not foreclose such a policy and may indeed have invited something like it. It is not true that the Framers intended the Fourteenth Amendment to outlaw segregation or to make applicable to the states all restrictions on government that may be evolved under the Bill of Rights; but they did not foreclose such policies and may indeed have invited them.

The question forever before the Justices, the hard question that cannot be escaped, is what the words of the constituent document mean *today*, with reference to current public policy and current government actions. The Court is thus inevitably embroiled in all sorts of current controversy: always has been, and always will be. Hughes at a banquet once gave Chief Justice Taft's definition of a constitutional lawyer: "one who had abandoned the practice of the law and had gone into politics."

3

What it means in the end is that the Court cannot provide final determinations. The issues on which it must rule in constitutional cases are simply too big for judicial decision-making. As Jackson put it shortly before his appointment to the bench, "The vice of the litigation process in broad constitutional questions is that since we cannot expand the lawsuit process to include an era, a people, and a continent, we simply cut down the problem to the scope of a lawsuit." Yet the Court must deal with just these problems in just this way, and it is fearfully free to decide. Justice Harlan Fiske Stone, in his bitter dissent to the invalidation of the first Agriculture Act, said, "[W]hile unconstitutional exercise of power by the executive and legislative branches of the government is subject to judicial restraint, the only check upon our exercise of power is our own sense of self-restraint." Brandeis in 1927 sent along to his friend Norman Hapgood a quotation from Goethe: "Everything which frees our spirit without giving us control over ourselves is fatal."

Where the Court indulges in large generalizations, its critics condemn it for unnecessary lawmaking, for usurping the functions of Congress. Madison denounced Marshall's opinion in *McCulloch* v. *Maryland* in a letter: "The occasion did not call for the general and abstract doctrine interwoven with the decision of the particular case. I have always supposed that the meaning of a law, and for a like reason, of a Constitution, so far as it depends on judicial interpretation, was to result from a course of particular decisions, and not these from a previous and abstract comment on the subject." Or, as Frankfurter put it, "If judges want to be preachers, they should dedicate themselves to the pulpit; if judges want to be primary shapers of policy, the legislature is their place."

If, on the other hand, the Court persists in deciding cases simply on their facts, because this result seems fairer than that result, the critics denounce it for lack of what Columbia's Herbert Wechsler called "neutral principles." What the Court should produce, Wechsler said, is a decision "that rests on reasons with respect to all the issues in the case, reasons that in their generality and their neutrality transcend the immediate result that is involved." (Chief Justice Traynor, commenting on this statement, regretted that "Professor Wechsler has ignored the abundant opportunities available to a scholar with hindsight to compose a symphony of neutral principles that would improve on the judicial ballads emerged from the mud of immediate cases without adequate transcendental slime.") Pushed by those critics at the law schools whom the Justices most deeply respect, the Court swings back to the broad generalization.

The Reapportionment Cases are an excellent example of the troubles the broad generalization can create. Starting with *Baker* v. *Carr*, a Tennessee case in 1962, the Court has in case after case invalidated the lines state legislatures had drawn to determine the districts which elect state legislators or Congressmen. The reason for invalidation in every case has been a disparity in population among the districts: to be Constitutional, the Court has ruled, such districts must show "substantially equal" census returns. The argument has been rested either on the guarantee of "equal protection" in the Fourteenth Amendment or, by Justice Black (relying again on idiosyncratic readings of contemporary debates to determine the *true* intention of the Founding Fathers), on the statement in Article I of the Constitution that the House of Representatives "shall be . . . chosen . . . by the People of the several States." The most grandiloquent statement was by Justice Douglas, speaking for the majority: "The conception of political equality from the Declaration of Independence, to Lincoln's Gettysburg Address, to the Fifteenth, Seventeenth and Nineteenth Amendments can mean only one thing—one person, one vote."

In fact, the disparities the Court had found (especially in the original Tennessee case and in the Georgia case which provoked the Douglas opinion) were nothing less than scandalous. Real rotten boroughs with a few thousand votes were electing representatives whose voice in the legislature would be equal to that of the representatives of tens or even hundreds of thousands of city voters. Though some conservatives were shocked by the Court's intervention, and Senator Dirksen took a brief run at amending the Constitution to prevent any further such interference, the sentiments expressed by the Justices were popular. Now that the 1966 elections are history, and anyone can see that reapportionment does not necessarily benefit liberal causes or harm conservative causes, perhaps the Reapportionment Cases can be examined less emotionally as a particularly clear illustration of why broad generalizations do not solve specific problems.

The argument in its earlier stages ranged around questions of law and precedent, which was unfortunate both because these questions were irrelevant (the Supreme Court, taking jurisdiction, takes jurisdiction to be wrong), and because it was not Justices Warren, Black, Brennan and Douglas in asserting the Court's authority over apportionment but Justice Frankfurter in denying that authority who had departed from the weightiest precedents. In 1932 the Court had ruled that reapportionment legislation was legislation like any other, and came properly to Washington if it raised a federal question— and also, more significantly, that if a new census required the reduction of Minnesota's representation in Congress, and the legislature could not agree with the Governor on a redistributing, the Court could compel the state to elect all its Congressmen at large.

But by insisting on a single broad rule—indeed, a slogan—the Court in the Reapportionment Cases mapped a road which led fundamentally in a wrong direction and would be impossible to follow.

The direction was wrong, as Bickel pointed out, because the new neutral principle was based on a misunderstanding of the American political system: "The equal-vote premise ignores all that we have learned in a generation of fresh inquiry and reflection." The genius of the American system is its tripartite division into an executive elected on an essentially majoritarian basis, an independent legislature elected for deliberative purposes to reflect numerous minority interests and to compromise them, and an independent aristocratic judiciary. The essence of the legislative election is districting, and elections-at-large, meeting the equal-vote principle exactly, would be far more damaging to the sense of the system than even serious malapportionment. Districting, Justice Frankfurter pointed out, is "the vital political principle." To write as Justice Black did in his dissent from this opinion that an at-large election is superior to malapportioned districting because it "gives all the people an equally effective voice in electing their representatives" is to indulge legalism at the expense of all reality.

Indeed, the wording of the Supreme Court opinions in the Reapportionment Cases comes perilously close to leaving the Court quite defenseless against total disfranchisement of the Negroes of the South in state and national legislative elections. Phil C. Neal of the University of Chicago, in commenting on the first of the apportionment cases, pointed out that "in a state where Negroes comprised 25 per cent of the population an at-large system which resulted in no Negroes being elected to the legislature would be constitutional." Only districting can provide that representation of minorities which is essential to the workings of a democratic legislative process. Appealing to the Court to declare unconstitutional the referendum by which the voters of California had killed that state's open housing law, attorneys for the NAACP argued in early 1967 that all legislation by popular majority vote should be banned as inevitably unfair to minorities—only legislative deliberation by the representatives of districts, each with a log to roll, could assure a minority a voice in law-making. And once districting is accepted as a principle, it must always be true that 25.1 percent of the voters (50.1 percent in 50.1 percent of the districts) can theoretically control the legislature. At this point considerations others than numerical equality become highly significant: a legislator must have a meaningful constituency to which he is responsible.

Quite apart from the theoretical difficulty, Neal added, "No constitutional principle has been suggested by which courts can control the drawing of district lines so that even districts of approximately equal population cannot be used to achieve results similar to those produced by unequal districts." And this practical difficulty is *not* (as even Neal thought) merely a question of gerrymandered districts. If that were the problem, and no legal commentator has gone beyond it, then as a practical matter there would be much in favor of the proposal of Associate Dean Robert B. McKay of the NYU Law School, that districting be turned over to "a non-partisan apportionment commission at the state level."

For a start, on a fairly low level, there is the difficulty in defining "person." Obviously, "person" includes nonvoters (it always has—in the original version of the Constitution, slaves were counted as three-fifths of a person for apportionment purposes). And the census is the basis point.

James Weaver, who redistricted Delaware by computer, found the census definition a source of serious distortion:

The census as now gathered includes various types of people. When you start to think about it, you wonder whether they should be counted in voting districts: aliens, people like the large group at the Air Force base at Dover, who probably either vote by absentee ballot or don't vote at all, hospitals including mental institutions, prisons, etc. We happen to have a concentration of hospitals and prisons at one point in our state so they get a higher apportionment because of it. The census is taken in April, which means they pick up all the students at the University of Delaware.

In Connecticut a similar group of computer programmers found that the census had included students at the University of Connecticut (giving the town of Storrs pretty heavy representation in the legislature) but not students at Yale. Then there is this problem of the children. Weaver said, "This range is quite surprising—suburban areas as opposed to city, the percentage of children." One person—one vote?

Problems of definition are as nothing next to those of policy presented by the job of actually drawing district lines. As a member of the audience in the ALI-ABA computer symposium said, "It's the question of this doughnut problem, the doughnut with the hole. In the past a number of times, one county, for instance, deserves, on some kind of population basis, two representatives, and consists of one larger city and the rural area. They said, 'The city gets one and the rest of the county gets one.' So you have a doughnut-shaped district."

Now, the other accepted generalization in districting is that "districts shall be compact and contiguous." This provision is supposed to be the guarantee against the gerrymander; McKay specifically recommends it. But the moment of inertia of a doughnut is the center of the hole. The most compact and contiguous district will be one that divides the center of the city; indeed, the districts produced by the computers in Delaware and Connecticut did just that. Where a metropolitan area might be entitled to four or five seats, the computers drew neat little pie-shaped districts as the ones that best met neutral criteria. Where there is a ghetto area at the heart of a city, the computer instructed merely to divide a state into equal, compact and contiguous districts will deprive the ghetto of representation. One person—one vote?

"This," said a participant at the ALI-ABA symposium, "is a problem that the court isn't prepared to deal with. The legislatures—the political representatives of the people—have got to establish these criteria first. I think they have an impossible job to do." To which Bruce Stargatt, who represented the plaintiffs in the suit which forced the redistricting of Delaware, replied, "Nobody realizes that. Until you start to fiddle around with it this way, nobody understands the magnitude of the problem." This was a little unfair, because Justice Frankfurter had understood it throughout.

Again, Frankfurter was not necessarily right and Brennan and Black and Douglas were not necessarily wrong. What *was* wrong, and visibly wrong, was "one person—one vote." It established as *the* constitutional criterion an element in the situation that cannot be the most important element. What the Court was called upon to do here was not to lay down a constitutional principle but to decide specific cases in the same way that all "due process" cases have been decided over the years—by the visceral feeling of the Justices that on the evidence presented to them the malapportionment was simply too raw, too "unreasonable" to be tolerated. As the nonlawyer Anthony Lewis wrote in an article in the *Harvard Law Review* that paved the way for the Reapportionment Cases, "The benefit that the courts can bring to the [apportionment] process will follow from their merely taking jurisdiction and requiring argument on the merits."

From a series of such cases, meaningful guidelines to permissible and impermissible districting might have been developed. Instead, there were newspaper headlines and newspaper editorials; and six years later, after much reiteration of the principle, nobody has any real notion of what the decisions mean in practice.

Other broad declarations by the Supreme Court in recent years have not been so fully accepted as the reapportionment decisions. We have already noted the limited impact of the great declarations in the field of criminal law. That the decision prohibiting prayer in the schools in fact changed the morning rituals of many teachers is an opinion which cannot be shared by at least one reasonably close observer of what has been going on in the nation's classrooms. (The children everywhere still Thank You, God, for ev-eh-ree-thing. *De minimis,* anyway: the law should not concern itself with such trifles.) And resistance to the decision in the School Segregation Cases has been the national scandal for more than a decade.

What goes wrong is inherent in the choice of forum. Eugene Rostow, while dean at Yale, described as a "fascinating and fantastic essay in nihilism" Justice Jackson's dissent in *Korematsu* v. *U.S.*, where he refused to join the majority in approving the action of the military in sequestering Japanese-Americans in concentration camps, but also refused to attempt to order the release of the prisoners. By contrast, Dean Rostow found that "the action of Chief Justice Taney in *ex parte Merryman* is in a more heroic tradition of the judge's responsibility." In fact, Merryman, who had been trying to raise Maryland for the Confederacy, remained in military custody after Taney issued his futile writ of habeas corpus, because Lincoln ignored the writ. Some months later (on July 4—mastery of timing is not a modern invention), Lincoln asked Congress, "[A]re all the laws, *but one,* to go unexecuted, and the government itself go to pieces, lest that one be violated?"

Jackson could not have freed Korematsu any more than Taney could free Merryman, or Hughes could compel the payment of mortgages in Minnesota at the bottom of the Depression, or Marshall could compel the Jefferson Administration to issue judicial commissions under the terms of a hated law passed by the lame-duck Adams Administration and its Congress. "To withdraw [the courts] from such controversies," as Learned Hand once put it, "may in the end be the surest protection of their powers." Indeed, it was only by withdrawing his Court from the controversy that Marshall secured the doctrine of judicial review.

Judicial process cannot finally resolve a dispute when the public interests involved in a decision are far *wider* than the interests of the litigants. The *ratio decidendi,* the reason for the decision, affects only one facet of a social system. Rebuffed by the Court at this point in the maze, a vital social system with popular support will simply hunt out a new path to the same objective. The anthropologist Bronislaw Malinowski stated the point too strongly but not falsely when he wrote, "The true problem is not to study how human life submits to rules—it simply does not; the real problem is how the rules become adapted to life."

Let us suppose for argument's sake that the Supreme Court accepted the position of the American Civil Liberties Union and Justices Black and Douglas that public prosecution for obscene books is prohibited by the Constitution. By and large, rightly or wrongly, rationally or neurotically, the public seeks protection from obscenity. Among the first reactions to such a judicial decision would be a wave of popular support for vigilante groups, picketers of bookstores, boycotters and the like. No constitutionalist could require a law to prohibit such activities without abandoning that insistence on freedom of speech which was what led him into this snake pit. The end result, very possibly—indeed, very likely—

would be restriction on publication much more devastating than the results of a shrewdly administered law.

To claim that the Court should be (or is) unconscious of the impact of its decisions is to state a case that leaves credibility gasping in the distance, but Constitution worship is so widespread that perhaps a piece of evidence is required. A remarkable one is at hand in Justice Jackson's memo to Chief Justice Stone, about

the wisdom of having Mr. Justice Frankfurter act as the voice of the Court in the matter of Smith v. Allwright. It is a delicate matter. We must reverse a recent, well-considered and unanimous decision. We deny the entire South the right to a white primary, which is one of its most cherished rights. It seems to me very important that the strength which an all but unanimous decision would have may be greatly weakened if the voice that utters it is one that may grate on Southern sensibilities. Mr. Justice Frank-furter unites in a rare degree factors which unhappily excite prejudice. In the first place, he is a Jew. In the second place, he is from New England, the seat of the abolition movement. In the third place, he has not been thought of as a person particularly sympathetic with the Democratic party in the past. . . . With all humility I suggest that the Court's decision, bound to arouse bitter resentment, will be much less apt to stir ugly reactions if the news that the white primary is dead, is broken to it, if possible, by a Southerner who has been a Democrat and is not a member of one of the minorities which stir prejudices kindred to those against the Negro.

The Chief Justice reassigned the opinion to Justice Stanley Reed, a Kentucky Democrat.

Perhaps people shouldn't exalt their private notions of what the community should do over those of the Justices of the Supreme Court, but it is difficult to construct a constitutional theory by which dissent is permitted only to minorities, never to majorities. Vigorous majority dissent carries a wallop, and not only for practical reasons. Justice Jackson once (in a discussion of reapportionment, incidentally) described as "a doctrine wholly incompatible with faith in democracy" and "a vicious teaching" the notion that "it would be nice if there were some authority to make everybody do the things we ought to have done and leave undone the things we ought not to have done." Just as judges cannot escape making decisions, the citizenry in a democracy cannot escape the determination of what is to be done about those decisions. The coercive power of the courts—indeed, of law itself—comes to a stop at the gates of policy. Within those gates, no court can do more than persuade.

4

Yet one cannot end here. Felix Frankfurter liked to observe that "Chief Justices of the United States are rarer than Presidents." There have been only fourteen of them altogether, only ten since Marshall. To speak personally for a moment at the end of a long trail, it seems quite obvious to me that when men come to write the history of the quarter-century after World War II, they will find that the dominant figure in American life was Earl Warren, and that the nation was blessed by the accident of his presence as Chief Justice. Once a year, the Chief Justice by tradition reports on the progress of the federal courts to the American Law Institute. It is a moving experience to be in the room when Warren enters, and to feel the tide of affection that flows to him, even from men who disagree profoundly with his opinions. For Warren has ennobled their profession, and most of the best lawyers know it.

He has done so by reopening, in a harsh age, the old questions about justice and law. That the Chief Justice believes in law is, of course, beyond doubt; but he believes much more profoundly in justice, and in the use of law to achieve it. A few years ago I sat for the first time behind the pillars in the big ugly courtroom, where the press can move back and forth without disturbing anybody, and heard Warren read an opinion. He told the story of a company which had stalled off negotiations with the union that represented its maintenance employees until three days before the expiration of their contract—and had then informed the union that the work was being contracted out to a third party who could do it cheaper, and all the union members were out of jobs. The company had, of course, secured competent opinion that its course of conduct violated no laws; indeed, the first officer of the National Labor Relations Board to hear the case had thrown it out. Subcontracting work to an outsider to save costs is an almost minimum management prerogative in a competitive economy.

Warren, his massive head shaking as he spoke, summarized the facts in his earnest, rather heavy way; and what he was saying, really, was "They shouldn't have done this." As he neared the decision itself, his tone changed to "They shouldn't be *allowed* to do this." And when he came to the end, what he was saying was "Dammit, they're *not* allowed to do this." The union members were reinstated with back pay. (Or so the Supreme Court ruled; the incident was then already half a dozen years old, the men who had been fired didn't want their old jobs back, and a complicated negotiation and additional lawsuit—still not even near final decision in early 1967, almost a decade after the events—would be necessary to give the decision practical effect. Justice is easier said than done.) Warren carried the rest of his bench with him on the decision, though not on the opinion; Justice Stewart in particular was concerned about what the opinion might mean in less brutal circumstances. This was tricky law the Chief Justice was making in his outrage at the behavior of an employer; the accordion ought not to be opened too far. Confronted at conference with a less dedicated hatred of injustice than Warren's, some of the concurring Justices, one felt, might have decided to sacrifice the individuals in this case to the stability and rationality of law.

Justice dies with its beneficiaries, while law remains. Justice is always in large degree anarchic, dependent on the individual situations of the parties to the case. The only possible operational definition of the word says that justice is the visceral reaction of informed people.

We are told that the Supreme Court has an "activist" majority; and at least two members of that majority have in truth said very foolish things at informal gatherings of lawyers and law professors. But the Court does not—cannot—go out and seek its cases. Its most "activist" opinions were born in cases where lower courts had with varying degrees of concern declared themselves powerless to stop developments that were not only unjust but unreasonably unjust. School segregation, whatever the framers of the Fourteenth Amendment may have meant and whatever the precedents may have said, was an outrage in a nation which had sent all its races overseas to die in three great wars within fifty years. The refusal of the legislatures to reapportion themselves violated a fundamental logic of democratic government. No fair-minded man, judge or otherwise, could support a system that sought to solve the bitter problems of criminal justice on the cheap by permitting the police to abuse the poor. Nobody who could see—even glimpse—the faces behind the documents could passively accept an inevitable powerlessness to supply a remedy.

It is always important, of course, to articulate as carefully as possible the reasons for a decision—to remember, as Henry Hart wrote, that the Court is "a tribunal which, after all, does not in the end have the power either in theory or in practice to ram its own personal preferences down other people's throats." But when the justice of the case is so obvious to so many, it may in the long run be more important to get the decision right than to get the reasoning clear. "The state courts," says Traynor sadly, "should have protected the Supreme Court. There's a heavy responsibility that's been missed."

Warren alone among the men who have occupied this office— the point is crucial, and is rarely mentioned—made his career as a lawyer almost entirely in the criminal field. As District Attorney of Alameda County he had been forced every day, as appellate judges are never forced, to weigh the fates of individuals who were not symbols on pieces of paper but live prisoners many of whom he had met, beginning to rot in jails which were fundamentally under his control. As Attorney General of California, he had lived with the wartime persecution of the Japanese-Americans—the attainder of blood, as Justice Jackson called it. If the lower courts insisted on forcing to his attention cases where they had found the law unable to do justice in the lives of real people, he would see his duty clear. As a leader—and a political leader, at that—he could carry his Court with him.

No doubt there have been losses. Law serves better than justice to control that self-deception which is part of all mankind, including judges. Jackson was right to remind his brethren of the "treacherous ground we tread when we undertake to translate ethical concepts into legal ones, case by case." Moreover, the waters of public debate have been muddied. Because the Court's only weapon in many of these matters is the Constitution, its actions have reinforced that chattering about constitutionality which is the blight of American political life. "Preoccupation by our people with the constitutionality instead of with the wisdom of legislation or of executive action is preoccupation with a false value," Frankfurter wrote. ". . . [C]onstitutionality does not exact a sense of proportion or the sanity of humor or an absence of fear." Holmes once wrote that "It is revolting to have no better reason for a rule than that so it was laid down in the time of Henry IV"; and the circumstance is made only somewhat less revolting when the name of George Washington is substituted for that of Henry IV.

"John Marshall has made his decision," Andrew Jackson is reported (probably inaccurately) to have said. "Now let him enforce it." Except in the brief period directly following the decision, before the readjustments can be made, the Court has relatively little power. It has been a fairly consistent loser: as Justice Jackson wrote, "In no major social or economic policy has time vindicated the Court." It has not been a shield for liberty when liberty was seriously endangered, by the red scares after the two world wars, by the hysteria over the Japanese on the West Coast, by the draft boards. Henry Hart and Herbert Wechsler are undoubtedly correct in their insistence that "as a matter of the hard facts of power, a government needs courts to vindicate its decisions." But an even harder fact of power is that a popular government, sooner or later, and probably sooner, will find courts to vindicate its decisions. "The ultimate reliance for the deepest needs of civilization," Frankfurter wrote, upholding the conviction of the Communists under the Smith Act, "must be found outside their vindication in courts of law."

There remains the delay: the Supreme Court can make the nation stop and think, and sometimes it can make the nation ashamed of itself. If the Supreme Court cannot actually make national policy on the issues that have come before it during Chief Justice Warren's incumbency, it can deny the legitimacy of drifting without policy in such areas as segregation, criminal justice, civil liberties and apportionment. Those who support the Court's decisions in these areas have had to learn a bitter lesson in what Roscoe Pound called "the limits of effective legal action." But those who oppose these decisions have learned the more important lesson that they cannot simply ignore the Court: there is no status quo ante available for a comfortable return after the Court has spoken. The Chief Justice and his brethren have demonstrated rather surprisingly that their Court can cure one of the ills of society: paralysis. Those who remember the mood of the American community in 1953 will not underestimate the accomplishment.

Cardozo saw a "wide gap between the use of the individual sentiment of justice as a substitute for law, and its use as one of the tests and touchstones in construing or extending law." We see a continuum rather than a gap, and we can easily place the Warren bench toward one end of the continuum. It is the better end. Better the follies of "one person—one vote" than the stasis of dishonest apportionment; better the *ipse dixit* of *Miranda* than the bedeviling of suspects; better the agony of a society forced to confront its own bigotry than the hidden slaveries of segregation. Set in motion, even in blind motion, the society will save itself if it is worth saving. Among the more obvious phenomena of our time is the fact that the areas on which the Court has (however imperfectly) spoken now command the talents of men much more able than those who were working on these problems before.

Meanwhile, the Court has improved the *tone* of the legal profession. The rest of us, after all, put up with the arrogance of the lawyers—accept their rigidities, their partial perceptions, their occasional corruption, their portentous self-praise, their cant, their infernal waste of our time—not because we care about the niceties or even about the creative accomplishments of the legal system, but because we sense, we hope, that the law seeks justice. That law must be stable to permit people to base their plans on it is not a theory which impresses us much when the plans produce visible injustice. We see little harm and much good in making lawyers analyze the facts of a case as they will appear not only to the law but also to the public. A layman, McGeorge Bundy, once suggested to a rather annoyed audience of law professors that "the fundamental function of the law is to prevent the natural unfairness of human society from becoming intolerable." What we value in the best of the lawyers is not their technical skill, their ability to manipulate the system, but their feeling for fairness, for the realities of a conflict not only of interests but of principles. Lawyers themselves, off duty, usually reserve their highest respect for other lawyers who radiate this sense of equity. It is comforting for us, and salutary for the profession, to feel that the Chief Justice agrees.

NOTES

PREFACE

Page
xi   Francis Bacon quote: Bacon, *Novum Organum*, in Kuhn, *The Structure of Scientific Revolutions*, Phoenix ed., p. 18.
xiii It is unprofessional to solicit: Drinker, *Legal Ethics*, pp. 316–318.
xiii A law firm may not acquiesce: *Ibid.*, p. 288.
xiii The duty of publicity: Brandeis, letter to his wife, in Mason, *Brandeis: A Free Man's Life*, p. 94.

CHAPTER 1.   A NUMBER OF LAWYERS: THE PROFESSIONAL FROM A DISTANCE

3   John W. Davis quote: *The Association of the Bar of the City of New York* (pamphlet, 1958), p. 30.
3   Lord Melbourne quote: Cecil, *Lord M.*, p. 161.
3   Harrison Tweed quote: Botein, *Trial Judge*, Cornerstode ed. p. 149.
4   Plato quote: *Theaetetus*, Jowett trans., Vol. II, pp. 177–178.
4   Louis D. Brandeis quote: Mason, *Brandeis: A Freeman's Life*, p. 86.
4   Kingman Brewster, Jr. quote: *Yale Law Report*, Spring, 1966, p. 5.
6   Elihu Root quote: Jessup, *Elihu Root*, p. 133.
6   Felix Frankfurter quote: *Felix Frankfurter Reminisces*, p. 128.
6   And he shall be thy spokesman: Exodus 4:16.
6   Hubert J. O'Gorman quote: O'Gorman, *Lawyers and Matrimonial Cases*, p. 112.
7   Michael Musmanno quote: Prentice-Hall, *Lawyers' Encyclopedia*, p. 1141.
7   George Wharton Pepper quote: Pepper, *Philadelphia Lawyer*, p. 59.
7   John C. Johnson quote: Acheson, *Morning and Noon*, p. 213.
7   Carl Sandburg poem: "The Lawyers Know Too Much," cited in Llewellyn, *The Bramble Bush*.
8   Public opinion polls invariably show: Prentice-Hall, *A Lawyer's Practice Manual*, p. 20.
8   Of those laymen interviewed: *Ibid.*, p. 30.
8   A Survey by Columbia's Bureau of Applied Social Research: Hunting and Neuwirth, *Who Sues in New York City?*, pp. 81, 73.
9   Karl Llewellyn quote: Llewellyn, *The Bramble Bush*, p. 142.
9   Learned Hand quote: Hand, "The Deficiencies of Trials to Reach the Heart of the Matter," 3 *Lectures on Legal Topics* 89, p. 105.
9   Tocqueville quote: Tocqueville, *Democracy in America*, Knopf ed., Vol. I, p. 278.
10 George Wharton Pepper quote: Pepper, *op. cit.*, p. 384.
10 The corporation president with whom you work: *A Lawyer's Practice Manual*, pp. 90–91.
11 Erwin Griswold quote: Berman, ed., *Talks on American Law*, p. 190.

Page

11   Robert P. Patterson quote: Blaustein and Porter, *The American Lawyer*, p. 118.

11   Jean Monnet quote: Acheson, *op cit.*, p. 146.

11   John J. McCloy quote: McCloy, "The Extracurricular Lawyer," 15 *Washington and Lee Law Review*, 171, pp. 182–183, 179.

12   In 1958 a county attorney in New Mexico: *Hanagan v. Board of County Commissioners of the County of Lea*, 32 P2d 282.

12   Daniel Webster quote: Hurst, *The Growth of American Law*, p. 367.

13   Felix Frankfurter quote: Love and Childers, eds., *Listen to Leaders in Law*, p. 8.

14   Charles Belous quote: *Case and Comment*, November-December, 1955, p. 3.

14   A federal court, refusing to give the government: *U.S. v. U.S. Shoe Machinery Corp.*, 89 F Supp 357, p. 359.

15   The minimum tolerable level of performance: Johnstone and Hopson, *Lawyers and Their Work*, p. 235.

16   Internal Revenue Service data: Smith and Clifton, "Income of Lawyers 1962–1963," 52 *American Bar Association Journal* 1043.

17   An Indiana study in 1963: Indiana State Bar, *Economics of Law Practice*, 1963.

17   Jerome Carlin survey: Carlin, *Lawyers' Ethics*, p. 27.

20   A number of the firms have nicknamed: Practising Law Institute, *Managing Law Offices*, p. 3.

22   If packaging is important for commodities: *Lawyer's Practice Manual*, p. 149.

22   Another authority advises: Dinkel, "The Deduction for Legal Fees," 3 *Law Office Economics and Management*, p. 247.

22   The schedules are probably not enforceable: McKean, *The Integrated Bar*, p. 21.

22   The state bar of New Mexico comment: New Mexico, *Official Advisory Statewide Minimum Fee Schedule 1961*, p. 3.

22   ABA pamphlet statement: ABA Economics of Law Practice Series No. 2, p. 27.

23   Seeing an estate through a probate court: MacKinnon, *Contingent Fees for Legal Services*, p. 19.

24   The Commercial Law League of America: *Ibid.*, p. 25.

24   Harry Gair action: *Gair v. Peck*, 160 NE2d 43.

25   The busted issue point: PLI, *op. cit.*, p. 22.

CHAPTER 2.   A NUMBER OF LAWYERS: SKILLS AND FUNCTIONS

28   John K. Carlock quote: Love and Childers, eds., *Listen to Leaders in Law*, pp. 265–266.

28   Arthur E. Sutherland, Jr. quote: Hurst, *The Growth of American Law*, pp. 329.

28   The law is a profession: Tweed, *The Changing Practice of the Law*, p. 19.

28   Lawyers should pay some attention: *Ibid.*, p. 8.

29   Lon Hocker quote: Curtis, *It's Your Law*, p. 18.

30   Aron Steuer quote: Aron Steuer, *Max D. Steuer, Trial Lawyer*, p. 301.

31   Paul Carrington quote: Love and Childers, *op. cit.*, p. 142.

32   In January, 1966, Continental Casualty revealed: Richard M. Deybold, "Attorneys' Professional Liability Claims," 7 *Law Office Economics and Management* 57.

Page

32 The physical requirements of the advocate: Wellman, *A Day in Court,* pp. 25–26.

32 Edward Bennett Williams tells a prize story: Love and Childers, *op. cit.,* p. 125.

32 According to Wellman, an English barrister: Wellman, *The Art of Cross-Examination,* p. 40.

33 The New York firm of Milbank, Tweed: Pfeiffer, *Law Practice in a Turbulent World,* p. 190.

34 Charles P. Curtis quote: Curtis, *op. cit.,* pp. 25–26.

35 The British bar seems fairly: Quoted in R. E. Megarry, Q.C., *Lawyer and Litigant in England,* p. 18.

35 *The American Jury:* Kalven and Zeisel, *The American Jury,* pp. 371–372.

35 For criminal trials there are statistics: *Ibid.,* pp. 502–503.

36 Karl Llewellyn quote: Llewellyn, *The Bramble Bush,* p. 143.

36 James Willard Hurst quote: Hurst, *op. cit.,* p. 172.

37 About four out of five claims: Zeisel, Kalven and Buchholz, *Delay in the Courts,* p. 105.

37 These proportions vary erratically: Rosenberg and Sovern, "Delay and the Dynamics of Personal Injury Litigation," 59 *Columbia Law Review* 1115.

37 Abraham Lincoln quote: Angle and Miers, *The Living Lincoln,* p. 144.

38 Bernard Botein quote: Cited in Zeisel, Kalven and Buchholz, *op. cit.,* p. 108.

38 Hubert J. O'Gorman quote: O'Gorman, *Lawyers and Matrimonial Cases,* pp. 107, 109.

39 An attorney would file the necessary pleadings: Brigitte M. Bodenheimer, "The Utah Marriage Counseling Experiment, an Account of Changes in Divorce Law and Procedure," 7 *Utah Law Review* 443, pp. 443–444.

46 In *Lawyers and Their Work:* Johnstone and Hopson, *Lawyers and Their Work,* p. 127.

47 Harrison Tweed quote: Love and Childers, *op. cit.,* p. 313.

48 Karl Llewellyn quote: Llewellyn, *Jurisprudence,* p. 257.

48 Benjamin Cardozo quote: Cited in Tweed, *op. cit.,* p. 35.

49 David Riesman quote: Riesman, "Toward an Anthropological Science of Law and the Legal Profession," in *Individualism Reconsidered,* Free Press ed., p. 442.

50 Reed Dickerson quote: Dickerson, "The Diseases of Legislative Language," 1 *Harvard Journal on Legislation* 1, pp. 1, 5, 7.

52 Henry J. Friendly quote: Friendly, "The Gap in Lawmaking—Judges Who Can't and Legislatures Who Won't," 63 *Columbia Law Review* 787, p. 792.

53 Missouri bar study quote: Prentice-Hall, *A Lawyer's Practice Manual,* p. 55.

54 G. E. Hale quote: G. E. Hale, "Preventive Law: Experience in the Antitrust Field," 38 *Southern California Law Review* 391, p. 393.

55 The Missouri Bar study of the 1960s: 39 *Journal of the State Bar of California* 658.

55 The School of Business at the University of Washington study: *How Small Business Firms in the State of Washington Cope with Their Legal Problems* pp. 23, 24, 29.

56 The New York Stock exchange: *Lawyer's Practice Manual,* p. 78.

57 Nationally, of lawyers twenty-eight and under: *The 1964 Statistical Lawyer Report,* Tables 3, 8.

60 Jerome Carlin quote: Carlin, *Lawyers on Their Own,* pp. 13–14.

61 Robert H. Jackson quote: Jackson, "The County-Seat Lawyer," 36 *American Bar Association Journal* 497.

Page

62 The California Supreme Court once found: *Hildebrand* v. *State Bar of California,* 117 P2d 863.

63 Boswell's *Life of Johnson:* Cited in Cheatham, ed., *Selected Readings on the Legal Profession,* p. 91.

64 Johnstone and Hopson write that Wall Street's: Johnstone and Hopson, *op. cit.,* p. 144.

64 There has never apparently been any extensive attempt: Drinker, *Legal Ethics,* p. 48.

64 Unauthorized practice of law is a swindle: Otterbourg, *A Study of Unauthorized Practice,* p. 4.

65 Chief Justice Taft quote: *Green* v. *Huntington National Bank,* 212 NE 2d 585.

65 Karl Llewellyn quote: Llewellyn, *Jurisprudence,* p. 253.

66 Jack L. Bernstein quote: 49 *New Jersey Bar Journal* 57, pp. 57, 58; adapted by the author from his article in January, 1936, *American Mercury.*

66 Of 2,325 law graduates of June, 1948: 28 *Personnel and Guidance Journal* 554.

66 The first such was signed: Johnstone, "The Unauthorized Practice Controversy: A Struggle Among Power Groups," 4 *Kansas Law Review* 1, p. 23.

66 These treaties have relaxed: Indiana State Bar, *Economics of Law Practice in Indiana,* 1963.

67 The way out has been pointed: *Brotherhood of Railway Trainmen* v. *Commonwealth of Virginia ex rel. Virginia State Bar,* 377 US 1.

68 These people do not want cut rates: "Group Legal Service," 39 *Journal of the State Bar of California* 639, p. 688.

68 The committe also noted that: *Ibid.,* p. 714.

68 Burnham Enerson quote: 51 *American Bar Association Journal* 1068.

69 An Illinois survey in 1959: 6 *Law Office Economics and Management* 346.

CHAPTER 3. THE LAW SCHOOLS: WHERE THE LAWYERS COME FROM

71 Louis M. Brown quote: Brown, "Law Offices for Middle-Income Clients," 7 *Law Office Economics and Management* 43, p. 55.

72 Joseph N. Welch quote: 58 *Harvard Law Review* 1136.

74 It comes as a distinct surprise: Warkov, *Lawyers in the Making,* p. 73.

74 Frank C. Newman quote: Newman, "The Public Responsibilities of the Academic Law Teacher," 14 *Journal of Legal Education* 105, p. 106.

76 David Riesman quote: Riesman, "Law and Sociology: Recruitment, Training and Colleagueship," 9 *Stanford Law Review* 643, p. 648.

76 Karl Llewellyn quote: Llewellyn, *The Bramble Bush,* p. 12.

77 Maitland quote: Maitland, *The Forms of Action,* p. 2.

78 William Blackstone, then a disappointed barrister: *The Maitland Reader,* Oceana ed., p. 129.

79 Maitland quote: *Ibid.,* p. 54.

80 Charles W. Eliot quote: Harno, *Legal Education in America,* p. 56.

80 Jerome Frank quote: Frank, "A Plea for Lawyer Schools," 56 *Yale Law Journal* 1303.

81 Louis D. Brandeis quote: Mason, *Brandeis: A Free Man's Life,* p. 35.

81 Jerome Frank quote: Frank, "Why Not a Clinical-Lawyer School?," 81 *University of Pennsylvania Law Review* 907, p. 911.

82 Warren Seavey quote: 79 *Harvard Law Review* 1333, p. 1339.

84 F. W. Maitland quote: *The Maitland Reader,* p. 228.

84 Dean Griswold quote: Griswold, *Law and Lawyers in the United States,* p. 52.

Page
85 Karl Llewellyn quote: Llewellyn, *op. cit.*, p. 133.
85 David Riesman quote: Riesman, "Law and Social Science: A Review of Michael and Wechsler's Casebook on Criminal Law and Administration," 70 *Yale Law Journal* 636.
86 Thomas Reed Powell quote: Arnold, *The Symbols of Government*, Harbinger ed., p. 101.
87 Justice Holmes quote: Holmes, "The Path of the Law," 10 *Harvard Law Review* 457–478, in Henson, ed., *Landmarks of Law*, p. 49.
87 Henry Stimson quote: Bundy and Stimson, *On Active Service in Peace and War*, p. xv.
88 David Cavers quote: Berman, ed., *Talks on American Law*, p. 204.
90 Lasswell and McDougal quote: Lasswell and McDougal, "Legal Education and Public Policy," 52 *Yale Law Journal* 203, pp. 206, 207, 212, 214, 215.
90 McDougal speech: 56 *Yale Law Journal* 1345, p. 1346.
91 Criticizing the case method twenty-five years ago: Riesman, "Law and Social Science," *op. cit.*, p. 651.
93 A 1947 sample survey of Harvard Law School: *Preliminary Statement of the Committee on Legal Education of the Harvard Law School*, 1947, p. 26.
94 About one-fifth of entering law students: Rogers, "Continuing Education of the Bar," 28 *Tennessee Law Review* 445, p. 453; Vanderbilt, "A Report on Pre-Legal Education," 25 *New York University Law Review* 199.
96 Karl Llewellyn quote: Llewellyn, *op. cit.*, p. 135.
96 Louis Toepfer quote: Warkov, *op. cit.* p. xviii.
97 In a speech to the Association of American Law Schools: Clark and Callahan, 17 *Journal of Legal Education* 250.
104 Alfred Z. Reed quote: Reed, *Training for the Public Profession of the Law*, p. 57.
106 Johnstone and Hopson quote: Johnstone and Hopson, *Lawyers and Their Work*, pp. 558–559.
107 Sidney Post Simpson quote: Simpson, "Continuing Education of the Bar," 59 *Harvard Law Review* 694, pp. 694, 700.
107 A New England group queried: Goodman and Rabinowitz, "Lawyer Opinion on Legal Education: A Sociological Analysis," 64 *Yale Law Journal* 537, pp. 540–541.
108 Felix Stumpf quote: Stumpf, "What You Should Know About Continuing Legal Education," 39 *Los Angeles Bar Bulletin* 42.
110 Karl Llewellyn quote: Llewellyn, *op. cit.*, p. 105.
110 Felix Frankfurter quote: Phillips, *Felix Frankfurter Reminisces*, p. 27.
112 Dean Harno quote: Harno, *op. cit.*, p. 194.
113 Roger Traynor quote: Traynor, "The Right Honorable Law Reviews," 10 *UCLA Law Review*, November, 1962, p. 26.
116 Kenneth Pye quote: Department of Health, Education and Welfare, *The Extension of Legal Services to the Poor*, p. 179.

CHAPTER 4. JURISPRUDENCE: WHERE THE LAWS COME FROM

119 Oliver Wendell Holmes, Jr. quote: Holmes, "The Path of the Law," in Henson, ed., *Landmarks of Law*, Beacon ed., p. 43.
119 Sir Henry Maine quote: Maine, *Ancient Law*, Beacon ed., p. 348.
119 Spinoza quote: Spinoza, *Tractatus Theologico-Politicus*, in Cohen and Cohen, *Readings in Jurisprudence*, p. 633.
119 H. L. A. Hart quote: Hart, *The Concept of Law*, p. 1.
120 In 1944 a lady fortuneteller: *Ibid.*, p. 60.
121 Archaic procedure shows us: Pollock, *Jurisprudence*, Macmillan ed., p. 13.

Page
121 Paul Bohannan quote: Bohannan, "Primitive Law," in Bohannan, ed., *Law and Warfare*, p. 20.
121 Holmes quote: Holmes, *op. cit.*, p. 42.
121 To conceive of any part of human conduct: Pollock, *op. cit.*, p. 14.
121 The anthropologist E. Adamson Hoebel: Hoebel, *The Law of Primitive Man*, p. 28.
122 Henry M. Hart, Jr. and Albert M. Sacks quote: Hart and Sacks, "The Legal Process" (mimeo, 1958 ed.), p. 4.
122 Frederick Pollock quote: Pollock, *op. cit.*, p. 15.
122 Benjamin Cardozo quote: Cardozo, *The Nature of the Judicial Process*, Yale ed., p. 103.
123 Blackstone quote: Cited in Biddle, *Justice Holmes, Natural Law and the Supreme Court*, p. 17.
124 A brooding omnipresence in the sky: *Southern Pacific* v. *Jensen*, 244 US 205, p. 222.
124 Benjamin Cardozo quote: Cardozo, *op. cit.*, p. 33.
125 Harlan Fiske Stone quote: Stone, "The Common Law in the United States," 50 *Harvard Law Review* 4, p. 36.
125 John Chipman Gray quote: Gray, *The Nature and Sources of the Law*, Beacon ed., p. 280.
126 In 1928 the Supreme Court found: *Long* v. *Rockwood*, 257 US 142.
126 Four years later, the Court overruled: *Fox Film Corp.* v. *Doyal*, 268 US 123.
126 The New York courts not only held: *People ex rel. Rice* v. *Graves*, 273 NYS 582.
126 Gray quote: Gray, *op. cit.*, p. 99.
127 Lord Radcliffe quote: Radcliffe, *The Law and Its Compass*, Faber and Faber ed., pp. vii, 11.
127 Benjamin Cardozo quote: Cardozo, *The Growth of the Law*, p. 62.
128 Chancery had three great advantages: Louisell and Hazard, *Pleading and Procedure*, p. 34.
129 Learned Hand quote: Hand, *The Bill of Rights*, p. 39.
129 Of average vigour and obstinacy: Bramwell, cited in Fuld, "Address to the New York State Bar Association," January 29, 1949, pp. 8–9.
129 Blackstone quote: Ehrlich, *Blackstone*, pp. 55, 15.
130 The barons of the Exchequer in Elizabethan England: "Heydon's Case, 76 Eng. Rep. 637," in Cohen and Cohen, *op. cit.*, p. 498.
130 James C. Carter quote: Carter, "The Proposed Codification of the Common Law," in Cohen and Cohen, *op. cit.*, p. 393.
131 The high point of this judicial sabotage: *Johnson* v. *Southern Pacific*, 117 F 462.
133 Roscoe Pound quote: *The Spirit of the Common Law*, pp. 21–22.
133 Sir Henry Maine quote: Maine, *op. cit.*, p. 13.
134 Arthur Vanderbilt quote: Vanderbilt, *Men and Measures in the Law*, p. 82.
134 Henry J. Friendly quote: Friendly, "The Gap in Lawmaking: Judges Who Can't and Legislators Who Won't," 63 *Columbia Law Review* 787, p. 793.
134 Holmes quote: *Southern Pacific* v. *Jensen*, 244 US 205, p. 221.
134 Gray quote: Gray, *op. cit.*, p. 173.
135 Lon Fuller quote: Fuller, *The Morality of Law*, Yale ed., p. 111.
135 In the United States lawyers found: Frankfurter, "Some Reflections on the Reading of Statutes," in Henson, ed., *Landmarks of Law*, p. 225.
135 Robert H. Jackson quote: *Schwegmann Bros.* v. *Calvert Corp.*, 341 US 384, p. 396.

Page

135 Hart and Sacks quote, Hart and Sacks, *op. cit.*, p. 1201.

136 The flagellant theory of statutory interpretation: *Ibid.*, p. 99.

136 Roger Traynor quote: Traynor, "No Magic Words Could Do It Justice," 49 *California Law Review* 615, p. 620.

136 Emerging problems of social maladjustment: Hart and Sacks, *op. cit.*, p. 186.

139 He then had to face the fact: *Swift* v. *Tyson*, 16 Pet. 1, in Hart and Wechsler, *The Federal Courts and the Federal System*, p. 612.

140 Karl Llewellyn quote: Llewellyn, *The Common Law Tradition: Deciding Appeals*, p. 414.

140 Gray quote: Gray, *op. cit.*, p. 253.

141 Holmes quote: *Black and White Taxicab Co.* v. *Brown and Yellow Taxicab Co.*, 276 US 518, p. 532.

141 At least one modern historian has argued: Crosskey, *Politics and the Constitution in the History of the United States*, Vol. II, pp. 900–902.

141 And the same men who wrote the Judiciary Act: Warren, "New Light on the History of the Federal Judiciary Act of 1789," 37 *Harvard Law Review* 49.

142 Justice Brandeis quote: *Erie Railroad Co.* v. *Tompkins*, 304 US 64; in Hart and Wechsler, *op. cit.*, p. 626.

143 Joseph C. Hutcheson, Jr. quote: Llewellyn, *op. cit.*, p. 417.

143 Henry J. Friendly quote: Friendly, *op. cit.*, p. 789.

143 An injured Californian was permitted: *Grant* v. *McAuliffe*, 264 P2d 944.

143 In 1957 Minnesota courts held: *Schmidt* v. *Driscoll Hotel, Inc.*, 82 NW2d 365.

143 In 1963 the Courts of New Hampshire: *Thompson* v. *Thompson*, 193 A2d 439.

143 The fastest motion (forward and backward): *Kilberg* v. *Northeast Airlines*, 172 NE2d 526.

143 Similarly, New York approved of an award: *Babcock* v. *Jackson*, 191 NE2d 279.

144 The New York court held that a Colorado: *Dym* v. *Gordon*, 16 NY2d 120.

144 Judge Friendly quote: Friendly, "In Praise of Erie—and of the New Federal Common Law," 19 *Record of the Association of the Bar of the City of New York* 64, p. 80.

144 Justice Brandeis himself brushed aside: *Henderlider* v. *La Plata River and Cherry Creek Ditch Co.*, 304 US 92, p. 110.

CHAPTER 5. CRIMINAL MATTERS: THE WAY IT IS NOW

149 G. K. Chesterton quote: Cited in Kuh, *National Conference on Bail and Criminal Justice*, p. 240.

149 Edward L. Barrett, Jr. quote: Cited in Jones, ed., *The Courts, the Public and the Law Explosion*, p. 87.

153 In Britain the circumstances: Metropolitan Police Courts Act, Section 24.

156 Charles P. Curtis quote: Curtis, *Lions Under the Throne*, p. 256.

159 A Midwestern prosecuting attorney told: Newman, *Conviction*, p. 74.

160 Recently, the Las Vegas courts: Virtue, *Survey of Metropolitan Courts*, p. 327.

160 In Wisconsin the newspapers had some fun: Newman, *op. cit.*, p. 101.

161 The National Crime Commission reported: *The Challenge of Crime in a Free Society: Report of the President's Commission on Law Enforcement and the Administration of Justice*, p. 129.

Page
165 Since a Supreme Court decision in 1963: *Douglas* v. *California*, 372 US 353.
166 Karl Llewellyn quote: Llewellyn, *Jurisprudence*, p. 400.
166 Montesquieu quote: Montesquieu, *L'Esprit des Lois*, cited in Ploscowe, "Criminal Process," 48 *Harvard Law Review* 433, pp. 453–454.
166 Holmes quote: Holmes, *The Common Law*, p. 75.
167 Jerome Hall quote: Hall, "Ignorance and Mistake in Criminal Law," 33 *Indiana Law Journal* 1, p. 22.
167 It is a principle of English law: *Rex* v. *Haddock*, CCA Miscellaneous Cases, *Criminal Law* 31 (1927).
167 Justice Johnson quote: Hart and Wechsler, *The Federal Courts and the Federal System*, p. 1086.
168 Circuit Judge Simon E. Sobeloff: Sobeloff, "Appellate Review of Criminal Sentences," 41 *American Bar Association Journal* 13, p. 15.
168 The thief caught in the act in Rome: Maine, *Ancient Law*, Beacon ed., p. 366.
168 When the state forced the criminal: Pound, *The Spirit of the Common Law*, Beacon ed., p. 85.
168 Holmes quote: Holmes, *op. cit.*, p. 42.
169 In Macaulay's nineteenth-century: *Ibid.*, p. 40.
169 Karl Llewellyn quote: Llewellyn, *op. cit.*, p. 408.
170 Francis Allen quote: Allen, *The Borderland of Criminal Justice*, pp. 3–4.
171 There is a value in getting these things: Barrett, in Jones, ed., *op. cit.*, p. 109.
177 The central assumption of the system: Denning, *The Road to Justice*, p. 34.
177 Chief Justice Warren quote: *Miranda* v. *Arizona*, 384 US 436, p. 469.
178 There is a German case: Sobel, *Selected Materials on New York Criminal Practice*, Practising Law Institute, ch. 5, p. 17.
178 Sir Frederick Pollock quote: Pollock, *The Genius of the Common Law*, p. 16.
179 Karl Llewellyn quote: Llewellyn, *op. cit.*, pp. 402–403.
180 The most recent full report: *Report of the District Attorney, County of New York, 1949–1954*, p. 16.
181 William McAdoo quote: "New York City Board of Aldermen Committee to Investigate the Police Department, 1913," transcript, pp. 3910–3911.
181 In *Garrison* v. *Louisiana*: 379 US 64.
182 Impressed with the improvement: Goldstein, "The State and the Accused: Balance of Advantage in Criminal Procedure," 69 *Yale Law Journal*, p. 1149.
182 Roscoe Pound quote: Pound, "The Future of the Criminal Law," in Cohen and Cohen, *Readings in Jurisprudence and Legal Philosophy*, p. 309.
183 One study has estimated that 56 percent: Silverstein, *Defense of the Poor in Criminal Cases in American State Courts*, table, p. 8.
183 A court official in Cheyenne: Virtue, *op. cit.*, p. 326.
184 In one recent year: Rubin, *Crime and Juvenile Delinquency*, pp. 122–123.
184 Irving R. Kaufman quote: *U.S.* v. *Bonanno*, 180 F. Supp. 71, p. 83.
185 The innocent suffer with the guilty: *People* v. *Cahan*, 44 Cal. 2nd 434, p. 447.

CHAPTER 6. CRIMINAL MATTERS: THE SEARCH FOR SOMETHING BETTER

186 Mr. Dooley quote: Dunne, Bander ed., *Mr. Dooley on the Choice of Law*, p. 1.

Page

186 Roscoe Pound quote: Pound, "The Future of the Criminal Law," in Cohen and Cohen, *Readings in Jurisprudence and Legal Philosophy*, p. 311.

187 The Supreme Court upheld the arrest: *Trupiano* v. *U.S.*, 334 US 699.

187 In the case of a crooked rare-stamp dealer: *U.S.* v. *Rabinowitz*, 339 US 56.

187 The case in which the doctrine was most seriously: *Jencks* v. *U.S.*, 353 US 657.

188 New Federal Rules allow limited access: *The Challenge of Crime in a Free Society*, p. 138.

188 The time a defendant needs counsel: *Ex parte Sullivan*, 107 F. Supp. 514, p. 517.

188 A dissent to one of them said: *Escobedo* v. *Illinois*, 378 US 478, p. 494.

189 The victims, later released, sued: Rudé, *Wilkes and Liberty*, p. 28.

189 If the government was prohibited: *Weeks* v. *U.S.*, 232 US 383.

189 Benjamin Cardozo quote: *People* v. *Defore*, 242 NY 13, p. 21.

189 In 1949, largely to eliminate the silver platter: *Wolf* v. *Colorado*, 338 US 25.

190 *Mapp* v. *Ohio*, in 1961: 367 US 643.

191 If one is indicted or appealed of felony: *Wigmore on Evidence*, Nos. 816–817.

191 And in the nineteenth century: *Ibid.*, Nos. 544–557.

191 Toward the end of the century, a six-man: *Bram* v: *U.S.*, 168 US 532.

191 John H. Wigmore quote: Wigmore, *op. cit.*, No. 823, n. 1.

191 Federal crimes, except for prohibition offenses: Hart and Wechsler, *The Federal Courts and the Federal System*, pp. 1024–1068.

192 The Supreme Court of Mississippi: *Brown* v. *Mississippi*, 297 US 278.

192 In a Texas case the state: *Ward* v. *Texas*, 316 US 547.

192 A rape-murder in Indiana: *Watts* v. *Indiana*, 388 US 49.

192 Illinois police told a lady: *Lynumn* v. *Illinois*, 372 US 528.

193 The Court in a bootlegging case: *McNabb* v. *U.S.*, 318 US 332.

193 And then in a rape case: *Mallory* v. *U.S.*, 354 US 449.

193 Year after year, the Court denied: American Law Institute, *A Model Code of Pre-Arraignment Procedure*, Tentative Draft 1, p. 183.

193 And then, in 1964, there arrived: *Escobedo* v. *Illinois*, 378 US 478.

194 William Brennan quote: *Haynes* v. *Washington*, 373 US 503.

196 Criminal justice is not a sport: American Law Institute, *op. cit.*, pp. 171, 173.

196 Nice people have some rights: *Killough* v. *U.S.*, 315 F2d 241, p. 265 (dissent).

197 James Vorenberg quote: *New York Times*, June 15, 1966, p. 1.

199 A local judge commented: Uviller and Lang, "Miss Mapp and Society's Search for Justice," 60 *Legal Aid Review* 13.

200 Defense counsel often present: LaFave and Remington, "Controlling the Police: The Judge's Role in Making and Reviewing Law Enforcement Decisions," 63 *Michigan Law Review* 987, pp. 1003–1004.

200 Thurman Arnold quote: Arnold, *The Symbols of Government*, Harbinger ed., p. 155.

201 Nearly thirty years after *Nardone* v. *U.S.*: *Nardone* v. *U.S.*, 302 US 379.

201 Walter Gellhorn quote: Gellhorn, *When Americans Complain*, p. 32.

202 In Chicago investigators found: LaFave and Remington, *op. cit.*, p. 1006.

203 Nathan Sobel quote: Sobel, *Selected Materials on New York Criminal Practice*, Practising Law Institute, ch. 3, p. 70.

203 Pressure to deal with the situation: American Law Institute, *op. cit.*, p. 174.

203 Defenders of exclusion can: Rogge, "Of Pleas and Confessions," 23 *Bar Bulletin* 49, p. 58.

204 Nathan Sobel quote: Sobel, *op. cit.*, ch. 5, p. 3.

Page
204 Roscoe Pound quote: Pound, *The Causes of Popular Dissatisfaction with the Administration of Justice*, pp. 10–12.
205 Abraham Goldstein quote: Goldstein, Book Review, *New Republic*, August 27, 1966, p. 28.
205 Justice Douglas quote: *McCray* v. *Illinois*, 1966 October Term, No. 159, p. 3 (dissent).
210 A parallel study of accused felons: Rankin, "The Effect of Pretrial Detention," 39 *New York University Law Review* 641, p. 642.
212 Roy Harper quote: *National Conference on Bail and Criminal Justice*, p. 193.
212 Rupert Crittenden quote: *Ibid.*, p. 199.
212 Finally, bail is used for purposes: Botein and Sturz, "Report on Pre-Trial Procedures," 5 *Journal of the International Commission of Jurists* 203, p. 211.
213 Francis Allen has said that it does: *Report of the Attorney General's Committee on Poverty and the Administration of Criminal Justice* (1963), p. 60.
215 Maitland quote: Maitland, *Domesday Book and Beyond*, Fontana ed., pp. 56–57.
215 As late as 1771 a French criminologist: Goldstein, "Police Discretion Not to Invoke the Criminal Process: Low-Visibility Decisions in the Administration of Justice," 69 *Yale Law Journal* 543.
216 What lawyers call "the insanity defense": Allen, *The Borderland of Criminal Justice*, p. 104.
217 Indigent defendants have already appealed: *Defender Newsletter*, November, 1965, p. 10.
217 David T. Bazelon quote: *Durham* v. *U.S.*, 214 F2d 862.
217 Herbert Wechsler quote: Paulsen, Reporter, *The Problem of Responsibility*, p. 9.
218 Monrad Paulsen quote: *Ibid.*, p. 1.
218 Chief Justice Weintraub quote: *Ibid.*, p. 78.
218 Herbert Weshcler quote: *Ibid.*, p. 19.
218 Garofalo quote: Allen, *op. cit.*, p. 81.
219 When a jury find that an accused person: Friedmann, *Law in a Changing Society*, Penguin ed., p. 149.
219 All acts—healthy, sick, or not-sure-which: Gaylin, "Psychiatry and the Law: Partners in Crime," *Columbia University Forum*, Spring 1965, p. 25.
219 Wolfgang Friedmann quote: Friedmann, *op. cit.*, p. 150.
219 Pointing out that there is no purpose: Birnbaum, "Primum Non Nocere: How to Treat the Criminal Psychopath," 52 *American Bar Association Journal* 69.
220 It has been estimated that one-ninth: *The Challenge of Crime in a Free Society*, p. 55.
220 A study by the Institute of Judicial Administration: Virtue, *Survey of Metropolitan Courts*, pp. 183–184.
220 But the rules are fairly uniform: Rubin, *Crime and Juvenile Delinquency*, p. 107 n.
220 Roscoe Pound quote: Rubin, *op. cit.*, p. 27.
221 Almost all of us are criminals: *Ibid.*, p. 27.
222 Half had no college degree: *The Challenge of Crime in a Free Society*, p. 80.
224 Perhaps the most upsetting single piece: Wald, "Pretrial Detention and

Page

Ultimate Freedom, a Statistical Study," 39 *New York University Law Review* 631, pp. 638–639.

224 Harry W. Jones quote: Jones, ed., *The Courts, the Public and the Law Explosion*, p. 140.

225 The factors which determine this difference: Paulsen, Reporter, *The Problem of Sentencing*, pp. 64, 66, 67.

225 The National Crime Commission has recommended: *The Challenge of Crime in a Free Society*, p. 146.

226 War or surgery for homicides: Cited in Cohen and Cohen, *op. cit.*, p. 293.

226 Morris Raphael Cohen quote: *Ibid.*, p. 360.

227 Norval Morris quote: Morris, "Prison in Evolution," *Federal Probation*, December, 1965, p. 22.

227 Marchese de Baccaria quote: Cohen and Cohen, *op. cit.*, p. 347.

228 Bruce Jackson poem: Jackson, "Prison Folklore," 78 *Journal of Folklore* 317.

CHAPTER 7. P. I. AND OTHER WRONGS

230 Samuel P. Sears quote: Sears, "In Defense of the Defense," 25 *Insurance Counsel Journal* 428, p. 429.

230 Oliver Wendell Holmes, Jr. quote: Holmes, *The Common Law*, pp. 111–112.

230 Montaigne quote: Cited in Curtis, *It's Your Law*, p. 33.

231 He that smiteth a man: Exodus 21:12, 19.

232 Sir Henry Maine quote: Maine, *Ancient Law*, Beacon ed., p. 358.

232 That felt need for vengeance: Holmes, *op. cit.*, p. 2.

232 In Exodus the ox that gored: Exodus 21:28.

232 Plato quote: *Laws* 14, in Jowett Plato, Vol. II, p. 618.

232 As late as 1842 a locomotive: *Queen v. Eastern Counties R. Co.*, 10 M & W 58, cited in Gray, *The Nature and Sources of the Law*, Beacon ed., p. 47.

232 Pollock and Maitland quote: Pollock and Maitland, *History of English Law*, Vol. II, pp. 470–471.

233 If a man is damaged: J. Littleton, cited in Holmes, *op. cit.*, p. 86.

233 As late as 1616 English courts; *Weaver v. Ward*, 80 Eng. Rep. 284.

233 Holmes quote: Holmes, *op. cit.*, p. 86.

234 Lord Ellenborough quote: *Butterfield v. Forrester*, 103 Eng. Rep. 926, cited in Prosser, "Comparative Negligence," 51 *Michigan Law Review* 465, p. 467.

234 Nobody has ever succeeded in justifying: Prosser, *Comparative Negligence*, p. 469.

234 Sir Frederick Pollock quote: Pollock, *The Genius of the Common Law*, p. 118.

235 This cruelty, like contributory negligence: *Baker v. Bolton*, 1 Campbell 493.

235 William Prosser quote: Prosser, *Torts*, 1964 ed., No. 12, cited in Speiser, *Recovery for Wrongful Death*, p. 10.

235 In 1867 the Supreme Court of Michigan: *Hyatt v. Adams*, 16 Michigan 180, cited in Speiser, *op. cit.*, p. 9.

236 The case of man who had thrown a lit firecracker: *Scott v. Shepherd*, cited in Holmes, *op. cit.*, p. 88.

236 Again, a court ruled that a drug supplier: *Thomas v. Winchester*, 6 NY 397.

236 Finally, in a decision by the house of Lords: *Rylands v. Fletcher*, 19 LT 220.

236 Benjamin Cardozo quote: *MacPherson v. Buick*, 217 NY 382.

238 Decisions in Texas and Tennessee: Kalven, "The Jury, the Law and the Personal Injury Damage Award," 19 *Ohio State Law Journal* 159, p. 171.

238 The decision that withdrew the immunity: *Silva v. Providence Hospital of Oakland*, 97 P2d 798, p. 800.

Page

239 In 1961 Chief Justice Roger J. Traynor: *Muskopf* v. *Corning Hospital District*, 359 P2d 457, p. 459.

240 Max Radin quote: Radin, "A Speculative Inquiry into the Nature of Torts," 21 *Texas Law Review* 697, p. 704.

240 Guido Calabresi quote: Calabresi, "The Decision for Accidents, An Approach to Nonfault Allocation of Costs," 78 *Harvard Law Review* 713.

240 David F. Cavers quote: Cavers, *The Choice of Law Process*, p. 144.

241 Blum and Kalven quote: Blum and Kalven, "Public Law Perspectives on a Private Law Problem; Auto Compensation Plans," 31 *University of Chicago Law Review* 641, p. 700.

242 Prosser quote: Prosser, *Comparative Negligence*, p. 486.

242 Liability is routinely imposed: "Report of the Committee on Personal Injury Claims," 40 *Journal of the California State Bar* 148, p. 202.

242 Holmes quote: Holmes, *op. cit.*, p. 144.

242 In Massachusetts . . . personal injury claims: Projected from *Insurance Facts 1966*, Insurance Information Institute.

244 Holmes quote: Holmes, *op. cit.*, p. 96.

244 In 1911 the New York Court of Appeals: *Ives* v. *The South Buffalo Ry. Co.*, 201 NY 271.

244 Justice McKenna quote: *Arizona Employers' Liability Cases*, 250 US 400, p. 436.

244 Robert Keeton quote: Keeton, "Conditional Fault in the Law of Torts," 72 *Harvard Law Review* 401, p. 441.

244 Blum and Kalven quote: Blum and Kalven, *op. cit.*, pp. 662, 681.

245 [T]*he question for decision today:* Report of the Committee, *op. cit.*, p. 200.

245 Fleming James, Jr. quote: James, "An Evaluation of the Fault Concept," 32 *Tennessee Law Review* 394, p. 398.

251 *Kilberg* v. *Northeast Airlines:* 9 NY2d 34.

255 Harold A. Smith quote: Smith, "The Role of the Lawyer in a Changing World," 33 *Indiana Law Journal* 198.

256 A Connecticut study in the early 1930s: Corstvet, "The Uncompensated Accident and Its Consequences," 3 *Law and Contemporary Problems*, 466, p. 470; percentages recalculated to eliminate incomplete cases.

256 In Pennsylvania in 1959: Morris and Paul, "The Financial Impact of Automobile Accidents," 110 *University of Pennsylvania Law Review* 913, p. 916.

256 In Michigan in 1960: Conard, "The Economic Treatment of Automobile Injuries, 63 *Michigan Law Review* 279.

256 Even in New York: Franklin, Chanin and Mark, "Accidents, Money and the Law, a study of the Economics of Personal Injury Litigation," 61 *Columbia Law Review* 1.

256 The operating costs of the damage system: Conard, *op. cit.*, p. 290.

256 A quick browse through a recent issue: *1963 Iowa Academy of Trial Lawyers Bulletin*, pp. 8, 5, 6.

256 Only in New York do insurance companies: Jaffe, "Damages for Personal Injury and the Impact of Insurance," 18 *Law and Contemporary Problems* 219.

257 In a recent year in California: Judicial Council of California, *18th Biennial Report*, p. 143.

257 Two and a half years is the normal wait: Zeisel, Kalven and Buchholz, *Delay in the Courts*, p. xxiii n.

258 A study in Philadelphia indicated: Levin and Woolley, *Dispatch and Delay*, p. 14.

258 David Peck quote: Peck, *Do Juries Delay Justice?*, 18 FRD 455, p. 460.

Page

258 *Delay in the Courts* . . . and the opposing comment: Zeisel, Kalven and Buchholz, *op. cit.*, pp. 191, 191 n. 192, citing *Gray* v. *Gray*, 128 NE2d 602, pp. 604–605, and Dworkin, "Let's Arbitrate," 29 *Cleveland Bar Association Journal* 107.

258 The world's record is apparently held: *Ibid.*, pp. 196–197, citing memo of Chief Judge Reardon of Massachusetts Superior Court.

260 But the poorer the victim: Morris and Paul, *op. cit.*, p. 923.

260 A Pennsylvania survey found: Levin and Woolley, *op. cit.*, p. 15.

261 Reginald Heber Smith quote: Smith, *Justice and the Poor*, p. 86.

261 California courts have held: *Jones* v. *Martin*, 256 P2d 905.

262 MacKinnon quote: MacKinnon, *Contingent Fees in Legal Services*, p. 204.

263 Joseph C. Hutcheson, Jr. quote: Hutcheson, "The Judgment Intuitive: The Function of the Hunch in Judicial Decision," 14 *Cornell Law Quarterly* 274, p. 282.

263 Henry Charles Lea quote: Lea, "The Wager of Battle," in Bohannan, ed., *Law and Warfare*, p. 234.

263 David Peck quote: Peck, "Court Organization and Procedures to Meet the Needs of Modern Society," 33 *Indiana Law Journal* 182, p. 193.

264 On the alleged ground: Judicial Council of California, *op. cit.*, p. 45.

264 Hans Zeisel quote: Zeisel, Book Review, 8 *Stanford Law Review* 730, p. 738 n.

264 Among the hypothetical situations: Carlin, *Lawyers' Ethics*, pp. 251, 48.

265 [T]he law as it now stands: Report of California Committee, *op. cit.*, p. 219.

267 Jack Ladinsky quote: Ladinsky, "Careers of Lawyers, Law Practice and Legal Institutions," 8 *American Sociological Review*, February, 1963, 47, p. 54; italics in original.

268 The Pennsylvania survey showed: Morris and Paul, *op. cit.*, p. 924.

268 In a New York sample of cases: Franklin, Chanin and Mark, *op. cit.*

269 Judge Botein estimates that the average: Botein and Gordon, *The Trial of the Future*, p. 106.

270 Walter Schaefer quote: "Remarks of Walter Schaefer," 39 *Chicago Bar Record* 265, pp. 266–267.

271 Lord Denning quote: Denning, *The Road to Justice*, p. 51.

CHAPTER 8. THE IDEA OF JUSTICE AND THE POOR

272 Benjamin Cardozo quote: Cardozo, *The Growth of the Law*, p. 87.

272 Mr. Dooley quote: Dunne, Bander, ed., *Mr. Dooley on the Choice of Law*, pp. xxii–xxiii.

273 Max Weber quote: Gerth and Mills, ed., *From Max Weber*, Oxford University Press ed., p. 185.

273 Roscoe Pound quote: Pound, *The Spirit of the Common Law*, Beacon Press ed., pp. 135, 124.

274 Lord Devlin quote: Borrie and Diamond, *The Consumer, Society and the Law*, p. 48.

274 Justice Reed quote: *Dalehite* v. *U.S.*, 346 US 16, p. 42.

275 As late as the 1950s New Haven: Brownell, *Legal Aid in the United States*, p. 190.

275 That every poor person or persons: 11 Henry VII, cap. 12.

275 Reginald Heber Smith quote: Smith, *Justice and the Poor*, p. 9.

276 Our productive procedure ought to be based: *Ibid.*, p. 42.

277 Eustace Seligman quote: 21 *New York State Bar Bulletin* 90.

281 David Caplovitz quote: Caplovitz, *The Poor Pay More*, p. 21.

Page
282 Hire purchase consists in being persuaded: Borrie and Diamond, *op. cit.*, p. 140.
283 In 1938 a British judge: *Ibid.*, p. 35.
285 In 1948 a survey by the Iowa Bar: Brownell, *op. cit.*, pp. 77–78.
285 Raynor Gardiner quote: Gardiner, "Defects in Present Legal Aid Services and the Remedies," 22 *Tennessee Law Review* 505.
285 Ten years later, Brownell: Brownell, *Supplement*, pp. 46, 69, 70.
286 Only one such program was set up: *New York Times*, September 2, 1966, p. 16.
287 [F]inancial dependence on local business: Carlin and Howard, "Legal Representation and Class Justice," 12 *UCLA Law Review* 381, p. 415.
288 One of the principal drawbacks: *Ibid.*, p. 432.
288 William R. Vance quote: Cited in Brownell, *Legal Aid*, p. 60.
289 As a Legal Aid lawyer told: *New York Times*, September 20, 1966.
291 This process of proving and maintaining eligibility: Greenleigh Associates, *Report to the Moreland Commission* (1962), p. 78.
292 [H]earing decisions do not always have: Department of Health, Education and Welfare, *The Extension of Legal Services to the Poor*, p. 34 n.
293 Wolfgang Friedmann quote: Friedmann, *Law in a Changing Society*, Penguin ed., p. 158.
293 Carlin and Howard quote: Carlin and Howard, *op. cit.*, p. 424; from Caplovitz, *op. cit.*, p. 155.
293 Marvin Frankel quote: Frankel, "Experiments in Serving the Indigent," 51 *American Bar Association Journal* 460, pp. 461–462.
294 Charles Reich quote: Reich, "The New Property," 73 *Yale Law Journal* 733, p. 786.
294 Harry W. Jones quote: Jones, "The Rule of Law and the Welfare State," 58 *Columbia Law Review* 143, p. 154.
296 Judah Gribetz and Frank P. Grad quote: Gribetz and Grad, "Housing Code Enforcement; Sanctions and Remedies," 66 *Columbia Law Review* 1254, p. 1290.
298 The unscrupulous loan company: Brendes and Schwartz, "Schlockmeister's Jubilee: Bankruptcy for the Poor," 40 *Journal of the National Conference in Bankruptcy* 69.
298 Nicholas deB. Katzenbach quote: HEW, *op. cit.*, p. 13.
300 The opinion by Judge Charles Breitel: "Application of Community Action for Legal Services, Inc.," 274 NYS 2d 779, p. 789.
300 Marvin Frankel quote: Frankel, "The War Against Poverty: A Challenge to Legal Aid," 63 *Legal Aid Review* 14.
300 Pollock quote: Pollock, *Jurisprudence*, p. xl.
300 Walter Gellhorn quote: Gellhorn, *When Americans Complain*, p. 44.
301 Charles P. Curtis quote: Curtis, *It's Your Law*, pp. 60–61.
301 One of the neighborhood lawyers was consulted: HEW, *op. cit.*, Parker, *The New Haven Model*, p. 91.
301 Neighborhood groups reacted with hostility: Cahn and Cahn, "The War on Poverty: A Civilian Perspective," 73 *Yale Law Journal* 1317, p. 1348.

CHAPTER 9.   PIECES OF PAPER

305 Mr. Dooley quote: Dunne, Bander, ed., *Mr. Dooley on the Choice of Law*, p. 36.
305 Elihu Root quote: Jessup, *Elihu Root*, Vol. II, p. 472.
305 Robert T. Swaine quote: Swaine, "The Impact of Big Business on the Legal Profession," 35 *American Bar Association Journal* 89.

Page

307   Harrison Tweed quote: Love and Childers, *Listen to Leaders in Law*, p. 313.

307   Arthur A. Ballantine quote: *The Bulletin*, internal publication of Root, Clark, Buckner & Howland, February 14, 1920.

308   Lawrence Boonin quote: Joint Committee on Continuing Legal Education (ALI-ABA), "Law and Computers in the Mid-Sixties" (study transcript), p. 245.

308   Paul D. Cravath quote: Swaine, *The Cravath Firm*, Vol. II, p. 266.

309   Robert Swaine quote: Swaine, "The Impact of Big Business," *op. cit.*, pp. 370–371.

310   Blackstone quote: Blackstone, *Commentaries*, Ehrlich ed., p. 100.

311   Before 1800 there were only 213: Warren, *The Supreme Court in United States History*, Vol. I, p. 491 n.

312   Roger Taney quote: *Ibid.*, Vol. II, p. 24 n., citing *Ohio Life Ins. v. Debolt*, 16 Howard 435.

312   Banjamin Tappan quote: *Ibid.*, Vol. II, pp. 96–97.

312   Elihu Root quote: Jessup, *op. cit.*, Vol. I, p. 207.

312   Marshall quote: *U.S. v. Devaux*, 5 Cranch 61, 86.

313   In 1844 the Supreme Court: *Louisville, Cincinnati & Charleston RR v. Letson*, 2 Howard 497.

313   Herbert Wechsler quote: Hart and Wechsler, *The Federal Courts and the Federal System*, p. 894.

314   Joseph James quote: James, *The Framing of the Fourteenth Amendment*, Illini Books ed., pp. 31, 194.

320   The largest specialized law firm: David T. Link, in "Law and Computers," *op. cit.*, p. 160.

321   Timothy Pfeiffer quote: Pfeiffer, *Law Practice in a Turbulent World*, pp. 185–190.

324   Phil E. Gilbert quote: Practising Law Institute, *Managing Law Offices* (forum transcript), p. 213.

324   Harrison Tweed quote: Tweed, *The Changing Practice of the Law*, p. 14.

325   Robert T. Swaine quote: Swaine, *Cravath Firm*, Vol. II, p. 712.

326   Erwin O. Smigel quote: Smigel, *The Wall Street Lawyer*, p. 37.

327   I would like to see our firm adopt: *Managing Law Offices*, p. 162.

329   James B. Tucker quote: *Ibid.*, pp. 147–148.

329   D. Nelson Adams quote: *Ibid.*, p. 135.

330   Hoyt A. Moore quote: Swaine, *Cravath Firm*, Vol. II, p. 143.

330   Harrison Tweed quote: Love and Childers, *op. cit.*, p. 313.

331   A lot of men who lost their partnership: Smigel, *op. cit.*, p. 75.

332   Lawrence B. Morris quote: *Managing Law Offices*, p. 98.

333   We focus on technical things: *Ibid.*, p. 198.

334   If there is an opening: *Ibid.*, pp. 195–196.

337   Frank Dewey quote: *Ibid.*, pp. 206, 205.

337   Outside of New York City: Johnstone and Hopson, *Lawyers and Their Work*, p. 241.

337   Clarence Seward quote: Swaine, *Cravath Firm*, Vol. I, p. 447.

338   Milbank, Tweed, Hadley & McCloy recently: Pfeiffer, *op. cit.*, pp. 311–312 n.

339   Harlan F. Stone quote: Stone, "The Public Influence of the Bar," 48 *Harvard Law Review* 1, pp. 6–7.

339   Ferdinand Lundberg quote: Lundberg, "The Legal Profession—A Social Phenomenon," *Harper's Magazine*, December, 1938, p. 4.

340   Brandeis quote: Mason, *Brandeis: A Free Man's Life*, p. 103.

340   Roscoe Pound quote: Pound, *The Lawyer from Antiquity to Modern Times*, p. 232.

340   Marshall quote: *McCulloch v. Maryland*, 4 Wheaton 316, 431.

Page
340 Justice Holmes quote: *Pan-handle Oil Co.* v. *Mississippi,* 277 US 218, p. 223.
340 *Ex parte Young:* 209 US 123.
340 According to a debate in Congress: Hart and Wechsler, *op. cit.,* p. 848.
341 John Foster Dulles quote: Dulles, "Administrative Law, a Practical Attitude for Lawyers," 25 *American Bar Association Journal* 275, p. 277.
341 Cravath quote: Swaine, *Cravath Firm,* Vol. II, p. 97.
341 Elihu Root quote: Jessup, *op. cit.,* Vol. I, p. 435.
342 Karl Llewellyn quote: Llewellyn, *The Bramble Bush,* pp. 149–150.
342 Charles Horsky quote: Horsky, *The Washington Lawyer,* pp. 125–126.
343 Charles W. Davis quote: *Managing Law Offices,* p. 204.
343 Robert T. Swaine quote: Swaine, *Cravath Firm,* Vol. II, p. 149.
343 Joseph Borkin quote: Borkin, *The Corrupt Judge,* p. 177.
344 We disapprove of a partner: *Managing Law Offices,* p. 73.
344 Our experience has been that the corporations: *Ibid.,* p. 72.
345 Horsky quote: Horsky, *op. cit.,* p. 127.

CHAPTER 10. BUSINESS IN WASHINGTON

346 Lee Loevinger quote: Loevinger, "Regulation and Competition as Alternatives," 11 *Antitrust Bulletin* 1, p. 17.
346 M. J. Rossant quote: Rossant, "Defect in Fund Survey," *New York Times,* December 7, 1966.
347 Maitland quote: Maitland, *The Forms of Action at Common Law,* p. 15.
349 *Munn* v. *Illinois:* 94 US 113.
349 Louis L. Jaffe quote: Jaffe, "An Essay on the Delegation of Legislative Power," 47 *Columbia Law Review* 359, p. 360.
350 Learned Hand quote: Hand, *The Spirit of Liberty,* Dilliard ed., Vintage, p. 14.
350 The high point in judicial prohibition: *Reploge* v. *Little Rock,* 267 SW 353.
350 Elihu Root quote: Frankfurter, *Law and Politics,* Capricorn ed., p. 258.
351 Among them Van Devanter: Jaffe, *op. cit.,* II, 47 *Columbia Law Review* 561, p. 567.
351 Felix Frankfurter quote: Frankfurter, *op. cit.,* pp. 321–322.
351 Chief Justice Taft quote: *J. W. Hampton Co.* v. *U.S.,* 276 US 394.
352 An 1895 notice in a legal directory: Horsky, *The Washington Lawyer,* p. 19.
353 Felix Frankfurter quote: Frankfurter, *op. cit.,* pp. 247–248.
356 James M. Landis quote: Landis, *Report on the Regulatory Agencies to the President-Elect,* December, 1960, p. 71.
357 Charles Horsky quote: Horsky, *op. cit.,* pp. 160–161.
358 Horsky quote: *Ibid.,* p. 32.
359 Lee Loevinger quote: Loevinger, "The Administrative Agency as a Paradigm of Government—A Survey of the Administrative Process," 40 *Indiana Law Journal* 287, p. 292.
360 The Supreme Court held that as the law was written: *Federal Radio Commission* v. *GE,* 281 US 464.
361 By far the most significant for the industry: *NBC* v. *U.S.,* 319 US 190.
363 When the Commission tried to dump: *Melody Music, Inc.,* v. *FCC,* 345 F2d 730.
365 Writing about this question recently: Loevinger, "Program Regulation," 20 *Federal Communications Bar Journal* 14.
365 One of the Commissions's very few efforts: *FCC* v. *ABC,* 347 US 284.
366 But in these areas, as a network official: Tribune Co., 9 *Radio Regulations* 719, p. 770 n., cited in Friendly, *The Federal Administrative Agencies,* p. 72.

Page

368 Judge Friendly has commented acidly: Friendly, *ibid.*

368 The FCC processes almost 3,000: Loevinger, "Paradigm," pp. 300–301.

368 This administrative Board . . . is the last stop: Woll, *Administrative Law: The Informal Process*, p. 151.

368 Loevinger quote: Loevinger, "Paradigm," p. 305.

369 Louis J. Hector quote: Hector, "Problems of the CAB and the Independent Regulatory Commissions," 69 *Yale Law Journal* 931, pp. 932–934.

369 The Board had in its own thinking: Subcommittee on Administrative Practice and Procedure of the Committee on the Judiciary, US Senate, 86th Congress, 2nd Session, *Hearings, Federal Administrative Procedure*, p. 231; in Woll, *op. cit.*, p. 173.

370 A disgusted trucker in Chicago: ICC Docket No. M-19432.

371 The National Recovery Administration: Jaffe, *op. cit.*, p. 570.

371 Even then, Professor Jaffe reports: *Ibid.*, p. 570.

371 The case in which most of this came out: *Panama Refining Co. v. Ryan*, 293 US 388.

371 Professor Jaffe recalled a dozen years later: Jaffe, *op. cit.*, p. 571.

371 Justice Brandeis quote: Pusey, *Charles Evans Hughes*, Vol. II, p. 734.

372 Justice Traynor quote: Traynor, "Some Open Questions on the Work of State Appellate Courts," 24 *University of Chicago Law Review* 211, p. 211.

372 Hector quote: Hector, *op. cit.*, p. 947 n.

373 Landis quote: Landis, *op. cit.*, p. 55.

373 The Commission would . . . continue to adhere: "*Eine Kleine Juristiche Schlummergeschichte*," 79 *Harvard Law Review* 921, p. 924.

374 [C]ourts are not charged with: *FCC v. Pottsville Broadcasting Co.*, 309 US 134, p. 146.

375 Kenneth Culp Davis quote: Davis, *Administrative Law*, p. 82.

375 Justice Frankfurter quote: Frankfurter, *The Public and Its Government*, Beacon ed., p. 160.

375 In dealing with tires and canned milk: "*Eine Kleine Juristiche*," p. 928.

375 Justice Harlan quote: *FTC v. Sun Oil Co.*, 371 US 505, p. 530.

376 A Court of Appeals has commented: *Borden Co. v. FTC*, 339 F2d 133, p. 139.

376 Henry Friendly quote: Friendly, "The Gap in Lawmaking—Judges Who Can't and Legislators Who Won't," 63 *Columbia Law Review* 787, p. 794.

376 Lee Loevinger quote: Loevinger, "Paradigm," p. 303.

376 You know . . . we keep talking about philosophy: Friendly, *The Federal Administrative Agencies*, pp. 97–98.

377 [E]ven our adversary or "cease and desist": "*Eine Kleine Juristiche*," pp. 925–926 n.

378 Loevinger quote: Loevinger, "Paradigm," p. 310.

378 Administrative agencies are creating: Friendly, *The Federal Administrative Agencies*, p. 174.

378 What would you think of a court: Friendly, "A Look at the Federal Administrative Agencies," 60 *Columbia Law Review* 429, pp. 437–438.

378 Wolfgang Friedmann quote: Friedmann, *Law in a Changing Society*, Pelican ed., p. 316.

378 In Europe, the business community: "*Eine Kleine Juristiche*," p. 931.

CHAPTER 11. A SMALL BAG OF SPECIALISTS

384 Archibald Cox quote: Cox, "The Place of Law in Labor Arbitration," 35 *Chicago Bar Record* 205, p. 210.

Page
385 Sylvester Garrett quote: Garrett, "Are Lawyers Necessarily an Evil in Grievance Arbitration?," 8 *UCLA Law Review* 535, p. 544.

385 Paul Bohannan quote: Bohannan, "Primitive Law," in Bohannan, ed., *Law and Warfare*, p. 16.

386 When I was comparatively new at arbitration: Hays, *Labor Arbitration— A Dissenting View*, pp. 62–63.

386 The rigged award . . . is a shocking distortion: *Ibid.*, p. 65.

387 The common law of the shop: *United Steel Workers* v. *Warrior & Gulf Navigation Co.*, 363 US 475, p. 582.

390 Mark Sullivan credited this Act: Sullivan, *Our Times*, Vol. I, pp. 201, 219; in Finkelstein, "The Copyright Law—A Reappraisal," 104 *University of Pennsylvania Law Review* 1025, p. 1027.

391 Learned Hand quote: *Sheldon* v. *Metro-Goldwyn Pictures Corp.*, 8 F2d 49, p. 54.

391 Unsuccessful playwrights, the Court of Appeals: *Christie* v. *Cohan*, 154 F2d 827, p. 828, in Finkelstein, Review, 72 *Yale Law Journal* 844, p. 847.

391 Justice Holmes quote: *Hadley P. Hanson* v. *Globe Newspaper Co.*, 159 Mass 293, in Lerner, *The Mind and Faith of Justice Holmes*, p. 99.

392 Potter Stewart quote: *Jacobellis* v. *Ohio*, 378 US 184, p. 197.

392 William Brennan quote, *Roth* v. *U.S.*, 345 US 476, p. 484.

393 Leon Friedman quote: Friedman, "The Ginzburg Decision and the Law," 36 *American Scholar* 1, pp. 81, 85.

394 Learned Hand quote: *U.S.* v. *Levine*, 83 R2d 156, p. 157; citation omitted.

394 The leading case involved an opera singer: *Lumely* v. *Wagner*, 42 Eng. Rep. 687.

397 Advising "the general practitioner" to be sure: Werner, "Protecting Your Client's Invention," *Wisconsin Bar Bulletin*, August, 1965, in *Case and Comment*, March–April, 1966, 1, p. 4.

399 Invalid patents, in the hands of unscrupulous: Kitch, "*Graham* v. *John Deere Co.*: New Standards for Patents," *1966 Supreme Court Review*, p. 343 n.

400 Patent infringement suits . . . cost: *Ibid.*, p. 343.

401 In the period 1953–63: Dearborn and Boal, "Adjudication by Circuits and Arts Involved," in Calvert, *Encyclopedia of Patent Practice and Invention Management* (1964), pp. 22–23.

401 In 1850, in the "doorknob case": *Hotchkiss* v. *Greenwood*, 52 US 248.

401 Giles Rich quote: Rich, Kettering Award Address, in *Proceedings, 8th Annual Public Conference*, PTC Research Institute, George Washington University, 1964, p. 141.

401 In 1941 Justice Douglas raised: *Cuno Engineering Corp.* v. *Automatic Devices Corp.*, 314 US 84.

401 The roadblock was the word "invention": *Walker on Patents*, Deller ed., Vol. I, p. 110.

402 Finally, in 1952, a new patent act: *House of Representatives Report*, 82nd Congress, 2nd Session, May 12, 1952, p. 1923.

402 *Graham* v. *John Deere Co.*: 383 US 1, p. 17.

402 In 1966, for the first time: *U.S.* v. *Adams*, 383 US 39.

403 A 1965 report from the Department of State: McKitterick, *East-West Trade*, Twentieth Century Fund, pp. 57–58.

405 A law review article was written a dozen years ago: Carey, "Pressure Groups and the Revenue Code: A Requiem in Honor of the Departing Uniformity of the Tax Laws," 68 *Harvard Law Review* 745.

405 Judge Friendly quote: Friendly, "Satisfaction, Yes—Complacency, No," 51 *American Bar Association Journal* 715, p. 719.

Page

410 In Connecticut, for example: Countryman, "The Bankruptcy Boom," 77 *Harvard Law Review* 1452, p. 1455.

413 Herzog quote: Herzog, 39 *Journal of the National Conference of Referees in Bankruptcy*, p. 110.

414 One referee, from Detroit, wrote: Katchen, "The Image of the Bankruptcy Court, 40 *Journal of the National Conference of Referees in Bankruptcy*, p. 7.

CHAPTER 12. WHO HAS SEEN THE LAW? BOOKS, BINDERS AND BITS

418 Arthur Vanderbilt quote: Vanderbilt, *Men and Measures in the Law*, p. 6.

421 The Supreme Court ruled rather reluctantly: *Wheaton* v. *Peters*, 8 Peters 591.

423 David Mellinkoff, *The Language of the Law*: pp. 279–281.

425 Delmar Karlen quote: Karlen, *Appellate Courts in the United States and England*, pp. 87, 89.

432 David Riesman quote: Riesman, "Law and Sociology: Recruitment, Training and Colleagueship," 8 *Stanford Law Review* 643, p. 653.

432 Craig Spangenberg quote: ALI-ABA Joint Committee, *Law and Computers in the Mid-Sixties*, p. 81.

437 Arthur Vanderbilt quote: Vanderbilt, *op. cit.*, p. 19.

443 Writes the profession's leading authority: Drinker, *Legal Ethics*, p. 273.

444 Horty's example is a search for laws: Commerce Clearing House, *Computers and the Law*, pp. 50–51.

446 David T. Link quote: ALI-ABA, *op. cit.*, pp. 162–163.

CHAPTER 13. THE BUSINESS OF THE COURTS

451 Plato quote: *Laws*, VI, Jowett trans., Vol. II, p. 527.

451 George Washington quote: Washington, letter to Edmund Randolph, in Warren, *The Supreme Court in United States History*, Vol. I, p. 32.

451 David Peck quote: Peck, "Court Organization and Procedures to Meet the Needs of Modern Society," 33 *Indiana Law Journal* 182, pp. 186–187.

452 In 1943 an appellate court in Pennsylvania: Vanderbilt, *Men and Measures in the Law*, p. 137.

452 Louis D. Brandeis quote: Mason, *Brandeis*, p. 580.

453 Maitland quote: Maitland, *The Forms of Action at Common Law*, p. 4.

453 Pollock quote: Pollock, *Jurisprudence*, Macmillan ed., p. 13.

454 [T]he physical-power theory: Jones, ed., *The Courts, the Public and the Law Explosion*, p. 19.

454 Paul R. Hays quote: Hays, *Labor Arbitration*, p. 23.

454 Justice Stone quote: *U.S.* v. *Morgan*, 307 US 183, p. 196.

454 The Permanent Representative of Chile: *Friedberg* v. *Santa Cruz*, 86 NYS2d 369, in Hart and Wechsler, *The Federal Courts and the Federal System*, p. 272.

455 Chief Justice Chase noted that the Constitution gave: Constitution, Article III, Section 2.

455 We are not at liberty to inquire: *Ex parte McCardle*, 7 Wall 506, in Hart and Wechsler, *op. cit.*, pp. 291-292.

456 In some states . . . it is not unusual: Institute of Judicial Administration, *A Guide to Court Systems* (1966), p. 19.

457 A study of the Detroit courts: Virtue, *Survey of Metropolitan Courts*, p. 46.

457 Kalven and Zeisel quote: Kalven and Zeisel, *The American Jury*, p. 13.

458 Kalven and Zeisel in their survey: *Ibid.*, pp. 418–420.

Page

458 Harry W. Jones quote: Jones, ed., *op. cit.*, p. 136.

458 Arthur Vanderbilt quote: Vanderbilt, *Men and Measures in the Law*, p. 114

459 Baron Martin is reputed once: Shientag, *The Personality of the Judge*, p. 61 n.

459 Vanderbilt quote: Vanderbilt, *op. cit.*, p. 99.

459 As the California Judicial Council admitted: California Judicial Council, *18th Biennial Report*, p. 94.

460 No standard descriptions exist: Association of the Bar of the City of New York, *Bad Housekeeping*, p. 9.

460 After much research and investigation: *Ibid.*, p. 49.

460 A typical answer came from Newark: Virtue, *op. cit.*, p. 227.

461 John J. Parker quote: *Bad Housekeeping*, p. 16.

462 Even the loyal, ABA-sponsored Survey: Virtue, *op. cit.*, p. 164.

462 A professor at the Texas Law School: Smith, "Court Administration in Texas: Business Without Management," 44 *Texas Law Review* 1142, p. 1168.

464 [T]he major number of claims: IJA, *Small Claims Courts in the United States*, p. 5.

466 A recent law review note says: Finley, "Judicial Administration: What Is This Thing Called Legal Reform?," 65 *Columbia Law Review* 569, p. 582, cited in IJA, *The Justice of the Peace Today*, p. 117.

466 The Institute of Judicial Administration in 1965: IJA, *The Justice of the Peace Today*, p. 2.

466 In 1927 it was necessary for the Supreme Court: *Tumey v. Ohio*, 273 US 510.

467 The National Crime Commission says: *The Challenge of Crime in a Free Society*, p. 129.

467 In response to a question as to how the justice: *The Courts of New Mexico*, p. 1.

467 In New Mexico the JPs perform: *Ibid.*, p. 2.

467 A JP, who handles about 1,200 cases: *Ibid.*, p. 3.

468 A JP, who grossed: *Ibid.*, p. 4.

468 There is no intention here of supplying a manual: *Ibid.*, p. 39.

468 Until recently, few JPs bothered: *Ibid.*

468 A. . . . she peeled the five off: *Ibid.*, pp. 40–41.

469 Many of the minor courts which were created: IJA, *The Justice of the Peace Today*, pp. 2–3.

469 Lawrence G. Brooks quote: Brooks, "The Citizen and the District Court," *Harvard Alumni Bulletin*, April 18, 1964, p. 549.

469 Maitland quote: Milton, *In Brief Authority*, p. 24.

473 David Peck quote: Peck, *op. cit.*, p. 187.

475 A fundamental cornerstone of the Federal Rules: Quoted in Virtue, *op. cit.*, p. 245.

475 [T]his fish-market pretrial: *Bad Housekeeping*, p. 17.

476 After 14 years at the bar: Virtue, *op. cit.*, p. 270.

477 A THOUGHT TO START: Hunting and Neuwirth, *Who Sues in New York City?*, p. vi.

477 Maurice Rosenberg quote: Jones, ed., *op. cit.*, p. 55.

477 In Philadelphia the Municipal Court: Rosenberg and Schubin, "Trial by Lawyer: Compulsory Arbitration of Small Claims in Pennsylvania," 74 *Harvard Law Review* 447.

477 Zeisel has described arbitration: Zeisel, "Delay by the Parties and Delay by the Courts," 15 *Journal of Legal Education* 27, p. 30.

478 Court Administrator advises: Institute of Judicial Administration, Calendar Status Study 1966, p. 11.

Page

478 This idea was tried out for Zeisel: Zeisel and Callahan, "Split Trials and Time Saving, a Statistical Analysis," 76 *Harvard Law Review* 1606.

478 Definitely not defensible: Jones, ed., *op. cit.,* p. 49.

479 Joseph M. Proskauer quote: *A Segment of My Times,* p. 141.

479 Kalven, Zeisel and Buchholz calculated: *Delay in the Courts,* p. 78.

479 Dean Griswold quote: *Dean's Report, 1962-3,* Harvard Law School, pp. 5-6.

479 David Peck quote: Peck, *op. cit.,* p. 189.

479 Prosser quote: Prosser, "Comparative Negligence," 51 *Michigan Law Review* 465, p. 506.

481 Bernard Botein quote: Botein, *Trial Judge,* Cornerstone Library ed., p. 190.

483 The juries "legislate interstitially": Kalven, "The Jury, the Law and the Personal Injury Damage Award, 19 *Ohio State Law Journal* 158, p. 161.

483 California, thanks to "reforms": Annual Report of the Administrative Office of the California Courts, Fact Sheet 1966, pp. 1-2.

484 An observation by a Chief Justice of Pennsylvania: Levin and Woolley, *Dispatch and Delay,* p. 119 n.

484 And now I fear that in doing so: Botein, "The Case Against Instant Justice," *American Business Law Journal,* Vol. 4, No. 1., Spring 1966, pp. 23-24.

484 Among the costs of the obsession: Jones, ed., *op. cit.,* p. 58.

484 The judge becomes sucked into: Botein, "The Case Against Instant Justice," p. 24.

484 Cognizance of the litigants' desire: Virtue, *op. cit.,* pp. 272-273.

485 Learned Hand quote: Hand, "The Deficiencies of Trials to Reach the Heart of the Matter," 3 *Lectures on Legal Topics* 89, pp. 104-105.

486 An article by a *plaintiff's* lawyer: Cohn, "Medical Malpractice Litigation: A Plague on Both Houses," 52 *American Bar Association Journal,* 32.

486 Judge Botein has noted: Botein and Gordon, *The Trial of the Future,* p. 99.

487 Llewellyn quote: Llewellyn, *The Bramble Bush,* p. 43.

CHAPTER 14. THE PERSONALITY OF THE JUDGE

488 Eugen Ehrlich quote: Ehrlich (Bruncken trans.) *Judicial Freedom of Decision,* 9 Modern Legal Philosophy Series, pp. 65-66.

488 Samuel I. Rosenman quote: Rosenman, speech to American Judicature Society, August 14, 1964.

488 Learned Hand quote: Hand, Dilliard, ed., *The Spirit of Liberty,* Vintage ed., p. 33.

489 Mr. Dooley quote: Dunne, Bander, ed., *Mr. Dooley on the Choice of Law,* p. 37.

489 Kierkegaard quote: Bretall, *A Kierkegaard Anthology,* p. 34.

490 Judge Botein quote: Botein, *Trial Judge,* Cornerstone ed., p. 53.

490 Joseph C. Hutcheson, Jr. quote: Hutcheson, "The Judgment Intuitive: The Function of the Hunch in Judicial Decision," 14 *Cornell Law Quarterly* 274, p. 287.

491 Five Justices of the Supreme Court in 1935: *Dimick v. Schiedt,* 293 US 474.

491 Jerome Frank quote, Frank, *Courts on Trial,* Atheneum ed., p. 117.

492 Judge Botein quote: Botein, *op. cit.,* p. 315.

492 Lord Hewart quote: Shientag, *The Personality of the Judge,* p. 50.

493 Charles E. Wyzanski, Jr. quote Wyzanski. *Whereas: A Judge's Premises,* p. 21.

494 If it is the King's wish: Lloyd, *A Book of Wales,* pp. 272-273.

494 When Chancellor Lyndhurst was asked: Shientag, *op. cit.,* p. 27.

Page
495   Curtis Bok quote: Bok, *The Backbone of the Herring*, p. 3.
495   Justice Lummus quote: Lummus, "The Trial Judge," in Vanderbilt, *The Challenge of Law Reform*, p. 28.
496   When, however, it is necessary for judges: Drinker, *Legal Ethics*, p. 334.
497   Timothy Pfeiffer quote: Pfeiffer, *Law Practice in a Turbulent World*, p. 148.
497   Harry W. Jones quote: Jones, ed., *The Courts, the Public and the Law Explosion*, p. 137.
497   Judge Burnell . . . apparently delights in exhibitions: *Podlaski v. Price*, 196 P2d 608, p. 619.
498   The bench clearly is not getting the lawyers: Winick, Gerver and Blumberg, "The Psychology of Judges," in Toch, ed., *Legal and Criminal Psychology*, p. 129.
498   Felix Frankfurter quote: Frankfurter, *Of Law and Men*, p. 133.
499   One out-of-state administrator had been: American Law Institute, *Division of Jurisdiction*, Tentative Draft 1, Commentary, p. 47.
500   Quite a number of New York lawyers: Borkin, *The Corrupt Judge*, pp. 38–39.
501   Estes Kefauver as chairman of a House: *Ibid.*, pp. 157, 182, 187.
501   Only twice in the twenty-year period: Schroeder and Hall, "25 years of Experience with Merit Judicial Selection in Missouri," 44 *Texas Law Review*, 1088, p. 1093.
502   The Supreme Court in 1920 upheld them: *Evans v. Gore*, 253 US 245.
502   A rather embarrassing opinion overruled in 1939: *O'Malley v. Woodrough*, 307 US 277.
502   Learned Hand quote: Hand, *op. cit.*, p. 60.
503   Riesman quote: Riesman, "Toward an Anthropological Science of Law and the Legal Profession," in *Individualism Reconsidered*, Free Press ed., p. 441.
503   The plebiscite in which the voters are given: Wormuth and Rich, "Politics, the Bar and the Selection of Judges," 3 *Utah Law Review* 459, in Murphy and Pritchett, *Courts, Judges and Politics*, p. 109.
504   Justice Traynor quote: Traynor, "The Unguarded Affairs of the Semikept Mistress," 113 *University of Pennsylavnia Law Review* 485, p. 504.
504   Jefferson quote: Borkin, *op. cit.*, p. 187.
504   Karlen quote: Karlen, "Three Quarters of a Century in Judicial Administration," 32 *Tennessee Law Review* 412, p. 416.
505   Chief Justice Traynor quote: Traynor, "Rising Standards of Courts and Judges: The California Experience," address at summer meeting of Pennsylvania Bar Association, June 24, 1965, p. 14.
506   Delmar Karlen quote: Karlen, "Judicial Education," 52 *American Bar Association Journal* 1049.
507   Virgil Thomson quote: Thomson, *Virgil Thomson*, p. 226.
508   Riesman quote: Riesman, *op. cit.*, p. 441.
508   Lord Jowitt quote: Jowitt, New York University Law Center dinner, September 26, 1947, in Vanderbilt, *Men and Measures in the Law*, p. 149 n.
508   John W. Davis quote: Davis, "The Argument of an Appeal," 26 *American Bar Association Journal* 895, in Gerhart, *The Lawyer's Treasury*, pp. 44, 43.
509   The purpose of a hearing is: Jackson, "Advocacy Before the Supreme Court: Suggestions for Effective Presentation," 37 *American Bar Association Journal* 801, pp. 803, 804.
509   [T]here should be some comfort derived: *Ibid.*, p. 862.
510   The public output of the appellate courts: Hamley, "Selecting Cases for Appellate Review," Institute of Judicial Administration (mimeographed), p. 17.

Page
510 Delmar Karlen quote: Karlen, "Cost of Appeals Study," Institute of Judicial Administration, cited in Karlen, *Appellate Courts in the United States and England,"* p. 162.
511 Learned Hand quote: Hand, *op. cit.,* p. 162.
511 Chief Justice Hughes quote: Pusey, *Charles Evans Hughes,* Vol. II, p. 710.
511 Joseph Weintraub quote: Newark *Star-Ledger,* January 7, 1966, p. 8.
512 Traynor quote: Traynor, "Some Open Questions on the Work of State Appellate Courts," 24 *University of Chicago Law Review* 211, p. 217.
513 Cardozo quote: Cardozo, *The Growth of the Law,* p. 58.
513 Arthur Vanderbilt quote: Vanderbilt, *Improving the Administration of Justice,* p. 106.
513 Frederick Hamley quote: Hamley, *op. cit.,* p. 5.
513 Harrison Tweed quote: Tweed, *The Changing Practice of the Law,* p. 8.
514 Karlen quote: Karlen, *Appellate Courts in the United States and England,* pp. 154–155.
515 Justice Brandeis quote: Wyzanski, *Whereas: A Judge's Premises,* p. 61.
516 Justice Jackson quote: Jackson, *The Supreme Court in the American System of Government,* pp. 14–15.
516 Justice Frankfurter quote: *Dick* v. *N.Y. Life Insurance Co.,* 359 US 437 pp. 458–459.
516 Henry M. Hart, Jr. quote: Hart, "The Supreme Court, 1958 Term. Foreword: The Time Chart of the Justices," 73 *Harvard Law Review* 84, pp. 100, 101.
517 Justice Frankfurter quote: *Cobbledick* v. *U.S.,* 309 US 323.
517 Geoffrey Hazard, Jr. has suggested: Jones, ed., *op. cit.,* pp. 83–84.
518 Each dissenting opinion is a confession: Jackson, *The Supreme Court in the American System of Government,* pp. 19, 18–19.
518 The division be forthrightly exposed: Jackson, "Advocacy Before the Supreme Court," p. 863.
518 I give up: Fuld, "The Voices of Dissent," 62 *Columbia Law Review* 923, p. 925.
518 It is perfectly apparent that the majority: *Ibid.,* p. 924.
518 Holmes was in the public mind: ZoBell, "Division of Opinions on the Supreme Court, a History of Judicial Disintegration," 44 *Cornell Law Quarterly* 186, pp. 202 ff.
518 Charles Evans Hughes quote: Hughes, *The Supreme Court of the United States,* p. 68.
518 Traynor quote: Traynor, *op. cit.,* pp. 218, 219.
519 Karl ZoBell quote: ZoBell, *op. cit.,* p. 212, 212 n.

CHAPTER 15. THE SUPREME COURT: A CONCLUDING UNSCIENTIFIC POSTSCRIPT

520 Learned Hand quote: Curtis, *Law As Large As Life,* pp. 156–157.
520 Karl Llewellyn quote: Llewellyn, *The Common Law Tradition: Deciding Appeals,* p. 24 n.
502 Robert H. Jackson quote: *Brown* v. *Allen,* 344 US 443, in Hart and Wechsler, *The Federal Courts and the Federal System,* p. 1295.
521 Edward H. Levi quote: Levi, *An Introduction to Legal Reasoning,* pp. 58–59.
522 A Supreme Court Decision in 1912: *Yazoo & Mississippi Valley RR Co.* v. *Jackson Vinegar Co.,* 226 US 217.
522 Another in 1960 reversed: *Thompson* v. *City of Louisville,* 362 US 199.

Page

523　James M. Landis quote: Frankfurter and Landis, *The Business of the Supreme Court*, p. 65.

524　Hughes is supposed to have: Pusey, *Charles Evans Hughes*, Vol. II, p. 664.

525　This statement makes me sick: *Ibid.*, Vol. II, p. 671.

527　The judicial branch of the Government has only: *U.S.* v. *Butler*, 297 US 1, p. 62 (AAA Case).

527　When a state came in here: Cited from Raymond Clapper in Mason, *Brandeis*, p. 572.

527　Frankfurter quote: Frankfurter, *Law and Politics*, Capricorn ed., p. 25.

528　Hughes quote: Hughes to annual meeting of ALI, May 10, 1934, in Hart and Wechsler, *op. cit.*, p. 1396.

528　Chief Justice Vinson quote: Vinson to American Bar Association, September 7, 1949, in Hart and Wechsler, *op. cit.*, p. 1404.

528　Holmes quote: Hart and Wechsler, *op. cit.*, p. 890.

529　Learned Hand quote: Hand, *The Bill of Rights*, p. 55.

529　The answer to this attack: Holmes in *Otis* v. *Parker*, 187 US 606, p. 609.

530　The First Amendment, for example: Black, Commencement Address at Swarthmore College, June 6, 1955, cited in Cahn, *Confronting Injustice*, p. 155.

530　Edmond Cahn quote: Cahn, *Confronting Injustice*, pp. 92, 93.

530　Learned Hand, *op, cit.*, p. 63.

530　Holmes quote: *Missouri* v. *Holland*, 225 US 416, p. 433.

531　Jefferson quote: Jefferson to Abigail Adams, September 11, 1804, in Cappon, *Adams-Jefferson Letters*, p. 279.

532　Justice Black quote: *Adamson* v. *California*, 332 US 46, p. 74.

532　Justice Pitney quote: *Prudential Insurance Co.* v. *Cheek*, 259 US 530, p. 538.

532　For present purposes we may and do assume: *Gitlow* v. *N.Y.*, 268 US 652, p. 666.

533　Charles Curtis quote: Curtis, *Lions Under the Throne*, p. 282.

534　Any legal proceeding enforced: *Hurtado* v. *California*, 110 US 516.

534　Sifting evidence is the everyday business: Fairman, "Does the Fourteenth Amendment Incorporate the Bill of Rights? The Original Understanding," 2 *Stanford Law Review* 6, p. 80.

534　Stanley Morrison quote: Morrison, "Does the Fourteenth Amendment Incorporate the Bill of Rights? The Judicial Interpretation," 2 *Stanford Law Review*, p. 162.

535　Alexander Bickel quote: Bickel, *The Least Dangerous Branch*, Bobbs-Merrill, paper ed., p. 103.

535　Hughes quote: Pusey, *op. cit.*, Vol. II, p. 625.

535　Jackson quote: Jackson, *The Struggle for Judicial Supremacy*, p. 299.

535　Harlan Fiske Stone quote: *US* v. *Butler*, 297 US 1, p. 79.

535　Brandeis quote: Mason, *Brandeis*, p. 554.

536　Madison quote: Warren, *The Supreme Court in United States History*, Vol. I, p. 517.

536　Frankfurter quote: Frankfurter, *Of Men and Law*, p. 29.

536　Wechsler quote: Wechsler, "Toward Neutral Principles of Constitutional Law," 73 *Harvard Law Review* 1, p. 19.

536　Chief Justice Traynor quote: Traynor, "No Magic Words Could Do It Justice," 49 *California Law Review* 615, p. 624.

536　*Baker* v. *Carr*: 369 US 186.

537　Justice Douglas quote: *Gray* v. *Saunders*, 372 US 368.

537　In 1932 the Court had ruled: *Smiley* v. *Holm*, 285 US 355, p. 374.

Page
538 The equal-voice premise ignores: Bickel, *Politics and the Warren Court,* p. 184.
538 Justice Frankfurter quote: Hart and Wechsler, *op. cit.,* pp. 206-207.
538 Phil C. Neal quote: Neal, *"Baker v. Carr:* Politics in Search of Law," *1962 Supreme Court Review* 252, pp. 279-280.
539 Neal quote: *Ibid.,* p. 278.
539 Robert B. McKay quote: McKay, *Reapportionment,* p. 270.
539 James Weaver quote: *Law and Computers in the Mid-Sixties,* p. 388.
540 It's the question of this doughnut problem: *Ibid.,* p. 391.
540 McKay specifically recommends it: McKay, *op. cit.,* p. 270.
541 Anthony Lewis quote: Lewis, "Legislative Apportionment and the Federal Courts," 71 *Harvard Law Review* 1057.
541 Dean Rostow quote: Rostow, *The Sovereign Prerogative,* pp. 226–228.
542 Lincoln quote: Angle and Miers, *The Living Lincoln,* pp. 416–417.
542 Learned Hand quote: Hand, *The Spirit of Liberty,* Vintage ed., p. 22.
542 Bronislaw Malinowski quote: Malinowski, *Crime and Custom in a Savage Society,* p. 127, cited in O'Gorman, *Lawyers and Matrimonial Cases,* p. 20.
543 The wisdom of having Mr. Justice Frankfurter: Mason, *Harlan Fiske Stone, Pillar of the Law,* p. 641.
543 A doctrine wholly incompatible with faith: Jackson, *The Supreme Court in the American System of Government,* p. 55.
544 Felix Frankfurter quote: Frankfurter, *Of Law and Men,* p. 157.
546 Henry Hart quote: Hart, *The Supreme Court 1958 Term,* p. 99.
546 Treacherous ground we tread: *Jordan v. De George,* 341 US 223.
547 [C]onstitutionality does not exact: *Dennis v. US.,* 341 US 494, p. 556.
547 Holmes quote: Holmes, *Collected Legal Papers,* p. 187.
547 Justice Jackson quote: Jackson, *The Struggle for Judicial Supremacy,* p. x.
547 Henry Hart and Herbert Wechsler quote: Hart and Wechsler, *op. cit.,* p. 336.
547 The ultimate reliance for the deepest needs: *Dennis v. U.S.,* 341 US 494, p. 556.
548 Cardozo quote: Cardozo, *The Nature of the Judicial Process,* Yale ed., p. 140.
548 McGeorge Bundy quote: Bundy, "A Lay View of Due Process," in Sutherland, ed., *Government Under Law,* p. 366.

INDEX

Format by Mort Perry
Set in Linotype Baskerville
Composed, printed and bound by The Haddon Craftsmen, Inc.
HARPER & ROW, PUBLISHERS, INCORPORATED